SHAKESPEARE ON SILENT FILM

A Strange Eventful History

ROBERT HAMILTON BALL

Illustrated

THEATRE ARTS BOOKS
NEW YORK

FIRST PUBLISHED IN 1968

*This book is copyright under the Berne Convention.
Apart from any fair dealing for the purposes of private
study, research, criticism or review, as permitted
under the Copyright Act, 1956, no portion may be
reproduced by any process without written permission.
Enquiries should be addressed to the publisher.*

© *Robert Hamilton Ball 1968*

*First published in the United States
by Theatre Arts Books, 333 Sixth Avenue, New York 10014.
Library of Congress Catalog Card No. 68-14014.*

PRINTED IN GREAT BRITAIN
in 11 point Ehrhardt type
BY C. TINLING AND CO. LTD
LIVERPOOL, LONDON AND PRESCOT

TO MY WIFE

'O give thyself the thanks, if aught in me
Worthy perusal stand against thy sight'

SONNET 38

CONTENTS

A

ILLUSTRATIONS

ILLUSTRATIONS

'What's dumb in show, I'll plain with speech.'
Pericles

TO THE READER

'Dost thou love pictures?'
The Taming of the Shrew

THIS book might be called a diversion. Certainly it deals with a subject which is unconventional for an academic who has spent much of his life teaching English literature to college and university students and whose publications, until he began gathering material for the book, had little to do with films. It has been a diversion in another sense too, a distraction from other and more customary forms of research and writing, a recreation, and on the whole great fun. It has led to a series of adventures and detections which have provided the thrill of the chase and the satisfactions of discovery over a considerable period of time. It has taken me to places to which I would not otherwise have gone and introduced me to some delightful people I would not otherwise have encountered.

Yet it is not so much a diversion as might be thought. I have been teaching Shakespeare for forty years and writing about the drama and stage for almost as long, and I have seen a great many films from the early days of cinema to the present. What more natural than that Shakespeare, the history of theatre in its inclusive meaning, and film should at some time come together.

Finally – for this play on a word – this book should not be considered a diversion in the sense that it is meant as mere entertainment for the reader, though I hope he will find it entertaining too. It is an attempt to show a relatively unconsidered way in which the influence of Shakespeare has been pervasive and through to me a fascinating if imperfect medium how Shakespeare reached a different and wider public by whom he was generally ignored. It is my hope therefore that what I have written will appeal to Shakespeareans, to specialists and enthusiasts in film, and to others who are interested in knowing more about a segment of history and the activities of a group of men and women who were doing strange or remarkable things in the period from the beginning of the twentieth century to the end of its third decade. A volume now in preparation will continue the story with Shakespeare on sound film.

Recognizing, however, the probability that whatever appeal this history has may be to different types of readers, I have divided it into two sections.

The first is a fairly straightforward narrative, uninterrupted by elaborate detail and documentation, which treats more or less chronologically what was done with Shakespeare on the silent screen. Here too, I have tried to put the subject in perspective by showing briefly how Shakespeare on film was related to other film, who were responsible and how they went about it, and how film itself fit into a world which has now passed. The second section, which I have called, 'Explanations and Acknowledgments', is for the film buffs and the scholars. Here each film treated in the main text is given additional comment or elucidation with particulars, even minutiae, not necessarily important to the general reader but of interest to specialists in film. Here too will be found specific indications of my indebtedness to many people and publications, my sources of information on the individual films covered in both parts. Those who wish to read the text and then immediately the subsidiary material in the second part on the same film are referred to the Index, where the page numbers for main treatments are italicized. I realize that for some readers this division may prove an inconvenience or an annoyance, but is the best arrangement which, after consideration, I have been able to contrive under the circumstances.

It has been suggested to me by my good friend, Ernest Lindgren, of the British Film Institute, that I should say something somewhere about the difficulties of film research. This book and the subsequent one planned have occupied me, not of course uninterruptedly, for over twenty years. In the first place, scholarship in the history of film has with notable exceptions, been shockingly bad. I enthusiastically indicate my debt to Harold Leonard's remarkable *Film Index* and to historians such as Terry Ramsaye and Lewis Jacobs for the United States, Rachael Low for Great Britain, Georges Sadoul for the world but especially for France, Jay Leyda for Russia, and Maria Adriana Prolo for Italy; the recent Wiesbaden brochure, *Shakespeare im Film*, has been useful and the *Enciclopedia dello Spettacolo* invaluable. But most of the books and articles which refer to Shakespeare film are inaccurate or contradictory and have proliferated error upon error. Films are listed which were never made or with credits which are incorrectly assigned or with wrong dates. Such publications can only serve as leads to be investigated; what they say can only be true if found to be true.

Essentially there are only three ways to achieve anything like accuracy; I do not pretend to complete accuracy and I have no doubt missed films I should have named. The first is to find the films, if they are extant. A surprising number have indeed survived, but they are scattered over the world, some in archives, some in private collections, some in the hands of distributors or makers or renters, some in storage vaults, some in junk shops. The archives are the places to start and they usually have lists, though not always complete ones, and sometimes facilities for screening or examination, but after onerous tracing, a film I have wanted to see turned out to be non-existent or in deplorable condition, or a piece of property 'unavailable for examination'. Another difficulty is that archives, especially those on the Continent and in South America, are frequently unwilling or unable to answer letters of inquiry. Nevertheless films turn up like the recently re-discovered Forbes-Robertson *Hamlet*. One never knows where, however: an American *Twelfth Night* in London, an English *Taming of the Shrew* in up-state New York, a French *Macbeth* in California, an Italian *Julius Caesar* in Cornwall. All this search takes time and travel, funds, and particularly when films are in private or company ownership, sometimes argument and tact. Yet if the films are available, one cannot write about them without seeing them. Moreover, they cannot properly be judged without viewing other films contemporary with them.

The second major source of information is the trade journals which describe the production, distribution, and nature of the films at the time they were made and released. It means reading or at least paging through all you can locate in several languages, not only English, but French, German, Italian, and so on. But these like the films are widely dispersed. Even the best or the most specialized libraries do not have complete files. Trade journals were highly ephemeral; they were meant principally for distributors or exhibitors who tossed them away when the films they mention were out-of-date. Maddeningly the particular issue you want often cannot be discovered or is so distant you cannot get at it. Because they are so rare and are in their way authentic (not, however, in their synopses of films), I have quoted from them at length, even to the point of repetition. Besides they are not unin-teresting in their own right; they show the commercial aspects of movie making as no other source can, and without the business there would be no Shakespeare films.

The third method of research is tracing people who were directly or indirectly involved with the films themselves, and this is real detective work. It means finding out whether they are still alive, who knows where they now live, writing endless letters, arranging for interviews. In the case of this volume most of these people are veterans to be questioned about films made many years before, few of them still connected with motion pictures. Unless they have personal records, many have hazy memories which must be checked by other data. One prominent actress gave me lucid details which turned out to be wrong from beginning to end. Others in their efforts to be helpful think they remember but they do not. On the other hand, the hunt is exciting and the rewards often large. It took me months to follow various hints as to the whereabouts of Edwin Thanhouser in America and Europe; it turned out his residence had been a mile from mine. The first screen Romeo in the United States, Paul Panzer, had batches of stills in cartons in his garage. I could not have put together what one film was like without talking with Edmund Gwenn and A. E. Matthews, nor dated another without finding its cameraman. In a way it is fortunate that this study has taken so long. I was able to meet and talk with Albert E. Smith, Godfrey

Tearle, Theda Bara, now all dead, but Arthur Kingston I did not discover until 1965.

In short, research in the history of film is likely to be lengthy and at times arduous and exasperating, but the pursuit of Shakespeare in this medium has provided more than a recompense if it shows the breadth of the trade in his name, the adaptation of his plays for the screen, indication of which of his plays were most used, and who participated in and enjoyed the results. I am quite aware that there are inconsistencies in treatment, but I have not been able to avoid them. The amount of space or the kind of analysis given to a picture, for example, frequently depends not on my own judgment of its importance but to the information available or to the conditions under which the picture was examined. It makes a difference whether a film was screened, shown on an Editola, examined in a hand viewer, or peered at, frame by frame, through a magnifying glass. In some cases there was time for repetitions, notes on each sequence, copying of all subtitles; in others, all I could do was to scribble in the dark and put down my recollections as soon as possible after projection. My judgment also may have been at fault in including so many inconsequential films to demonstrate the nature and breadth of Shakespeare's sway; all I can say is that they interested me and therefore may interest others. Finally, though I have learned a good deal about film, I do not consider myself a technical expert, and I offer apologies if I have made mistakes in describing the processes employed. I shall be happy to receive corrections in these and other misapprehensions or errors.

My obligations to those who assisted me in obtaining information about specific films is expressed in the second section of this book, but organizations and individuals also encouraged and supported me over long periods of time. Much of the research was enabled by the award of a fellowship of the John Simon Guggenheim Foundation, and I owe much to Dr Henry Allen Moe, its then President. I am also indebted to the Rockefeller Foundation and Mr John Marshall for a grant for another purpose which sent me abroad for eighteen months and allowed me a third of that time to conduct research. At the beginning of the work I received helpful endorsements from Arthur H. DeBra, Director of Research, Motion Picture Producers and Distributors of America; Iris Barry, Curator of the Film Library, Museum of Modern Art; the late Barrett H. Clark, Executive Director, Dramatists Play Service; George Freedley, Curator, Theatre Collection, New York Public Library; Dr Louis B. Wright and Dr James G. McManaway of the Folger Shakespeare Library; and Mr John Gassner, then of the Play Department, Columbia Pictures Corporation, late Sterling Professor at Yale University. I make grateful acknowledgment to the staffs of the Museum of Modern Art, especially to Mr Bernard Karpel and Miss Margareta Akermark; to Mr Freedley and to Mr Paul Myers of the New York Public Library Theatre Collection; to Colonel Willard Webb and members of the staff of the Library of Congress; to Mr John E. Allen for hunting out and screening for me Shakespeare films in his collection; to Mr Jay Leyda who has gone out of his way to send me many useful contributions; and to too many to name who have written me and assisted me as company executives, interested individuals, and friends. I owe a huge debt of gratitude to Mr Ernest Lindgren, O.B.E., F.B.K.S., Curator of the National Film Archive of the British Film Institute, who, for three long periods gave me free run of the resources of the Archive and allowed me to use it as a base for European operations, and to members of his staff who could not have been more kind on my behalf: Mr David Francis, Mr Roger Holman, Mr Liam O'Leary, Mr Harold G. Brown, Mrs Kristen Brockman, and Mr John S. L. Barnes. I am particularly indebted to Mr Martin Quigley, Jr., President of the Quigley Publishing Company and Editor in Chief of the *Motion Picture Herald* for permission to use material from its predecessor, the *Moving Picture World*. I wish also to express my appreciation to Mr Robert M. MacGregor, my friend and American publisher, and to Mr Philip Unwin and Mr Peter Leek of George Allen and Unwin, Ltd., for all their care and courtesies at Ruskin House.

Queens College of the City University of New York

CHAPTER I

Pioners and All:

THE BEGINNINGS OF SHAKESPEARE FILM
(1899–1907)

IT WAS bright in London on that day towards the close of the nineteenth century – or at least there were bright intervals. In the early morning the sun sparkled on the silver Thames, and as one strolled north along the Victoria Embankment from Westminster Bridge, Wordsworth's sonnet came to mind. Farther north still, as the river turned more and more to the east above Charing Cross it was pleasant to wander in the gardens. This was historic ground. At the foot of Buckingham Street was the seventeenth-century Water Gate of York House and then the region known as the Adelphi, built by the brothers Adam. It had once been the site of Durham House, the home of the fourteenth-century Bishop of Durham, and later of Lady Jane Grey and of Sir Walter Raleigh. Adelphi Terrace, looking on the Thames, had been inspired by Robert Adam's visit to the palace of Diocletian at Spalato though remodelling had now altered its original design. Robert and James Adam had resided at No. 4; Thomas Hardy had worked at No. 8; the Savage Club occupied Nos. 6 and 7. There were dramatic associations too. David Garrick had lived and died at No. 5; Richard D'Oyly Carte was in the Adam residence; and Bernard Shaw had recently moved into No. 10.

This particular day was also to be in a peculiar way historic. If Shaw stood at his window contemplating Cleopatra's Needle and glanced obliquely elsewhere, he saw a curious sight. There were groups of people in elaborate and antiquated costumes who walked and gestured in a strangely theatrical manner and who appeared to be enacting a scene from a play. Two individuals were in charge. One was a man who stood at a tripod surmounted by a black box with a crank and whose dress contrasted with that of the others by being more or less what one might expect to see along the Embankment in 1899. The other, a tall, lanky man with a personality obviously more buoyant and dominant, wore, of all things, a robe and a crown. The name of the first man has vanished but what he was operating was a motion picture camera. The second man Shaw might have recognized – he had indeed known him for some years. It was Herbert Beerbohm Tree, and he wore the crown of King John. This was the first Shakespeare film.

In 1897 Tree had opened Her Majesty's Theatre, where he was to produce thirteen of Shakespeare's plays with unusual splendour. His first real success there had been the presentation in 1898 of *Julius Caesar* with scenery and costumes by Laurence Alma Tadema. *King John*, which he put on earlier for special matinees at the Crystal Palace Theatre in 1889 – 1890, was his second Shakespeare production at his new theatre. It began on September 20, 1899, achieved its hundredth performance on December 16, and was then withdrawn until Boxing Night, when it was resumed until January 6, 1900. Supporting Tree as King John were Julia Neilson as Constance, Louis Calvert as Cardinal Pandulph, and as Faulconbridge, the Bastard, Lewis Waller, who was especially applauded. Quite clearly the presentation was a distinct hit, and the business phenomenal. The review in the *Era* of September 23rd indicates some of the reasons. The play itself is 'without central purpose, but very eventful; and Mr Beerbohm Tree has done the best thing possible, in the circumstances by cutting away the superfluous matter, arranging the piece in three acts, and, by a succession of splendid tableaux, giving us a grand idea of the pomp and circumstance of war and politics in the thirteenth century. . . .' Of all the tableaux the one which was most noticed was an insertion of 'the granting of the Magna Charta . . . represented by Mr Walter Hamm in a stage picture of elaborate pictorial arrangement.' Evidently there was material here which could be caught by a motion picture camera.

Nevertheless it is remarkable that even a primitive Shakespeare film should have been made so early. This is hardly the place to present the arguments of those who claim to have 'invented' the motion picture. Moreover, the whole matter has been confused by national pride, the dates of patent registrations, and the equity of legal decisions. But Edison's peep show Kinetoscope, though demonstrated in 1889, had no commercial presentation until 1894, when it also reached London, and there was nothing like what we call the motion picture until successful screen projection in 1895. In England Robert W. Paul first demonstrated his projector on February 28, 1896, and it was in that year that the British public became aware of projected films. It was then only five years after the peep show type and three years after projection when Tree was photographed in motion in *King John*. Moreover, unless one counts Joe Jefferson, who had acted bits from *Rip Van Winkle* for the Mutoscope in 1895, there was no precedent for so eminent an actor to allow himself to participate in a medium which was hardly regarded as respectable by the cultured public.

The explanation lies largely in Tree's character, his boyish light-heartedness, his impulsiveness, his willingness to be considered eccentric, his energy and his vision. He was always eager for experiment, and he enjoyed the excitement of taking chances. He had made a risky gamble when he assumed the management of the failing Haymarket Theatre in 1887 and challenged the rivalry of Henry Irving. There he dared to produce special performances of plays which he admired but which were not expected to prove financially successful. He showed his recognition of the new drama by producing Maeterlinck, Wilde, and Ibsen, later Shaw. His own acting roles were deliberately varied rather than chosen for comfortable success. He acquired the site of Her Majesty's and built his theatre there with a pocketbook frequently almost empty. He was to found the Academy of Dramatic Art and to institute an annual Shakespeare festival. This was not the kind of a man to let slip the opportunity to try a new medium.

Unfortunately it is not clear for what purpose the experiment was made, nor who suggested it. Later, Tree was to be involved in three other Shakespeare films, in two of which he both acted himself and made money. There is no evidence he made money here, and it is more likely that he lost. In 1899 films were very short indeed, but it took some time to arrange and take the picture, and there was the expense of transporting actors and appurtenances from the theatre. There is no record, moreover, that the finished product was ever publicly exhibited or brought in any returns. It seems probable either that Tree was caught by the excitement of active participation in a new sort of enterprise or that he realized – he did of a later film – that the camera could be used to make a kind of record in motion of a successful performance which would remain after the theatre production had vanished into limbo, a record which might in addition, at some time in the future, afford a few minutes' amusement to him and his friends.

It is improbable that much of the play was photographed. Perhaps the site on the Embankment gives the clue. Here was greenery and the Thames, an approximation to Runnymede. The tableau of the granting of the Magna Charta needed no words, only pantomime for its effect. This may have been all. If so, it is ironic that the first film of a performance of a Shakespeare play was of a scene which Shakespeare did not include. At any rate the characters were Shakespeare's, and Tree's King John was there in part, and to Tree's other efforts in pioneering must be added that he became a motion picture actor in 1899 in a part created by Shakespeare.

The casual itinerant who happened upon Tree's filming of *King John* became more purposeful the next year. He crossed the Channel to attend the Paris Exposition, grandly open from April 15th through October of 1900. One of its wonders was sound film, first commercially exploited at the Olympia two years before, but still a wonder nevertheless. At one pavilion a demonstration of *phonorama* presented hand-coloured scenes of Parisian life accompanied by street cries, and at the Théâtre de la Grande Roue there were audible and visible sketches with original dialogue, one of which presented a comic scene of a pretty wife and her angry husband preparing for bed (*rien d'indécent*, however). Yet these were perhaps too tame as attractions. On the other hand at the beginning of the Rue de Paris near the Pont des Invalides there were crowds before the Phono-Cinéma-Théâtre. Here there was a poster, designed by François Flameng, on which a beautiful lady in modish costume pointed winningly with a long cane to the bill for the day. It included the clowns Footit and Chocolate; Emilio Cossira from the Opéra singing a tenor aria from Gounod's *Roméo et Juliette; L'Enfant Prodigue*, three tableaux by Mlle Félicia Mallet; the celebrated comic, Little Tich; Polin in an air from *La Fille du Régiment*; and two duel scenes from celebrated plays. In the first Cyrano de Bergerac in the person of the elder Coquelin discomfited the Vicomte de Valvert. The second was last on the programme and calculated to send patrons away from the theatre with gasps of pleasurable astonishment, Sarah Bernhardt in *Hamlet*.

The sound films at the Phono-Cinéma-Théâtre had been made by Clément Maurice. It was he who had introduced Antoine Lumière to the Kinetoscope in 1894, an event which started the Lumière sons, Auguste and Louis, on the road to screen projection. When they were ready it was to Maurice they turned for public exhibition. As concessionaire he found a billiard room, the Salon Indien, which had been closed by the police, in the basement of the Grand Café, 14, Boulevard des Capucines, near the Opéra, and opened it to show Lumière films on December 28, 1895. In addition he was a still photographer of some reputation who specialized in theatrical portraits. His work naturally brought him into contact with people of the stage and gave him opportunities to persuade various celebrities to appear in his films for the Exposition, where they were shown five or six times a day. Later he was to found two important companies, Radios, which combined with Eclipse, and Eclair; both companies made Shakespeare films.

Maurice's system was simple enough. First the performers played before his motion picture camera; then retaining so far as possible the same cadence, they recorded song, words, or other sounds on the wax cylinders of a phonograph. Warned by a red light, the projectionist in his booth listened by telephone to the sound of the phonograph near the screen and adapted the speed of his hand cranking so as to make sound and visual images as far as possible coincide.

Since he had been involved with *phonorama*, the projectionist at the Phono-Cinéma-Théâtre was probably not that extraordinary cameraman, Félix Mesguich, but after the Exposition closed Mesguich took Maurice's films on tour, and on his return presented them at the Olympia. In his memoirs he describes some of the hazards of operation. Synchronization in any case must have been nerve racking and imperfect, but it was also complicated by the tactics of competitors who resorted to sabotage. On one occasion while the room was in darkness, a malevolent hand cut the telephone wire which permitted Mesguich to follow the sound of the phonograph and to communicate with its operator, Jacques Berst (later Director-General of Pathé in New York). Fortunately Mesguich was by then so experienced in maintaining the proper pace that the audience was never aware of the difference. Exit villain, foiled.

This Mesguich is worth noting. An Algerian, he had been a Zouave before he found his *métier* with the brothers Lumière. He was one of the operator-projectionists whom they sent to the United States in June, 1896 to show their cinematograph at the Eden Musee and B. F. Keith's Union Square Theatre in New York, and in other principal cities. In competition with Edison's Vitascope, which had begun exhibition at Koster and Bials' (now the site of Macy's) on April 20th, and outmanoeuvred by American interests, Lumière's representatives had to flee in disorder. Mesguich returned to Paris by way of Canada, and in 1897 was sent to Russia, where he shot and projected Lumière films, in Yalta before Nicholas II, and in Moscow before the Grand Duke Michael. He made a film of the crowning of the czar. At the fair in Nijni-Novgorod in July, 1898 he showed this and other Russian pictures before a stupified public which suspected diabolical agency and had to be dispersed by the police. Ultimately his installation was burnt out, excellent publicity for the engagement which was to follow at the summer theatre of the Aquarium in St Petersburg. At this cabaret, two entertainers were at each other's throats, Lina Cavalieri, not yet an opera singer nor publicized as 'the most beautiful woman in the world' (she starred in films from 1914 to 1921), and the Andalusian-born dancer, Caroline (La Belle) Otero, whose successes included appearance *au naturel* on a silver platter. The latter by way of squelching her rival asked Mesguich to make a film of her dances. In her *Valse brisante* her partner was a young Russian officer. When the film was shown, it was interrupted by whistles and the police, and the next day Mesguich was accused of insulting the army and ordered to leave on the Paris express. Since the Lumières had now decided to give up the business of exhibition, Mesguich with a Lumière camera he had bought was on his own. After an interval he filmed the scenes of Parisian life for *phonorama*. La Belle Otero, now remembered primarily as a subject of Toulouse-Lautrec, turned up at the Exposition in a film of her Spanish dance.

After the Exposition closed, Mesguich took the films and cylinders of the Phono-Cinéma-Théâtre through provincial France to Switzerland, Germany, Austria, and Spain with what he called lively success. After their showing at the Olympia in 1901 he was reaffiliated with Lumière and was the projectionist there for Méliès' famous *Voyage dans la lune*, but he was never really happy unless pursuing *actualités*. 'Tourneur de manivelle à travers le monde,' he called himself. He took pictures of the coronation of Edward VII, followed the Russo-Japanese War, was in St Petersburg for the beginning of the Revolution in 1905, caught President Loubet donning his hunting breeches at Rambouillet – the film was shown at the Folies Bergère while an orchestra played 'Le bon roi Dagobert a mis sa culotte à l'envers' – filmed the Olympic Games in Athens in 1906, the marriage of Alfonso XIII, and in 1908 became the first aerial film photographer, in the plane of Wilbur

Wright. He crowned his career as a news and documentary cameraman by a trip around the world. An unusual man, this Mesguich. What, one wonders, did he think of that other pioneer, Sarah Bernhardt?

At the turn of the century, Bernhardt was much in the public eye, no less because of her decidedly controversial interpretation of Hamlet. There was difference of opinion about her merits as an actress, almost universal recognition of her determination, her waywardness, her vitality, and her brilliance. What Henry James called her 'génie de la réclame,' her skill in self-advertisement, together with the adulation of her devotees, had made her not only a celebrity but an institution. Playgoers everywhere knew of her fractious temper and unpredictable temperament. Her early and not particularly successful engagement at the Comédie Française had been terminated when she boxed the ears of an elderly colleague, and she had built her reputation at the Odéon before she returned to the national theatre in 1872. Here too, after eight years, she broke her contract and had to pay substantial damages. Thereafter she acted when she wished, managed her own theatres, toured all over the world. Her quarrels and her caprices were common gossip and excellent publicity, a publicity not contradicted but augmented by her personal magnetism. At various times she made balloon ascents, stood on a captive whale, and kept a collection of unlikely animals. Her bedroom contained a skeleton as a reminder of mortality, and she slept and learned her parts in the coffin she was finally buried in. So tempestuous a personality and so energetic a seeker of attention would not fail to embrace the opportunity to appear in a filmed duel as Hamlet, a part she had recently added to her repertory.

Sarah had played Ophelia as early as 1886, but it was not until 1897, when she was fifty-three, that she decided to act the title role in her own production of *Hamlet* and commissioned a new prose translation. By 1899 she took over the Théâtre des Nations and renamed it the Théâtre Sarah Bernhardt. It was here that her presentation greeted an astonished and on the whole, delighted audience on May 20th. On June 12th she appeared in the part at the Adelphi Theatre, London, and later at the Memorial Theatre in Stratford. She reopened her own theatre in Paris on December 16th with President Loubet, he of Mesguich's enrobement scene, in a stage box. New York did not see her as the Dane until after the film, at the Garden Theatre on Christmas Day, 1900, during a repertory presentation of five plays with Coquelin aîné. Coquelin, who was in the other duel on the same bill at the Phono-Cinéma-Théâtre, was the First Grave Digger.

Bernhardt's conception of Hamlet evoked heated controversy. There was nothing new about an actress playing the part. Mrs Siddons had done so in 1777 and was followed by a spate of female princes in Great Britain and the United States in the nineteenth century. In France, Mme Judith had appeared as Hamlet in 1867. It was not primarily a matter of sex but of interpretation. The French take their theatre seriously and as a subject of discussion and argument. Bernhardt's Hamlet was both admired and disputed, but it was accepted as a revelation. Rostand said she made him comprehend Hamlet for the first time; two journalists, one of them Catulle Mendès, fought a duel over whether Hamlet was fat. In England, though Walter of the *Times* thought the play 'acted to perfection,' most of the comments were satirical. 'Where everything is necessarily wrong,' said the *Athenaeum,* 'nothing can be right,' and Max Beerbohm in the *Saturday Review* of June 17th wrote of 'her aberration at the Adelphi. Had she for one moment betrayed any faintest sense of Hamlet's character, the reminiscence were less painful.' In New York, William Winter of the *Tribune* was bitter: 'Her superficial and expiditious performance' was a 'dreadful desecration.'

Why? Bernhardt played Hamlet as 'manly and resolute, not a weak or languid person' but 'firm and logical' a 'young strong determined character' of 'great power of mind.' There was no mental shock, and difficulties, including the ghost, were encountered with equanimity. This Hamlet knocked together the heads of Rosencrantz and Guildenstern, and kicked Polonius in the shins. To people to whom Hamlet was associated with imagination, sensibility, nobility, and melancholia, Bernhardt was a shock. Nevertheless the vigour must have made an effective duel scene, and it was the duel scene which was filmed.

Reviews and illustrations of stage and film performances convey some idea of what a visitor would have seen at Mme Marguerite Chenu's little theatre at the Paris Exposition. On the stage, Winter tells us, 'at the climax of the duel Hamlet's sword-hand was made to show a trace of blood, and the Prince's face and person were made to reveal pathological symptoms of the approach of death by poison. Mme Bernhardt's Hamlet died standing, and his reeling body was caught by Horatio . . . .' In the photograph of film frames, Bernhardt appears at one side crossing rapiers with Laertes on the other. Laertes was Pierre Magnier, an 'élegant jeune premier' and frequently Bernhardt's leading man; she had engaged him for her company in 1898. Behind the duellists stand two 'valets d'armes' in lieu of a court, and a page, Suzanne Seylor, who had been with Bernhardt as early as 1892 and become her inseparable companion. Bernhardt herself is sprightly, graceful, and slender. (The figure was padded on the stage to reduce her femininity.) She wore a belted black silk tunic, a white ruffle around the neck; black silk tights; a black cloak which hung from her left shoulder; a wig of fair, waved, bobbed hair. The setting is simple, an archway supported by columns and a painted backdrop. After the duel the body of the Prince is carried away on a shield. The whole action took perhaps three minutes. Various writers speak of the sound effects, the clash of weapons, the stamp of feet. These were probably recorded, but the scene required little or no speech, and Henri Cossira is explicit that the *voix d'or* was unheard. Still, much could be enjoyed for the twenty sous admission price.

Unlike the reviews of Bernhardt's stage performances, comments in the

journals on the Phono-Cinéma-Théâtre are chiefly on the scientific achievement and the entertainment provided thereby. Since some of the remarks
are clearly publicity, it is not easy to judge their critical accuracy, but *Le
Figaro* of June 8, 1900 congratulates Clément Maurice for a combination of
cinematograph and phonograph which is 'complète et absolue' and a
'résultat de rare perfection'. It constitutes a real artistic progress and will
have considerable documentary value in the future. And on September 8th,
it adds that Sarah Bernhardt has been admirably caught in the duel scene
from *Hamlet*, and that 'la reconstitution de cette scène est une merveille
d'art en même temps qu'un chef-d'oeuvre d'exactitude.' *Le Gaulois* of
September 9th speaks of the combination of sight and sound in respect to
Coquelin as prodigious, but notes we go from marvel to marvel for here is
Sarah Bernhardt with Magnier. And it was reported in the second *Figaro*
article that the artists themselves came to the theatre to see and hear themselves, and what is 'bien agréable', to hear themselves applauded as if they
had actually appeared before the public. According to one report, however,
possibly apochryphal, seeing herself on the screen so shocked the divine
Sarah that she fainted.

All due allowance made for uncritical enthusiasm, there is no doubt of the
contemporary popularity of the films at the Exposition and later on tour and
at the Olympia, as Mesguich testifies. Evidently Mme Chenu was still the
proprietor of the films, because he says he and Berst did the bill posting on
their travels in order not to increase her expenses. As late as 1908 George
Kleine in the United States announced that he had received from Urban-
Eclipse in London and Paris 'a remarkable assignment of film subjects . . .
depicting famous French actors and actresses in their most popular plays,
such as Bernhardt and her company [a slight exaggeration] in *Hamlet* . . . .
It is of peculiar interest that the films were taken *eight years ago* and only
now has permission been obtained for their public exhibition [i.e. in
America].' There is no evidence, however, that these primitives then
attracted any attention.

In 1930 the films and cylinders of the Phono-Cinéma-Théâtre were
discovered in the archives of the Compagnie de Tirage Maurice, owned by
Mesguich and Clément Maurice's son. In 1933 Pathé-Cinéma showed some
of the films as reconstituted by Roger Goupillières at a new theatre on the
Champs-Elysées where they provoked some nostalgia. Articles of the
period credit Mme Chenu with having originated the idea of the sound films,
no doubt with the collaboration of Clément Maurice, for her theatre at the
Exposition. She has other reasons to be remembered. In World War I she
was a nurse who founded a hospital; later she was sent by France to the
United States on a propaganda mission. A woman, said Robert Destez, with
a head and a heart. A worthy pioner!

It could be said that all periods of the motion picture, including our own, have involved experiment, but the older the medium became, the more it tended to fall into definite norms. At the beginning it struggled to find out what it was and what it was for. At first an invention, it soon grew to a business, a means of providing entertainment, and only gradually to pretentions of art. The *King John* of Tree, and Bernhardt's duel scene from *Hamlet* showed one direction which it could take, the reproduction of stage scenes, and this tendency was to continue, but from 1901 to 1907, there were other gropings too. With some of these we are not concerned; the filming of actualities which results in news or documentary pictures, for example, has little or nothing to do with Shakespeare. Any films relating to Shakespeare have at least a basis in literature or the theatre, that is, in art, though their ultimate aim may lie in amusement or the box-office. The problem was how Shakespeare's name and plays could be employed to draw and hold audiences who found pleasure in the relatively new experience of watching moving images on a screen.

During these eight years of cinema such Shakespeare film was used to accompany recitation and music, to reproduce stage scenery, and to tell briefly the story or show a bit of action of certain of the plays. In addition, titles and subjects from Shakespeare were adopted or adapted for non-Shakespearean films. Finally one man used Shakespeare material to suit his vision of what a film should be. Except for the last it was all very crude; with the last, however primitive, there were glimmerings of understanding of the nature of the new medium.

To follow a strict chronology is here neither possible nor desirable. Some of the films cannot be accurately dated, some of the references are highly questionable. I have no confidence in the authenticity of a statement that 'Shakespeare was first put on the screen by the Vitagraph Company, *Othello* having been released in 1902, and *Romeo and Juliet* in 1903.' Vitagraph was an important American company, and in 1908 it made films of these plays, but it seems altogether unlikely that it made versions so early. I am almost equally doubtful about a hand-coloured *Cleopatra* (Pathé) purportedly of 1903, which even if it did exist may not have been in any sense Shakespearean, and an Italian *King Lear* of 1905 to which all my references are German. There is, however, good evidence for a nevertheless vague *Othello* in 1907, put out by the Cines company which had been founded in Rome in 1905. A British distributor indicated that, 'the grand tragedy of William Shakespeare [was] retold with glorious effects. The canals of Venice beautifully tinted, the strong dramatic story of the jealous Moor, the lovely Desdemona and the wicked adventurer, Iago, culminating in the smothering of Desdemona, the death of Othello. 540 feet.' Such films as were actually made must have been attempts to recount the familiar tales.

In some cases the telling of the story itself was not the purpose, rather the depiction of an episode from it. A manuscript notebook in the Museum of Modern Art, New York, a record of the American Mutoscope and Biograph

Company for the years 1903 to 1912, lists as Film No. 3063, a *Duel Scene from Macbeth*, photographed on July 15, 1905. This company had been in business from the middle nineties, and produced both apparatus and films for peep show (Mutoscope) and projection (Biograph). The *Macbeth* duel was probably shot on the roof of the Hackett-Carhart building in New York, which it called its studio. The manuscript at any rate says 'taken in studio', and the company had not yet moved to the brownstone house in Fourteenth Street which was to become famous. The operator of the camera is listed as G. W. Bitzer, the Billy Bitzer also to become famous as the cameraman for David Wark Griffith. The length was 53 feet. In mutoscope or on the screen – it was made for both purposes – Macbeth and Macduff fought for less than a minute. Nevertheless the film was copyrighted and two copies were deposited in Washington. Motion pictures were copyrighted, if at all, as photographs in those days. The subsequent history of the *Duel* is also recorded in the manuscript. Evidently Shakespeare's characters were to lose their individualities, for the bit became Scene 3 in Negative No. 3272. Negative No. 3272 was *Fights of Nations*, otherwise shot in 1907, also by Bitzer, and presumably in Fourteenth Street, whither the company had moved in 1906. *Fights of Nations* was 750 feet long, but the original duel was not extended. Evidently a specific Macbeth and a specific Macduff did not longer 'lay on', but I cannot help wondering whether a property head was used to illustrate a characteristic finale of duels in Scotland.

Another kind of action was also recorded on film in 1905, and apparently for a somewhat different purpose, at least originally. The event reintroduces Herbert Beerbohm Tree, and if the evidence is authentic, shows him pioneering in a new direction. In March, a London trade journal announced: 'Mr Charles Urban, never behind in seizing every opportunity that presents itself for making the Bioscope popular, has by means of his splendid lens used on his recent trip to America, successfully photographed the ship scene in Mr Tree's play, *The Tempest*. As the company now tour the country, there will be no need to carry the cumbersome property belonging to the scene. The Bioscope will do the work of depicting the scene by projections from behind the screen. The audience, however, will not be made painfully conscious that they are looking at animated pictures, as the colouring of the films and various other technicalities we need not mention, serve to produce the illusion of reality, equal if not better than did the original mechanical contrivances.' Though I find no evidence that Urban's film was ever used on tour in an actual production of what the journal naively but not entirely inaccurately calls Mr Tree's play, *The Tempest*, there is at least here an indication of intention in Tree's mind, and it is the first instance I know of where the motion picture was envisaged as a means of painting moving scenery with light. It could possibly have been the enterprising Urban's suggestion.

A shrewd organizer and astute business man, Charles Urban, after becoming a salesman for Edison films and the Edison Projecting Kinetoscope in America, had developed his own projector, the Bioscope, came to London in 1897 where he organized the Warwick Trading Company for export and import trade, brought out the Warwick camera and settled down to his special interest, the documentary film. Some of his factual films were not as factual as they might have been. In 1902 he presented pictures of the coronation of Edward VII; the exterior scenes were authentic but the coronation itself was a reconstruction made in Paris by Georges Méliès, of whom more shortly. However, most of his actualities were dignified and informative records. He founded the Urban Trading Company in 1903, retaining his own patents and contracts, and distributed not only his films but those of various foreign manufacturers. Mesguich, and W. G. Barker, who was to make Shakespeare films, were at various times his cameramen, though not, I think, for *The Tempest*. He is best remembered as the exploiter of a colour film called Kinemacolor, developed by an associate, G. A. Smith. Later Urban's career turned to France and then back to the United States, but during the first decade of the century he headed one of the largest and most far reaching motion picture organizations in England.

At any rate, Tree's presentation of *The Tempest* provided material spectacular enough for independent exhibition as well. It had opened on September 14, 1904, ran for a hundred forty-three performances, and was subsequently revived. 'In the production at His Majesty's,' wrote the *Era* of September 17th, 'modern science has enabled Mr Tree to fairly stagger us by some wonderful storm effects and to produce a magnificent realization of the shipwreck that opens the play. The vessel takes up the whole of the stage . . . Amid the shrieking of the wind and the roaring thunder we hear faintly the voices of the ship's master and the boatswain; the very timbers seem to creak; the mainmast snaps like a piece of matchwood; and the spectacle is really awesome. In the triumphs of modern stagecraft nothing quite so fine as this shipwreck has been seen, and it will be the talk of London.'

Urban's catalogue and that of George Kleine, who brought the film to America, are more graphic about the storm and more explicit about the film, which was 'photographed through the courtesy of Mr Beerbohm Tree by special and exclusive arrangement. This remarkable picture, taken under the ordinary conditions of stage lighting during representation, illustrates the great advances in animated photography which the motion camera has rendered possible. The shipwreck with all its intense realism is reproduced with startling detail. The lightnings flash, the billows leap and roll, and break, until on the tossing ship, where the terror-stricken voyagers can be seen wildly rushing about the mast snaps and crashes to the deck. Three views are given in the film, each from a more distant point as the wreck recedes, and as the film is issued tinted to the suitable weird moonlight color, the effect obtained is very fine. It is also issued artistically colored, which greatly heightens the wonderful effect of what is unquestionably one of the greatest triumphs of stage production ever attempted.' The film storm was 100 feet in length, and was over in less than 2 minutes. Tree was not in the picture – he played Caliban – and I hope Viola Tree's Ariel did not flame amazement, but presumably 'wildly rushing about' and visible for $13.00, Kleine's price for the film, were J. Fisher White as Gonzalo, S. A. Cookson as Alonzo, Lyn Harding as Antonio, W. A. Haines as the Boatswain, Basil Gill as Ferdinand, and assorted mariners, howling inaudibly, 'All lost!'

Nevertheless this is all comparatively sublime. On the other hand Shakespeare was in this period forced to lend his name or his weight to the ridiculous. The 'Edison Films' Catalogue No. 135 of September 1902 lists under 'Imported Films' a *Burlesque on Romeo and Juliet*, 75 feet, $9.00. The story detailed makes no sense and has nothing to do with Shakespeare except for the inclusion of a kind of balcony scene. I make no apology for failing too to summarize two American films, *A Midwinter Night's Dream*, or *Little Joe's Luck* (Vitagraph, 600 feet, 1906) and *All's Well That Ends Well* (Selig, 760 feet, 1907) which show no Shakespearean influence whatever except in their titles.

In these absurdities, the camera was clearly the whole show, but it was also used as an accompaniment to sound. It had been employed originally for the still pictures of optical lantern days to form illustration to song or recitation. In 1901, for example, Harbach and Co., film and photographic supply dealers, were offering a 'grand recitation, with ten exquisite coloured slides' of *The Merchant of Venice*, priced at $5.00. A favourite was the 'Seven Ages' speech of Jaques from *As You Like It*. I suspect the *Seven Ages* motion picture offered by Edison in 1905 was used as a background for oral delivery; at least it is difficult to see how it could have been effective in silence. Perhaps, however, the eight views copyrighted February 27 were part of an early sound film. Synchronization of motion picture and the phonograph had been achieved in Edison's West Orange workshop as early as 1899; in fact the invention of the motion picture as we know it today sprang from attempts to do for the eye what the phonograph did for the ear. Indeed Edison was supplying to exhibitors synchronized films and recordings.

Synchronization of visual images and music ran parallel to silent films. Cossira, we recall, had sung an aria from Gounod's *Roméo et Juliette*, probably 'Ah! Lève-toi soleil,' in Maurice's sound films at the Phono-Cinéma-Théâtre in 1900. Some years later, perhaps in 1907, primitive sound film was to introduce Germany's first film star, Henny Porten. The daughter of an actor and singer, she mimed for the camera with her father, Franz, and sister, Rosa, appropriate action for the illustration of excerpts of opera played on records. One of the records was the 'Death of Othello' from Verdi's *Otello*. A picture in her autobiography shows Fräulein Henny 'in den letzen Zugen' on a draped bed, Franz in the leading role standing at its foot about to stab himself, five supernumeraries raising their hands in protest, and Rosa as Emilia (?) seated in front of them in the right foreground. Such scenes were photographed in the Berlin studios of the pioneer of German cinema, Oskar Messter, who had begun making films with a camera of his own devising in 1896. The décor was simple and hasty, the costumes rented for the occasion. The camera ground while the record played, and the film was of course of the same duration. The usual procedure was one film before breakfast as soon as the sunlight was suitable, and one or two afterward. The direction was handled principally by Franz Porten, but Carl Froelich, who had been a cameraman with Messter since 1905 may well have assisted. The synchronization process was known as Biophon; it had been developed by Messter as early as 1903 before he opened the first really commodious cinema theatre in Germany on Unter den Linden in 1905. He and Henry Porten were to be associated for many years. Such was the début of the girl who was to become not only the most popular film actress in Germany but a symbol of German womanhood.

But though experiment was frequent, sound film was not in the main stream of development; like the photographs of stage action, the recitation and musical pictures were aberrations. They were aberrations because they showed no recognition of the unique and special capabilities of the motion camera as an interpreter nor of cinematic ideas. One man, however, who incidentally concerned himself with Shakespeare, did have a real, if limited, creative vision, and if it could not at this period be used successfully because of the limits of duration and the absence of lines, to present on the screen anything which allowed a significant presentation of the dramatist's plays, there was at least a realization of the need under these conditions of adaptation to the new medium rather than a mere reproduction of another art. That man was a Frenchman, Georges Méliès.

The versatile Méliès was at the time of the exhibition of the Lumière films at the Grand Café a professional magician and the proprietor of the Théâtre Robert-Houdin near the Opéra, where he presented his transformations and feats of prestidigitation. Excited by what seemed to him a revelation of possibilities, he acquired a camera and began photographing in motion the familiar sights of Paris streets. On one occasion his film jammed in the camera. When he later projected it, he discovered to his surprise that a bus he had been shooting had suddenly turned into a hearse. By an accident he had achieved a new kind of transformation. Realism could be turned into film fantasy. He had already tried some experiments in this direction but now he saw his path more clearly. In 1897 he built a practical studio behind his house at Montreuil and turned in earnest to the production of films suitable not only to his own predilections but to presentation at the Théâtre Robert-Houdin, scenes of magic, stories of the supernatural, subjects already prearranged. For these films he made his own designs, with assistants constructing the settings, hired performers from the music halls, and directed and photographed them – or when he was in them, had them photographed –

B

on the stage he had constructed at one end of the studio. In the process he discovered many of the techniques of the camera which would further his aims of mystifying spectators and transporting them to a world that never was: stop, slow, fast, and reverse motion; double exposure and animation; fades and dissolves. For a decade Méliès' fantastic and trick films enjoyed enormous success not only in Paris, but elsewhere in Europe and in America.

Méliès was an intelligent and well-read man in both French and English, and if he turned naturally to Jules Verne, it was also to be expected that he would dabble with Shakespeare. His 1899 film inaccurately titled *Cléopatre* showed no such dabbling, but in 1901 he made a picture, *Le Diable et la statue*, which included two Venetian lovers, Roméo and Juliette, and a balcony scene. Otherwise the story had nothing to do with Shakespeare. Another early Méliès film also bears some relationship, probably equally slight, to Shakespeare, *Le Miroir de Venise* (*Une Mésaventure de Shylock*), but of this there is no extant scenario. So far there is nothing that could really be called adaptation of Shakespeare; there is merely borrowing of the names of characters or a setting or a situation.

In 1907, however, Méliès came out with a *Hamlet*, and though this is not a particularly characteristic Méliès film nor probably one of his best, it does show him deliberately cutting and rearranging the story in order to make it intelligible within the compass of 570 feet of film by means of flashbacks and visions. Of this *Hamlet* we fortunately have a full summary in the delicious English of Gaston Méliès, Georges' brother, who was his representative and general manager in the United States.

'The melancholy disposition of the young prince is demonstrated to good advantage in the grave-yard scene where the diggers are interrupted in their weird pastime of joshing among the tombstones by the appearance of Hamlet and his friend. After questioning them he picks up one of the skulls about a newly-dug grave, and is told that it is the skull of a certain Yorick who was known to Hamlet in his natural life. Hamlet slowly takes up the skull, and his manner strongly indicates, "Alas, poor York, I knew him well!" The following scenes combine to show the high state of dementia of the young prince's mentality. He is seen in his room where he is continually annoyed and excited by apparitions which taunt him in their weirdness and add bitterness to his troubled brain. He attempts to grasp them but in vain, and he falls to brooding. Now is shown the scene in which he meets the ghost of his father and is told to take vengeance on the reigning monarch, his uncle; but not content with this, Hamlet's fates tantalize him further by sending into his presence the ghost of his departed sweetheart, Ophelia. He attempts to embrace her as she throws flowers to him from a garland on her brow, but his efforts are futile; and when he sees the apparition fall to the ground, he, too swoons away, and is thus found by several courtiers. He is raving mad and storms about in a manner entirely unintelligible to them; but they calm him gradually. The last scene shows the duel before the King, when Hamlet returns from the fool's errand upon which his royal uncle had sent him in order to get rid of him. The word is passed, and the well-known story of the duel before the King takes place in pictures which show the Prince's antagonist as he falls after a fierce combat. Now the episode of the poisoned drink, which the King has prepared for Hamlet, is depicted; his villainous mother takes the drink instead, and falls lifeless. Hamlet is now desperate, and bidding the courtiers to stand aside, he ends the life of his wicked uncle with one thrust of his sword, and then turns the weapon on himself; before dying he tells the secret of his terrible enmity toward the King, then sinks to the ground. Lying upon his shield, he is carried off on the shoulders of the courtiers.'

It is easy to brand this ten-minute film an absurd simplification, and one which could not fail to tickle the risibilities of a sophisticated audience. But Méliès audiences were not sophisticated, and the film was a primitive of 1907. It may not have been, as it was advertised, 'An artistic film reproduction for lovers of the great playwright,' but it was nevertheless a distinct advance over anything which had heretofore been achieved in Shakespeare film. Here was a picture which contained at least three scenes, in those scenes told the story of the main external action in *Hamlet*, attempted to convey some of the perturbation of the Prince's mind, and did these things by using the camera to create effects proper to itself, and difficult or impossible to realize satisfactorily on the stage. It eschewed the chronological method for a kind of montage, partially escaped from mere realistic reproduction, and concentrated on major scenes at the end of the plot. In other words, this film is basically an adaptation of Shakespeare's play in cinematic terms. As stills make clear, Méliès himself acted Hamlet; he was shortly to play Shakespeare himself.

Méliès' last Shakespeare film, also of 1907, stemmed not from a play but the creation of one. It was called *Le Rêve de Shakespeare* or *La Mort de Jules César*, or more frequently in English, *Shakespeare Writing Julius Caesar*. It showed according to an advertisement; 'How Shakespeare conceived his world-famed death scene. An elaborate reproduction costumed and staged according to the history of ancient Rome.' Shorter than *Hamlet*, it was in 344 feet. Again the *Star* Film Catalogue comes to the rescue with details.

'The idea of the film is a novel one. It shows the bard of Avon seated in his study, trying to devise the scene in which Caesar is murdered by the conspirators. He makes several attempts, but apparently the results are unsatisfactory to him. He reads them over and over and then begins to pace the room impatiently. At his wits' end, he sits down in an armchair, crosses his legs, and leaning on his hand prepares for a good, long think. Suddenly his thoughts take life, and right before him appears an old Roman forum. Shakespeare is still seated in his armchair and now watches all that occurs.

Several classical female figures appear and one of them burns incense; after stepping around the small flame, they take their leave. Now the conspirators – Brutus, Cassius, Casca and the others enter, debating hotly on what action to take against their dictator. After an argument, they draw swords and pointing them to the ground together they swear that Julius Caesar shall die. While this is going on Shakespeare is an interested spectator – it seems to be just what he had been striving for. Now Caesar enters with two consuls, and all three seat themselves. Now the conspirators one at a time lay their grievances before the dictator. The first two do naught but speak, but the third, in his frenzy, raises his dirk. Caesar, however, envelopes his face in a fold of his tunic, and the would-be assassin desists from striking the defence-less man; but the next conspirator is quicker, for he suddenly draws his sword and Caesar falls from one stroke. The scene now changes to Shakespeare's study again; the poet recovers himself, realizes that he at last has come upon the required idea and begins to stalk about excitedly, going it all over for himself. While he does this his servant enters with a tray of food, but Shakespeare pays no attention to him but keeps on tearing and ranting about the room in his passion. Alone he goes through the entire scene and winds up by raising a knife and plunging it furiously into the loaf of bread which was on the table. Realizing the humour of the situation he now joins in a hearty laugh with his servant, but is unable to eat from enthusiasm. When the servant leaves the room he steps back and folds his arms, and the scene dissolves into a bust of William Shakespeare, around which all the nations wave flags and garlands.'

The dissolve unfortunately shows the author of a pleasant little scenario yielding to the magician and the need for a transformation, however inappropriate. Evidently Shakespeare made some slight changes in his plans before *Julius Caesar* was given to the world.

Méliès' Shakespeare films show both his virtues and his limitations. He was full of ideas and he was a man of great technical resources. He was aware that the camera could do something more than take pictures of whatever was at hand or convenient, that it could be used creatively. His careful pre-arrangements led to considered results and in his fairy tales and planetary travels there was something both childlike and poetic or occasionally satiric. But his ingenuity was not always tastefully applied, and his vision was curtailed by his delight in magic. The purpose of his films was too frequently not to convince but to baffle. His shooting of scenes on a stage led often to *tableaux vivants* rather than to cinematic action. Nevertheless he made great advances and was much imitated. Unfortunately by 1907 he had reached his peak and a decline had started in his fortunes. Méliès lived in a world of his own. He did not or could not adapt to whatever progress was being made by others; the others learned from him. He sold his positives outright long after most manufacturers were using a system of rental distribution. He stayed indoors when others went out. His fantasies were too much alike and began to pall. When he turned to other subjects, he illustrated rather than re-created them. Though he continued to make pictures until the War, he could not keep up with competition and had to make an unfortunate alliance with Pathé. He lost his home, his studio, and his films. For fourteen years, he all but vanished. In 1928 he was recognized selling toys and candy at the Gare Montparnasse. He was helped by friends, tendered an elaborate banquet, decorated with the Cross of the Legion of Honour. In 1932 the Chambre Syndicale Française du Cinématographe arranged for him to pass his last years at the chateau d'Orly. He died in 1938. Méliès had founded the Chambre in 1897 and for ten years been its president. On fortune's cap he was not the very button, but he did have dreams.

CHAPTER II

What, All in Motion?

SHAKESPEARE BY VITAGRAPH (1908-1911)

AND suddenly there was a march of Shakespeare on film. 1908 was the key year, 1908 through 1911 the period. The United States led the way; with somewhat different impulses, Italy and France joined the parade. In four years, not counting minor adaptations and petty pilferings, almost fifty new productions of Shakespeare were on the screens in America, England, and on the Continent. They included seventeen of Shakespeare's plays, seven of the tragedies, six of the comedies, two each of the dramatic romances and English histories. Most of them were in one reel, approximately a thousand feet of film; some spilled over into two; one anticipated the feature picture of a later era. Why were more Shakespeare films made in this period than in any comparable span later, more in 1908 than in any subsequent year?

There were no doubt cross-influences from one country to another. This was the period of the 'art film' in France and Italy and the stage-film in England. But these films with theatre actors, though they represent something pervasive in the air – and the air was international – do not for the most part explain what lay behind the work and the choices of the studios in New York. The American films tended to get off the stage and go outdoors; they made little appeal to the intelligentsia; they did not employ known writers or name actors from the theatre – indeed, it was only gradually that companies revealed the identity of their mimers, and to movie audiences they were with a few exceptions merely familiar faces. In order to explain why there were ten American Shakespeare films in 1908, it is necessary to know what was happening in the United States.

By 1908 the story picture had become general. News items, local events, vaudeville skits, and comic episodes were no longer sufficient. For camera narratives, people were now writing scenarios as fast as they could but there were not enough. It was natural to borrow from literature and the stage, and surely Shakespeare himself would have approved. Moreover his variety of scenes fitted in well with new conceptions of scenario structure, with cutting and editing. For some years the major companies had been copyrighting their films in Washington, but for their scripts they went to whatever literary sources were handy or would be effective. Surely photographs could not be considered a means of plagiarism from written words, and no acknowledgments were necessary. But in 1907 the Kalem Company produced a *Ben Hur*, and was promptly sued by its publisher, the producers of a stage version, and the administrator of the estate of Lew Wallace's heir. Though the suit was not settled against Kalem until 1911, it had to be defended, and it frightened the major producers. One way of avoiding legal difficulties was to disguise their reconstructions, but another was to make use of authors not protected by copyright. Shakespeare was not concerned with rights and royalties.

An additional drive toward Shakespeare stemmed from the need for respectability. When the motion picture was an infant phenomenon, it impressed because it was a novelty and because it moved. Few cared what it said or implied. But narratives involve people, and people, conduct and morality. Favourite subjects were portrayals of crime, or risqué situations (at least according to the titles). There were sordid settings exemplifying a crude realism. The attraction of the *vulgus* could be maintained by vulgarity. In 1907 there were the first serious attacks from outraged society. The movies it was said in print, appealed to the baser passions, caused juvenile delinquency. Though the industry martialled its forces in reply, it knew the opposition had both power and justice on its side. It joined in 1909 in the formation of the National Board of Censorship of Motion Pictures, which later became the National Board of Review. Meanwhile no one could object to Shakespeare. It is ironic that someone did. In Chicago the police censor called the Vitagraph *Macbeth* 'worse than the bloodiest melodrama' and ordered the deletion of the stabbing of Duncan, the brandishing of a bloody dagger, and the duel between Macbeth and Macduff.

The enormous expansion of the industry in America invited the search for the untried. From 1903 the exchange system brought wider distribution, increased profits, and the clamour for more pictures. By 1907 there were over a hundred film exchanges. Renters and distributors not content with their own incomes went into manufacture to supply the demand. The major companies left the streets for roof-top stages, and in 1906 for permanent and specially constructed studios where they could use the newly developed mercury-vapour lamps. By 1908 there were close to ten thousand nickle-odeons, five-cent 'theatres', mostly in stores. In 1905 Kalem had been founded on $600; three years later it was making a net profit of $5,000 a week. The larger Vitagraph was filming four pictures a week, twice as many as Kalem. The competition among companies was incessant. Much of it was quantitative, but it was also qualitative. The better the pictures, the better the profits. How could their films be improved? Well, Shakespeare was the best dramatist in the world, wasn't he? People spoke well of him. And finally, there were some concerned with the production of films who had read Shakespeare and acted in his plays. In at least two cases, they could urge, and even more important, act as directors of Shakespeare films.

One of those men was to come in 1908 into the Vitagraph company, the producer of the largest number of Shakespeare films ever made by one company: not counting a title-borrowing for an otherwise non-Shakespearean *Comedy of Errors*, ten of them within less than two years. Vitagraph, one of the earliest and largest of the producing organisations, was found in 1899 in William T. Rock's billiard hall on 125th Street by combining the interests of three people who had already been making or exhibiting films. 'Pop' Rock had bought in 1896 from Edison a Vitascope, one of the prefected Kineto-scopes, with territorial rights for the state of Louisiana, where he exhibited films. In the same year J. Stuart Blackton, usually Jimmy, a free-lance sketcher, entertainer, and newspaper writer, had been sent by the New York *World* to interview Edison about his new machine. Edison told him that his latest, the Projecting Kinetoscope, would soon be on the market. Blackton and a friend, Albert E. Smith, who was clever with his hands, acquired one and began giving shows. The ingenious Smith shortly turned the apparatus into a camera and they began to take pictures, first on the pavements, and then on the roof of the Morse Building on Nassau Street. They called themselves Vitagraph. When Rock, now a free lance as well as the operator of the billiard parlour, began to take away their customers, they joined in partnership rather than fight each other. The combination pros-pered and in 1906 the firm acquired property in western Flatbush and built a studio. It was here that Vitagraph assembled a kind of stock company of actors and here or from here that they made their Shakespeare films. Blackton was in charge of the choice and direction of films but the rapidly expanding business needed additional assistance. An advertisement in the New York *Clipper* brought to the studio one William V. Ranous.

'Billy' Ranous had been in the theatre since childhood in a variety of capacities. Actor, stage manager and director, he is nevertheless difficult to trace because he was so frequently 'out-of-town' with minor companies. He made a kind of speciality of copying New York hits and jumping to the sticks with a scrub group of players until the law caught up with him. In more legitimate activities, he played 'heavies' or character parts and stage managed road companies. In New York his roles were usually bits, which he acted competently. He played unimportant characters in plays starring Fanny Janauschek, as early as 1874, and was at various times with Salvini, George Rignold, Genevieve Ward, Ernesto Rossi, Frank S. Chanfrau, Margaret Mather, Kyrle Bellew and Eleanor Robson. Some of his parts were in Shakespeare. He had done some acting in moving pictures made by the Edison company. If published theatre annals say little about him, he was obviously a man of wide experience, and a valuable acquisition for Vitagraph. Ranous was a theatre man; Blackton was not. Ranous had played Shakes-peare, and probably also stage managed and directed some of Shakespeare's plays. It seems reasonable to suspect that now the time was ripe, he urged or supported Blackton in the decision to film Shakespeare at Vitagraph. In any case he directed most of the Shakespeare films made by the company and acted in some of them. When he left Vitagraph in the fall of 1909 to become the first director for the newly organised Imp, the Independent Motion Picture Company of Carl Laemmle, the number of Vitagraph's Shakespeare pictures dwindled.

Paul Panzer, later the villain of the famous serial, *The Perils of Pauline*, reminiscenced in 1917 about Shakespeare film production at Vitagraph and gives us a valuable picture of activity in the studio.

'And it was when we began work in Flatbush that we had our first salaried director – the late William V. Ranous . . . . He was a Shakespearean actor of the late Salvini school and a most capable man. Under his direction, Vitagraph produced *Macbeth*, *Richard the Third*, *Othello*, *Romeo and Juliet*, *King Lear* and other Shakespearean plays. They were all in one reel each. Those are the days that I remember best. We built our own scenery and props, and we certainly must have presented an incongruous sight, doing carpenter work and painting canvas while we were dressed in the costumes of Shakespeare's time. After we had built a set we threw saw, hammer and paint brush aside and stepped on to the stage and assumed the characters drawn by the immortal Bard.

'In this connection there is one thing that stands out with cameo clearness in my memory. There was a happy trio at the studio – a little girl named Florence Turner, a young man named Hector Dion and myself. Mr Dion and I built our own frames for the scenery, and Miss Turner sewed the canvas together on a borrowed sewing machine. When all was ready, we three would tack the canvas on the frame. For these services we received the magnificent salary of $14 a week; but we got $3 a day extra when we played in pictures. As a memento of those times Mr Blackton still has one of the rough battle axes that I made of wood for the production of *Macbeth* . . . .'

Macbeth was indeed the first of the plays to be filmed by Vitagraph; 835 feet long, it was released on April 17, 1908, and could be obtained 'beautifully tinted'. It contained at least seventeen sequences with the emphasis on the first part of the play. The witches are shown before an effectively atmospheric studio backdrop of gnarled trees; they hail Macbeth and Banquo; Macbeth is informed that he is now Thane of Cawdor; Duncan names Malcolm his heir; Lady Macbeth receives her husband's letter; Duncan arrives at their castle; Macbeth sees a supernatural dagger; Duncan is dispatched; his murder is discovered; Banquo meets his death; his ghost appears at the feast; Lady Macbeth sleepwalks; Birnam Wood comes to Dunsinane; Macbeth is finally killed. There were other scenes too, but the rest are difficult to identify.

It is necessary to warn the reader of the uncritical enthusiasm displayed by trade papers, but the review in the London *Kinematagraph and Lantern Weekly* of May 14 shows not only that the Vitagraph *Macbeth* was almost immediately exhibited abroad but also something further about the film.

'This firm are to be congratulated on the masterly way in which they have staged Shakespeare's tragedy. The famous play contains many situations which lend themselves admirably to effective treatment in picture form, and the company have made the most of them. Thus in the first scene, when the three 'Weird Sisters' prophesy that Macbeth shall be King we are shown him as in a vision, in the King's robes and crown. Another effective scene reveals Macbeth on his way to murder the King, the appearance of the dagger being cleverly represented. Then in order are pictured the other famous scenes of the play, culminating in Macbeth's death at the hand of Malcolm [?] . . . . Each scene is cleverly set, the costumes are accurate and the acting good and we shall be surprised if this does not prove one of the most successful of recent subjects.'

Two stills show Macbeth killing Duncan and Banquo's ghost at the banquet, the latter confirming the hint of double exposure in the review. Other details of the film are pointed out in the published remarks of the unfortunate Police Lieutenant who censored it in Chigaco. He rules especially against its realism. It is difficult to have much sympathy with censorship, but the point of view becomes understandable.

'I am not taking issue with Shakespeare. As a writer he is far from reproach. But he never looked into the distance and saw that his plots were going to be interpreted for the five-cent theater.

'Shakespeare has a way of making gory things endurable, because there is so much of art and finish. But you can't reproduce that. The moving picture people get a bunch of Broadway loafers in New York to go through the motions and interpret Shakespeare . . . .

'The stabbing scene in the play is not predominant. But in the picture show it is the feature. In the play the stabbing is forgotten in the other exciting and artful and artistic creations that divert the imagination. On the canvas you see the dagger enter and come out and see the blood flow and the wound that's left.

'Shakespeare is art, but it's not adapted altogether for the 5-cent style of art.'

If the Lieutenant was right, the picture did not live up to its subtitle: 'Shakespeare's Sublime Tragedy,' though Billy Ranous, who played Macbeth, made the most of his opportunities. A Miss Carver was the Lady Macbeth, Panzer was the Macduff, and I suspect Charles Kent doubled as Duncan and Banquo, thereby being killed twice.

> 'The time has been
> That when the brains were out, the man would die'

As far as one can gather, *Macbeth* was largely taken in the studio; for its next Shakespeare film, *Romeo and Juliet*, Vitagraph shot much of the action outdoors. The evidence is conclusive, for this is one of the films which has survived. In addition there are more stills to examine, and much more was published about it than for *Macbeth*. The balcony scenes for example, utilized a house near Fort Hamilton, Brooklyn. The duel between Romeo and Tybalt was fought on the paved terrace at the south end of the Boat Lake in Central Park, close by the tiered Bethesda Fountain surmounted by the winged Angel of the Waters. The figures on the fountain of Temperance, Purity, Health and Peace are perhaps only ironically suitable to the atmosphere of street fighting in Verona, but they were well in the background, and there is at least a tenuous appropriateness in that they, as well as the Angel, had been executed by the sculptress, Emma Stebbins, who at the time of their completion in 1865 was living in Rome in the home of Charlotte Cushman. The outdoor contestants were Paul Panzer as Romeo, and John G. Adolfi as Tybalt, both later with Warner Bros, the one as actor, the second as director. The Juliet of this film was Florence Lawrence. Others recognizable are Ranous as the apothecary – he also directed – Charles Kent as Capulet, Charles Chapman as Montague, William Shea as Peter, and Miss Carver as the Nurse. Josephine Atkinson, who the next year was to become Mrs Panzer, had a bit part. *Romeo and Juliet* was 915 feet in length, could be had tinted, and was released on June 2, 1908.

Romeo and Juliet was advertised by Vitagraph, not quite accurately as in nine scenes:

'Scene 1—Capulet introduces his daughter, Juliet, to Paris, her future husband.
Scene 2—Romeo, son of Montague [Capulet's enemy] enters Capulet's house during a masked ball and there meets Juliet.
Scene 3—Love at first sight. [The wall-leaping and balcony scene.]
Scene 4—The secret marriage of Romeo and Juliet in Friar Lawrence's cell.
Scene 5—Infuriated by the death of his friend, Mercutio, Romeo fights and kills Tybalt, a kinsman of Juliet, and is banished by the Prince.
Scene 6—Capulet insists on Juliet's marriage to Paris.
Scene 7—'Take this potion and for two days you will be as dead, then I will come to the tomb and awaken you [used as a subtitle].'
Scene 8—Hearing of the supposed death of Juliet, Romeo buys poison and prepares to kill himself.
Scene 9—Juliet recovers from the effect of the potion and, finding that Romeo is no more, joins him in death.'
[The reconciliation between the two houses follows].

This summary omits the picture of Juliet drinking the potion, a shot of

breaking in the door of Juliet's room, and the scene of the discovery by
the Capulets and Paris of the supposedly dead heroine. It is worth noting
that the door shot here provided a visually effective bit of excitement which
is not in Shakespeare, or at least it would have if Capulet had not succeeded
with ridiculous ease in shattering an apparently massive portal. Roughly
speaking, the motion picture followed incidents and suggestions in Shakespeare's I, 2 (though Paris is actually introduced to Juliet); I, 4 and 5; II, 1
(in the picture Romeo leaps onto a porch and hides from his friends behind
a pillar); II, 2 (the balcony is on the second floor of one wing of a fairly
spacious, modern, stucco house); II, 3 and 6 combined (Romeo, Friar
Lawrence, and the marriage); II, 4 (the Nurse and Peter deliver Juliet's
message to Romeo, not mentioned in the scenario because it is combined
with: III, 1 (the duel); III, 5 (Romeo's departure from Juliet by rope ladder,
not listed as a scene by Vitagraph, and Capulet's insistence on the marriage
to Paris); IV, 1 (Juliet's visit to Friar Lawrence); IV, 3 (the drinking of the
potion); IV, 5 (the discovery of Juliet apparently dead); V, 1 (the apothecary
scene); and V, 3 (played entirely within the tomb).

The film is in its way surprising. The essentials of the story are told, on
the whole clearly, and the viewer is assisted by leaders which correspond
to the items of the Vitagraph synopsis already quoted. Naturally one cannot
hope for much in fifteen minute Shakespeare, but less than might be expected
is there a feeling that the story is absurdly compressed. The Vitagraph
comment said; 'This, the most beautiful of Shakespeare's plays, has been
magnificently staged, gorgeously costumed, and superbly acted by a large
and competent cast. Particular attention has been given to detail and scenic
effects.' If all due allowance is made for partiality, there is some truth in
the statement. There is no real historical authenticity in the picture, but
the anachronism of setting and costume are not bothersome and would be
unnoticed by a movie audience of 1908. A modern audience might wonder
why there was a 'V' on the canopy of Juliet's bed and another over the
Gothic doorway which is the entrance to Friar Lawrence's cell; this was
not for Verona but an attempted protection against illegal duping by the
display of the Vitagraph trademark in various sequences. Some parts were
played in a sort of court with a portico in the background, and both the
Central Park and the tomb scenes, the best in the film, have architectural
quality and are by no means unimpressive. On the other hand the apothecary scene is played before an elaborate but obviously painted backdrop.
The costumes are on the whole satisfactory, if nothing more. The acting
is less flamboyant than in most pictures of the period. Juliet's tumble onto
her bed after drinking the potion is rather violently comical, and Romeo at
his demise settles himself too comfortably at the base of the steps before
the bier of Juliet. Nevertheless the effects are not entirely theatrical. The
camera remained stationary but there is cinematic movement and the pace
is good. There is even some deliberate cross-cutting, so as to convey the

story by alternation. Any attempt to compare Vitagraph's *Romeo and Juliet* with a modern film would be ridiculous, but this movie version of the star-crossed lovers is for 1908 remarkably successful.

I am glad to know that it did not, like *Macbeth*, displease the Chicago censor.

'*Romeo and Juliet*, on the other hand is different. There are violence and suicide and duelling there, too. But the manager knows that the love element, not the fight element, predominates, and he knows that when anyone pays 5 cents to see *Romeo and Juliet* films, he pays to see love. When he pays 5 cents to see *Macbeth* he pays to see a fight. So love is the feature of the *Romeo and Juliet* films, and love is fit for children to see, if kept within reason.'

Whatever one may think of this as Shakespearean criticism it should be noted that the fights in the Vitagraph *Romeo and Juliet* were very good indeed.

For some reason there is little information to be had about Vitagraph's *Othello*, which I take to be next in order. It was not copyrighted; the trade journals carry no summaries or reviews; there is no announcement of the date of release. However in a general article by W. Stephen Bush in the *Moving Picture World* of September 5, 1908, an *Othello* is mentioned in the same breath as films of *Macbeth* and *Romeo and Juliet*, and the reference is all but certainly to this series. Mr Panzer's recollections and stills which we examined together in 1949 confirm 1908 and indicate that Ranous directed and played *Othello*. The Iago was Hector Dion; the Cassio, Panzer. Adolfi may have been the Roderigo – at any rate it is apparent from a faded photograph that he was in the cast – and Charles Chapman and Ralph Ince can be made out as soldiers. A still reproduced in an article by Blackton in *Photoplay*, July 1919, and its caption establish that Desdemona was impersonated by Julia Swayne Gordon, and confirm Ranous as the lead. Othello is in a gondola on the Grand Canal before a door at which stands Desdemona. The gondola was actually on wheels in a wooden trough. The 'V' over an adjoining window is not for Venice, any more than it was for Verona in *Romeo and Juliet*.

For its next Shakespeare pictures, Vitagraph shifted to history, first English, then Roman. *Richard III* in 990 feet was released on September 22, 1908. Ranous no doubt directed and probably played the lead in a film adapted from the Cibber version. It is difficult to assign others, but two of the ladies were Florence Turner and Julia Swayne Gordon, and a third, Florence Auer, we meet for the first time. Linda Griffith places her there, and also adds to the cast Thomas H. Ince, who was as a director to be a major force in the development of the American film. They were not regular members of the company; Miss Auer played character comedy at Biograph.

I distrust summaries by the producers but in that supplied by Vitagraph, if it is accurate, there is some indication of what was included:

'*Exterior of the Tower of London*. Tressel brings to the dethroned King Henry the news of the loss of the battle of Tewksbury and the death of the King's son. "Now is the winter of our discontent." The Duke of Gloucester (afterward King Richard III) enters the tower and kills the imprisoned King Henry VI. "Down to hell, and say I sent thee there." The Duke of Gloucester stops the funeral procession of Henry VI, woos and wins Lady Anne. Inside the palace, Queen Elizabeth and the Duchess of York are weeping over the death of Edward IV. To this Gloucester remarks, "These tears look well; sorrow's the mode. With all my heart I'll not be out of fashion," and he weeps too.

'*Plotting for the Crown. Crosby Palace.* – The Little Prince of Wales on the throne is visited by his brother, the Duke of York. He jokingly makes a lamb of the Duke of Gloucester, who advises the two princes to live in the tower until the Prince of Wales is ready to be crowned Edward V, but privately intends that they shall never leave the tower alive. The Duke of Gloucester, now married to Lady Anne, wishes that she were dead. The Lord Mayor of London, urged by the Duke of Buckingham, offers Gloucester the crown, which he accepts, and immediately after orders the two princes in the tower to be separated from their mother. The Duke of Gloucester, as King Richard III, is now seated on the throne of England. He endeavors to persuade the Duke of Buckingham to consent to the murder of the two young princes. Buckingham refuses and he bribes Sir James Tyrell and two of his followers to smother them. Buckingham now claims his reward for assisting to make Richard the King of England, but Richard, in a rage, replies, "I'm busy, thou troublest me. I'm not in the giving vein."

'Richard, with his army on the way to battle, is halted by his mother and the Duchess of York and Queen Elizabeth, and cursed for his evil deeds. Catesby brings news of the loss of Buckingham's army and the capture of Buckingham. "Off with his head; so much for Buckingham." While Richard sleeps in troubled dreams the spirits of those whom he has killed visit him and call upon him to "despair and die". They vanish and he wakes in terror.

> Hence, bubbling dreams,
> You threaten here in vain;
> Conscience, avaunt!
> Richard's himself again.

'Closing scene, battle of Bosworth Field, showing death of Richard III and the crowning of the Earl of Richmond as Henry VII, King of England.'

If the summary is to be taken in good faith, it suggests a fairly crowded story of complicated relationships, difficult to follow in a one-reel picture. If the quotations signify subtitles, it may be a new departure. Nothing is said about either by a reviewer who saw the film at Keith's. 'It is high praise when I say that this film is equal to the other three Shakespeare films which have been put out by this company. The acting of the principal characters ... is all that can be desired, the only blemish in this respect being in the battle scene, where the smiles on the faces of the actors are ill-timed. The staging and scenery is well handled and the film took well with the audience.' Apparently, one may smile and smile, and be an extra.

Did the supernumeraries behave themselves, I wonder, in *Antony and Cleopatra* which was released in 995 feet on November 3rd? Mr Panzer told me that the director was Charles Kent. Apparently Ranous was not available. On the New York stage at least, Kent was better known as an actor than Ranous and had played more important parts. Born in England, he had played in the United States in Shakespeare from 1875 – with Thomas Keene, Barry Sullivan, Rignold, Rossi, and Edwin Booth when the last was supported by the Boston Museum company. He had also performed with Robson and Crane, had indeed created the role of the unscrupulous son in Bronson Howard's enormously successful, *The Henrietta*. I find him on the stage until 1906, but he lost his voice and turned to acting in motion pictures. I know nothing about him as a director of what I very tentatively take to be Betty Kent as Cleopatra, Charles Chapman as Antony, and William Phillips as Octavius. I gather there was some departure from the play in making Antony 'a dashing soldier in the heyday of early manhood.' A summary of this 'stupendous production, a fine picture of Roman pride and Eastern magnificence, elaborately staged, superbly acted' – a summary quite obviously furnished by Vitagraph, in listing the scenes, shows what other departures there were from the text.

'Scenes: Antony's meeting with Cleopatra. Rome and Caesar forgotten. Love at first sight. [What? Again? Compare *Romeo and Juliet*]. Caesar hears of Antony's love for Cleopatra. Antony returns to Caesar. Caesar's anger at Antony. They are reconciled by Antony's marriage to Caesar's sister, Octavia. Cleopatra's wild jealousy on hearing of Antony's marriage. Longing for Cleopatra, Antony leaves Octavia and returns to Egypt. Antony's Defiance to Caesar. The battle lost, Antony asks Eros to kill him. Cleopatra dies by the sting of the deadly asp.'

The sequences in the Library of Congress indicate thirteen scenes, say, a quarter of the number Shakespeare used, and without the poetry. There was some attempt in the background to contrast Roman austerity with Egyptian splendour, but all the photography was in the studio and the barge was clearly a stage contrivance. Yet the film pleased reviewer and audience.

'If Shakespeare could only realize the fate of the works he left behind, the modern use of them would cause his prophetic soul to weep. Just think of it! Antony and Cleopatra given in its entirety, with the vocal parts and other details [! ! !] of the regular production cut out, in less than twenty minutes! What a vast difference between the older presentation and that represented by the modernized form of amusement. But with all the condensation, the magnificence was retained, and I heard several in the audience say the film had created in them an appetite for more of the same kind. The Vitagraph Company can take pride in the production. The elaborate stage effects and superb costumes, together with the magnificent manner in which the parts were played, is a credit to the company. The story was told in a concise manner that threw the condensing of the scenes into the shade. The audiences were liberal in expression of appreciation.'

I can only say, 'The man hath seen some majesty, and should know.'

The success achieved in *Antony and Cleopatra* was not maintained in *Julius Caesar*, released by Vitagraph in 980 feet on December 1, 1908. Ranous, according to Mr Panzer, played Antony, and probably directed. But Panzer left for Europe late in 1908; without his presence I have less information on the casts of this and later productions, and I have seen no stills. Charles Kent had played the part of Julius Caesar on the stage in 1888 with Robson and Crane in a benefit for Tony Hart, and may have repeated it here. William Shea was the First Citizen 'and led with the "shouts".' He lets us in on the sort of detail which enlivens the account of production: 'During the taking of this picture a dog spoiled two hundred feet of film by walking into the scene during Antony's oration. *Julius Caesar* was also the means of my getting a raise in salary, because of money I saved the firm. I was sent to town for 100 pairs of brown tights, with instructions to get them in a hurry. Unable to locate more than seven pairs, I conceived the idea of using brown paint. This saved the firm about $60, but lost them the service of a number of actors who had been inveigled into using the paint on their limbs in lieu of tights.' The scene-by-scene synopsis of sequences supplied by Vitagraph of its 'elaborate production' in this case is completely confirmed by the paper film-strips in the Library of Congress.

'Scene 1.—Street in Rome. Casca and Trebonius upbraid the citizens for praising Caesar.

Scene 2.—The Forum. A soothsayer bids Caesar "beware the ides of March."

Scene 3.—Mark Antony wins the race and "thrice he offers Caesar a crown".

Scene 4.—Cassius tempts Brutus to join the conspiracy against Caesar.

Scene 5.—Brutus' garden. Meeting of the conspirators.

Scene 6.—Caesar's palace. Calphurnia tells Caesar of her dream and begs him not to go to the senate. The conspirators enter, laugh at his fears, urge and get his consent to go.

Scene 7.—Street near Capitol. The soothsayer again warns Caesar.

Scene 8.—The Capitol. The assassination of Caesar.

Scene 9.—The Forum. Brutus addresses the mob. Antony enters with
  Caesar's body.
Scene 10.—Brutus' camp near Sardis. Cassius upbraids Brutus.
Scene 11.—Brutus' tent – quarrel – Caesar's ghost.
Scene 12.—Plains of Philippi. Armies of Mark Antony and Octavius Casear,
  and Brutus and Cassius.
Scene 13.—The Battle. "Caesar, thou art revenged even with the sword that
  killeth thee."
Scene 14.—Brutus slays himself. "Caesar, now be still. I killed not thee
  with half so good a will."
Scene 15.—Brutus' funeral pyre. "This was the noblest Roman of them all."'

Almost all of this could have been photographed in the open air but the
incomplete film-strips do not depict the race and the dog apparently
wandered into the studio, for the Forum scene was taken indoors. However,
it is clear that of the last six scenes, all except that in Brutus' tent achieved
some variety and mobility by being shot outdoors, and the funeral pyre
is a deliberately visual addition. Where Brooklyn supplied Sardis and
Philippi, I do not know. A French trade journal thought the mise en scène
'splendide', as well as applauding 'la qualité dramatique' and 'l'esprit de
fidèle reconstitution.' It praised 'ses beaux films . . . dans la série de ses
drames shakespeariens'. In England it was characterized as 'full of life
and splendidly staged, and Scenes 8 and 9, the assassination of Caesar and
Brutus' address to the mob are fine pieces of pantomime'.

But in America commentators either pulled their punches or delivered
them soundly. 'A historical film of some interest. The action is weak,
Caesar especially, but the staging seems to be as nearly correct as possible.
It is, however, marred in some instances by weak photography and an
attempt to tone the film some colour other than black and white. . . . From
the first scene to the death of Brutus the film is watched with eagerness
proving beyond question that almost any audience can be interested in this
class of films. The Vitagraph Company are aiming high, and that alone is
commendable.' For a trade journal, intent on retaining the good will of
producers at the same time as advising potential exhibitors, this is indeed
damning with faint praise. W. Stephen Bush is decidedly more explicit.

'To render *Julius Caesar* into moving pictures, following the outlines of
the Shakespeare play, was a grave and difficult problem. In such a case, a
critic has need to be lenient, and it would be perfectly absurd to apply the
highest standard of criticism. I am inclined to hold that on the whole the
problem has been fairly well solved, and it is surely better that the lovers of
the moving picture have a faulty or imperfect rendering than no rendering
at all. *Julius Caesar* is not up to the standard of *Antony and Cleopatra*,
Richard III, *Macbeth*, and *Othello*. Of course none of these plays without

a lecture are more than a bewildering mass of moving figures to the majority of the patrons of electric theaters, but none stands more emphatically in need of a good lecture than *Julius Caesar*. The adapter has done clever work, the acting of Cassius is superb, that of Antony and Brutus good, but of the Caesar only fair. The scene showing the assassination is excellent, the scene in the forum likewise, and is an exact representation of the famous painting by Gerome [Jean Léon Gérôme (1824–1904)]. The get-up of Antony is burlesque; he looks far too old and resembles a waiter in a French restaurant far more than a dashing Roman [Alas, poor Ranous?] It would be well for all makers of films to bear in mind that the American audiences have a finely developed sense of humor, and there were some broad smiles at the thought of this Mark Antony winning the race at the Lupercal; either the rest of the runners had leaden shoes or the contest was not honestly run. . . . If you want to shoot high it is always well to aim high. The constant offering of swords by Brutus and Cassius to their retainer[s] with a request to be killed is out of place in the film and not a bit necessary, and poorly done at that. When Brutus starts in to do the Roman harikari by proxy, people who have just seen Cassius do the same thing either get tired or begin to laugh. The ending is poor, dramatically and every other way; the "funeral pyre" had a fatal resemblance to a Rhode Island clambake.'

It is a pleasure to run on criticism which is both honest and sprightly, but I doubt if Vitagraph enjoyed it as much as I do. However, it was probably able to laugh off the objection of a 'Reverend Gentleman' who thought that the shortness of Caesar's tunic was proof that 'the movies were an immoral influence'.

The Merchant of Venice, released on December 22nd, concluded Vitagraph's Shakespeare year. Were the productions going down hill or reviewers becoming more critical? There is nothing like the objections to *Julius Caesar*, but an overtone of condescension:

'An ambitious film. The staging is exceptionally good, and this includes the costumes and all accessories. But some of the characters are weak. Shylock himself is not up to standard, though perhaps he is better than some of the others. Nevertheless, the fact that others are weak does not affect the play as much as it does if Shylock is weak. It is a little difficult to follow the thread of the play through some of the scenes, but this is due to necessary elimination. In the main, however, the film is good and deserves a long run. It is a good representation for the money.'

For five cents, that is. Do I detect an unbecoming sneer? And who was the Shylock? Ranous? Portia was Julia Swayne Gordon; and Jessica, Florence Turner. Despite nineteen scenes – the number apparently increases – a clue to the reviewer's failure to mention the ladies may be due to the 'elimination'. The scenes were principally chosen for the Shylock story: about three quarters of them deal with the preliminaries of the loan, his domestic relations, the signing of the bond, the theft of his money chest, and the elopement of his daughter with Lorenzo, the discovery of his loss, his own frantic reaction to it and the mockery of others, and the court scene. In the last of course Portia plays her part, but her wooing is confined to the casket scene, and the last act is entirely omitted. The length, however, was much as usual, 995 feet. Evidently Venice presented an exterior problem which Vitagraph could not easily solve in the vicinity of Brooklyn. All the scenes seem to have been shot in the studio before painted drops, natural enough for the interiors, but somewhat obvious for the backgrounds of St Mark's and the Grand Canal, and there is no evidence at least even for the wheeled gondola used in *Othello*. The principal open air scenes were acted in a street before Shylock's balconied house; the indoor scenes, except for the casket and court scenes, within it. The suspicion arises that the picture was more than usually static and stagy.

This tendency unfortunately continued in Vitagraph's first Shakespeare production of 1909, released on March 27th. One would have thought that *King Lear* offered ample opportunity for outdoor scenes, but there were none; even Gloucester at the cliff and Lear on the heath were played before painted decorations, the latter a simulacrum of Stonehenge. The picture too was subject to a criticism met with earlier, unintelligibility, as a review implies.

'The commendable ambition of the Vitagraph Company to adequately produce classical plays in motion picture pantomime, is not as happily realized in this subject as in previous efforts along the same line. *King Lear* is not an easy subject to handle, and we think the Vitagraph adapters have made the mistake of trying to adhere too closely to the book, instead of taking only the principle incidents of the plot and making these clear in a connected story. The result is that the picture fails to hold the interest of the spectators. The costumes and scenery are faithfully represented, but the photography is dim in parts.'

Insufficient light must have added to the confusion of audiences trying to follow the complicated double plot on 960 feet of film. Evidently an innovation at the beginning of the film to obviate this confusion was insufficient, though it shows the director aware of the problem. This was the introduction of four sequences depicting the principal characters on a kind of dais with name labels. King Lear and the fool, the three daughters, the Earl of Kent, Gloucester and his two sons are each successively shown and identified without action before the play starts with the distribution of the Kingdom. There is even some apparently deliberate differentiation of costume. Thus Regan is in a dark robe, Goneril in light, Cordelia also in light but wearing long braids. As near as can be guessed from the film strips which provide the only basis for estimating the content, the film included the rejection of Cordelia, the perfidy of Edmund, Lear's rejection by Goneril and Regan, the blinding of Gloucester, Lear and the fool in the storm including a hovel scene, Gloucester's attempted suicide, the reunion of Lear and Cordelia and their ultimate deaths, all with intervening intrigue and perhaps other bits as well adding up to seventeen or more sequences. Small wonder if picture theatre patrons gathered little of what it was all about. Of all the plays *King Lear* seems least suited to radical condensation without audible language. Ranous probably directed and may have played Lear. Florence Auer was one of the wicked sisters, Florence Turner the other; Thomas Ince was apparently in it, and Julia Swayne Gordon may perhaps be recognized as Cordelia. It is a pity that the introductory labels did not identify the actors as well as the characters.

Whether or not Vitagraph was disturbed by the adverse criticism or grudging praise which had been greeting its latest Shakespeare films, it now turned not only to lighter subject matter but to freer and less theatrical production methods. *A Midsummer Night's Dream* in 991 feet, made during the summer of 1909 but held for supposedly more appropriate release on December 25th, was one of its most successful films. The reasons are not far to seek, though the first notice in the *Moving Picture World*, December 31st, looks suspiciously as though it stemmed from company publicity: 'The Christmas Day release of the Vitagraph, Shakespeare's *Midsummer Night's Dream* is said to be a charming and magnificent adaptation of the great bard's most poetic play. The outdoor scenes were chosen with a special view to their harmony with the theme. Fortunately the weather and atmospheric conditions were perfect for superb photography so that a series of art pictures have been produced that should attract wide attention.' If 'art pictures' produces a slight shudder both by its self-consciousness and its hint of a comparable European trend, there is at any rate indication here of a deliberate choice of suitable locale and an awareness of the inherent qualities of the play which should somehow be transmitted.

Evidently the *Moving Picture World* of January 8, 1910 had a new critic for in an article on 'Shakespeare on the Screen', the writer starts his review by saying; 'Shakespeare is a dramatist for the moving picture screen as well as for the ordinary stage,' goes on to wonder who will be the first to use this material, to congratulate Vitagraph for its picture, and to add he would like to see all the dramatist's plays adapted into motion pictures, apparently unaware that the company had now filmed nine and showed no particular sign of stopping.

'It was therefore with special interest that we braved the Arctic weather Christmas night for the purpose of seeing the Vitagraph *Midsummer Night's Dream* in a New York moving picture theater. . . . Of course the personal equation must enter very largely into the interpretation of the Shakespearean text. Then again, in such a play . . . the producer is called upon to exercise great skill and judgment so as to compress the scenes into a continuous and intelligible story which does not destroy the narrative – which makes the narrative clear, even to a moving picture audience, which can hardly be supposed to be following the piece on the screen with the text of the play in its hands. Out of the somewhat trying ordeal the Vitagraph people came with great success. They told the story in a word as Shakespeare told it – clearly and intelligibly. None of the salient points of this delightful fairy comedy were missed.

'Something of the atmosphere of the play . . . was imparted to this beautiful film, a marvel of decorative richness, with well drilled crowds of actors and actresses, a veritable Christmas story and unquestionably a real Vitagraph triumph. The changes marking the appearance and disappearance of the fairies or immortals were managed with singular skill. Indeed, the fairy part of the story was everything that was graceful and charming. Real true comedy marked the acting of Bottom the Weaver and his associates in arranging the play to be performed on the marriage of the Duke. And then again, when Bottom was changed into an ass and Titania the Queen of the Fairies was made to fall in love with him, we seemed to be looking upon the scene from the very play itself as we remembered it when seen on the ordinary stage. The acting seemed to be so naturally, drily humerous.

'The court scenes of this magnificent film were superb, but what pleased us as much as anything were the open air scenes. . . .

'We should like to hear the opinion of qualified Shakespeareologists on this picture. . . . For ourselves, speaking generally, the picture is full of poetical beauty. The Vitagraph actors and actresses have risen to the occasion. The photograph of the subject, too, is so good that we seemed to feel that the end of the matters [sic] showed a marked advance – a picture having a rich deposit free from mechanical and chemical defects. We look forward to other Shakespearean products from the Vitagraph Company and altogether to our mind the *Midsummer Night's Dream* stands out as the Christmas success of the moving picture stage of the last days of 1909. Bravo, Vitagraph Company!'

The London *Bioscope* said 'Bravo' too in its own way:

'The versatility of the Vitagraph company of actors is never better displayed than in this charming Shakespearian comedy. Students of the great dramatist's works will thoroughly enjoy the careful pictorial presentation of the many scenes, while the whole play is so cleverly portrayed that it will not fail to delight the spectator who is not familiar with the works of Shakespeare.'

Perhaps the appeal of Vitagraph's *Midsummer Night's Dream* dictated the manufacture of more than the usual number of prints to surmount the hazards of time, decomposition, and fire. At any rate it is one of the three of the company's Shakespeares in this period which have survived, and the best. Some of the praise heaped upon it by reviewers is justified. The story is fairly intelligible, the photography unusually clear and sharp, and it does achieve a kind of charm, an atmosphere of romantic fantasy.

In the extant positive there is no introductory title or identification, and a first sequence with the situation of the two pairs of lovers and the interference of Egeus and Theseus seems to have been lost. The casting of the mechanicals' play, the quarrel of Oberon and Titania were deliberately cut from the scenario. There is, indeed, no Oberon in the entire film, his place being taken by a fairy, later designated Penelope. The present opening corresponds in part to II, 2. Titania falls asleep, and Penelope drops in her eyes the enchanting juice of love-in-idleness. There follows a subtitle which explains the second sequence: 'The eloping lovers become weary in the forest. Puck places the magic herb upon the eyes of Hermia and Lysander. Lysander awakes and falls in love with Helena.' The title is not entirely accurate; Puck does not anoint Hermia; moreover the episode includes the business where Hermia asks Lysander to sleep farther off, the rejection of Helena by Demetrius and his departure, her awakening of Lysander and exit, Lysander's rejection of the sleeping Hermia, and his exit in pursuit of Helena. A caption now introduced several sequences: 'The tradesmen come to the forest to rehearse their play. Puck changes the weaver into an ass. Titania awakes and falls in love with him.' In the third sequence, Puck watches the rehearsal with manifest enjoyment; Bottom throws down his script but is persuaded not to quit, and leaves with the part in his hand. In the fourth, Bottom is shown reading his part. Puck enters, waves his wand, and Bottom's head is transformed. In the fifth sequence, Bottom returns to the tradesmen, who flee. In his wanderings in the sixth he comes upon Titania, sleeping, as Puck watches. Titania wakes to fall in love with the weaver and introduces him to two child-fairies. The seventh sequence is not entirely clear, but apparently Penelope explains to Puck his error in enchanting the wrong lover. The eighth sequence is preceded by a title: 'Puck puts the herb upon the eyes of Demetrius who awakes and falls in love with Helena. Demetrius and Lysander quarrel over Helena.' In more detail, after Hermia leaves the scene, Demetrius falls asleep and is anointed by Puck (and apparently Penelope, who exit.) Lysander enters, pleading with Helena. Demetrius wakes and also sues. When Hermia reenters, the men quarrel and exeunt, and the girls do likewise. In the ninth episode, Puck, waving his wand, separates and misleads the men, and in the tenth the sleeping Titania and Bottom are disenchanted respectively by Penelope and Puck. There is evidently a lacuna where the young lovers are likewise disenchanted, for the eleventh sequence shows a kind of procession including Theseus and Hippolyta, Egeus, and the two pairs of lovers, who are forgiven and pair off. The twelfth sequence depicts Bottom describing his experiences to the rehearsing mechanicals. It is followed by a title: 'The Duke, Hippolyta and the lovers are married. The tradesmen give their play in honor of the occasion', but the marriage is not pictured. In the thirteenth scene, Theseus and his guests are shown possible programmes for their entertainment; in the fourteenth, the crowd and principals stand awaiting the play. The performance of *Pyramus and Thisbe*, with part of the audience watching and laughing, occupies the fifteenth and seventeenth. In between is cut in a sequence giving further detail of the audience participating and finally there is a title: 'End'. The picture made use of parts of Shakespeare's play included in II, 2; III, 1, 2; IV, 1, 2: and V, 1.

Though there is a certain ingenuity in the compression and adaptation of the story, it might still have resulted in an inferior film. What gave *A Midsummer Night's Dream* its comparative distinction was that it was more of a movie than a photograph of a play. Only the last episodes at the court smack of the stage or the studio with painted backdrop. The parts in the wood near Athens, twelve of the sequences, were shot outdoors in an attractive locale, actually a now vanished chestnut forest in the southern part of Flatbush near the old village of Greenfield, and in some cases where a pond appears at the old Gravesend water works. The natural backgrounds allow actors to group themselves before trees or hide behind them, to move through scenery which seems more varied than it is, and to blend in with the sylvan mystery of light and shade. The result is that the film does achieve a kind of pictorial poetry appropriate both to the fairy atmosphere and the lunacy of the lovers. It is interesting too that while the enchantment of Bottom, emerging from the rehearsal, was photographed in woodland, his pantomimed recital of his experiences to his fellows, after his return to reality, was taken with the background of fountain and stone columns at the Ocean Avenue entrance to Prospect Park. Of course this was the period of the stationary camera, and medium shots are employed exclusively; the camera was not used for dissolves. Nevertheless, the transformations, though instantaneous, were managed neatly by cutting and are surprisingly effective. The players are at least appropriately dressed, even if their acting is with a few exceptions negligible by present day standards, and the children are delightful. As a whole then the picture manages a certain grace and jollity. Someone in charge was using his imagination.

Whether it was Ranous is doubtful. He had not yet left the company, but unless he made an abrupt change in his methods, the qualities of *A Midsummer Night's Dream* are not his. Maurice Costello, who was in the film, told me the director was Charles Kent, and this is more likely. Kent had now been with Vitagraph for some years, had directed one of the Shakespeare films which was praised, and may well have replaced the erratic Ranous, whose last Shakespeare films had met with adverse criticisms. Moreover it is definite that Kent later did another Shakespeare film for Vitagraph. I do not know whether he acted in *A Midsummer Night's Dream*;

as the father of a long line of Vitagraph heroines, he might have been disguised as Egeus. About some of the cast it is possible to be sure. Costello, who had come to Vitagraph from the Spooner Stock Company of Brooklyn via Edison pictures was Lysander. He achieved double fame, first by refusing to build sets and paint scenery, second by becoming a cinema matinee-idol. His two children, Dolores and Helene, were the fairies to whom Bottom was introduced; they too were to achieve some fame. The Puck, however, ran away with the show with an obvious delight in the whole lovely foolishness and had to be identified for a fan who wrote in to a trade journal; she was Gladys Hulette, who a year later was to be Tyltyl in the New Theatre's production of Maeterlinck's *The Bluebird*. Almost as surely we can find Billy Ranous as Bottom, Charles Chapman as Quince, Walter Ackerman as Demetrius, and Julia Swayne Gordon as Helena. Rose Tapley was in the picture and may have been Hermia, Titania was possibly Florence Turner, and one of the mechanicals surely Will Shea. 'The best in this kind are but shadows; and the worst no worse if imagination amend them.'

Twelfth Night, released on February 3, 1910 and the last of Vitagraph's one reel Shakespeare films unless one counts a later *Cardinal Wolsey* as Shakespearean, has also survived but in a less satisfactory print than *A Midsummer Night's Dream*. Originally of 970 feet it has dwindled to 743; there is no title; parts are missing at the beginning, the ending, and no doubt elsewhere; and the sequences are not always in the proper order. Moreover examination of it had to be in a viewer, and low magnification is not as conducive to descriptive detail or identification as projection on a screen. Nevertheless its content can be reconstructed with reasonable confidence, and the synopsis in the *Moving Picture World* of February 12th seems fairly accurate:

'Viola and her twin brother Sebastian, while on a sea voyage, are shipwrecked. Viola is rescued and Sebastian is supposed to have been lost. Among the wreckage on the coast, Sebastian's trunk is found by Viola. When she opens it and sees her brother's clothing, she decides to disguise herself as a boy. Learning that she is within the realm of the young Duke Orsino, she repairs to his castle, where she is employed as his page.'

In the film as it stands there is an initial caption: 'Viola, separated from her twin brother Sebastian by a shipwreck finds herself in the realm of Duke Orsino. She dresses herself from her brother's trunk, cast up by the sea and finds her way to the Duke's palace where she is believed to be a young man and meets with strange adventures.' Viola is not shown being rescued but on shore with rescuers and trunk. A second caption says: 'Sebastian rescued', and the next sequence illustrates this. He is shown being supported from sea to shore. An old hulk appears in the background. It either stands for the ship which was wrecked or indicates that the landing was at a different place, and it is possible that this sequence is misplaced. Both shots are external. Three sequences, one of them now out of order, show Viola dressed in Sebastian's clothing, and approaching and arriving at Orsino's palace. The summary continues:

'The Duke is apparently very much in love with Olivia, a rich Countess. Nothing daunted, Viola falls in love with the Duke, who adds to her discomfiture by sending her as his page, with a message of love to Olivia. As soon as Olivia beholds the handsome page, she falls in love with Viola, thinking that she is a boy. She presents the page with a jewel, and later, through her pompous steward, Malvolio, with a ring.'

This section is depicted in the film by three subtitles and four sequences, one of which is misplaced. A subtitle, 'One week later. Viola believed to be a boy is admired by the Duke, becomes his page and is sent by him with a message to his sweetheart, Olivia', is followed by a picture of Orsino surrounded by his courtiers in a not unattractive structural set with a painted backdrop. He sends for Viola, who is shown arriving. Now a caption gives the content of his letter: 'My dear Olivia: – Though oft times scorned by you, I send my best beloved page once more to plead my cause. I follow her to learn thine answer. Orsino.' Two sequences in the film as it stands include the delivery of instructions and a scroll to Viola, but since the second is misplaced at the end of the picture, they may have coelesced into one. Subtitle: 'Viola arrives at Olivia's court where Olivia, believing her a young man, falls in love with her, arousing the jealousy of Olivia's courtiers.' In a pretty, though artificial setting with a painted backdrop of a gate and distant scenery in an architectural frame, Sir Toby is shown introducing Sir Andrew to Olivia, who is surrounded by her attendants, girls, Feste, and Malvolio. Maria announces the arrival of the page, and Malvolio is sent to admit him. When Viola arrives, it is clear that Olivia is smitten. She dismisses the others and unveils her face. Viola delivers the scroll and departs. Malvolio is summoned to deliver a ring to the page, as Olivia leaves the scene. Malvolio calls to Viola, who has left the range of the camera. She reappears, is given the ring on Malvalio's staff, and they exeunt severally. I see nothing here about an additional 'jewel,' though there is later a necklace.

The rest of the summary has to be given entire since the events described in the last paragraph are not in order:

'Sebastian, in search of his sister, meets Viola by chance at the house of Olivia and the two are once more united. Explanations follow, and Olivia finds it an easy matter to transfer her affections to Sebastian, who falls madly in love with Olivia.

'Orsino finds Olivia in the embrace of Sebastian. Viola now appears before the Duke as herself – a sweet and attractive girl. She tells him of her impersonation of her brother and the page. Orsino is so struck by her beauty and cleverness that he declares his love for her and asks her to become his wife. "All's well that ends well" and everybody is happy.

'A delightful touch of comedy is introduced in this play in the scene where Maria forges an affectionate note to Malvolio, imitating Olivia's handwriting and leading the arrogant steward to believe the Countess in love with him. Malvolio is so puffed up and elated when he gets the note that he cannot contain himself, much to the amusement of Sir Toby, Maria, and Sir Andrew, who are watching him and greatly enjoying the stroke.'

The last incidents in the summary occur next in the film. Maria, Sir Toby, and Sir Andrew are not named in the captions and their relationship may have been somewhat difficult to follow. The next subtitle says: 'Olivia's maid plans a joke on Malvolio, the supercilious steward by addressing a love letter apparently written by her mistress. Malvolio thinks Olivia is in love with him and becomes more pompous than ever.' After a shot of Viola departing through a garden, another outdoor scene, Maria enters followed by Sir Toby and Sir Andrew. They pantomime the letter plot and hide behind the bushes. Malvolio arrives, finds the letter, and reacts appropriately, while the others laugh. The characters here are well acted, and the scene is a good one. Three subtitles now give the text of the letter, with, for the first time, Shakespeare's own words, somewhat adapted and much truncated: 'To the unknown beloved – Malvolio, who doth sway my life.' Malvolio reads, astonished. 'Be not afraid of greatness. Some are born great, some achieve greatness and some have greatness thrust upon them.' Malvolio continues to read. 'She thus advises thee that sighs for thee. If thou entertainest my love let it appear in thy smiling. Therefore in my presence still smile, dear my sweet, I pray thee. Thine own, Olivia.' In two sequences, Malvolio postures, and the plotters laugh and embrace in their glee.

The first part of the next sequence is confusing but apparently Viola, seated on a bench, is approached by Olivia. The plotters see the page kissing her hand and receiving a necklace. Olivia throws Viola a kiss, as the page departs. Malvolio, in this garden scene, now poses as the supposed loved one before Olivia; he smiles and is cross-gartered, though there was no direction for the latter. Olivia thinks him mad and leaves. Malvolio continues to posture as the plotters laugh. Still in the garden but in a new sequence, Sir Toby tries to foment a duel between Viola and Sir Andrew, both present. Little was done with Shakespeare's complications of this incident, or else parts here are missing. At any rate there is no Antonio in the film, and I do not find the reappearance of Sebastian, his recognition by Viola, or the mistaking of his identity by Sir Toby and Olivia despite the next subtitle: 'Sebastian is mistaken for Viola by Olivia. The twins are reunited. The Duke finds a sweetheart, and Olivia, discovering that she has been in love with a girl finds consolation in the arms of Sebastian.' In the final two sequences, one sees first Olivia and Feste. Sebastian enters and embraces Olivia. The entrance of the Duke and his train is followed by recognitions. Malvolio demands an apology and the letter is explained. Another scene shows the happiness of Olivia and Sebastian, and the reappearance of Viola as a girl before Orsino. It is all very huddled up, either because of the need for compression into one reel or, more probably here, because of lost footage.

It should be plain that under the circumstances it is difficult to judge the quality of the film in comparison with, say, *A Midsummer Night's Dream*. The backgrounds are well used; the constructed ones are not obtrusive; the outdoor scenes on shore and in the garden are effective; the photography is good for the period. The acting is adequate, with the comedy characters best, especially Malvolio and Maria. The story told by the film in its present state is not particularly clear, and without the fairly elaborate titles would be unintelligible, but one cannot be sure that this is fair criticism of the original. The picture narration seems crowded but this objection would apply to most of Vitagraph's other Shakespeare films; it took suggestions and situations from I, 2, 4, 5; II, 1, 2, 5; III, 1, 4; and V, 1, omitting in the version described at least seven scenes, though some of the material is covered in subtitles, and wisely including at the beginning incidents which Shakespeare did not show. The cuts are judicious; for example, there is nothing here of Malvolio in confinement, nor the purse business. On the whole my impression is that though *Twelfth Night* in its original form was less imaginative and atmospheric than *A Midsummer Night's Dream*, it ranked fairly high in the series, and this impression is supported by a reviewer in the *Moving Picture World* of February 19, 1910.

'Another of the ambitious releases by this house. This reproduction of one of Shakespeare's most pleasing comedies is satisfactory in every particular. The staging is according to the best traditions of Shakespeare's time [whatever that means!] and the acting is in harmony with the modern understanding of the piece. . . . Of course much must be eliminated, otherwise it would be impossible to make any adequate reproduction of the play. The condensing has been done by a master hand, however, and does not mar the piece itself. In some degree, perhaps, it is an improvement, since it eliminates many of those portions which illuminate the main story, though they are not essential to its development, nor to an understanding of it. Manufacturers who endeavor to place such pictures before audiences numbering in the aggregate many thousands scattered through the country are to be commended. It brings to the many who really enjoy the drama an opportunity to see it adequately performed, and at a nominal cost. It elevates and improves the literary taste of the great mass of the people, performing in this way service which cannot be measured in material terms. Such work is in the nature of an educational service, which is deserving of the heartiest support of all who are working for the improvement of humanity.'

Who were the individuals who helped to improve humanity here? I suspect Kent as director, though there is no evidence except his association with other Shakespeare films, and the previous departure of Ranous from Vitagraph. Blackton some years later wrote that Florence Turner played Viola, and Edith Storey, Sebastian. Julia Swayne Gordon is recognizable as Olivia, Tefft Johnson as Orsino, and Charles Kent was Malvolio. I wish I knew who was the Maria who adds sprightly humour to what must have been a pleasing picture.

CHAPTER III

Cranks and Offices

WHILE Vitagraph was producing its long series, other American companies also made some Shakespeare films. With two exceptions, none is extant in any form. Moreover about the production of smaller firms, there is not so much information. About a *Julius Caesar* copyrighted by Lubin on March 16, 1908 before the appearance of the first Vitagraph Shakespeares, there is just no information at all. What was Sigmund Lubin of Philadelphia doing in that galley? It is the more odd because he was inclined to follow others rather than to step out on his own.

About a Kalem *As You Like It* there is more. Kalem had been founded in 1907 by George Kleine, Samuel Long, and Frank Marion, whose initials gave the firm its name. It had a studio in New York on 21st Street, but much of its reputation was gained by the outdoor scenes it shot on location. An advance announcement of August 1, 1908 indicates that this was the practice here:

'The Kalem Company announces the completion of a magnificent production of Shakespeare's *As You Like It* done by an experienced Shakespearian cast on the splendid estate of Mr Ernest Seton Thompson, Windygoul, Cos Cob, Conn. In photography, scenic effects and beautiful costuming the new production is easily a masterpiece.'

Here was nature with a vengeance, nature supplied by a naturalist. Ernest Seton-Thompson, later Ernest Thompson Seton, was a friend of Frank Marion's. He 'placed at our disposal', wrote Gene Gauntier many years later, 'his extraordinarily beautiful' property to provide the background of the picture and give it a proper local colour, surely a hopeful sign. Yet when it was released in 915 feet on September 11 it did not entirely please a commentator:

'Kalem Company's rendering of this charming comedy is not what I hoped to see. It comes so near to being a success that it is a pity that it had not received the finishing touches. In filming this story the minor characters should have been eliminated and the unity of design better adhered to. The story of Rosalind and Orlando should have been brought out more strongly. . . . The love scene in the forest between Rosalind and Orlando is acted in a lame manner. I have seen people hold hands in that fashion on the last Coney Island boat of a Saturday night, but in a Shakespeare play – never.'

And we learn that for the picture Kalem supplied a lecture. 'With the average audience the delivery of a lecture on this film would make it a big success, otherwise the situations would be unintelligible to many.' An ununified and confusing story in 'elaborate scenic surroundings', and what about the unidentified but 'experienced Shakespearian cast'? The picture was still rentable in 1910 but one wonders why.

Kalem's one contribution to Shakespeare film was followed by the only similar picture by Biograph, a *Taming of the Shrew* released on November 10, 1908, which is of special interest because of the personalities connected with it. The American Mutoscope and Biograph, in business since 1896, was the chief rival of the Edison and Vitagraph companies. Beginning in 1906 a stream of films flowed from its studio at 11 East 14th Street. To it, after some experience at Edison, came a young man from Kentucky who had been salesman, reporter, hop-picker, actor, and most of all wanted to be a writer, especially a dramatist. To tide him over frequently lean periods, he had acted in and written for some Mutoscope films, an occupation he and others considered so thoroughly unrespectable that he used a stage name rather than his own. One of the camera men, Arthur Marvin, was sufficiently impressed with his ideas to recommend him to his brother, H.N., who was vice-president. H.N. in June 1908 offered him a job as director, which he was reluctant to take until promised that he would be retained as an actor if he failed. He signed his first contract under the name he had already used and expected to continue to use until he became famous, Lawrence Griffith. It was not until his third yearly contract that he signed himself David Wark Griffith.

As a 'literary' man, Griffith was brought up on the Victorians and Shakespeare. It was then natural enough that he should make films based on Browning, Kingsley, Tennyson, and Hood; Reade, Dickens and Scott; and *The Taming of the Shrew*. But if his sources were sometimes from the classics, his ideas were cinematic, and it was by virtue of the last that he became the most influential director in America. With his later development we are not here concerned. *The Taming of the Shrew* opened up no new vistas; it belongs to his fumbling experiments to express himself artistically in a new form. Yet it is not without significance that it was photographed by the encouraging Marvin and the still sceptical Billy Bitzer, who gave him the opportunities he needed to develop new camera techniques of far reaching importance, and that he used for his principals a young woman he had enticed from Vitagraph who was to become so famous as 'the Biograph girl' that there was publicity value in identifying her shortly as Florence Lawrence, and an actor, whom he had in June persuaded off the streets for his first film, Arthur Johnson, who came to be almost equally idolized. Griffith understood the new medium as no one had done before him; he also knew picture personalities when he saw them.

The Taming of the Shrew, released in 1048 feet, was filmed in the studio on October 1st and on location at Coytesville, New Jersey on October 7th. No doubt the adaptation was made by Griffith himself. The summary prepared by Lee Dougherty, who was Biograph's scenario and publicity department, and printed in the Biograph Bulletin No. 136, is not particularly helpful in showing the arrangement but it does indicate contemporary attitudes in film advertising:

'If we could see ourselves as others see us what models we would become. Shakespeare doubtless had this in mind when he wrote this masterpiece of comedy, evidently taking his inspiration from Dekker's comedy, *A Medicine for a Curst Wife* [a play, not extant, later than Shakespeare's; both may have derived suggestions from an earlier ballad, *A Merry Jest of a Shrewd and Curst Wife*]. One may readily conceive the wonderful possibilities for spirited motion picture situations in such a theme, and the Biograph has availed itself of every chance, the result being one of the snappiest, funniest films of the kind ever made, besides being most elaborate in detail. Following the example set in the production of "Ingomar" [an earlier Griffith 'literary' film with Florence Lawrence based on Maria Lacy Lovell's *Ingomar the Barbarian* from the German], only the stirring interesting portions of the play are depicted; at the same time, the story is clearly, though concisely told. It starts just before the arrival of Petruchio to sue for the hand of Katherine, the shrew; contrasting her nature with that of her sister, Bianca, the gentle. Petruchio woo's and wins Katherine in spite of herself, and at once sets out to curb her headstrong humor. This he does by becoming a veritable tyrant himself, and ostensibly all for love of her, showing her first of all how despicable the ill-tempered, restive being is, and finally teaching her that a wife's duty is obedience to her husband, all of which is accomplished, but not until his poor servants are beaten black and blue and heads nearly broken in punishment of pretended offenses and short-comings. The cook is accused of burning the meat and gets the joint at his poor head; the baker has made the tart too sweet and receives it full in the face; the chamber attendant has not made the bed properly and so is made to feel the sting of the whiplash; in fact the whole household is ruled with extreme despotism and all in pretension of pleasing her ladyship Katherine, until finally we see her pleading for mercy for the poor servants. However, she fully realizes what she herself has been guilty of in the past, and it effects a permanent cure, transforming her from the shrew and froward woman that she was to a meek and amiable being. It is indeed an object lesson – "See ourselves as others see us".'

Though he is accurate enough in his way in describing this moral custard-pie comedy, fortunately we do not have to depend entirely on the floridities of Mr Dougherty, for the film exists, photographed on a paper roll, in the Library of Congress. It is unfortunate, however, in determining its continuity, that it has no titles, that some parts of it have stuck together, that it cannot be screened, and that manual examination is hardly satisfactory. It is clear that Christopher Sly is, as frequently, entirely eliminated, that the Bianca plot is not carried very far, and that the emphasis is on Katherine and Petruchio. I take it that there are ten sequences as follows:

1. Apparently shows the arrival of Petruchio at Baptista's house, a room of tapestried walls and a bit of furniture. He is ushered in through curtains at the back, and is greeted by Baptista and another, perhaps one of the suitors. Bianca's entrance is followed by conversation at which point Kate enters, berates a servant (in either the Elizabethan or modern sense) and chases him out. Bianca, it seems, paints at an easel. Kate turns out the other characters. Re-enter Baptista with a music teacher (Hortensio?) and then exit. Kate breaks the lute and a picture (?) over the teacher's head. This is part of II, 1, much adapted.

2. An anteroom, with Bianca and a lover seated and various other unidentifiable characters. I do not follow the business but it is climaxed by Petruchio's kicking a servant in the posterior. Possibly part of III, 1.

3. Same set as 1. I gather Petruchio is talking with one of Bianca's lovers (concocting plans?) when Baptista enters and Petruchio asks for Katherine's hand. Baptista's exit is followed by the entrance of Kate, and a wooing scene in which she storms at Petruchio. When she hits him with a pillow, he laughs at her. Baptista re-enters. Petruchio accepts Kate, forcibly embraces her, and leaves her, raging. This is also from II, 1.

4. Same set as 1. Petruchio arrives for the wedding in comic attire and tempestuous mood, brandishing a whip; he manhandles someone unidentifiable, terrifies Kate with his whip, and goes out with her. Based on III, 2.

5. Same set as 2. A strewing of flowers, evidently prepared for the reappearance of the bride and groom. Not in Shakespeare.

6. Same set as 1. The sequence is hard to follow, but it is evidently based on III, 2 also. Petruchio storms, picks up Kate, and carries her off.

7. The dining room at Petruchio's house, with Kate, Petruchio, and servants. Kate turns on the servants, and then Petruchio becomes more violent than she, as Kate tries to calm him. He storms and chases out the servants while she hides under the table. He prevents her from

1. Magna Charta scene from Tree's *King John* at Her Majesty's Theatre (1899). Theatre Collection, New York Public Library

2. Clément Maurice films at the Phono-Cinéma-Théâtre (1900). *L'Illustration*, April 1, 1933

a Sarah Bernhardt in the duel scene from *Hamlet*

c Emilio Cossiri as Romeo in Gounod's opera, *Roméo et Juliette*

b Poster announcing Bernhardt film

3. Henny Porten as Desdemona (Messter, ca. 1907) Porten, *Vom "Kintopp" zum Tonfilm . . .*, Carl Reisner Verlag, Dresden, 1932

4. Georges Méliès as Hamlet in his own film (1907). Museum of Modern Art Film Library

eating. At this point the paper roll is in bad condition, but after a break Kate is shown alone with nothing to eat. The business with the tailor follows, and Petruchio leads Kate away. She sneaks back to a servant who leads her to the kitchen, Petruchio following. Adapted from IV, 1, 3.

8. The kitchen, an effective set. Petruchio takes the food away, and berates the servants with much slapstick. Kate pleads for mercy. More of IV, 3.

9. Same as 7. I gather that Baptista has come to see his daughter. She embraces him, but is now tamed and embraces Petruchio too, as Baptista approves and exit. A suggestion from V, 2 but mostly new.

10. An outdoor scene, the only one in the picture, a garden with shrubbery, flowers, and a stone wall upon which Kate is seated. Petruchio appears from behind her; there is an exchange of flowers, an evident intention to indicate the happiness of the lovers, a wholly new scene, except for the suggestion 'Come on, and kiss me, Kate' at the end of Shakespeare's play.

Griffith then has followed Shakespeare's order chronologically but used only five or six scenes for central incidents and suggestions. Visually the strewing of flowers in the anteroom, the kitchen set, and the final garden scene are new but he has tried to tell the story in a few backgrounds, shifting from one to another as needed to emphasize, sometimes by contrast, the physical and boisterous comedy which would appeal to the eye. Yet, though explanatory titles might have helped some, and screening might make some of the action more intelligible, there is still too much meaningless conversation, the Bianca plot at the beginning gets lost, and some scenes are over-crowded by minor characters. The violent bits are best, and Florence Lawrence and Arthur Johnson act them with a pleasant zest. There are no real innovations in camera technique. The indoor sets are hardly adequate, and the last sequence, though pretty, is too long for the simple meaning it conveys. On a paper roll it is difficult to judge the quality of the photography, and to compare a film examined by hand magnification with a contemporary one seen on the screen hardly provides a proper basis for critical estimate, but my impression is that *The Taming of the Shrew* does not equal in quality Vitagraph's *Romeo and Juliet* of the year.

W. Stephen Bush's verbose review in the *Moving Picture World* is hardly acute and certainly over-enthusiastic:

'Too much praise cannot be bestowed on this picture. To tell the story of the taming of the shrew in moving pictures is a task from which the cleverest of film makers might shrink without discredit, for it is a tale of emotion mainly with but a few dramatic situations, and these very difficult to render. No actor or actress has ever dared to enter the charmed circle without

c

trembling and none except the divinely gifted have acquitted themselves in a manner worthy of the great poet. After seeing the play in moving pictures my first duty is to speak in unreserved praise of the lady who took the part of the shrew, and the gentleman who portrayed Petruchio. There is not a false move anywhere. The staging is good and the costume nearly faultless, high praise for such a play. A word of acknowledgment is also due to the adapter, who has done his work well. As the subject is here presented it would please an audience of Shakespearean scholars and at the same time delight the humblest intelligence. The power of Shakespeare lies in his appeal to the human heart and it makes no difference whether that heart beats under the longshoremen's coat or under a multicolored vest of satin and velvet.'

Another comment is more to the point:

'A rather confused film, presented on an overcrowded stage. I cannot say that the film was well received by the audience, and it is a rather brutal subject in which the lash has too much play. The last scene calls for a special mention, as the most beautiful composition with very fine photographic effects.'

I think we can accept Florence Lawrence's charm and expressiveness, and Arthur Johnson's manly attraction and vigorous action; the compositional arrangement of two or three of the scenes; the adequacy of the costuming, but the brief comment in a Biograph manuscript notebook in the Museum of Modern Art is apt enough: 'Value – Fair.'

1909 brought forth no American Shakespeare films other than those by Vitagraph, though three short ones used Shakespeare's titles for stories not his. There was a Lubin *Measure for Measure*, an Essanay *Much Ado About Nothing*, and *A Winter's Tale* by Edison. For its story of two husbands who carry their wives' pictures in overcoats they accidently interchange in a restaurant, and the discovery of the wrong pictures by the wives, Essanay at least acknowledged the debt: 'To our friend, William Shakespeare, we owe apologies only for the title of this amusing little skit, and great humorist that he was, we do not think he could have developed a funnier situation than in this story.' Be that as it may, I doubt if Shakespeare was restless in his grave.

Imp, Selig, and Edison glanced at the perennial favorite, *Romeo and Juliet* in 1910 and 1911, the first with *A Rural Romeo*, where Romeo probably stands for no more than lover, the second with *Romeo and Juliet in Town*, characterized as 'a modern burlesque, roughly paralleling the plot of Shakespeare's tragedy'. The parallel consisted only in the unfriendly relations between two families who are finally reconciled by the sweethearting of their respective offspring, Romeo Brown and Juliet Smith. Edison's *Bumptious as Romeo*, released on February 1, 1911 in 975 feet, was also a travesty. This was part of a Bumptious series featuring a rotund comedian, John R. Cumpson, who played a character aptly named. He organizes a dramatic club for a performance at the Town Hall of *Romeo and Juliet*, in which he is to play the male lead. The picture utilizes the familiar device of a show in which everything goes wrong. The climax comes in a balcony scene where the entire palazzo collapses on the unfortunate actor. Upbraiding the stagehands, he looks through the curtain peep-hole and discovers that the theatre is empty of audience. The film ends with Bumptious demolishing a bust of Shakespeare and resolving never to act again. This is not quite on the same level as the artisans' Pyramus and Thisbe play in *A Midsummer Night's Dream*, but it was funny, visually effective, and was evidently enjoyed by the public, for it turns up shortly in England and Scotland.

The Taming of the Shrew probably suggested another comedy which Sidney Drew, lately from the stage and vaudeville, both sketched and acted for Kalem in 1911. It was the kind of domestic fun-making which he and his wife were later to popularize on the screen. Called *When Two Hearts Are Won*, it parallels Shakespeare in dealing with the curbing of an ill-tempered wife by the tactics of her husband. In this case, however, she insists on taking her pet dog on their honeymoon with resultant complications. The husband retaliates successfully, the lady yields, and all ends happily.

Thus the bowl should run,
And not unluckily against the bias.

Perhaps Kate's misfortunes with a horse suggested to Drew the dog which in a certain sense proved the *pièce de resistance*. The comedy was highly praised in the *Moving Picture World* of September 2nd. All these citations of adaptation or adoption prove nothing except the filmic usefulness of Shakespeare and the pervasiveness of his reputation with scenarists and presumably the public.

Since I have already scrambled strict chronology in order to treat comic derivations, I may in turning to films which are more truly Shakespearean be forgiven for commenting briefly on a Selig, *Merry Wives of Windsor* before a group of films, one of which is earlier in time, but which can more usefully be discussed together. There is, in any case, precious little to say about the Selig picture released November 24, 1910 and certainly no paean of praise from a reviewer:

'One of the most amusing of all Shakespeare's comedies, this picture necessarily has to confine itself to Falstaff's doings principally. A thousand feet of film is scarcely capable of containing more. In the film Falstaff is crowned with an ass's head where the text calls for a buck's head. This can be easily remedied, but as it is presented it makes an incongruity which is like a discord in music. It jars upon the nerves of one who is familiar with

Shakespeare. Aside from this one defect, the film is a relatively satisfactory presentation of Falstaff's doings, and markedly appreciated by the audience.'

Obviously the head had more of an effect on the reviewer than the body of the film, but I gather from the unreliable pre-release summary supplied by the company, which incidentally mentions 'buck horns' rather than ass's head, that the underplot of rivalry for the hand of Anne Page was cut, though she is present for Falstaff to flirt with at the beginning, and that Fenton, Shallow, Slender, Sir Hugh Evans, Dr Caius, and Mrs Quickly are entirely absent. Selig was one of the pioneers. The Colonel had begun in Chicago before the turn of the century with the Selig Polyscope Company, but though the truncation is explicable enough, Shakespeare was hardly his forte – nor that of Francis Boggs who probably directed; his specialty on the stage had been acting in melodramas like *Why Girls Leave Home*.

Edwin Thanhouser, however, was neither a pioneer like Selig nor unfitted by his background and sensibility to produce Shakespeare on the screen. On the stage from the 1880s, he turned to stock company producing in Milwaukee and organized his film company in 1909 in the East. He brought with him actors he had worked with in stock, his wife who as Gertrude Homan had been a child star, and persuaded to join him his brother-in-law, Lloyd Lonergan, a newspaper man and feature writer, to prepare scenarios. His company was then neither haphazard nor unprofessional in experience; this was indeed the first American company planned and operated by members of the theatrical profession. At the same time Thanhouser was aware that making good films was a different problem from producing plays on the stage. He experimented carefully and thoughtfully before venturing into Shakespeare with *A Winter's Tale* in 1910.

The film occasioned preambles in the *Moving Picture World* which are worth noting both because they indicate a planned series, and for the first time in this history announce publicly the names of the actors:

'The Thanhouser production, *The Winter's Tale*, is now definitely announced for release, and scheduled for Friday, May 27. The manufacturers have spared no expense to make it a notable issue. The success of the "Thanhouser Classics," as they are called, that have gone before, has caused the New Rochelle manufactory to inspect Shakespeare with a view to picture production and a strong series of Shakespearean releases are in order, of which *The Winter's Tale* is the first. Miss Rosemund portrays the Queen of Sicilia, Martin Faust the King of that country, Frank Crane the King of Bohemia, Amelia Barleon the Princess of Sicilia, and Alfred Hanlon the Prince of Bohemia.'

And an advertisement the next week gives the length as 1000 feet and proclaims that the film cost three times as much as 'an ordinary picture'.

It is a pity that no print of this picture, adapted from Shakespeare by

Lloyd Lonergan and Mrs Thanhouser and probably directed by Barry O'Neil, has survived, for in its time it evoked unusual enthusiasm. One special article is really an extended puff for the daring of Edwin Thanhouser and this 'Thanhouser Triumph':

'Dealing with kings and queens, of course, it gives an opportunity for magnificence of mounting, costumes, and the like of which Mr Thanhouser has taken full advantage.

'We come now to the acting and for this we have none but the highest praise. We have never seen better acting in any motion picture that has come before our eyes. All the parts struck us as properly cast and throughout the entire production we thought, nay, we are sure, we saw the hand of an accomplished producer. Every movement, every action, was suited to the text of the story. From the point of view of film production we regard the Thanhouser *Winter's Tale* as a masterpiece. And think of it now, the man who made and produced this picture was absolutely unknown in the moving picture field three months ago. [He had begun actual production in a converted skating rink in New Rochelle only in March.] The record then assuredly belongs to Edwin Thanhouser, whom we cordially congratulate on his triumph. . . .

'We have seldom looked upon a moving picture film which gave us greater pleasure in respect of its photography. . . .'

The formal review two weeks later of this 'excellent' piece of work could add little by way of appreciation.

'The pictorial characteristics of the film are made a prominent feature and are never lost sight of. Every scene was set with fidelity to the original, but always with the development of the pictorial feature as an important factor. Then the acting. It would be captious critic, indeed who could discover a flaw in it. . . . Seldom, indeed, is the final scene, where the supposed statue comes to life, so well done, and involuntarily one rejoices with the King of Bohemia [Sicilia] in the return of his lamented queen. Few, indeed, will be the releases of the month, to surpass this, and few, indeed, are the pictures that seem so complete and in every way satisfactory. Mr Thanhouser deserves the heartiest congratulations on his success.'

One would like more detail about the adaptation and the arrangement of the pictorial images but there can be no doubt that this was an unusual film. A summary in a trade publication seems to be largely based on Shakespeare's play rather than the picture, but for what it is worth I note no reference to Mamillius, the consultation of the oracle, Autolycus, the Shepherd's son, or the rustic feast. A still shows a simple court set with apparently Paulina presenting Hermione, a statue come to life but still in chains, to Leontes and Polixenes. Unfortunately, however, questions of inclusion and exclusion cannot be answered since 90% of the Thanhouser product was destroyed by fire in 1917, *A Winter's Tale* included.

1911 was both lean and transitional in America for Shakespeare films, but one picture was of considerable importance. This was not Thanhouser's *The Tempest*, released on November 28th, which added nothing to the reputation of the company. There is little about it in the trade papers, and the cast is not even identified.

'This photoplay has a sketchy outline of the scenario of Shakespeare's play. At times there is much commendable suggestion in the scenes, some of which are very pretty. It now and then seems crude. The player who takes Miranda's part fills it, so far as physical requirements went, very well indeed. But Ariel is, perhaps, the only truly well-acted part in the picture. It is taken by a young lady who has put something of sprightliness and mystery into it, with the help of some well chosen backgrounds. As a whole, the film will please, not only because of its subject, but for the sake of the prettiness of parts of it.'

The adaptation and direction were probably by the same people who had worked on *The Winter's Tale*, but quite clearly without the same success, and the mysterious Ariel singled out for spriting is no longer correspondent to command.

However, before *The Tempest*, Thanhouser had made another Shakespeare picture, one which for various reasons it is again suitable to discuss outside of strict chronology. It marked a new departure in advertizing, foreshadowed a different system of distribution, and paved the way to a new tendency in production. One reel films of course continued to be made but 1912 begins in the United States an era of longer Shakespeare films. The Thanhouser *Romeo and Juliet* in 1911 serves as the transition to greater footage and complexity.

Romeo and Juliet was actually a two-reeler, but since the exchanges were not equipped to handle a picture of 2000 feet, it was produced in such a way as to make each reel capable of independent showing and was distributed one reel at a time. Part 1 was released on Friday, September 1st; Part 2, on September 8th. The *Moving Picture World* of August 12th explains the system:

'The reels are so constructed that each tells a complete story. Giving a half hour's show as they do, when they are used together, they will enable exhibitors to give a "Romeo and Juliet Night" that affords all manners of opportunity for feature advertising. Many managers will use them as they appear for the first showing, and book them together for the return date.'

And in the same periodical under date of September 9th:

'In addition to the extra lobby display matter on *Romeo and Juliet* Thanhouser has been offering exhibitors gratis, they announce that three-sheet posters, and special booklets for theatre distribution are now available to exhibitors who wish to spend a little money in featuring the picture. This makes *Romeo and Juliet* the first film issued as a regular release on a manufacturer's regular release day, to be honored with a three-sheet poster, or indeed anything over the size of a one-sheet. The departure, since it is made in behalf of a Shakespearian production a "classic", would seem to prove that the best classes of people are being drawn to the moving pictures.'

The review in the issue of August 19th, evidently based upon a private screening, is not only enthusiastic but shows something of how the story was cut in half, for separate exhibition or later combination.

'The film of the Vitagraph Company possesses rare merit, but the present production has a great advantage – it has more space for the telling of the story, two thousand feet instead of only one thousand. Nothing could better illustrate the advantage of the two-reel over the one-reel film than a comparison between the production of these two companies. The Vitagraph story was exceedingly well told, the acting was superb, the settings magnificent, the adaptation clever. The two-reels production, however, makes the story plainer to a person who has never read the classic tragedy.

'It is creditable to the maker of this present film that each of the reels tells a story of its own; one the love story, the other the tragedy. As the reels are issued at different times this will help the exhibitor. Someday it is to be hoped that arrangement will be made which allows of such productions being released at the same time – the only sensible and logical way.

'The Thanhouser adaptation is the work of skilled and conscientious effort and makes the story very plain to every grade of intelligence, a merit which cannot be estimated too highly. All the classic figures in the play are well individualized, from Romeo and Juliet to the smallest character. The individualization extends to the matter of costumes as well; indeed, in this regard the present production leaves no room for adverse criticism. This is much to be lauded, for in a Shakespearian classic above all things, proper costuming is an essential part of the right atmosphere. The settings, especially the outdoor scenes, are very happily chosen and arranged and lend much charm to the production. Owing to the fact that the film maker had two reels to tell the story, he was able to give much space to the opening scenes, which makes it so much easier to grasp and follow the story. The choosing of these scenes was dictated by art and good taste. Just praise must be given to the acting, which was well up to the general fine standard of the whole production.'

Synopses of *Romeo and Juliet* prepared and released by the company are confusing and misleading; as usual they were prepared before the picture was distributed. Moreover they do not indicate where in the story Reel 1 ended. However, Reel 2 luckily is still available. Its opening with the Tybalt-Mercutio duel and other scattered gleanings imply the content of the first reel. It apparently included the initial brawls, the Prince's edict, the invitation to the Capulet's ball, Romeo's unwilling attendance at the festivities, the meeting of Romeo and Juliet, the first balcony scene, and the marriage at Friar Lawrence's cell, in other words, the essentially pictorial material of the first two acts. There may have been more, for unlike the practice of many early companies, Thanhouser production used carefully prepared continuities for all their pictures, and Mrs Thanhouser and Lloyd Lonergan were both intelligent and experienced script writers, who would have utilized whatever was best at their disposal to clarify the incidents and characterizations. The greater length of the film would have been a challenge also to its probable director, Barry O'Neil.

The extant Reel 2 is an excellent print probably from the original negative; it is about 950 feet in length – a final sequence is missing. The photography is unusually good for the period, sharp and well composed, though the camera remains stationary. The first shot of the duels which result in the deaths of Mercutio and Tybalt is taken on a terrace of a rather handsome country mansion with spacious grounds in or near New Rochelle. In the next sequence Friar Lawrence in his cell advises Romeo to flee to Mantua. The third is in Juliet's bed-chamber and includes Romeo's reluctant departure. The Capulets enter and her father bids her to marry Paris, who is present. Her pleading is in vain. She is now shown in an exterior shot on the way to Friar Lawrence's cell, during which she repels the suggestions of the Nurse. In the cell itself she receives the vial from Friar Lawrence who blesses her. After she leaves, the Friar writes a letter to Romeo and sends it by Friar John whom he summons. On her way home, Juliet evades the nurse by hiding in shrubbery, a visual indication of her attitude. Back in her room, she prays, drinks the potion, and is discovered apparently dead by the Nurse, the Capulets, and Paris. The next sequence shows them laying her in her tomb. In Mantua Romeo is told by Balthazar that Juliet is dead. It is a street scene, just outside of an apothecary's shop, so labelled over the door. Romeo knocks, the apothecary appears, receives a purse, re-enters his shop, and returns with the poison he gives to Romeo. We now shift to outside Juliet's tomb. Paris arrives to visit Juliet, but hides at the approach of Romeo and his servant. As Romeo uses a crowbar to force entrance, he is accosted by Paris, whom he kills. Romeo crosses himself and reapplies himself to the task of gaining admittance. In the next sequence, Romeo in the tomb finds Juliet, kisses her, takes the poison, and falls. There is a cross-cut to Lawrence receiving in his cell the news from Friar John that he was unable to deliver the message to Romeo. In the tomb, Juliet wakes (rather quickly), and at first does not see Romeo (a bit ludicrous since he is so obviously there). When she does, she takes Romeo's dagger, stabs herself (unconvincingly down and inside the neckline of her dress), and falls on Romeo's body. Outside the tomb Friar Lawrence discovers the dead Paris (after practically falling over his body) by means of torches (which quite obviously are burning in broad daylight). As he enters the tomb, the reel closes, with the final sequence of reconciliation unfortunately missing.

My summary has already indicated that final sequences in graveyard and tomb obviously could have been improved. For the rest, however, the presentation is for the period good, the acting rather better than what would be expected for 1911. Julia M. Taylor was a sweet and pretty Juliet, George A. Lessey as Romeo competent though rather too old and unromantic for the part. The unidentified Friar Lawrence is effective, most of the minor characters without much individuality, including the Nurse, Mrs George W. Walton. It was a pleasure to see no backdrops; the sets were solid when interior and appropriate where external. The costuming was good, and all in all the film contains considerable significant visual movement, and avoids the unintelligible talkiness we have met before partly by the inclusion of explanatory subtitles, a few of which are Shakespearean.

In view of the characteristics and the success of *A Winter's Tale* and *Romeo and Juliet* and despite the relative failure of *The Tempest* which followed, Edwin Thanhouser's contribution to the development of Shakespeare on film was of considerable importance. Vitagraph must be given credit for pioneering, for the number of films in its Shakespeare series, and for individual triumphs, such as its *Midsummer Night's Dream*. They led the way and Mr Thanhouser told me that one of the reasons why he pictured Shakespeare – others were his personal interest and his stock company experience – was that other such films had recently been made. But he thought he could do better. For *A Winter's Tale* he dignified his cast by announcing the names of his actors; whether or not this impressed a reviewer, he was able to say he 'had never seen better acting in any motion picture. . . .' For *Romeo and Juliet* he doubled the customary footage, 'a great advantage . . . for the telling of the story', and introduced three-sheet advertising and 'special booklets' for feature presentation. In addition he had prepared carefully detailed continuities, and gave proper attention to architectural backgrounds for indoor shots and suitable locales for those outdoors. His costumes were chosen both with an eye to their appearance within the settings and to their photographic effectiveness on the actors in relation to each other. Though the training of his players was theatrical rather than cinematic, he was able to present Shakespeare's stories without meaningless harangues and in terms of visual movement. In short, if Vitagraph had shown the possibilities, Thanhouser was making the advances. He went on making Shakespeare films into 1916. By 1912, multiple reels could be distributed simultaneously; by 1916 he could use five.

CHAPTER IV

Inexplicable Dumbshows

ENGLISH FILMS (1908–1911)

THE development of the film industry in Great Britain after an auspicious beginning had by the period treated in the last chapters lapsed into a distressing stagnation. It has been estimated that in 1909 not more than 15% of the films exhibited in London and the provinces were home products, whereas pictures from France and the United States where the enterprise had been continuously vigorous accounted for 70%. Part of this failure to grow was due to the unwillingness of English producers to run the risks of vigorous experiment and speculation. Symptomatic were its dependence on literary sources and, even more revealing, its treatment of those sources. While America was going outdoors and France was promoting the so-called art film, England too often stayed in the studio or on out-door stages and either repeated the methods of an earlier era or followed at second hand the trends inaugurated by others. It is not that the United States and France did not along with other parallel growths use literary sources, but that they tried, however primitively, to translate those sources into essentially pictorial terms. Great Britain's tendency, however, was to reproduce without words what appeared on page or stage. With a few exceptions, it is so with her Shakespeare films from 1908 to 1911. Nowadays they may have some value as records of theatrical practice, but they can hardly be considered good films as films.

Nevertheless, these pictures have their interest both in their own right and as part of this chronicle. The irrepressible Tree whom we saw pioneering with *King John* and the storm scene of *The Tempest* is to be involved with a much longer photograph of a stage performance than any which had yet been tried. W. G. Barker develops new methods of production, and initiates amid startling publicity an altogether heterodox system of exhibition. F. R. Benson pictures some of the Shakespeare performances of his company, and Godfrey Tearle, already known on the stage, begins his career on the screen.

Tearle came first, and with two stimuli, though it is difficult to tell exactly what individuals supplied the impetus. With his wife, Mary Malone, he had been touring in repertory in the provinces, a repertory which included as a curtain-raiser the balcony scene of *Romeo and Juliet*. In London, Matheson Lang and Norah Kerin had, beginning March 14, 1908, been playing the lovers in a successful production at the Lyceum which ran over a hundred performances. The Benvolio was Lauderdale Maitland, whom we shall later meet, as we will Lang. Through some concatenation of circumstances, Tearle, the Lyceum, and the Gaumont Company agreed to make a film of *Romeo and Juliet*. Tearle and Mary Malone were to act the leads but some of the actors and appurtenances were from the London stage performance, 'by special arrangement with Mr Ernest Carpenter of the Lyceum Theatre'. It is possible too that there had been international cross-fertilization. An Italian *Romeo and Juliet* film had appeared earlier in the year, and the Vitagraph picture was distributed on June 2nd, shortly before the British venture was released on June 17th, although I cannot find that either of these had been shown in England. It seems more probable that the Gaumont film was independently conceived as a result of Tearle's experience and the success of the Lyceum production of what, after all, was a popular love-story suitable for romantic appeal.

Gaumont's 'studio' was an open-air platform at Fellow's Cricket Field, Champion Hill, Dulwich. To it presumably were brought the Lyceum scenery and costumes. Whoever was responsible for the direction did little directing. The actors were reminded that they knew the play and their parts, and told to proceed. A good deal of the play was filmed, but later much cut. Between shots, the cast relaxed by using the field for the purpose for which it had been intended; they played cricket – in full costume. Mr Tearle retained a photograph, much faded, 'of himself as Romeo putting in some fielding, with Mercutio batting and Juliet at point!' I hope there was no dispute between Gordon Bailey, from the Lyceum production, who was the Mercutio, and J. Annard, the Tybalt.

Gaumont advertised *Romeo and Juliet* with flourishes:

'The sensation of 1908. . . . We have eclipsed all previous efforts, and the tragedy has been produced on a scale never before attempted. The results are beyond expectation. . . . Over 40 of London's Foremost Artists have taken part in this representation, the majority of which were engaged in the recent Lyceum Theatre Production. The Dances and Fights are Triumphs of Grouping and the Tragedy teems with irresistible movement and life. . . .'

The 'scale never before attempted' was 1240 feet, the price, £20 13s 4d net; England was still selling some prints outright.

The review in the *Kinematograph and Lantern Weekly* of June 18th echoes the enthusiasm:

'Each year sees an advance in the methods of staging for film subjects. It might indeed almost be said that the contrast between present day film productions and those which satisfied audiences in the early days of the trade, is at least as great as that between the methods of the Stage in Shakespeare's time and those which distinguish for instance, a Shakespearean revival by Mr Tree at His Majesty's. We have an illustration of this progress in the film of *Romeo and Juliet* issued by the Gaumont Co. this week.

'The production of *Romeo and Juliet* is so finely accurate in its leading details, and the scenery, costumes and acting so realistic that we sit and forget for the time that we are looking at the kinematograph art, but fancy ourselves seated in a theatre. In fact, the actors in Gaumont's Triumph are well known in the world of theatricals; many of them were in the recent Lyceum Theatre cast. The acting of the several artistes is superb, the scenery is magnificent and the photographic quality is perfect.

'The scenery cannot be praised sufficiently. The balcony scene is a masterpiece of realism. In the fine bedroom scene the bed and several of the draperies are those that were actually used by the Lyceum Theatre in their recent representation of the tragedy. The duels are most effective, and the picture teems with spirited movement and life. A further addition to Gaumont's Triumph is the important fact that all the artistes who have taken the different parts are highly trained and well-tried in their profession, everyone beautifully acting his own part. . . .

'Living records such as the one we have before us can only in their production and in public estimation (which is so essential to success) bring forth unstinted praise to the producers. . . .'

But the reader will note that this review is not soundly based criticism. Whatever one may think of Tree's elaborations compared to Elizabethan staging, a film should not ignore its own qualities and it is quite wrong to wish or seem to be transported to the experience of the theatre. The reference to accuracy is ominous, to theatrical acting wrong-headed, to stage realism dangerous. And though a record of a stage production can be valuable for an historian, it cannot thereby be called properly cinematic. It shows film going in a wrong direction when the issue of June 25th could report that this *Romeo and Juliet* 'has proved a tremendous attraction. The first batch of copies issued were immediately disposed of, and orders were received with a rapidity that speaks well for the success of this film production.' Nevertheless, *Romeo and Juliet* is important in its way as the first English picture which exploited stage personalities and in permitting those who were not able to attend the theatre some glimpse of what a Lyceum production was like.

Shakespeare's *The Tempest* also suffered some kind of a sea-change, probably not rich and rare, in 1908. At least the trade papers in November and December listed a Clarendon picture of that name, and one in reviewing

The Martyrdom of Thomas à Becket said: 'The Clarendon Company are to be congratulated on the manner in which they have recently staged a number of the most famous scenes of English history, Shakespeare's plays, etc.' Otherwise I would doubt if this *Tempest* were Shakespeare at all, especially since I know of no other Clarendon films of Shakespearian plays. This one was 780 feet, and that is the sum total of my knowledge about it. The picture was not reviewed, and Clarendon did not advertise in the trade papers. It was, however, one of the more important English companies of the period, had a studio on Lymes Road, Croydon, and rejoiced in some literary pretensions since it later counted Low Warren and the Marchioness of Townshend among the authors who wrote scenarios for it.

However, the weight of this chapter properly belongs not to Gaumont and Clarendon, but to William George Barker, who was concerned with all the rest of the films to be treated. Will Barker, unlike many of his British contemporaries, was not content to follow the practices of others. If there had been more like him, there might not have been better pictures during the period, but there certainly would have been more life in the industry. Born in 1867, he saved enough money from his income as commercial traveller for a German firm which made gold paint to buy in 1896 a box camera, and with it to make some amateur films which photographed his own children at Hackney. By 1901 he was in the picture business. In that year he started the Autoscope Company and built a primitive outdoor stage at Stamford Hill. Most of his pictures were, however, topicals, that is newsreels and documentaries, on which he built his reputation.

In 1906 Autoscope was absorbed by the Warwick Trading Company, in business since the late eighteen nineties, of which Barker became Managing Director. Three years later he resigned to form his own company, Barker Motion Photography, opened offices at 1 Soho Square in March 1910, and began making his own pictures in a studio at Ealing Green. There was soon evidence that the vigorous Barker was to parallel his filming of actualities and narrative incidents with features and spectaculars. On Armistice Day of 1918 he turned his back on what had become for him a worrysome business, and retired with a comfortable income.

It was sometime shortly after Barker went into independent production in 1910 that he made England's first *Hamlet* film, and at the same time showed by his production methods, how expeditiously and cheaply it could be done. Barker's property consisted of a house, West Lodge, in which he lived, five acres of suburban ground, and a brick and glass 'studio' like a glorified greenhouse. All three were used or adapted for backgrounds for various pictures. The studio, except for one scene, was used for *Hamlet*. The construction of the sets and furnishings by carpenters, painters, and property men occupied about three weeks. The sets were built so that they could be arranged inside one another; after one scene was shot, the background was struck, and the stage was ready for the next sequence. Meanwhile Charles Raymond, an actor and pantomimist from the Alhambra and the Palace Theatres, was hired to play the title-role. Now notification was sent to people who had applied for work at not more than 10s. per diem; they were told to report, if the weather was fine, at 8.00 a.m. on a certain day. The actors are come hither. Barker mounted a chair and looked over the group which had assembled. The casting was not based on professional ability. A tall man was picked to play the Ghost; the Ophelia was selected because she could swim. The successful applicants dashed to the dressing rooms, and shooting began before ten o'clock. About one, there was a twenty-minute break for bread and cheese, and coffee. Before 4.00 p.m. the photography was complete, and the cast had been paid off and dismissed. Except Ophelia; on the next day, she floated down the Thames on a raft of flowers in a backwater at Shepperton. Except for this sequence, the picture was shot in less than the six sunlit hours appropriate for cinema photography. Barker said the total cost, including the carpenters' wages was £180, and that he made £600 from the film.

Something have you heard of Hamlet's transformation. Though it was also shot in one day and to some extent in the same way, the energetic Barker's next film was considerably more ambitious and in many respects it was altogether exceptional. Beerbohm Tree, now Sir Herbert, had opened his elaborate production of *Henry VIII* at His Majesty's on September 1, 1910, playing Wolsey himself, and with Arthur Bourchier as the King, Violet Vanbrugh as Queen Katharine, Henry Ainley as Buckingham, and Laura Cowie as Anne Bullen. It was a striking production, swift in pace, enlivened by pageantry, rich scenery and costumes, masses of super-numeraries, dancing, and Tree's own interpretation of the Cardinal, 'coarse, cunning, ostentatious, arrogant, avaricious, unscrupulous, an astute politician, a greedy nest-featherer'. It was obviously to be a success and was to play for over seven months. Well before it closed, Barker persuaded Tree to transport the stage production to his Ealing studio for filming.

Barker must have seen the cinematic possibilities in its visual effects; he was certainly aware that the picture would be not only a feather in his cap, but with Tree in it, a source of considerable gain; he was prepared to cope with the enormous difficulties of so grandiose a project; and Tree, after all, had shown himself nothing loath to experiment with film. With Tree, he worked out an agreement which was entirely unprecedented and which marked the first English 'feature' picture and the first Shakespeare 'exclusive'. Tree was to be paid the unprecedented sum of £1000. Only twenty prints were to be made, ten for London, ten for the provinces. These prints were not, as was customary, to be sold to a dealer, but leased for special exhibition as an 'exclusive'. Lest the film prove unsatisfactory, deteriorate, or interfere with the ticket sales of the theatre presentation, after six weeks the prints were to be called in and destroyed. The contract not only showed the way for the expansion of the somnolent British film industry, but was excellent publicity. Season your admiration for a while with an attent ear till I may deliver this marvel to you.

The story of the filming on February 9, 1911 is best told, complete with journalistic flourishes and spelling errors, in the *Kinematograph and Lantern Weekly* of February 16th; it is headlined '*Henry VIII* Successfully Filmed. Barker's Fine Picture of Sir Herbert Tree in His Greatest Production':

'All things come to him who waits, so after being very badly used by the weather on several occasions where arrangements had been made to take the films of Sir Herbert Beerbohm Tree's great production *Henry VIII* . . . the Clerk of the Weather at last relented, and favored Mr Will L. Barker with atmospherical conditions which enabled him to bring this great undertaking to a successful issue. Mr Barker is to be all the more congratulated as the excellent photographic quality of the film secured on Thursday last is such as to more than compensate for the delay. That this film would be a great artistic triumph was a foregone conclusion, and the interest it will create, coupled with the great influence it will have on the uplifting movement, will, we are certain, more than come up to our anticipations.

'The Barker studios at Ealing were a veritable hive of industry from a very early hour on Thursday, and when Sir Herbert Tree, Mr Bouchier, Miss Violet Vanbrugh and the others arrived about 10.30, very little preparation was necessary before the filming of the subject began. [Barker explained the limits of the acting area, marked off by white tapes, in which they could work before the stationary camera; the actors within these limits gave their usual stage performance.] Once under way, it proceeded from 1.30 until about 3.30 in the afternoon without a hitch, a tribute to the careful rehearsals at His Majesty's Theatre. . . . Each scene was gone through once only before actually being taken, and Mr Barker, at the camera, had the satisfaction of knowing that none of the 5000 feet or so of film was wasted.

'The subject consists of five scenes: The Cloisters, the Banqueting Hall, the Trial, the Ante-Chamber to the King's Room, and the Coronation.

'In all, a caste of some 200 were employed with an effectiveness of which our illustrations give but a very faint idea [each scene except the Ante-Chamber.]

'Some idea of the "props" necessary for such a piece as this may be gained when we state that there were loads of "hand props" brought from His Majesty's in addition to the stage settings, which were a replica of those at the theatre, specially prepared for Barker Motion Photography, Ltd.

'It was five o'clock before Mr Barker and his assistants reached Soho Square with the film. This was immediately developed and a complete print of the subject, toned throughout, was prepared and shown to Sir Herbert, Lady and Miss Viola Tree, Mr Bouchier and Miss Violet Vanbrugh and other members of the cast at midnight.

'We reserve a detailed criticism of this subject until the Press view of the film. The Terms upon which it is exhibited have already been published, and unless we are very much surprised, Barker and Co. will be inundated during the next few days with applications from showmen anxious to secure this advantage of exclusively showing the film of the year – *Henry VIII.*'

Tree's arrangement of the play for the theatre had been in three acts, divided into eleven scenes. The five scenes Barker photographed presented the enmity between Buckingham and Wolsey, the King's infatuation with the charms of Anne, the trial of Queen Katharine, Wolsey's downfall, and the coronation. These scenes correspond to I, 1 and 3; II, 4; and III, 2 and 4 of the adaptation for His Majesty's, and omitted I, 2 (The Council Chamber), II, 1 (The River Gate), 2 (The Gallery), and 3 (The Plesaunce, Windsor); and III, 1 (also The Plesaunce) and 3 (Kimbolton). Tree's stage adaptation had already eliminated from Shakespeare all the scenes which had to do with the intrigues against Cranmer and the christening of Elizabeth. Barker's descriptive booklet advertising the film was accurate enough; on the cover was the title 'Scenes from Shakespeare's *King Henry VIII* As Given by Sir Herbert Tree at His Majesty's Theatre.' Nowhere, however, do I find any explicit statement of the length of the finished film. Nevertheless it was quite clearly not what we would call a short but a feature.

Barker's exploitation of the Tree film exceeded anything heretofore attempted. His pre-release publicity was followed by consistent and elaborate advertising. His announcements of the limitation of exhibition brought in immediate orders, which were handled in strict rotation; provincial managers were in haste to secure the film for their districts. He prepared an illustrated booklet which showmen could obtain at £1 per 1000 for sale to their patrons, and a frame containing photographs of the chief scenes for theatre display. He encouraged managers to embellish their performances with special orchestras and choruses in accordance with the importance of the occasion, and 'personally supervised rehearsals of special music which he thinks important in adding to the effectiveness of the subject'. Exhibitors caught the spirit. One of them, at Ipswich, was not only to add a recitation of Queen Katharine's speech at her trial but offered 'two half-guinea prizes to the boy and girl who writes the best 200 word essay on the subject of *King Henry VIII* as presented in the pictures', a device frequently used later as a means of attracting children and schoolteachers. At Bath tea was provided at the matinées. As a result of the exploitation, four days after *Henry VIII* was first publicly shown, the company which handled for Barker the provincial rentals announced to disappointed applicants that the film was 'fully booked for the stipulated six weeks,' and apologized because no further requests could be honoured. Nothing like this had ever happened before.

After an interval for private and trade exhibition, *Henry VIII* made its official début on February 27, 1911 in various theatres, London, suburban, and provincial, 'the exclusive right of display in so far as West-End audiences are concerned, having been acquired by Mr Alfred Butt for the Palace, and Messrs Horace Sedger and Edward Laurillard for other areas covered by their group of electric palaces, of which the Marble Arch Hall is, perhaps, the best known.' Despite prices of admission which were higher than normal, queues formed early and many were unable to obtain entrance. The theatres were continually full. From the exhibitor's point of view, the picture was clearly a huge success. A. E. Taylor writing from London for the American trade was only one enthusiast. 'The great event in the Moving Picture World this week has been the production of *Henry VIII*. . . . Words fail one to adequately describe this great triumph of the kinematographers' art. The picture is without doubt the greatest that has ever been attempted in this country, and I am almost tempted to say in any other. . . . In it we have the best of dramatic talent, and consequently the acting surpasses anything ever seen in moving pictures before. Mr Will Barker, in inducing Sir H. Tree to allow his company from His Majesty's Theatre to be filmed, has placed kinematography under an obligation to him which it will be hard to repay. The effect on the moving picture industry here will be enormous.' The non-technical press, not accustomed to taking films seriously, at least praised the picture as a record of the stage performance.

A sampling from the reports of managers will show what happened in their theatres. There were 'immense crowds all week' at the King's Hall, Shepherd's Bush. 'Hundreds had to be turned away nightly, and the general impression of those fortunate to gain admission, was that it was the finest picture ever thrown on a screen.' At the Picture House, Leicester, the film was 'an astounding success, and owing to its popularity has been prolonged for two weeks.' The Highgate Electric Palace said it 'had a tremendous reception.' 'Immense queues thronged to all parts of the house' at the New Picture Palace, Plymouth. There was 'extraordinary business' at the Bijou, Camberwell. The Premier Electric Theatre, Harringay, reported that *Henry VIII* was 'not only drawing local people, but those from distant parts'. At Bath, the picture was 'a big money taker'; and all records were broken at Plymouth and South Shields. There is no doubt that patrons flocked to see the film.

Audience reaction, however, is more difficult to gauge. The response seems to have been mixed. Individuals showed enthusiasm; there was even some cheering at the conclusion. On the other hand, the typical motion picture spectator accustomed to different fare must have been somewhat baffled. The prestige would hardly have sufficed to please him at a film which he could not understand both because of its subject and its treatment as an incomplete reproduction of a stage play he had never read. The more sophisticated spectator felt that much had been left out, and one gentleman, evidently more accustomed to His Majesty's than to motion pictures, rose in the stalls at the beginning of a performance and complained audibly, 'I say, you know we can't hear a word!' Nevertheless, six years later, at the death of Tree, a reporter for the *Cinema News and Property Gazette* recalls the film as 'one of the finest picture plays ever produced, and really the origin of the super-films. . . . [It] will never be forgotten by those who had the good fortune to see it.'

Tree's feelings too seem to have been divided. His enthusiasms were often short lived, and besides he must have received a good deal of ribbing from his friends. Low Warren says he 'was never proud' of the film.

'I once asked him, at the time it was showing, how he felt when he first stood before the camera. We were seated in the Dome, his famous den at His Majesty's Theatre. His reply was typical.

' "Well," said Tree with a smile, "one throws oneself into the thing as one goes into a submarine. You take a dive – a plunge as it were – into the unknown, and calmly await the result. It was a strange experience for me, I admit. I found in it a novel form of expression, and as a new sensation, I embraced it. I fell into it quickly enough. Before the film was finished I wondered if I had not deteriorated – whether, like playing the pianola, I might lose my touch. In playing before the camera I found an entirely different method is required, as different as sculpture is from painting. Still, I was greatly interested and pleased to see the result. In fact, looking at what was on the film", said Sir Herbert laughingly, "I thought I was quite passable – thanks to the operator." '

And Warren adds, in an account which it must be said is not completely accurate, that Tree was ' "not anxious that his art should be perpetuated in celluloid", as he put it.'

Certainly Tree did not alter his agreement with Barker, for at the end of the stipulated period the prints were called in, and on April 13th the press and various other visitors saw at Ealing an unusual ceremony which I wish had never taken place. After the prints had been counted and checked, they were unwound into a loose pile on an iron sheet. Barker himself applied a match to the films; as the flames shot up, everyone retired to a cooler distance and watched – all except a cameraman for the company who shot a new film of the burning of *Henry VIII*. How typical of Barker not to let an opportunity slip! In a minute or two all that was left was a heap of ashes. Sir Herbert was not at the execution; it was understood that he would be given as a memento a print of the new film. If he was, what happened to it? The rest is silence.

Barker's *Henry VIII* and the British distribution during this period of American and European Shakespeare films gave impetus to a series of pictures presenting Frank Benson and his company. Barker too was involved with them but in a less conspicuous way. In 1911, the Co-operative Cinematograph Company, which had been formed out of the remnants of the defunct London Cinematograph Company, began production under the management of G. W. Jones, who had been in the earlier concern, with *Julius Caesar*: 'As Played by the famous F. R. Benson Company, at the Shakespeare Memorial Theatre, Stratford-on-Avon.' The idea just possibly originated with Benson, more probably with Jones, who was aware of the excitement generated by Barker's and other Shakespeare films. Certainly the publicity had none of the fanfare of Barker, who must have been sub-contracted to do the photography; his name was not mentioned in any of the advertising for the series. No doubt he was as a consequence of *Henry VIII* sought out as the current expert in the field.

Julius Caesar, said Co-operative in advance of release, 'is superbly acted and produced with wonderful realism, being a subject which is specially adapted to the kinematograph. It is doubly interesting owing to its historic nature and having a complete plot which is easily followed throughout, and is also well-known as one of Shakespeare's most successful works. A classical subject that will be appreciated by all'. This 'classical subject' was released at 4d for each of its 990 feet on March 25th. Benson played Mark Antony; his wife, Portia. The others listed were Guy Rathbone as Caesar, Murray Carrington as Brutus, Eric Maxim as Cassius, and Nora Lancaster as Calphurnia.

There was no doubt a trade screening before the picture was shown to the public but the comments in the journals were apparently based on company hand-outs before release.

'*Julius Caesar* is well adapted for film production there being so many in-dividuals that can be intelligently portrayed in pictures, and in this version, that master of the legitimate, Mr F. R. Benson, has certainly accomplished wonders in regard to stage management with the result that many tableaux are of a most convincing and intelligent character, the most notable scenes being the murder of Caesar in the Senate, Marc Antony's oration over Caesar at the Forum, with the subsequent burning of Caesar's body, the great quarrel scene between Brutus and Cassius, the battlefield at Philippi, and the dramatic ending of Brutus and Cassius on the field of battle. We have selected these scenes at random as being vividly and intelligently given, but the minor scenes are of an equally complete character, and con-tribute materially to a successful production. Additional interest is given to the subject by the fact that Mr Benson and his clever company were filmed in the Memorial Theatre, Stratford-on-Avon, which is closely identified with the life of the great bard.

'Everything possible in the way of acting, grouping, scenery and dressing was done to make the production worthy of the occasion, consequently, there is little doubt but that it will receive a ready appreciation at the hands of exhibitors.'

At least this gives us some of the content of the picture, and *Bioscope* listing the same scenes as the *Kinematograph and Lantern Weekly* can only add that the film is 'well acted and adapted'. Evidently exhibitors took the bait for the last journal carries a Co-operative advertisement on March 30th which announced that *Julius Caesar* had been received 'very favourably by buyers', and that the next productions would be *Macbeth*, *The Taming of the Shrew*, *Richard III*, *The Merry Wives of Windsor*, and *Twelfth Night*.

The last two were never made, but the first three proceeded in order. Co-operative was publicly confident: 'Another Great Production/Shakespeare's *Macbeth*/Look out for it/Released April 8th/Length 1260 feet. . . . Shakespearian Revivals are the best attraction you can put before your patrons. See these two [*Macbeth* and *Julius Caesar*] and you are certain to buy, as they are each of distinctive merit and certain money-makers.' The journals in review use the stock phrases: 'faithful representation. . . graphically given in a thoroughly intelligent and convincing manner . . . plot easy to follow, the acting being excellent throughout . . . effective groupings'; 'wonderfully and vividly portrayed.' The undiscriminating praise must have made it difficult for exhibitors to choose pictures in those days. However, 'all the familiar incidents' were included, 'from the Witches' Scene in the first act to the death of Macbeth,' and 'the murder of King Duncan by Macbeth, and the subsequent terror-stricken murderer and his wife flying from the scene of their crime' is singled out for particular mention. 'This is a vivid piece of acting, that even without words tells the gruesome story in every detail. The Banquetting Scene, and appearance of Banquo's Ghost is another realistic and impressive scene. The death of Lady Macbeth and the great Battle Scene, terminating with the fierce encounter between Macbeth and Macduff, are also both worthy of special commendation.' Is it noteworthy that the film was longer than *Julius Caesar*, to depict 'all the familiar incidents'? Benson was of course Macbeth, Mrs Benson, Lady Macbeth, and Rathbone, Carrington, Maxim, and Miss Lancaster reappear.

No doubt the same were in *The Taming of the Shrew*, released on April 29th in 1120 feet, but do we need details? It was, says *Bioscope*, 'remarkable for its fine acting and vigor throughout the well-staged scenes', but the summary is brief and useless, despite the proclamation earlier by Co-operative that it was 'Our Next Great Production'.

The final Benson Shakespeare, *Richard III*, was released in 1385 feet on June 12th after a postponement from June 1st, and since the film is extant one can say with confidence and even apply the comment to the other Co-operative films that it was a 'most arch deed of piteous massacre'.

A list of the scenes and titles captioned on the film will show the general structure of the story and the proliferation of information which the makers thought essential for the clarity of viewers:

'Scene 1. The Battle of Tewksbury. Henry VI defeated and crown passed to Edward IV. [This is a kind of amalgamation and simplification of material from *Henry VI*, Part III, V, 5 and 7, the defeat of Queen Margaret and the Lancastrian forces, and Edward's resumption of the throne.]

Scene 2. Murder of King Henry VI in the Tower of London by Richard, Duke of Gloucester, afterwards Richard the Third. [*Henry VI*, Part III, V, 6.]

"I'll throw the body in another room
And triumph, Henry, in the day of doom."

Scene 3. King Edward IV orders arrest of Clarence, at Gloucester's instigation. [*Richard III*, I, 1.]

"Go tread the path that you shalt ne'er return,
Simple, plain Clarence! I do love thee so,
That I will shortly send thy soul to heaven."

Scene 4. Richard woos Lady Anne over King Henry's corpse [I, 2.]

"Was ever woman in this humour woo'd?
Was ever woman in this humour won?
I'll have her but I will not keep her long."

Scene 5. Murder of the Duke of Clarence in The Tower. [I, 4.]

"A bloody deed and desperately dispatched!
How fain, like Pilate, would I wash my hands
Of this most grievous guilty murder done!"

Scene 6. News of the death of Clarence brought to King Edward. [II, 1.]

[Unnumbered scene.] Gloucester prevents coronation of the Prince of Wales. [III, 1.]

Scene 6a. Lord Hastings visits Princes in the Tower. [This is transitional, a visual adaptation of III, 2 where Hastings is about to go to the Tower.]

[Unnumbered scene.] Lord Hastings sent to execution. [III, 4.]

"Come, lead me to the block; bear him my head;
They smile at me, who shortly shall be dead."

[Unnumbered scene.] Lord Mayor of London offers crown to Richard, which he reluctantly accepts. [III, 7.]

"Then I salute you with this Royal title,
Long live King Richard, England's worthy king."

Scene 8. Coronation of Richard and death of his Queen (Lady Anne). [IV, 2, but in Shakespeare Anne is *reported* sick, and *reported* dead in IV, 3.]

Scene 9. Murder of Princes in the Tower. [IV, 3, but shown instead of described.]

> "The most arch deed of piteous massacre
> That ever yet this land was guilty of."

Scene 10. Arrival of Richmond in England. Nobles rally round his standard. [Shakespeare does not show Richmond on the stage until V, 2, well after arrival, and Richmond's speech is still later in V, 3.]

> "O thou whose captain I account myself,
> Look on my forces with a gracious eye."

Scene 11. Richard starts to meet Richmond, is cursed by his mother, Queen Margaret, and Queen Elizabeth. [IV, 4.]

> "Therefore take with thee my most heavy curse
> Which in the day of battle tire thee more
> Than all the complete armour that thou wear'st."

[Unnumbered scene.] Buckingham captured and sent to execution. [In Shakespeare, Buckingham is reported captured at the end of IV, 4, and led to execution in V, 1.]

Scene 12. Richard's dream, the night before the battle. [V, 3.]

> "O coward conscience how dost thou afflict me."

Scene 13. Battle of Bosworth Field. Death of Richard. Richmond offered the crown. [V, 4 and 5.]

> "God and your arms be praised, victorious friends;
> The day is ours, the bloody dog is dead." [V, 5.].
> "Now civil wounds are stopped, Peace lives again:
> That she may long live here, God say – Amen."'

Anyone who has tried to make a brief summary of Shakespeare's play will realize how difficult it is to cover the many active characters and the complicated series of turnabouts and intrigues in such a way as to convey to someone who has not read it the full story-line of the complete *Richard III*. What has made it over the centuries an extremely successful stage play has been not the plot but the characterization of Crookback and the opportunities it offers to a star actor, particularly one of the old school. Nevertheless upon first consideration one who has not seen the film might reasonably think that the scenario provided by the explanatory titles and Shakespearean quotations was a passable job. To use Shakespeare's own words seems reasonable; to make clearer the action by indication of place or episode sensible. There is even here some attempt at appropriate adaptation. Material from the last act of *Henry VI*, Part III is turned into staged action by way of exposition; what is in Shakespeare described is depicted; there is even some transposition of episode from the end of *Richard III* to alternate the gathering of opposing forces in the impending conflict. But a further glance should begin to raise doubts. What happened to Edward IV? Why was Hastings decapitated for visiting the Princes? What brought about the demise of Lady Anne – for that matter, why did Richard woo her at all? Why was Buckingham 'captured and sent to execution'? And even before seeing the film, one might wonder why the quotations so frequently repeat the substance of the episodic designations in bare prose, and are there not an awful lot of them anyway?

The truth is that the story is not at all clear, even with captions that take up almost half of the film footage, leaving, say, 700 feet and ten or twelve minutes to do what silent cinema should do, tell its story through significant moving pictures in a continuity which can be followed. Here what is visualized is, as Miss Low has perspicuously observed, merely 'a number of illustrations' of what has already appeared on the screen as titles, in short, 'a number of tableaux.' Even if the titles are carefully noted, what is shown in action would be largely unintelligible to one who has not read the play, and to a Shakespearean merely an exasperation. Benson's Richard is recognizable as a villain, but the others are vague shadows without definition or real identity. It is often difficult even to decide who the characters are, much more why they do things, or indeed what they are doing. They 'seem to consist of unwieldy groups of unrecognizable people brandishing swords, arguing and moving about on their own obscure business.'

Why is this so? Miss Low explains with here and there a minor assist from me. In the first place, the rigidly stationary camera is so far from the fully pictured stage that the stage becomes the focus for the eye, and the characters cannot easily be distinguished. The stage scenery and appurtenances become obtrusive. A viewer sees the front line of the floor cloth and recognizable boards between it and the footlights even in supposedly exterior scenes, and the floor line of the backdrop. Second, the groupings are stage groupings, so that essential action which the camera should interpret is not centered immediately before it. The foreground is left empty, and principals are obscured by other characters in the background. One cannot see with the camera eye. Third, the exaggeration of gesture is stage gesture amplified, and it is appropriate neither to the theatre nor to the screen; the overregistration of emotions with no suitable aesthetic distance becomes ridiculous. Fourth, even the one scene which might have offered the necessary variety, the appearance of the ghosts of Richard's victims, is botched. Here surely the long known techniques of fades, dissolves, and double exposure should have been used. Nothing of the kind. The ghosts appear successively pictured by Richard's bed, make their apparently violent speeches, and one is instantaneously cut to another without transition. This is not movie technique; it is not even good stage technique which might have called for the backlighted appearance of the ghost *behind* Richard's tent.

This film, then, is stage film at its worst, theatrical rather than cinematic in its methods and effects, a series of incomprehensible illustrations of subjects described by titles, of unrecognizable people doing unintelligible things. One might go further: it is not in any true sense a movie at all, nor is it, as stage films can be to a certain extent, a record of theatrical performance from which one can gather an acting style, a characteristic bit of business, or the interplay between performers. It may well have been so with the other Co-operative films too. If Barker photographed this one as well as the others, it makes one wonder whether his *Henry VIII* was any better. By its very nature it must have had many of the same faults, and Barker was best known for his reproduction of actualities, rather than his imaginative rearrangement of materials. Yet *Henry VIII*, for all its duplication of stage action, was longer, and had at least more time to be clear. Moreover, though it was photographed on a stage, it was on the more flexible studio stage, not that of the Memorial Theatre, and Barker himself had much more of a stake in it. Personally concerned and with his experience and flair, perhaps *Henry VIII* was the high point, though not very high, of British Shakespeare films of the period, and the Benson films an unhappy retrogression.

Even though the English films of 1908–1911 are dominated by the unfortunate misunderstanding of their medium which led to unoriginal reproduction, without proper transformation, of stage action and stage business, quantitatively there were eight home products based on Shakespeare which film-goers could, if they chose, go to see, and one of them at least, *Henry VIII*, involved new procedures of manufacturing and distribution, if not aesthetic principles, which were startling and on the whole, healthy for growth. There was too, at least a minimal conception that film might be used as a means of recording for posterity the performances of actors and companies who would soon vanish, and though film as reproduction of theatre cannot be film as film, yet even skimpy records can be valuable for future generations. The period therefore has some importance.

Yet it is meaningful that almost three times as many Shakespeare films from other countries were exhibited in London and the provinces during this span. The United States sent over the Vitagraph pictures of *Antony and Cleopatra*, *Julius Caesar*, *Macbeth*, *The Merchant of Venice*, *A Midsummer Night's Dream*, *Richard III* and *Twelfth Night*, and Selig's *Merry Wives of Windsor*. From the continent, mostly from France and Italy came *Antony and Cleopatra* (called *Cleopatra*), a *Brutus*, several *Hamlets*, *Lear*, *Macbeth*, *The Merchant of Venice*, a *Merry Wives of Windsor* labelled *Falstaff*, *A Midsummer Night's Dream*, *Othello*, *The Taming of the Shrew*, and *A Winter's Tale*. Imports from the United States equalled in number the Shakespeare films of British making; the nearer continent exceeded them by at least five.

I have taken these figures from announcements of release and from reviews in trade journals, but since policy is inconsistent, there may well have been more. One does not know whether to welcome the opportunity the British Isles had to see so much Shakespeare on the screen even in highly primitive form – I count not less than thirty films in four years – or to condemn the sterility and the wrongheadedness of the British products which with perhaps one exception could not compete. No one of course can make any claim for the Shakespeare films yet made on the basis of true artistic merit, but judging from those I have seen and what I have learned, the British films do not compare favourably with what was brought in from across the ocean and the Channel.

CHAPTER V

Strange Motions

THE Shakespeare films produced in the United States between 1908 and 1911 inclusive were essentially a part of the vast business of popular entertainment. They were that too in England, but with a difference in that they tended to reproduce and record the stage performances of actors of the theatre, whereas the American companies used their own motion picture players. On the Continent, however, there was a definite and conscious movement, however disappointing, toward the 'art film.' It was to be concerned with authors as well as stage actors, literature as well as theatre. Its aim, no longer casual but based on serious critical theory, was to use what it called noble subjects and the most distinguished actors it could employ to interpret those subjects in a form, not so much theatrical as cinematic. That it rather badly failed to achieve its objectives was partly the fault of the theory, partly its failure to realize it in the relatively new medium.

Shakespeare was not originally involved with this movement, but as a noble subject it was inevitable that he would be included, and there were in consequence a considerable number of Shakespeare films in this period, though it is fair to say that some would have been produced without the particular impulse. They were made principally in France and Italy; Denmark also participated. The theory and the impetus came from France.

The production organization which was to give shadowy substance to the art film was itself called Film d'Art. Founded on March 25, 1907, with a capital of 500,000 francs, it was presided over by the brothers Lafitte, who knew the value of publicity. It was to make full use of the talents of great writers and great actors: Sardou, Rostand, Capus, Donnay, and Lavedan were mentioned among the former; Bernhardt, Réjane, Mounet-Sully, Coquelin, Le Bargy among the actors. Henri Lavedan of the French Academy and Charles-Gustave-Antoine Le Bargy from the Comédie Française were to be immediately concerned as literary and dramatic directors. Early in 1908 a studio was built at Neuilly, and an agreement was signed with Pathé for exclusive rights for distribution and exploitation. On

November 17, 1908, specially invited spectators saw among other pictures the first presentation of what has become an historic film, *L'Assassinat du duc de Guise*, scenario by Lavedan, direction by Le Bargy, who also acted Henri III, and his assistant, André Calmettes, a cast which included Albert Lambert as the duc de Guise, and music by Camille Saint-Saëns. Nothing like this had ever happened in film before, and the repercussions were enormous. It was not that this was a great film, nor though since much maligned a particularly bad one for 1908, but that it opened up opportunities not heretofore realized. Its ultimate influence was more important than the immediate effects which concern us here. The practical Charles Pathé shortly after the initial manifestoes of Film d'Art and before waiting to see its first films founded S.C.A.G.L., the Société Cinématographique des Auteurs et Gens de Lettres, with plans to produce such proven authors as Daudet, Zola, and Victor Hugo under the direction of Albert Capellani, an actor formerly with André Antoine and theatre administrator who had also made films. Pathé in March 1909 was also to found in Rome Film d'Arte Italiana with separate direction. Other companies followed suit. If the idea of original scripts by famous authors and a cast of well known theatre names under a theatre director was shortly abandoned, at least we would have famous stars in famous plays but not photographs of stage performances. This was where Shakespeare came in. The new evolution can be traced with the decline of the original Film d'Art company.

The *succès d'estime* of *L'Assassinat* was soon accompanied by a serious financial deficit, which increased with the next releases. *Le Retour d'Ulysse* with a scenario by Jules Lemaître interpreted by Paul Mounet and Julia Bartet and directed by Le Bargy, assisted by Calmettes, was flat and academic, and though *Le Baiser de Judas*, written by Lavedan and with Mounet-Sully and Lambert fortunately went to Fontainbleau for its backgrounds, a *Tosca* with Sarah Bernhardt, Lucien Guitry, and Paul Mounet was at Bernhardt's insistence not even distributed. Contracts with noted writers and actors were proving too expensive, the Lafittes were replaced by Paul Gavault, Le Bargy departed, Pathé as distributor was succeeded by Mono-film, but deficits mounted. The stars of the Comédie Française were little used.

Nevertheless Film d'Art did present Paul Mounet in a *Macbeth* film usually dated 1909, but probably of early 1910, directed by Calmettes, with Jeanne Delvair as Lady Macbeth. Mounet was born in 1847. After studying medicine, he decided to become an actor, and made his official début at the Odéon in 1880 as Horace in Corneille's play of that name. Ten years later in 1889, he moved to the Comédie, where he became a sociétaire in 1891. There he was to achieve 'vif succès' as Macbeth on May 30, 1914, but I do not find he had played the part before the film. He was a fine actor but never achieved the high reputation of his older brother, Jean-Sully Mounet, known as Mounet-Sully, who has wrongly been assigned to this film. Jeanne

Delvair was of the same theatre, where she had made her debut in 1899. Calmettes, formerly Le Bargy's assistant, had acted and directed at the Odéon and the Théatre Sarah-Bernhardt, and was in 1911, when Film d'Art was under the direction of Charles Delac, to direct Réjane in the film version of her great theatrical success, *Madame Sans-Gêne*. Much could have been made of *Macbeth* if the picture had been longer, but though the story is remarkably full, the many scenes had to be short and swift to fall within the compass of one reel.

The title of the film in one of the extant prints is 'MACBETH/Tragédie de W. Shakespeare/Interprètes M. Paul Mounet de la Comédie Française/ Mlle Delvair de la Comédie Française.' The film opens with a fairly close shot of Mounet in costume, a sort of tunic; his glance is piercing, his chin bearded, his wig somewhat unkempt with hair falling almost to his shoulders. A similar shot of Mme Delvair shows an oval face, hair partly plaited and thrown forward over her breasts; her robe is light coloured, trimmed with dark, bejewelled down the front. Both actors are identified in subtitles immediately before they are pictured. The first explanatory caption is 'Une sinistre forêt. Des sorcières s'y livres à de singulières pratiques. Macbeth survient.' The witches are now shown in a glade; they light a fire, the smoke rises, the fire dies down and is rekindled. Macbeth watches through shrubbery, is seen by the witches, and appears before them. 'Macbeth rencontre des sorcières qui lui prédisent qu'il sera roi.' He wears a helmet, a cloak over his tunic, dark boots; the upper parts of his legs are white. Banquo and others enter and with Macbeth hear the prophetic greetings. The fire which has died down comes up again, its smoke blotting out the central figure and allowing a transition to a view of Macbeth as King, seated on a throne. Obviously this is an attempt to show what Macbeth is thinking. It is black on blank stock, contains no movement, and looks like a cut-out. After this interpolation we return to the glade; Macbeth and his friends are there but the witches have vanished. The cross-cut made their disappearance simple. Macbeth and Banquo show astonishment. A subtitle rams home the point: 'Puis elles disparaissent. Macbeth est très impres- sionné.' The astonishment continues as Macbeth and Banquo talk with much gesturing. They and their retainers leave the scene empty as they go off, as if leaving the stage of a theatre. With another subtitle we shift to 'Le camp du roi d'Ecosse,' where Duncan, crowned, sleeps before a tent with shields stacked against the tent pole. From the tent come Malcolm and Donalbain (not identified) who assist Duncan, evidently quite old, to rise. Macbeth enters, announces the victory (which we have not seen), is embraced by the King. Banquo is also present. There is a good deal of unheard talk after which all characters depart.

The next shot shows Macbeth's castle, twin arches at the rear, table and chair to the right, a chair left back of which stands Lady Macbeth. Guards are in the right arch through which we see vague mountains. As Lady

Macbeth, followed by attendants, comes downstage, a title is inserted. In one print it reads, 'Lady Macbeth reçoit Duncan et sa suite,' in another, 'Lady Macbeth donne l'hospitalité à Duncan, roi d'Ecosse.' The pictures show Lady Macbeth surprised by a soldier's announcement of the impending arrival. She retires to contemplate the mountains. Macbeth enters, followed by Duncan. There is general congratulation. Lady Macbeth motions to Duncan, who is tired, to sit down in the chair right; she kneels before him, then pours wine. Duncan rises; escorted by Lady Macbeth, he leaves. Macbeth stands before the chair the King has vacated, as the room clears and Lady Macbeth reappears. 'Elle suggère le régicide à Macbeth pour s'emparer du pouvoir.' Macbeth holds Duncan's crown; Lady Macbeth takes it and crowns Macbeth, hastily removing it as there is a sign of someone approaching, perhaps Banquo with a message or a request for the crown. The next shot shows a rearrangement of the stage. The left arch has become the guardroom which is now central, a bench left, table and stools right. (A draw curtain is available to close off an arch when it is not in use or to be masked.) Two guards are in the background; one leaves, the other takes off his cloak and puts his sword on the table. Lady Macbeth and servants bring wine which is put on the table; they depart. The other guard reappears from Duncan's room, off left; then both guards go to Duncan. Lady Macbeth re-enters, listens carefully, dopes the drink. She exits, and the guards reappear. The second removes his cloak; both drink and show signs of sleepiness. One flops onto the bench; the other goes rear, staggers, and falls. On the full stage, Lady Macbeth persuades Macbeth to murder Duncan, gives him a dagger, urges him roughly through the door left. In the guardroom, Lady Macbeth and Macbeth check on the sleeping guards. He departs for Duncan's room as Lady Macbeth waits. When he returns without the dagger, she retrieves it and does something obscure to the guards, and exeunt. There enter unidentifiable figures who show consternation at the condition of the guards and leave to discover the death of Duncan. There are so many persons in the scene at this point that it is difficult to determine what anyone is doing but Macbeth after consoling Malcolm and Donalbain, still, so far as the spectators are concerned, unidentified, stabs the guards as Lady Macbeth reappears. 'Les fils du roi echappés au carnage vont demander l'appui du roi d'Angleterre.' Cut to the outside of the castle. Malcolm and Donalbain reappear and since the drawbridge is up, jump into the moat and are seen escaping. In the guardroom again Macbeth is apparently explaining his hasty stabbing of the guards.

All this is, I suppose, straightforward enough in its presentation of the action of Shakespeare's play – if one knows the play – but the next scene is a bit of a surprise. It is preceded by a title: 'Le couronnement. Banco refusant de reconnaître Macbeth pour roi.' Macbeth is on the throne surrounded by courtiers. Various people bow before him, but Banquo declines to do so.

He complies only when the angry Macbeth stands and threatens. Even so, Banquo turns his back on the King before leaving. It looks as though Macbeth gives a murderer a dagger and orders him after Banquo. In the outdoor scene which follows, however, there seem to be not one or three but four murderers, skulking under a tree. Banquo and Fleance approach with others behind them. The murderers attack, kill Banquo; Fleance escapes. The shift is to the banquet scene. There is an arch to the left, but all are at table right, until the murderer enters. Macbeth gets up, goes to him, is shown a bloody dagger, gives him money. As the murderer leaves, the Queen holds out her hand for Macbeth to return to his place beside her. 'Le spectre de Banco.' In a double exposure, as Macbeth starts to do so, Banquo is shown seated in Macbeth's chair. Macbeth recoils, starts away, but Lady Macbeth goes to him and shows him the empty chair. As Macbeth starts to sit again, the ghost of Banquo reappears. Lady Macbeth attempts to calm her husband, as Banquo vanishes, and the party breaks up.

In one print the next title is thoroughly confusing: 'Les fils de Duncan implorent Malcolm, roi d'Angleterre, le châtiment du coupable. Il le leur promets.' But this must be an ignorant substitution for the title in an earlier print, which quite properly reads, 'Le secours du roi d'Angleterre.' The scene is external but the King's throne is under a canopy which itself is under an archway. The sons implore, a messenger enters (to report the death of Banquo?), the King comes down from the throne and promises help. 'Macbeth retourne consulter les sorcières.' This seems to be a new set, perhaps an entrance to a cave, artificially constructed. One witch has a skull and bones beside her. Macbeth literally kicks her out of the way. Out of a smoking fire appears a sheet of scroll in Old English script, which a title interprets: 'Macbeth / tu n'auras rien à craindre / du roi d'Angleterre tant que / la forêt de Birnam ne se / mettre pas en marche.' Macbeth, pleased, goes out along with a guard who has stood watch. The next scene, within Macbeth's palace, shows the familiar double arches at the rear, with the right arch curtained. 'Les remords de Lady Macbeth.' She enters in a dark nightgown, hair loose. The doctor and her waiting gentlewoman watch behind and then in front of the curtain. Lady Macbeth rinses her hands as she sleepwalks. The minor characters retire, but Macbeth enters, hides behind a central pillar to observe Lady Macbeth who exits. Some persons appear excitedly with information for Macbeth, presumably news of the attack. All leave hurriedly, and we ponder another caption: 'La ruse de Malcolm / La forêt qui marche.' The final battle scene is huddled; if footage has not been lost, the action was hurried to get it into one reel. Despite the small number of participants, it is difficult to follow. One sees a glade with several dead soldiers, figures which appear individually and depart un-recognized, but it is clear that Macbeth and someone accompanying him, as they turn from the camera, see Birnam Wood approaching. The branches are thrown down. There is a hand-to-hand fight between Macbeth and, I guess, Fleance, in which Macbeth is killed, and the battle over, Fleance crowns Malcolm. I do not find Macduff anywhere in the film, but with unidentified characters it is impossible to be sure. The last title is appropriately: 'Fin.'

The no doubt wearisome detail of this summary demonstrates, however, how much the Film d'Art production made use of the conventions of the theatre. Actors are forever entering or leaving the scene as if they were on a stage, and the frequency with which the technique is used makes identification of characters in the rapidly paced and shifting episodes at times impossible. Talk and gesture which would interpret a play become empty or extravagant when there is no sound. Scenes with many characters would have some effect on a stage reasonably large but within the focus of the fixed camera the persons merely mask each other and confuse the spectator. The indoor scenes are played in stock sets, adapted by curtains, and with stage properties. And there is so much crammed into one reel as to make the action unintelligible to one unfamiliar with Shakespeare's play. It is probably not necessary to indict the captions which are meant to assist; without them the action is merely confusing. Respect for Shakespeare no doubt contributed to the intention to photograph all the major scenes, but any emotional participation would surely be achieved in such brief compass only by rigid selection and more prolonged concentration on the scenes chosen, and an attempt to convey continuity between them.

Yet this film is no worse than most primitives and in some respects is better. Some values are cinematic. The photography itself is admirably clear. Cross-cutting conveys simultaneous action, and double exposure gives reality to the appearance and disappearance of Banquo's ghost and makes Macbeth's perturbation intelligible. Macbeth's desire for sovereignty is shown by an episode in which he imagines himself on the throne, and the scene in which he tries on the crown at his own castle is a bit of visual business which conveys the direction of his thoughts. Fire effects are visual, and the appearance of the prophetic scroll in the smoke of the witches' fire is proper to the camera. The scenes in outdoor settings are divorced from the theatre, and the fairly architectural structure of the indoor scenes conveys less of paint and canvas than might be expected. There is some ingenuity in what simplification and compression are attempted, for example, the scene of Banquo's unwilling obeisance before Macbeth, and Macbeth's immediate reaction of anger and retaliation, and the development of Fleance as opposition. Finally the action, especially that of Mounet, is fresher, more his own, less conventional in either a stage or a motion picture sense than most other performers could have managed. His and Mme Delvair's introduction in costume, the same technique used in the probably earlier Vitagraph *King Lear*, is not of the cinema nor indeed of the stage, but at any rate establishes their identity as Macbeth and Lady Macbeth for the spectator and gives some pleasure, not necessarily intended, to the historian who wants to know how they appeared in motion. If *film d'art* is not art, it is by no means uninteresting.

There was another Film d'Art production which had a relation to Shakespeare, however muzzy. This was *The Children of Edward*, based on a once popular romantic tragedy (1833) by Casimir Delavigne. Delavigne's play simplifies Shakespeare's *Richard III* by concentrating on incidents and situations involving the characters of Gloucester, Queen Elizabeth, the two princes, Buckingham, and Tyrrel and their conflicts, external and internal. The stress is on the emotional engagement of mother and children, the wavering of Tyrrel who before becoming a profligate had lost a son, the calculated heroics of Buckingham to preserve the royal succession, and of course the insinuating perfidy of Richard. In the last scene the princes are murdered as the audience hears outside the tumult of Buckingham's attack on the Tower, where they have been confined. It is a sensational and sentimental piece, freighted with false psychology and execrable poetry, and now as deservedly forgotten as its author. How much of it the scenarist used I do not know, nor in this second-hand Shakespeare much care. Film d'Art was evidently proud of the picture. In an advertisement in the *Moving Picture World* of June 4th, 1910, it indicates the 'cast includes Garnier, Krauss and Demidoff. The settings and costumes are wonderfully brilliant, and the leading thespians of France furnish epoch-making acting.' In another in *Ciné-Journal* of June 25th it plumes itself and identifies further: 'Il y a des Films "ARTistiques" / Il y a des Films "EsthetiQUES" / Il y a toutes sortes de Films "ART" et en "IQUES" / Il n'y en a qu'UN seul qui soit "Le Film d'Art".' In a following list is included *Les Enfants d'Edouard*, with Philippe Garnier of the Comédie Française and Mme Demidoff of the Porte-St Martin. Garnier, Demidoff, and Henri Krauss were not of the same stature as Mounet and Delvair; the budget was pinching and economy was necessary.

It is difficult to know how far announcement of the plans of Film d'Art in 1907 affected the production elsewhere of films based on literature, specifically on Shakespeare, but I doubt for reasons already presented if there was immediate influence in English speaking countries, nor on Méliès, who had his own ideas, nor on the isolated Cines *Othello*. After all Film d'Art's first exhibition of *L'Assassinat* was not until November 17th, 1908, and its first Shakespeare film probably early 1910. Before the latter date, whether in part determined by rumors or announcements of plans or by developing production independent of them, there were other Shakespeare films on the continent, though exact dates of month and day are elusive. In 1908 Cines had produced in Italy a *Romeo and Juliet* by April and a *Hamlet* by May. Cines, founded in Rome in 1905 had by 1908 not only become the principal cinema company in Italy but the chief rival of Pathé and Gaumont for the European film market. In 1907 Mario Caserini, up to that time a painter, had become its artistic director, and he had a predilection for the

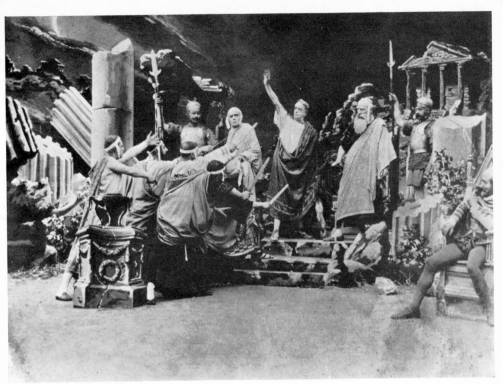

5. Georges Méliès as Shakespeare watches his conception of the murder of Caesar, from *Shakespeare Writing Julius Caesar* (1907). Museum of Modern Art Film Library

6. Romeo (Paul Panzer) and Juliet (Florence Lawrence) say good-bye as the Nurse listens for intruders in Vitagraph's *Romeo and Juliet* (1908). "*Pic,*" August 23, 1938

7. Paris and Capulet (Charles Kent) find Juliet apparently dead in Vitagraph's *Romeo and Juliet* (1908). "*Pic*," August 23, 1938

8. Desdemona (Julia Swayne Gordon) beams at Othello (William V. Ranous) in a gondola on wheels in Vitagraph's *Othello* (1908). *Photoplay*, July 191...

he mechanicals rehearse, Bottom (William V. Ranous
Quince (Charles Chapman) in the foreground, while
k (Gladys Hulette) looks on

b The two fairies watching Titania and Bottom are Helene
and Dolores Costello.

elena (Julia Swayne Gordon) and Demetrius (Walter
erman)

d Lysander (Maurice Costello) and Hermia (Rose Tapley)

Film frames from the Vitagraph *Midsummer Night's Dream* (1909). Courtesy of James Card

10. The final scene in Vitagraph's *Twelfth Night* (1909), Viola (Florence Turner)
and Orsino (Tefft Johnson) at left, Sebastian (Edith Storey) and Olivia (Julia
Swayne Gordon) at right. Louis Reeves Harrison, *Screencraft*, Chalmers
Publishing Co., 1916

11. The *Biograph Bulletin* No. 186 includes a picture of the wedding procession of Katherine (Florence Lawrence) and Petruchio (Arthur Johnson) in David Wark Griffith's *Taming of the Shrew* (1908). Museum of Modern Art Film Library

12. Paulina presents Hermione (Miss Rosemond) to Leontes (Martin Faust) and Polixenes (Frank Crane) in the final scene of the Thanhouser *Winter's Tale* (1910). *Moving Picture World*, May 21, 1910

so-called noble subjects. He directed the *Romeo and Juliet*; though probably he did not actually stage the 1908 *Hamlet*, he was certainly ultimately in charge and later was to direct a *Hamlet* himself.

The first news I find of the Cines *Romeo and Juliet* is in the American *Moving Picture World* of April 11th and 18th. In the second of these issues a Cines advertisement indicates release on April 6th of 'A Shakespearean conception of the Italian legend, done with a purity and vigor which easily marks the master film production of the year,' but I find no reviews to support Cines's enthusiasm, except an unidentified and somewhat equivocal newspaper comment quoted in the same periodical on May 2nd: 'The possibilities of motion pictures seem to have been reached in the successful representation of the drama.' A French journal, *Argus Phono-Cinéma* on May 16th gives its length as 225 metres, and George Dureau in the *Ciné-Journal* on September 15th, listing with other films what is apparently this picture, praises the rapprochement between film and theatre: 'Il y a là une dignité nouvelle pour le cinéma, naguère attardé dans de médiocres inspirations.'

Hamlet must have followed hard upon *Romeo and Juliet*. Williamson and Company, a British distributor, advertised in the *Kinematograph and Lantern Weekly* of May 14th a *Hamlet* in 855 feet for sale at £14 5s. which evidently refers to the Cines film, since it was 'Acted by a cast of well known Italian actors.' It was reviewed in the same issue:

'The difficult task of staging *Hamlet* so as to preserve the continuity of the narrative and at the same time include all of the most famous scenes has been attempted successfully. . . . The film begins with the appearance of his father's ghost to Hamlet and his two companions. Hamlet follows when the spirit (which is very cleverly represented in the film) beckons him. The figure leads Hamlet past a waterfall (a charming scene) to a rocky cavern and there reveals how he was killed . . . a vision appearing against the black background showing the poison being poured into his ears. This vision determines Hamlet to seek revenge, but he first seeks confirmation of what he has witnessed by having the scene re-enacted before the King by a troupe of strolling actors. The obvious discomposure of the King confirms his suspicions. Following this we witness the killing of the eavesdropping Polonius, the madness of Ophelia, the return of Laertes, the scene at the graveside, and last the duel between Laertes and Hamlet. Both are mortally wounded but before he expires Hamlet stabs the King. The subject is acted and staged throughout in masterly fashion and should be a feature in many programmes.'

We are indebted to the reviewer for the exceptional detail in his summary of the content, but there seems to be a great deal to force into 855 feet of film. On the other hand I am pleased to learn of the 'charming scene' of the waterfall and rocky cavern, implying outdoor photography, and the 'cleverly

D

represented' ghost of Hamlet's father and the vision of his murder, which sounds like double exposure though, alas, the critic does not particularize. These parts at any rate indicate adaptation to the visual medium.

There were other Italian Shakespeare films in 1908, though I do not know whether or not a Cines picture titled in French *Un drame judiciare à Venise* was based on *The Merchant of Venice*. There is less doubt about another *Hamlet*, and a *Taming of the Shrew*. The first was made by Milano, founded by Luca Comerio in this year, and probably directed by that former photographer of actualities. I know as little about *La Bisbetica Domata* of 187 metres put out by the Società Italiana Fratelli Pineschi; the *fratelli* were Lamberto and Azeglio; Lamberto seems to have been the more active, and, at a guess, directed. I cannot find more and can only say with Kate:

> Fie, fie, unknit that threat'ning unkind brow
> And dart not scornful glances from those eyes. . . .

If you wish music, Pathé made in Austria a sound film of *Othello*, 'gesungen und gespielt von Kammersänger Erik Schmedes'; if a laugh, a comic *Othello* from Nordisk in Denmark in 277 feet, which showed an actor, played by Carl Alstrup, studying the main role; he 'becomes so imbued with his part that he deals violently with any caller, and in the end is pursued and subjected to rough treatment.'

It is extremely difficult to date accurately continental films within the period covered by this chapter, but some can reasonably be assigned to 1909. Pathé listed an *All's Well That Ends Well* for release on March 8th, but this was only a title borrowing. Also in France, Eclipse by autumn had a picture called *Henry IV*, but I suspect the King was Henry of Navarre rather than Lancaster. Gaumont's *Les Filles de Shylock*, a sound film, would seem to be equally peripheral, and Knaur's reference under Shakespeare to a *Henry III*, directed in Italy by Giovanni Pastrone, is a misunderstanding; Pastrone directed for Itala which made a *Henry III*, presumably about the King of France. As with other films of 1909 there are many perplexities, but at least some are more Shakespearean.

Of an Italian *Julius Caesar*, produced by Itala, I first catch sight in the *Ciné-Journal* of October 11–18th where it is listed merely as an historical drama in 255 metres and not reviewed, but the summary and comment in the *Moving Picture World* of November 20th and December 24th make clear that this picture released in America on November 18th in 850 feet was Shakespearean enough, if not therefore very satisfactory. Since I analyse shortly an extant positive print in the National Archive of the British Film Institute I reproduce only the *World*'s criticism in the second issue:

'Perhaps this picture is in some ways as good as anything this firm has done The dramatic possibilities in this historic scene, the assassination of Caesar, are great and perhaps will never be wholly exhausted. It is a touch of the romance of history that appeals very strongly to the imagination, and naturally has its effect on the reproduction of the story, no matter what medium is employed. The Caesar here is reasonably dignified, and the conspirators perform their parts with reasonable fidelity to the ordinary interpretation of the story. It doesn't seem that the company rises quite to the possible dramatic heights, and it does so well that one wishes it had done better. But however these slight shortcomings may arouse a desire to see some of the work a little better done, one may thoroughly enjoy the film and see again the murder of the great statesman and soldier re-enacted with sufficient fidelity to make it seem real. The picture as a whole is to be commended, and for such an ambitious attempt holds its quality well from beginning to end.'

This vague and vapourish review manages neatly however in showing a certain disapproval without offending the distributor.

The incomplete print I have examined justifies the disapproval. The story has at least ten scenes:

   I Calphurnia in her home is told by her attendants, who hear the tumult outside, of the arrival of Caesar from Gaul. In joy she rushes to an archway, rear, her arms outspread. Caesar enters and they embrace. The action is too far upstage to be a good shot, and the soldiers who accompany Caesar only clutter the scene in miming their triumph.

  II Subtitle: 'Brutus surprises the tyrannical aspirations of Julius Caesar his anger for the attempt against the liberty of the Republic.' (Is this bad translation?) Caesar is in conference with someone unidentified. Brutus enters and overhears what he takes to be Caesar's 'tyrannical aspirations' and designs against the state. This strip is largely unheard conversation.

 III Subtitle: 'Mark Antony obtains from the Senate the triumph and the crowning of Caesar notwithstanding the opposition of Brutus and his friends.' The scene is the Senate; the argument is evident but unintelligible, partly because this sequence has badly faded. I discern no crowning but the opposition is clear.

 IV Subtitle: 'The Triumph.' The street procession moves through an arch at rear toward the camera. The *Cinema News and Property Gazette* was to call this 'a magnificent spectacle, splendidly staged,' but the scene is so crowded that characters cannot be picked out.

  V A street scene with a slave apparently asleep on some steps. Two conspirators enter talking, decide the slave will not overhear. They are joined by two more conspirators. The assassination is apparently planned and exeunt. The slave rises and runs off. It would help if we knew who in addition to Brutus the conspirators are. The summary in the *Moving Picture World* mentions Cassius and Casca, but there is no such identification in the film.

VI Subtitle: 'Calphurnia's dream. Scorning the warnings and the prayers Caesar faces fearlessly his destiny.' The scene is Caesar's house as in I, with Calphurnia asleep on a bench. Her dream is shown in a double exposure back left, the conspirators enacting Caesar's murder. As they dissolve, Calphurnia starts up in terror. The slave comes to tell what he has overheard. He leaves as Caesar enters. Calphurnia urges Caesar not to go to the Senate. Two conspirators come for him. He apparently decides to remain, changes his mind, picks up his cloak, and follows them off. This scene is at least cinematic and the action is clear, if the photography is not.

VII Subtitle: 'Death of Caesar.' Amid palaver in the Senate House, Caesar enters and talks to Antony as the conspirators prepare. They rush upon Caesar and stab him. The Senate empties except for Brutus, who stands alone. The populace pour into the building. Subtitle: 'Mark Antony excites the people against the murderers.' There are perhaps two sequences here, one inside the Senate and one outside, but it is impossible to know since the sections covering the actual assassination and Antony's speech are lost, though the subtitles are present. Much of the strip has faded.

VIII Brutus, at first alone in his garden, is joined by conspirators who report that they are to be driven from Rome. All leave in haste.

IX The same street scene and arch as in IV. The conspirators are pursued by soldiers and populace.

X Philippi. The entrance to the tent of Brutus who talks to two soldiers, perhaps conspirators but not identified. At the rear is a painted backdrop of a landscape. The soldiers salute and leave upstage on horseback. Brutus turns and walks into his tent, as the camera pans, 'a piece of clever staging,' says the *Cinema News*. Within the tent, Brutus lies down on a couch and goes to sleep before a black background. There may well be a sequence missing here; the *Cinema News* says, 'While he sleeps the camp is attacked, and a stirring encounter follows.' If so, there is a cut-back to the tent, rather than a continuous scene. Soldiers rush in to wake Brutus, presumably announcing the attack. As they leave, Brutus accompanies them to the entrance, then returns within and is confronted with the ghost of Caesar against the black curtain. The supernatural appearance is not, so far as I could make out, handled by double exposure, odd since it was used in VI and would have been more effective. A subtitle, 'The Death of Brutus' is illustrated. He draws a sword and stabs himself, falling to the ground at Caesar's feet. There is evidently cross-cutting here; we are shown soldiers fighting in the camp between tents. When we return to the tent, the ghost has disappeared. Antony arrives on horseback, dismounts, enters the tent, finds Brutus dead. There are soldiers with Antony, and to them he makes an unintelligible speech, presumably;

'This was the noblest Roman of them all.' What I have designated the tenth scene at Philippi is actually a series of sequences, the number of which is not determinable. At any rate, according to the *Cinema News*: 'It is a strong and dramatic conclusion to a most excellent historical subject.'

However, as a whole the picture is disappointing. Its best scenes are Philippi and Calphurnia's dream. Even allowing for the wretched condition of the print and the difficulties of seeing clearly what was actually in the film, the crowds are poorly handled so as to minimize the importance of central characters, who are often too far away from the camera and cannot be recognized or identified. The painted backdrop at Philippi is notably out of place, especially since there are outdoor scenes elsewhere. Some of the invented action is unnecessarily obvious, particularly the episodes involving eavesdropping; the discussion of the conspiracy before a slave, even if he is pretending to be asleep, makes the plotters seem remarkably unintelligent. And in general the photography and the acting are primitive. I do not know who was involved. Itala, though it had a progenitor, was founded in 1908 in Turin. Its producer was the youthful Giovanni Pastrone, who in 1914 was to make the famous *Cabiria*, but he was administrator, inventor, and supervisor more often than director, and what his actual connection was with *Julius Caesar* is problematic. Itala made no other film closely related to Shakespeare.

Cines of Rome which had already produced an *Othello* in 1907, and a *Romeo and Juliet* and a *Hamlet* in 1908 may have produced another *Othello* in 1909, and certainly was responsible for a *Macbeth* in the same year. On the first I find no information and basically only one source. More is available on the *Macbeth*. Caserini had a penchant for the production of, for the time, fairly elaborate historical subjects with of course costumes and extras and monumental backgrounds; some of these films were based on literature. His *Macbeth* was reported to have cost about $10,000 for 1460 feet of film and much of its wide success was attributed to its spectacle and crowd effects. The Film Import and Trading Company which handled its distribution in the United States, where it was released the week of December 6th, advertised that it was 'a very special feature and your exchange will doubtless ask an increased rental for it, as it costs them more than the regular program.' Some of this may be revealed in the unfortunately incomplete description in the *Moving Picture World* of December 11th.

'The play [that is, the picture play] opens with the scene on the wild heath where the witches appear to Macbeth and Banquo, as they are returning from their victorious battle with the rebels. They predict the kingship of Macbeth with the words "All Hail, King, that shall be hereafter." They show him a crown, and having also predicted that he shall be created Thane of Cawdor, and that the sons of Banquo shall be Kings of Scotland and not those of

Macbeth, the witches fade away, to the utter dismay of the two generals. Then follows a series of very fine tableaux, showing King Duncan conferring upon Macbeth the dignity of Thane of Cawdor, thus verifying the prophecy of the witches, the evil councillings of Lady Macbeth and the visit of King Duncan to Macbeth's castle accompanied by his two sons, Malcolm and Donalbain, with a numerous retinue. The King is received with gracious smiles by Lady Macbeth, who is still urging her husband to kill him so that they both attain to royal state. Macbeth's honorable aversion to so foul a deed, and the constant promptings of his wife, are finely portrayed. The murder of the King is finally accomplished, and Lady Macbeth is seen to place the drug stained daggers in the belt of one of the royal attendants, to divert suspicion. Macbeth is crowned King. The assassination of Banquo follows, and his ghost is seen to appear to Macbeth at the great feast.

'Macbeth's second consultation with the witches in their cave is shown, and he is told to beware of Macduff, the Thane of Fife, and that he should never be vanquished until the wood of Birnam should move.'

At this point the description just stops, perhaps because the reviewer had rather spread himself on the first part of the picture and had no more space. If, however, there were 'very fine tableaux' and a 'numerous retinue,' if the crowning is actually depicted, surely one of Caserini's big scenes must have been Birnam Wood coming to Dunsinane. Alas, there is no evidence, for this is the only review of the film I have been able to find, though it also was shown in England and France, and won some sort of a prize at Milano. The Macbeth, I gather, was Dante Capelli; the Lady Macbeth, Maria Gasperini, the wife of Caserini.

Othello was evidently Shakespeare's most popular play in Italy; there were two more presentations in 1909. One, however, was a parody, adapted and directed by Yambo for the Società Anonima Pineschi which in July became Latium Film. Yambo was the pseudonym of Giulio Enrico Novelli, son of the great Ermete Novelli who will short reappear in this chronicle and to more purpose. Enrico Novelli produced for Latium a series of noble subjects with actors from the theatre. Did his *Othello* turn into parody during production?

The other Italian *Othello* was far more serious, though its production had humorous overtones. In March 1909, Charles Pathé, who not only had the original distribution of Film d'Art but had set up in France a competing organization, S.C.A.G.L., to make art films, founded in Rome Film d'Arte Italiana for the interpretation of famous writers by well known actors, many of them from the theatre. The heads of this organization were Re Riccardi, Gerolamo Lo Savio, and Ugo Falena. Its films were of course handled by Pathé. Its first production, under the direction of Lo Savio, was *Othello* with Ferruccio Garavaglia as the Moor, Cesare Dondini as Iago, Vittoria Lepanto as Desdemona, Alberto Nepoti as Cassio, and A. Pezzaglia as the Doge.

Much of the film was shot in Venice, thus inaugurating a new development in natural and authentic background. To Venice the company went, actors and actresses, technicians and assistants with the intention of remaining a week or so. Venetians were of course utterly bewildered to see men and women dressed in costumes of brilliant colours, apparently half a hundred of them if courtiers, soldiers, and principals were included, some with false beards and wigs, proceeding through the piazza of San Marco, through the streets and byways, and for a while assumed this was some sort of a carnival. They were followed by amazed youngsters, and greeted by people at doors and windows. Garavaglia, wearing sword, breastplate, and helmet, with complete aplomb dumbfounded a tobacconist by entering his shop and buying cigars. Pezzaglia in red accompanied by senators and footmen appeared in a gondola and was identified as Don Carlo with his suite. Obviously amid crowds who had never seen a filming before it was difficult to maintain order, and even when the circumstances were understood, there were those who broke the bounds of decorum. In one sequence, Vittoria Lepanto was to lean over the parapet of a bridge, while Iago passed beneath in a gondola. Lepanto's beauty, enhanced by silver and gold brocade, attracted the attention of a young elegantly bedecked youth. As she mounted the stairs to the bridge she did not notice, or pretended not to notice the unknown admirer. As she bent over to assume her pose he gave her an unexpected pat on that portion of her anatomy which was then most prominent. Lepanto turned suddenly and slapped him, whereupon the too audacious admirer unfortunately was heard to say that after all she was only an actress. This was adding insult to injury. Lepanto was furious, and the whole company took umbrage. Garavaglia and Pezzaglia, both big men, instantly and as if on command picked up the young coxcomb by his armpits and tossed him into the canal, while the crowd applauded. As he struggled in the water and swam to a ladder, the camerman recorded his discomfiture, and Desdemona was vindicated.

Garavaglia's heroism was not known to English audiences in 1909 but his performance of Othello was. *Bioscope* on November 11th, which devoted to him most of its review of what was listed merely as a Pathé film of 1105 feet, was unenthusiastic.

'If this is not exactly an ideally Shakespearian performance, it is at least vigorous. In any case, it seems to be rather a hopeless business to attempt a wordless Shakespearian performance. It is very hard for any actor to invest Othello with due dignity and greatness by gesture alone. For the production of this new *Othello*, as regards scenic effect, there can be nothing but praise; seldom can a stage court have sparkled with brighter lustre than in this picture, but by the acting one can scarcely be so moved. [The reviewer says nothing about Venice, and in his naming of the star and its release by Pathé evidently assumed it was French.] M. Garavaglia obviously has not a personality to embody those tremendous storms of love and jealousy which shook the Moor. He acts well, and laughter is as far from us as tears; but he is simply unconvincing, and an unconvincing Othello is as bad as a gentlemanly Hamlet. However, it is an interesting production on the whole, and its scenic beauties should gain it much popularity.'

No cigars for Garavaglia! Yet Louis N. Parker, who had met him in 1904, called him 'one of Italy's greatest actors.'

In the United States, where *Othello* was not released until April 20, 1910, Pathé trumpeted the film in the *Moving Picture World* on March 19th.

'Pathé Frères will release, in the near future, a film of exceptional strength and merit – Shakespeare's *Othello*. The story of the famous Moor of Venice will be released as a film d'art. The pictures were taken in the famous Queen of the Adriatic, and all the exquisite beauty of the famous palaces of Venice are all shown in the picture, in addition to the marvellous pantomimes executed by the leading actors of Italy. Many have seen *Othello* but never in such a setting. The stage has been noted for wonders of scenic fidelity but to enact this marvelous tragedy along the very waters and in the very gardens and palaces as the immortal Shakespeare pictured them with his versatile pen, is to add an interest which could not be obtained in any other way. We are shown Othello and Desdemona in the palace. We see Iago going to the palace of the Doge, along the Grand Canal, and we seem to be in the gondola with him as it sweeps steadily along, propelled by the muscular gondolier who so duly handles his oar. Imposing facades, beautiful colonnades, magnificent porticos and marvelously wrought gateways, all come under our view as we pass from one scene to another of this great play. The film is colored with the usual Pathé excellence, and it is well to note that the costuming and the interior decorations are absolutely correct to the period.'

If *Bioscope* stressed the acting, it is evident that Pathé wished to stress the Venetian settings. In the United States, the review in the *Motion Picture World*, April 30th, was both vaguer and different from both.

'A successful attempt to reproduce Shakespeare's greatest plays in motion pictures. Looking at a picture of this character one must recognize the limitations of the motion picture and realize that Shakespeare may suffer more than a drama written especially for the films. On the other hand, certain great qualities, perhaps one might say personal qualities, stand out in strong relief in Shakespeare's tragedies, and here there is no mistaking the lesson which the play itself teaches. To successfully present a drama of this importance argues a company capable of interpreting the great emotions of the human mind. The tragedies represent these emotions so clearly that once seen they can never be forgotten. And here the characteristic of the Moor of Venice, jealousy, is so plainly represented that it impresses one in an oppressive way. If the overmastering emotion or the personality of the principal character be sympathetically developed what the accessory characters do is of little importance. In this play Desdemona and Iago are successively important and it is essential that the parts be well taken. That a play of this character can be so satisfactorily placed on the screen is strong evidence of the progress of the motion picture. It enables thousands to become acquainted with great dramatic masterpieces who would never otherwise know about them. One may read them many times, but not until they are produced by competent actors does one comprehend their meaning, or appreciate their marvelous delineation of human passion. To have successfully performed that is sufficient honor; and it has been done in this instance.'

Evidently, the play's the thing in America – and the lesson. Was there slight cutting? The same journal says 1043 feet, some 60 feet shorter than in England. Nevertheless I should like to have seen this film, the first in which the actual locale was used for a Shakespeare play and in colour too of a sort. It was a feature which Italian films were to stress more and more. Whatever they did with Shakespeare, they realised that motion pictures were pictures.

The two other Shakespeare films which were certainly of 1909 are relatively unimportant but not without interest. Deutsche Vitascope made a brief sound film of *Romeo und Julia* with Luisa Tetrazzini as 'Julia.' This was perhaps a presentation of the Valse from Gounod's opera; we have already found another selection from it at the Paris Exposition. And a performer in the same Phono-Cinéma-Théâtre at the Exposition, Footit, turns up in a French version of *A Midsummer Night's Dream*, not this time with Chocolate, but with his sons. The announcement came in the *Ciné-Journal*, December 20–26th, in an advertisement by Le Lion: 'Le songe d'une Nuit d'été, d'après Shakespeare, 309 m. Scènes cinématographiques, interpretées par Footit et ses Fils (du Nouveau-Cirque); Mlle Napierkowska (de l'Opéra-Comique). Affiche artistique.' Footit, a Manchester born Englishman named Tudor Hall, was, as you have gathered, a clown and a fairly famous one. Stacia Napierkowska was a dancer arrived from Russia, where she is reported to have pleased the Czar before she came to Paris to be *première danseuse* at the Opéra-Comique and to make a number of French films. She was in the United States in 1913, and was hailed into court by Anthony Comstock for dancing without sufficient clothing; when the charge was dismissed, she left these shores. Footit and Napierkowska seem an oddly assorted couple for *A Midsummer Night's Dream*, but what fools these mortals be.

If 1909 could be designated the year of *Othello*, 1910 seems to have been the year of *Hamlet*, though admittedly it is difficult to be certain about dates and even identifications. A Lux *Hamlet* in 950 feet, for example, may have been made late in 1909, since it was reviewed in the London *Bioscope* on January 13, 1910, where it was called 'extremely fine . . . bids fair to become

D*

as much a classic amongst films as the immortal play of the same name. The various indoor scenes are well staged, and those taken out of doors are amongst romantic woodland scenery.' The American *Moving Picture World* of February 12th did not agree with *Bioscope*'s nomination of it as 'one of the best films of the year.'

'To adequately represent Shakespeare's greatest drama in a motion picture is a difficult task, and though in this instance the producer has done well, one must say that it is a great pity he has not done better. Improvement in the interpretation would, perhaps, make amends, at least in some degree, for the deficiencies in the photography. There are too many weak spots in the film, detracting from its mechanical beauty, though one must say that the improvement in photographic quality of this firm's work is marked. One wishes, however, that they might have gone a little farther in this direction and have made the picture clearer and better through its entire length. The staging is perhaps adequate. Staging in Shakespeare's time was not the elaborate operation it is now, and what appears to be meager settings often represent fidelity to the original. The acting has weak points, yet it is, perhaps, a reasonably satisfactory reproduction of the play as it is likely to be understood by a majority of readers. Pictures that urge actors and reproducers forward by the necessity of producing something out of the ordinary unquestionably exert a beneficial influence and assist materially in both dramatic and photographic development.'

It is annoying that no details are given, the more so because I cannot find any French review of this French picture.

In the Film Library of the Museum of Modern Art there is an incomplete film which is catalogued as Lux. I confess to doubts; there is no woodland scenery in the Museum's film, and my recollection and notes of the screening do not match a still in *Bioscope*. However, the outdoor scenes could be among the portions missing, and if the Museum film is not Lux, I cannot identify it. It is, in style, almost certainly French or Italian, but carries no marks which would permit recognition. There are six scenes in the extant 16 mm positive:

 I A corridor, where Hamlet is brought by Horatio and the soldiers. The beginning is abrupt and parts may be lost.

 II The ramparts. Horatio sees the ghost and follows him off, despite the objections of his friends.

III Another part of the ramparts. The ghost shows Hamlet (through an arched door) a vision of Claudius killing his father. Hamlet swears revenge.

IV The home of Polonius. Laertes departs for France, and Ophelia is warned against Hamlet.

 V A room in the castle. Rosencrantz and Guildenstern greet the King and

Queen and receive instructions. In the same setting, there is a cut to Hamlet reading a book, the banter with Polonius, the greeting of Rosencrantz and Guildenstern, the arrival of the players, and the arrangements for the play-within-the-play.

VI A room of state, with a throne at the right, a curtained picture-frame stage rear. Hamlet advises the players. The court arrives. He sits at Ophelia's feet. The play is incredibly brief. An actor enters the stage and lies down; another comes in and pours poison in his ear. The King shows consternation and leaves hurriedly with the court. Hamlet stabs wildly at the empty throne, is then summoned by Polonius to go to his mother.

The print ends here. What titles there are, are in English: designations of place, garbled or cut quotations from Shakespeare, some not Shakespearean at all. The action is staged as if it were a play and photographed with a fixed camera. The sets are largely painted backgrounds. The third scene is at least partly architectural, and it is only in this scene that there is any real adaptation. Despite some fluidity, the story would be unintelligible to anyone who did not know the play. Nothing is made of the love-affair, but this may be lost. There is no real chance for characterization, and the acting is florid and stagy. The names of the personnel are a mystery, but Lux had been founded in Paris in 1907, and its artistic director, who may have staged this film, was Gérard Bourgeois, formerly an actor at the Porte-St Martin.

If the film just described is not the one by Lux, it could be the earlier Milano or a new *Hamlet* by Cines in 1910. This was directed by Caserini and emerged in 325 metres. The title role was taken by Dante Capelli, an actor of considerable stage experience with Eleuterio Rodolfi and Ferruccio Garavaglia. Capelli, who had already acted in the Cines *Macbeth*, played in films in 1909 and 1910 and occasionally thereafter, and also directed, but he was primarily of the theatre where he was associated later with Italia Vitaliani, Emma Gramatica, and again Garavaglia.

Another stage actor, Jacques Grétillat, who had been with Antoine for five years at the Odéon, also played *Hamlet* in pictures about this time. He was later to alternate between the two media and had a long professional career. Since he had been born in 1885 he was at least a young Hamlet. Gertrude in this presentation was Mme Colonna Romano, who was even younger; she too was from the Odéon but was to be engaged by the Comédie Française in 1913. The identities of the producing company and the director, and the exact date are far from clear, since I find no reviews or advertisements in the trade papers which would settle the issues. On the weight of secondary evidence, the scales balance in favour of Eclipse, a firm founded in 1906, which by this time had a 'série d'art,' and a director, Henri Desfontaines of long experience in one capacity or another at the Théâtre Libre, the Odéon, the Folies Bergère, and with Pathé's S.C.A.G.L.

While I am on French *Hamlets*, I should mention that sometime or other Mounet-Sully made an excerpt of the graveyard scene. The excerpt was included in Nicole Vedrès' *Paris 1900* (1948), a recreation of Paris from 1900 to 1914 which included clips of over seven hundred films in private collections and public archives. Where she obtained this particular bit I do not know, but it is now in the Cinémathèque, which lent it to a Unesco Shakespeare Celebration in Paris, where it was screened on November 14, 1964. In the scene Mounet-Sully, with an Horatio, was shot outdoors with moving trees and a tombstone in the background, Yorick's broken stone and a grave with a grave-digger in it and bones in front in the left foreground. Hamlet holds Yorick's skull in both hands, then rolls it on the ground as if he were playing bowls. The scene is so brief as to tell little about Mounet-Sully's conception or acting, but the actor's majestic stature and controlled gestures are plain. I do not know whether this scene was all that was made or whether it is the only surviving part of a fuller film, but it is valuable to have even a short sequence of the greatest French actor of the period in *Hamlet*. Born in 1841, trained at the Conservatory, he first was at the Odéon, then made his début at the Comédie Française as Oreste in *Andromaque*. He had already indicated his preference for Shakespearean characters such as Macbeth and Othello; indeed he played Lear at the Odéon, and was to appear as Hamlet, one of his great parts, and Othello. Now an officer of the Légion d'honneur and the *doyen* of the Comédie, he was much praised for 'his fine physique, beautifully modulated voice, and sombre, penetrating gaze, added to fiery impetuous acting, and great originality. . . .'

I can be much more circumstantial about a Danish *Hamlet* made in 1910. Denmark's film studio, Nordisk, was not particularly interested in Shakespeare, and its founder in 1906 and president, Ole Olsen, detested costume films. It is not surprising therefore that the idea for the picture did not originate with the studio. It was the brain-child of Oluf Jensen, editor of the Helsingör *Avis*, who had read in a newspaper that an English company planned to produce *Hamlet* in Wales and would build in preparation a small Kronborg castle there. Of course, he thought *Hamlet* ought to be filmed at the real Kronborg of Helsingör, Shakespeare's Elsinore, the castle built in Gothic-Byzantine style about 1580 by Frederick II, which was already a tourist attraction. A film in its grounds and with its background would bring more people to the city. Jensen therefore took pen in hand and wrote a film play of *Hamlet*. The problem was to put the play within reasonable compass, omit Hamlet's reflective scenes, and concentrate on the plot and the setting. His script he published in the *Avis* where it occupied sixteen pages. Permission for a production at the Castle was obtained because the officers in charge agreed that it would be a tourist inducement. Through intermediaries, one of whom was Jacques Copeau, an approach was made to Pathé in Paris for a feature film with Sarah Bernhardt as the star. Pathé applauded the idea, but felt that it would be too costly to send the famous lady and a supporting company to Denmark. Jensen then turned to Nordisk. Olsen was not enthusiastic but was finally persuaded by August Blom, who was to direct the film. Weapons of the late sixteenth and early seventeenth centuries were borrowed from the Töjhuset in Copenhagen, and in the summer the company and crew arrived in Helsingör. The garrison from Kronborg was sent away for manoeuvres, but a half a hundred soldiers in training stayed to don the costumes and take part in the picture. The section of the moat where Ophelia was to drown was cleared of brambles and mud by the castle superintendent, and a raft was anchored a metre below the surface of the moat to prevent accidents. Then the filming started. In the first scene, the ghost appeared to Hamlet and the soldiers on the west rampart. Ophelia drowned in the moat and was pulled out shivering from cold. When Hamlet rode over the drawbridge on his way to England, he was followed by fifty halberdiers, swordsmen, and ladies and gentlemen of the Court, all in period dress. The graveyard scene including Hamlet's first encounter with Laertes were shot in the courtyard of the Carmelite monastery attached to the Church of St Mary, dating from 1430. The final scene of the play was taken in Valby. In one of Ophelia's mad scenes, Blom copied the grouping in John Boydell's engraving.

August Blom was enthusiastic about his film and in spite of admonitions from Olsen to keep it short took in a few days what is variously reported as 12,000 feet and 3000 metres of negative. If he had been permitted to use it all, this *Hamlet* would have been the longest film yet made or to be made in the near future. But alas, Olsen insisted that the finished product must be in one reel. The length of the picture as it was finally distributed in one hundred prints, depending no doubt on titling, was indicated as 420 metres in France, 1200 or 1128 feet in the Nordisk advertisements in England, and 972 feet or 300 metres in Denmark.

The Hamlet of this film was a German-born actor named Alwin Neuss. Neuss had studied acting under Josef Kainz, who himself was a famous European Hamlet. No doubt Neuss's interpretation owed something to Kainz; at any rate Neuss was a well known Hamlet on the stage. He made a number of Danish films in this year. Aage Hertel's Claudius was particularly praised in Denmark. Ella la Cour played Gertrude; Emilie Sannom, Ophelia; Einar Zangenberg, Laertes; and I gather from captioned stills that Oscar Langkilde was Horatio. Additional members of the cast were Carl Rosenbaum, Axel Mattson, and Rigmor Jerichau. American announcements stress the cooperation of the Royal Theatre company of Copenhagen. The film was shown however in England before its release by the Great Northern Company, Nordisk's affiliate, in the United States.

In London, a representative of the *Kinematograph and Lantern Weekly* reported in the issue of January 19, 1911: 'We have been favored with an early view of a splendid Shakespearian production ... to be put on the market by the Nordisk Company. In quite manageable length ... all the principal parts of the great tragedy are adequately dealt with, and the film has this striking recommendation – it was taken on the grounds of Elsinore. The acting and photography are first rate, and the staging on a scale worthy of the piece.' He goes on to mention 'the very appropriate subtitles, all taken from the play.' On January 26th and thereafter Nordisk gives it lead advertising as 'Our Great Production' and announces its release date as March 18th. On February 9th, 'Stroller' in his 'Weekly Notes' says, 'Having seen the film I can confidently recommend it to buyers and exhibitors. The acting is good, the effects are splendid, and the photographic quality is all that can be desired.' In the same issue Nordisk went farther: 'Surpasses any previous Shakespearian Production in acting, natural scenery and ensemble. . . . Although a classical subject, appeals forcibly to every class of audiences.' Someone was getting cold feet about the breadth of appeal.

The full length review in the same journal appeared on March 16th:

'Shakespearian productions are, at the present time at any rate, the rage, and the Nordisk Film Company's release of Hamlet on March 18th, comes, therefore at an appropriate moment. If only for the fact that the representation of the Immortal Bard's play took place at the original castle of Cronenberg, the production would have been a notable one, but when in addition one is able to chronicle that the setting is in itself most charmingly picturesque and appropriate, whilst the acting is of the highest order of merit, the Nordisk Films Company are justly entitled to their Hamlet film the superlative adjective "Masterpiece".

'The story of Hamlet is too well known to all lovers of the drama to need recountal here, suffice it to say, therefore, that the portrayal follows the Shakespearian text religiously. Notable among the many beautiful scenes must be placed those depicting the wanderings of Ophelia, especially that in which she falls into the river and meets her death. The play scene, the burial of Ophelia, the slaying of Polonius, the departure of Hamlet for England, and the fight between Laertes and Hamlet with the tragic ending of the death of the King and Queen, after imbibing the poisoned potion.

The photographic quality of the film is excellent, and the length is sufficient without being tiring. No show for the next few weeks can be considered complete which does not include in its programme the Nordisk Films Company's Hamlet.'

Whether exhibitors took this advice to heart or not, I find it within the next two months at the Ardwick Picture Hall, Manchester, 'a magnificent show'; the Picture House, Leicester; King's Hall, Newcastle; the Central Hall, Hastings; and the Assembly Hall, Darlington.

I do not find reviews in France – only a reference in the *Ciné-Journal* a year later, March 30, 1912, to the theft of a print in Marseilles – but there is considerable information from the United States. Someone who wrote under the name of Lux Graphicus for the *Moving Picture World* of April 8,

1911, vapourizes about 'the immortal story' and the ambition of every actor to play Hamlet, and sketches in background information already presented, but he adds that 'the scenery around the castle is beautifully portrayed. We are told that the King of Denmark was an interested spectator of the proceedings and aided the Great Northern Company in every way to make the filming of this great drama a masterpiece of realism. The text is closely followed and the action clearly conveys the meaning.' I doubt if the writer had seen the film, and most of his screed sounds like company publicity. In the next issue a London Letter by A. E. Taylor mentions 'a boom here in Shakespearian films,' naming Tree's *Henry VIII* and Benson's *Julius Caesar* as well as the Nordisk *Hamlet*, which is 'exceptionally fine'; and a Great Northern advertisement gives the release date as April 15th. The review came on April 22nd, and is as illiterate as the earlier London one.

'Artistically, as a picture of much beauty, but especially as a picture of very excellent acting, one feels on seeing a private view of it that it is indeed a notable success. The mechanical work of the Great Northern Film Company deserves high praise and this picture seems very well done.

'The film impresses one most as a picture of the histrionic art of Herr Neuss. It would be delightful if one could compare its excellencies with films showing the Hamlet of Booth, of the elder Sothern, of Kean, of Irving. The pleasure of comparing many great Hamlets will belong to the critics of the following generations. But the Great Northern Company is to be congratulated on having the photograph of so interesting a Hamlet as Herr Neuss', and he is to be congratulated on having so clear a picture of his representation of this strange but very human prince. [Omitted is a paragraph on the character of Hamlet.]

'In watching this film, I was anxious to discover how much of Hamlet's character could be revealed apart from the words that bear witness to his thoughts. Of course I was hindered by this that I remembered many of his words, and, so, was likely to see qualities in the picture that otherwise would not have been so plain. As I watched the scenes unrolled, the picture gave me thoughts that did "often lie too deep for tears."

'Herr Neuss' Hamlet of the film vividly accents the heart qualities of the character when he first comes out on the castle's platform – it is the actual Castle Cronsberg (Elsinore) – he places his hands on the shoulders of Horatio and Marcellus in a way that suggests how much his affection leaned upon their friendship, yet it was the gesture of a prince, too, of one who in the supreme moment will not be ruled but be the ruler. Again, when he advises Ophelia (Fraulein Sannom) to enter a nunnery, his gestures convey so deep a tenderness that the scene is poignantly affecting.

'In this Hamlet nothing could be plainer than the quickness of his perceptions. In the scene where King Claudius (Herr Aagel Hertel) is overcome with remorse and Hamlet comes upon him as he prays on the steps of his throne, the prince, now sure of his guilt, is about to stab him. The dagger is raised. As he bends over to strike, he sees the King's face. The dagger is caught half-way in its descent and Hamlet tiptoes away.

'Fraulein Sannom makes a very beautiful Northland Ophelia; she seems a true princess; but on the screen she is perhaps more poetic than mad. In other words, she wasn't as pathetic as she might have been. The acting of all the characters is very intelligent and dramatic.'

We are grateful at least and at last for a little something about the interpretation and the stage business. The stills extant show a bit more and for indoor scenes reveal theatre groupings and crowded scenes. Yet there must have been some impressive moments of action in Kronborg and cloister, and it is a pity that no print is available.

If *Hamlet* predominated in 1910, it was not by any means the only Shakespearian subject filmed on the Continent in 1910. Perhaps the Pathé *Cleopatra*, released in its Série d'Art in 1170 feet, is not however a particularly good example, since its story is a mixture of Shakespeare, Plutarch, Sardou, and invention. Publicity and reviews indeed do not mention Shakespeare at all, though the influence was inevitable. A comment on it appears in *Bioscope* on January 27th; since the same is reprinted in the *Moving Picture World* of May 14th, it probably issued from the company rather than from an independent reviewer, and its impartiality is suspect.

'. . . as fine an example of the producer's skill as we have seen. The management of the riotous crowds, the costly splendor of the costumes, and the perfectly artistic spirit in which the whole is carried out, are worthy of the finest productions of the "legitimate" stage, and for one, in all sincerity, the voice of criticism must be more or less silent. . . . In this film the whole history of [Antony and Cleopatra's] passion to its tragic end is depicted.'

'Arrangement and management' are praised, as well as 'the playing of those who take the principal parts. . . . We feel confident in prophesying full and enthusiastic houses for all managers who are wise enough to secure this film.'

The Pathé Notes in the *Moving Picture World* of March 26th, are more specific.

'The approaching release of "Cleopatra" is a stupendous production, staged by M. Zecca in the Pathe studios, France. The cost of the stage setting, costumes and scenery was enormous, and the production bids fair to be one of the most pronounced successes which Pathe Freres have released. The beauty of the scenery, which includes some water views, is striking, and the characters in this great tragedy have been played with consummate skill by some of the leading players in France. A notable incident in the production is the scene of the death of the messenger who bears to Cleopatra the ill news of Antony's defeat and who, as you all know [*au contraire*], was poisoned by Cleopatra for being the bearer of such bad news. The part of the messenger is played by Mlle Napierkowska, of the Opera, and her work is extremely clever. Cleopatra and Antony are both parts which provide an opportunity for the greatest play of feeling, and this opportunity is realized and properly grasped by Madaline Roche, who proves herself a great tragedienne in the part of the powerful and cruel queen.'

Probably Zecca supervised or produced rather than actually directed; this kind of film was not his dish of tea. And Napierkowska was hardly one of 'the leading players of France'. Madeleine Roch, however, was. She had made her début at the Comédie Française in 1903 in *Andromaque* and was a notable interpreter of French classic rôles. 'On lui trouve,' said Antoine, 'une belle voix et un masque énergique.' The voice, alas, would be useless here, but one could appreciate her expressive features. She evidently dominated the unnamed Antony.

Pathé had no qualms about further puffery in the *Pathé Weekly Bulletin* of May 9th, where it is called Film d'Art – which, with capitals at least, it was not. It was to be released on May 11th in the United States, this coloured art film that 'overshadows all others in point of conception, magnificent staging, irreproachable and beautiful coloring.' At any rate there is, along with a still, a detailed account of the episodes.

'The opening scene is Cleopatra's court. The beautiful and imperious sovereign is in the act of declaring to her courtiers her intention of penetrating into the camp of Mark Antony, the conqueror of her land.

'The next picture shows her in most gorgeous robes, floating down the Nile in a galley with silver oars and silken sails. Little wonder that the vision of this beautiful woman should dazzle the rough soldier.

'Octavius Caesar and Octavia, Antony's wife, bitterly reproach him for his desertion but the infatuated conqueror enraged at their daring to dictate to him banishes them both for their interference.

'Next we see a feast in progress at the Palace of Tarsus, Cleopatra's home. Such magnificence; such brilliancy is hardly conceivable at this distant date.

'In the midst of all feasting and gaiety, a messenger arrives from Octavius Caesar, who has declared war against Mark Antony. The latter realizing that the time for pleasure is now at an end, hastens to gather together his forces while Cleopatra, knowing Octavius to be her bitter enemy, encourages Antony to meet him on the battlefield and speeds him on his way.

'Moody and pensive in the extreme do we find Cleopatra in the next view for the absence of Antony has been long indeed. Her pensiveness is turned to despair however, as a messenger arrives bearing the evil tidings of the defeat of Mark Antony and the rapid approach of Octavius Caesar. So grieved and enraged is the beautiful Egyptian that even the innocent heralder of the bad news becomes hateful to her and she orders a poisoned drink to be prepared for him.

'Eagerley the unfortunate youth takes the goblet from the servant's hand and drains it to its dregs and in a second he is writhing at the foot of the queen.

'The defeated and humiliated Antony soon returns to Egypt a prisoner of war, and with a heartbroken [but inaudible] moan he kills himself at Cleopatra's feet. The latter not wishing to grace the triumph of Octavius Caesar willingly dies by the bite of a wasp brought to her in a basket of figs.

'When Caesar and his train force their way into the Queen's apartments great indeed is their surprise and sorrow to behold only the lifeless body of the beautiful Egyptian, who preferred death to humiliation.'

The 'wasp', I am happy to say, was a misprint, as the *Bioscope* article shows.

There is evidence apart from Pathé's own exploitation that *Cleopatra* was successful. The *Moving Picture World* of May 21st, in addition to some omitted flourishes about the historical Cleopatra and the nature of imagination, found the various scenes 'magnificently set and beautifully photographed. . . . It is one of the most satisfactory films of the sort the Pathes have ever produced.' It inspired a sequel called *Caesar in Egypt*, in the announcement of which in the same journal, June 25th, there was reference to the 'extensive approval' *Cleopatra* had received. In England, the *Kinematograph and Lantern Weekly* of April 21, 1910, called it a 'superb production', and its popularity penetrated to Russia. The *Pathé Weekly Bulletin* of May 30th quoted the New York *Telegraph* of May 15th as saying: 'Such a stupendous production is not produced every day. It is by far one of the greatest film productions ever seen. What added to the richness of the settings and scenery generally was the fact that the film was beautifully colored. The action of the principals could hardly be excelled. Cleopatra with her winning ways, Mark Antony, the victim of her beauty, showed remarkable skill in handling their parts.' If the *Bulletin* can be trusted to quote accurately, one can gather from it and previous citations that what especially appealed in this only semi-Shakespearean film was its spectacular settings and action in colour, and the attraction of Madeleine Roch's Cleopatra.

There were films in this period which have Shakespearean titles or characters in the titles which otherwise are not even semi-Shakespeare. A Pathé *All's Well That Ends Well* (1910) turns out to be a Max Linder comedy with no doubt a different French name. Another film with this evidently popular proverbial title (1911) I cannot even identify, but its connection with Shakespeare is equally nebulous. The *Ciné-Journal* of August 5, 1911, lists a Cines *Une Aventure de Henry IV*, but an English journal is careful to explain that the title character is Henry IV of France. A 'jolie comédie en couleurs' about Henry IV put out by Pathé in 1911 deals with the story of the King and the wood chopper from La Fontaine. A film about the English Henry VIII which was playing in Newcastle and elsewhere in January 1911 had various titles including just *Henry VIII* but the key one is *Katherine Howard and Henry VIII*, which removes it from the Shakespearean category. Henry's relations with his ladies served again for a Pathé *Une intrigue à la cour d'Henri VIII d'Angleterre* (1911), but this is equally un-Shakespearean; it dealt with the attempt of Jane Seymour to supplant Catherine of Aragon. In 1910, the German firm, Messter, had a film titled in English *Romeo and Juliet at the Seaside*; I doubt its relevance. On the other hand Pathé's *Romeo Turns Bandit* of the same year has a bowing acquaintance with Shakespeare in that a modern Romeo climbs a garden wall and appears in a balcony scene with his Juliette. There was *A Modern Shylock* (France, 1911) which deals with a village money-lender in Brittany who sees an accusing vision and falls over the cliffs, and a Danish *Taming of the Shrew*, also of 1911, which if it resembles a later Nordisk picture so named, has borrowed only a Shakespearean title. It is a relief to turn from films which might be misunderstood to be Shakespearean to films of Shakespeare's plays, even to an Italian *Racconto d'Inverno* by Cines, released in London, May 11, 1910, 'a magnificent series of pictures dealing with episodes in Shakespeare's wonderful tragedy. Acted in the most perfect manner, and amid scenes of splendor that bewilder . . . and charm the eye,' or so at least Cines said. I cannot find that anyone else says more, or indeed anything at all.

After *Hamlet*, the story of Brutus and Julius Caesar was more popular in 1910–11 than any other treated by Shakespeare, but it is sometimes less than clear how far films on this theme derived from or were influenced by the English dramatist. There is record of both a *Bruto I* and a *Bruto II* (1910) which stemmed from the company named Milano, now reorganized under aristocratic sponsorship. Its director and leading actor was Giuseppe De Liguoro. Prolo cites the first film as having a length of 163 metres but assigns no responsibility. For the second with no indication of length she says that the subject and direction were by De Liguoro but names no actor. Just how far De Liguoro participated and how much, if anything, was owed to Shakespeare are doubtful.

Even more mysterious is a film made in Nice at approximately this time and released by Kineto, an English subsidiary of the Charles Urban Trading Company. The part of Julius Caesar was taken by a Dutch actor, Theo Frenkel, Sr. A Frenkel scrapbook in the Nederlands Filmmuseum contains stills: one shows Caesar as haughty soldier, cape on his arm, his hand on his sword; another a crowned emperor threatened and warned by two prominent characters, perhaps Cassius and Brutus, while others, male and female, black and white, crowd around. The stills are labelled in Frenkel's handwriting Nice, Kineto Film Co. but without date. Other stills in the scrapbook are marked Kinemacolor. Urban, who used the old Williamson studio in Brighton, also established in 1910 another studio in Nice where most of the Kinemacolor films were produced, sometimes with black-and-white versions, but I find no record of a *Julius Caesar* other than these stills. Frenkel directed Kinemacolor films under the name of Theo Bouwmeester.

In 1910 Cines brought out a more important picture than any of the Julius Caesar films just treated. Called *Brutus*, it was directed by Enrico Guazzoni, who had been designing settings for Caserini and no doubt designed some here. I do not have Italian announcements or reviews, but a Cines advertisement in the *Ciné-Journal* of October 28, 1911, heralds it with capitals which I reduce, 'cette semaine le plus beau film de l'histoire romaine qui ait jamais été édité par la Cinès (Série Princeps) . . . 362 mètres.' The *Kinematograph and Lantern Weekly* of October 12, 1911, noticed 'This great Shakespearian masterpiece' would be released on November 18th in 1187 feet and provided a long summary and review which must have pleased the Italian firm and sent exhibitors scurring for prints.

'Amongst Shakespeare's immortal works, there are few that possess more dramatic interest than the play of *Julius Caesar* in which Brutus plays such a prominent part. It is from this popular tragedy that the Cines Company have taken the incidents which provide the story of this powerful subject. That it is one of the best and most magnificent productions the firm have yet given us we have no hesitation in saying, for every scene is a masterpiece of acting, staging and dramatic interest. There is not a dull moment from the opening scene where the conspirators decide upon the death of Caesar, to the final battle scene and the defeat and death of Brutus. Indeed the battle scene is one of the greatest and most realistic pictures ever attempted, and it is depicted with a realism that is awful in its grandeur and convincing in its delineation. It is a scene to live long in one's memory, and conveys the horrors of war in all its hideousness. The murder of Caesar at the Senate, the lying in state, the funeral, the oration of Marc Antony, the wrecking of the houses of the conspirators, the apparition of Caesar to Brutus and the many minor scenes and incidents are all depicted with a fidelity to the text of Shakespeare, and a strict adherence to all that perfection of detail in dress, scenery and appointments for which the Cines Company have become so deservedly popular. Every scene being taken in the open air, the photographic quality is perfect throughout. The action is brisk and easily followed and without a single foot of unnecessary padding, the result being a set of perfect pictures that cannot fail to interest and impress every class of audience.

'The story opens with a meeting of the conspirators, who have become dissatisfied with the rule of Julius Caesar, and after an excited and heated discussion, the edict goes forth that Caesar must die. A view of the home life of the noble senator introduces us to Calphurnia, Caesar's wife, who, full of forebodings, begs her husband not to go to the Senate. He, full of his duty to his country, resists his wife's pleadings and goes forth to meet his doom. The senators are next seen in full conclave and an altercation

arising, the malcontents rush upon Caesar and stab him to the heart. Marc
Antony swears by the body of Caesar to avenge his dastardly murder, and
when Caesar's body is laid in state, he rouses the immense concourse of
people to the point of fury by his impassioned oration. The funeral of Caesar,
and the reading of his will, leaving all his possessions for the good of the
populace, with the inspiration of Antony, cause the Roman citizens to wreck
the houses of the known conspirators, and put to death all with whom they
come in contact. Brutus, at the earnest solicitations of his friends, flies to save
his life. He raises his standard, and a numerous army is soon in the field to
do battle with the regular troops commanded by Marc Antony. A grand
review of the troops takes place, and after many skirmishes with the enemy,
a decisive battle at Philippi is decided upon. The eve of battle sees Brutus
alone in his tent preparing for the fray. The shades of night are falling, and in
the darkening gloom, the shade of Caesar appears to Brutus, and uttering
the warning "We shall meet at Philippi", disappears. Brutus, with a fore-
boding of his fate is filled with horror at the apparition and calls in his
officers to keep him company until the break of day, when the battle commences. The armies meet and soon the field is strewn with the dead and
dying. All the crude implements of war are requisitioned, and both sides
strive for victory. A final charge and Brutus and his army are defeated,
flying in all directions and pursued by the adherents of the victorious Antony.
Brutus seeks safety in flight, and deserted by all but one faithful friend, in
his despair calls upon him to kill him. His friend, hesitating to commit so
foul a deed, Brutus seizes his sword, upon which he impales himself as the
victorious Antony appears upon the scene. Full of horror at the sight of the
dying Brutus, the scene closes with Antony kneeling by his one-time friend's
side and stricken with grief at the fearful termination of a noble career.'

Bioscope of the same date gives much the same summary, indulges in a good
deal of unnecessary quotation from the play, but adds some useful comments: 'Wonderful adaptation . . . vivid historical portrait. . . . Some of the
scenes are quite exquisite in their artistry, notable so the "raid on the house
of the conspirators", which is purely classical in its setting and entirely
Roman in its style. Shakespeare's play has been faithfully followed throughout, and there is no well-known passage or traditional situation which has
not here its dumb counterpart . . . here is a subject which will offer [the
showman] an opportunity to appeal with no uncertain call to the most
cultivated audience. . . .' Finally the reviewer suggests encouraging educational visits from schools and the substitution of explanatory quotations from
Shakespeare for the present ordinary subtitles.

From these summaries, and others to be mentioned which essentially
agree, it is evident that one of the virtues of *Brutus* was the clarity of its
story line. Shakespeare's play, if one is not primarily interested in interpretation of character or the delineation of minor figures, presents a relatively

simple plot; even so it was no mean feat to present in one reel a story which could be 'easily followed' in pantomimed action. It is not quite true that 'there is no well-known passage or traditional situation which has not here its dumb counterpart.' The Portia scenes are not there, for example, nor the significant quarrel between Brutus and Cassius. Indeed the conclusion might be drawn so far that Cassius does not exist as a character, since he is never named, and that his rôle as an individual has been watered down to being one of the vague and unidentified conspirators. Actually other evidence will show that while he is not as important as in the original, he is easily recognizable. What the scenarist has done is to eliminate Act I, and draw material in chronological order from parts of II, 1, 2; III, 1, 2, 3; IV, 2, 3; and most of V, while adding the flight of Brutus at the urging of his friends, the actual destruction of the conspirators' property, the 'grand review' of Brutus's troops, and the fighting *en masse* at the Battle of Philippi, all material which lends itself readily to pictures, and to the crowds and spectacular features which Guazzoni was in a few years to develop in pictures which no longer had to be confined to one reel and which made his name and films famous.

When George Kleine imported *Brutus* to America in 1912, the film was reviewed by James S. McQuade in the *Moving Picture World* of January 12th. His article provides the kind of detail which helps us to visualize the way various sequences were presented in this 'Extraordinary One-Reel Picture Based on Shakespeare's "Julius Caesar".'

'This great one-reel subject will bear the strictest criticism with credit to the makers and with pleasure to anyone who, while ready to praise its beauties, is on the lookout to discover any marring defects . . . the scenes in the film enable one to follow clearly the march of events that led to the assassination of "the foremost man in the world" and the death of the two arch conspirators, Brutus and Cassius. . . .

'The opening scene . . . shows Cassius and other conspirators in a room awaiting the arrival of Brutus. The setting of this scene and the posing and acting are highly artistic. When Brutus arrives, he is shown to a seat at a large table, with Cassius immediately to his left, as one views the picture from the audience. The conspirators, seated, listen to Cassius, who speaks with vehemence. Suddenly he rises and confronts Brutus, and, drawing his dagger, makes a downward thrust through the air to illustrate the spoken words that mean death to Caesar.

'Brutus, with a look of horror on his face, expostulates, but is gradually led to embrace the decision of the others. The impersonation of Brutus in this scene, and throughout the film, shows great histrionic merit and a fine conception of the character. Cassius also is strongly sustained, and the grouping and acting of the conspirators show patient rehearsal and a careful aiming at realistic effects.

'Next we are in a room in Caesar's home, where we see his wife, Calpurnia, vainly endeavoring to keep him from going to the senate on this particular day. She thinks her pleadings have succeeded, when a messenger from the senate appears and Caesar goes to his doom. This scene affords a pleasant glimpse of the love prevailing in Caesar's domestic life, and gives us a close view of the furniture and tapestries used in the first homes of imperial Rome at that period.

'The killing of Caesar in the senate chamber follows. Intently one watches the proceedings leading up to the tragedy. To the left of the picture, as viewed from the audience, stands Cassius, a few feet behind Caesar. We watch his lips curl in a cruel smile as a senator makes a motion, and a parchment scroll is handed the First Consul. Caesar glances at it and throws it on the floor with imperious gesture. As he does so Cassius snatches the robe from his shoulders. Caesar springs up and faces Cassius. He immediately receives several downward dagger thrusts from the senators behind him. As he turns toward them, Cassius drives another home, and so it is until that sacred body receives the knives of all. Brutus is the last to inflict a wound; but he does it from the front, and the look that Caesar gives him – of reproach and surprise – shows that no other bolt from Jove can hurt either body or soul. Then Caesar covers his face with his garment and sinks to the floor. Not one vestige of shrinking is shown by him throughout the ordeal, not a trace of fear, on face or in action. The actor who took the character of Caesar merits much praise for preserving so thoroughly the dignity of the part.

'The funeral of Caesar in the Cines film is a most imposing spectacle. The site chosen by the producer is most probably on the very spot overlooking which Mark Anthony made his moving speech to the populace of Rome. In the picture the rostrum occupied by Anthony's impersonator has a commanding view of the surroundings, and looks down on the altar on which is placed the catafalque which bears the mortal remains of Caesar. In the midst of the speech we watch the excitement of the assembled multitude, stirred by the fierce desire for revenge on the murderers. As the torches are applied to Caesar's brief resting place and his remains are being consumed, Anthony stirs the minds of all to immediate action, and we see them rush off to the homes of those responsible for the deed.

'We view the flight of Brutus, who obstinately refuses to move and is determined to meet the mob and take the consequences, until his wife and friends finally urge and drag him to safety.

'We next visit the camps of the two armies before the battle of Philippi, and we see Brutus in his tent engrossed in studying the plans of battle. Influenced by some unseen power, he looks up, and beholds the ghost of the murdered Caesar, who speaks to him the familiar words, "We shall meet at Philippi", and then vanishes. His guilty soul cowers at the sight and fearful forebodings of the morrow seize him.

'The battle of Philippi that follows is a really remarkable massing and engaging of a multitude of soldiers in close action. It is a thrilling sight, full of the incidents of a hand-to-hand combat. Then the flight of Brutus, his discovery of Cassius dead on the field, and his own ignominious death.

'The photography is in keeping with the other high merits of the production.

'It will be wise to have a lecture on this film prepared and delivered by a competent man, as its educational value will be greatly increased thereby.'

It is rare that, so early, a review is found which gives the kind of particulars which McQuade presents – the gestures, the expressions, the groupings of actors, the settings and even properties. I wonder only why the raid on the conspirators' houses is not detailed, and why there is no mention of the review of the army. Kleine's release was on January 20th in 1065 feet, somewhat shorter than the English footage; perhaps there was some cutting.

I can add, however, a bit of detail, since fragments of this film are extant. All the shots are medium to long. The outdoor pictures of Brutus's flight after the loss of battle, and particularly of the forum scene are good. The camera pans from the crowds to Antony ascending the rostrum. There are no dissolves or double exposures. In the ghost scene, the film is stopped, the actor impersonating the ghost comes on the set, photography is resumed; at the end of the confrontation, the process is followed in reverse. On an Editola it is difficult to judge the acting because the frame is so small, and in this case critical episodes are missing. It is clear that Brutus dominates the action both in the presence of the impersonator and the concentration on the character – the film is accurately titled – but who the actor was, I have not been able to discover. 'According to his virtue let us use him. . . .'

When all the evidence is assembled, however, there can be no doubt that Enrico Guazzoni saw *Julius Caesar* in cinematic terms, so assembled his story, and produced in *Brutus* which was for the time an impressive film.

Italy mostly preferred Shakespeare's tragedies to his comedies. So far we have had, among the latter, films only of *The Taming of the Shrew* and *A Winter's Tale*, while *King Lear*, *Romeo and Juliet*, *Hamlet*, *Othello*, *Macbeth* and *Julius Caesar* have been made for the screen, three of them more than once. There were two more Italian *Lears* in 1910. Giuseppe De Liguoro added to his *Bruto* a *King Lear* for Milano, both adapting and directing; he may have acted in it as well. There is fortunately more information about a production in 1072 feet by Film d'Arte Italiana, which had already presented *Othello*. Again the director was Gerolamo Lo Savio, but the star this time was the most distinguished tragedian in Italy, Ermete Novelli, and Cordelia was acted by a young woman who was to become the most popular film star in Italy, Francesca Bertini. One of the other sisters was impersonated by Giannina Chiantoni, who had been leading lady for Novelli on the stage since 1902; this was her first film.

A surviving print of this *King Lear*, though truncated and in parts in poor condition, is worth analysis.

    I Lear calls on his daughters to express their love for him before the court. There are arches in the background. Goneril (tinted green) kneels and makes appropriate gestures, while Cordelia (tinted pink) stands aloof. The Fool is at the King's feet. Regan (tinted brown) now makes her protestations of affection. Cordelia refuses. Lear, angry, turns Cordelia over to France who takes her off.

       Subtitle: 'Goneril shamefully drives her father from her home. He leaves to seek revenge with Regan, his second daughter.'

   II Goneril and then shortly Kent. Lear arrives and sits, is insulted by Oswald. Kent's objection is approved by Lear. A hunting dog and the Fool are at Lear's feet. Goneril reenters, remonstrates. Lear, furious, leaves. Goneril sends Oswald to Regan.

       Subtitle: 'The Earl of Kent, servitor to King Lear hastens on in advance to inform Regan of her father's coming. On his arrival he is treated with scant ceremony and put into stocks. King Lear goes mad from excess of grief.'

  III At Regan's, a grass terrace and sentry box. Kent arrives and fights with Oswald. Regan enters, and Kent is stocked as she leaves. Lear arrives; Kent is freed; Regan reappears, then Goneril. Lear goes insane because of their attitudes. If Regan's consort is in this scene, he is too vague to be recognized.

       Subtitle: 'In his childish madness Lear compares the heart of his daughter to a stone.'

  IV The Fool is with Lear in a reasonably wild place of grass and trees, – and a stone. Kent enters and with the Fool tries to calm Lear. Servants, probably of Cordelia, arrive and take Lear off. This whole sequence is foggy and meaningless with much rant and gesture. There is no storm. Probably the next subtitle should have been inserted in the middle of this scene rather than at the end.

       Subtitle: 'Cordelia and her husband hearing of the misfortunes of the King send their officers to seek him.'

   V Kent describes Lear to the grief-stricken Cordelia.

       Subtitle: 'King Lear is taken to his daughter Cordelia.'

  VI Lear sweeping with a broom, haystacks in background. Various servitors enter, including Kent, who persuade Lear to accompany them.

       Subtitle: 'In the presence of his daughter, King Lear recovers his reason.'

 VII Lear is on a bed in a tent. Cordelia, accompanied by Kent, approaches, kisses her father. He wakes and recognizes her. Exeunt.

       Subtitle: 'Cordelia and her father are made prisoners. Cordelia is killed by her sisters' orders and King Lear expires in despair.'

VIII Cordelia and Lear are led off. There are soldiers under a background
arch. Some business with Kent is inexplicable. Lear enters with dead
Cordelia, puts her on the ground, bends over her, making unintelligible speeches. Possibly the feather business is included, but the rest
of the film is missing.

It should be apparent that the FAI *King Lear* has used, at least in what is
left of this print, parts of I, 1, 3, 4; II, 2, 4; III, 2,; IV, 3, 6, 7; and V, 3.
The only real adaptation is the complete elimination of the Gloucester plot
and all its connections with the Lear plot, and as a result the introduction
of means to get Lear to Cordelia. But unlike the simplicity of Shakespeare's
Julius Caesar of which Cines could take advantage, even the Lear plot of
King Lear is complex. Without subtitles this film could not be understood
at all; with them including the highly elaborate one between sequences II
and III, which is a story for rather than a mere direction to the viewers, it
can be only partly understood. One sees only tirades and movements which
baffle. With little comprehension, little emotion can be conveyed. Novelli
was a great actor, but he is not a great actor here because he has been unable
to adapt himself to the ruthless eye of the camera. What emerged was
melodramatic rather than forceful, gesticulation rather than expressive
mobility. Whoever the Kent was, he is much more restrained, and Francesca
Bertini shows why she will be a film actress. The settings are neither bad
nor good; they are just not much of anything. The tinting may help to
separate the identity of the daughters, but it does little more. I am sorry
not to have seen the complete film. No doubt those portions which are lost
might have helped somewhat. But I cannot believe that even in its entirety,
this is a film of any real significance except perhaps to give to the curious an
unkind glimpse of Ermete Novelli.

Novelli also starred as Shylock, like Lear one of his famous rôles on the
stage, in a Film d'Arte Italiana *Merchant of Venice* which must have followed
closely upon *King Lear*. Francesca Bertini played Portia, and Olga Giannini
Novelli, Ermete's wife, also took part, presumably as Jessica but possibly as
Nerissa. It was a better film than *King Lear* and was almost immediately
popular in England, where it was released on March 8, 1911, in 890 feet.
The *Kinematograph and Lantern Weekly* of February 23rd says of the Pathé
distributed film: 'The difficult task of putting forward a kinematograph
adaptation of *The Merchant of Venice*, has been well undertaken in the
present instance; the various scenes are fully played out, and the advantages
afforded by the natural background of Venice must be obvious to all.'
Bioscope of the same date merely summarizes and says 'the adaptation . . .
has been carried out in a very artistic and faithful manner.' I doubt if either
commentator had yet seen the film. However reports from theatre managers
in later issues – it was first shown at the Grand Central, Tottenham Court
Road – talk about 'good draws', 'greatest satisfaction to crowded houses',

'has created much admiration', 'brings the house down', etc. In Paris, the *Ciné-Journal* announced the film and the release by Série d'Art-Pathé Frères in 270 metres on April 8th, and on the 15th speaks of Ermete Novelli as 'l'admirable Artiste'. It is worth noting too that in England at least, the picture was reissued in 1913, though probably to pick up some money from confused patrons who thought they would be seeing a current French film of the same subject.

About two thirds of the original film remain today for the curious to examine.

Subtitle: 'Lorenzo who is in love with Jessica, daughter of Shylock the Jew, arranges to come for her.'

I This is shown but the characters and characterization are not clear. The arrangement is apparently with Launcelot Gobbo. A short sequence in a street.

Subtitle: 'Bassanio who is in love with Portia, begs his friend Antonio for a loan to enable him to ask for her in marriage.'

II The sequence however first shows Portia and Nerissa in a garden watching someone (Bassanio?) depart. Portia and Nerissa exeunt with attendants. Then Bassanio and Antonio as in the subtitle. Obviously much of the first part has been lost, and we never learn of Bassanio's choice of caskets or his marriage.

Subtitle: 'Antonio having all his fortunes at sea, takes Bassanio to Shylock.'

III The scene is authentically in Venice, a canal with bridge in background and a street in front of Shylock's house down scene. Shylock comes out of his house down steps, and the matter of the loan is put before him by Antonio and Bassanio. There is a long sequence of talk which would be meaningless without the subtitle. They all go into the house. Cut to a room which they enter. Antonio and Shylock sit at a table.

Subtitle: 'I give my bond that I will pay Shylock the Jew, the three thousand ducats that he promises to lend to my friend Bassanio, and that the forfeit of my bond when it expires, shall be Shylock's right to a pound of flesh taken from any part of my body he pleases. / Antonio / Merchant.'

IV This is really spelling it out. Bassanio makes objections but Antonio accepts. Shylock takes the document which Antonio has written at the table, goes to a chest through an arch at the rear, returns with a money bag which he puts on the table. At this point Novelli accidentally dropped it on the floor and had to pick it up. The bag is given to Antonio who passes it to Bassanio. As they leave the room, Shylock, alone, gloats and retires. Cut to Antonio and Bassanio outside Shylock's house, where Shylock joins them. He turns back to tell Launcelot to guard the house and to speak to Jessica at the top of the stairs, and then goes off arm-in-arm with Antonio and Bassanio. Launcelot and Jessica wave goodbye. Launcelot explains the plans for elopement to Jessica, who reads a letter from Lorenzo.

Subtitle: 'Pretty Jessica / My friends Antonio and Bassanio have business with your father and he will leave with them soon. Be prepared and as soon as they are gone I will come for you / Lorenzo.'

V Jessica continues to read and then retires with Launcelot into the house. Lorenzo arrives with friends. Jessica joins them and exeunt.

Subtitle: 'Shylock discovers the abduction of Jessica.'

VI This is a long and perfectly understandable sequence, and we might have been spared the subtitle. Shylock returns with someone, probably Tubal, who tells him something. Shylock discovers the keys dropped by the elopers, enters his house, returns distracted. People on the street laugh at him. He falls to the ground.

Subtitle: 'Antonio's ships having been wrecked he is ruined, and he is unable to pay the three thousand ducats for which he has given his bond. He is taken before the court of justice.'

VII Antonio with someone (Bassanio?) in a street scene, bridge over canal, receives word of his losses and is apprehended by soldiers.

Subtitle: 'Portia learns of the arrest of Antonio and resolves to save him.'

VIII The scene is in a courtyard. Present are Portia, Jessica, Nerissa and others. Portia hears the news from Bassanio, sends for her hat, dons it, and they all leave.

Subtitle: 'Portia disguised as a lawyer saves Antony by reminding Shylock of the law of Venice making confiscation of lands and goods the penalty for the shedding of a drop of Christian blood.'

IX In view of the next subtitle, this one seems unnecessary and would destroy any suspense created. Was it in the original film? This is the court scene, with Shylock, the Duke, and others. There is announcement of the arrival of a lawyer. Nerissa (?) enters and explains. Portia comes in and reads from a book. This sequence is jumbled and confused, and I suspect loss of footage.

Subtitle [an open book]: 'The penalty for the shedding of one drop of Christian blood is the confiscation of lands and goods, and the punishment for an attempt by an alien upon the life of a citizen of Venice shall be at the discretion of the Duke of Venice.'

X Shylock reacts, holds his head in his hands. At this point the print ends. The *Bioscope* summary adds, 'The Duke of Venice begs Antonio to decide what Shylock's punishment is to be, and Antonio declares that one half of his fortune shall be forfeited, while the other shall go to his daughter, but that he, Shylock, must become a Christian.'

It seems probable that this film eliminated entirely the casket plot and the ring plot, since they are not mentioned in any summary and do not show up in the fragmented print. Story line and suggestions have come from Shakespeare's I, 1, 2 (possibly), 3; II, 4, 5, 8; III, 1, 2, 3, 4; and IV, 1. The last act is not included. There has been some adaptation. The picture adds the scene in Shylock's house where the loan transaction occurs; also a scene where the people in the street laugh at Shylock, which is merely mentioned by Shakespeare. I see nothing about Jessica's theft of money and jewels from her father. In other words the main story has been much simplified and some thought has been given to the visualization of scenes. Yet this film has many of the same faults as *King Lear*. Too often the pictures merely illustrate the subtitles, and some of the subtitles seem unnecessary. Without subtitles, however, the story could not be followed, and is still unintelligible in parts. There is the repeated unheard conversation. Yet this is a better film than *King Lear*, despite the cutting of much of Portia's part for Bertini, who might have given it more verve. Novelli has an opportunity here for a wider range of emotions, and though there are violently gesticulated scenes, he is more impressive. The chief virtue of the film, however, is that all or most of it is shot in Venetian backgrounds. It is not that authenticity is in question, but that they provide meaningful and varied architectural backgrounds which could not be presented by conventional rooms, painted curtains or relatively inconsequential outdoor views. We shall see whether there was progress in FAI's soon to follow *Romeo and Juliet*.

There was certainly progress of a kind and considerable development. *Romeo and Juliet* was longer than the earlier Film d'Arte Italiana Shakespeares; there was more opportunity for the budding Francesca Bertini, who was Juliet to the Romeo of Gustavo Serena; there was considerable adaptation, though no print apparently has survived for analysis in detail; and for what it is worth in considering range of appeal, the picture was released in the United States, as *King Lear* and *The Merchant of Venice* had not been.

Romeo and Juliet must have been made late in 1911, though I find no contemporary references to it until it was shown in foreign countries early in 1912. In London, *Bioscope* of January 25th indicates it is to be released on February 7th in 2342 feet, and an advertisement in the *Kinematograph and Lantern Weekly* adds that it is issued by Pathé in colour. In Paris, the *Ciné-Journal*, March 16th, carries Pathé's advertisement, 'Vendredi prochain 22 mars Pathé Frères editent le plus pur Chef d'Oeuvre de Shakespeare, Roméo et Juliette, Film d'Arte Italiana, Joué à Verone sur les lieux où vécurent et moururent les deux Héros,' and elsewhere in the same issue it is listed in colour in 725 metres. In the United States it was not, according to the *Moving Picture World* of December 21st, to be released officially until January 3, 1913; the length is given merely as two reels. What is most important here is that we are again at the end of an era. Two reels or more gave film makers much greater opportunity to develop story and character-ization than the conventional one-reeler. Lo Savio must have welcomed the advantage.

Without the film itself, however, it is impossible to say what expansion there was, and we have to be content with summaries to show the adapta-tions. *Bioscope*'s review, already referred to as an announcement, is in fact merely a summary. Condensed it shows that at the beginning Romeo and Juliet have already met and that the first sequence was the balcony scene. There is no Paris, and Tybalt becomes the lover she refuses to marry, though preparations continue for that wedding. Romeo, determined to prevent it, attends the Capulet ball, where he speaks to Juliet, is discovered by the Capulets, and has to leave abruptly. Irritated, the Capulets provoke the Montagues, and there is now Shakespeare's opening brawl followed by the Duke's decree. Romeo persuades Juliet to marry him secretly, and the ceremony takes place in Friar Laurence's cell. There is apparently no consummation of the marriage. Romeo is now challenged to a duel by Tybalt and wounds rather than kills him; Mercutio is not in the film. Romeo is taken before the Duke, who banishes him. He takes secret leave of Juliet. Because Capulet presses her marriage to Tybalt, Juliet goes to Friar Laur-ence, obtains the potion, and on the day of Tybalt's marriage she is found apparently dead and is interred in the Capulet vault. Romeo hears the news, returns to Verona, penetrates the vault, and stabs himself. Juliet awakes in time to see him expiring and kills herself with the dagger dropped by Romeo. Rather than expanding the opportunities of showing more of Shakespeare's narrative than a one-reel film could cover, by its rearrangement and elimina-tion of characters this scenario actually simplified it. Of course it also meant that scenes and shots could be more detailed and of greater length with greater concentration on the two principals, who are introduced as lovers before any untoward external events and whose course of true love can be clearly followed. I hope therefore there were fewer purely explanatory sub-titles and more attention was given to the action and the actors. Unfortun-ately there is not much to show. The review in the *Moving Picture World* of January 18, 1913, says, 'Here are beautiful illustrations of Shakespeare's tragic story that are gracefully, rather than powerfully acted. The back-grounds are fine and with the furniture, costumes and all that are usually grouped under "staging", are very commendable. It was put on or seems to have been put on in a magnificent palace and is one of the prettiest pictures we have seen in some time. Both reels [are] full of poetry.' The background was, as we have seen, Verona, and the palace was perhaps the Palazzo della Governo, built by the della Scala family, where Dante and Giotto stayed. A week later the same periodical mentions 'two reels of surpassing beauty. The procession that followed the bier of Juliet formed a picture that is rarely equalled.' Evidently the pictorial quality of the picture was high. I wish I knew whether the mention of 'reels full of poetry' meant that subtitles were

Shakespearean or that the film had poetic quality. Either would be an advance.

For the comedies, we must go to France, where Eclipse produced in 1911 a *Falstaff*, based on *The Merry Wives of Windsor*, and a *Taming of the Shrew*, both directed by Henri Desfontaines. The *Ciné-Journal* announces the first on April 8th: 'La Societé des Films "Eclipse Radios" a très heureusement interprété cette éternelle aventure avec un soin de mise en scène et une ingéniosité remarquables. Les artistes choisis pour incarner les person-nages, semblent avoir été crées pour eux et M. Degeorge de l'Odéon est un Falstaff idéal.' An Eclipse advertisement in the same issue gives an addi-tional cast, unfortunately without indicating the assignment of rôles, of MM. Coste, Bacqué, Denis d'Inès, and Mme. Barjac, all of the Odéon, and Mme. Louise Willy of the Théâtre du Palais-Royal. Françoise Rosay, who did not appear again in motion pictures until 1922, should also be included among the players. The approximate length was 325 metres. There is no real review, but in London where the film was released on May 10th in 1025 feet, *Bioscope* on April 20th said: 'The facial expressions and delightful by-play are really excellent.' The *Kinematograph and Lantern Weekly* of same date headlines 'A Magnificent *Falstaff* Film / Urban Trading Com-pany's Shakespearian Triumph' and continues, 'We may assert without the slightest hesitancy that in *Falstaff* adapted from *The Merry Wives of Windsor*, which the Urban Trading Company are releasing on May 11th..., the Company, thick as its honours are, has made an achievement which is entitled to rank amongst the greatest successes. Nor is the reason hard to find, for the principal character, that of the title part, is sustained by Mr Degeorge of the Theatre National de l'Odeon, than whom we can imagine no more ideal exponent of the role. [The other actors are named.] Con-sequently we have acting of the highest order, and when added to this there is the fact that the photographic quality has seldom been equalled and never surpassed, even in the films released by this company, we have all the necessary concomitants that go to make up that which only the phrase, "A Shakespeare Masterpiece", fittingly describes.'

George Kleine imported *Falstaff* to the United States for release in 1000 feet on June 14th. The *Moving Picture World* of June 24th tempers its praise: 'The story of Shakespeare's *Merry Wives of Windsor* is well acted in this picture. We have the story plainly enough and it's an amusing one, but very little of the fun that is in the original comes over. We should have liked to have seen [Falstaff] get ducked, if it took four men to carry the basket, but behind a screen of bushes he seems to have saved himself a com-plete immersion. Excellent facial expression saves the picture. It accom-plishes a great deal, but it can hardly make a picture of so merry a play as *Falstaff* come up to our expectations.'

A George Kleine press sheet in the New York Public Library outlines the 'action as shown in the film':

'I At the wedding of Miss Anne Page, Falstaff is attracted by the wealth of Mrs Page and Mrs Ford.

II He covets their fortunes and pretends to love both of them.

III He sends a letter to each lady.

IV They agree to punish him by encouraging his suit.

V He visits Mrs Ford and is forced to hide in a laundry basket.

VI The basket is thrown into the river.

VII The second appointment.

VIII When discovered Falstaff disguises himself as an old woman.

IX Mr Ford and his friends discover the fraud and punish Falstaff.

X Ford apologizes to his wife.'

The 'scenes' are listed as: 'I The Banquet Hall; II An Ante Room; III Public Room at Dame Quickly's Inn; IV The Ford Residence; V The Rendezvous; VI The Inn; VII The River; VIII Before the Inn; IX The Ford Home; X Finale.' The first five scenes evidently provide the settings for the first five pieces of action, but from there on until the end there is some variation. The summaries in the trade journals indicate that Falstaff writes his letters to Mistress Ford and Mistress Page at the Garter Inn; that the rendezvous of Falstaff and Mistress Ford is interrupted by Mistress Page, who reports the arrival of Ford, informed in advance; that the second appointment is with Mistress Page, who sends for Falstaff at the Inn, where he is trying to warm himself after his ducking; that in this appointment, Falstaff is disguised as the Witch of Brentford and is beaten with a stick. I distrust the accuracy of these summaries, but one includes what is apparently a subtitle, a short version of the letter in Shakespeare's II, 1: 'Ask me no reason why I love you. Let it suffice thee, Mistress Page, if the love of a soldier can suffice, that I *love* thee. I will not say pity me, but love me. Thine own True Knight, By day or night, for thee to fight, John Falstaff.' This is the letter which the two women compare in section III of Kleine's 'action' list.

What does this add up to in relation to Shakespeare's play? Anne is married at the beginning of the film, perhaps to Fenton, who is however not named. Mistress Quickly is the proprietress of the Garter Inn, and the Host disappears. A good many characters are probably eliminated, at least by their Shakespearean appellations, Shallow and Slender, Sir Hugh Evans, Dr Caius, and various servants. The first scene is invented; Shakespeare is picked up at I, 3; the scenario then jumps to II, 1, then to III, 3; the ducking is depicted; the second interview is adapted from IV, 2, and the beating is staged; the reconciliations follow, as in IV, 4; and the rest of the play in Windsor Forest has been eliminated. If this be accurate, the scenario is reasonable, and the story must have been clear, even in one reel, even if not as funny as in the original. With good acting and photography, *Falstaff* must have been a picture worth seeing in 1911.

13. Juliet (Julia M. Taylor) and Romeo (George A. Lessey) in the Thanhouser version of 1911. *Moving Picture World*, August 26, 1911

14. Scenes from Barker's film production of Sir Herbert Tree's presentation of *Henry VIII* (1911). Compare the Banquetting Hall still with the almost identical illustration from the production at His Majesty's, which opened September 1, 1910. *Kinematograph and Lantern Weekly*, February 16, 1911, and *Playgoer and Society*, September 15, 1910, 'Daily Mirror' Studios

15. The wooing of Lady Anne, and Richard cursed by Queen Margaret, from the Benson *Richard III* (1911). Rachael Low, *The History of British Film 1906-1914*

16. Paul Mounet as Macbeth, a frame enlargement from the Film d'Art picture (1910). National Film Archive.

17. Calphurnia dreams of Caesar's murder, a film strip from the Itala *Julius Caesar* (*Brutus*) (1909). National Film Archive

18. Ophelia in her madness distributes flowers in the Lux *Hamlet* (1910). *Ciné-Journal*, January 3-10, 1910

Société "LUX

32, rue Louis-le-Grand

HAMLET

Film Artistique, d'après Shakespeare

A l'heure où le public parisien est appelé par M. Camille de Sainte-Croix à applaudir sur un théâtre spécial les grands drames du « divin » Shakespeare, la **Société Lux** offre à sa clientèle cinématographique une reconstitution d'*Hamlet*.

Certes l'œuvre a déjà été traitée, mais jamais elle n'avait présenté plus de simplicité dans l'action, plus de vérité dans le costume et les décors. La mise en scène particulièrement soignée. le jeu excellent des interprètes, assureront à ce film un succès durable.

Nous n'avons pas besoin de raconter ici l'histoire universellement connue d'Hamlet. Le drame de Shakespeare et l'opéra sont dans toutes les mémoires. Qu'il nous suf-

fise de rappeller que le nouveau d'œuvre de la **Société Lux** suit pa les scènes du dramaturge anglais. L de côté la partie purement psycho qui échappe nécessairement à la cir graphie, le metteur en scène a reter tion seule, les gestes explicatifs de la les péripéties matérielles du drame l'apparition du spectre jusqu'au d'Hamlet après la mort de la douce lia.

Et la suite des événements est ains parfaite clarté : le public retrouve charme et émotion les figures qu'il et qu'il aime.

Tous les directeurs de *Cinéma-* passeront l'*Hamlet* de la **Société L**

19. Hamlet (Jacques Grétillat) sees his father's ghost in the closet scene (Eclipse, 1910); the Gertrude is Colonna Romano. *Le Crapouillet*, November 1932

I am not so sure that *The Taming of the Shrew* was, and I begin to suspect that the Shakespeare series of Eclipse was running out its apparent popularity. Curiously, it was released by Kleine in the United States on June 28, 1911, more than three months before it was presented in France and England. The footage was announced in the *Moving Picture World* of July 1st as 1000 feet; a week later this journal reviews: 'This picture is very interesting. It is well acted and beautifully staged and also the story is made clear. It might be best characterized as graceful and dignified. It is highly commendable.' I rather doubt whether this comment would sell the picture to exhibitors, and *The Taming of the Shrew* is hardly a play which should emerge on film as 'graceful and dignified'. In England, the *Kinematograph and Lantern Weekly*, September 14th, is so content with laudatory generalizations that I believe the reviewer is working from company hand-outs rather than from a press showing of the film itself.

'On October 4th, the Charles Urban Trading Company are releasing another of their remarkable series of Shakespearian subjects, which have proved so popular in the past, and in *The Taming of the Shrew*, they have once again shown the world at large how the Immortal Bard's plays should be produced kinematographically. When one talks of Urban Trading Company quality, one recognises that to pay compliments is but to gild refined gold or paint the lily. Quality and the Urbanora trade-mark ever go hand in hand. And to attempt to criticise the acting of the exponents of histrionic art whose actions and gestures have been preserved by the company for all futurity, would be superfluous. Everyone knows that only actors and actresses of the front rank of the profession are considered good enough to appear in Urbanora subjects, whether Shakespearian or otherwise. In the 1060 feet to which *The Taming of the Shrew* runs, there is not a single inch of padding, the film is real sterling value and excellence every inch of it, and is one of a kind which all who have the true interest of the electric theatre at heart, must wish there were even more of.'

This effusion really says nothing about the film, and *Bioscope*, if one omits equally useless generalizations, says merely, 'No praise can be too high . . . the finest film ever put out by the Company.'

France does it with more grace but no more detail. So the *Ciné-Journal* on September 23rd:

'En verité, si l'on peut appeller film d'art une oeuvre dramatique empruntée à la littérature et jouée, dans des décors artistiques, avec des costumes exacts, par des comédiens de valeur, *la Mégère Apprivoisée* que l'Eclipse doit sortir le 5 October prochain mérite cette flatteuse dénomination.

'Continuant avec un rare bonheur la traduction cinématographique des oeuvres de Shakespeare commencé par l'admirable *Falstaff* [What about *Hamlet*?], l'Eclipse n'était pas sans audace de s'attaquer à cette jolie fan-

E

taisie bouffonne qui s'appelle *la Mégère Apprivoisée* et qui pourrait être aussi bien baptisée: 'L'Art de dompter les femmes par l'amour'. Nulle tâche n'était plus delicate.

'L'excellente Societé de la rue de la Michodière a perfaitement réuisi, grâce au talent de son metteur en scène et au concours très artistique des interprètes.

'L'oeuvre comptera parmi les meilleures et la faveur de tous les amis de la Cinématographie artistique lui est acquis. Son succès sera très vif.'

The French footage was announced as 328 metres, but the personnel were not. However from other sources it is clear that the *metteur en scène* was Desfontaines, and that the 'concours très artistique des interprètes' included Barjac and d'Inès, who had been in *Falstaff*, and that others were Romuald Joubé, Jean Hervé, and Cécile Didier.

Kleine's press sheet lists ten settings: 'I Baptista's Home in Padua; II Lucentio's Rooms in Pisa; III Music Room at Baptista's; IV The Wedding at the Church; V Another Hall of the Church; VI Petruchio's Palace, the Dining Hall; VII A Chamber in Petruchio's Palace; VIII Audience Room in the Same; IX A Room in Lucentio's House; X Banquet Hall after his Wedding.' This outline is probably more accurate than the summaries, often prepared from the play rather than the film, but with them and the scene plot, one can gather fairly accurately what was included in the film. It opened with Petruchio's application to Baptista for Katherina's hand (II, 1). I do not see why there is a scene in Lucentio's Rooms in Pisa unless there is a cross-cut to show him preparing to woo Bianca and disguising himself (I, 1). The next episode must be a sequence in which is depicted Katherina breaking the lute over Hortensio's head, the interview between Katherina and Petruchio, and Baptista's acceptance of the marriage proposal. Evidently Scene IV includes Petruchio's arrival in fantastic dress but in this case at the Church, where the wedding is pictured rather than described (III, 2). The wedding feast is dispensed with, and bride and groom depart on horseback for Petruchio's 'Palace', a scene probably filmed and perhaps starting from the Hall of the Church (described in part in IV, 1). The Dining Hall scene must be the unsatisfactory meal which Katherina is not allowed to eat (IV, 1), and the Chamber scene, the disarrangement of the bed (also described in IV, 1). The tailor business (IV, 3) follows. The plan to go to Baptista's house is abandoned as a result of the disagreement about the identities of the sun and moon (IV, 5), but Katherina and Petruchio go to Lucentio's where both bring their brides for the wedding feast and the clear evidence of the taming of the shrew (V, 2). The characters in addition to the principals include Petruchio's servants, the tailors, and Hortensio and his widow at the end; in other words, Shakespeare's tale is simplified and compressed into one reel, but with certain scenes shown which Shakespeare only described. This is one way to adapt Shakespeare, but there were others.

It became apparent in 1911 that the impact of *film d'art* was largely spent. Films with literary backgrounds and Shakespearean subjects continued to be made, especially since multiple reels offered opportunities for more detailed treatments than had hitherto been possible. Stage actors continued to appear in screen productions but for some time there was no Mounet-Sully, no Ermete Novelli. Scripts by well known authors gave ground to scenarios by writers essentially trained by their experience in the studios. *Film d'art* probably had had more influence in Italy – witness the number of Italian Shakespeare films – than it had had in its country of origin. Now directors in both countries were interested in pursuing different paths, paths which led more and more to contemporary subjects and less and less to the conventions of the theatre. One such director in France was Louis Feuillade who was influenced by the realism of Antoine and the naturalism of Zola, and by the production methods of Vitagraph.

Feuillade, who had been with Pathé, went in 1906 to Gaumont as a scenario writer. He was soon building a stock company and directing as well. He had tried films of various types, including Films Esthétiques, influenced by Film d'Art, when in 1911 he launched a series called 'La Vie telle qu'elle est', which was to present slices of life, moments of truth. He devised his own scenarios, more or less in his head, jotting down notes as he worked, improvising as he directed his actors and Charles Guérin, his cameraman. The reader might well wonder what all this had to do with Shakespeare if he did not know that one of the first pictures in the new series was *Le Roi Lear au Village*, *A Village King Lear*.

Le Roi Lear au Village was listed in the *Ciné-Journal* on May 20th as of 360 metres, and in the *Kinematograph and Lantern Weekly* on May 11th for release in 1235 feet on June 29th. It was brought to the United States by Kleine, where it was made available on July 18th in 1010 feet. There is a summary in the *Moving Picture World* of July 8th.

'A blind father is prevailed upon to transfer his property to his two daughters, who promise to look after him properly. The elder daughter, with whom he first makes his home, is kind for a short time, but attending to the requirements of a blind man soon becomes irksome, and she gradually relaxes her attentions and finally looks upon the old man as a great nuisance, and neglects him. After a time she loses all patience with his infirmity, and rather than be troubled with him any longer, takes him to the house of her younger sister. The younger sister is equally unwilling to give him the attention he needs, and heartbroken by the base ingratitude of his daughters, the old man leaves the house and his servants find him wandering helplessly about the village. Knowing the conditions upon which the gift was made, they take him to the solicitor's office, where a meeting is arranged with his daughters. The elder daughter, in order to avoid the scandal which is otherwise bound to arise, puts the best face she can upon the matter and takes him home again, where, perhaps feeling some small amount of remorse on account of what has transpired, she treats him with more compassion.'

The same journal on July 22nd gave the picture a mixed review: 'This is a very intelligently produced picture of a tragic incident. It doesn't seem as effective as it ought to be. It is an extremely difficult situation to picture adequately, for the bitterness in such an old man's heart at being ill-treated by his two daughters, to whom he has given everything he owns, needs words to express it. The village Lear has to sit in judgment on himself and his daughters before he can feel all their sharp-toothed unkindness. These are things that cannot be expressed by gestures alone. The acting is very good, but though the picture is interesting, it doesn't get across powerfully.' The review is probably just. What is more important is that this film is a new way of presenting Shakespeare, and one typical of Feuillade. It is very different in treatment from Eclipse's *A Modern Shylock* where a miser is treated sentimentally and conventionally. It is equally different from Shakespeare's *King Lear* in its handling of the mixed motives of the daughters who are exasperated rather than cruel and in its level ending which has elements of tragedy in it but is not tragic. There is if not happiness at the end, at least compassion in the Goneril, and a better understanding of himself in the Lear. Feuillade's film illustrates one way in which a basically Shakesperean story is treated by methods at utter variance from the ideals of *film d'art*, to become 'la vie telle qu'elle est', not poetry in motion but prose.

Another kind of modernized use of Shakespeare was attempted in Denmark. Nordisk in the person of Ole Olsen was neither much influenced by *film d'art* nor, despite its *Hamlet*, by Shakespeare, but it made a *Desdemona* in 1911 which it advertised in the *Kinematograph and Lantern Weekly* on February 22, 1912, as 'a thrilling portrayal of the terrible vengeance a husband exacted from his erring wife', to be released on March 30th, in 1797 feet. Its length again shows that we are at the beginning of the two-reel era. The same journal on March 7th carried another Nordisk advertisement of this 'thrilling modern drama': 'Not the unadulterated Desdemona of Shakespeare, but a good modern play with a plot not too deep but just deep enough for mental exercise without effort, while interest and excitement are sustained throughout.' Accompanying this remarkable statement is a still of a recognizable Othello beside a bed with Desdemona on the floor, so we may expect something more than was contained in Nordisk's comic *Othello* of 1908. This one too, however, was to include histrionics, as a long summary in the London trade paper shows.

'There are, of course, many lovers of Shakespeare in a pure and unadulterated form, but there are countless hordes to whom the Bard's plays do not appeal in the remotest degree. Bearing this in mind, the Nordisk Films Company have written, so to speak, around the tragedy of Othello a thrilling

drama, the plot of which is enacted largely behind the scenes of the legitimate theatre and the *mise en scene* of which is a portrayal of the tragic death
of Desdemona at the hands of her lover. . . . Ejnar and Maria, husband and
wife, are artists in a forthcoming production of *Othello* at the Rococo
Theatre. Maria leaves her husband, for whom she has but little love, to
attend a rehearsal at the theatre. Preben, an actor, tries to force his attentions
on her, but repulsed, vows vengeance. A bouquet comes for the woman from
her admirer, Count Brisson, and in it is enclosed a note appointing a *rendezvous*. Preben obtains possession of this and when Maria meets Brisson,
follows the pair to a restaurant. There he sees them engage in loving embraces and subsequently sees Brisson present Maria with a locket containing
the Count's portrait. Soon after they leave, and Maria arrives home just as
Ejnar, who has become impatient at her absence, is preparing to go in search
of her. Asked where she has been, she declines to explain her absence, and
pleading headache, goes to lie down in her bedroom. Close upon her foot-
steps comes the revengeful Preben, who discloses to the husband his wife's
perfidy, and in proof produces the note that was affixed to the bouquet.
Ejnar goes to his wife's room, and finding she has fallen asleep, gently
disengages the locket from about her neck. Gazing at it he is struck by the
similarity between the features of the Count and himself, and conceives the
idea of disguising as Brisson. Now follows a series of pictures showing the
gradual transformation of Ejnar into the likeness of Brisson. Satisfied that
his disguise will not be penetrated, he returns and awakens Maria. She is
entirely taken in by the disguise and proceeds to give her husband all the
necessary proof that she is a dishonoured woman. Tearing off his disguise,
despite her appeals, he turns her out of house and home. That evening Maria
receives a message from her admirer arranging another meeting. News of
this is carried by Preben to Ejnar, and he, almost driven mad, vows to effect
retribution. In the play Maria sustains the role of Desdemona, whilst Ejnar
appears as Othello and Preben as Iago. The play steadily progresses, and
throughout its course Desdemona bestows many smiles on Brisson, who is
occupying one of the boxes. This is all that is needed to destroy the last
threads of control remaining in Othello, and in the final scene when he is
supposed to kill Desdemona, the audience wonders at the realism of the
acting. Seizing her by the neck, Othello crushes the life out of her body,
then turning to the footlights, he dramatically points to Brisson, crying:
'He has taken away my happiness.' Seeing that the sympathies of the
audience lie entirely with the actor, the Count silently withdraws. The
police are hastily summoned and arrest Ejnar, who breaks away and falls
upon the body of his wife.'

I have given the whole extent of the summary, even though it describes a
film which is not of Shakespeare's *Othello*, because the scenario could not
have been written without the original, and to demonstrate another and

different way in which Shakespearean material was adapted, adulterated if you will, instead of being condensed and duplicated. In *A Village King Lear* Shakespeare's story, transferred to a modern milieu, was essentially retained, but in *Desdemona*, a story has been written around the original play. I suppose this elaborately devised scenario to give Shakespeare to the masses without provoking any unnecessary thought was someone's pride and joy. It was to appear later in a number of films, such as *The Mad Lover* (1917), originally called *A Modern Othello*, *Carnival* (1921, 1931 with sound), and *A Double Life* (1947), in all of which there is a frame story around a performance of *Othello* in which the characters in the frame participate in the play. As the length increases, the plots become more and more complex. *Desdemona* indeed could hardly have been done in one reel, if it was to become what used to be called 'strong drama', because the complications were necessary to its effect. The Nordisk people in England were a little worried about its length; the summarizer concluded with giving its footage, but added about the picture that it 'is one therefore which can be included in any programme without unduly encroaching upon it.' The feature film was not yet generally accepted. It soon will be, and with it comes the end of *film d'art*.

CHAPTER VI

Increase the Reels

1912 TO WORLD WAR I

As the impulses which had led to the many productions of films which were directly based on Shakespeare's plays (and were advertised as such) declined, as the footage increased beyond one reel with consequent increases in elaboration of settings and cost, there was at first an immediate diminution of the number of such films. In 1912, there were only three pictures which purported to be Shakespearean, all of them adaptations from comedies, two made in the United States, one in France, all three in two or three reels. 1913 was, however, a big year; there were, even if allowance is made for doubtful dating, at least seven, and they included history and tragedy as well as comedy, and were of varying footage from two up to six reels; moreover, figures prominent on the stage reappeared in leading roles, Frederick Warde, Arthur Bourchier, Forbes-Robertson; and England, Italy, and Germany joined America and France as countries of origin. In 1914 we are back to three, one made in the United States, two in Italy, in lengths from four to seven reels. And by way of preamble to the next chapter, there were in 1915 no Shakespeare feature pictures at all.

Concomitantly there were of course in this span a considerable number of films which borrowed in one way or another from Shakespeare, by adapting story to modern or at least different *milieux*, by including Shakespearean material in pictures which were essentially not Shakespearean at all, by using Shakespeare's titles or characters because they were proverbial or catchy or symbolic. If this group is combined with the first, it will be found that *Hamlet* and *Romeo and Juliet* were the plays most often bowed to. 1913 was again a peak year. Most of this sort of adoption resulted in one-reel films, or in relatively small segments of longer pictures. Finally there was the usual planning for films with stage stars – Tree, Salvini, Sothern and Marlowe – films which were never filmed.

Vitagraph in the United States was the company most concerned in 1912. It made two pictures partly Shakespearean and one straight adaptation, an *Indian Romeo and Juliet*, a *Cardinal Wolsey*, and *As You Like It*. The scenario of the first was by Hal Reid, the father of the soon-to-be popular Wallace Reid. How far he borrowed from Shakespeare is evident in the summary of the story in the *Moving Picture World* of January 27th:

'Oniatare, a young brave of the tribe of the Hurons, and Kowa, a chief of the Mohicans, are in love with Ethona, or "The River Flower", an Indian Princess. The Hurons and the Mohicans are sworn enemies. The young brave and "The River Flower" meet from time to time. Kowa notices this and in plaintive song would lure the fair Ethona to him. But it is of no avail. The Great Medicine Man of the Mohicans prescribes rest and a sleeping potion, which she takes and falls into a deep sleep. Both Oniatare and Kowa meet at her uncovered pyre. They fight a duel unto the death. Oniatare slays the older man, and then plunges the dagger deep into his own breast, dropping lifeless. The falling of his body across hers arouses her from sleep and she awakens to behold his self-sacrifice, a still stronger evidence of his love for her. Seizing the blood-stained dagger from his breast, she thrusts it into the heart which goes out to his.'

The comment on this 'very pretty picture in beautiful Mohawk Valley backgrounds' in the issue of February 17th adds other details of the story: the Capulet Mohawk, Ethona's father, has destined her for Kowa; the lovers meet and are married by stealth; and Ethona procures the potion from the medicine man on the eve of her marriage to Kowa. The comment concludes inexplicably, 'The ending scene is exactly almost like the old ending. . . . It will be a good feature picture although the story is not very vital. The photographs are very beautiful.' I like the 'suggested press announcement' in the *Vitagraph Bulletin* of January 17th–February 1st that the film is 'far more Shakespearian than Shakespeare . . .' and the piling up of adjectival puffery in the company's advertisement in the *Moving Picture World* of February 3rd: 'Shakespeare's *Romeo and Juliet* is great; the Indian version of it makes a superb picture of sublime art and dramatic finish – exquisitely impressive in majestic scenery and tableaux.'

The *Indian Romeo and Juliet* was directed by Laurence Trimble and featured the Vitagraph Girl, Florence Turner; they were to be long associated, but not hereafter with Shakespeare. William Wallace Reid – he soon dropped his first name – was the Romeo; Harry Morey, Kowa; James H. Reid, Rohowaneh (Capulet); Mrs Adelaide Ober, Neok (Nurse); Harold Wilson, Oyenkwa (Friar Lawrence). The film, which was released in England on April 15th was considered by *The Cinema News and Property Gazette* of the same month 'quite out of the ordinary, considering that it has strong romantic and poetic tendencies. It is an attempt to translate poetry into cinematography'. Not having seen the film, I am at a loss how the 'poetic tendencies' were conveyed.

Cardinal Wolsey was considerably farther from Shakespeare's *Henry VIII* than the *Indian Romeo and Juliet* was from its source. Here Hal Reid took from Shakespeare suggestions for scenes and incidents and a quotation used as a subtitle, but the motivations are so simplified and the plot made so essentially domestic that the effect is not really Shakespearean at all. An incomplete print in the National Archive of the British Film Institute can be pieced out with various summaries to indicate the coverage and something of the nature of the film itself. Material in the summaries but not in the print is included in parentheses, titles in the print in quotation marks. The general title is missing, and the first shot is of Julia Swayne Gordon as Queen Catherine. Subsequent pictures using the same technique identify Anne Boleyn as Clara Kimball Young (her début) and Tefft Johnson as Henry VIII. There probably should be one of Hal Reid as Cardinal Wolsey.

   I (At a royal audience, Henry sees Anne Boleyn, lady-in-waiting to the Queen and is at once attracted to her.) The print shows only Henry with Queen Catherine and Wolsey. As the King leaves the scene, there is a title: 'Henry VIII sees Anne Boleyn, the new lady-in-waiting.'

  II A sycophantic courtier, in whom Henry has confided, enables the King to catch a glimpse of Anne at her toilette in her boudoir.

 III 'The King prepares to masquerade'. The preparations are shown.

 IV 'The King becomes more infatuated with Anne Boleyn.' At the masquerade, Anne is introduced to the King. Wolsey joins Henry as Anne leaves.

  V 'Queen Catherine learns of the King's affair with Anne.' It is Wolsey who tells her in a private chamber. Her distress is mimed as Wolsey leaves.

 VI The scene is a corridor. Anne and her attendant are greeted by the King. Henry dismisses the attendant, embraces Anne, with his arms around her walks with her to a bench. Wolsey and the Queen see the love-making.

 VII 'The Queen's accusation – Henry is defiant.' This action is presented.

VIII (Henry appeals to Cardinal Wolsey to allow his divorce from Catherine. Wolsey refuses, to the anger of Henry.) 'Cardinal Wolsey excommunicates the King because he seeks a divorce from Catherine.' The scene is shown, with the Queen present at the beginning of it.

 IX 'The Archbishop of Canterbury agrees to help the King.' (The Archbishop is to call a special council, by order of Henry, which will authorize the divorce.) Not shown.

  X 'Catherine takes council of the Cardinal.' He writes a letter to Rome. The letter is filmed but is indistinct. It is given to a priest who will act as messenger.

 XI 'The Cardinal's letter is intercepted.' The interception is by a courtier, who notifies the King. The scene is in the corridor as in VI. Wolsey sees the interception, is denounced by Henry. As the others leave, the courtier bows ironically to the Cardinal.

E*

XII 'Catherine sees the coronation procession of Henry's new wife.' Her view is from a window into a courtyard, the only outdoor shot in the film. The Cardinal is with her as she watches the procession, comforts and blesses her. Anne is crowned.

XIII 'Cardinal Wolsey denounces the altered Bible which Henry has changed to permit of his divorce.' In fact, Wolsey knocks the Bible out of the hands of the priest who carries it. Henry cringes but orders Wolsey's removal.

XIV (The Cardinal is exiled to Leicester Abbey. He is a sick man and dies three days after his entrance to the monastery.) 'Had I but served my God with half the zeal I served my King, He would not in mine old age have left me naked to mine enemies.' 'Old' is an addition to the passage in Shakespeare's III, 3; the title is not lined as poetry. The film in its present form shows only Wolsey at his desk with light from a window at the right. He bows his head. 'The End.' This sequence, in yellow tint, is photographically the best in the film.

Hal Reid has taken from Shakespeare, in addition to the quotation, the masquerade (I, 4), the King's infatuation with Anne (I, 4; II, 2), the approval of divorce by the Archbishop of Canterbury (II, 4), a suggestion for the comforting of Katherine (III, 1, with change of spelling of the Queen's name), the discovery of Wolsey's letter to the Pope and his learning of the discovery (II, 2), the idea of the procession and coronation of Anne (III, 3), the departure of Wolsey (IV, 1), and, if it is in the complete film, the death of Wolsey at Leicester (IV, 2). Much of the derivation is of course of incidents reported by Shakespeare but not actually depicted. The rest is Reid's invention or taken from other sources. There is nothing in Shakespeare of Wolsey's denunciation of the altered Bible, or the observation of Anne at her toilette, or Wolsey's excommunication of Henry, or the witnessing by Katharine of the coronation procession, scenes shown in the film, and the position and site of the masquerade are changed. Shakespeare's speech for Wolsey, partly used as a subtitle, comes at the end of the film instead of before the Cardinal's departure from the Court. It is unnecessary to detail the multiplicity of incident which is omitted.

Despite the simplification and omissions, the story of the film is not altogether clear. Since Henry is made an unsympathetic intriguer, and Wolsey heroic in his opposition, the final quotation is not apt. The position of Anne is decidedly equivocal. There is nothing about the King's 'conscience', nor of the need for an heir, and Katharine becomes merely pitiful. Some of the confusion is obviated by the over-numerous subtitles, and the introduction of the actors in costume at the start of the picture, a device which Vitagraph had used before in its *King Lear* but not, so far as I know, elsewhere. Evidently the director of the film, again Laurence Trimble, was aware of the difficulties, even if he could not altogether solve them. The film is somewhat static because there is so much conversational incident. Yet the picture is not altogether bad, at least for its period. The photography is satisfactory, though unimaginative except in the final scene, and confined to indoor shots, largely of medium length, except in the scene of the procession and coronation. The costumes are good. The acting of the principals is even better, though of 1912 in its elaboration of gesture and facial expression. All the leads were experienced, except Clara Kimball Young, whose appeal is apparent in her début. In addition to those already named, Logan Paul was the Archbishop of Canterbury; Robert Gaillard, the King's secretary; Harold Wilson, the King's friend; and 'Mr Ober', the Bishop of Essex, roles so small I have not detailed them.

The review of *Cardinal Wolsey* in the *Moving Picture World* on March 5th, the date of release, is on the whole favourable and just:

'This historical, dramatic series of scenes suggested by Shakespeare's *Henry VIII* is the week's big release. It is in one reel (1000 feet); but it is so magnificently acted, costumed, set and pictured that it leaves a very deep impression. The great cardinal is played with most remarkable success by Mr Hal Reid. This portrayal, we believe, reaches a very high plane of art and is very worth while seeing. Even if he were not Cardinal Wolsey, he was every inch a cardinal. Catherine of Arragon is played by Julia Swayne Gordon, who shows the outraged queen in a dignified, royal way that stirs our sympathy. Anne Boleyn is played by Clara Kimball Young, who makes the pretty young lady-in-waiting a bit frightened at first, yet not very reluctant. She seemed somewhat awed by her honors as she passed in the coronation pageant. This out-of-doors parade is the picture's only weak point. It wasn't very suggestive, hardly could be; because the cast couldn't fill the space and there were no spectators, no citizens crowding for a look at their new queen. It would have 'got over' better if it had passed through the hall-setting used in other scenes. Teft Johnson played King Henry, and, at moments, looked very much indeed like this King's portrait. The picture is a big educational feature. By the way, the reviewer got four people who were sitting near him into a discussion of it. They seemed to lose it altogether. One young boy of about eighteen seemed to think the cardinal was making love to the queen whom he was comforting.'

Apparently education could be confusing in those days too.

Vitagraph's third contribution to Shakespeare film in 1912 was more direct and more pretentious. The company engaged, perhaps under the impetus of European practice and certainly contrary to its own, a famous star of the stage, Rose Coghlan, to appear as Rosalind in *As You Like It*. Moreover it lengthened the footage for the first time in its Shakespearean productions to three reels. The adaptation by Margaret Birch was photographed under the direction of Charles Kent in the Flatbush woods during the summer, screened for reviewers in August, but not released to the public until October 7th, no doubt to allow time for exploitation. The rest of the cast was made up of Vitagraph players with Maurice Costello as Orlando, Rosemary Theby as Celia, Robert Gaillard as Oliver, Kent himself as Jaques, Tefft Johnson as Duke Senior, Robert McWade, Sr as Touchstone, Harry Morey as Duke Frederick, Rose Tapley as Phoebe, Kate Price as Audrey, George Ober as Adam, George C. Randolph as Charles the Wrestler, Charles Eldridge as Corin, James Morrison as Silvius, Frank Mason as Amiens, Hugh McGowan (Hughie Mack) as William, and Leo Delaney as Jaques de Bois. James Young, the husband of Clara Kimball Young, was either Le Beau or Sir Rowland de Bois, whose part is written into the script.

The structure of Vitagraph's *As You Like It* is best shown by a list of the titles which encumber it to the extent of 472 feet, a total of almost half a reel. The first two give the general title and name the actors of the principal parts.

Reel I

3 'Duke Frederick usurps his brother's power and banishes him from court.' (Before scene 1)

4 'Rosalind begs to accompany her banished father but is detained by her uncle, Duke Frederick, as a companion for his daughter, Celia.' (Cut in scene 1)

5 'Sir Rowland, a friend of Rosalind's father, urges his oldest son to care for his younger brothers.' (Before death scene)

6 'Orlando, Sir Rowland's youngest son, learns that he is entirely dependent on the bounty of his brother, Oliver.' (Before scene where will is read)

7 'Orlando pleads for his rights.' (Before scene at sundial where he talks to Oliver)

8 'Orlando challenges Charles, the Duke's wrestler.' (Before scene where he challenges him)

9 'Oliver bribes Charles to kill his brother, Orlando.' (Before scene where he gives him money)

10 'The banished Duke is joined by loyal followers in the forest of Arden.' (Before scene where they are crowded around him)

11 'Duke Frederick urges Orlando not to fight Charles.' (Before he advises him not to fight)

12 'The Contest.' (In jump)

13 'The champion.' (In second jump)

14 'The Duke learns that Orlando is the son of his banished brother's friend and therefore, his enemy.' (Cut in before he asks him who he is)

15 ' "We must rid our kingdom of this Orlando!" ' (Before scene of Duke talking to courtiers)

16 ' "Cupid have mercy! I am mad with love for Orlando!" ' (Before scene with Celia)

17 'Fearing Rosalind's allegiance to his enemies, her uncle banishes her.' (Before scene where he tells her to go)

18 'Orlando is warned that his life is in danger.' (Before scene where servant tells him)

19 'A plan to escape in disguise.' (Before scene where girls plan)
20 'The jester agrees to go as escort.' (Before garden scene where they talk to him)
21 ' "Therefore look you, call me *Ganymede* and you, as my sister shall answer to *Aliena*!" ' (Before scene where they enter in disguise)
22 'Part II of AS YOU LIKE IT will follow immediately,

Reel II

1 (Title) AS YOU LIKE IT. PART II.
2 'The flight is discovered. (Before scene 1)
3 'Orlando joins the followers of Rosalind's father, the brother of Duke Frederick. (Before scene where he joins them)
(3½) 'The Duke requests Jacques to relate the story of "The Seven Ages".'
4 ' "All the world's a stage,
    And all the men and women merely players:
    And one man in his time plays many parts,
    His acts being seven ages.
    At first the infant,
    Mewling and puking in the nurse's arms:" '
5 ' "Then, the whining schoolboy with his satchel,
    Creeping like snail unwillingly to school." '
    (Before scene of man reciting second verse)
6 ' "And then the lover,
    Sighing like furnace, with a woful ballad
    Made to his mistress' eyebrow." '
    (Before third verse)
7 ' "Then, the soldier:
    Full of strange oaths and bearded like a pard
    Seeking the bubble reputation even in the cannon's mouth." '
8 ' "And then, the justice
    In fair round belly, with good capon lin'd
    Full of wise saws and modern instances,
    And so he plays his part." '
9 ' "The sixth age shifts
    Into the lean and slippered pantaloon;
    And his big manly voice,
    Turning again toward childish treble, pipes
    And whistles in his sound." '
10 ' "Last scene of all.
    That ends this strange eventful history,
    Is second childishness and mere oblivion;
    Sans teeth, sans eyes, sans taste, sans everything." '
11 'Suspecting that Orlando knows the whereabouts of the girls, Duke Frederick sends for his brother Oliver.' (Before messenger tells Oliver to come)
12 ' "Find your brother, Orlando, or your lands will be seized!" ' (Cut in where Duke tells him)
13 'In the forest of Arden.' (Before scene of girls in the woods)

14 'Phoebe, the shepherdess, scorns Silvius' vows and falls in love with Rosalind, whom she supposes to be a man.' (Before scene where she scorns Silvius)

15 ' "We'll buy this shepherd cote for home!" ' (Cut in)

16 'Orlando, who has never forgotten Rosalind, spends his time penning verses to her.' (Before scene in woods where he puts verse on tree)

17 'Celia finds the verses.' (In jump)

18 'Believing Rosalind is a man, he confides his love story.' (Before scene where he tells her his story)

19 'Rosalind promises to make Orlando's love come true if he will court her as his "Rosalind".' (Cut in)

20 ' "By two o'clock, I will be with thee again!" ' (Cut in before he leaves)

21 'Orlando saves the life of his brother, Oliver.' (Before scene where he slays animal)

22 'Part III of AS YOU LIKE IT will follow immediately.'

Reel III

1 (Title) AS YOU LIKE IT. REEL III.

2 'Thinking Rosalind is a man, the infatuated Phoebe sends a love note.' (Before she sends note)

3 'Phoebe's letter is delivered.' (Before he gets the letter)

4 'Orlando's bloody handkerchief explains the broken appointment.' (Cut in)

5 'Realizing that he owes much to his brother, Oliver offers Orlando half of his estate.' (Before scene of brothers talking)

6 'Rosalind teaches Orlando how to make love to his lady when he meets her.' (Before scene where she teaches him)

7 'Rosalind obtains her father's permission to give his daughter to Orlando if she comes to the forest.' (Before scene with father)

8 'Phoebe's promise. "If I ever change my mind about you, I will marry Silvius!" ' (Cut in)

9 'Prepared to make the Duke keep his promise.' (Before they come down stairs dressed as girls)

10 'Duke Frederick recalls his brother from banishment.' (Before last scene)

11 'Epilogue.' (Before it begins)

12 ' "It is not the fashion to see the lady the epilogue; but it is no more unhandsome than to see the lord the prologue." ' (Cut in first of prologue)

13 ' "If I were a woman, I would kiss as many of you as had beards that pleased me, and I am sure, as many as have good beards, will for my kind offer, when I make courtesy, bid me farewell." ' (Cut in toward last of epilogue)

The author of the photoplay shows considerable ingenuity in adapting *As You Like It* into silent photographic action. The first four sequences depict scenes which are only narrative exposition in Shakespeare, and the reading of the will is an invention. The fifth and sixth are from I, 1, and 2. I, 1 suggests the seventh but the persuasion is handled by a visual bribe. Sequence eight is Shakespeare's II, 1; nine is a new scene suggested in I, 1. The wrestling in ten and eleven and its consequences in twelve and fourteen are again from I, 2, but the intervening thirteen is an innovation. The fifteenth, sixteenth, and seventeenth sequences are respectively from I, 3; II, 3; and I, 3; and the eighteenth, where Touchstone consents to accompany Rosalind and Celia is suggested in I, 3 but turned into a new scene. Part 1 ends with further presentation of I, 3.

The first two sequences of Part 2 are based on II, 2, and 7. The Duke's request for 'All the world's a stage', provides somewhat surprisingly for sequences actually picturing each of the seven ages, and with omissions here and there uses Shakespeare's lines. Sequence ten is action suggested by II, 2, and eleven is from III, 1. Twelve and fourteen are prompted by II, 4; but the Phoebe-Silvius material which is interposed is III, 5. III, 2 in narrative provides the action for sequences fifteen and sixteen, and Shakespeare's action in the same scene is the basis of seventeen and eighteen. Nineteen is suggested by IV, 2, and the final sequence of Part 2 turns Oliver's narrative in IV, 3 into a shot of Orlando rescuing his brother from the lion's attack.

The first sequence of Part 3 is Shakespeare's III, 5; the next two sequences, IV, 3. V, 2 suggest the action of sequence four. Rosalind's instruction in love-making (IV, 2) becomes sequence five. All the rest of the photoplay is from V, 4, with the recall from banishment, told by Shakespeare, presented on the screen in an episode with Duke Frederick. The beginning and end of the playwright's Epilogue provides the titles and picturization of the end of the film.

The freedom exercised by the scenarist in changing order, in turning exposition into action, and in inventing connecting scenes might well lead to the assumption that structurally at least the play has been turned into a successful film story. But, as a viewing of the film makes clear, the assumption is wrong. The Forest of Arden is pictorially attractive in the Flatbush woods, and vague porticos on some estate or other provide appropriate enough backgrounds for the other scenes and lend variety to the outdoor settings, but one is chiefly conscious of a not very interesting story, somewhat difficult to follow and rather hard to accept anyhow, accompanied by far too much title-explanation, far too much unheard dialogue and monologue, and gestures and postures which do not make clear what the characters are saying. Jaques' *Seven Ages* turned into pictures provides amusing individual shots – a cute schoolboy, a soldier with a cannon, a justice dozing in a chair – but it interrupts the narrative and slows its pace, and the Epilogue which might have been turned into pairings and pageantry merely allows Rose Coghlan to take a stage bow. Since Touchstone is inaudible, he becomes only a jester accompanying the girls except for one brief and entertaining scene with William and Audrey in Reel III, not suggested by the captions. I had had great hopes for the rescue scene, but the direction gave Costello too much leisure to divest himself of hat and tunic, thereby killing any possible suspense, and Vitagraph had no lion except a face in the bushes. In short, Shakespeare's *As You Like It* does not depend on story for its appeal, and this transcription necessarily has to emphasize story and therefore cannot, certainly does not succeed.

Louis Reeves Harrison in his review of the picture in the *Moving Picture World* of August 10th devotes more time to Shakespeare and extraneous matters than he does to the film, and while he praises the 'many and varied views' of the Forest of Arden with its 'softening and radiant effect . . . felt by those in front,' and 'the incalculable advantages moving pictures have in the background over legitimate productions', puts his finger on the non-structural weakness of this 'wordless' film:

'Losing so much in the dearest of all court fools, we lose still more in constructing a perfect egg shell for the character of Rosalind that it may represent the real article. Without the youth demanded of the role, Rosalind is not Rosalind to those who sit in front and no effort of the imagination, nor kindly feeling toward an actress who was at the zenith of her powers a score of years ago can make it so. No amount of fine acting, fine staging, fine directing, fine photography, and all else that is really fine in the production can compensate for a loss of personality in the heroine . . . the girlish spirit of frolic. . . .'

'The part of Jacques is admirably portrayed, and many of the minor roles flash forth with star-like brilliancy at moments,' said Harrison. I agree, though less flamboyantly, but the camera was cruel to Rose Coghlan's face and figure, and to her outmoded histrionics, unmodified by any training or experience in cinema acting. When she played Rosalind with Lester Wallack's company in 1880, William Winter said 'her voice, which she knew how to use, was strong and melodious', and in 'garb of slate-colored cloth and leather, with a red cap, she was a bewitching figure'; she was 'agreeably piquant, but neither poetical in spirit nor flexible in style'. J. Ranken Towse thought her 'deficient in poetic imagination and tenderness of female spirit,' but praised this Rosalind's brilliancy and charm'. But alas, in 1912, Rose Coghlan's voice was not heard, the red cap was not seen, the piquancy was gone, and she was sixty-one years old; no amount of make-up or corseting could hide the lines in her face or the dumpiness of her figure. On the screen she was an old woman, absurdly arch in her efforts to be a young girl, so awkward in her sprightly movement that at one point she fell against Costello, who visibly staggered at the impact. All the rest of the cast were better than Rose Coghlan, who starred; though most of them had had stage training, they were comfortable and sufficiently expert because of their experience before the camera. Costello hardly had the physique to wrestle Charles, but he made a handsome Orlando. Rosemary Theby's Celia and Tefft Johnson's banished duke were charming and effective, and Charles Kent's Jaques was indeed outstanding, even if parts of his role were unnecessary. His direction did what it could with the unwieldiness of cast and story. It probably was not his fault that parts of the picture were shot during a disturbing wind.

The English journals were kinder to the film than I have been, or Harrison. It was announced before its release on February 8th in 3115 feet – were there still more titles? – in the *Cinema News and Property Gazette* of January 1, 1913.

'One of the keynotes of the success of the Vitagraph Company is the lavish scale upon which they handle everything they touch, and in the film now under notice this note is again most pronounced. The quality of the photography is magnificent, and when we mention that one of America's most celebrated actresses, Miss Rose Coghlan [English born, she had made her reputation in the United States, and became an American citizen in 1902], together with Maurice Costello, the people's idol, figure in the cast, which is a remarkably strong one, we have said sufficient to set exhibitors and picture theatre patrons alike agog with a desire to see the picture on the screen.'

The *Kinematograph and Lantern Weekly* on January 16th makes it apparent that someone has seen more than a summary. The reviewer calls it:

'. . . pictorially one of the films of the season, the many fine opportunities for open air settings . . . having been developed in a manner which could hardly have been bettered. The scenes which show large companies of gaily dressed characters in the clearings and glades of the forest form a series of the most delightful stage pictures we remember.

'Miss Rose Coghlan . . . plays in a vein of broad comedy, which, if not quite in harmony with the usual rendering of the plot as seen on the English stage, gives full value to the many amusing scenes in which Rosalind has a part – the fooling with Silvius in particular is made most diverting. . . . Mr Maurice Costello has, in Orlando, a part differing widely from those in which he is usually associated, but does full justice to the character of Rosalind's love-sick swain. All the scenes which are most popular on the stage are suitably emphasized in the film. . . . An interesting point of novelty is the illustration of Jacques' long speech . . . [all the characters described], being suitably pictured.

'*As You Like It* makes an obvious appeal to the better-class public and, suitably advertised, the film will undoubtedly fill the theatre which features it. . . .'

The last paragraph of course is a warning, and the picture was as unsuccessful in Great Britain as it had been in the United States. The 'better class public' would have been disappointed, and the rest of the audience thought it a ridiculous bore. I rejoice only in the fact that I shortly spot what must have been the first Shakespeare film festival. 'British Notes' in the *Moving Picture World*, April 19, 1913, is the source: 'A Shakespearean revival by kinema is being projected in the north of England by a Shakespearean Society. The films are to include *As You Like It*, by the Vitagraph Company, as the premier item. In fact from the list of films I have received eighty per cent of those to be shown are Vitagraphs.' The Vitagraph Shakespeares had made a reputation, but *As You Like It* did not add to it. Despite its backgrounds and photography, and the general competence of its regular players, it could not carry Rose Coghlan to any but a preposterous conclusion.

Thanhouser was the only other American company which had acquired a certain prestige for its Shakespeare films. It made its contribution in 1912 with a two-reel version of *The Merchant of Venice*, announced for release on July 30th. The director was again probably Barry O'Neill working from an adaptation by Lloyd Lonergan and Mrs Thanhouser. The outdoor scenes were photographed near New Rochelle; the Italian garden may have been that belonging to a friend of Thanhouser's, E. M. Benedict. William J. Bowman played Shylock; Florence LaBadie, Portia; Harry Benham, Bassanio; William Russell, Antonio; and Mignon Anderson, Jessica. The review by Louis Reeves Harrison in the *Moving Picture World* is largely a discussion of Shakespeare's Shylock, anti-semitism, modern applications, and the moral, but fortunately there is something about the film:

'The types are well chosen, the men being especially good, but Portia lacks repose of manner and is entirely too gay at the moment when her lover's life is at stake. She displays little of the fullness of power which enabled Portia to extend protection to those less able to care for themselves in a trying emergency. She should have enforced a contrast with Jessica . . . her [Jessica's] weakness affords opportunity for Portia to show her strength instead of her pretty teeth and dimples on the eve of a horrible tragedy.

'The interior settings are as near perfect as they could be made – even Shylock's iron chest of ancient design is a real one – and the exteriors are a delightful surprise. It would be impossible to reproduce Venice in any part of this country, but the palace is superb and so appropriate that I noticed a pretty Italian garden peering over the walls in one scene. The deep scenes at the masque are a delightful relief. The characters are well posed in several of the interiors where studio limitations make it difficult to handle any number of people in action.

'The general conception of the play is correct, and it affords me pleasure to say so. It opens as a comedy and ends as one with Shylock's dark mental working injected in the middle. . . . Whether to credit Mr Thanhouser or his director or both I am in doubt, but I must compliment the ruling spirit for the delightful and scholarly interpretation.'

The same issue prints the company's summary, which I distrust for the usual reasons, but it does indicate that the first reel ended with Bassanio's successful choice of the right casket, and that Part 2 begins with Portia and

Bassanio happily married and the receipt of Antonio's message of his predicament.

Notice of *The Merchant of Venice* first appeared in England in an advertisement of the Western Import Company in the *Kinematograph and Lantern Weekly* of December 19th; release was announced for February 8, 1913. A week later, that journal reported that the film 'gives all the leading incidents of the play . . . and the acting of the company, its staging and costuming will meet with general approbation. . . . Among the most striking scenes we may include that which shows the choice of Portia's suitors between the three caskets and that which illustrates Portia's successful defense of Antonio and the turning of the tables on Shylock. Throughout the quality of the film is magnificent and the whole subject with its brilliant scenes of Venetian life forms a veritable feast for the eye.' Since the Venetian life was in New Rochelle and a recollection of the play would denominate the two big scenes, the reader may suspect, as I do, that this information has not been supported by much more than the importer's publicity. *Cinema News and Property Gazette* on January 1, 1913, at least implies a viewing: 'The version which the Thanhouser company has given us is the finest it has ever fallen to our lot to witness, and we doubt whether this company, masters as they are in the art of film production, can ever go one better than their present attempt.' The accompanying summary does not include the Lorenzo–Jessica plot, odd since we know Jessica was one of the characters. *Bioscope* of January 9th is of the English journals the most informative. It praises the adaptation in preserving salient features and omitting non-essential characters such as Gratiano and Launcelot Gobbo, indicates the picture included a scene in which Portia consults the learned Bellario and subtitles which were condensed quotations from Shakespeare, and is favorably impressed by the settings, the gondolas, the picturesque Italian seamen, the richly dressed characters, 'acted with commendable earnestness'. Maybe Venice in New Rochelle was vivid after all. At any rate *Photoplay* in December 1912 was hopeful about improved conditions in the character of motion pictures. It quotes the Portland (Maine) *Telegram* in noting crime, violence, and exploits as disappearing subjects: 'The new rule is the presentation of excellent picture plays and of standard plays done pictorially. Shakespeare is being done in pictures in precincts where his words have rarely been spoken.'

What is one to do, I wonder, with Helen Gardner's mammoth, or perhaps colossal, *Cleopatra*? It was announced in the *Moving Picture World* on June 15, 1912, as 'a free and liberal adaptation of Shakespeare and Victorien Sardou' and copyrighted on December 17th as in six reels. The title on the film, which I have seen, says it was 'adapted from the play by Victorien Sardou' and does not mention Shakespeare at all. In truth, the adapter and director, Charles L. Gaskill, freely adapted Sardou, added a good deal of his own, and bowed to Shakespeare only for several incidents and the names of two characters. The issue is complex, since Sardou also borrowed from

Shakespeare, but is not really important. This picture is essentially Sardou, and does not need extended treatment.

Helen Gardner was a teacher of pantomime who, after appearing in small parts for the screen, had attracted attention as Becky Sharp in Vitagraph's *Vanity Fair* (1911). Financed by her mother, she founded the Helen Gardner Picture Players and built an outdoor studio at Tappan-on-the-Hudson, where *Cleopatra* was filmed. She later made a couple of other pictures and then vanished from sight, except for re-issuing a somewhat remodelled *Cleopatra* in 1917, an obvious attempt to draw customers from the Theda Bara *Cleopatra* of that year. The cast of the Gardner film were relatively unknown and since their first names were not given, are largely unidentifiable; the settings, though there are a few natural backgrounds, were largely built on a somewhat confined area; the effects are stagy and obvious; and Helen Gardner, to modern eyes, a well upholstered pantomimist but without the variety of a good actress, certainly without the 'infinite variety' of Cleopatra. Yet the picture had in 1913 enormous success in the United States and abroad. Lewis Reeves Harrison thought Helen Gardner's performance would 'rank as one of the greatest ever shown on the screen up to the present time'. Warren Hastings Abbott in the *New York Dramatic Mirror* called the film 'probably the most stupendous and beautiful picture ever produced'. To David Warfield it was 'the greatest moving picture ever made', and to the artist, Harrison Fisher, 'a most wonderful production'. When *Cleopatra* opened in Denver, the manager of the theatre reported 'nine thousand four hundred admissions despite blinding snow storm', and in Dallas, business was greater on the third day than on the first and 'thousands turned away'. In England, where it ran three weeks at the Theatre de Luxe on the Strand, reviews were enthusiastic. Territorial rights were sold for Russia, Germany, Austria, Switzerland, Rumania, Italy, Belgium, Australia. What a triumph for Sardoodledum and a play which Odell, thinking of Bernhardt and Fanny Davenport, remarked 'no critical asp had been able to kill'. Fortunately, time has.

But what of Shakespeare? There is a Diomedes in the film but he is not Shakespeare's; on the contrary, an aspirant for Cleopatra's hand and a rival of Pharon, a fisherman-slave, who is entertained by Cleopatra for ten days on condition he then destroy himself but who has a somewhat miraculous life throughout. There is a barge, pushed in from the wings, upon which Cleopatra arrives to meet Antony in Cydnus. Antony's chief lieutenant is a Ventidius, who is not in Sardou though he assumes functions distributed among several characters in the French play; in the film, Ventidius announces Fulvia's death and the impending war with Pompey and pleads with Antony to leave Egypt; later, at Actium, he agrees to kill Antony, should the battle be lost, thereby taking over the function of Shakespeare's Eros, and like Eros stabs himself rather than Antony. Antony is shown being drawn up to Cleopatra's monument, an incident not in Sardou. As in Shakespeare, the Queen offers jewels to Octavius. The bringing of the asp is in both Shakespeare and Sardou. There are no Shakespearean subtitles. What emerged is not Shakespearean, but a complicated story of various loves and honours without real depth and with somewhat incomprehensible characters, indeed a sorry mish-mash.

The rest of American Shakespearean film production for 1912 is even less exciting. The *Moving Picture World* of April 20th reported 'a story is going the rounds of the daily press to the effect that Mr E. H. Sothern and Julia Marlowe, now appearing in repertoire, contemplate giving a performance of *The Taming of the Shrew* for pictures. It is said that Miss Marlowe has become a regular picture "fan", visiting the "movies" whenever the opportunity is offered.' It can also be said that, true or not, no such film was ever made. I hear too of Alla Nazimova in a film version of *Hamlet*, variously dated, but though I should like to be undeceived, I think this is a myth. Lubin pictures included a *Love's Labour's Lost*, *A Modern Portia*, and *A Midwinter Night's Dream*. The second deals with a woman lawyer who unwittingly defends her own father who has lost his memory and assumed another identity, but this is the extent of the borrowing – from Shakespeare. Solax made a *Comedy of Errors*, which was released in England by American and Continental in 1913, but this too is merely a title-borrowing. The contribution of Rex was equally insignificant, a *Taming Mrs Shrew* about 'a nagging wife', but except for her shrewishness, this has nothing to do with the case. The Knickerbocker film, distributed in England by R. Prieur and called *The Taming of the Shrewd*, had to do with a woman who neglects her housework to attend suffragette meetings. Her husband arouses her jealousy by taking another lady to one of the meetings. This seems to me neither shrewish nor shrewd.

Europe did this sort of thing too. For variety, I proceed alphabetically. There was an Urban–Eclipse–Radios *All's Well That Ends Well* about mixups in an inn room; a Cines film with the same title with money-lending and misunderstanding; and an Eclair ditto, which was a romance of the Middle Ages. Another Cines film, a *Comedy of Errors*, embroiled two army recruits with the same name. I am very curious about *The Jewish King Lear* which was filmed and shown in Commercial Road, London, but there is no information. It was reported that 'Sir Herbert Tree's production of *Macbeth* is about to be "filmed" for the cinematograph and that the fee to be paid is $20,000. . . . The fee seems enormous, but it must be remembered that all the scenery and fittings must be transported to a daylight theatre specially built for the business.' Was this an abortive brain-storm of Will Barker's? At any rate, Tree did not make a *Macbeth* film until 1916, and then in America. The report appears in a 'London Letter' in the *Moving Picture World* of April 13th. The famous *Queen Elizabeth* in which Sarah Bernhardt watched the Falstaff-basket scene and was afterward introduced by Essex (Lou Tellegen) to Shakespeare is, I suppose worth noting. It was based on a play by Émile Moreau (who had collaborated with Sardou on *Cléopatre*), directed by Louis Mercanton in London, and launched in the United States Adolph Zukor's fortune and Famous Players. A picture, called in England *The Vengeance of Iago*, was described as 'an original drama'; it bears little resemblance to Shakespeare but deals with rivalry for a girl's hand and the attempted vengeance of the unsuccessful lover. The name, the revenge theme, and the setting – it takes place in Cyprus – are, however, suspicious. I take this to be an Italian film, *Lo Spettro de Iago*, made by Aquila in 800 metres. Tommaso Salvini, by the way, was asked in this year, though he was eighty-three, 'to present his sublime portrayal of *Othello* before the camera', – so, at least Robert Grau in *The Stage in the Twentieth Century* (New York, 1912, p. 69) – but he declined, no doubt wisely.

Europe did, however, produce in 1912 one film which purported to be Shakespearean. This was a French version of *The Tempest*, made by Eclair, a company founded in 1907 with a studio at Epinay. It had made a great success with a *Nick Carter* series and at first specialized in the *genre policier*, but it broadened its interests into other types, and imitative of Film d'Art, launched Théâtro-Film under the patronage of Maurice de Féraudy of the Comédie Française. This in turn was replaced by A.C.A.D. (Association des Comédiens et Auteurs Dramatiques); the principal director of this *série d'art* was Émile Chautard of the Odéon. Adaptations followed of de Musset, Balzac, and Molière, and of *The Tempest*.

The Tempest shows considerable adaptation but, unlike Eclair's earlier *All's Well That Ends Well*, it is undeniably based on Shakespearean story. It opens in Milan, where Prospero is a student of the occult. Antonio wins Alonso to the idea of usurpation, and Gonzalo is sent to expel Prospero and Miranda. Set adrift in an open boat, they drift to an island, inhabited by Caliban, who looks on in dismay, and Ariel, whom Prospero releases from imprisonment in a tree. At command, Ariel transforms a cave into a sunny apartment and summons a vision showing Antonio's treachery. Sixteen years pass before Prospero, recognizing the royal galley of the King of Naples, blows up a storm and shipwreck. The royal party, safe ashore, finds Ferdinand missing. He meets Miranda, they fall in love, and Prospero consents to their betrothal. Ariel leads the royal party to the abode of Prospero, but the culprits do not recognize him until he puts on his ducal robes and accuses them. They plead for mercy, as Ferdinand and Miranda are disclosed, and are forgiven. Prospero leads them through an enchanted garden where spirits dance, a suggestion from the Shakespearean masque though transferred to a scene following the reconciliations. Subsequently the party all return to Naples where the court celebrates the marriage. The film consequently has pictured the beginning and end of the story, emphasized the magic, dropped the comic characters, and more or less ignored Caliban and his plot. Flashback has been used to give Prospero recognition of the treachery of his brother and the King of Naples, and evidently the ship-wreck was pictorially emphasized.

I do not know when *The Tempest* was released in France, but it was available in 1885 feet through the Tyler Film Company in England on December 22nd in time for Christmas spectators. The *Kinematograph and Lantern Weekly* on November 28th announced that it was 'a splendid representation of one of Shakespeare's most famous plays. The dresses and staging are perfect in every detail. The scenes in Prospero's island are just as one would imagine them to be.' This may have stemmed from a reviewer but more probably from Tyler, which in its advertisement in the same issue emphasized that the picture was 'presented in popular style, with magician feats, sumptuous staging, fine natural scenery, perfect acting. . . .' It was shown also in Germany and the United States, but I find no reviews. Our revels now are ended for 1912.

The seed of experimentation with multiple reels in 1912 flowered in 1913, particularly in England and Italy. France was content with two and the United States began with this limit. At the same time there are films, planned or realized, to star well known actors from the stage. Features were catching the public eye, and the evidence of Helen Gardner's *Cleopatra* and Bernhardt's *Queen Elizabeth* showed they might also open the public purse. In the United States, Famous Players on December 21, 1912, announced in the *Moving Picture World* plans for 1913 which were to include a *Julius Caesar* with William Faversham and his wife, Julie Opp, and a special version of Shakespeare's *Seven Ages* with Henry E. Dixey. The first was obviously spurred by the actor-manager's currently successful production at the Lyric Theatre in which he played Antony. Dixey's *The Seven Ages* was an amusing extravaganza which the popular comedian had first played in 1889; in it he enacted the various ages from infant (in a perambulator) to slippered pantaloon as described in Jaques' speech; it was hardly Shakespearean, though a bronzed actor appeared as Shakespeare in the prologue. Nothing came of either project, though the Faversham *Julius Caesar* was reconsidered in 1914, if we accept the *Kinematograph and Lantern Weekly* of January 29th. Helen Gardner, still emulating Bernhardt, decided to play *Hamlet* in a five thousand feet picture to be released by the Charles L. Fuller Distributing Co. – so at least the *Moving Picture World* of May 31st and June 7, 1913 – but by July there is no further public reference to any such ill considered scheme.

As heretofore, the far seeing Edwin Thanhouser made the first real breakthrough. Though he stuck to the two-reel footage which he had used for his 1912 *Merchant of Venice*, he chose to make a picture of *Cymbeline*, a Shakespearean play never before filmed, and, as far as I know, never since. Moreover, if statements in both American and English trade journals are accurate, he chose to produce his film in California, presumably in that suburb of Los Angeles called Hollywood. Though he retained his New

Rochelle studio, the choice of locale was perspicacious. Thanhouser was one of the group of Independents who were fighting the claims of the Motion Picture Patents Company, which was seeking by fair means or foul to monopolize the production and distribution of motion pictures. In 1913 the trust was sued for violation of the Sherman law by William Fox, one of the Independents. Some of the Independents had already moved to the West Coast to avoid legal action and soon discovered the advantages of freer atmosphere and more varied topography. Apparently Thanhouser was willing at least to try a change as an experiment.

The personnel for *Cymbeline* were, however, mainly from the East. Flo La Badie, who played Imogen, and William Russell we have met before, and William Garwood had already played at New Rochelle. Others were Jean Darnell, and a young man who was to be decidedly conspicuous as the director of *The Covered Wagon*, James Cruze, who took the part of Posthumus Leonatus. Barry O'Neil, who had been responsible for the earlier Thanhouser Shakespeares was directing for Lubin in 1913; in charge of *Cymbeline* was a newcomer from the British Isles, Frederic Sullivan. The picture was released on March 28th and noticed in both comment and review in the *Moving Picture World* of April 5th.

'The Shakesperian drama is here worked out in two reels, with good scenic effects. Flo La Badie and James Cruze play the parts of Imogene and Leonatus, but the whole Thanhouser Company joins forces to make the cast a balanced one. The costuming is sumptuous and the scenes pleasing throughout because of the clean-cut staging. The visit of the Roman officer to Imogene's bed chamber, where he takes the bracelet from her wrist as she sleeps, was artistically presented. The battle scenes in the second reel hold the interest well; also the manner in which the separated family of Cymbeline finally becomes united. A good offering.'

And again:

'This two-reel production of the Shakespearean play, *Cymbeline*, taken in California, shows a praiseworthy ambition on the part of the producer. *Cymbeline* is singularly well adapted to rendition in motion pictures, and the director has presented some of the dramatic moments in the play with a fair degree of success. Much pains was evidently taken in a laudable endeavor to be correct in historic details. The scene in Rome where the wager is made between Leonatus and Iachimo to test the fidelity of Imogen was rendered not without skill. Another scene deserving of some praise is the entrance of Iachimo into the bedchamber of Imogen. The situation is handled with great delicacy and follows the spirit of the Shakespearean play. The groupings in the scenes showing the court of Cymbeline seem to lack artistic arrangement. . . . Some of the outdoor settings are beautiful, but in one of them the intrusion of a decidedly modern house tends to destroy the illusion.

On the whole I think that this picture ought to be acceptable to the average motion picture audience, and the producer deserves very great credit for seeking to aim high. Such pictures, though there may be blemishes in the execution, strengthen our hope in the future of kinematography.'

A praiseworthy effort, shall we say? At any rate, it was one of the films featured in London and the provinces during the week ending June 21st.

Almost miraculously in view of the Thanhouser fire a print of *Cymbeline* has just recently been discovered. Screened, it is not only a praiseworthy effort but an attractive and in part a rather pretty picture. Shakespeare's complex and intricate story is, quite properly, much simplified. The exposition is turned into explanatory captions and visual sequences. Unless a sequence has been misplaced, the film starts with Belarius, Guiderius, and Arviragus before their cave, identified as 'the King's sons', as they eat, drink, and prepare for hunting (III, 3). Their names are never given; indeed no characters are given names except Imogen, Leonatus (his given name is not used), Iachimo (only in a written wager agreement), Pisanio (called Pisano in the signature of his letter to Leonatus), and Cymbeline, who curiously is not identified as the King until well into the second reel, and not as a King of Britain until even later. The significance of the general title of the film therefore must have been a mystery to most of the spectators throughout Reel 1, and the opening puzzling since the characters of the first sequence are not shown again in Reel 1, which is otherwise wholly devoted to the story of Imogen and Leonatus. We see scenes at court with Cymbeline, his Queen (jealous of Imogen's favour), Cloten (not established as the Queen's son), and Imogen herself. Leonatus makes love to Imogen in a pleasant garden; Cloten becomes a suitor approved by Cymbeline; 'Imogen refuses to marry one she does not love', to Cymbeline's displeasure; and is shown being secretly married in an outdoor setting to Leonatus, after which they hold hands (the bracelet is visible) in the garden, where the Queen sees them. She brings Cymbeline, who banishes Leonatus, who after leave-taking departs. Imogen, alone in the antechamber of her bedroom kisses the bracelet which Leonatus has given her. These pictures take the place of material presented largely as exposition in I, 1, and Shakespeare's next two scenes are omitted. Leonatus and others are entertained before an outdoor Roman bath by a dancer and entertain themselves by drinking wine. They are not drunk but the implication is that Leonatus is provoked in an unguarded moment into the wager by Iachimo. Leonatus' boast of his wife's devotion is specified in a subtitle, but the wager has to be made clear by the action of a scribe, who records the agreement on a scroll, which is then shown to the audience. The ring is made significant when Iachimo points to it. All this is Shakespeare's I, iv; I, v is dropped, eliminating here and hereafter all the business of the drug and the Queen's intrigues with it. Adapted from I, vi is Iachimo's presentation of himself at Cymbeline's court with a letter of introduction from Leonatus, his introduction to Imogen, and in the garden his attempted and quite unsuccessful seduction. Imogen and her lady attendant pass through the antechamber to her bedroom, where the waiting woman begins to prepare Imogen for bed. Iachimo steals into the ante-chamber, peeks into the bedchamber, disappears as the attendant comes and leaves. He emerges from a trunk which he has not been shown entering, and which is a part of the furniture of the room, not as in Shakespeare his own device for concealment. He goes to the sleeping Imogen, puts her hair away from her neck and shoulders (if there is a mole it is decorously above a tight bodice), take the bracelet from her wrist, and departs exultant. This is Shakespeare's II, 2; II, 3 has been omitted; and both Cloten and the Queen have disappeared from the action, never to return, alive or dead. In the same Roman setting as before, Iachimo reports his success to Leonatus, who receives the bracelet, gives his ring, and indicates his perturbation (II, 4). Leonatus' soliloquy of II, 5 is of course dropped. Imogen and her women search her bedroom in vain for the lost bracelet (II, 3). Pisanio, vaguely present before but without function, now gives Imogen in the antechamber Leonatus' letter, asking her to join him at Milford Haven, and that night they both leave on horseback, she already disguised as a page (III, 2, with the disguise earlier than in Shakespeare). We see nothing of Lucius and his embassy to claim tribute (III, 1), and the departure is the end of Reel 1.

The second reel begins at Milford Haven where on the coast, Pisanio, sword in hand, shows Imogen the letter from Leonatus ordering Pisanio to kill her. Several shots and a title demonstrate her grief and his refusal to obey. This is III, 4, but there is nothing about joining Lucius. Instead we see Belarius and the two sons leaving to hunt, a continuation of the opening sequence of Reel 1. After their departure, the famished Imogen as a page comes before the cave, investigates, eats food she has discovered, and falls asleep. The hunters return, do not recognize but welcome her (III, 6). Scenes 6 and 7 are omitted, as is most of Act IV. Cloten, no longer in the script, is not beheaded, Imogen is not found apparently dead, neither is prepared for burial, there is no mistaken identity, nor soothsayer. What we see next is Leonatus' receipt of Pisanio's letter about the death of Imogen, and his repentant reaction, but there is no bloody handkerchief (V, 1). There is a shift to Cymbeline receiving the news of Roman invasion, our first knowledge that the two countries are at odds. The Britons wave defiant swords. Now the Romans enter Britain and are shown marching through open country. There is a general corresponding to Lucius, but there are very few soldiers. Imogen leaves her succorers, is captured by the Romans, and becomes Lucius' page. Act V is much compressed, but Leonatus is seen as a peasant fighting for the Britons (1, 2), Cymbeline's sons join his army 2, 3), Iachimo is also there. Armies march and fight; Imogen is shown with Lucius before his tent watching the battle; the Romans are winning until Belarius and the sons save the day; Lucius is surprised and taken (V, 3).

Leonatus is not arrested and put in prison, and there are no apparitions, dumb show, or masque (V, 4). Cymbeline thanks his sons and Leonatus for their valour; and Belarius reveals that the sons are the King's, somewhat ridiculously in a subtitle, 'Sir, I stole your sons as babes – I give them back to you', after which Cymbeline embraces them and Belarius for having stolen the boys. Iachimo is discovered wounded, pronounces his guilt, and gives the ring to Leonatus, who tries to stab himself with his sword, but Imogen now reveals herself, and there is general reconciliation and rejoicing. The reel ends with Imogen and Leonatus kissing in a close-up. All this is a simplified adaptation of V, 5, with considerable omission. On the whole the continuity has been sensible; the action, supported by thirty subtitles, usually but not always clear; the ending somewhat huddled.

In addition to an interesting story, it is the outdoor scenery which lends the film a kind of charm. Indoor scenes, Cymbeline's court and Imogen's apartments, are made deliberately and somewhat too obviously primitive to accord with the era in which the action is supposed to take place, and the costuming consists for the Britons mostly of rude furs, though the women wear simple gowns, but most of the pictures are outdoors where garden, sea coast, open country, mountains and rocks are attractively photographed, sometimes at long range. Most of the shots, however, are medium to close with a few close-ups to emphasize Imogen's bracelet or give the final clinch. There is some cross-cutting, especially in Reel 2 where we shift from one army or person to another and back. There are twenty-one scenes in Reel 1, thirty-five in Reel 2, but some of these scenes are really part of the same sequence, interrupted by such cutting or by titles. A few titles lend a touch of Shakespearean poetry, for example, 'But that it eats our victuals, I should think / Here were a fairy', 'Stand by my side, you whom the gods have made / Preservers of my throne', and 'Hang there like fruit my soul / Till the tree die!' The acting is better than might be expected, no worse than in similar films of 1913. Florence LaBadie makes a pretty Imogen and manages to convey emotions simply if conventionally. James Cruze is an effective Leonatus. The film lists no credits except to the Thanhouser Film Corporation, but Jean Darnell must have impersonated the Queen, the only other principal female role in the story, and I think William Garwood played Iachimo. At least the clean-shaven Iachimo looks like Garwood as he appears in other photographs. Since most of the other main characters are disguised by abundant whiskers, I cannot even guess William Russell's contribution.

A much longer American film, this time of *Richard III*, apparently was exhibited before *Cymbeline*. Plans for it, still untitled, loom first in 'Weekly Notes' by 'Stroller' in the London *Kinematograph and Lantern Weekly* of September 26, 1912: 'I understand that Frederick Warde, the renowned American tragedian and portrayer of Shakespearean roles, will shortly appear in a five-reel classic production, the name of which is at present withheld. These pictures will be disposed of by Mr M. B. Dudley, a newspaper and theatrical man of long experience. Several other notable actors are on Mr Dudley's list to appear in pictures. The scenarios for these pictures will be arranged by Mr James Keane [Keene, late of Selig] . . . who will also stage the productions.' *Richard III* was probably not staged by Keene, however, but by Dudley, who also produced it. The film was, I gather, being shown in January 1913, though it had not yet been copyrighted, and advertisements do not appear in the *Moving Picture World* until April 12th when the Shakespeare Film Co., New York, announced it as in 4400 feet starring 'America's Greatest Tragedian', Frederick Warde and including in 'M. B. Dudley's $30,000 Production', a thousand people and two hundred horses. The May 3rd issue carries another advertisement which prints a cabled puff from a British exhibitor. On September 27th, after copyright on the 9th, the firm name is changed to the Broadway Film Company, which offered *Richard III*, 'in which Frederick Warde, the old time tragedian, appeared, to state rights buyers. The subject is in four reels – 4000 feet – and is said to be fairly descriptive of the stirring events in the life of one of England's earliest kings, as told in history and by Shakespeare'. The copyright however names the producing company as the Sterling Camera and Film Co., which had the same address as the Broadway Film Co. I mention these details because some writers have postulated several *Richard III* films in 1913, when actually there was only one production.

A programme in the New York Public Library has an insert of the Olympic Theatre at Broadway and 107th Street carrying the date of March 22, 1914, and adds other not necessarily reliable details: 'A Genuine Novelty and Triumphant Success / The Eminent Tragedian / Mr Frederick Warde / in Shakespeare's Historical Play / Richard III / Five Reels – 5000 Feet / A Feature Costing $30,000 to Produce . . . / 1500 People, 200 Horses / 5 Distinct Battle Scenes. A Three-Masted Warship, Crowded with Soldiers, on Real Water. Architecture, Costumes, Armor, All Historically Correct in Every Detail'. This elaboration also quotes from three newspapers. According to the New York *Times*,

'The presentation of *King Richard III*, which Frederick Warde is giving at the Academy of Music this week, is a revelation in many ways. As a picture of conditions as they existed in England . . . it is far and away ahead of any possible stage presentation. The camera mellows acting, as it were, adding to its gracefulness. Not only that but the scenic effects are incomparably better through the moving pictures than they ever are in real life.'

The New York *Globe* makes an interesting comparison:

'Although it is announced that Edison is ready to make motion pictures talk . . . Frederick Warde's wonderful photographic masterpiece of himself in *Richard III*, as now being produced at the Fulton Theatre, illustrates that Mr Warde has anticipated the great Wizard of electricity.'

If Warde's 'presentation' and the references to sound film are less than clear, they will shortly be elucidated. Meanwhile the Boston *Herald* remarks that

'There will hardly ever be a stage presentation – indeed, it would be impossible to stage one within any opera house – comparable with Richard III, as it is shown in picture form, while the scope is so vastly broader that the entire scheme is given to the audience beyond the possibility of stage acting. This particular attraction is a far greater conception of Shakespeare's play than anything heretofore produced in Boston, and is worthy of an unlimited attention.'

Exactly what was going on here becomes manifest if we know something about Frederick Warde. If his name means little to the present generation, he was at one time known as a distinguished interpreter and scholarly gentleman. Born in Oxfordshire in 1851, he had appeared on tour and in stock with Adelaide Neilson and Henry Irving before coming to the United States in 1874 where he acted with John McCullough, Charlotte Cushman, Edwin Booth and other stars. In 1881 he formed his own company in which for many years he played leading roles, especially Shakespearean ones, including Richard. He retired from the stage in 1919 and for his services to literature was awarded an honorary D.Litt by the University of Southern California. He died in 1935, having published two books, *The Fools of Shakespeare* (1913) and his autobiography (1920).

If the award of a doctorate does not seem from this brief sketch an inevitable outcome of his career, it becomes more understandable when we learn that from 1907 he was, in addition to being an actor, a public lecturer on dramatic subjects. His lecture on 'The Wit and Wisdom of Shakespeare's Fools' was immensely popular. His talks were accompanied by histrionic recitation and interpretation. When the reviews talk about his 'presentation', this is what is meant. Whether *Richard III* was originally intended to be accompanied by his own physical presence on the platform and appropriate recital is not made clear in his autobiography, which does, however, contain details about the making of the film:

'A company had been incorporated to present Shakespeare's tragedy of *Richard the Third* in pictures and I was selected to play the Duke of Gloucester.

'*Richard the Third* had been one of the popular plays in my repertoire for many years. I had played Gloucester frequently and the idea of recording it by motion photography interested me greatly.

'An unoccupied estate on City Island, New York, was the location of our labors. There the Tower of London, Guildhall, and other historic buildings were reproduced, and the charming landscape of Westchester County served as the green fields of midland England.

'I found the action of the camera necessitated entirely different methods of acting from the stage. Spontaneity must be replaced by deliberation and concentration take the place of words. I had much to learn and considerable to unlearn but the director and photographers were very considerate, lt hough my ignorance of the camera must have tried their patience almost to the limit.

'Many vexatious yet humorous incidents occurred. A picture of Gloucester's ride from Tewkesbury to London was required. Most of the roads in Westchester county are flanked by telegraph and telephone poles. That would not do for England in the fifteenth century, but our director discovered a lane that had not been disfigured by modern utilities, and would serve the purpose. A negative was taken, but a refractory horse made several retakes necessary; however, we finally secured a very good picture only to find on examination, a modern nursemaid wheeling a baby carriage, with two small children, had come into the background unseen by the director but largely in evidence on the screen.

'In spite of many discouraging conditions, the picture was completed and my first appearance in moving pictures was voted a success.'

There is nothing here about personal presentation along with screening, but if it were not so planned, it is quite clear from a programme for an illustrated lecture in the copyright file that the film was so used. The presentation was called an 'Illustrated dramalogue / of Shakespeare's historical play / *Richard III* / Illuminated by five reels of moving pictures of the play in which Mr Warde posed himself, comprising 77 scenes and incidents.' The entertainment, headed 'The Spoken Word and the Picture', began with an overture which was followed by 'Introductory Remarks by Mr Frederick Warde'. Next were presented 'Pictures Introducing Prominent Characters':

1 Mr Frederick Warde in person.
2 Mr Warde as Richard, Duke of Gloucester.
3 Mr Warde as King Richard III.
4 Mr Warde as Richard the Warrior.
5 Mr Gomp as King Edward IV.
6 Prince Edward of Lancaster.
7 The Earl of Richmond.
8 Sir Richard Catesby.
9 The young Princes.
10 Queen Elizabeth, their mother.
11 Lady Anne Plantagenet, wife of Prince Edward.
12 The Princess Elizabeth.

These shots were apparently introductory sequences of the film itself, when it was shown separately, or clips from parts of the film which served the lecturer by way of introduction to the narrative. After them came a 'Des-

criptive Recital by Mr Warde', perhaps commenting on the various characters or appropriate lines from the play. After each of the first four reels of the
narrative, there was a 'recital by Mr Warde'. Included in the copyright file
are what purport to be four newspaper comments. That labelled Charleston
News and Courier, January 12, 1913, has a first paragraph identical with
what has already been quoted as from the New York *Times*, but the second
is illuminating about the performance:

'Mr. Warde offers five reels of moving pictures, depicting the great play,
King Richard III. While the eyes rest in the intermissions between the
showing of the reels, Mr. Warde entertains the audience with a dramatic
recital of famous passages in the play, elucidating them at the same time.
During the showing of the pictures he explains the situations. The result is
amazingly good. In educational value, from the historical viewpoint, it is
better than the presentation of the play itself. Indeed the offering is the best
combination moving picture entertainment that has yet been brought to this
city. It is truly wonderful.'

The rest is merely further praise, but the nature of the performance, a
combination of film, lecture, and recital, is firmly established. The other
three newspaper pieces are from '*The Metropolis*, Jacksonville, Florida,
January 7, 1912', which presents word for word the same matter as that
quoted from the New York *Globe* – the date is manifestly wrong, – the
Savannah *Morning News*, January 4, 1913 (by Marion Lucas), and the
Augusta *Chronicle*, January 22, 1913 (an editorial), but they add nothing to
our comprehension except that Warde's entertainment was enthusiastically
praised by the press. I should be suspicious about the dates, did not the
programme show that Warde was presented at the Prince Theatre, city not
known to me, for the 'week commencing Monday, May 5th'. May 5th fell
on a Monday in 1913. Evidently he must have taken the film on tour very
shortly after its completion, before it was advertised in New York and before
it was copyrighted. The copyright was apparently entered to protect the
company when the picture was offered for sale in September. And I begin
to wonder whether the recital-picture combination had not been contem-
plated when the film was made, though Warde does not say so.

The scenario of *Richard III*, as far as it can be gathered from the list of
episodes in the programme of May 5th, shows much adaptation, transposition, and invention with apparently the elimination of many of Shakespeare's characters.

Reel I

1 King Edward's tent, after Tewksbury. Death of Prince Edward of Lancaster.
2 Richard of Gloucester on his way to London.
3 Richard at the Tower of London.
4 Richard demands admission to King Henry's prison.
5 The passages of the Tower.

6 King Henry's prison. Death of the King.
7 Edward of York enters London in Triumph.
8 The end of the house of Lancaster.
9 Richard leaves the Tower.
10 Lady Anne Plantagenet receives the body of King Henry for burial.
11 The road to Chertsey. Lady Anne is wooed and won by Richard.

Of the eleven sequences, the first nine, following the tradition of the Colley Cibber adaptation, are from *Henry VI*, Part 3, or are invented. The first is from V, 5; at the end of it Clarence announces that Richard has left for London. The film picks up this information and provides the next four sequences, which are not in Shakespeare's play. Episodes 6 and 7 are from V, 6 and 7; 8 and 9 are invented. The second scene of Act I of *Richard III* provides the material for the last two scenes of the reel. Thus in the first reel four scenes of Shakespeare provide four sequences of the film, with a fifth sequence suggested by narrative.

Reel II

1 Court of Edward IV. Quarrel with the Duke of Clarence.
2 Exterior. Scroll of alleged prophesy thrown in at window.
3 Edward orders arrest of Clarence.
4 Clarence and friends leaving Palace.
5 Arrest of Clarence.
6 Richard visits Clarence in the Tower.
7 Richard and Catesby leaving Tower, plotting death of Clarence.
8 Richard urges Edward to sign warrant for death of Clarence.
9 Warrant delivered to murderers.
10 Murderers demand admission to Clarence.
11 Dream and death of Clarence.
12 Catesby pays the murderers.
13 Death of King Edward on learning of his brother's death.

Almost all of this is invention or derived from report, suggestion, or implication in Shakespeare. Episodes 9–11, though order is changed, are from the end of I, 3, and I, 4 of the play. In Shakespeare's I, 1, Clarence has already been arrested, and Edward's death is reported in II, 2.

Reel III

1 The young Princes, at their country home.
2 Departure of the Princes for London.
3 Arrival of the Princes in London, welcomed by Richard.
4 Court of the young King. Richard as Lord Protector.
5 Guildhall. The Duke of Buckingham urges the Mayor and citizens of London to demand Richard to become King.
6 Mayor and citizens assemble in court-yard of Palace.

20. Mounet–Sully in the graveyard scene from the Film d'Art *Hamlet*. The date is doubtful.
Cinémathèque Française

21. Hamlet (Alwin Neuss) drags forth the dead Polonius; Ella la Cour played Gertrude (Nordisk,
1910). *Moving Picture World*, April 22, 1911

22. Theo Frenkel, Sr. (Bo
meester) as Julius Caesar
Kineto film of about 1
Nederlands Filmmuseum

23. Scenes from the C
Brutus (1910), dire
by Enrico Guazz
Barnes Museum
Cinematography

Opposite: 24. Lear's rec
nition of Cordelia, a
strip from the Film d'A
Italiana *King Lear* (19
with Ermete Novelli
Francesca Bertini. N
ional Film Archive (
column)

25. Film strips from
Film d'Arte Italiana *M*
chant of Venice (19
1911), Ermete Novelli
Shylock. National F
Archive (2nd and
columns)

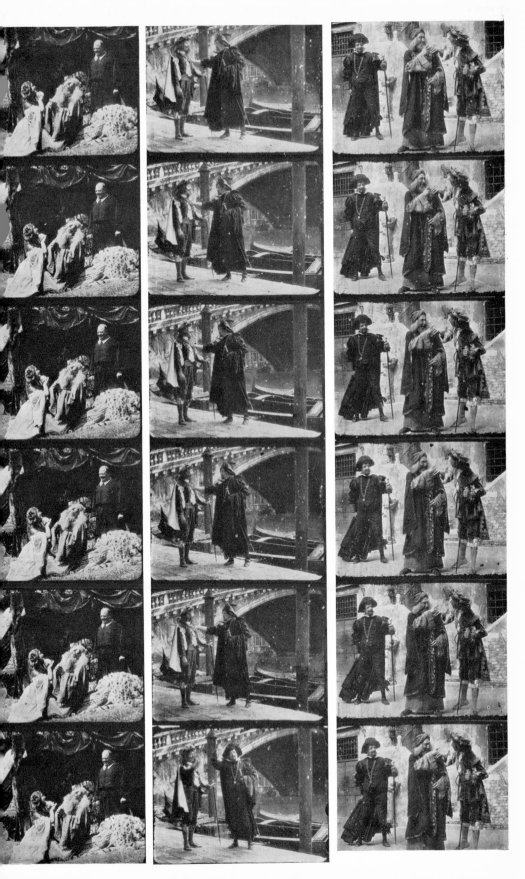

26. Paris, Capulet, and Juliet (Francesca Bertini) in the Film d'Arte Italiana *Romeo and Juliet* (1911). *Motion Picture Story Magazine*, September 1912

27. Degeorge as Falstaff in the Eclipse version of Shakespeare's *Merry Wives of Windsor* called *Falstaff* (1911). *Motion Picture Story Magazine*, July 1911

7 The Oratory. Richard's hypocrisy.
8 Buckingham conveys Richard's refusal to the citizens.
9 Buckingham induces Richard to meet citizens.
10 Richard, with apparent reluctance, accepts crown at the appeal of the Mayor and citizens.
11 Dismissal of priests.
12 The Princes are ordered, by Richard, to the Tower.
13 Richard directs the abduction of the Princes.

Shakespeare shows nothing corresponding to the first two sequences, and the Princes do not arrive together, but they are both welcomed by Richard in III, 1, where they are also sent to the Tower (Episode 12) by the Lord Protector (Episode 4). Buckingham's and Catesby's narratives and other suggestions in III, 7, are turned into visual action for sequences 5–10. Episode 11 is invented and there is no abduction in Shakespeare.

Reel IV

1 Richard crowned King of England.
2 The Princes in the Tower.
3 Richard urges Buckingham to murder the Princes.
4 Murderers seen at exterior of Palace.
5 Richard instructs Tyrrell to employ murderers. Quarrel and defiance of Buckingham.
6 Tyrrell gives instructions to murderers.
7 The Princes in the Tower.
8 The murder of the Princes.
9 Burial of the Princes, at base of White Tower.
10 The murderers are rewarded.
11 Death of Princes reported to Richard.
12 Queen Elizabeth summons the Earl of Richmond from France to protect her daughter from Richard.
13 The expedition of Richmond discovered by Catesby.
14 Arrival of Richmond and his forces on the shores of England.
15 Departure of Catesby with the news.
16 Richard urges his wife, Lady Anne, to commit suicide.
17 Death of Lady Anne.
18 Richard learns of Richmond's invasion and prepares for war.

The first sequence shows what Shakespeare has had reported in IV, 1. Episodes 2 and 4 are invented; 3 and 5 are from action in IV, 2. Episode 6 is an invention, and the next three sequences and Episode 11 provide scenes which derive from Tyrrel's soliloquy and report in IV, 3, which also contains the news of the invasion (Episode 13). Episodes 10, 12, 13, and 15 are invented. Shakespeare does not show the landing of Richmond (14) but has him near Tamworth in V, 2. Episode 16 is not in Shakespeare, nor is a scene

F

of Anne's death, which is, however, reported in IV, 3. The fourth scene of the fourth act provided the last sequence of the reel.

Reel V

1 Richmond visits young Elizabeth, to whom he is betrothed.
2 Richard departs from London with his army.
3 Exterior of Richard's tent on Bosworth Field.
4 Interior of the tent. Richard's dream.
5 Exterior of the tent. The summons to battle.
6 7 and 8 [so grouped on the programme]. Episodes of the battle.
9 The battle of Bosworth Field. Combat and death of Richard.
10 The last of the Plantagenets.

Shakespeare announces the betrothal in IV, 5, but this episode and the next are invented. Episodes 3, 4, and 5 are from V, 3, but did the ghosts not appear to Richmond in the film? All the rest of the reel is from V, 4 and 5, but visualized.

I see no evidence in the picture of the presence of Rivers, Dorset, Grey, Hastings, the widow of Henry VI, or the Duchess of York. Buckingham's role is somewhat cut, and Catesby has been elevated to chief henchman. The young Elizabeth betrothed to Richmond has been added and of course various supernumaries, doubtfully however to a total of a thousand. If there were two hundred horses they must have got in each other's way. What the continuity writer has done is to take the outline of the narrative, eliminate a good many of the unintelligible court intrigues thereby simplifying the story line, stress some of Shakespeare's big scenes, especially those which involve Richard, rearrange to show oppositions, allowing in some cases for alternation between characters, and invent freely to connect major episodes with each other, to indicate localities or allow travel between them, and to feature crowds and the spectacular. Since the film is not extant and there are no detailed reviews, it is impossible to know what success was achieved, but there can be no doubt that this picture with a well known actor in the lead was one of the most elaborate of its time. Whether it could have stood on its own feet without Frederick Warde's explanatory intercessions is highly questionable.

If the sound effects of *Richard III* were personally supplied, there was an attempt in 1913 to record sound along with sight. Hints have already been given in the reviews quoted about what Edison was doing. On January 25th, the *Moving Picture World* carried an advertisement by the American Talking Picture Co. for Edison Kinetophone. On the afternoon of February 17th there was a demonstration of sound films at four New York theatres, the Colonial, the Fifth Avenue, the Union Square, and the Alhambra. Among Edison's films was a Brutus–Cassius scene from *Julius Caesar*, the fourth act quarrel. The invention was not a success and was shortly withdrawn from the market.

If we took the trouble to hunt in the theatres of 1913, we could have seen seven other American pictures which show the pervasive influence of Shakespeare upon producers, if not upon viewers. Mutual Educational – how educational? – released on January 30th *All's Well That Ends Well*; probably only the title was borrowed. *Alas! Poor Yorick* by Selig, released on April 21st, perhaps lasted long enough to compete with Essanay's *Something Rotten in Havana* of July; there is no evidence of *Hamlet* except in the quotation and the mangling of another. *Much Ado About Nothing* usually means just that, but Crystal's picture available on September 2nd included a possibly successful attempt to bring two lovers together after a misunderstanding. Edison's *Othello in Jonesville*, released on June 9th, was an evidently successful brief burlesque which dealt with an out-of-work actor and a gawky stage-struck girl. He teaches her family acting for his keep, and they try to give a performance of *Othello* at the town hall, no doubt with lamentable, if amusing results. I can cite the titles of *Romeo in Pajamas*, *A Would-be Romeo*, and *The Galloping Romeo*, which seem to run the gamut of something or other. The first was a one-reeler by Solax, June 18th. It did include parental objections to a youthful romance, but the comedy consisted of the hero's holding up a rival to ridicule by removing some of his clothes. The second was another comedy, this time by Punch in 533 feet, in which an actor follows directions in a faked mash-note and ends up first meeting a veiled negress and then having to walk twenty miles back to New York. There are at least scenes at a window and an attempted elopement in the third, by Selig, but it is wholly farce; the lovers' run-away is mixed up with attempted burglary, burglar alarms, the arrival of the posse, and of course mistaken identity. A plague, I say, on all your houses!

Europe too had its Shakespearean trivia in 1913. In England three films borrowed or truncated titles without adopting the earlier stories. Cricks and Martin showed a penchant for this device with a *Much Ado About* without the *nothing*, released in 460 feet on January 18th, and an *All's Well That Ends Well* in 850 feet on April 19th; the first was a comedy, the second, a 'drama'. Gaumont gave to the world another comedy, *Love's Labour Lost*, in 490 feet on January 23rd. There was the usual planning of pictures which were not realized, pictures with stars. Zenith specialized in filming stage successes and persuaded Seymour Hicks and his wife, Ellaline Terriss, to consider a *Richard III*. The *Cinema News and Property Gazette* on January 29th said that 'the interest of this picture will be immensely increased by the fact that it will be taken actually on the Field of Bosworth, with the armour, dresses, &c., historically correct. . . .' On May 29th Hicks himself was quoted in the *Kinematograph and Lantern Weekly* as saying that 'all our arrangements are complete for the production of "Richard III".' By July, however, other subjects were decided upon, and Shakespeare was abandoned in favour of *David Garrick* and *Scrooge*, trade shown in September. On October 25th, J. B. Sutcliffe in the *Moving Picture World* could announce that Sir George Alexander was to film *Much Ado About Nothing*; the plan turned out to be only much ado.

Far more interesting is what I think is the first amateur Shakespeare film. The Picture House, Stratford-upon-Avon, had some success with local topicals. Among these, I learn, were a hockey match between Stratford and a theatrical touring company, and – can this cockpit hold the vasty fields of France? – *Henry V*, acted by the boys of Shakespeare's school. No doubt the spectators pieced out imperfections with their thoughts. Another school in its way had something to do with *Henry V*. Eric Williams, quondam headmaster of Worthing Collegiate, turned professional elocutionist and in 1911 began reciting to pictures made at his instance. I am by no means sure of the original date of his 'synchronized speaking excerpt from *King Henry V*', or, as it was also called, *England's Warrior King*, nor which of the various firms which made his pictures was responsible for this one, but they were very popular. As late as 1919 at the Cinema Hall, York, his performance of *Henry V*, originally produced in the museum grounds and St Mary's Chapel ruins of that city with 'the whole of the cast made up of men drawn from the Royal Scots Greys, who were stationed at York at the time the film was done . . . was honoured by the attendance of the Lord Mayor and Lady Mayoress of York (Sir Foster and Lady Todd) and a municipal party, and a very large and most appreciative audience.' Gaumont in 1913 made his excerpt from *King John* called *Hubert and Arthur* in which he 'acted the leading characters. This adds a great piquancy to the entertainment, for the audience behold in flesh and blood, the actor on the picture, and also hear him reciting the words to fit in with his gestures on the screen.' *Hubert and Arthur* was, as might be expected, full of pathos. Edison was not the only one to use sound pictures in 1913, but these, more primitive, hark back to the slide recitations of earlier in the century.

Films having a possible or not close relationship with Shakespeare were longer on the Continent in 1913. Since Laura Cowie had played Anne Boleyn in Tree's *Henry VIII* we might suspect that a three-part *Anne Boleyn* with her in the title role would have some discernible reference to Shakespeare. This was a French picture, made by Eclipse, but the review in the *Kinematograph and Lantern Weekly* on December 18th shows that Max Pemberton, who wrote the scenario, had quite other fish to fry. And was *Dente per Dente* produced by Latium in 850 metres with Mignon Vassallo, Lidia Gauthier, and Ubaldo Pittei really based on *Measure for Measure*? There were two nods to *The Merchant of Venice*, one French, one German. Pathé's *A Modern Portia*, released in the United States in two reels on December 11th by the General Film Company, involved a woman lawyer who presses a court action against her lover and convicts him of stealing from another woman. Projections–A.-G. Union filmed *Der Shylock von Krakau* in '4 Akten', 'Ein

Mimodrama von Felix Salten', in which the daughter of a pious Jew steals money from her father and elopes with her lover who has been borrowing from the Jew. The latter's pursuit ends with a mental breakdown, recovery, the rejection of his deceived daughter and her death. Rudolf Schildkraut played the character corresponding to Shylock; Beata Ehren, his daughter; and Karl Wilhelm, her lover. *Othello* too played its part. In Italy, Pasquali presented its contribution to the experimental sound films of the year with a fifteen hundred metre *Bianco contro Negro*, music by Verdi but with the actors Alberto Capozzi and perhaps Mary Cleo Tarlarini in leading roles. The German company, Continental Kunstfilm produced a series of short comedies featuring a character called Bumke. Among them was *Bumke as Othello*, released on April 18th, and in England on June 12th in 590 feet by the Elite Sales Agency. This one concerns the trite situation in which an ambitious but incompetent actor makes himself ridiculous by playing a Shakespearean hero and has to flee from his outraged spectators. The Italian *Iago's Inheritance* on the other hand was a thriller based on a novel by Charles Darlington, produced by Savoia in 2630 feet, and distributed by Eclair in England for release on February 12, 1914. Here a confidential secretary steals from his employer, is suspected by his employer's wife, and sends to her husband an anonymous letter accusing her of infidelity. The husband returns from a pretended journey to see his drugged lady at a window in a confederate's arms. Perhaps Darlington borrowed from *Much Ado About Nothing* as well as from *Othello*. When the duplicity is discovered and the secretary is dismissed, he sets lions free in the husband's grounds but dies himself when the animals get into the house, knock over a lamp, and burn it down. My, oh my! This seems to be the first time when the popular 'fauves' films get tangled up with Shakespeare.

Somewhere between European films which obviously borrow from Shakespeare and those which are basically transmissions of his plays are two treatments in 1913 of the story of Antony and Cleopatra. The first was issued by Pathé in France in two reels, the second of much greater length and scope by Cines of Italy. It seems probable that the second was respons- ible for the first. Indeed it may well be that Pathé's film called *Cleopatra* in England, and *Antony and Cleopatra* in the United States is a padded remake or reissue of its 1910 film already discussed. When I first catch sight of it in a pre-release announcement in the *Kinematograph and Lantern Weekly* of July 31st it is listed as among 'Pathé's Latest Productions', to be released on August 31st in 1070 feet. Now this is very curious indeed. The 1910 film was in 1170 feet, and either the journal is in error or Pathé was at this point contemplating a reissue without enlargement, in fact a hundred feet shorter than it had been. Cines's announcements had already begun to appear in the same paper on February 27th for release in May, later delayed until autumn. Yet by the time Pathé's film reaches the United States on May 21, 1914, it is clearly described as in two parts. It seems to me probable that Pathé put out something longer than its 1910 film in order to profit by natural confusion with a rival film.

Pathé's 1913 release had, so far as one can discern from unreliable summaries, much the same story and coverage as in 1910: Antony's enslavement to Cleopatra, their love affair, the objections of Octavius, the battle between Antony and Octavius, the messenger bearing ill news who is poisoned, Antony's return, his suicide at Cleopatra's feet and her own suicide by the bite of an asp. The only thing I note as hitherto unrecorded is that 'the return across the desert on camels was particularly striking'. This is from the *Moving Picture World* on June 6, 1914, which emphasizes that this picture is 'an elaborate staging of the great drama of Egypt's wondrous Queen. The scenic investitute is very complete and carries with it the heroic atmosphere of the times depicted. . . . A fine spectacular number.' Three weeks before, Pathé's advertisement had called it 'a massive and glittering production showing the barbaric splendor of the Great Queen's court'. Perhaps all this means that Pathé had dusted off its 1910 picture and inserted enough spectacular sequences to give the impression that it was a new film.

The Cines *Antony and Cleopatra* was altogether a different matter. When Enrico Guazzoni had made his *Brutus*, his flair for the massive and the spectacular had to be confined to one reel. In 1912 he produced a stupendous and extraordinarily successful *Quo Vadis?* in eight reels. The next year he again undertook the production of a subject also treated by Shakespeare, *Antony and Cleopatra*, released in the United States by George Kleine in eight reels but probably even longer in its original Italian version; at any rate this is the longest film yet treated. Guazzoni details an enormous amount of research, planning, and construction to obtain historical accuracy, and acting as designer and script writer as well as director, he made a picture at an expense which was reported in England as £40,000. In France it was said the cast included two thousand persons, not to mention 'lions et tigres'. Exclusive distribution rights for the British Isles were sold at auction for £8,100; there was a similar disposal for Australia, Asia, and Africa. Four Paris theatres showed it at the same time. In London it was first revealed to the public on Christmas Eve, 1913; in the United States, it was playing in January 1914 in Chicago, San Francisco, Seattle, Nashville, Columbus, Buffalo, and Dayton, in February in Springfield (Ohio), Memphis, Savannah, Atlanta, Detroit, and Indianapolis. The New York opening was delayed until the completion of the new Candler Theatre, partly controlled by Kleine. From May 5th it ran five weeks with two performances a day. Audiences were no doubt encouraged or stimulated by a 2,000,000 lot printing by Kleine of an eight-page booklet 'on a good grade of India tint paper, profusely illustrated with dainty vignetted cuts'. Reviewers used only superlatives to praise the historicity, the imaginative creation of atmosphere, the lavish settings, the battle and crowd scenes, the moonlight effects, the acting of Amleto Novelli and Gianna (Giovanna) Terribili Gonzales as the principals, Ignazio Lupi as Octavius, Elsa (Léna?) Lenard as Octavia, and Matilde di Marzio as a character called Hagar or Agar in Europe but Charmian in America. The last identification should give us pause. How far was this picture Shakespearean?

Some of Kleine's publicity and one of the London trade papers indicate that Guazzoni's film was based on Shakespeare. There is little enough in the story to demonstrate this provenance, as a synopsis will show. Antony successfully attacks Egypt and sends for Cleopatra. She consults a seeress in a cave, an old woman attended by a huge snake, who leads her to a sacred flame, and tells her she can do what she will with Antony. Sending gifts ahead of her, Cleopatra sets out on her barge down the Nile. Antony, much impressed upon her arrival, promises to visit her in Alexandria. There he becomes infatuated. Octavia appeals to Octavius and is advised to go to Egypt and reclaim Antony, who, against the will of Egyptian advisers, has been made joint ruler with Cleopatra. Octavia in Egypt pleads with Antony to return to Rome but is violently rejected. She appeals to Cleopatra, who, strong in her assurance of his love for her, says Antony may go if he wishes. Octavia leaves, threatening Rome's vengeance. Hagar (Charmian), a slave girl, smitten with Antony, trespasses in his quarters, is caught and is about to be punished, but Antony saves her and allows her to go free. Egyptian nobles meet in council and ask Cleopatra to throw off the yoke of Rome and bid Antony go, but she rejects the request, asserts her will, and warns against interference. As Hagar watches, they leave defiantly. After praying to Isis, they conspire to kill Antony. Hagar, overhearing, is recognized, pursued, apprehended, and imprisoned. Antony is given a sleeping potion. Hagar makes a rope out of her clothes, overpowers a jailor, and escapes to inform Cleopatra. The conspirators approach the sleeping Antony. As they are about to dispatch him, Cleopatra interferes and dismisses them. Antony thanks Hagar so emotionally that Cleopatra's jealousy is aroused, and when Hagar declares her love for Antony, Cleopatra has her chained, whipped, and then thrown by a negro slave to the crocodiles. (In a later version, Hagar is inappositely forgiven.) Octavia's return to Rome is followed by a meeting of the Senate to judge Antony. He is declared a traitor, but when this action is reported to him, declares his intention of remaining in Egypt. The Senate decides to bring Antony back in chains and sends a fleet under Octavius to Egypt where Antony is seen revelling. The fleet arrives and the warriors disembark, wading ashore with armour and supplies. The news of the invasion interrupts the revels. Confusion, the battle, and Antony's defeat follow. Eros kills himself rather than end Antony's life, but Antony stabs himself with a dagger. Cleopatra faints on being brought to him, shown on a bier. Octavius mourns Antony's death but is impervious to Cleopatra's attempt to win him over. Fearful of being taken as a prisoner to Rome, the Queen decides to commit suicide. She goes to the seeress for means and is given both poisons and an asp in a bag. The wild beasts of the palace are restless. Octavius sends Cleopatra a message to prepare to go to Rome. She lets the asp bite her. Octavius discovers her dead and returns to Rome in triumph. In detailing the story line, I have omitted a scene where Cleopatra does a 'danse de ventre' and another where she tries the effect of poisons on her slaves.

Though the Cines picture is sometimes listed as Shakespearean, it clearly is not. There is no scene closely paralleling the play until the Eros business (IV, 14), but this is also in Plutarch. Plutarch indeed is the well from which the water ran, obviously mixed with other chemicals, mostly devised by Guazzoni. The oracular enchantress of serpents and the story of Hagar derive from a 'poema drammatico', Cleopatra (1876) by Pietro Cossa, a mediocre poet but good dramatic craftsman, remembered outside of Italy because he was the subject of an essay by Benedetto Croce. There is therefore no point in this book in detailing shots and effects of mass marchings, Egyptian revelry, and palatial architecture, impressive as they are in their way. If Shakespeare had any influence it was slight. It is perhaps this disappointment which makes me recall Vachel Lindsay's criticism of Guazzoni's film: 'It is equivalent to waving the Italian above the Egyptian flag, quite slowly for two hours. From the stage standpoint, the magnificence is uncompromising. Viewed as a circus, the acting is elephantine in its grandeur. All that is needed is pink lemonade sold in the audience.'

Italy did, however, produce more authentic Shakespeare films in 1913. Two of these shadows are very shadowy indeed. For a Gloria Giulio Cesare, I have only one unauthenticated reference, and of a Midsummer Night's Dream, parts of which I have seen, I can only guess at the date. The second, unrecorded by screen historians, is a pleasant surprise. In three reels, 800 feet, of 16 millimetre stock, it gives credit only to Socrate Tommasi as Lysander and Bianca Maria Hübner as Helena. The English subtitles are Shakespearean quotations. All the camera work was done out of doors, and the scenery is lovely and charmingly rustic. Remarkably for its period, the photography is technically advanced; it uses iris outs, dissolves for vanishings, and double exposures. There is cross-cutting with, for example, interspersed cloud shots to indicate mood and time. The acting is unimpressive but not stagy; evidently the participants knew how to underplay, even if the resulting pace is slow. The Theseus–Hippolyta framework is not in the film, whether or not it was originally, and Titania has almost no role, but she is shown surrounded by girls and small children, her train, who do considerable and rather awful dancing. There are no artisans or play-within-the-play. The whole presentation consists of the mix-ups of the two pairs of lovers, their embroilment by Oberon and Puck, and the ultimate pairings, but the Oberon–Titania quarrel is not in the film as it now exists. There is an unusual shot of Theseus and his huntsmen superimposed in the upper right of some of the frames and kept squarely distinct from the young lovers scene which is the centre focus. Egeus appears briefly at the beginning and end of the picture; it concludes with the suggestion of a feast, and Puck, a tiny, winning youngster who obviously was having the time of his life, speaking part of the epilogue. I wish I knew more about this curiously refreshing film, which may be somewhat later than 1913.

There is fortunately more about an Ambrosio *Taming of the Shrew*, but unfortunately no surviving print. Arturo Ambrosio had begun filming actualities as early as 1904, and became a producer of comedies in 1906 in Turin. His success was rapid, and he soon turned to serious subjects as well; by 1911 his company produced more films than any other Italian firm, many of them of the first quality. One of his scenarists was a lawyer, Sebastiano Ferraris, who wrote under the name of Arrigo Frusta a prodigious number of scripts. It was he who made the adaptation for *La Bisbetica Domata* in 1913. It was advertised in England on August 21st by the New Agency Film Co. for release on October 2nd in two reels, totalling 2200 feet. As far as can be gathered from a summary-review, the film 'of peculiarly good quality' followed the principal episodes of Shakespeare's play fairly closely and gave 'rare opportunity' to 'two accomplished performers', '[Eleuterio] Rodolfi and Mdlle Louise'. Indeed, 'the film has the advantage over the play' in that some parts which we only hear about in the stage version are 'actually illustrated. Thus, for instance, the moonlight journey to Petruchio's house gains vastly in humour as the picture shows it to us.'

'The subject opens with a picture of the distracted household of Baptista Minola, who is blessed with two daughters of a sweetness of temper and docility of disposition beyond reproach. [Did Hortensio's 'widow' become a member of the family?]. Their virtues have been appreciated by others beside their father, and each is pledged to a gallant. Their happiness is wormwood to their elder sister, Katharina, whose furious temper and frightful disposition have kept all possible courtiers at a safe distance. Katharina forcibly parts her sisters from their lovers and dragging them before Baptista demands why they should be allowed to take husbands while, she, the eldest sister, is still a spinster. In despair at her 'frowardness' Baptista declares at last that a husband she shall have, and to hasten the happy day when his house shall be rid of her declares that her sisters shall not wed until she is matched.

'Then comes the appearance of Petruchio, son of an old friend, who learns of the state of affairs, learns also that, cross-grained though she be, Katharina will bring her husband a handsome dowry. Straightway he declares himself a suitor for her hand, and in that character blithely announces himself to the shrew when he encounters her. Her biting contempt, her blows, her anger are disregarded. Petruchio announces, to the equal surprise and delight of her father and her sisters' suitors, that he will marry Katharina in ten days.

'The wedding day dawns, Katharina, half-dazed by the furious wooing

F*

of which she has been the object, permits herself to be dressed for the ceremony. Petruchio keeps the company waiting and in the end appears in a dirty, tattered suit, which he refuses to change for the ceremony. The wedding over, the guests, preparing for the banquet which should follow, are amazed by the newly-made husband forcibly carrying his wife away to her new home in a broken-down wagon before she can eat or drink.

'On the road the bridegroom maintains his methods of violence, quarrels punctuate the journey, and Katharina arrives at her husband's house exhausted and hungry. But the sumptuous meal which awaits them does not recommend itself to Petruchio, who, under the pretence that the food is not good enough for his wife, throws one dish after another across the room. Katharina retires to her chamber fasting – even here her troubles are not at an end. The couch excites the bridegroom's ire and he will not let her rest on it. She passes the night in a chair and in the morning the taming is well on its way.

'Its triumphant completion is revealed when Baptista, with his younger daughters and their husbands, come to visit Petruchio and his wife. The once uncontrollable Katharina is now the model of a quiet even-tempered wife, obedient to her husband in all things. Petruchio wagers with the other young husbands that his wife will prove the most obedient of the three. Each sends a message to his lady asking her to come to him. Two return pert answers – Katharina alone obeys, and the climax of the comedy is reached when she lectures her sisters upon their duty to their husbands.'

The elimination of the induction and all of the disguisings and strategems of Bianca's lovers, the secondary plot that is, the concentration on the main plot of the taming and its visual possibilities such as the journey and the chamber scene have resulted in a straightforward story with plenty of opportunity for comedy which the actors can mime and the camera can catch. This is one film which the spectators should have had no difficulty in following and enjoying. The next year Ambrosio was far more ambitious.

Late in 1913 there is word of an Italian screen adaptation of *The Winter's Tale*. *La Cinematografia Italiana* on November 25th reprints comment from *Le Ciné-Journal* on *Le Conte d'Hiver* 'qu'elle vient d'editer' by Milano-Film and is 'une merveille de gout et de sentiment. La mise en scène fait grand honneur à celui qui l'a reglée et l'interprétation est des plus heureuses. Tous nos compliments à M. L. Sutto qui fut le directeur artistique de cette belle oeuvre. . . .' *Le Courier Cinématographique*, three days before, had run an advertisement of the General Film Agency, Ltd., which indicated that the length was 1000 metres and that the adaptation to the screen had been under the direction of L. Sutto; a superb brochure was available on demand. In Germany, *Der Kinematograph* carried publicity on November 26th, and in England notice appeared in the *Kinematograph and Lantern Weekly*, January

29, 1914, that Milano had 'just finished' the film. On March 15th, the same journal announces that 'the sole United Kingdom rights for the Milano masterpiece, *A Winter's Tale*, have been secured by the Exclusive Supply Co. . . . The film (which is 3000 feet in length) has a plot that is melodramatic in intensity and many of the scenes have rarely been equalled for beauty'. Exclusive's advertisement on April 2nd commends not only the photography but 'the remarkable command of gesture revealed by the Artistes who take part in this fascinating production', and on April 16th announces a trade showing for the next day. The same issue reviews 'this cleverly edited version of one of Shakespeare's immortal dramas'.

'From whatever point of view one looks at it the production pleases, and pleases all the more because the company have not spared themselves to give it all the wealth of circumstance and pageantry it demands, with at the same time a general accuracy of detail that will act as a sort of benison to those who are inclined to look askance at the tendency to "adapt" anything associated with the name of the "immortal bard" . . .

'We do not say for a minute that this version of *The Winter's Tale* is perfect. It would be absurd to express such an opinion, for there are incidental pegs on which criticism could be hung were one inclined to be captious. But in the face of what we have said of its general accuracy of detail and indisputable excellence, such criticism is almost tantamount to looking a gift horse in the mouth.

'Were we inclined we might launch into a phillipic against the non-inclusion of Autolycus . . . but how could this merry pedlar and pickpocket be possibly introduced – for it must be remembered that action and not character study is the mainspring of picture plays. . . .

'As the Milano Company have interpreted this admirable work it is made even attractive and intelligible to childhood, and that is something warranting cordial praise. . . . But what we should be concerned with is this: Is the Milano production worthy of the material taken in hand? And the answer, to all who see the film, we believe, will be an emphatic affirmative. In one or two instances the country of origin is clearly attested, but only a company with the big resources of this Italian one could have presented the "Tale" as it is. It is splendidly acted, magnificently staged, and photographically beautiful.'

On the same date the *Cinema News and Property Gazette* heads its review 'Shakespeare That Will Pay' and praises the film as 'an artistic triumph of no mean order'; two weeks later in this journal, Exclusive Supply quotes the *Cinematograph Exhibitors Journal* as saying 'its excellence is such as to merit unstinted praise. . . . All lovers of Shakespeare will welcome the opportunity to see it screened', and the *Westminster Gazette*: 'The production is thoroughly engrossing, well acted, and magnificently mounted.' Fortunately, *Bioscope* on April 16th gives more detail:

'The version produced by the Milano Company . . . is necessarily condensed to bring it within the limits of three reels. . . . The adapter has the choice of two themes, and in this instance he has done wisely in keeping more strictly to the story of the jealousy of Leontes and his unreasonable persecution of Hermione, though in condensing the story of Perdita . . . it is inevitable that much must be sacrificed that one regrets. For this reason we miss that drollest and most genial of rascals, Autolycus, though it is doubtful if a character which is so entirely Shakespeare's own could be represented adequately without the aid of words. . . . There are one or two slight departures from the text, which in some instances are entirely justified by the result. After Antigonus deserts the child he is set upon by robbers and hurled into the crater of a volcano. This produces a scene which is sufficiently effective and spares us the episode with a bear described with such evident relish by the shepherd's son. . . . There is one departure from the original by which the producer seems to us to have missed a great opportunity. One of the most beautiful scenes in the play is that at the end, where Hermione is revealed to her repentant husband 'standing like a statue', and one which seems particularly well adapted for effective treatment on the screen. This, however, is not attempted. . . . The mounting throughout is brilliant, and the costumes are rich and picturesque. . . . The scenes in the palace of Leontes are magnificently mounted, and some beautiful landscapes are shown with fine effects of light and shade, greatly enhanced by the perfect quality of the photography. . . . The acting is of . . . high standard . . . , and the outstanding figure in an exceptional cast is that of Madame Fabbri, who plays the part of Paulina. . . . Madame Fabbri has grasped the possibilities of the part, and if the prominence this figure acquires alters the balance of the play, it is more than compensated for by her dramatic and impressive rendering of the character. . . . This version is the most satisfactory film rendering of Shakespeare that we have yet seen. It is concise, dramatic, and artistic in every detail.'

I do not know how many Shakespeare films the reviewer had seen, but it is indeed visually handsome, as is testified by a print on 1919 stock in the National Archive of the British Film Institute. It partakes perhaps rather more of the spirit of Robert Greene's wonder-tale than of Shakespeare's play, partly because the English titles in this version are not Shakespearean. The acting, especially of Leontes, is stagy, and none of it is distinguished. Introductory credits assign Leontes to V. Cocchi, and Paulina, obviously the principal part, to Pina Fabbri. The director is listed in the Archive's records as Baldassare Negroni. An opening section shows above-waist close-ups of the named actors, separately, in costume and character, crown and mail-cloth for Leontes, black cape and hood for Paulina. The next sequence, preceded by an explanatory sub-title, shows Shakespeare reading *The Winter's Tale* to his friends. In well arranged composition, Shakespeare and four others sit at a table, drinking wine, as the playwright reads. The story proper begins with the next frames:

1 Subtitle: 'King Leontes, at the Court of Socilia, asks his wife Hermione to request their guest, Polixenes, King of Bohemia, to prolong his stay.' The action is depicted in an attractive interior. Leontes follows Hermione and Polixenes, as they leave. (I, 2)

2 Subtitle: 'King Leontes feast in honour of his guest.' This crowded scene, shown in both long and middle shots, was evidently introduced for spectacle and dancing. The emphasis, however, is on Hermione and Polixenes talking and drinking.

3 Subtitle: 'The King of Sicilia misinterprets his guest's courtesy to Queen Hermione and is tortured by jealousy.' The focus shifts to a balcony. Leontes leaves the feast and is shown at the railing, looking out over the water, then in a new sequence walking along the bank where he is joined by Camillo, talks with him and shows his irritation. They leave the scene. The jealousy is adapted from I, 2, but the rest is invented.

4 Subtitle: 'Leontes orders Camillo to poison his guest.' In an indoor set, the event is accompanied by much argument and pleading by Camillo, who then departs. (I, 2)

5 Subtitle: 'Camillo warns Polixenes.' Thus, with Polixenes protesting his innocence. (I, 2)

6 Subtitle: 'Two Lords of the Court observe Polixenes and Camillo's flight.' A happy visualization, merely spoken in Shakespeare (II, 1). The scene is a rocky coast, a rowboat leaving with Polixenes and Camillo. The Lords watch from the shore. The camera moves to show the rowboat approaching a ship. The sequence is on green stock to simulate night.

7 Subtitle: 'Leontes, believing his suspicions confirmed by the flight gives orders for the Queen to be thrown into prison.' Paulina and Hermione talk. The Lords report the escape. Hermione, accused, protests her innocence, but is removed. Paulina is shocked. (Adapted from II, 1)

8 Subtitle: 'Paulina, who is devoted to her Royal mistress, craves mercy for her.' She kneels in this invented scene.

9 Subtitle: 'Upon the advice of faithful Antigonus, the King sends two messengers to consult the oracle in Apollo's temple as to the fidelity of his wife.' A visual adaptation of Leontes' own speech in II, 1. There is a cut to Paulina approaching the prison, bribing the warder, and being admitted, adapted from II, 2. We see Paulina and the warder entering the prison; an interior scene on green stock for darkness. The warder raises by a winch the grating to Hermione's cell. The interior scenes, which conclude Part I of the four parts of this particular print, are new.

10 Part II begins with more invented scenes. Hermione is shown on a bed, attended by two women, one of whom holds her baby. Paulina enters the cell, holds up the child for the audience to see, hands her back to the nurse, goes to Hermione and kneels before her, takes the baby again, wraps her in

her cloak, and leaves. Cut to the outside of the prison, where we see Paulina leaving with the concealed baby. We move to the Court, where Paulina shows his daughter to Leontes, who gives her to Antigonus. (II, 3)

11 Subtitle: 'Leontes commands Antigonus to take the child out of his dominions and to abandon it to the elements.' Antigonus kneels in expostulation, but has to obey and retires. Cut to a ship at sea, transporting the baby, held by Antigonus. (II, 3, then new)

12 Subtitle: 'A month later. The trial of the Queen.' The King sits on his throne in a crowded courtroom. Hermione protests her innocence. (III, 2)

13 Subtitle: 'The two messengers return with the oracle.' They are seen on a ship. (Adapted from III, 1.) There is a cut to the court scene where the judges confer on the message from the oracle. There are no judges in Shakespeare.

14 Subtitle: 'Hermione is chaste; Polixenes blameless; Camillo a true subject; Leontes a jealous tyrant; and the King shall live without an heir, if that which is lost is not found', an adaptation of Shakespeare's own lines. The King is conscience-stricken. (III, 2)

15 Subtitle: 'The Queen, grieving for her child, is threatened with madness.' Adapted from a suggestion in III, 2. Hermione is shown on a four-poster, two attendants by her. (New)

16 Subtitle: 'The potion.' In a market place, Paulina buys a potion from a woman. With the potion concealed in her cloak she enters Hermione's bed chamber, dismisses an attendant, and goes to the Queen. (New)

17 Subtitle: 'Paulina administers the potion to save the life and reason of her mistress.' (New)
This action ends Part II.

18 Subtitle: 'Paulina declares the Queen to be dead and upbraids Leontes for his cruelty.' The scene is still in Hermione's cell. The King, who has entered just before the subtitle, is scolded, and kneels by Hermione's bed. This is based on dialogue in III, 2, but the setting is different.

19 Subtitle: 'The burial of the Queen.' A burial vault is entered through a cave, shown on green stock. In the burial chamber itself is a tomb with an open side. Hermione's body is brought in on a stretcher, inserted in the tomb. Flowers are put on the body. (New)

20 Subtitle: 'Grief.' The body is shown in the tomb, which is closed, as Leontes shows his sorrow. Paulina comforts him but orders him to leave. This action has been suggested by III, 2.

21 Subtitle: 'Antigonus arrives in Bohemia and is watched in landing by robbers.' The robbers from a cave spy an approaching rowboat, a good shot. Antigonus arrives on the beach with the baby. (New)

22 Subtitle: 'The babe deserted.' Antigonus leaves the child in a wood and retires (III, 3). Cut to Antigonus in another part of the wood, where the robbers attack him. (New)

23 Subtitle: 'The robbers demand the treasure which they believe Antigonus to have carried under his mantle.' Thus. (New)

24 Subtitle: 'Antigonus is cast into the burning crater of a volcano.' This shot was meant to be spectacular but it is not very effective in business or photography, despite shifts from yellow to red stock. (New)

25 Subtitle: 'Shepherds find the child.' And money. (III, 3)

26 Subtitle: 'The robbers burn the vessel and destroy all traces of their crime.' This new scene is on red stock; smoke is shown rising; it is not convincing, especially since the same ship turns up later. With a shift to green stock, Father Time walks across the screen with a scythe, waves it once. (IV, 1)

27 Subtitle: 'The deserted child under the care of the shepherds has grown to be a beautiful girl and is called Perdita.' A pleasant rural scene; we cut to Florizel watching. (New)

28 Subtitle: 'Florizel, the King of Bohemia's son, dressed up as a shepherd woos Perdita.' He goes to her; medium and then close shot. (IV, 4)

29 Subtitle: 'King Polixenes and Camillo follow him in disguise to ascertain the reason for his frequent absences.' A pleasant woodland road, then a cut to close-up of a decorous wooing. (IV, 4)

30 Subtitle: 'A rustic betrothal.' A very pretty scene with dancing and merrymaking on a lawn surrounded by woods, too pretty to be really rustic. (IV, 4)

31 Subtitle: 'The King angrily declares his son shall not marry a shepherdess.' He interrupts the frolicking. End of Part III. The shepherds run up to see what is happening. (Adapted from IV, 4)

32 Subtitle: 'Threatened with punishment, the shepherds disown any blood tie with Perdita and the secret of her birth is discovered.' The true identity is established by a coin left with Perdita as a baby. There is a close-up of the coin which carries on it a picture of Leontes, and the motto, 'Leonte Rex Siciliae'. Perdita rushes into Florizel's arms. The discovery of Perdita's identity at this point is new, as is the means by which the discovery is made, but the first part of the scene is from IV, 4.

33 Subtitle: 'The King of Bohemia promises to take Perdita to her father.' This action is a substitute for the function of Autolycus. A rather handsome open piazza, then cut to Bohemians riding through their city gate. (New)

34 Subtitle: 'The arrival on Sicilia.' A shot of the ship with a rowboat putting off with the principals, then a cut to the landing. (New)

35 Subtitle: 'Camillo and Perdita find Paulina.' Camillo leads Perdita to Paulina's house, leaves her outside picturesque sculptured pillars. He enters alone and is shown telling Paulina the news. (New)

36 Subtitle: 'Thoughts of the past.' More of the same. Camillo leaves. Cut to outside. Camillo takes Perdita in. Paulina is convinced of Perdita's identity and they embrace. (New)

37 Subtitle: 'Paulina tells Perdita how her mother died.' What is the point under the circumstances? We see them leaving after this conversation. (New)

38 Subtitle: 'The meeting of the two Kings.' This is V, 1, made visual, instead of being described. Paulina is seen watching the reunion from behind black curtains. She returns to Perdita, and they go aside.

39 Subtitle: 'Leontes meets his daughter.' Again adapted from V, 1. The King enters with Camillo, staggers at the recognition.

40 Subtitle: 'Leontes wishes to show his daughter once the face of her mother.' This is described in V, 2, pictured here. The scene is the burial chamber. The tomb is opened. There is nothing there but a robe. Paulina shows signs of trepidation, the King of amazement. Paulina directs them out. (New)

41 Subtitle: 'An appeal to Paulina to reveal the truth of the mystery.' Apparently, a room in Paulina's house. Curtains are drawn aside, showing Hermione seemingly dead, an adaptation of V, 3, but with no statue.

42 Subtitle: 'The awakening of Hermione.' As the print stands, most of the sequence is devoted to Leontes and the three women, but the actual awakening is not there, and part of the sequence must be lost. (Adapted from V, 3)

43 Subtitle: 'Reunion.' A longer shot showing all the characters. (New)

44 Subtitle: 'Epilogue.' Shakespeare finishes his reading of *The Winter's Tale*. (New)

With the detail thus spelled out, no elaborate comment on the adaptation is necessary. The principal changes from the story told by Shakespeare are that Autolycus has been dropped, and the recognition of Perdita therefore takes place in Bohemia; Antigonus makes his exit in a volcano, where he is tossed by robbers, rather than being 'pursued by a bear;' and Paulina, given more to do than Shakespeare had in mind, evidently secretes Hermione in her own quarters, thereby eliminating the statue business. The last change with its suggestion of the Resurrection seems unnecessary, but the other two are understandable. The many subtitles make the story clear, if only too clear; but I do not know what they were like in the Italian original. The photography is unusually good, though the colour processing is primitive. What one remembers most indeed is the scenery and backgrounds surrounding the highly romantic but entertaining and visually told tale. Milano's film is, and quite properly, a motion picture, and one of the best so far on a Shakespearean subject.

Germany, content so far with comic insert or operatic excerpt, produced in 1913 *A Midsummer Night's Dream*, but it, alas, was a kind of perversion from the pen of a third-rate romancer, Hanns Heinz Ewers. Notices of the Deutsche Bioscop film, based on an earlier theatre presentation which must have attempted to rival Max Reinhardt's revival of his production of Shakespeare's play in the same year, stress that the picture was freely adapted from Shakespeare's ideas, was not a realization of Shakespeare's work, and was modernized so as to present characters and attitudes of the twentieth century. The plot on first reading seems harmless enough: 'A gentleman living with his daughter and niece at his country place expects the visit of two young men who are engaged to the niece and daughter. They come and their arrival is celebrated with a supper on the lawn. There is plenty of wine and the old gentleman becomes drowsy and falls asleep and dreams. The photoplay shows his dream. The dream embodies the frolics of the different characters from Shakespear's *Midsummer Night's Dream*, viz. - Puck, Oberon, Titania, fairies, satyr, etc. In his dream he sees these different lovers chased by Puck and the fairies. He finally wakes up and thinking that his dream is a reality he goes to hunt the intruders and all that he finds are the different couples sleeping on the lawn.'

Yet the un-Shakespearean satyr, the pursuit, and the sleeping lovers, as well as some knowledge of the participants in the production raise doubts about the innocence. Ewers, strongly influenced by E. T. A. Hoffman and Poe but without their ability, wrote fantastic, grotesque, sensational and erotic narratives about mirror images, doppelgängers, and abnormal creations; his imagination revelled in sex, horror, and psychological symbolism. Later he did not endear himself to the western world by writing the script of the official Horst Wessel film. In 1913 Ewers was in charge of production at Deutsche Bioscop. Stellan Rye, who collaborated with Ewers on the screen play of *Ein Sommernachtstraum* and who directed it was a Dane, who after being in jail on a morals conviction, left Copenhagen for Berlin. He staged the theatre presentation of Ewers' play, and the association continued at Deutsche Bioscop where the two men made *The Student of Prague* (1913) about a young man who sells to a sorcerer his reflection in a looking-glass and is destroyed by it. The success of this film prompted others in the same vein and *A Midsummer Night's Dream*. Grete Berger, who played Puck, presented that character with lickerish leers. In short, the playful fantasy of Shakespeare must have become a grotesquerie with sensual implications, and quite possibly a gross and nasty distortion, ill met by moonlight or any other time.

On January 25, 1913, *Ciné-Journal* announced with delicious incongruity that 'La "Radios" qui se recueillait depuis quelque temps, vient de créer une très belle bande artistique, adapté de Shakespeare: *Shylock, ou le More de Venise*.' This film of *The Merchant of Venice*, to be released on February 21st, was surely the last Shakespearean gasp of French *film d'art*, the last too of Eclipse's series of Shakespeare pictures. It was also the only straight adaptation in France of a Shakespeare play in 1913, and the last straight adaptation before 1916. The commentator continues:

'Traitée avec un soin scrupuleux de la verité dans le décor et dans les costumes, interprétée par les meilleurs artistes: MM. Harry Baur, Joubé, Hervé (de l'Odéon), et Mlle Pépa Bonafé - notre nouvelle étoile cinématographique - cette oeuvre d'art s'annonce comme un gros succès.

'Action claire, bien composé, d'un intêret soutenu, sur six cents mètres à peine, *Shylock* fait le plus grand honneur à la Radios-Eclipse.

'Ce sera le triomphe de nos écrans dans quelques semaines.'

The issue of February 8th gives the length more exactly as 642 metres in two parts, and further identifies cast and characters: Baur, of the Athenée, as Shylock; Joubé, of the Odéon, as Antonio; Hervé, of the Odéon, as Bassanio; and Pépa Bonafé, of the Apollo, as Portia. The director must have been Henri Desfontaines, who was responsible for earlier Shakespeare films by Eclipse.

George Kleine brought *Shylock* to the United States, where it was released in two reels as a 'special' on March 3rd. The *Moving Picture World* reviewed on February 22nd a trade showing.

'After introducing the leading characters in costume, utilizing some very clever dissolving effects, the film opens, showing us the scene of the Rialto in Venice, where Bassanio is relating to his friend Antonio, the merchant, of his love for Portia, a rich heiress dwelling in Belmont. The story then progresses much the same as the original text, with several of the minor details, which would only tend to confuse those not very conversant with the story, eliminated.

'The principal scenes have been admirably handled. The gorgeous interior of Portia's home, where the suitors come to try their fortune at the test for the hand of the beautiful heiress, is a picture of great magnificence, and is carried out with all the necessary dramatic effects. . . . It is interesting to note the proud bearing and extreme confidence of the two haughty suitors, the Prince of Morocco and the Prince of Aragon, and their utter consternation when they in turn select the gold and silver caskets and discover their complete failure, as is the pleasure expressed by Portia when Bassanio, her favorite suitor, wisely selects the leaden casket, which proves to be the one containing her portrait. . . .

'The famous trial scene marks the climax of the play, and is always thrilling, as few more dramatic situations in a play have ever been developed.

'The part of Shylock is ably taken by Mr Harry Baur. . . . His interpretation of the role is somewhat different from those we have seen in America, inasmuch as he portrays a less dignified Jew, yet it is done with a remarkable skill, and shows what a finished actor he is. . . . Miss Pepa Bonafe makes a beautiful and bewitching Portia. Mr Herve . . . portrays a gallant Bassanio.'

The English importer and distributor, the Globe Film Co., blew flourishes in the *Kinematograph and Lantern Weekly* on June 12th: 'A Stupendous production staged with wonderful skill, and giving a remarkably thrilling picture interpretation . . . Portia [is] a charming and beautiful actress. . . . You will get your pound of flesh and MORE if you screen this latest Globe exclusive. . . . The crowds and the money will simply roll in. You have never seen anywhere finer photography or more perfect staging and acting than you get in this brilliant production. Your patrons will be enchanted . . .'

I omit the discussion of Shakespeare's characters in the review on June 26th, but the critic was indeed enchanted: 'Here, it will be generally agreed, is a production that not only helps to make film history, but during the coming summer should pack houses with patrons from all classes.' The acting is uniformly praised, and so is the adaptation. 'The setting, too, is quite magnificent, and the quality of the photography worthy of the subject. Need more be said?' Decidedly! Has he seen it? The reviewer in the *Cinema News and Property Gazette*, June 11th, says he has, with a combination of ecstasy, unhelpful generalization, and very long summary, but I detect the press agent.

'If there is one play in the book of Shakespeare which is more popular with theatre-goers than any other, it undoubtedly is *The Merchant of Venice*. Cinema theatre proprietors will, therefore, hail with satisfaction the news that the Globe Film Co. are placing at their disposal a 2040 feet film under the title of 'Shylock', of remarkable quality. Not only is it entitled to rank among the best photographically, but the display of histrionic talent which it contains is of the highest order. The name-part is sustained in a manner worthy of an Irving; indeed it is quite one of the best portrayals of this character it has ever been our lot to witness. We do not wonder that this is so, nor do we marvel at the real excellence of the acting, when we bear in mind that the characters were sustained by some of the most noted members of the legitimate art in Paris.

'There are occasions when to bestow praise on a film is but to paint the lily or to gild refined gold. Such is the case in regard to the picture now under notice. Were we to devote columns of our space to criticising the production, we would be able to say but half the good things about it that it deserves; indeed, the English vocabulary does not contain the adjective which would fitly describe this film or to convey to the reader any real idea of its magnificence. We therefore content ourselves by stating that of its kind it is the most praiseworthy attempt that has ever been made to give upon the magic screen an adequate representation of what Shakespeare intended the play to be.'

Never mind the vocabulary; let's get to the detail. Fortunately *Bioscope*, June 12th, has it, as well as some criticism both favourable and adverse. The favourable is but repetitive or general: 'the most satisfactory adaptation of Shakespeare's work that we have seen.' But some of the rest is more informative.

'. . . the film producer, by not making the greatest possible use of natural outdoor effect, deprives himself of one of the greatest advantages he possesses over the regular stage . . . M. Baur would seem to have gone back to earlier traditions for his impersonation of Shylock, reviving memories of the time when the Jew was regarded more or less as an object of ridicule and mirth rather than sympathy. His performance is full of comedy, occasionally striking a somewhat commonplace note, as in his huckstering with Antonio over the bond, and his business with the knife in the court scene, when he takes off his shoe and uses it as a strop, squatting on the floor with all the appearance of a wayside cobbler. In the main, however, it is exceedingly effective, and his gesture and facial expression are wonderfully illuminative. The long dramatic speeches are wisely dispensed with, and the few quotations which are needed to tell the story are well chosen and carefully condensed. ...'

Pépa Bonafé, it was reported, made 'a stately and beautiful Portia . . . at her best in the scenes . . . with the caskets; these scenes, with the reception of the three suitors and their attendants, being magnificently staged.'

'In the endeavor to give some plausibility to her disguise in the trial scene, Mlle Bonafé is almost too conscientious. In her white wig and spectacles she bears a stronger resemblance to Lady Isabel, in *East Lynne*, than to a young Paduan advocate. . . . The trial scene is as effective as it possibly can be without the words. . . . [The] restoration of Bassanio's ring . . . takes place in a room adjoining the court, instead of at Belmont, and here Shylock is introduced, being left to the tender mercies of the crowd, whose invective has had full play throughout the entire trial.'

But the photography is 'admirable' and 'the play is produced with a lavish richness and artistic taste which reflect the greatest credit on those responsible for it.'

An analysis of a print of the film in the National Archive of the British Film Institute will clarify the structure and allow for occasional additional comment. Following the main title is an identification of the major dramatis personae, Baur as Shylock, Joubé as Antonio, Hervé as Bassanio, and Bonafé as Portia. The first picturization is

1 Harry Baur in evening clothes. Dissolve to

2 Baur in costume, bowing.

3 Subtitle: 'Mr Herve as "Bassanio".' Cut to

4 Herve in costume, bowing. Cut to

5 Subtitle: 'Mdlle Pepa Bonafe as "Portia".'

6 Bonafé in costume.

7 Subtitle: 'Venice on the Rialto. / In Belmont is a lady richly left: / And she is fair, sometimes from her eyes / I did receive fair speechless messages: / Her name is Portia.' (I, 1, cut)

8 People on a stage street, painted backdrop. Business of everyday life. Bassanio waits for Antonio, who arrives and greets him. There is long and meaningless talk, presumably related to the previous subtitle. Shylock enters from upstage, the crowd hooting at him. Antonio greets him, evidently at his door. but Shylock rejects his advances and enters his house. (Adapted from I, 3),

The crowd indicates someone's approach. It is Portia, accompanied by attendants and suitors. She is greeted by Bassanio who kisses her hand and converses with her at undue length. She leaves, followed by attendants, and suitors who glare at Bassanio. This is a new scene. As Bassanio and Antonio talk, cut to

9 Subtitle: 'Thou knowest that all my fortunes are at sea / Try what my credit can in Venice do.' (I, 1)

10 Antonio's house, interior, where Antonio and Bassanio discuss obtaining money. Bassanio receives a letter from Portia. (New)

11 Subtitle: 'If I live to be as old as Sybilla, I will die as chaste as Diana, / unless I be obtained by the / manner of my father's will.' (I, 2)

12 Bassanio reads the letter, passes it to Antonio to read. Some rather silly acting: business of leaning on the mantle looking elaborately thoughtful about where to obtain credit. They leave the scene. Cut to

13 Subtitle: 'Three thousand ducats; well / For the which as I told you Antonio shall be bound.' (I, 3)

14 Shylock at a chest in his house. Since there is a black curtain in back of him and he is dressed in black, it is difficult to see what he is doing, possibly counting, tallying, worshipping his gold. He hears a noise, goes to the door, listens, returns, closes the chest, again goes to the door, goes out, returns with Antonio and Bassanio, sits on the chest. There is discussion about money, some mutual revulsion, then an agreement under conditions before the preparation of a document. There is good business here, and good playing. This sequence is a sweeping adaptation with interior scene of I, 3.

15 Subtitle: 'If you repay me not on such a day / In such a place such sum or sums as are / expressed in the condition, let the forfeit / be nominated for an equal pound / Of your fair flesh to be cut off and taken / In what part of your body pleaseth me.'

16 Bassanio reads the bond, objects; Antonio laughs, pulls it away, signs. Shylock sees Antonio and Bassanio out, returns, and shakes his fist at them. (Adapted from same)

17 Portia's house, a stage set. Portia and attendants have some meaningless business, a bit of a solo dance, etc. From a window, Portia and one attendant, a counterpart of Nerissa who is not named and has no part in the plot, see Bassanio arriving. In their excitement, Bassanio enters, bows; attendants retire as he talks to Portia. She motions him out. Portia and attendant embrace. (An adaptation of the end of II, 9, and the beginning of III, 2) Cut to an empty room.

18 Subtitle: 'End of Part One.'

19 Subtitle: 'Part Two.'

20 Subtitle: 'Behold, there stand the caskets, noble Prince: / If you choose that wherein I am contain'd, / Straight shall our nuptial rights be solemnized.' (II, 9, 4–6, but addressed to Morocco rather than Arragon.)

21 An aisle of people, the caskets on the right, Portia up rear. Morocco enters with attendants, makes his choice – wrongly. The scene is overcrowded, and details are less than clear. (II, 7)

22 Subtitle: 'All that glitters is not gold.'

23 Arragon makes his choice.

24 Subtitle: 'What's here? The portrait of a blinking idiot / Presenting me a schedule!' (II, 9)

25 Bassanio chooses successfully. He kneels as Portia comes downstage, kisses his forehead. He rises, leads her upstage. (III, 2)

26 Subtitle: 'This house, these servants, and this same myself, / Are yours, my lord: I give them with this ring: / Which, when you part from, lose or give away, / Let it presage the ruin of your love.' (III, 2)

27 The end of the marriage ceremony in a chapel, including the giving of a ring. As Portia and Bassanio approach the camera from the rear, Bassanio receives a letter. The onstage ceremony is new, the receipt of the letter from III, 2.

28 Subtitle: 'Dear Bassanio / My ships have all miscarried, my creditors grow cruel and my bond to the Jew is forfeit. If your love do not persuade you to come, let not my letter / Antonio.' (III, 2)

29 Antonio leaves. Apparently Portia plans something but what is not clear. (Based on III, 4) She leaves. Cut to

30 Subtitle: 'I am sorry for thee: thou art come to answer / A stony adversary, an inhuman wretch / Uncapable of pity, void and empty / From any dram of mercy.' (IV, 1)

31 The court scene, with the Duke speaking, upstage; tables on left, people on right, forming an aisle. The learned doctors in robes. Antonio and Bassanio are at the left. This is a peculiarly rigid, crowded, and unsatisfactory setting. Dark costumes are against a dark background. It is difficult to pick out the principals or follow the action. (IV, 1) Cut to

32 Subtitle: Bellario's letter. (IV, 1)

33 Shylock enters and sits on floor, right, while spectators shake their fists at him. Portia and Nerissa appear. There are no subtitles here in the Archive print; apparently they have been lost. The Kleine title list has six, dealing with the proceedings up to the judgment, the most relevant are a part of 'The quality of mercy . . .' speech; 'A pound of that same merchant's flesh is thine. / The court awards it, and the law doth give it.' 'Tarry a little; there is something else. / This bond doth give thee here no jot of blood; the words expressly are "a pound of flesh".' The Archive print resumes with

34 Subtitle: 'Take then thy bond, take thou thy pound of flesh: / But in the cutting it, if thou dost shed / One drop of Christian blood, thy lands and goods / Are, by the laws of Venice, confiscate / Unto the State of Venice.'

35 The reactions of the participants. Shylock is violent and vengeful. Portia is thanked.

36 Subtitle: 'And, for your love, I'll take this ring from you.'

37 Bassanio, urged by Antonio, reluctantly gives the ring to Portia. She leaves as the two friends talk. (End of IV, 1)

38 Subtitle: 'Give him this, / And bid him keep it better than the other ... / By heaven it is the same I gave the doctor.' (V, 1)

39 Portia in an anteroom; she takes off her cloak. Shylock is dimly seen as a mass on the floor upstage; around him, Bassanio, Antonio, and others enter. Portia's demand for her ring is followed by explanation and expostulation until she shows her lawyer's gown, and all is forgiven. Shylock rises and comes forward. Why is he there unless to give the character and actor the end of the film? He grovels, falls flat, picks himself up, and leaves. (A bit of V, 1, except Shylock.)

40 Outside scene, where Shylock is reviled by the crowd. He pushes his way through, staring down those who intercept him, and leaves, apparently into his own house. Shylock shows a certain fierce dignity here, but he is otherwise wholly unsympathetic. (New)

41 A final shot as at the beginning of the film, with Baur as Shylock in costume. Since he is laughing, the sequence is either misplaced or wholly out of key.

Lopped, then, in the adaptation of the play are both the subsidiary love affairs, Launcelot and Old Gobbo, Jessica's flight from her father's house, the masquers, Shylock's relation to Tubal of the theft of his property, Antonio's arrest, and most of Act V. The story has essentially been simplified to the involvement of Shylock with Antonio and the love tale of Bassanio and Portia. For a length of two reels, this paring is sensible enough, and if some scenes are not clear, it is not the fault of the scenario. The direction is ordinary or worse: there are too many people masking the principals; there is too much action at a distance from the camera; there is too much stage convention in the arrangement of the players. The photography is clear, but the settings, indoors and in the simulated outdoors, are theatrical or badly planned in terms of light and dark, and the costumes do not stand out from the scenery. What is lacking is cinematic sense and taste. What is best about *Shylock* is a pretty heroine and the impressive characterization which Harry Baur in his first film was able to build. Already the actor could demonstrate both personality and vitality, and could adapt his theatre training into appropriate cinematic projection. In his case at least the end of *film d'art* demonstrated possibilities for the future of Shakespeare films.

In England prominent Shakespearean actors, following the lead of Tree and Benson, continued to appear in films of plays in which they had achieved a reputation on the stage. 1913 saw two such pictures, *Macbeth* with Arthur Bourchier and his wife, Violet Vanbrugh, and Sir Johnston Forbes-Robertson's *Hamlet*. The success of the first was indifferent. Early in the year, Ludwig Landmann, who had represented Nordisk in London, established in the outskirts of Heidelberg a large studio for a company called the Film Industrie Gesellschaft which was to specialize in 'classical and romantic subjects of a convenient length'. According to first reports he brought to Germany a company of English actors, and chose for performance, *Macbeth*, *Hamlet*, *King Lear*, and *The Merchant of Venice*. One trade paper by July 24th could announce that Bourchier and Violet Vanbrugh 'are said to have been engaged . . . at a fee of £1,000, to be filmed in *Macbeth*. They will speak English, but the rest of the cast will render the German translation.' If the company was English, why would they speak German? Another, a bit later, was more circumstantial:

'The visit was arranged by Mr Acton Bond, the director of the British Empire Shakespeare Society, of which Mr Bourchier is a vice-president.

'"Mr Bourchier is the first of a series of 'stars' who, it is hoped, will go out to be filmed," said Mr Bond to a representative. "He will be supported by an all-British company, which has been at Heidelberg for some weeks. Arrangements have been made for producing the play in the same manner as at the Garrick Theatre. It is quite possible that after *Macbeth* has been 'filmed', other plays will be arranged for. The event is notable in that it is the first time an all-British company has been invited to Germany for the purpose." '

By September 4th, however, when the company itself advertised the film, it was indicated that the 'other principal parts [were] played by leading German actors.' I can only conclude that Bourchier, who was easily dissatisfied, did not like the English actors Landmann had engaged before he was approached, or that their maintenance abroad was too expensive, and consequently they were replaced by Germans.

In August, production was under way. Macbeth's castle was a conversion from ruins near Bad-Dürkheim, but parts of the film were shot at Hardenberg, now Neviges, southeast of Velbert. Rain, however, spoiled the sequence of the meeting between Macbeth and Lady Macbeth (I, 5), and this was reshot in England 'at Lululand, the beautiful home of Sir Hubert von Herkomer at Bushey. . . .' The scene was photographed outside the painter's house, and an anachronistic water pipe made necessary a later cutting of those frames which showed it. Such doctoring postponed the release of the film by A. E. Abrahams of Stratford from late September until November 17th. The footage was variously announced as 4200, 4500, and 4700 feet, and the production 'as played at His Majesty's Theatre'. Bourchier, his wife, and Mr Bond all professed delight in the new film. The reviewer in the *Kinematograph and Lantern Weekly*, October 9th, on the whole did too:

'The filmed version of *Macbeth* may prove to be one of the outstanding successes. ... We were permitted to have a private view of the film . . . , and found that all the trumpetings which had preceded its introduction are in no measure unjustified.

'*Macbeth* . . . offers difficulties in the way of adaptation for pictures because of the vastness of the canvas on which the happenings are pictured, and because of the strong individuality of the outstanding characters who figure in the scenes.

'But the producers have surmounted the imposing difficulties in a way warranting the warmest praise. They have contrived to give us a . . . version of the story which is tense with dramatic power, which grips the imagination, which is set with singular success, and acted with rare discrimination. It is full of Shakespearean detail, is rapid in action, possesses no obvious anachronisms, and photographically is admirable. Evidently considerable trouble has been taken by the company to ensure *vraisemblance* with the background. . . . Equal trouble, too, must have been taken to ensure the most careful reproduction of the domestic court life of the half-barbaric times . . . and the conviction carried by this effort is naturally emphasized by the exactitude with which the uniforms and liveries have been copied.

'Mr Arthur Bourchier and Miss Violet Vanbrugh play the two principal roles . . . magnificently. Mr Bourchier's acting on the legitimate stage is invariably characterized by a quiet subtlety which it would be impossible to efficiently translate through the medium of pictures, but in acting before the camera he has broadened his style, amplified his gesture, and developed increased facial expression, with the result that his success is far more pronounced than that which has attended several other of our eminent actors who have sought to act for pictures. Miss Violet Vanbrugh has that virile style and strong dramatic resource which makes her ideal for a tragic role, but if she has done anything more instinct with graphic power than her Lady Macbeth, we have not had the privilege of seeing it. In conjunction with her husband, she scores in *Macbeth* an undoubted triumph, naturally overshadowing the achievements of the rest engaged in the production, although their capabilities are beyond question. In some of the fighting scenes – they are somewhat unequal in quality – there is a vim and *abandon* about those engaged that is refreshing to see, and the final combat between Macbeth and Macduff is done with fine fervour. Again the art of the subordinate actors is fully attested in the scene round the witches' cauldron, which has a weirdness that cannot fail to impress, the 'visions' being secured particularly well here – much more felicitously, in fact, than when Banquo's ghost appears to Macbeth.

'It would be idle to deny that the production is not perfect. The lack of any ceremonial in the burial of Lady Macbeth and the death struggles of Banquo are two small blemishes, but they are, indeed, so small as not to warrant undue emphasis. What might be emphasized, however, is the able way in which the murder scenes are enacted. They are not shown either in the case of the murder of the King or of Banquo, but they are implied in an unmistakable way, without anything that might be considered gruesome.'

In view of the faults observed, I suspect the reviewer is rather too polite, though the *Cinema News and Property Gazette*, October 15th, mentions the 'lifelike and spirited elaborations of the siege of Dunsinane Castle', Miss Vanbrugh's 'feline', 'seductive', and 'comprehensibly dominating' Lady Macbeth, 'the barbaric in Mr Bourchier's make-up ... [which] quite belongs to the age mirrored in the architecture', and 'the movement and excitement' of the banquet scene. 'After the sleep-walking scene ... comes a succession of bright landscapes culminating in the numerous phases of the assault. ... The advance of the attacking forces beneath the branches from Birnam Wood, their scaling the sheer rectangular keep, the desperation of the defense, the hand-to-hand fighting along the mural chambers and galleries are all most vivid. Macbeth's final combat is robust and archaic enough for patrons of films anywhere – his knowledge of distance and a certain little side-step have charms of their own.' Evidently Bourchier thought so. Never a modest man, he thought 'the production really magnificent'. On the other hand a piece in the *Moving Picture World* on November 15th, though calling *Macbeth* 'a most sumptuous production', said 'the effective work was not done by the stars but by the photoplayers employed in their support. These expressed the story in action where the stars adhered to stage methods. ...'

Three years later there is no doubt about American opinion. The picture was copyrighted in the United States on March 7, 1916, by Lucky Film Producers, and distributed in five parts by the Big A Film Corporation in an obvious effort to cash in on Tree's *Macbeth* made in California. Apparently meant to be accompanied by dramatic readings to cover the mouthed, but unheard speeches on the screen, and advertised as 'played on the historic ground at Dunsinane Castle', it was called in the *Moving Picture World* of July 8th 'an entirely inadequate production of Shakespeare's tragedy. ... Arthur Bourchier, as Macbeth, and Violet Vanbrugh as Lady Macbeth, are unimpressive. The picture was cheaply staged and poorly photographed.' There was amplification a week later:

'Pictures such as this five-part version of *Macbeth* might be passed by as harmless save that they tend to create a false idea of what is being accomplished in the handling of classical subjects. Anyone seeing this production and taking it as an example of what Shakespeare on the screen means would be careful to avoid Shakespearean pictures in the future, thereby reducing the patronage for commendable works. The Big A Film Corporation is distributing old trash on the strength of a great name, trusting in its power to draw a public that does not discriminate between the products of various manufacturers.

'The version of *Macbeth* under consideration is so ridiculously inadequate in every respect that one may seek in vain for a redeeming quality. Apparently the picture was made a number of years ago by a director unversed in the finer points of photoplay construction. The plot is followed accurately enough, but never for a moment does one sense even a suggestion of the spirit of the tragedy, either in the performances of Arthur Bourchier as Macbeth and Violet Van Brugh as Lady Macbeth, or in the atmosphere of the production. To make the unpleasant impression complete, there are five reels of poor photography.'

Granted that the reviewer has the superior advantage of looking scornfully at a film which was three years old, and that a good deal had been accomplished in the interval in the United States, not yet directly involved in the War which had stifled European production, the least one can say is that the English reviews of 1913 were over-flattering, and that in any case the film did not wear well. I find no mention of Macbeth by English handlers after June 14, 1914, and no public distribution in America after the *débâcle* of 1916, when it was first introduced there after being significantly ignored.

It is impossible to be accurate about what was in the film except for the information conveyed by the reviews and a synopsis, no doubt untrustworthy, in the copyright file. One may surmise from these that the picture began with Macbeth's encounter with the witches (I, 3), that he may have been shown dispatching a letter to Lady Macbeth (if so, new), that the meeting of Macbeth and Lady Macbeth follows I, 5, that Macbeth commits the murder off-stage and that Lady Macbeth takes the daggers back to the drugged servants (II, 2), that Macduff discovers the crime and gives the alarm (II, 3) but escapes with Malcolm to England rather than going to Fife. Subsequently we see Macbeth's feast with or without the plotting with murderers, Banquo's death throes but not his murder, and Banquo's ghost (a combination of III, 1, 3, and 4); the cauldron scene (IV, 1); possibly but only possibly the murder of Lady Macduff and her children (IV, 2), and Macduff's reception of the news (IV, 3). Shown too are Lady Macbeth's sleep-walking (V, 1), perhaps her suicide (reported in V, 4), and her burial (invented). The rest of the photoplay elaborately included Birnam Wood coming to Dunsinane, the attack, the fighting, and the death of Macbeth (some combination of V, 4, 5, 6, 7). Without the film, without any knowledge about the cutting, with confusion between what was recited and what was pictured, one can say no more.

Bourchier, of Eton and Oxford, where he was one of the founders of the University Dramatic Society and acted in its productions, married Miss Vanbrugh in 1894, and from 1900 to 1906 managed the Garrick Theatre. He first played *Macbeth* there with her in December 1906. He joined Tree at His Majesty's in 1910, and was Macduff in Tree's *Macbeth* in 1911. He had already appeared in Tree's picture of *Henry VIII* as the King along with his wife as Queen Katharine. With his experience he probably directed the film himself. He was a good actor, devoted to his chosen profession, but difficult to get along with, conceited, and truculent. Violet Vanbrugh, a fine actress and a distinguished Lady Macbeth on the stage had much to do with

Bourchier's success on the stage. I cannot conceive that with their lack of experience in film, their pictured *Macbeth* could bear any relation to this success. None of the other planned Shakespeare films was ever made.

Not planned until after the Bourchier–Vanbrugh *Macbeth* was being made but released before it, was another and much more important production which reflected the éclat of the British theatre. The finest Hamlet of his time was Johnston Forbes-Robertson. Urged to play the part by Sir Henry Irving, advised by George Bernard Shaw in a letter which unfortunately has been lost, Forbes-Robertson had opened in *Hamlet* at the Lyceum on September 11, 1897. Though he did not follow all of Shaw's recommendation, that critic in his pronouncement in the *Saturday Review* of October 2nd called the presentation 'a prodigious success. . . . Nothing half so charming has been seen by this generation. It will bear seeing again and again. . . . Mr Forbes-Robertson's own performance has a continuous charm, interest, and variety which are the result not only of his well-known grace and accomplishment as an actor, but of a genuine delight – the rarest thing on our stage – in Shakespeare's art, and a natural familiarity with the plane of his imagination.' After its Lyceum run, Forbes-Robertson took the play on tour on the Continent and in America and kept it in his repertory. His formal farewell to the English stage in a series of performances began at Drury Lane on March 22, 1913, and ended on June 6th. Fittingly enough the series both opened and closed with *Hamlet*. The actor was knighted during the final week.

The prestige accompanying Forbes-Robertson's English farewell led naturally enough to a desire to make some permanent record of his *Hamlet* and to make some money out of it. Less than a week later, on June 12th, the *Kinematograph and Lantern Weekly* announced: 'The Gaumont Company were able to persuade the eminent actor, Sir J. Forbes-Robertson, on the eve of his retirement, to allow his magnificent production of *Hamlet* to be perpetuated on the screen. The work of preparing and taking the picture has been entrusted to the Hepworth Company. . . . Beautiful scenery . . . has been made for the production, and will be used for all the interior scenes, whilst the principal studio has been specially enlarged for the occasion, and will be used for no other work until the picture is completed. Elaborate preparations are being made at Bushey, where there is some beautiful natural scenery peculiarly suitable, and a temporary outdoor studio has been erected there. . . . In addition to this, a magnificent castle on the cliffs of Lulworth Cove is being built, an exact replica of the famous old castle still standing in Denmark. . . .' Two weeks later, the cost was estimated at £10,000, and it was noted that Forbes-Robertson would have the Drury Lane Company of seventy in support. On July 24th, a special supplement supplied by Gaumont identified the cast which included Forbes-Robertson's wife, Gertrude Elliott, as Ophelia:

Claudius	Walter Ringham
Horatio	S. A. Cookson
Polonius	J. H. Barnes
Laertes	Alex Scott-Gatty
Ghost	Percy Rhodes
Fortinbras	Grendon Bentley
Rosencrantz	Montague Ruthurford
Guildenstern	E. A. Ross
Osric	George Hayes
Marcellus	A. Roberts
Bernardo	G. Richards
Francisco	R. Ericson
Reynaldo	Eric Adeney
First Player	Robert Atkins
Second Player	R. Andean
First Gravedigger	J. H. Riley
Second Gravedigger	S. T. Pearce
Priest	R. Montague
Gertrude	Adeline Bourne
Player Queen	Olive Richardson

There was some doubling here. A. Roberts was really Robert Atkins; G. Richards, Richard Andean; R. Ericson, Eric Adeney; and R. Montague, Montague Rutherford. Why Gaumont felt it necessary to be excessively moral about *Hamlet*, it is difficult to ascertain, but along with the cast it printed the following remarkable comment, later reproduced in the souvenir programme:

'In this play we see exemplified the proverbial saying "Murder will out", for by introducing the ghost of the murdered King, Shakespeare intended, no doubt, to intimate that though secrecy may veil the deed of the murderer for a time, Providence, that "suffers not a sparrow to fall to the ground unnoticed", will by supernatural agency both expose and punish the aggressor.

'In the death of the queen we are warned against participation in the fancied success of villainy, and in that of Laertes against suffering our passions perfidiously to lead us to seek a secret revenge without a regard to either justice or our own honour. He has our contempt but might have commanded our pity and admiration.'

How this would have delighted Shakespeare, and Forbes-Robertson, if he ever saw it! The same supplement announces the release date and footage as September 22nd in 6000 feet, and quotes the Bristol *Evening News* of June 23rd as saying that the garden and graveyard scenes were taken at the home of Maxine Elliott, Gertrude's sister, Hartsbourne Manor, Hertfordshire. 'The grave was dug in the ground and an old Norman church erected in solid wood.' Other locations were specified in the *Illustrated London News*, which carried two pages of stills on July 5th. Ophelia did wander into the lake at Hartsbourne Manor but natural scenery was also used at Halliford-on-Thames and Walton-on-Thames. At the first it was an orchard supposedly adjacent to Claudius' castle; at the second, the Queen watched Ophelia gather flowers. Interiors by Hawes Craven were staged at the Walton studio. The director was E. Hay Plumb, who had been one of Hepworth's actors; the supervision, by Cecil Hepworth himself.

Forbes-Robertson had agreed to an engagement with Hepworth for three weeks. His reluctance was due to his shyness; he dreaded being watched by bystanders, and must have had some agonizing moments. Plumb reported that the star's dressing room at Walton was across from the studio. 'Sir Johnston used to wrap his *Hamlet* coat about him, resign himself to the inevitable, and walk straight across the road, removing any odd stones with his foot or sword. ... [He] ... was quite shy of being seen by the outside world until we took him to the Castle of Elsinore at West Lulworth, where he didn't mind anything. ... [He] ... invariably greeted ... [his] own appearance in black and white with shrieks of laughter during the most serious moments. ... "I've got a mouth like a cavern", while Miss Gertrude Elliott's contribution to the general flow of comment during the graveyard scene (with a fairly strong wind blowing) was: "Just look at your hair". In filming well-known actors in plays they have become famous in, I have always found it difficult to persuade them of the necessity for slight additions. ... Forbes-Robertson was quite averse to Ophelia picking flowers by the willow that "grows aslant a brook", but to do [him] ... justice, [he] ... liked and agreed with it when the finished production was shown.'

Hepworth indicated, however, that, though it was necessary to convince Forbes-Robertson of the value of what then were considered close-ups, the actor understood the need to adapt himself to the new medium. His own aim he saw as to produce a fair representation of *Hamlet* as played on the stage, but not just a photograph of a theatre performance, to give the impression which an audience would receive in the theatre but in a different way. Words were, so far as possible, to 'be translated into action'.

'It was necessary to interpolate all sorts of scenes visualizing episodes which are merely described in the play. The Queen's explanation that she has seen Ophelia gathering flowers by the side of a glassy stream, is, for instance quite useless for the purpose of the pictorial vision; we had to show the incident in actuality. Wherever possible, we took the beautiful scenery painted by Hawes Craven for Forbes-Robertson as our model for the special cinematograph scenery which it was necessary to construct, but where he had used flat cloths, we had to use solids, including huge carved Norman columns 2 ft 6 ins in diameter. Then ... we built a complete reconstruction of Elsinore Castle at Lulworth Cove. It took us a week to find a suitable spot, and it was so secluded that all the building materials had to be carried over a sort of rugged mountain pass. As the plaster required alone weighed two tons, you can imagine this was no light business.'

Hepworth had used Lulworth Cove since 1910 as a background for short subjects; he was to use it again. For the ghost scenes at the Cove he converted the balcony, by velvet drapes, into 'a dark room in which the ghost could be filmed to the exact count that had been used in filming the other actors in the scenes'. According to one report, he took almost three miles of film before cutting to manageable size. Among scenes which the world never saw were the complaint of the Ghost that the real rocks on the Dorset coast hurt his feet, and a part of the graveyard procession in which the mourners were overcome with hysterical laughter.

There may, or may not, have been a press screening of the film by July 24th when 'Stroller' in the *Kinematograph and Lantern Weekly* said he could not 'speak too highly of it. It is a most perfect production, with photography of the very best description, and is a worthy souvenir of a great actor's farewell to the stage'. We learn a fortnight later that special music was being arranged, but not until September 11th that it was 'arranged from Tschaikovsky by Professor Henry Gibson, of the Guildhall School of Music.' With or without accompaniment there is a review of breathless extravagance on August 21st of what must have been a private showing which proclaimed the picture 'perfect in every detail'. Forbes-Robertson's Hamlet was 'ideal', and Gertrude Elliott's Ophelia 'a beautiful representation'. The 'appearance and disappearance of the uneasy spirit [was] a really graphic and realistic representation. . . . This great work, expounded by the foremost artistes in the dramatic profession, cannot fail to receive public approval and should prove one of the greatest financial successes we have had for a long time.' On August 30th, Gaumont could announce in the *Moving Picture World* that 'Sir Johnston and Lady Robertson both witnessed the production a week or two ago and were highly delighted at the success of their first appearance in a picture play; and well they might be so, for the acting, staging, and whole construction of Shakespeare's tragedy is absolutely superb throughout. . . . The scene on the battlements, where the ghost of Hamlet's father appears, is a veritable *chef d'oeuvre*, and will cause boundless wonder from audiences in every portion of the civilized globe.'

Sir Johnston and Lady Robertson were on the *Mauretania*, bound for New York, when the gala premiere of *Hamlet* took place at the New Gallery Kinema, Regent Street, on September 22nd where the picture was scheduled for four weeks, but they sent a Marconi message which was flashed on the screen. 'A packed house sat enraptured for an hour and forty minutes, and watched the gradual unspooling of this beautiful and artistic rendering of Shakespeare's immortal play', said the *Kinematograph and Lantern Weekly* on the 25th; 'at the close there was enthusiastic applause for what must be looked upon as a unique achievement.' The next week 'Stroller' was 'delighted to find that Sir Johnston Forbes-Robertson's *Hamlet* has so far been a triumph for everybody concerned. The New Gallery Kinema are drawing record houses. Every paper is speaking in the highest terms of the clearness, steadiness, and altogether magnificent quality of the picture, and of the beautiful and effective settings that have been chosen, which in my opinion are the chief points of the film. . . .' The same number quoted with careful selectivity from journals which did not usually notice the cinema. The *Times*: 'The pictures were beautifully prepared, and where the play demanded action, it has been, of course, admirably supplied.' No mention was made of the *Times*'s comments on the limitations of the medium, the lack of voice and verse especially. The *Standard* noted the star 'was no less successful before the whirr of the cinema than before the glare of the footlights. His acting was most dramatic, yet pleasantly restrained – and restraint is a quality much needed on the film.' The *Daily Chronicle* called it 'perhaps, the most completely artistic picture which has so far been seen', and the *Daily Telegraph* remarked that 'It was a good thing to do, and it has been done most thoroughly and effectively. . . .' The *Morning Advertiser* said that it was 'reproduced before a large and equally enthusiastic house, including playgoers drawn from all quarters. Indeed, a proportion of the audience consisted of persons who usually pay attention only to what might be termed the theatre proper. Their applause, it may be noted, was even longer than that of the regular *habitues*. . . . Sir Johnston's facial expression and the movement of his hands are brought out in the most lifelike fashion possible, while the rapidity with which each scene is "played" and the novelty of the whole thing invests the drama with an interest which the ordinary stage performance of the play lacks. Indeed *Hamlet* on the film looks very like cutting out *Hamlet* in the flesh.' This must have seemed preposterous to the *Pall Mall Gazette*: 'To most people it will be obvious that to essay the representation of *Hamlet* without the words is to attempt the impossible. . . . Certain of the scenes gained enormously in vraisemblance by having been taken in the open air – on the seashore and in the woodland glade, and in the portrayal of the ghost, photography lent an artful aid that had a strangely thrilling effect. For the rest, one could only be grateful to the new mechanical device, which by its application lends some degree of permanency to the essentially personal ephemeral art of the actor.'

Outside of London, where *Hamlet* was being presented at the same time reports were similar. 'It is a most fascinating production' (Dublin *Daily Express*); 'The cinematograph has seldom offered more welcome artistic entertainment' (Birmingham *Gazette*); 'The resources of the cinema are indeed well-nigh inexhaustible . . . and it is by means of the camera that posterity will judge the merits of Sir J. Forbes-Robertson's *Hamlet* (Manchester *Courier*). The Newcastle *Daily Chronicle* thought the scenic arrangements 'as near perfection as possible. Of the acting it is sufficient to say that

28. Baptista introduces Katherina to Petruchio in *The Taming of the Shrew* (Eclipse, 1911). *Motion Picture Story Magazine*, July 1911

. The King (Tefft Johnson) greets a startled Anne Boleyn (Clara Kimball Young) in Vita-aph's adaptation of Shakespeare's *Henry VIII* called *Cardinal Wolsey* (1912). National Film chive

30. Rosalind (Rose Coghlan) recites the epilogue of *As You Like It*. At left, Orlando (Maurice Costello); centre rear, Oliver (Robert Gaillard) and Celia (Rosemary Theby); at right, Silvius (James Morrison) and Phoebe (Rose Tapley). (Vitagraph 1912). *Moving-Picture World*, August 10, 1912

31. A scene from Thanhouser's *Merchant of Venice* (1912). The Shylock is William J. Bowman. *Moving Picture World*, July 20, 1912

32. Leonatus (James Cruze) receives Imogen's bracelet from Iachimo in the Thanhouser *Cymbeline* (1913). *Cinema News and Property Gazette*, April 30, 1913

II visiting King Henry in the Tower of London.

Court of Edward IV.

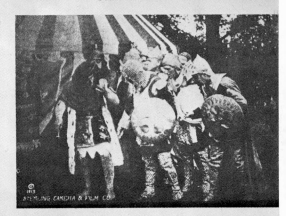

Richard III On the Way To the Battle of Bosworth Field.

Richard III and His Staff at Bosworth Field.

nes from *Richard III* in which Frederick B. Warde starred as Crookback (Sterling 1913)
Picture World, October 11, 1913

34. Petruchio (Eleuterio Rodolfi) and Katherina (Gigetta Morano?) in the Ambrosio *Taming of the Shrew* (1913). *Cinema News and Property Gazette*, September 3, 1913

35. Paulina (Pina Fabbri) presents Hermione's child to Leontes (V. Cocchi); a film strip from the Milano *Winter's Tale* (1913). National Film Archive

in the filmatised version the art of the great tragedian is enhanced, because the success of the picture necessarily depends upon the gesticulation and facial expression. . . .' Finally, the Liverpool *Evening Express* spoke of 'the high degree of excellence to which the cinematograph art has attained. . . . The production was a fine one, the many enthralling scenes in the drama being shown with remarkable effect. Particularly so was this the case in the mad wanderings of Ophelia; while the ghostly appearances of the King of Denmark were depicted with thrilling effect.' I hear three notes, however, in one way or another discordant. B. Nichols, a London film handler interviewed by the *Moving Picture World*, November 15th, said the star was not effective because he 'fitted the gesture to the speech, as Shakespeare advises, instead of suiting the gesture to the action as advised by the director.' Whether this was the reason or not, the film was not taken to the United States until 1915, when Forbes-Robertson was better known there. Finally, I cannot resist the report of a Birmingham correspondent that 'on the occasion of *Les Miserables* showing at New Street Picture House . . ., a near-by bookseller sold 2000 extra copies of various editions of the book.' He made similar inquiries while *Hamlet* was being shown, 'and learned that only 50 extra copies of the book had been sold'. Perhaps there were more copies of Shakespeare than Victor Hugo in the homes, or perhaps the exhibitor did not, like the manager of Cinema House, Rye Lane, Peckham, advertise by having a suitably dressed melancholy Dane outside the theatre, lost in the contemplation of Yorick's skull.

In September of 1913 Forbes-Robertson's *Hamlet* was shown successfully in Germany, and in India in July 1915. In the latter month it reached the United States, where the prestige of the actor, who had just finished a tour, had been firmly established and might in theory draw audiences for the film. On the 7th it was released on its regular programme by Knicker-bocker Star Features, which announced that: 'This picture alone remains to please his many followers.' It may have been cut, for a summary indicates that it was in three parts; on the other hand there is evidence to the contrary, and three parts may merely mean that a part consisted of a double reel. Evidently the film made little stir, for after July 10th, when it was reviewed by Hanford C. Judson in the *Moving Picture World*, there is scant reference to it in the trade papers, and I find nothing after October in those of a more general nature. The review by Judson, who had seen Forbes-Robertson's *Hamlet* on the stage, is complimentary enough but tends to be general.

'If ever a great play with a well known star had advertising possibilities, Forbes-Robertson in *Hamlet* should draw from the start. The picture of the powerful player over the name *Hamlet* should and probably will draw many passers to enter and see the picture. . . . It illustrates Robertson's acting very well and is surely a valuable contribution to stage history. The person who cares nothing for Shakespeare, or Forbes-Robertson, or for good acting, will be entertained not by a powerfully moving story clearly told, but solely by the inherent grace of the illustrations such as an artist might place in a book. *Hamlet* is a play that should never be put into pictures for the gallery, but there is justification enough in Robertson's acting of Hamlet, in Gertrude Elliott's playing of Ophelia, and in the support that the Drury Lane players give these two stars.

'There is no actor today whose playing of this character reaches so noble a height as Forbes-Robertson. The things that he brought out of the spoken stage play absolutely astounded this reviewer when he first saw him in the part and the play is so tremendous that, see it as often as you please, the mind is not able to grasp it all at once. The depth, of course, is not in the story, but in the poetry and in the humanity, which in this play reveal themselves in the rhythmic lines themselves, then in the interpretation and finally in the stage sets and background illustration. The picture gives the backgrounds as no stage could; it also gives that part of the acting which is not dependent on the words of the poet, but solely on the actor's knowledge of their meaning. This is only a part of the whole.

'There are scenes in the picture of special excellence and two that are particularly beautiful and effective. The first of these, in which there is undeniable poetry, is the mad scene where Ophelia distributes flowers. In this scene, set in a church yard, the center that catches and holds the eye is the face of the actress, Gertrude Elliott, full of meaning and subtlety, pathetic in all its changes, showing both the lovely garden of the soul that was and the ruin that is; as true to madness as sweet chords mixed with discords. The last group of scenes, beginning with the duel of Hamlet with Laertes and closing with the coming of Fortinbras, is impressive and dramatic, though silent. The acting of Robertson rises to its height, and the Queen, the King, Horatio and Laertes are all human and convincing. It seems to be an exact replica of the stage business and is thoroughly worthy. It is an offering especially made for lovers of the stage and admirers of Robertson, of whom there are many.'

Unfortunately, perhaps, those who had seen the actor on the stage did not go to the film, and American filmgoers of 1915 were not much interested in *Hamlet* or Forbes-Robertson or stage-history.

Two specifications in the review just quoted are of considerable interest since they demonstrate that the motion picture *Hamlet* followed recommendations made by Shaw for the stage version. One was that Ophelia's mad scene be played in a garden setting; here, as we have seen, it was an actual garden. The other was the restoration of Fortinbras's appearance in the final scene, action which had not appeared in the theatre for generations because stars preferred not to have at the end a competing character and speeches which might draw the attention away from Hamlet to the summary of past events and the question of the succession. Shaw had also urged the inclusion of IV, 1, in which Fortinbras's appearance prompts the soliloquy, 'How all occasions do inform against me ...' because he wished to emphasize the contrast between the personalities of the two men, but Forbes-Robertson did not follow this suggestion. The actor did, however, take Shaw's advice on emphasizing in appropriate scenes Hamlet's urbane humour and on presenting the play in a brisk tempo. On the stage Hamlet did not show an awareness of the eavesdroppers in the nunnery scene, again following Shaw's views, but the film includes the traditional business. Forbes-Robertson's stage arrangement of *Hamlet* followed with few exceptions Shakespeare's text. The ambassadors in I, 2 and II, 2 were cut, as were some of Hamlet's obscenities and the dumbshow in III, 2. Act IV was shortened and the two scenes between Claudius and Laertes (IV, 5, 7) were telescoped into one. An examination of the film version will show how closely Forbes-Robertson followed his own text, and what adaptations were made for the film.

The extant version opens with a Prologue introducing Forbes-Robertson and Gertrude Elliott. Hamlet is shown writing in his 'Tables' (I, 5), and Ophelia with flowers (adapted from IV, 5). I am not positive the original film had this prologue, which may be made up of clips from later scenes. The picture continues with action sequences numbered in their order of appearance.

1 The court scene. Laertes, with the permission of Polonius presents his petition to leave for France. Hamlet is visible throughout the scene and bows farewell to Laertes. Claudius urges Hamlet not to return to Wittenberg; Hamlet accedes to the Queen's wish that he stay. As throughout, the speeches are much shortened, especially Hamlet's soliloquy after the others go out. (I, 2, with the first part omitted.)

2 A platform outside the castle of Elsinore (Lulworth). The Ghost appears to Horatio, Marcellus, and Bernardo. Double exposure is used on the whole effectively, but somewhat awkwardly since the Ghost is not always in the right place for the actors' gestures and address to him. (I, 1)

3 Back to the court. Hamlet, alone, is greeted by Horatio and the soldiers. Horatio informs Hamlet of the Ghost's appearance. Hamlet plans to watch. There is just a suggestion of the soliloquy. This is, however, a good scene, where action and expression adequately convey the meaning. (I, 2)

4 Laertes warns Ophelia. Polonius enters and advises Laertes, who departs. Polonius counsels Ophelia. (I, 3)

5 The platform. Hamlet and Horatio see the Ghost, which Hamlet follows. (I, 4)

6 On the rocky shore. The Ghost reveals Claudius' perfidy. Hamlet faints, as the ghost vanishes. Enter Horatio and Marcellus. Hamlet recovers consciousness and swears them to secrecy. The actors have some trouble with their footing. (I, 4, 5)

7 Ophelia reports Hamlet's strange behavior to Polonius. I do not find Reynaldo in the scene. (II, 1)

8 The interior of the castle. The King asks Rosencrantz and Guildenstern, identified by a subtitle, to try to discover why Hamlet acts so strangely. Rosencrantz and Guildenstern leave. There is no report from the ambassadors, who are not in the film. Polonius enters; indicates he has found the cause of Hamlet's madness and shows to the King and Queen the letter Hamlet has written to Ophelia. Exeunt Claudius and Gertrude. Enter Hamlet, who reads at a lectern, with his back to Polonius, whom he scarcely bothers to notice. Polonius leaves as Rosencrantz and Guildenstern enter and talk briefly with Hamlet. As Rosencrantz and Guildenstern leave, Polonius enters, is befuddled by Hamlet, and announces the arrival of the Players, who enter. Hamlet's plan to re-enact his father's murder is made intelligible only by a subtitle, and the final soliloquy is meaningless. (II, 2)

9 The King and Queen receive the report of the two spies, who leave. Claudius and Polonius plan to observe Hamlet with Ophelia. Exit Gertrude. Polonius instructs Ophelia. He and the King hide behind a curtain, stage right. The soliloquy is very brief, but the interview between Hamlet and Ophelia fairly full. She is seated in a chair at a table, Hamlet behind her. He reaches out as if to stroke her hair, when a hand grasping the curtain reveals the presence of the eavesdroppers. Hamlet's tenderness turns to repulsion. They leave severally. I do not find the ensuing conversation between Claudius and Polonius. (III, 1)

10 The instruction to the Players is not included. Hamlet enters with the Court. The King and Queen sit on a kind of bench-throne stage left, Ophelia in a chair, stage right. The play-within-the-play is presented upstage centre in a raised area behind an arch. Hamlet on the floor gradually creeps from Ophelia's feet to the King. Claudius' consternation is followed by his departure along with the rest of the Court. Hamlet's triumphant conversation with Horatio is curtailed. Exit Horatio as Rosencrantz and Guildenstern enter and are taunted by Hamlet. Horatio enters with a Player carrying a recorder. Exit Horatio. The pipe scene is given in full. Polonius re-enters to tell Hamlet his mother wishes to see him, and after Polonius leaves, Hamlet himself departs. (III, 2)

11 The King tells Rosencrantz and Guildenstern that they are to accompany Hamlet to England. The Polonius bit is cut. The prayer scene is effectively mimed, though the speeches are unintelligible. (III, 3)

12 The closet scene is shown complete. Polonius hides. Hamlet upbraids his mother and kills Polonius. The Ghost appears. Gertrude believes Hamlet mad. Hamlet comforts the Queen. (III, 4)

13 In a garden. Enter to the King and Queen, Laertes threatening. Ophelia, mad, appears and offers flowers. She wanders off through a wood by a brook. Of Act IV, scenes 1, 2, 3, 4, the beginning of 5, and all of 6 are omitted. (IV, 5, much adapted)

14 The messenger hands Claudius Hamlet's letter. This is odd, since we do not know of his departure. The pirate ship business may have been shown in the original film, as is intimated by the summary in the *Kinematograph and Lantern Weekly*, August 21, 1913. (IV, 7)

15 A cross-cut shows Ophelia continuing to wander, picking flowers (visually an original scene but based on the Queen's speech at the end of IV, 7).

16 The King and Laertes plan Hamlet's death. (IV, 7)

17 The Queen, standing by the side of the brook, gives a violent start, apparently to indicate she has seen Ophelia's body in the water, but if there was in the original film a scene of the drowning it has been lost. Gertrude rushes away. (New)

18 The Queen brings to the King and Laertes the news of Ophelia's death. Laertes mourns. (End of IV, 7)

19 A churchyard, a Celtic cross in the background. The Gravediggers at work. The second Gravedigger is sent off. Hamlet and Horatio appear. Hamlet talks with the first Gravedigger. There is little comedy in the scene, which is used largely for the business of Yorick's skull. The funeral procession enters. The grave is now seen to be near a church. Hamlet and Laertes have their brief encounter, not in the grave, and are parted. (V, 1)

20 In a wood, heavily ferned. Hamlet's and Horatio's conversation is interrupted by Osric, who delivers the challenge. The 'Lord' is omitted. (V, 2, beginning)

21 Really three shots, close up, against black background. These are the only close-ups in the film. The first shows a rapier being unbated by a hand; the second, a hand putting poison on the rapier; the third, poison being poured in a cup. The first two are original, the third from V, 2.

22 The final Court scene. The apology is minimal. The foils are selected. The duel begins with Hamlet upstage facing the camera, Laertes downstage, Horatio with his back more or less to the audience. The King and Queen are on thrones, stage right. The many courtiers make a crowded scene. Hamlet wins the first bout, is offered the cup, and declines. He wins the second bout; Gertrude wipes his face and drinks the poison. The third bout is won by Laertes, not while Hamlet is off-guard, but Hamlet recognizes from the nature of his wound that there has been treachery. Laertes is hit by the poisoned foil. The Queen dies. Claudius' guilt is proclaimed. Horatio supports Hamlet. Hamlet does not kill Claudius on his throne or use the poisoned cup. He is given a rapier, and the actual killing is masked by the crowd downstage. The extant version ends with Hamlet's being pulled up to the throne, where, seated, he dies. Horatio puts the crown in Hamlet's hands on his lap. All kneel in homage. The summary in the *Kinematograph and Lantern Weekly* says, 'The concluding scenes show us the death of Rosencrantz and Guildenstern and the selection of the new King of Denmark', but these scenes have been lost. (V, 2)

The deficiencies of Forbes-Robertson's *Hamlet* film are easy to specify. The essential problem remains of the presentation of Shakespeare without the poetry. The interior shots are more theatrical than cinematic, though the area of action is even more confined than it would be behind the proscenium arch, and there is no sense of depth. The grouping of actors is stage grouping, and in the limited space, scenes are often crowded with characters who interfere with a focus on the principals. Main characters edge off the lateral sight lines and are cut in two or vanish, as for example in the final scene where Claudius is at times almost a nonentity. In one case the exasperated cameraman, who could not pan, apparently twisted the stationary apparatus during the action to keep a character in focus. The properties are few, chairs, table, lectern, fur rugs. The star was sometimes noticeably careful not to trip over the rugs. The studio shot decor consists generally of a one-level floor, curtains as backdrops (or sidedrops which provide wings), and massive plaster or papier-maché Norman pillars. The last are about the only means to provide solidity for the interior of Elsinore. The shots with the few exceptions noted are medium, so there can be little variety or cinematic rhythm. Finally Forbes-Robertson was sixty years old, though he looked younger, and Gertrude Elliott nearing thirty-nine, hardly suitable for an inexperienced Ophelia, though appropriate enough for this more than mature Hamlet.

Yet assets more than match liabilities. Hepworth's exterior shots at Lulworth Cove, in garden and churchyard are interesting and effective to the eye, and modify the monotony of the shooting distance and the stage arrangements. They provide scenes which are more than a cramped recording of a Drury Lane production. The supernatural element is better handled than it usually was on the stage. Some of the action here and elsewhere comes through without the words. If the film did not vastly appeal to typical motion picture spectators of 1913, it is a remarkable record of a remarkable performance for those who know the play. And the age of the star, as we watch the reels unroll on the screen, becomes less and less noticeable. The day after the film was revived at the National Film Theatre on April 24, 1960, the *Times* said accurately that it was 'far in advance of its time', and 'the performance a resurrection astonishing in its vigour'.

The truth is that Forbes-Robertson triumphed over his medium. Some of the roles other than Hamlet are well played. J. H. Barnes's Polonius is not a fool but a sensible white-bearded patriarch who will stand no nonsense; his garrulousness is minimized in silent action. S. A. Cookson makes Horatio considerably more than a character for Hamlet to talk at. He is solid, sensible, and devoted. Gertrude Elliott in her outdoor scenes conveys Ophelia's madness with affecting simplicity and economy of means. But Forbes-Robertson is necessarily the centre, and one cannot come away from a screening without recognizing that here was a great Hamlet. Unlike most stars of the period who made films, he never gives the impression of tearing a passion to tatters. Partly because it was his own style, partly because he was able to make some adjustment for the camera, he underplays; the result is that expression and gesture and bodily movement convey nuances of character with extraordinary effectiveness. His Hamlet is not mad, nor overtly feignedly mad, but marked by a courtly dignity; he is a lonely intellectual caught in a dilemma. Naturally one wishes for the voice, and I have heard it on records, the advice to the Players, and the 'O, what a rogue . . .' soliloquy. It is a fine voice, a deep baritone; the articulation is precise and the tone and pace capable of dramatic variety; the voice itself becomes an interpreter to the thought. But these speeches are absent or unimportant in the picture, and film was unfortunately not yet ready for sound. However the rugged, though sensitive face, the deepest piercing eyes, the grace and significance of the figure in action create a sustained intensity in the film. An interpretation created from the poetry strangely enough adds a kind of poetry to the visual medium. If silent film could not encompass Shakespeare, Forbes-Robertson's *Hamlet* reaches toward a fuller recognition of the possibility.

The films of 1914 did little to encourage that possibility. There was the usual traffic in Shakespeare's name, one spectacular picture which was only partly dependant on *Julius Caesar*, and three more or less direct adaptations of his plays. Among the trifles, a Hepworth *Princes in the Tower* may serve as a transition since the castle built for the Forbes-Robertson *Hamlet* was used for some of the scenes, but I do not know its exact date, nor how much it was Shakespearean, or if it was at all. Hepworth himself said 'little Reggie Sheffield (Eric Desmond) [was] one of the victims'.

However, *Romeo and Juliet* takes the usual precedence in popularity in offering suggestions or descriptions of 1914 films, and three of these were made in the United States. The earliest was a Keystone comedy called *A Robust Romeo*, released on February 12th, with Fatty Arbuckle as a swain who covets his neighbour's wife and is properly punished; 'Romeo' equals 'lover', and there is nothing more. Biograph came ridiculously closer with a *Romeo and Juliet*, exploiting a modern Irish–Italian feud, a fight at a quarry between Mike Montague and Pete Capulet, and an escape by Romeo and Juliet in Romeo's rag wagon. A half-reel, it was released on May 21st, and was characterized as a 'rattling good burlesque'. American Kinema contributed *A Modern Romeo* in 1225 feet in which the hero's fiancée is attracted to an actor. The hero enlists the assistance of the actor, who plays drunk. Disillusion of heroine; clinch. This is T. W. Robertson's *David Garrick*, not Shakespeare – except for the title. *Rural Romeos*, made by Luna but released by Warner Features on December 17th was equally distant; it featured Dot Farley. The foreign product, made by Comica, I find only with a German title, *Romeo geht ins Kino*. The Comica studio was a Pathé establishment on the Côte d'Azur directed by Roméo Bosetti, who also played in a Romeo series. The Romeo of the title may not be Shakespeare's Romeo at all.

The distribution of borrowings from other plays is sufficiently wide to make an alphabetical listing as good a procedure as any. Shakespeare, bandied about in so many other ways, got into a serial, *Nina of the Theatre*, which Kalem issued by two-reel instalment. The first, reviewed in the

Moving Picture World on May 30th, has an irrelevant story about an actress (Alice Joyce) who is in love with an actor (Tom Moore), but includes two stage scenes in at least one of which the actress played Rosaline in *As You Like It* to the actor's Orlando. In England, Bransby Williams was photographed in the impersonation of his stage success, *The Seven Ages of Man*; the film was produced for Planet by Charles Vernon, no doubt as he liked it. At least a reviewer said: 'These seven little studies in make-up and expression are swift, terse, complete and altogether delightful'. *All's Well That Ends Well* seemed at the time doubly newsworthy. The British rights to a picture with this title credited to the Tyler Film Co. were sold at auction in January, but Tyler was more renter than producer, and this film was probably Eclair's un-Shakespearean comedy of 1912 with which its footage checks. Princess Films produced another *All's Well That Ends Well* for release on February 20th but this American product about the misunderstandings of two suitors for the hands of a widow and her daughter was not at all well in its 'broad humor without finesse' and knew nothing of Helena and Bertram. I am more pleased by Thanhouser's *Two Little Dromios*, if only because this is the first film which has a relation beyond title to *The Comedy of Errors*. Released on January 11th, 'this single reel works up so entertainingly that the story could well be carried through a second reel. Mignon Anderson plays the double part of a country and city girl, double exposure being used to advantage. The country girl comes to the city; the city girl goes to a masquerade as a country girl and they are thus confused.'

Does *Hamlet*, planned but unreleased, or used for comedy, or excerpted for an actor's recital in a modern story deserve a new paragraph? Vitagraph in the *Moving Picture World* announced the first on May 23rd to be directed by James Young with Young in the title role and his wife, Clara Kimball Young, as Ophelia. By August 8th the cast had been selected for this 'magnificent production', and the director was 'busily engaged with rehearsals of what is expected to be the most pretentious film story of a classic ever filmed. . . .' L. Rogers Lytton was to portray Claudius; Lionel Belmore, King Hamlet; Julia Swayne Gordon, Gertrude; Charles Kent, Polonius; and Arthur Cozeng, Laertes. It would be a pleasure to see again the old familiar faces, but somehow or other the film died. If it was rehearsed, it was never produced or released, and I suspect that James Young, who had played Hamlet on the stage, aroused company enthusiasm only temporarily. The records in the hands of the Vitagraph custodian show only that the picture was assigned to him, not that it was conducted to termination, and it was not copyrighted. The vacuum is hardly supplied by *Martin as Hamlet*, produced in Germany by Neue and distributed in England by Cosmopolitan for June 1st release in 715 feet. 'Martin is to play Hamlet. He commences to rehearse at once. Donning a very unique costume and picking up his part, he starts. The servants, however, are quite convinced that he is mad and have him conveyed to the police station. Here the chief official is also addressed in language which is strange to him, and our hero is cast into gaol. . . . Fortunately for him, his wife turns up, he is released and all ends well.' More serious is *La maschera che sanguina*, produced by Pasquali in 1000 metres. An actor recites a *Hamlet* soliloquy to applause, and the daughter of a rich banker falls in love with him. The rest of the picture deals with their romance and despite opposition their marriage. The actor was interpreted by Alberto Capozzi, whom we have met before.

Once more remove, good friends, first to a *Love's Labour Lost*, a drama of 998 feet, released in England on October 19th, about a smuggler who gives himself up to revenue officers in order to save his sweetheart from drowning, and dies in the process, and then far away from the coast to Snakeville. *When Macbeth Came to Snakeville* was one of a series of rural Western comedies featuring Victor Potel as Slippery Slim, Margaret Joslin as Sophie Clutts, and her husband, Harry Todd, usually, though not here, as Mustang Pete. 'Snakeville is all in a whirl, the world's greatest tragedian is to appear in *Macbeth* at the "Opry House". The "Tank Town" troupe arrives and stops at Slim's boarding house. Slim discovers his wife, Sophie, paying attention to the leading man and that evening at the performance she goes into hysterics at the marvellous acting of her ideal. That night she walks in her sleep, and imagining herself to be Lady Macbeth, gets a butcher knife and enters the room of the "Would-be Macbeth". The actor is frightened nearly to death. Sophie finally awakens, but it is not in her power to persuade the actor to remain in town another day, so he leaves, much to the satisfaction of Slim.' Essanay was responsible for this picture, released September 3rd, or irresponsible. If *Macbeth* could be turned into comedy so could *Othello*, twice in 1914. *Leonce Plays Othello* was also one of a series of film comedies made by Gaumont featuring Léonce Perret. This picture of causeless jealousy in 955 feet was released in England on July 9th, but except for the *motif* had no relation to Shakespeare. Nor did *A Modern Othello*, produced by American Beauty and released in 990 feet on September 1st, in which Marguerita Fischer and Harry Pollard appeared. It was a comedy of modern life involving a jealous husband. If Romeo means lover, Othello means jealous husband. That is all ye know and all ye need to know. On the other hand *The Taming of the Shrew* means the taming of the shrew, as in a modernized comedy of that name which stemmed from Denmark's Nordisk. In three reels, it starred the dancer, Rita Sacheto, under the direction of Holger Madsen, but the story is irrelevant. *The Tempest* of July 13th in 224 feet was only a tempest, a topical of a storm at sea, released in England as a reissue by R. Prieur. About *Das Wintermärchen* in three reels with Senta Söneland, Albert Paulig, and Richard Senius, released in Germany by Belle Alliance, I know nothing but it could be anything.

Two films somewhat more pretentious than these short or hazy ones appeared in 1914. One was a remake but not a reissue of *Les Enfants d'*

G*

Edouard; the second, inspired no doubt by this being the sesquicentennial of Shakespeare's birth was a film about Shakespeare himself, which included excerpts from his plays. Since *The Children of Edward* is an adaptation by Paul d'Ivoi of Delavigne's adaptation of Shakespeare, it need not occupy us further, but it was three or four times as long as the Film d'Art version of 1910, with which it has often been confused, and had a different cast. An advertisement by Le Cosmograph, 'Exclusivité de France-Cinéma-Location', in *Ciné-Journal* of March 14th calls it a 'Grand film inspiré du Général [in later issues fortunately corrected to 'génial'] Shakespeare et du Grand Poète, Casimir Delavigne. Adaptation de M. P. d'Ivoi. Mise en scène de M. Andréani. Mlle Delvair, de la Comédie Française = La Reine Elisabeth / M. (Jean) Toulout, du Théâtre Antoine = Le Duc de Buckingham / Mlles Suterre, du Théâtre Sarah Bernhardt, et Marcelle Fleury, de l'Opéra = Les Enfants d'Edouard / M. Vague [Georges Wague], mime de l'Opéra = Le Duc de Gloucester / Mlle Maipolska [Maiapolska], de l'Olympia = La Sorcière Rahel / M. Jacquinet, mime de l'Opéra = Le Roi Edward.' The story and nature of Delavigne's play have already received sufficient comment, but d'Ivoi added 'La Sorcière', an attendant of Queen Elizabeth who disguises herself as a sorceress, Rahel, to penetrate the intentions of the Duke of Gloucester, there are further complications to the intrigue, and the battle of Bosworth Field occurs in the city streets and Richard's death in the Queen's palace. In England, Cosmograph advertised the picture, there called *The Princes in the Tower*, in *Bioscope*, on April 2nd, with remarkable inaccuracy as 'adapted from the work of William Shakespeare' and a 'faithful reproduction of the English historical episode'. The review of May 7th praised the picture as 'a very effective and beautifully mounted drama', but properly noted that M. Paul d'Ivoi 'with somewhat inaccountable modesty has shared the credit with Shakespeare, though the film has no more in common with Shakespeare's play than the ever-popular "Jane Shore".' It was not historically accurate either, but the attribution of a Shakespearean source was Cosmograph's, not d'Ivoi's. In any case it is not a Shakespeare film, and therefore something too much of this.

The Life of William Shakespeare, a new aspect of film's Shakespeare industry, was made between December 1913 and February 1914 by British and Colonial. The interior and London scenes were photographed at the company's studio, Hoe Street, Walthamstow; the open-air scenes, at Stratford. There was considerable insistence on authority and accuracy by J. B. McDowell, the managing director. Names dropped in the announcements included Sir Sidney Lee, Halliwell (without the Phillipps), Capt. Curling, the unidentified Mayor of Stratford, Flower (Chairman of the Shakespeare Memorial Theatre), Sir Henry and Lady Fairfax-Lucy of Charlecote Hall, the Rev. Hodgson of Clopton Hall, Canon Melville of Stratford-on-Avon Parish Church, and Mr Wellstead, librarian of the Trust at Shakespeare's House. The cost was estimated at £4,000, the cast named as

Albert Ward (Shakespeare), Eva Bayley (Shakespeare's mother), Sybil Hare (Anne Hathaway), Miss Bennett (Charlotte Clopton), Aimée Martinck [Martinek?] (Queen Elizabeth), Gray Murray (Hugh Clopton), and George Foley (Sir Thomas Lucy). Frank Rawlings, a former Benson actor, was identified as co-producer. The picture was to contain one hundred and fifty scenes, one of which would represent the Globe Theatre, and furniture for studio scenes was to be brought from Anne Hathaway's cottage. By February 12th there had been a trade screening which was reviewed by 'Stroller' in the *Kinematograph and Lantern Weekly*:

'I am about the last person who should review a film of Shakespeare, for I do not possess an atom of poetry in my nature, and am apt to look for the practical and financial aspect of a subject in preference to the aesthetical and poetical. Still, I found yesterday, when I saw 'Shakespeare' run through . . . for the first time, that we had a subject containing both attributes. I wondered how so vast a subject would be dealt with and now do not know which to congratulate most – those who provided the scenario, and so cleverly chose and interwove the interesting points in the life of the Bard, or the producer, who has chosen the scenery and interior views, which, to my mind, are some of the most beautiful and typically English scenes we have yet filmed.

'The subject is lavishly sprinkled with titles, but instead of the usual monotonous descriptions we had carefully selected quotations from Shakespeare's works, which, because of their peculiar aptness, add materially to the interest in the story of his life. . . . The film has plenty of variety in its incidents and gives a wide scope. . . . Mr Albert Ward in the title role fits the various phases of the poet's life in a thoughtful manner, without obtrusiveness or self assertion.

'Altogether the subject deserves the most careful attention of the renter. . .'

Another commentator – in the *Cinema News and Property Gazette* of February 19th – notes that 'in the final stages of the film, Shakespeare is seen dreaming of his plays. They are superimposed on the picture and represent scenes from *The Merchant of Venice*, *Macbeth*, *Hamlet* and *The Merry Wives of Windsor*.' In France, Monatfilm, its distributor, calls the picture on March 7th a 'reconstitution historique absolument remarquable', notes that it was given a private showing at the West-End Cinema to Shakespeare admirers and authorities, and quotes rave reviews from English newspapers.

With all this fanfare we shall want the story, and the best summary of it in English is to be found in the *Moving Picture World* of June 13, 1914. The American importer of the six-part picture was Trans-Oceanic Films, which no doubt supplied the distressing detail about what was later titled in the United States *The Life of William Shakespeare: His Intrigues and Romances* or *The Loves, Adventures and Life of William Shakespeare*.

'The romantic attachment which the humbly born William Shakespeare had for the beautiful and gentle Charlotte Clopton, of Clopton Hall, is authenticated by the letters of many people of the period, and as it is one of the most potent factors in the development of the genius of Shakespeare, it is very appropriate that the film should open with the first meeting of the future playwright and the beautiful young girl. This acquaintance always remained a romantic one on the part of young Shakespeare, but Charlotte felt the attraction more seriously.

'Meanwhile, Sir Hugh Clopton, Charlotte's father, who is an ardent Catholic, shelters in his house a man named Parry, who is a traitor to the Queen; he does this at the command of Pope Gregory XIII, not knowing the character of the man he is harboring. Shakespeare, pursuing the apparently gay and thoughtless tenor of his career – but in reality training the great qualities of mind which were to make him famous – displeases a lawyer [his name was Grasp] in whose employ he has been, and while he is trying to explain this to his mother, a tragic scene takes place in the assassination of the traitor Parry. Too late, Sir Hugh Clopton learns of Parry's treachery, through Shakespeare's employer, who informs Sir Thomas Lucy of the plot, and also accuses Sir Hugh of being in it.

'Sir Hugh's celebration of his daughter's birthday is rudely interrupted by the arrival of soldiers, who are come to arrest him for complicity in the treasonous design. The Queen pardons Sir Hugh, but his lovely daughter falls ill of a mysterious malady, which is wrongly diagnosed as the Plague, but which is a fatal one, nevertheless despite the great danger of infection, Shakespeare bids her a passionate farewell before she dies. Some months later Shakespeare – now beginning to be the great man of his village – champions pretty, shy Anne Hathaway at the Twelfth Night Revels. Their acquaintance ripens, and their courtship is played out in the beautiful environs of Stratford and about the Anne Hathaway cottage.

'In sharp contrast to the idylic Anne Hathaway of the courtship, the wedded wife of Shakespeare is undoubtedly the shrew, whose tongue drives Shakespeare to the distractions of the 'Lucy Arms'. This condition of things, added to the fact that Shakespeare has incurred the displeasure of Sir Thomas Lucy by his poaching exploits, drives the young man to leave home. He decides to try his fortunes in London, so takes leave of Anne and his child and starts away. In London, Shakespeare views the great crowds of richly dressed people with astonishment, but he soon wins friends. The theatre, of course draws him, and outside the historic old Globe Theatre he looks upon the scenes of his future triumphs.

'The genius of the young dramatist is soon discovered by the great Lord Southampton, who becomes his generous patron and introduces him to the court of Queen Elizabeth, where he meets Raleigh, Drake, the Earl of Essex, and all the famous political and social figures of the time. The command performance of *Romeo and Juliet* in the Blackfriar's Theater which is attended by the Queen and all the Court, marks the beginning of that triumph which was, through the following year, to be the great crescendo of English literature.

'The final stages of the film show Shakespeare in the glow of middle age. He is dreaming of his past successes, scenes from his great plays visioning themselves before him. The film closes with the fading in and fading out of the bust of Shakespeare [à la Méliès, 1907], which is in the Parish Church of Stratford-on-Avon.'

This farrago of largely invented nonsense was advertised by Sawyer, the American distributor, with the assertion that 'the great bard's life was one long series of adventures, romances and intrigues; far surpassing the imagination of modern scenario writers are the facts that history has brought down to us, and which are so strikingly recorded in this picture'. I doubt if Shakespeare ever turned in his grave, but if he did, this film must have provided the impulse.

The *Moving Picture World* evidently thought a special review was advisable, and assigned the task to E. Boudinot Stockton, S.T.B. He pointed out in the issue of October 24th that the Sawyer release was 'in no sense a biography of Shakespeare, but as its [American] title indicates rather a portrayal of the romance and poetry of his youth and early manhood.' This deviation, however, bothered him less than certain religious implications.

'. . . the undertaking is a most ambitious one and on the whole the results in production are remarkably good, despite the fact that the story is a little too long drawn out and sketchy in the last two reels and that the photography might have been better. The papist plot against the life of Queen Elizabeth has also been handled crudely and inaccurately and in such a way that it is likely to shock Roman Catholics of today both here and in Canada. . . . We understand, however, that the print we saw was an imperfect copy of the original negative. . . . A careful revision of this negative is now being made so as to adapt the story to American and Canadian ideals and way of looking at things, and as all the blemishes, except perhaps some of the photographic ones, can easily be remedied in this way, the story promises to be one of the best of the many good things put on the market by that company. . . . The greatest pains have been taken to reproduce in costumes, properties and settings the actual atmosphere of the old Elizabethan life . . . when its revision . . . is completed . . . the picture should rank as one of the great productions of a great year.'

Was there a similar reaction in France? It was announced there on May 2nd that public presentation of the film would be postponed to September. The reason given, however, was 'la température réelment trop clémente qui rend aléatoire les grosses transactions. . . .' At any rate neither clemency or inclemency made the film a success in either country, and in England, the

Kinematograph Year Book of 1915 under December 1914, is content with calling it 'an immense costume and spectacular drama' – this and nothing more. It *was* nothing more.

Late in 1913 Rex released a picture called *The Jew's Christmas* about a rabbi who having disowned his daughter for marrying a gentile, is reconciled by a Christmas Eve meeting with a child who turns out to be his granddaughter. The scenario had been concocted by Lois Weber, who with her husband, Phillips Smalley, both directed the film and acted its leading roles. *The Jew's Christmas* particularly interested Carl Laemmle, whose Universal group included Rex, and led to the production by the same team of *The Merchant of Venice*, presented as a Universal Special Feature in four reels. Made at recently acquired studios in Hollywood it was heralded as 'one of the most elaborate, from the point of costly costumes and scenery, that the Universal has ever turned out. So careful have the Smalleys been to render the production technically correct that many of the Venitian street scenes were repainted four and five times before they would answer the specific requirements of the producers.' In an interview with George Blaisdell after a screening in New York of *The Merchant of Venice*, Smalley revealed that he thought this 'was the best work he and Miss Weber had done for the screen'. Blaisdell comments:

'In all truth, it is beautifully staged and costumed, well acted, and a remarkably faithful adaptation of Shakespeare's text . . . he expressed a belief that of all the plays of Shakespeare there was none containing less action than *The Merchant of Venice*, especially for screen adaptation. When we suggested to Mr Smalley that the Shakespearean subject from a pictorial viewpoint was splendidly conceived and executed and that from a dramatic standpoint apparently nothing worth doing had been overlooked, still from the human side, in deep appeal to the sympathy and in pathos, it did not approach *The Jew's Christmas*, . . . [he] admitted that he enjoyed portraying the rabbi a good deal more than he did Shylock. "The rabbi was much more human than Shylock", he said. . . .

'Surely in Mr Smalley's interpretation of the dramatist's great tragic figures there is much material for pleasurable study. It is a portrayal that one will want to see more than once. Miss Weber, in writing the text, is said to have aimed to bring to the play a slight modern touch, but the language of the twenty-one players was the language of Shakespeare. Miss Weber made a charming Portia. Mr Smalley was advantaged in making the production by the fact that he had seen Irving play Shylock forty-seven times and has also witnessed the performance of Forbes-Robertson and Sothern.'

Among the 'twenty-one players' were Rupert Julian as Antonio, Edna Maison as Jessica, and Douglas Gerrard as Bassanio.

The Merchant of Venice was released during the last week in February but reviewed by Hanford C. Judson in the *Moving Picture World* on February 14th with the heading 'Full of Dignity and Scholarship', which for a romantic comedy with serious overtones sounds somewhat ominous.

'Shakespeare could be a careful weaver of plots and many of his plays are perfect in the artistic setting forth of the story, but his mind was so rich that he often makes story overlap story. In *The Merchant of Venice*, there is the interest of which Shylock is the center, and there is Portia's love story, with the relief and criticism that it gets from Jessica's adventures in love, and besides these, one or two smaller stories such as the comedy episode of the rings. In making a picture of the play for the average spectator, it is inevitable that the love story, with its broad emotional appeal, should be prominent, and in producing this picture, the Smalleys have fortunately done just this. In doing so they have brought out much of its wonderful significance. It is hard to estimate the value of this picture to the thoughtful mind or to praise it too highly as interpretation, for thus setting it so clearly forth leaves us free to catch the deeper significance of the different threads that are fed into it. These things are subtle, and, in their scholarly and dignified production, the mind will catch glimpses of things that a newspaper reviewer of the picture cannot stop to develop. Suffice it to say that it is very rich in sidelights on Shakespeare's human truth, and has value aside from its entertainment.

'As an offering of entertainment to the public, the picture has many fine qualities. While the love story is being developed, it is deeply absorbing, the more so because Jessica's love affair in the narrower compass of four reels is brought in closer relationship to Portia's romance and greatly enhances its value. The center of this is Lois Weber as Portia. The charm, the dignity, the womanliness that are needed to make the spectator feel the great value of the prize Bassanio has at stake are all there. The courtliness of her surroundings is not overdone. Her palace, her attendants, etc., are reflections of herself; it shows art that they are only what is needed. She is not well supported in Bassanio, whose lovemaking is unfortunate. The choosing of the caskets in each of the three cases has been made into an impressive ceremony, and in each case it is done slowly enough so that the significance of it can sink into the mind. We want to repeat that the whole picture gets its peculiar quality from the fact that the condensation helps us to see the whole at a glance, so to speak. The author of the scenario, Lois Weber, shows wisdom, too, in the quick strokes with which she has drawn Jessica's elopement with her father's jewels and ducats. It is like a flash to one side, as though one said, 'See how others, under other circumstances, enjoy their romances'. Jessica is played by Edna Maison, who, without attaining any passion, has given an even, pretty portrayal. The episode is light and acceptable rather than especially praiseworthy. Antonio, the merchant, is convincing in both affection and dignity; is a man of worth and honor; but we are not made deeply interested in his fate, for the terror that Shakespeare put in the play is not brought out strongly.

'The role of Shylock is played by Phillips Smalley, and while it is certainly a good, human piece of work, it hardly does justice to the skill of the actor. In make-up, in bearing, in the self-respect due his grey hairs and keen mind that has carried him successfully through one long battle against great odds, the Jew is all that could be desired; but the bitterness of the struggle is not there. Even when he sharpens the knife there is no real ferociousness in him. This is not to be wondered at. The poet's lines carry, when spoken, continual suggestions to the heart of the player and to spectator alike. In drawing such a character, the living vibrations between these two must count for much. Here, the whole scheme of the picture makes it hard for the spectator to understand the attitude of Shylock. He is not likely to fear the kindly eye under Mr Smalley's bushy eyebrows. Thus the pert mocker of the 'A Daniel Come to Judgment' episode rather hinders than helps.

'The ending of the story which gives us the story of the rings is a bit obscure. Such as do not remember the story will be apt to miss some of it. Of the staging the highest praise is due. Many of the scenes make lovely pictures, and none of them is awkward. Grace, dignity and charm are found all through the offering.'

Universal's *Merchant of Venice* was then careful, respectful, dignified but lacking in passion and poetry. One reason why emotion was underplayed may be revealed by the difficulty the picture had in passing the censors. A prominent rabbi in Chicago strenuously objected to its approval on the ground that the play, 'more than any other book, more than any other influence in the history of the world, is responsible for the creation of a world-wide prejudice against the Jew'. He thought the picture 'not fit to be shown to children' and found especially repugnant 'the scenes showing Shylock groveling on the ground and clutching his beloved money'. The Board overrode these criticisms but they would hardly have promoted the success of the film. In addition it is apparent that the cast with the exception of Lois Weber was not really up to interpreting Shakespeare on the screen. It was reported that Smalley had played leading Shakespearean parts on the stage. That may be but I do not find him doing so in New York, where he had been in relatively minor roles with Mrs Fiske and in a musical farce with Raymond Hitchcock. Moreover, since *The Merchant of Venice* was a 'special feature' rather than a release on the regular programme, exhibitors had to pay extra for it. Their reluctance probably contributed to the swift demise of the only American direct adaptation of Shakespeare in 1914.

In such adaptations of the year, Italy led the way, though one of its three films could hardly be designated as direct. Guazzoni's *Julius Caesar* for Cines was like his earlier *Antony and Cleopatra* an historical spectacular with only minor borrowing from Shakespeare. The two films indeed were of the same sort in their elaboration and their appeal. *Julius Caesar* was reported as being eighteen months in production and as having a cast of 20,000. There was extensive promotion before the picture was completed. George Kleine in the United States copyrighted it on May 12th by depositing in Washington title, description and 146 prints, but re-entered on October 21st after publication. He announced it as to be ready about June 15th, but there was delay; on September 19th it was 'nearing completion' and was to include 'a miniature city of Rome covering six square blocks, and a stone fortress built after the Gallic fashion of the times more than a mile in length. . . .' Guazzoni was said to have had eleven assistant directors, the advice of two professors of archaeology, and to have spent $750,000. Trade reviews stressed the adjectives powerful, spectacular, impressive, brilliant, lavish. We learn that eighteen seamstresses worked five months on costumes, and that Victor Emanuel visited the studio during the staging. A play was made for the academic audience. In December it was scheduled for private showings at the University of Pittsburg and by Professor D. Armes of the University of California in the 'magnificent ballroom of the St Francis Hotel at San Francisco', where those attending included 'more than three hundred professors' from leading educational institutions, not to mention 'artists and musicians of note'. It was 'without doubt the greatest gathering of cultured folks ever assembled here to view a moving picture. Included in the assembly were representatives of the American Philological Association and of the American Historical Association, and many scientific bodies . . . [who] . . . thunderously applauded'. In Portland, Oregon, the local distributor offered 'a complete set of Shakespeare's works to the school boy or girl who wrote the best essay on "Caesar" from the film portrayal'. *Julius Caesar* was first publicly shown at the Butterfly Theatre, Milwaukee, on January 11, 1915. Spectators by this time must have felt they would get their money's worth for the general admission of ten cents; box seats, evening only, twenty cents.

In England reports on the film begin in June 1914, but it was not given private screening until almost a year later. Walturdaw, securing the British rights, announced it for release on October 11th. The journals called it 'the most remarkable and striking production yet given us . . . an intellectual treat', 'greatest triumph', 'the most enthralling film ever produced. . . .' A tie-up was made with the *Teacher's World* with the hope that *Julius Caesar* would be a 'special lesson in all the schools throughout the country'. By July 22nd it had already been booked for India. In Italy the picture, there called *Cajus Julius Caesar* was advertised in November 1914 with credits: 'Ideato dal Prof. Raffaello Giovanoli [Raffaele Giovangnoli], messo en scena dal Cav. Enrico Guazzoni . . . interpretato dai celebri artiste: Sig. E [Amleto] Novelli, Sig.*ª* [Gianna] Terribili-Gonzales, Sig.*ª* Mastripietri, Sig. [Ignazio] Lupi, Sig. Ricci. . . .' Prolo adds Lea Orlandini to the cast, and gives the operator as Antonio Cufaro. In Germany notices began to appear in July 1914, and a long series of ecstatic reviews in December. War delayed any showing of the film in France, but it was ultimately received there with great enthusiasm. Like his *Antony and Cleopatra*, Guazzoni's *Julius Caesar* was a triumph.

But not a Shakespearean triumph, as a brief synopsis will show. For five of its six reels it was not based on Shakespeare at all, and it may well be that Kleine's prints of the sixth reel with their Shakespearean subtitles tended to over-emphasize the indebtedness even there. The film shows Caesar's love for Servilia, of the house of Cato, who marries Marcus Junius and bears Brutus. Caesar marries Cornelia, daughter of Cinna. The displeasure of Sulla, the dictator, is followed by Caesar's exile and divorce. Twenty years elapse before Caesar returns to seek the consulship; opposed by Cato, he is championed by Calphrunia, whom he marries, and Pompey. Cato denounces Caesar to the senate and implants his hatred in his nephew, Brutus. Caesar plans to conquer Gaul, and is saved by Calphurnia from being stabbed by the Priestess of Gaul. The Romans rout the Gauls and capture Vercingetorix. 'Veni, vidi, vici'. Pompey announces the victory to the senate. Three years later, Pompey is Caesar's enemy and opposes a proconsulship for him. Antony warns Caesar of the senate's hostility. When its wishes are communicated by Brutus, Caesar's soldiers plan to kill Brutus, but Caesar saves the son of the woman who was his first love. He decides to march on Rome and crosses the Rubicon. The senate proclaims him a traitor but the citizens applaud him. Caesar opposes Pompey, robs the Temple of Saturn to pay his soldiers, routs Pompey who flees to Africa, returns to Rome in triumph, and is made dictator. Cato hatches a conspiracy which Brutus is chosen to head. So far, allowing for invention, compression and adaptation, the Giovangnoli script is based on Plutarch and Caesar's *Commentaries*. With the sixth reel there is detail provided from Shakespeare to illustrate subtitles or which the subtitles illustrate. Brutus receives the anonymous letter: 'Brutus, awake'. The soothsayer warns Caesar to beware the Ides of March. Caesar refuses guards. The soothsayer again warns Caesar that the Ides of March are 'not gone'. Caesar in the senate refuses a petition and is assassinated: 'And thou too, Brutus.' Antony says, 'Thou art the ruins of the noblest man. . . .' Antony's forum speech, interlarded with Shakespearean quotations, is given in more detail than classical sources provide. The riot and the deaths of some of the conspirators are shown. The picture concludes with mourning. Guazzoni's film is in short a spectacular presentation of the life of Caesar from youth to death, brilliant in its handling of crowds, somewhat floridly acted by Amleto Novelli as the hero, well photographed, presented on prints washed in different colours (mostly sepia), and one of the most remarkable products of 1914, but it is not essentially based on Shakespeare and borrows from him only for the conspiracy, the killing of Caesar, and the immediate consequences of it.

The other two films, both by Ambrosio, were in one case surely, in the other probably, more faithful to Shakespeare's text. In 1914 George Kleine joined with Ambrosio personnel in the formation of a company called Photodrama and erected a large studio near Turin at Grugliasco. The corporate arrangements were complex and at this distance are confusing, since there were several Photodrama companies with different functions, including one in Paris and another in Illinois. One purpose was to film in Italy American and English actors in their dramatic successes. Included was Mrs Leslie Carter in her highly popular part in Belasco's *DuBarry*, in which she continued to play for years. In the Ambrosio film her chief support was A. Hamilton Revelle, who acted in a number of Italian features during 1914. Revelle, the son of an officer in the Royal Horse Artillery and a Spanish mother from whom he took his stage name, was born Arthur Louis Hamilton Engström in Gibraltar in 1872. At the age of fifteen and for six years he was with Augustin Daly's company in the United States. In 1891 he returned to England, became an understudy for H. B. Irving, and subsequently played Horatio in one of Tree's revivals of *Hamlet*. He made his reputation as the handsome leading man of Olga Nethersole, alternating between England and America and becoming a matinee idol. He vanished from the English speaking stage in 1912, appeared in continental films and was engaged in 1914 by Ambrosio to star in twenty productions. Only a few were made before the onset of war cancelled the others, and in December Revelle was back in New York. He retired in 1921 to private life but did not die until 1958 at the age of eighty-five.

One of Revelle's Italian films was apparently a *Hamlet*, and since George Kleine did not import it, it was probably made after the other Ambrosio-Photodrama Shakespeare of the year, *Othello*, which Kleine did distribute. Probably Arrigo Frusta had made the adaptation, but because of the confusions of the time, reliable records are hard to come by, and this film has passed into limbo.

Fortunately, *Othello* has not. It was copyrighted on March 16, 1914, by George Kleine as 'manufactured by the Societa Anonima "Ambrosio",' Turin, with the deposit of a description, actually of Shakespeare's story, not that of the film, and 150 prints, but there was nothing in the *Moving Picture World* until May 30th when it was included among impending releases. On June 13th, it was announced as 'made at Venice, Italy, last winter by the Photo Drama Company', to be distributed by the General Film Company. 'This beautiful subject follows the Shakespeare version faithfully. The costuming, settings and photography are almost without rival. . . .' On July 4th we learn that it would be released in about five reels in the week of July 6th; on July 11th that it was 'probably the first Shakespearian story to be produced in the actual environment of the original', – which is not true; and on October 10th that its length was 4215 feet. It was reviewed as in five parts by James S. McQuade on August 1st as pure 'Ambrosia'.

'The production of *Othello* in films, as of any other of the Shakespearian tragedies, is a tremendous task that must be worthily done when once undertaken, so bright is the light of public opinion that is brought to bear on the result ... to carry the story clearly and to visualize the complex action of the characters intelligently.

'Take the character of Iago, for example. Without the spoken word it is impossible to judge the labyrinthic subtleties of his abnormally wicked soul.... The true nobility of Othello and the sweet gentleness of Desdemona can, indeed, be grasped through the medium of pictures, as is shown in these Ambrosia films, but the spoken word is also required. ...

'For what reason, I am unable to see, the Ambrosia treatment of the story makes it appear that Roderigo's suit for Desdemona's hand was fostered by Brabantio. ...

'As a whole, however, the picture story follows the Shakesperian account pretty closely.

'We are not favored with a list of the people in the Ambrosian cast, the oversight in a film of such prominence is rather unusual nowadays. Everyone will be attracted by the impersonators of Othello, Iago, Cassio, Desdemona, and Emilia.

'The "noble Moor" has been well represented, both in physique and mental parts. It is hoped that the swarthy features of his double in the pictures will not be mistaken for those of the African type. ... The gentleness, the noble-mindedness and the horrible fury of the man are well brought out. The death scenes of Desdemona and the Moor have been discreetly shortened.

'The commanding character, as seen in the films, is that of Iago. The part is excellently cast. The actor who sustains it has the face, the manner, and the youth essential, and is gifted with a fine appreciation and the art of expression.

'Cassio is also in able hands, and the artist has succeeded in conveying ... the reason for Othello's preferment of Cassio to the place of Iago. ... Roderigo is also very acceptable.

'The selection of Desdemona's representative was most happy. She is a charming woman, less attractive than Emilia in her physical beauty, but revealing a soul and devotion worthy of her great prototype.

'Great praise is due to Ambrosia for the artistic settings of the drama. The main scenes were laid in Venice by Shakespeare and the Ambrosia people took due advantage of that fact. The Grand Canal, the Palace of the Doges and other favored spots are given us as they are today. I understand that, in order to take the scenes on the Grand Canal, without having them marred by the busy rush of everyday life, all traffic was suspended by order of the municipal government for half a day.

'The attack on the Turkish fleet near Cypress is both picturesque and full of action. This scene is rendered more attractive for the educated eye by reason of the fact that the Venetian authorities loaned for the occasion galleys of the time now held guardedly as valuable relics of the fifteenth century. It will be noted in the pictures showing the engagement that a large Turkish vessel, dismasted, but still pouring shot on the Venetian fleet, is blown up. It will be remembered that in the Shakesperian story a great storm scattered the Turkish ships, many of them being sunk and others disabled. The showing of the disabled vessel in question was to conform as closely as possible to the original narrative, and this observance of history deserves due commendation.'

Exactly how this conforms 'to the original narrative' is difficult to see; there is no engagement in Shakespeare and no storm or engagement in Cinthio. However the wrong-headed but mild mannered prose of the reviewer is preferable to the lush purple of the Photodrama advertisement in the same issue which speaks of Venice as 'a very fountain-head of Romance and Adventure! The waterways of Historic Venice with its tales, ten centuries old of Passionate Loves, and Fierce Vendettas – the indolent dreamy sweep of these Gondola-ridden highways are scenes of the quaintest stories in any language!' As for the cast, it was indicated nowhere outside Italy, probably because the names would mean nothing. It is only an Italian trade paper which remedies the deficiency: Othello by Colaci; Iago by Tolentino; Cassio by Ubaldo Stefani; Desdemona by Léna Lenard. The cameraman was Beccaria. The film was released in Italy on October 19th.

In England, advertisements for *Othello* began appearing in the *Kinematograph and Lantern Weekly* on September 18, 1913, but on January 29, 1914, it was still in the making, and it was not trade shown in London by the Ideal Film Renting Co. until July 23, 1915, for release on September 20th. It was evidently a considerable success. It is nice to know that 'those who suppose that Shakespeare is not a popular draw in the picture house have evidently not gauged the attracting powers of his dramas. A conspicuous case is that of *Othello* . . . which gets a hearty welcome wherever it is shown. A typical working-class audience is that of Werkman's Hall, Ynyshir, and there *Othello* came in for great applause recently. The masses have a keener taste for classic drama than some of their destructors [sic] would have us believe.' And again: 'Who says Shakespeare cannot draw a crowd? That he can "pull" a Welsh crowd may be seen from the success which *Othello* met with at the Coliseum, Ystalyfera.' Since Ideal announced on July 20, 1916, that the film had been booked in 144 theatres, I suppose these reports do not merely represent the opinion of an enthusiastic Welshman. Across the Channel, *Ciné-Journal* began carrying the Photodrama Company's advertisements for *Othello* in 1450 metres on April 25, 1914, but the reception in France was not always the same as that in Wales. Nevertheless it was still news in August 1918 that 'the local censors of Villefranche-sur-Rhône have refused to allow the exhibition of *Othello* on the screen, because Desdemona is killed. . . .'

In addition to the hints derived from contemporary comment, it is possible to obtain some, though not exact, information about the content of the film from a surviving negative, unfortunately incomplete and badly disorganized. The picture probably began with Brabantio's recommendation of Roderigo to Desdemona or perhaps with Othello's colloquy with Brabantio, while Desdemona and Emilia listen unobserved. After Othello's departure there is evidently a time lapse. In a gondola, Othello approaches Brabantio's house to see Desdemona. Her hand is shown at a window, holding a rose. During their private meeting, Othello relates his adventures. She extends her hand to be kissed. Before a door on a canal, Othello takes his leave. He picks up the rose she has dropped, and steps into a gondola which moves off. Standing in its prow, he looks up to Desdemona at a window, and kisses the rose as she watches his departure. This shot is perhaps followed by a scene in which Desdemona displays emotion before Emilia. With Iago, Cassio, and others present, Othello and Desdemona are married. Up to here we have had a picturization of events described by Shakespeare in I, 3. Iago and Roderigo report the marriage to Brabantio, who appears on a balcony. Brabantio and others set forth to find Othello and to appeal to the Senate (I, 1, 2). Othello addresses the Senate and receives his commission for the Turkish war. At Brabantio's insistence, Desdemona is sent for and justifies her marriage to Othello. Iago plots with Roderigo (I, 3). There is a scene at the 'Osteria S. Marco', which without explanation, is incomprehensible. The naval engagement is missing, but Desdemona waves from the walls of Cyprus, as Othello approaches by ship and lands. Iago confers with Roderigo (II, 1). Cassio, drunk, fights with Montano. Othello quells the disturbance. Iago's explanation is followed by Cassio's demotion. Desdemona enters to fetch Othello, who departs with her. Iago advises Cassio to appeal to Desdemona (II, 3) and arranges with Emilia to take Cassio to her (III, 1). Inspection of the fortification may follow (III, 2). Desdemona is shown in a garden; to her come Emilia and Cassio, who asks for her intercession. Othello and Iago see Cassio kissing Desdemona's hand at his departure. She pleads to Othello for the restoration of Cassio to favor. Othello starts to follow her out, but Iago holds him back and plants suspicion. Re-enter Desdemona and Emilia. Desdemona renews her pleas, uses her handkerchief to wipe the brow of a now distraught Othello, and drops the handkerchief, which Emilia picks up. Iago takes the handkerchief from Emilia and uses its evidence and further insinuations to fan Othello's jealousy into a fury (III, 3). Desdemona again appeals to Othello for Cassio (III, 4). Iago's baiting of Othello is followed by the scene where Othello watches Iago's interview with Cassio about Bianca and the meeting between Cassio and Bianca. Desdemona's death is planned (IV, 1). No doubt there were scenes corresponding to the rest of Act IV but I can spot nothing until a conversation between Desdemona and Emilia, which may be from IV, 3. Desdemona, alone, prays. Othello accuses and then strangles her. Emilia and others, first shown outside the bed-chamber, are admitted. Othello draws a dagger and stabs himself (V, 2). Much of Act V has been omitted or lost.

The state of the negative makes futile any real criticism of the Ambrosio *Othello*. It is clear that the film followed Shakespeare's play fairly closely but must have depended upon captions for intelligibility. The interior scenes look stagy; the outdoor ones with canals, garden, and fortification, more cinematic. In general the latter derive from material which was only suggested by Shakespeare in incidental narrative. How much effect was achieved by deliberate transposition of shots or by cross cutting, the condition of the negative does not permit us to know. Some sequences show individuals alone and in movement, Othello, Iago, Cassio for example, but what they are doing or where they are going is mysterious, and the sequences cannot, nor can certain others, be properly assigned to their appropriate positions. The quality of the acting and interpretation is undetermined, and must remain so unless the negative is rephotographed, restudied, and reassembled into something like its original form. The film was probably no better and possibly much worse than the surviving Cines spectaculars which offered more opportunity for visual movement and masses, or the more closely Shakespearean pictures of 1913. It is not likely that it had the fluidity of the Milano *Winter's Tale*; it did not mirror a great performance like Forbes-Robertson's Hamlet. In its way, *Othello* probably marks the end of an era, but without more of its pattern, we cannot tell. At any rate the production of Shakespeare films was at this point disrupted by 'a pattern called a war'.

CHAPTER VII
These Visions did Appear
DURING THE WAR

AMONG the casualties of the War was film; among the film dislocations was Shakespeare on film. In combatant countries especially, there was constriction or concentration in particular areas. French cinema suffered an almost mortal blow. Studios closed or kept their doors open with difficulty or were used for other purposes. Newsreels of military action or personages and other recorded events superseded literary sources and native invention; entertainment came usually from abroad, Italy, Sweden, the United States. Italy made war pictures or continued with spectacle and sentiment. Sweden had no interest in Shakespeare, nor did Russia, Czarist or revolutionary. Germany, at first propped by Danish films, developed in isolation. In England, producers and exhibitors, hampered by taxes, regulations, and restrictions, sacrificed quality for a quantity not sufficiently supported by capital, and lost much of the market to American importation. On the other hand the industry in the United States made huge strides toward dominance. This was a major period for Griffith, Ince, DeMille, for Triangle, Fairbanks, Chaplin, and Pickford. As long as it was officially neutral, the United States emphasized its position, made pacifist pictures or ignored social trends entirely; just before and after its entrance into the War, the stress was on patriotic or propagandist films, with however the usual escape entertainment as well.

It is not surprising that under these conditions there were no strictly Shakespearean feature films in 1915, and that in 1916 such films were largely made in America: a *Lear*, a *Macbeth*, two realizations of *Romeo and Juliet*, and a picture celebrating the tercentenary of Shakespeare's birth, while only a *Macbeth* came out of France, and excluding adaptations only a *Merchant of Venice* from England. After 1916, there were before the Armistice only an Italian *Hamlet*, and doubtfully an Italian *Romeo and Juliet*. In 1918 there were no feature Shakespeares at all. It is, however, more remarkable that in the whole period between the onset of the War and the coming of sound there were fewer Shakespeare films than in either of the short spans, 1908–

1911 and 1912–1914. Clearly reasons other than the War and its aftermath inhibited Shakespeare films.

With the increase in middle class audiences which provided the profits came a decline in interest in the productions which might appeal to special ones. The rapid development and exploitation of stars with particular capabilities and appeal tended to limit the nature of the vehicles in which they appeared. Breadth of range was succeeded by typicality. When literature was adapted for the screen, it was not the classics which provided the stories, but more contemporary fiction and drama. In England, the *Kinematograph and Lantern Weekly* of April 9, 1914, headed an article, 'A Too Artistic Craze', and reported that managers and buyers complained about 'the tendency . . . to film subjects not only with which a vast number of picture theatre patrons are unfamiliar, but to sacrifice effectiveness to art. . . .' The journal objected to this view but thought that 'a little too much attention has been paid to Shakespeare lately.' The New York *Times*, November 21, 1915, indicated that William Fox, having secured the services of Robert B. Mantell, took a poll of exhibitors about their interest in having Shakespeare features. A large majority of those replying vetoed the idea. The reasons given were that costume movies were not popular, that what was wanted was society pictures, and, more sensibly, that Shakespeare should be heard. E. H. Sothern was engaged by Vitagraph in 1916 to appear in three feature films, but the *Moving Picture World* of March 11th was careful to explain that he 'will not be shown in any of his Shakespearean roles'. Sometimes producers or distributors were so chary of Shakespeare's name that adaptations of his plays were given under disguised titles. Who would recognize *Love in a Wood* as based on *As You Like It*? If early film adopted Shakespeare to be respectable, he was largely dismissed in this period as not only unsuitable but unprofitable.

There was, however, considerable filching of Shakespeare's good name in the War years, almost entirely for comic purposes. What would the film makers have done without *Romeo and Juliet*? The lovers were neither star-crossed nor piteously overthrown. Romeo's name led all the rest. There were at least nineteen short films that touched, however vaguely, on Shakespeare's play; eighteen of them were American. Sometimes the heroine's name was not Juliet, as in *Ethel's Romeo* or *Martha's Romeo*. The first was a one-reel farce which had no other discernible relationship to Shakespeare; the second, a boarding-house comedy in which an actor assumes Romeo's garb and climbs to a window to woo the cook. In *Her Romeo*, the balcony scene was drawn on for an undesignated romantic heroine, who having read *Romeo and Juliet* induces her lover to hire a Romeo costume and climb a clothes-line ladder. Discovered and pursued by her father, he is mistaken for an actor who is being chased by villagers after a poor local performance, but escaping decides that Romeo is not for him. *Her Rustic Romeo* borrowed nothing except the name. As in the last case, the title sometimes suggested locality or occupation: *A Seashore Romeo, Romeo of the Coal Wagon, A Tugboat Romeo, Two Small Town Romeos, Seaside Romeos, A Depot Romeo, A Prairie Romeo*. Only the first and the last hint at anything in Shakespeare's plot. In *A Seashore Romeo* the hero overcomes the opposition of his sweetheart's father by apparently saving her from drowning; in *A Prairie Romeo*, Billy Bones, a lovable old drunkard, serenades his love at her window and has potato peelings dumped on his head. There were *A Roaming Romeo* and *A Reckless Romeo*, and, to change the point of view, *Roping Her Romeo*, with a glance at a balcony scene in the first. Sometimes Shakespeare's title was used directly but with comic purpose. In England, Cricks and Martin produced two Shakespearean burlesques 'as performed by the "Mudford Amateur Dramatic Society".' One was a *Romeo and Juliet* which focused both on the audience – a bored schoolboy who sticks chocolates on the bare back of a lady in front of him, a footman who shouts details down the ear-trumpet of a deaf old gentleman – and on the performance, during which the struggling cast is deserted by stage hands and orchestra. There is no indication of the content of an American *Romeo and Juliet* except that it was a two-part comedy, but an earlier presentation with this title appears considerably more interesting. A review by Margaret I. MacDonald in the *Moving Picture World* of November 24, 1917, is headed: 'Prominent Sculptor in Film. Helena Smith Dayton Appears on the Screen Introducing an Animated Clay Figure Production of *Romeo and Juliet* Fashioned by Her Hand.'

'The production is a novelty in one reel. It repeats the pathetic story . . . and while it treats the matter in somewhat of a burlesque style, we can forgive this from the fact that the clay figures are necessarily more or less burlesque. All the emotions to which human kind are subject are well portrayed by these queer little figures; and in looking at the picture we are strangely conscious of the union of two of the greatest arts.

'Little need be said here of the wonderful talent of Helena Smith Dayton; her work speaks for itself. In the introduction to the picture we are privileged to watch her deft fingers fashion the form of Juliet from an apparently soulless lump of clay. This mere lump of clay under her magic touch takes on the responsibilities of life, and love, and sorrow which the play requires, and finally grasps in desperation the dagger with which it ends its sorry life, falling in tragic fashion over the already lifeless form of its Romeo.'

Another kind of animation was a split-reel cartoon film called *Romiet and Julio* but this was about a couple of cats. It included two balcony scenes, one when Julio sings from the back-fence an unmusical love-song to his inamorata who is prevented from joining him by being snatched up by her mistress, the other when Julio with the aid of toy balloons ascends to her window only to have them punctured by a vengeful magpie. This nonsense was probably more appealing than a picture with a non-Shakespearean title, *A Footlight Flame*, in which an actor is opposed in his love by the girl's father. He arranges that the girl pretend madness after seeing him play Romeo. The father calls in a hypnotist, who turns out to be Romeo, and the lovers escape by automobile in a chase ending.

After *Romeo and Juliet* it was *Hamlet* which was most pilfered. England did so twice for burlesques. Even before its Mudford Amateur Dramatic Society's presentation of *Romeo and Juliet*, Cricks and Martin had made *Hamlet*, the first of its series of 'Shakespeare Minced' comics. Here during the Society's theatricals, the village doctor (Claudius) is called away during the performance and changes his stage costume for everyday clothes in full sight of the audience; the Ghost sticks in a trapdoor; the scenery collapses and reveals Ophelia ungowned in her dressing room; the prompter falls asleep; Hamlet is unsuccessful in stabbing himself and is pelted with eggs by the gallery gods. The other burlesque was *Pimple as Hamlet* for which there is no synopsis. It was one of a long series of 'Pimple' films (1913–1916) which featured the comedian, Fred Evans, in historical or literary skits.

American comedies also contain intercalated performances of *Hamlet*. *To be or Not to Be* is about a ham actor in the sticks, who with his company leaves town without paying their hotel bill. Pursued by a constable, he takes refuge in a private house where he accidently finds long lost jewels and money, with part of which he is rewarded. The hotel bill paid, he and his troupe are at last able to give their serio-comic performance of Shakespeare. Another bad actor playing Hamlet appears in *Hamlet Made Over*. When the show fails, the manager insists on presenting a revised version to draw audiences and persuades a wealthy girl to play Ophelia. In the performance the Ghost does a song and dance with six little ghosts, Polonius wears a top hat and does a magic act, Ophelia is made up as Yum Yum and recites 'Curfew Shall Not Ring Tonight', the asbestos is lowered onto Hamlet's neck, pinning him to the stage and making him a target, and finally he is tarred and feathered. All this has an 'ancient fishlike smell'. In *Freddy Versus Hamlet*, Wiggins takes Mabel to the theatre, where they snub Freddy. Mabel flirts with the actor playing Hamlet and joins him for a soda at the drug store. Wiggins and the actor are both discomfited by Freddy. I gather that 'a remarkably active old cab-horse' stole the show, as well it might. There were also two American cartoons which bear dimly on the matter. One was part of a series, *Col. Heeza Liar Plays Hamlet*. The Colonel, in shock over an unfortunate investment, is invited to play Hamlet to the grave-digger of Charlie Chaplin at a million dollars a week. The graveyard scene drives the director into hysterics and wrecks the camera. After being kicked out of the studio, the Colonel wakes from what has proved to be a nightmare. The other was probably galline, *The Barnyard Hamlet*, content not indicated.

Comics also continue to borrow in one way or another from other Shakespeare plays, two each from *Antony and Cleopatra* and *Julius Caesar*. *Queenie of the Nile* involved the comedian, Billie Reeves, who was also the featured player in *Her Romeo* and *Hamlet Made Over*, already mentioned. Evidently Lubin's writers were ransacking Shakespeare for material which could be turned into farce. In this case Billie is persuaded by a doctor to play Antony to a woman who imagines herself to be Cleopatra, but he is attracted to her maid, Charmian, who doubles as a dancer. A jealous Cleo pursues Billie, who is protected by a policeman. In the struggle the policeman accidently clubs Cleo, who is thereby restored to sanity, as Billie and Charmian pair off. The picture was embellished by luxurious interiors and dancing girls, but 'was not as funny as it might be'. Settings were elaborate too, along with camels and supernumeraries in *Cleopatsy*, but this 'burlesque of *Cleopatra*' has no story-summary. Toto provided the laughs. The stories were probably even less related to Shakespeare in a *Julius Caesar* with Pimple, timely in relation to the English release of the Cines spectacle and the Cricks and Martin parodies, and *A Rural Caesar*, with Billy Bevan in a modern narrative.

The Comedy of Errors, *Love's Labour's Lost*, *The Taming of the Shrew*, *Richard III*, and *The Merry Wives of Windsor* all provided something, if only title or idea, to five more comedies of the period. *A Comedy of Errors* from a Yorkshire studio was built on a poet's embroilment with two girls who had the same Christian names, one 'the love of his life', the other a slavey. *Love's Labour Lost* was a cartoon about a man who, finding himself unable to write love letters, telephones instead with gratifying results. This is hardly Shakespeare's plot, and Judy's *Taming of the Shrew* may be equally distant. There was a Clarendon picture, *A Horse! A Horse!* which Richard Crookback would not have recognized. An actor rehearsing in *Richard III* is overheard by a charlady who takes him seriously enough to go looking for a horse for him, but only manages to bring a donkey onto the stage. And only someone with a summary could spot *The Lady Killer* as using some of *The Merry Wives of Windsor*. This one-reel comedy has Ralph Herz masquerading in feminine attire, hiding in a linen basket, and being dumped into the water.

The experiments with sound belong among the short films. In England, British and Colonial made a picture in 1915 of the wooing scene from *The Taming of the Shrew* in which the actors spoke the complete text. When it was presented in the theatre, the same actors, one at each side of the screen but unseen, repeated the words in what was supposed to be synchronization. It was expected that the operator after rehearsal would be able to project the film so that picture and voice would jibe. Arthur Backner, 'an actor of considerable West-End experience' did Petruchio, and his sister, Constance Backner 'from His Majesty's Theatre, Vaudeville Theatre, Haymarket Theatre, &c.' played Katherina 'to perfection'. According to Bertram Clayton, the results were disappointing: 'The poor mimes struggled bravely from their respective corners to create the illusion that the silent drama had become articulate; and when either of the shadowy characters happened to be situated on the side nearest his or her human impersonator, the coalescence of scene and sound had the effect of a moderately good bit of ventriloquism. But frequently, of course, the Petruchio of the film would dash over to the side where only Katherine's voice was heard, and *vice versa*. At such moments it would have been a charity if the orchestra had struck up and drowned all four of them.' The other two attempts at synchronization were German, and Shakespeare only at second hand. One was a picturization of incidents from *Die lustigen Weiber von Windsor* to the accompaniment of Otto Nicolai's music; the incidents may have been from Mosenthal's libretto. The other presented the choreography of Mary Zimmerman and the ballet of the Deutschen Opernhauses Berlin in the *elfenszene* of *A Midsummer Night's Dream* with Mendelssohn's score. Reports are not available on the success of either experiment, but it was a decade before film was ready for sound.

Other types of adaptation during the War were insertions of incidents into films not based on Shakespeare and modernizations of Shakespeare's plots. In the first group may be included Meyerhold's film, *The Picture of Dorian Gray*, which contained an original scene from *Romeo and Juliet* reflected in the morror of a theatre loge from a performance of the play on the stage. And Abel Gance had 'une forêt qui marche', adopted from *Macbeth* in his *Barbe Russe*. In the other category were treatments of *As You Like It*, *Macbeth*, *Othello*, and *The Taming of the Shrew*.

Two of these films of 1916 have titles so disguised as not to indicate their sources. Both were comedies and one at least must have been hilarious. *Love in a Wood*, 'A Modern Romance in Three Parts', produced by the London Film Company was an adaptation by Kenelm Foss of *As You Like It*; directed by Maurice Elvey, it featured Elizabeth Risdon, one of the most popular English picture actresses of the period, as Rosalind. Other members of the cast were also members of the resident stock company at St Margarets, Twickenham. Edward O'Neill played Squire Duke; Fred Groves, Fredericks; Kenelm Foss, Oliver; Gerald Ames, Orlando; Frank Stanmore, Mr Touchstone; Vera Cunningham, Celia. The relation of the film story to Shakespeare's play is made clear by a summary.

'Squire Duke owns a fine old mansion and estate. He falls on hard times, and, with the exception of a small entailed wood some distance away, sells his property to Fredericks, a common though rich neighbour. Fredericks promises the old man that he will allow him to remain on the land of his fathers till he dies. Squire Duke's daughter, Rosalind, and Fredericks' daughter, Celia, are great friends.

'Sir Rowland Boyse, a neighbour, is dying, and, when his two sons visit him, he shows preference for Orlando, the younger, at which the elder son, Oliver, is angry and jealous. When Sir Rowland dies Oliver makes it clear that *he* now is master on the estate.

'Fredericks attempts to close a right of way, but Squire Duke tells him it has always been open to the public. Orlando, finding the right of way barred, hastens off to tell the villagers. Oliver supports Fredericks in his attitude, and, when Orlando arrives with the angry villagers, his quarrel with Fredericks looks like ending in bloodshed.

'Squire Duke intervenes, and Fredericks turns him out. Meantime Oliver bribes a burly gamekeeper to thrash Orlando; but the gamekeeper's attempt to do so ends in a terrific wrestling bout with Orlando which is watched by the admiring Rosalind and Celia. Orlando wins to the delight of the villagers who now disperse.

'Rosalind, fascinated by Orlando, follows him to the Boyse mansion to congratulate him, and Celia accompanies her. Celia gets between Rosalind and Orlando, and Oliver, watching from a distance, thinks Orlando is making love to Celia and he is jealous. When the girls depart, he orders Orlando from the house. And Orlando, accompanied by his old manservant, goes.

'Fredericks now tells Rosalind and Celia that he has turned out Squire Duke, and the two girls set out together to look for the old man.

'Squire Duke is directed on his way to the entailed wood by some gypsies; and later Orlando is also directed by the same people. Then Rosalind and Celia arrive at the gypsy camp, and, thinking they will be safer in their wanderings if disguised, buy clothes from the gypsies. They go into the wood and change their clothes, Rosalind appearing as a gypsy boy and Celia as a gypsy girl.

'Meantime, Orlando, who has made it clear that he loves Rosalind, joins Squire Duke's caravan.

'After some amusing adventures, Rosalind and Celia discover Orlando carving Rosalind's name on a tree. He thinks Rosalind is a boy, and tells her she reminds him of his lady-love. Whereupon she mischievously undertakes to give him a lesson in love if he will meet her later. Orlando, agreeing, goes. Orlando keeps the appointment and has an amusing lesson. Then Rosalind calls Celia to play the part of clergyman in a mock marriage between her and Orlando, who still thinks Rosalind is a romantic boy.

'There is another right of way dispute and, to escape personal violence from the villagers, Fredericks and Oliver furiously drive away in a trap. Tearing through the gypsy camp, they run over a man. The gypsies give chase and Fredericks driving recklessly, causes Oliver to be jerked out; but he drives on. Oliver, badly shaken, rushes into the wood, closely followed by the gypsies. He breaks in on Orlando, Rosalind and Celia, and begs Orlando to protect him. Orlando beats off the gypsies; Rosalind, frightened, looks on, while Celia tends the exhausted Oliver, to whom she is soon engaged.

'Rosalind pretends to Orlando that by gypsy magic she will bring his lady-love to him at sundown.

'Meanwhile Fredericks' trap collides with Squire Duke's caravan, and

Fredericks is thrown to the ground. He is not badly hurt, and he and the Squire make friends again. The caravan is presently joined by Oliver and Celia, who announce their engagement and are generally congratulated.

'That evening, when the party is gathered round the camp fire they hear a call from the woods. They look and see Rosalind – now in her own dress – approaching. Orlando brings her into the camp, and there is another engagement and more congratulations.

'Rosalind and Orlando set out in the moonlight for a lovers' stroll. Their attempts to embrace are interrupted by other lovers; first by a shepherd and his lass; then by Mr Touchstone and a barmaid; and, finally by Oliver and Celia. . . . And then they climb up a tree and find seclusion for a kiss.'

This is ingenious enough but the film was not a success, despite 'Frank Stanmore's whimsical interpretation of Mr Touchstone, depicted as a subtle county-fair shill'.

It is not difficult to see why *The Real Thing At Last* made a much greater impact. After Sir Hubert Herkomer, President of the Royal Academy who made cinema his hobby, died in 1914, his motion picture studio at his castellated home near Bushey Heath was taken over by A. E. Matthews, who lived nearby. Matthews, with the support of other actors, formed the British Actors Film Company, with the intention of appealing to the market by producing stories by well known authors played by theatre luminaries. One of its pictures proved, in more senses than one, to be a diversion. Matthews asked Sir James Barrie to write a script. The enthusiastic Barrie the next evening turned over to the actor two pages of notepaper which contained a burlesque version of *Macbeth*, 'The Scottish Murder Case – Sensational Clue – Peculiar dagger found on floor', etc., or more specifically *The Real Thing At Last*, 'A suggestion for the Artists of the Future'. The *dramatis personae* in Barrie's handwriting listed four Murderers (Edmund Gwenn, Nelson Keys, Frederick Kerr, Gladys Cooper), two Murdered (Norman Forbes, Owen Nares), Willing to Murder (Marie Lohr), Page (Afterwards murdered) (Teddy Gerard), Her Murderer (Leslie Henson), His Murderer (Moya Mannering), Nearly Murdered (Godfrey Tearle), Not worth Murdering (But murdered) (A. E. Matthews), Expert in the old methods of murder (Frederick Volpe), Murder Specialists (George Tully, Paul Arthur, Caleb Porter). But this is not particularly helpful in identifying some of Shakespeare's characters, and indeed there are contradictions in evidence for the cast. It is clear that Edmund Gwenn played Macbeth; Nelson Keys, Lady Macbeth; Godfrey Tearle, Macduff; Leslie Henson, both Shakespeare and a page, and in addition Duncan, while Norman Forbes was temporarily ill. Godfrey Tearle told me that Owen Nares was Ross, but it seems more probable he was Banquo. Matthews had a bit part as a messenger, and there were more than the usual number of witches because there were two groups, British and American. Tearle named

Gladys Cooper; Matthews, in an interview, Moya Mannering, Fay Compton; in his autobiography, Gladys Cooper, Pauline Chase, and Teddy Gerard (American); Caleb Porter, George Kelly (Tully?), and doubtfully Ernest Thesiger (Paul Arthur?) (British). This omits from Barrie's cast Frederick Kerr, Marie Lohr, and Frederick Volpe, and I expect we shall never know exactly who played any but the major roles. At any rate the cast was more or less all-star, and confusion was part of the spirit of the film.

A motion picture professional, L. C. MacBean, was hired to direct, but upon first meeting Barrie was so overwhelmed that he backed into the camera and smashed it. After it had been repaired, the direction was collaborative but Barrie did most of it, changing his script, writing in bits, and finishing the picture in less than two weeks. Barrie thought Leslie Henson's profile was like Shakespeare's, so he added a frame story in which Henson, photographed in Shakespeare's house at Stratford, appeared as the dramatist, pacing up and down his bedroom and waiting for a telephone call from New York. In the finished picture, the conversation appeared in subtitles: 'Yes! Shakespeare speaking. How did they like *Macbeth* in New York?' '*Macbeth* is sure-fire! What price your next play?' Henson, who as a harlequin jumping through a hoop, provided the trademark shown at the beginning and end of the company's films, reports that among Barrie's interpolations for him were a page, a goblin, and a new kind of witch. It was Barrie who when Norman Forbes was indisposed suggested that Henson could substitute for him if he kept his head averted. As Duncan he climbed into bed in full regalia, sat up to remove his crown and hang it on a nail, at the arrival of the murderers hid under the four-poster, crawled out in their full view to get his crown, and slid under again. On the day when Macbeth and Malcolm were to fight on the flat roof of Herkomer's tower, it snowed. The roof had no railings, and Gwenn to the consternation of Tearle and watchers on the ground became so enthusiastic about his part that he frequently drove Macduff to the edge of the slippery surface. Tearle's expostulations, and yells from the spectators, were of no avail, and finally Tearle had to hurl his shield at the rapt but now astounded Gwenn to stop the battle. This was in the American version, where the action was supposed to take place on a skyscraper from which Macbeth was to be hurled to his death in Hollywood fashion. In the English version, the participants rolled around in a muddy ditch.

There were then two parallel stories as well as a frame. In the British story, Lady Macbeth had no difficulty in wiping away a small spot of blood from her hand; in the American, Nelson Keys, according to Matthews, 'covered in gore . . . tied himself in knots trying to clean up'. In the British, the witches stirred a very small cauldron; in the American, blondined and glamourous cuties danced around a huge one. The point of the film was to show by contrast how Hollywood would produce Shakespeare; whether or

36. Harry Baur as Shylock in the picture of the same name (Eclipse 1913); an enlargement of a film frame. National Film Archive

37. Macbeth (Arthur Bourchier) is worried by a dagger, as Lady Macbeth (Violet Vanbrugh) watches (Film-Industrie 1913). *Cinema News and Property Gazette*, October 9, 1913

38. Hamlet (Sir Johnston Forbes-Robertson) sees his father's ghost and with Horatio (S. A. Cookson) talks to the gravedigger (J. H. Riley) in the film made for Gaumont by Hepworth (1913). National Film Archive

39. *Nina of the Theatre* (K 1914) had Alice Joyc Rosalind in an excerpt fror *You Like It*. *Moving Pi World*, May 30, 1914

40. Lois Weber as Portia and Phillips Smalley as Shylock (inset, top left) were featured in Universal's *Merchant of Venice* (1914). *Universal Weekly*, February 7, 1914

41. Iago (Tolentino), Othello (Colaci), Cassio (Stefani), and Desdemona (Léna Lenard) in the signoria scene of Ambrosio's *Othello* (1914). Museum of Modern Art Film Library

42. Lady Macbeth (Constance Collier) and Macbeth (Sir Herbert Beerbohm Tree) at the end of the banquet scene in the Triangle-Reliance *Macbeth* (1916). Theatre Collection, New York Public Library

43. Romeo (Francis X. Bushman) takes his farewell of Juliet (Beverly Bayne) in the tomb (Metro, 1916). Courtesy of Beverly Bayne

not Barrie and the others knew that it was shortly to present Sir Herbert Tree in *Macbeth* does not particularly matter. A telegram delivered by Matthews on horseback was displayed in a caption, 'If Birnam Wood Moves, It's a Cinch'. A letter from Lady Macbeth to Macbeth read, 'Dear Macbeth, the King has gotten old and silly. Slay him. Yours sincerely, Lady M.' 'The elegant home of the Macbeths is no longer a happy one' contrasted with a final 'The Macbeths repent and all ends happily'.

The Real Thing At Last was first shown at a Royal Command Performance at the London Coliseum on March 7, 1916, as part of a charity show to provide funds for concerts for British troops. Barrie's set showed the front of a picture theatre with box-office and posters. The cast which had been seated in the front row of stalls filed up onto the stage and except for Irene Vanbrugh and Edmund Gwenn disappeared through the stage-door which was part of the set. A lot of old film had been jammed in a barrel with a cover on it. Miss Vanbrugh touched the barrel with a wand, and 'released' the film, which jumped out. When the lights were lowered and the screen dropped, Gwenn, overdressed as a flashy showman and with a large cigar, introduced the picture and gave a running comment on it in an exaggerated American accent to subdued accompaniment on a tinkling piano by Frederick Norton, who wrote the music for *Chu Chin Chow*, to be produced in August. The audience thoroughly enjoyed it. Matthews says the film made a profit and was shown all over the country, not of course with the elaborate presentation.

But the British trade saw little that was funny in this delightful spoof, and was righteously indignant.

'The idea of the piece is that the cinema actors are furious at not having been asked to help in the tercentenary celebrations, and the producer . . . with a fat swan for a trade-mark, asks us only to wait and see how much Shakespeare owes to them. Immediately you are plunged into a magnificent feast at King Duncan's palace, where lovely ladies and shaggy thanes engage in the turkey-trot and other delights of the kind. Then come the witches, lovely creatures, working up Macbeth, who hesitates as if he had conscientious objections to murdering, and then the murder itself. Duncan seems to have grown cautious with the passage of centuries; he distrusts the climbing Macbeths, and spends the night under his bed. Lady Macbeth gets a bucketful of blood to smear the pages and sleep-walks as she never did before. Then the screen warns Macbeth that General Macduff is after him. "If you see a wood moving, it's a cinch!" The wood moves, and Macduff is after him indeed. He falls from the top of the keep after him, over bridges after him, over a whole landscape, till every weapon is left behind, and they run at each other like buffaloes.

'And this is the kind of entertainment provided for royalty and society in war-time! Well! Well!

H

'I thought that the British Actors' Film Co. had intentions more serious than turning out sorry stuff of the above description.'

Two weeks later it took up the cudgels for America. Edmund Gwenn was 'superb' as a 'talking subtitle', but as a satirical attack 'this burlesque photo-play is ill-considered'.

'It is one of the most childish or primitive of errors to make sweeping generalizations on the foundation of a few particular cases, or, on the other hand, to particularize what are in reality general characteristics. In *The Real Thing at Last* Barrie has achieved the distinction of making both mistakes at once. The type of photo-play which he satirizes in this boisterous bur-lesque . . . as being characteristic of, and peculiar to, the United States, is in truth peculiar to no country, and is anything but characteristic of screen dramatic art.

'Still Barrie may be forgiven because it is all done in the jolliest way – the manner of pure lightsome fun. . . .

'It is not true that the dominant characteristic of American production is an irreverent modernization of the classics of the British stage. On the contrary the American feeling for our classics . . . errs if it errs at all, on the side of fanatically reverent worship. It is in England, and on the stage, that there have been productions of plays which Shakespeare worshippers have deemed mere displays of gorgeous scenery accompanied by extracts from the Shakespearean play.

'There is no reason (unless it be want of enterprise in the past) why British producers should not have undertaken years ago the putting of all Shakes-peare's great dramas, and many of the comedies, on the screen. . . .'

And it goes on to mention that it is an American company which is at present producing *Macbeth*. On the whole, this seems to be what Stephen Leacock described as riding a horse madly in all directions, when all that was necessary was to laugh and be silent about what must have been a cleverer Shakespeare burlesque than the professional film makers themselves had been able to devise and produce in the many examples which have already been described.

For four war-time modernizations, such detail is either unnecessary or unavailable. Two of them were American. The first, called in the United States, *The Iron Strain*, stemmed from the Thomas Ince section of Triangle, was written by C. Gardner Sullivan, and directed in four reels by Reginald Barker. In England, however, it was re-titled *A Modern Taming of the Shrew*, and a review points out the aptness of the change.

'If Shakespeare could have been at the Triangle show of *A Modern Taming of the Shrew*, how he would have revelled in its wit and homely truth. The great bard would have enjoyed, far more than any other feature, the daring manner in which his plot had been lifted and set within scenes and incidents unknown to his time. . . .

'The modern shrew is a petulant society beauty. Not until her spirit is tempered by rough usage with the world does she acquire the robustness of her prototype Katherine. She is a spoiled and petted darling of the money gods. Her father, a gold king, and one of Nature's gentlemen, maps out a married life for her away from the vapid, insincere social throng. He wants a real man to be her life companion, one who can mould her to tread paths of useful, womanly endeavour.

'The opening scenes show us social New York in all its grandiloquent splendour. Miss Enid Markey (the shrew) soon shows the mettle of her temperament. . . . She is taken on a trip to Alaska, sees real life for the first time, and she also sees a barbarian – at least she calls him one – a man in reality of her own social state, who has fled to the wilds to live a life of freedom. He sees and loves at first sight. She abhors, with haughty hate, this natural-living man. The story of how he conquers her to his will, whilst it follows closely the methods used by Shakespeare in his play, is given an added charm, because of the novelty of the situations, and the essentially modern activities of the actors.'

She is kidnapped, married by force, made jealous, but at last happily capitulates, and when hero and heroine go back to New York, they are accompanied by a future heir. The end of the review, however, is unfortunately a revelation of the state of film. 'It should prove a worthy play to give to audiences who can appreciate something out of the ordinary without that something being in any way a subject beyond their ideas of entertainment. . . .' Dustin Farnum was the counterpart of Petruchio; Charles K. French, the shrew's father; and Louise Glaum, the cause of jealousy.

A Modern Othello also underwent change of title, first to The Shadow of Night, then to The Lash of Jealousy, and finally to The Mad Lover. This Harry Rapf production in six parts was photographed at the Selznick studio in the Bronx, and in Richmond, Virginia, an odd choice for a story about a New England country gentlemen, played by Robert Warwick, and his wife, Elaine Hammerstein. The story was written and directed by Léonce Perret, he who had played the comic Leonce Plays Othello in 1914, now emigrated to America and using Othello for a supposedly serious film, though it appears too conventional to be taken seriously. The motifs of the virile young American who prefers the open spaces to the artificialities of the city, and the misunderstandings gladdened by the birth of a child are repeated. So are the over-familiar rehearsal of a play-within-the-play which has relevance to the feelings and attitudes of the leading character, and the employment of a dream. During the preparation of Othello for charity Robert is made jealous by the impassioned love made to his wife, Clarice, as Desdemona, by the impersonator of the Moor. Robert falls asleep and imagines himself in a rehearsal playing Othello to his wife, smothering her with a pillow, and taking his own life. When he wakes up, it turns out that Clarice is entirely guiltless and has been insulted by the original Othello. The hero ducks the villain in a muddy pond. Perret was an unimaginative director, and this must have been shoddy stuff, despite the appearance of the attractive and popular Robert Warwick and the beautiful daughter of Arthur Hammerstein.

Three European films were also probably modernizations. Enrico Guazzoni directed a *Lady Macbeth*, which at a guess might have been adapted from Nicolai Leskov's popular story, *Lady Macbeth of Minsk* (1865) which was later filmed and was the basis for Shostakovich's opera. Max Mack made an *Othello* from a script by Reinhard Bruck 'nach motiven von Wilhelm Hauff', with actors Beni Montano and Ellen Korth. Alex Heinz directed a five-reel farce, *Der Fliegentüten–Othello* for the antics of Paul Beckers, but are we interested in a 'flypaper' Othello? And at long last we can pass to activities connected with the Shakespeare tercentenary of 1916 and to films which are directly based on Shakespeare's plays.

1916 was the biggest of the War years for Shakespeare films and in one way or another a number of the American film colony participated. To open the Hollywood Stadium, Lillian Gish turned the first shovel for a live production of *Julius Caesar* in which five thousand were to take part. There were to be gladiatorial combats to precede Caesar's entrance, barbaric dances focused on Mae Murray, and a realistic battle of Philippi. In the play itself, Theodore Roberts appeared as Caesar, Tyrone Power as Brutus, Frank Keenan as Cassius, William Farnum as Antony, and Douglas Fairbanks as Young Cato. Someone sold to the World Film Company a plan for a film of *Romeo and Juliet* for Clara Kimball Young which introduced an elaborate fight between the two houses and the funeral of Juliet. Later the company was doubtful whether the Juliet should be Mrs Young or perhaps Gail Kane or Alice Brady or Kitty Gordon, or Jane Grey, or Ethel Clayton, or Gerda Holmes, and in this confusion the picture was never made. William N. Selig in Chicago said he was planning to produce Shakespeare pictures and therefore obtained an injunction against a publisher who was issuing a Baconian book which might hurt his business; he lost the case and he produced no Shakespeare but it was good publicity to try to protect Shakespeare's name. Edwin Thanhouser's contribution to the Shakespeare tercentenary was a film called *Master Shakespeare, Strolling Player*, which on the whole had very little to do with Shakespeare but more with the Bacon–Shakespeare controversy, in which the heroine is stoutly Baconian and the hero upholds Shakespeare's authorship. After a quarrel, the hero goes off to the Mexican War where he is reported wounded. The girl, played by Florence LaBadie, promptly falls into a delirium in which she is transported back to the sixteenth century, where she is saved from abduction by a man who remarkably resembles her lover, played by Robert Vaughn, and a stranger who turns out to be Shakespeare as impersonated by Lawrence Swinburne. Bacon in the person of Robert Whittier declares that the Shakespearean play being performed has been stolen from him and provokes a duel in which the lover is killed. When the girl comes to, she finds herself back at home, where she falls into the arms of her young lieutenant, now recovered from his wounds. Philip Lonergan wrote this farrago for direction by Frederic Sullivan. It seems an odd way to celebrate Shakespeare, but Thanhouser was to do better later in the year.

What was expected to be the big film event of 1916 was the recapture of the venturesome pioneer, Sir Herbert Beerbohm Tree. The *Moving Picture World* of November 6, 1915, had announced that the actor had been signed by Triangle to a contract which called for remuneration in excess of $100,000 to make pictures under the supervision of David Wark Griffith. *The Tempest* was mentioned as a possible subject, but three weeks later the same journal said the actor would appear as Cardinal Wolsey and probably as Bottom, and the London *Pictures and the Picturegoer* of November 20th had heard that *Richard II* would be included. Evidently Griffith was considering the suitability of various Shakespeare plays for cinematic treatment. Before Tree's arrival in the United States, however, Griffith and John Emerson, who was to write the scenario and direct the production, had decided on *Macbeth*, a choice which Tree after initial misgivings was to approve as 'an ideal one. . . . *Macbeth*, apart from the power and beauty of its dialogue, is a highly pictorial narrative. Its characterizations are strongly developed, and it is throughout a story of action'.

Meanwhile Emerson went to work on the scenario for a picture which was to include 250 shots and 1000 supernumeraries. This undertaking was to be no mere transcript of a stage performance. In an interview Emerson said that the plot of *Macbeth* lent itself well to the picture method of treatment.

'The supernatural atmosphere . . . is very difficult to realize on the speaking stage. . . . On the screen, with the aid of the camera, the witches are easily given supernatural quality. The same applies to Banquo's ghost. . . . The visionary dagger is also an impossibility on the stage, but on the screen we can show it in a very effective and mystical sort of a way. And don't forget that *Macbeth*, aside from its psychological aspects, is a rattling good melodrama. Another big thing in the favor of the *Macbeth* production is that scenery can be found in California almost identical with that of Scotland. We are considering doing *The Merchant of Venice*, and in that case shall build Venice on the canals at Santa Monica for the exterior scenes. . . . You can't successfully produce Shakespeare on a small scale; there is too much meat in his plots, so it was decided to produce *Macbeth* in nine reels and thereby avoid omitting any of the essentials of the play.

'When it came to preparing the screen scenario for *Macbeth*, the task was not so difficult as I had anticipated. In fact, it was surprisingly easy, as Shakespeare's dramatic structure is more near in form to that of the film than the modern play or novel. . . . We can not only do all the scenes Shakespeare provided for us in practically the same sequence, but are able to fill in the lapses of time by adding scenes merely described in the lines of the play. As, for instance, the fight between Macbeth and Cawdor and the execution of the latter.

'The coronation of Macbeth, which is completely jumped over in the play, will be one of the biggest scenes in the picture. . . .

'And another instance, where I elaborated on a line in the play, is Birnam Wood, which is merely spoken of; we show it moving toward the castle of Macbeth. . . .

'We found it much simpler on the screen to suggest the evil influence of the witches than on the stage. The opening scene of the picturization presents the witches in their cavern . . . they draw forth the fires of evil, which are thrown from their fingers down into the valley of destruction, where Macbeth and the traitor Cawdor are fighting for supremacy.

'It became necessary at times to take liberties with the text, in order to knit the story closely enough to be able to project it in the limits of two hours and yet retain all the incidents of the play. While taking these liberties, we have endeavored to show a spirit of reverence for the text and have consulted Shakespearian authorities for justification in every alteration we made. One change in particular was in the sleep-walking scene . . . in order to knit the photoplay structure together, it was essential that Ross and Lennox overhear this scene. . . .'

And, as usual, especially since Emerson, as did Orson Welles much later, conceived of the picture as set in Holinshed's eleventh century, there was much fanfare about consulting the archives of England and Scotland to achieve historical accuracy and detail. R. Ellis Wales, the studio librarian, quoted in the same article, gives some of the latter.

'In this photoplay panoramic scenes will be revealed, showing at one time five hundred camp-fires, thousands of torches, great cataracts of boiling pitch, marching masses of men at midnight, the terrific onslaught at Macbeth's castle, the weird, picturesque witches, who dominate the story, and Macbeth and Duncan walking directly out of the historic past. . . .

'Witches play dominating parts thruout the play, and in the cavern some of the most wonderful electrical and mechanical effects will be seen, and the apparition of the naked child, the tree and the crown, the skeletons, and the bubbles from the ground exploding in the air.

'On the heath the vivid display of storm and lightning, Macbeth riding in his own element. The battlefield – the beheading of Cawdor – the wild highlanders who fought in the old days stark naked. In the picture also are shown some wild dances of highlanders.

'We secured some special, large greyhounds, obtained at great rental expense. We reproduced accurately the great gate and portcullis of Macbeth's castle ... and the huge drawbridge of Dunsinane Castle and the terrific battle there, scores of men falling from high walls into the moat below.'

It may be added here that 'the mounting of the witches' scene, owing to the intricacy of the electric wiring to produce the weird lighting effects', was reported to have cost over $10,000.

The casting did not prove a difficult problem. Tree cabled Constance Collier, already in California where she had made several pictures, asking her to be his Lady Macbeth; she was able to accept by arrangement with Oliver Morosco. She had long been associated with Tree at His Majesty's and elsewhere. Emerson engaged the rest of the cast, twelve of whom, reportedly, had appeared on the stage in Shakespearean roles and all but two in *Macbeth*. Ralph Lewis became the Banquo; Spottiswoode Aitken, Duncan; Wilfred Lucas, Macduff. Griffith personally rehearsed the cast before any film was shot. It was his Reliance group which produced the Fine Arts picture for Triangle, but occupied with *Intolerance*, in which incidentally Tree was later an extra, he only supervised *Macbeth*.

The arrival of the British actor-manager in Los Angeles must have been something to behold. Certainly Tree himself could never have expected the kind of ovation he received. Conducted from the station to the studios, he was welcomed by cowboys shooting pistols into the air, and received an official greeting from a 'fair-haired little boy of five years . . . one of the most popular film actors. The infant phenomenon wore a long garment, on which was sewn in large letters the word "Welcome", and coming towards me with extended hand, at once put me at my ease by saying, "Pleased to meet you, Sir Tree".' It is Tree himself who tells the story in his *Impressions of America*, originally in the London *Times* of September 8, 1916. Griffith and his staff received the distinguished guest. Tree's sense of humour must have been tickled by the child, and he was to be good friends with the cowboys, to whom his daughter, Iris, who accompanied him, says, 'he repeated his most obscure epigrams.'

Sir Herbert began work on January 4, 1916. He left for New York in March to play Cardinal Wolsey at the New Amsterdam Theatre, with the picture about finished. In between many strange and wonderful things happened to him. After his first day at the studio, he said,

'It is quite wonderful . . . how many things can be done in pictures for the Shakespeare tales that cannot be done on the stage. With all due reverence to the master dramatist, it is possible to illuminate and accentuate many details so as to produce a marvellously truth-telling commentary on the text and at the same time heighten the dramatic values.

'That is what I have learned from my first day's work with Director

Emerson upon the scenario. The pictorial possibilities grow, as one studies it in the light of this strange new art, into something very beautiful and wonderful – not precisely a play in the Shakespearean sense, perhaps, but a dramatic narrative of great power.

'I should like to call this series of productions *Tales from Shakespeare*. If we can bring to the dramas some such reverent and illuminating interpretation as did Charles Lamb, I shall be happy indeed to have entered on this enterprise. The motion-picture studios are naturally strange places to me, but I am delighted with the kindly spirit of welcome and cooperation manifested, and the amazing vitality of the industry. I know that I am going to like it immensely.'

He did like it immensely. Griffith, Emerson, and Lillian Gish were kind to him. DeWolf Hopper borrowed Dorothy Gish's horse because it had a walrus-mustache similar to the one used by Tree for his hairy make-up as Macbeth and presented it to him. 'Tree accepted the recruit with crocodile tears and was astride the animal on his first appearance.' He rode with his daughter in the California hills on a wooden property saddle. And when he was working hard, sometimes as much as eighteen hours a day in the hot sun of a location or in the glare of studio lights, he could relieve his fatigue by laughing and making merry.

Tree himself specifies some of the difficulties.

'The mimic coronation of Macbeth at Scone took place about forty miles from Los Angeles at a place called Chatsworth. Thither the actors and hundreds of supernumeraries, together with the 'properties' of the occasion, were conveyed in motor-cars and motor-omnibuses. This scene was taken in brilliant sunlight, while the arrival at the King's camp of Macbeth and Banquo after the victorious battle was photographed at two in the morning, the scene being lighted by huge electric lights. Through the ranks of the cheering soldiers surrounding their camp fire and through the flaring lights projected on their faces, Macbeth and Banquo galloped with the news of victory. This nocturnal scene was deeply impressive. The interior of the Witches' Cavern was enacted in a scene built in the studio. One scene was photographed no less than a dozen times; this ordeal was a somewhat trying one in the watches of the night.

'Acting to the lens requires a peculiar temperament, and demands a much more "natural" method than that of the stage; the great requisite in the actor is the power of momentary self-excitation. A mere resort to the technique of the theatre would not "register" satisfactorily on the film – a relentless detective. To the new-comer it is somewhat disconcerting to act a scene of carousal immediately after your death-scene ... although I had little difficulty in acclimatizing myself to the new conditions. I confess I have not outlived my preference for the spoken drama. It is only by the exercise of one's imagination in visualizing the perspective of vast crowds of spectators that one can maintain the pitch of excitement necesssary for the fine frenzy of the scene.'

John Emerson said that despite Tree's inexperience, 'his adaptability and dramatic intelligence were of such a high order that, a week after the picture started, he was playing like a screen veteran', but this was probably too complimentary. Tree was considerate, willing, and assiduous but he really knew little about film acting; his earlier Shakespearean films had been transcripts of stage productions. Essentially he tended to do whatever he had found effective in the theatre. Otis Skinner, in California some years later, talked with studio people who had worked with Tree and found he had been difficult to direct. Heretofore he had used all the room on the stage he needed; he was always a mobile actor. Emerson found it almost impossible to keep him within the camera lines. Moreover, he wanted to recite all the words. 'He could not,' wrote his daughter, 'be cynical or merely clever in his acting, and . . . the directors were amused and slightly irritated by his insisting upon knowing his part perfectly, putting into his voice all the impassioned quality it had on the stage. "I could not act unless I *felt* the words", he said, "and they knew it was true".' Constance Collier relates how the exasperated cameraman – it was George Hill – solved the problem by a dummy machine which was not loaded with film. Sir Herbert, unaware, spoke the whole text, largely unphotographed; when the unnecessary speeches were over, the real camera took pictures. Tree wanted to be in everything – everything at least in which Macbeth was. Since the script called for some acrobatic horseriding, it was thought expedient to persuade him to be elsewhere while a double was substituted without his knowledge. Afterwards he was bewildered by seeing rushes of Macbeth doing things of which he had no recollection. The best story of all is also Constance Collier's and concerns the first showing of the whole picture at the private studio theatre. All the important people were there, including those who had been involved in the production; all waited eagerly to hear Tree's comments, but he said nothing during the projection. When the lights went up, there were murmurs of congratulation, but Sir Herbert still remained mute. For a very good reason – he was asleep!

Macbeth was publicly shown in June at the Majestic Theatre in Los Angeles, and in New York. Tree and Miss Collier, now playing *The Merry Wives of Windsor* at the New Amsterdam, attended the special *première* at the Rialto Theatre on June 4th. A sample of reviews from a general and a trade paper is sufficient to indicate the reactions of critics. The New York *Times* the next day called it 'a fine achievement, one that should be seen by everyone at all curious as to the progress the movies have made by this year of grace. It is a famous old story, told in moving pictures of a beauty worthy its associations. This beauty is not in any sense Shakespearean. To suggest for one moment that it derives to any appreciable degree from the essential

H*

beauty Shakespeare gave to *Macbeth* is to talk nonsense of a peculiar wild-ness. To say, however, that *Macbeth* should therefore not be given on the screen is to relapse into an equal absurdity.' Emerson was particularly praised for 'the imagination revealed, the impressive panoramas, the fine sense of composition, the cunning use of impressionism, the prevailing good taste. . . . The product is among the best things in motion pictures. All the detail of costuming and background is excellent, the vision of the weird sisters a triumph . . . the cave scenes are peopled with fine phantoms and the ghost of Banquo is more truly spectral than the stage can ever make him. . . . What is especially noteworthy is the suggestion of brooding night, the black, midnight quality which pervades all the picture . . . you see things of the director's invention, as when a vision of the luckless Duncan brings Macduff hurrying to Inverness on the morning after the murder, or when Macbeth, in feasting Duncan, winces at the sight of the little Fleance playing with the crown and trying its oppressive weight upon his own small head. You see the moonlit murder of Banquo, and the madness of Lady Macbeth. . . . For flashes Shakespeare's text has sufficed in nearly every instance, passage after passage being given just for its own sake even when it is scarcely necessary to advance the narrative. . . . *Macbeth* has been done handsomely for the screen' and elsewhere in the review, 'The shade Tree is effective', both because he weathered admirably the necessary athleticism and because he was literally a picturesque player.

The *Moving Picture World* had two reviews on June 24th. Lynde Denig found Tree 'a virile, compelling Macbeth, possessed of the rare art that makes possible the communication of emotional states. . . . There is infinite variety and subtle shading in the portrayal. . . . Judiciously used close-ups of his wonderfully mobile features enable Sir Herbert to reveal the ever-increasing torture that eats into the soul of the usurper. The Lady Macbeth of Miss Collier is no less impressive. . . .' Nevertheless it was Emerson's film, and 'his is the credit for the production of a picture that not only visualizes the dramatic incidents completely and convincingly, but makes clear the mental processes of Macbeth and Lady Macbeth.' In summary, 'it will win on its merits as an interesting, artistic photoplay, as a faithful representation of Shakespeare's tragedy. . . .' The other review was under the section labelled 'Motion Picture Educator, Conducted by Rev. W. H. Jackson and Prof. Hardin Lucas', who felt that 'this great subject in moving pictures has enriched the library of those films calculated to bring honor to the screen in general, and to the series dedicated to educational purposes in particular. . . . At the close of the first presentation . . . Sir Herbert, in thanking his admirers for their reception of his efforts, spoke of the "educational value behind the attempt of the producers to depict the classics through the instrumentality of the motion picture".'

But whatever its merits, *Macbeth*, alas, did not win, and the public did not want to be educated. Financially, the picture was a failure both in the

United States and abroad. The screen was inarticulate; the audiences lethargic or absent. Expected to run for ten weeks at His Majesty's in London, where it opened on June 22nd, it ran one and was shortly released for general showing as just another film. And now the studio was in a quandary. Tree's contract was for ten months. It seemed clear that neither he nor another Shakespearean film could draw. What to do with him? The obvious move was to find some way to make him abrogate his agreement.

The rest of the story, as it is told by Rupert Hughes, is not a pretty one. When Sir Herbert returned to Los Angeles in July, cancellation of his contract was suggested as mutually desirable. Tree, shocked and hurt, refused. Lawyers were consulted. Could Tree be asked to play a low-comedy Negro role in the hope that he would reject it and find it easier to depart? The lawyers thought not. 'Then', says Hughes, 'they cast the English knight as an American farmer in my Old Folks at Home, of all things! To their horror, he went through with it. To their even greater horror he played the part magnificently.' Hughes is contradicted, however, by the reviewer in the *Moving Picture World* of October 14th. He commended two other actors. Tree got no notice until the last half of the last sentence, which needs no analysis: 'Mr Beerbohm Tree is in the cast as the "Senator" and does fairly well.' Tree did not wait, though, for the release of the film; the handwriting on the wall was clear enough. Early in September he tore up his contract, and left for New York on his way to England. Still, in his characteristic way, the pioneer in Shakespeare film had the last word after his arrival. When Chance Newton expostulated with him for posing for a *Macbeth* without dialogue, Tree chuckled and replied, 'Well, you see, I thought I had reached the time of life when I ought to be seen – and not heard!'

Romeo and Juliet was clearly the most popular subject for Shakespeare film; it is equally clear that different distributors indulged in the practice of digging up old pictures in order to benefit from new products which dealt with the same or similar material. 1916 however saw a new phenomenon when one company deliberately and with whatever secrecy was possible brought out a Shakespeare film in order to compete with an already announced forthcoming release. William Fox had tried this method with success in 1915 when he produced a *Carmen* with Theda Bara to vie with a much publicized *Carmen* which starred the opera singer, Geraldine Farrar. The next year he made a *Romeo and Juliet* to challenge a more lavish presentation by Metro. The dates of preparation, manufacture, and release are therefore of some significance in revealing the strategy of competition. Metro announced on April 29th that it had a *Romeo and Juliet* in production and a week later that it was to be 'one of the most pretentious features ever offered on its programme'. By May 20th it was not only 'pretentious' but in six parts, and sensational announcements were to come shortly of Metro's contribution to the Shakespeare tercentenary. On July 1st the company was able to inform exhibitors that the stars were to be the extremely popular team of Francis X. Bushman and Beverly Bayne. On August 12th the film was nearing completion, and on September 9th it was announced that the $250,000 production was to be released in October but not on what day, perhaps because it was to be a 'special', more probably because Metro had by now become aware of a rival. A two-page spread on October 14th had seven illustrations, the information that the picture had been directed by John W. Noble and Bushman, assisted by Edward Elsner and Rudolph deCordova, and publicity: 'Metro believes its best service to the exhibitor lies in productions that guarantee great box office returns and offers *Romeo and Juliet* as the supreme profit maker of the year. Produced . . . with a cast of 600 chosen players, this, the Love Story of the Ages, eclipses the possibilities of the spoken drama . . . the most magnificent spectacle drama in the history of the screen.' All of a sudden the sly Fox came out on October 21st with a similar two-page advertisement of 'The Tragedy of Love. As his offering toward the Shakespeare Tercentenary William Fox Presents *Romeo and Juliet*. The sweetest story ever told. With that Renowned Screen Artist, Theda Bara. And an incomparable cast of more than 2500 persons.' It was to be released on the 'regular' programme, which therefore required no special arrangements, and on October 23rd, as directed by J. Gordon Edwards from a scenario by Adrian Johnson. Metro, which had been planning on October 29th, now put the release date forward to October 22nd; Fox riposted by bringing his film out on the same day. The houses of Metro and Fox from ancient grudge now broke to new mutiny. In screaming capitals, which I partially reduce, Metro advertised: 'Don't be misled. There is one and only one Special Production de Luxe of Shakespeare's Love Story of the Ages. . . . Don't be misled by inferior imitations of a masterpiece.' Fox, also carefully not mentioning the name of the other firm, asked: 'What is Your Verdict? Comparison is *now* possible between the William Fox production . . . and that of another producer *who invited* the parallel.' Metro countered with arranging personal appearances. The stars appeared on the second night at the Broadway Theatre, and received a 'Tremendous ovation . . . crowds of admirers filled the big theater. . . . Outside hundreds were waiting to gain admittance. . . . It took half a dozen attaches of the theater to keep the throngs away from them. . . . They were ushered to a box, where the spectators . . . applauded . . . and [were] dragged . . . onto the stage. Instantly there were cries for a speech. Mr. Bushman and Miss Bayne addressed the big house. . . . Altogether it was a big night.' Of course the clamouring crowds were photographed for publication. Thereafter the parents' strife was largely confined to announcements which emphasized how big the business was for each picture, not only in New York but all over the country; the children prospered.

Metro's *Romeo and Juliet* was evidently the more successful and the more artistic. It was shot largely at a studio in New York, and on location in Greenwich, Connecticut, where a partially completed structure provided architectural backgrounds, and in Brighton Beach, sets were constructed for the streets of Verona. Contrary to the usual practice, the cast learned Shakespeare's lines and spoke them in the film. Miss Bayne had always wanted to play Juliet, and it was she and Bushman who were responsible for choosing the subject in the first place. She even designed her own costume. The scenario was prepared by John Arthur, deCordova, and Noble. Though Noble received credit, he was undependable and a good deal of the direction was handled by Bushman and by the assistants already mentioned; Edward Elsner had for years staged plays on Broadway in close association with George Broadhurst. A score for theatre orchestras was compiled by Irene Berge and Samuel Berg from Gounod and Tschaikovsky. The picture which finally emerged was in eight reels, a fact which must have annoyed Fox, who had to reduce the seven he copyrighted to five to fit regular release on his programme. He therefore announced that 'the story has not been sacrificed in any attempt to obtain extra film footage'.

The review by George F. Blaisdell in the *Moving Picture World* on November 4th was highly laudatory and is rather more than usually revealing. He called it 'a great production and one that will easily rank with the best', and said why.

'It is a subject that should appeal alike to the Shakespearean student and the man to whom the linked names of Romeo and Juliet have only the remotest significance. Plainly, it has been the aim of the producers to visualize the story . . . just as it was planned by the hand of the master. They have neither subtracted from it in any substantial detail nor have they added to it.

'Best of all, the textual accompaniment to the photographed action is the language of Shakespeare. Right here is a good place to say that the leaders constitute of this picture a thing apart. We have all heard it said . . . the works . . . are not for the screen – that the "upright stage" robs them of their matchless dialogue. The Metro production measurably disproves the assertion. Elaborate use has been made of the text. Artistically and clearly presented are these gems of the world's literature; there is no possibility that their majesty will be marred by those who are "capable of nothing but inexplicable dumb-shows and noise".

'To the making of the picture Director John W. Noble has contributed his best work for the screen. . . . Francis X. Bushman and Beverly Bayne head the cast. It is an ideal combination. Mr Bushman, above all else, possesses the physique of a "well-governed youth", of "a man to encounter Tybalt"; he appears to unusual advantage in the scanted garb of the period – in the language of Juliet's Nurse, "his leg excells all men's". He fits the part, and he plays it. Miss Bayne is a rare Juliet. Kindly endowed by nature in figure and feature, she has entered into the interpretation of the role of the heroine with marked sympathy and feeling.

'Supporting these two is an excellent cast. . . . Space forbids mention of

more than a few. Robert Cummings is Friar Laurence, a fine performance.
Adela Barker is the portly nurse to Juliet. Joseph Dailey is Peter, the Nurse's
servant. These two contribute to the somber story the sole touches of lighter
color. W. Lawson Butt is Tybalt, a heroic figure; Edmund Elton and Helen
Dunbar are the Capulets, Eric Hudson and Genevieve Reynolds the Montagues, Horace Vinton is the Prince.

'*Romeo and Juliet* will appeal to picture lovers as an all-round production.
It will possess a distinct double appeal – to the eye and to the mind – that
of the action and that of the text . . . on the initial presentation, nearly two
hours and a quarter were devoted to the running of the eight thousand feet
of film; yet the movement at this normal speed is sharp, the best of evidence
the scenes have been trimmed to a hair. Approximately a full reel is devoted
to the single scene of the balcony. . . . Of the twelve thousand inches of film
devoted to the portrayal . . . not a single one is superfluous. It is the dramatic
height of the play as we see it on the screen. The remainder of the story holds,
but this particular scene markedly moves.

'As has been said, the story runs with fidelity to the text. It is told so clearly
that lack of knowledge of the book is no bar to full enjoyment of the production. Pictorially the subject is notable. The studio interiors and exteriors
– especially those of the streets of Verona – are unusually elaborate. For the
home of the Capulets Director Noble has employed a great castle which he
discovered in the neighbourhood of the metropolis, a setting which most
happily fits the requirements of the story.

'Metro has done the screen a distinct service. Not only has it lavished its
best on the adaptation of a great tragedy; not only has it brought it out in
all its strength and beauty, its glamor and romance, for the education as well
as entertainment of countless thousands who heretofore may have had slight
acquaintance with it or concern about it. It has demonstrated that Shakespeare dead three hundred years penned in his youth lines that stamp him
the greatest title builder in the world of to-day.'

Other journals were equally enthusiastic but not always so lucid. *The
Motion Picture News* said it was 'a picture of universal appeal . . . will live
forever as a classic masterpiece and a triumph of dramatic Screen construction', the *Dramatic Mirror* that it 'deserves to rank with the classics',
Billboard that 'all in the picture is wonderful', and the *Morning Telegraph*
that 'for the first time in the history of motion pictures Shakespeare has
successfully been immortalized'. Three out of four of these entertainment
journals were not confined to the cinema trade. More remarkable is that the
general dailies also approved. The *Tribune* found 'not a dull moment', Zit
in the *Evening Journal* thought it 'like a beautiful dream'. The *American*
characterized it as 'the most prodigal film spectacle ever seen', and the
Philadelphia *Record* as 'a masterpiece'.

Romeo and Juliet was released initially in forty-two cities, in some of them in direct clash with the Fox picture. It played, usually at advanced prices, to crowded houses. Seven prints went to the Pittsburgh office alone. Three theatres in Boston showed it at the same time; for two weeks it was in Cincinnati at a theatre which had never had a run of more than one; two theatres under the same management in Birmingham screened it because the crowds could not be accommodated in one. In England, where it was announced in April, it was extravagantly praised in the *Cinema News and Property Gazette* on November 30th as 'a realization in pictures fully entitled to rank with Shakespeare's immortal lines. . . .'

The Fox *Romeo and Juliet* received no such encomia. The original announcement on October 21st put the weight on the 'Famous Actress', Theda Bara.

'William Fox announces Theda Bara, the great emotional actress, in a magnificent and colorful picturization. . . . It will be shown to the public for the first time at the Academy of Music.

'This epochal film, which adheres precisely to the poet's masterly play, has been in work for many weeks at William Fox's studio in Fort Lee, New Jersey. Thousands of dollars were spent to insure absolute accuracy in details, as well as in essentials. From many standpoints the picture should prove one of the real triumphs recorded in the history of the silent drama.

'The settings throughout are entirely worthy of the production. Among those particularly attractive are the fateful masquerade ball, the beautiful balcony scene, and the city of Verona. . . .

'It is needless to dilate upon Miss Bara's fitness for portraying before the camera the intensely tragic character of Verona's fairest maid. Miss Bara's success as an emotional artist has been recognized internationally.

'Mr. Fox engaged a supporting cast which is strong and well balanced. Harry Hilliard gives a remarkable presentation of the role of Romeo.

'Among the principals in the cast Glen White, Walter Law and John Webb Dillion [Dillon] have acted in many of William Fox's recent releases. Einar Linden [he played Paris] will be recalled for his splendid performance of Don José in . . . *Carmen*. Alice Gale has a record of thirty year's success on the stage; for several seasons she acted the Nurse in the legitimate. Jane and Katherine Lee . . . have the parts of pages. The name of J. Gordon Edwards, who has made most of the Bara photoplays, guarantees the excellence of the direction.'

It is difficult for those of us who remember Theda Bara's early pictures to think of her as Juliet. She had been transformed two years earlier by some spectacular press agentry from Theodosia Goodman to a death-ly Arab (note the anagrams), photographed with skulls and snakes, and labelled vampire for and after *A Fool There Was*. After the venture into Shakespeare, she returned to being *femme fatale* as Cleopatra, DuBarry, and Salome. Apparently her conception of Juliet partook somewhat of her more familiar roles. An article signed by her explains that she 'gave the character a great deal of study, and perhaps in that investigation discovered that Juliet lived in a period of passionate abandon. Italy, in the days of *Romeo and Juliet* was no place for a Sunday-school girl.'

Hanford C. Judson, reviewing the film in the *Moving Picture World*, November 11th, headlines Theda Bara as 'Chief Treasure of the House of Capulet'.

'It is better to be young and Juliet than to be Sarah Bernhardt trying to be young when the cold screen refuses to be deceived. Theda Bara is young and her long dark curls make many a beautiful picture. . . . Harry Hilliard, as Romeo, also has the bloom of youth and an engaging personality that goes well with his role. It is a very worthwhile picture that anyone might be glad to see. If it doesn't reach those heights of beauty that gives to the critic who has seen great presentations of the richly magnificent play, it is beautiful enough to inspire many and give delight to them. It tells the story clearly. The story is full of suspense and that suspense remains in the picture. The scenes in which it is told are often glorious and hundreds seems to have been employed in making the full-manned scenes on street and in market place and in the funeral procession which was impressive till marred for one unhappy moment by the levity of one rose girl. The set scenes give a good suggestion of an Italian city and the chosen backgrounds are just about what was desired.

'The nurse is a "rich part" and a hard part to play even in the spoken drama with all the aid of the poet's wit and humor. In the picture the humor has largely to be created. Alice Gale deserves credit for her presentation of a humorously grumpy, but motherly old soul. Both Glen White, as Mercutio, and John Webb Dillon, as Tybalt, are as the real thing in the gentlemanly swashbuckler way and fill the bill to perfection. Helen Tracy, as Lady Capulet, is acceptable and more pleasing than the too stiff Lord, her husband, played by Edwin Holt. Lord Montague, by Elwin Eaton, has but a moment-ary part to play. Victory Bateman's Lady Montague is effective in the trial scene. Walter Law as Friar Laurence carries his part of the picture well.

The film stands as a pretty presentation. . . . It is a valuable offering that would please any audience. The director, J. Gordon Edwards, deserves more credit, perhaps, than anyone else interested in it. The scenario, by Adrien [Adrian] Johnson, ought also to be mentioned as economic, clear and able. It has drawn the story through many lovely scenes. It departs from the Shakespearean ending and follows the even more dramatic close of the original Italian.'

I derive the impression that Mr Judson is trying hard to say nice things without committing himself to any comparison with the Metro film reviewed a week before. Much of his criticism is strangely non-committal. Bara is young and beautiful. Hilliard is young and personable. The picture does not rise to the heights but is beautiful enough. The story is clear and suspenseful. The studio scenery – apparently the company did not go on location – is suggestive. There are some lovely scenes, and so on. But there is definitely no enthusiasm. The capsule summary, three pages before, calls it 'a pretty offering, full of lavishly put on spectacles. We feel sure that it will be thankfully accepted. ...' It did nevertheless sell for one reason or another, but the accounts of its success outside of New York have the same lack of specifics, except in Great Britain, where the star was advertised as 'Mlle Theda Bara, the famous Parisian actress'. The *Cinema News and Property Gazette* reporting on a trade showing says the picture 'Scored heavily ... its success was immediate', and in a review that it was 'a riot of action and a bounty of beauty', though the acting 'never rises out of a conventional groove'. It was booked to be shown at Stratford during the Shakespeare festival, and in Sydney did 'big business at prices ranging up to two shillings'.

The fourth American Shakespeare film of 1916 was a *King Lear* which starred the veteran Frederick B. Warde, already noticed for his *Richard III* of 1913. Warde had appeared in *King Lear* in 1880 when he was with John McCullough, but not in the title role until February 1896, in Salt Lake City, then in Los Angeles, San Francisco, Sacramento and Portland. The Salt Lake *Herald* called his 'achievement ... marvellous. The crucial test is, of course, the great curse scene, and in this he rose to great heights. The mad scenes were not less pathetic and powerful, and throughout Warde gave evidence of being entirely able to cope with the great character he has added to his repertoire.' In a following season his son, Ernest C. Warde, played the part of the Fool. Late in 1915, Edwin Thanhouser offered Warde a year's contract to appear in films directed by Ernest, who had gained considerable experience with Richard Mansfield. 'The offer', said Warde, 'was liberal, the association exceedingly pleasant, and the results very satisfactory. We made pictures of Shakespeare's tragedy ..., George Eliot's novel of *Silas Marner*, Goldsmith's *Vicar of Wakefield* and several modern subjects, all of which were popular successes ... the work that at first was not entirely to my liking became agreeable as the possibilities of the camera became apparent.' *King Lear* was the second of these films.

Filming began early in 1916; by October 7th the picture was nearly ready and to be distributed by the Pathé Exchange as a Gold Rooster Play; it was released on December 17th as 'Shakespeare in every detail, except that of course it is produced upon a vastly larger scale than ever was possible on the speaking stage ... never before has *King Lear* had such a mounting as is given Mr Warde's characterization. Castles were built [presumably in New Rochelle] and thousands of persons were employed. ... *King Lear* ... lends itself readily to the screen. The Battle ... is splendidly done. ...' The adaptation by Philip Lonergan was enacted by Ernest Warde as the Fool, Ina Hammer as Goneril, Wayne Arey as Albany, Edith Diestal as Regan,

Charles Brookes as Cornwall, Lorraine Huling as Cordelia, J. H. Gilmour as Kent, Boyd Marshall as the King of France, Hector Dion as Edmund, Edwin Stanley as Edgar, and Robert Whittier as Oswald. Edward Weitzel, reviewing in the *Moving Picture World*, pointed out that in a film version, Shakespeare's poetry was limited to brief subtitles, but thought this five-reel screen play was 'well acted and scenically effective'.

'The plot of *King Lear* when stripped of its wealth of marvelous verse, is a sordid story in which evil passion in many different forms is contrasted with the affection of the old King for his daughter, Cordelia, and her love for him. It is also worthy of note that, practically, the only physically revolting scene in all Shakespeare is found in this play – the scene where Gloucester's eyes are torn out – a scene, by the way, that is handled with becoming restraint in the version under discussion.

'In view of the conditions imposed upon the producer and his associates, it is only just to them to regard their efforts in but one light, to what degree have they succeeded in taking the bare plot of *King Lear* and clothing it with some of the poetry of thought and feeling that was given it by its creator. All of the outward accessories required by the undertaking have been provided. Correct costuming, impressive settings, and a thorough knowledge of the traditional "business" of the scenes are all in evidence. It remains for the art of the actor – the technique of the silent drama – to make the poetry of the play speak to the heart of the spectator. This it does, to a praiseworthy degree.

'Aided by a clear and concise scenario, Mr Warde and his fellow players throw many pictures on the screen by which the soul of the tragedy, as well as its physical action, finds expression. ... The Thanhouser version is an achievement to be thankful for; it may serve as a lamp to many who would otherwise never have their paths cheered and made radiant by the genius of the great Elizabethan. If such an experience leads them to a study of the poet's works, the picture will have vindicated its creation, upon this ground alone. To the student of Shakespeare and those familiar with Lear on the spoken stage, the screen version offers a novel and interesting means of visualizing the poignant scenes of the greatest of human tragedies.

'Frederick Warde is not new to the character of Lear . . . and is fitted by temperament and training for its impersonation. He has the grand manner necessary to the aged monarch, and indicates to the life the choleric old King, jealous of his dignity, brooking no insult, rash and impetuous, blind to everything but momentary feeling, and heedless of all results until, as Schlegel observes, "all that remains to him is the capability of loving and suffering beyond measure". Ernest Warde, who directed the play, is excellent as the fool.'

This sensible comment does not, however, tell much about the film, copies of which are still available. It opens with a long expository subtitle followed by character shots which identify actors and parts. The first reel is devoted to the division of the kingdom (I, 1). Goneril and Regan make their speeches of love to Lear on his throne. The inexpressive Cordelia is rejected; Kent intercedes and is banished; after Burgundy's refusal of Cordelia's hand, she is accepted by France. In Reel II, there is some vague business of Goneril and Regan plotting, and Goneril's rebuff of Lear (I, 1, 3) followed by Regan's arrival at Gloucester's castle (II, 1). Edmund plots Edgar's downfall with the forged letter and uses the business of drawing swords; Edgar flees (I, 2; II, 1). Shakespeare is followed very closely here (and elsewhere) to the confusion of clarity. In scenes of open country, Edgar disguises himself as a half-witted shepherd (II, 3). At Albany's palace Kent seeks service with Lear; there is a close-up of meat cutting for Lear's dinner; in fact close-ups are used frequently in this scene, which continues with Goneril's instructions to Oswald (I, 3), Oswald's impertinence and Kent's retaliation, the Fool's mocking, and Lear's departure (I, 4, 5). In Reel III Kent reaches Gloucester's castle, meets and beats Oswald, and is stocked by Cornwall and Regan (II, 2). Lear and the Fool arrive, Kent is freed (by Regan), Goneril approaches and is defended by her sister, the storm begins. There is an expressive shot here of Lear, Kent, and the Fool left outside, as the others enter the castle and the gates are closed. Edmund's plotting against Gloucester (III, 3) ends the reel. In Reel IV Edmund reveals Gloucester's apparent complicity (III, 5), and Goneril leaves for her palace, Gloucester's eyes are plucked out (not actually shown), Cornwall's servant is killed, Gloucester is left to smell his way to Dover (III, 7). An invented Edmund–Regan love scene is succeeded by Gloucester's recognition (by touch) of mad Tom as Edgar, not in Shakespeare. At the French court, Kent tells Cordelia of Lear's plight. France says he cannot leave his country but Cordelia shall go to the rescue, an invented scene suggested by IV, 3. There is a cut to the mad Lear with the Fool at Dover, not a visualization of any specific scene. The French cross to Dover. To Cordelia Kent brings Lear, who recognizes her (IV, 7). Note that the Gloucester story is dropped, and the Fool kept alive. Reel V is in the British camp. Edgar reveals to Albany the plot of Goneril to end his life, a scene not shown by Shakespeare. The battle begins, as Cordelia agonizes. Goneril poisons Regan, as suggested in V, 3. Cordelia and Lear are taken prisoner, and Edmund arranges for their deaths. Albany brands Edmund a traitor. Edgar appears and defeats Edmund in personal combat. Goneril, accused by Albany, stabs herself as Regan dies from poison. Kent seeks Lear and is sent by Edmund to rescue the King and Cordelia. The guards strangle Cordelia in prison. Lear carries out her dead body. The incomplete film ends abruptly without showing Lear's death, but the final episodes are all adaptations of Shakespeare's last scene.

As may be guessed, the film tells far too much of the complex story in detail, and the plot is hard to follow. Shakespeare has been treated with too much respect, but he has not been manhandled. Some but not all of the titles scattered throughout are cut or modified Shakespeare dialogue. Close-ups bring out character traits in physiognomies, and the make-up is impressive. Some of the tragic quality comes through in the performances of Ernest Warde, Gilmour as Kent, and the wicked sisters of Ina Hammer and Edith Diestal. Unfortunately, the Cordelia is rather dreadful; she does nothing but look heavenward in anguish and roll her eyes. Frederick Warde himself is surprisingly good, especially in the scenes of the division of the kingdom and the expulsion during the storm. He had learned something about acting before the camera and does not especially smack of the stage. If the film as a whole bears marks of the primitive, it is not dull or ridiculous. It does not rank with Forbes-Robertson's *Hamlet* because Warde was not as great an actor as Forbes-Robertson, but it is unquestionably the best silent version made of *King Lear*, even though it was advertised as 'A Drama of Powerful Heart Interest Staged in Barbaric Splendor'.

France's one contribution in 1916 was a short *Macbeth* film, 'featuring Madame Georgette Leblanc-Maeterlinck, the World-famous Belgian Prima Donna as Lady Macbeth.' So at least the *Cinema News and Property Gazette* had it in an Eclair advertisement. Its reviewer starts profoundly.

'What is the main theme of Shakespeare's noted tragedy *Macbeth*? Certainly it is not, as one might assume from a superficial survey of the story suppose, mere sensationalism. It is, in truth, a picture of character, the last stages of the degeneration of a noble man degraded by inordinate ambition. Though the Eclair photo-play is an extremely abbreviated edition of Shakespeare's story, yet it does effectively bring out the main idea. The most striking scene of all, perhaps, is that near the opening, where the three witches appear at the border of a wood and implant the first seeds of ambition into Macbeth's brain.

'This scene is produced with wonderful ingenuity. First smoke seems to rise spontaneously from the grassy ground, and then the witches, one by one, rise from the earth. After this the main outline of the story is followed fairly faithfully, and the principal scenes of the tragedy are effectively presented. In what the photo-play evidently sets out to be it is successful. It does not appear to claim to be a full presentation of the broad scenes and national events depicted in Shakespeare's play, and much of what, in a more ambitious production, would be actually depicted is told in quotations from the play, as in ordinary subtitles. Among the most notable things in the production is the acting of Georgette Leblanc-Maeterlinck as Lady Macbeth. . . . Her carriage and every gesture denotes majesty and force, so that one is compelled to respect the character in spite of its unscrupulousness. The character of Macbeth is also suitably represented by Severin-Mars; and all the other characters contribute to making a notable and impressive production of a very much abridged *Macbeth*.'

This picture was then a series of illustrative scenes from Shakespeare's play, only one of which is sufficiently described so that some idea is conveyed of a visual sequence. Nothing more is heard of it. Georgette Leblanc herself may have provided the momentum. That strange, obsessive, and effusive actress-singer from the Opéra-Comique and the Théâtre de la Monnaie had decided after reading his introduction to Emerson's *Essays* that she and Maeterlinck were natural affinities, deliberately arranged an introduction to him, and became his companion, mistress, mother, irritant, inspiration, and according to her, collaborator for many years. While they were living at the Abbaye de Saint-Wandrille in 1909, she had produced for private performance there Maeterlinck's translation of *Macbeth*, in which she played Lady Macbeth. Since her film of *Pelléas et Mélisande* was reviewed in the same issue, she may have decided to do both pictures during the same engagement with Eclair.

England unfortunately reverted to type in the 1916 Broadwest production of *The Merchant of Venice*, starring Matheson Lang. Lang, who had played Lorenzo as a schoolboy of sixteen and Shylock at nineteen, had been presenting the play with his wife, Hutin Britton, at the St James Theatre. But let him tell the sequel: 'When we were playing *The Merchant of Venice*, the Broadwest Film Company came along with a proposal that they should film the whole production just as it stood with my company and my stage scenery! . . . They transported the whole of the production to their premises in Walthamstow, set up the scenery in a glass-roofed studio and photographed most of it by daylight.' This primitive procedure is perilously close to that followed by Barker in filming Tree's *Henry VIII* five years back, though, as will appear, there was greater flexibility in the use of the more fully developed camera. Lang was quoted before the trade show on July 27th as being 'delighted with the production, which, he says, embodies the very spirit of Shakespeare's immortal masterpiece. The production is an elaborate one, and no expense has been spared to make it remarkable in the history of British films. Mr Walter West is responsible for the screening'. After the trade show it was reported that 'the film had a wonderful reception, and big bookings have resulted'. It was released on December 11th in five reels.

The *Cinema News and Property Gazette* was more explicit about the nature of the film itself.

'An exceedingly interesting educational experiment, combined with very fine acting was received with great enthusiasm by the large and distinguished gathering of spectators. . . . There is no doubt that, even amongst those who go to the cinema for mere amusement, many will be induced by seeing this production . . . to read the play from start to finish, and to go and hear the magnificent words when next Matheson Lang, with Hutin Britton, produce the play on the stage.

'The Broadwest *The Merchant of Venice* is not a photo-play, but a moving photograph of Shakespeare's stage play. If there had been any pretence that it was to be an 'adaptation of Shakespeare to the screen', there would have been room for disappointment in the fact that there is not one real exterior scene. But there has been no claim that it was to be a spectacular attraction. ... In short the Broadwest production is not a *translation* to the screen; the stage play has been transferred bodily or almost so. That is to say, Shakespeare's words have been skilfully abridged by Walter West, these forming the only subtitles [not true]; and the essence of the story thus thrown on the screen in words is illustrated by moving photography of the acting, with the scenery from St James's Theatre as a background. The total result is the conveyance of the spirit of the main part of Shakespeare's play to the great public in a quite novel and attractive form.

'In such a presentation the screen has two advantages over the stage – to compensate for the lack of the music of the words – first, that the play can be seen by a far larger number of people, including many in villages who never get the opportunity of going to a theatre, and, secondly, the facial expressions and actions of the artistes ... can be observed far more closely and minutely. As might be supposed, the special attraction is in the character study of Shylock by Matheson Lang. So fine and sympathetic is his presentation of the character that the spectator at times almost comes to feel that his wrongs are greater than the sin of his intense, revengeful, and temperamental hatred of the melancholy and rather priggish Antonio – in which part, by the way, George Skillan is made up to appear very like Shakespeare himself. One of the most effective pieces of acting is one of the very few scenes which are screen additions to the stage play; the actual giving of her mother's ring to Jessica by her father Shylock. Here Kathleen Hazel Jones shows something more than mere charm; there is a subtlety of acting which indicates that Jessica has a sweet simplicity of character, almost excusing her robbery. In fact, the whole of her acting seems to show a natural aptitude for screen work. The other characters all helped efficiently to fill in the picture, including J. R. Tozer as Bassanio, Terence O'Brien as Tubal, George Morgan as Lancelot, Ernest Caselli as Lorenzo, and Hutin Britton as Portia.'

Other trade show reports reveal further details. *Bioscope* thought 'Mr Lang's very popular conception of Shylock has been adapted to a new medium with remarkable skill and with a very great measure of success ... as a record of a fine performance.' It objected to adaptations of Shakespeare's lines in the subtitles which lost 'the poetry and rhythm and even the sense ... and the banality of such subtitles as "Visitors" and "Three Weeks Later". .... The childishness of Shylock's trap for the merchant, and the empty sophistry of Portia's legal quibble, seem more apparent when stripped of the magic of Shakespeare's verse, and the conclusion of the great trial scene is robbed of its dramatic climax by the necessary interposition of a subtitle.' It also remarks on 'the obvious artificiality of outdoor scenes' and the inadequacy of some of the make-up. The *Kinematograph Monthly Film Record* indicates that: 'The introductory scenes of the negotiations with Mr Lang at his private house were intended to interest the trade show audience', but should be cut for the general public, and is explicit on some of the camera effects: 'the wonderful power of the kinema to quickly produce an enlarged version of any scene. It is somewhat akin to watching the play as a whole, that is the whole stage, and then suddenly using a pair of opera glasses upon the chief characters alone. ... We have never seen the dissolving effect so cleverly carried out. ... The way in which Matheson Lang becomes Shylock and Miss Britton reveals Portia, and returning to their private characters without visible change in the opening or preliminary part, is a marvel of kinematographic dexterity.'

The buyers were enthusiastic. According to the *Evening News* of July 31st, they 'cheered this picture, a rare thing at any time and an unprecedented thing in the case of a Shakespeare film ... the only true successful version of a Shakespeare play. ...' Nestor in *Cinema News* on August 3rd reported that 'the film had a wonderful reception, and big bookings have resulted', on August 10th that representatives of Broadwest had shown him contracts, and that 'bookings are literally pouring in for this fine Shakespearean production, on August 31st that there were 'record trade shows' in Manchester, Liverpool, and Glasgow' which were received with 'enthusiasm, and resulting bookings ...', and on January 11, 1917, that 'wishing to renew my acquaintance with the Broadwest *Merchant of Venice* ... I visited one of my local cinemas ... where a good family business is the order of the day. Not a place where people go prepared to ... view the higher arts. It's a hall where amusement and entertainment are sought. Yet so great was the power of this excellent play that through the screening ... one could literally have heard a pin drop. The audience, a crowded one, were gripped and held entranced – a proof if such a thing were needed nowadays, that the cinema only has to show the highest expression of art to be appreciated. ... I said not a sound. ... There was, however, one great bravo from the darkness, forced from the throat of an enthusiast who could not restrain himself, when Bassanio chose the lucky casket.' Finally the same reporter, on July 12th, indicated that the picture had played in over eight hundred theatres.

Analysis of the extant Reels II and III will indicate why, though financially successful and a useful record, the Broadwest *Merchant of Venice* is an artistic failure.

Reel II

Title: Shylock: '... for an equal pound of your fair flesh to be cut off and taken in what part of your body pleaseth me.' (I, 3)
1 Shylock, Antonio, and Bassanio.
Title: Antonio: 'Content, i' faith I'll seal such bond.'

2 Objection from Bassanio.

Title: 'The Prince of Morocco . . . John Daly.'

3 Morocco enters to Portia and Nerissa.

Title: Morocco: 'How should I know if I do choose the right?' (II, 7)

4 Morocco with caskets. Portia explains.

Title: Portia: 'The one of them contains my picture, Prince. / If you choose that, then I am yours withal.'

5 Portia shows apprehension, as Morocco picks up the right casket and reads:

Title: 'Who chooseth me must give and *hazard* all he hath.'

6 Relief of Portia when Morocco rejects this casket. He reads the inscription on the second casket.

Title: 'Who chooseth me shall get as much as he deserves.'

7 Morocco puts back this casket, takes the third.

Title: 'Who chooseth me shall gain what many men desire.'

8 Morocco chooses the third casket.

Title: Morocco: 'Deliver me the key: / Here do I choose and thrive as I may!

9 Portia, relieved, smiles. She gives the key, hanging around her neck, to Nerissa, who gives it to Morocco. He opens the casket, and finds a parchment in the eye of a skull; shows distaste as he reads,

Title: 'All that glisters is not gold / Often have you heard that told / Many a man his life has sold / But my outside to behold / Gilded tombs do worms unfold / Had you been as wise as bold / Young in limbs in judgment old / Your answer had not been inscroll'd / Fare you well; your suit is cold.'

10 Morocco shows disappointment.

Title: Morocco: 'Portia, adieu. I have too grieved a heart / To take a tedious leave; thus – losers – part.'

11 He leaves as Portia and Nerissa curtsy.

Title: 'Shylock departs to the Merchant's house.' (II, 5)

12 Shylock, lantern in hand, leaving Jessica, gives her a ring from his finger. (Slight pan as he leaves)

Title: Jessica: 'Farewell and if my fortune be not crost, / I have a father, you a daughter lost.'

13 Shylock, outside, goes away. (But stage outdoors, not real.)

14 Young men, masquers, enter.

15 Jessica puts a necklace around her neck, packs jewels, money, luggage.

Title: Gratiano: 'This is the pent house under which Lorenzo desired us to make stand.' (II, 6)

16 Lorenzo enters.

Title: Jessica: 'Who are you? Tell me for more certainty.'

17 Jessica at window. Lorenzo, below, unmasks.

Title: Lorenzo: 'Thy love Lorenzo.'

18 Jessica at window, ecstatic, holds treasure.

Title: Jessica: 'Catch this casket it is worth the pains / I am glad 'tis night for I am much ashamed of my exchange. Cupid himself would blush to see me thus transformed to a boy.'

19 Jessica tosses down the casket, closes the window, as others wait below. Jessica comes out, embraces Lorenzo; the others retire.

Title: Jessica: 'O Lorenzo, if thou keep promise I shall end this strife. Become a Christian and thy loving wife.' (II, 4)

20 They kiss and depart.

21 Shylock and others bargaining. Shylock leaves the room.

22 Street scene (stage set). Shylock disperses a crowd, goes to his door, knocks, waits.

Title: Salanio: 'How now Shylock? What news among the merchants.' (III, 1)

23 Salanio and a friend (Salerio) talk to Shylock.

Title: Shylock: 'You knew, none so well as you, of my daughter's flight.'

24 Brief action, illustrating.

Title: Shylock: 'I say my daughter is my flesh and blood.'

25 Brief action, illustrating.

Title: Salanio: 'There is more difference between thy flesh and hers than between jet and ivory.'

26 Shylock threatens.

Title: Salanio: 'But tell us do you hear whether Antonio have had any loss at sea.'

27 Brief miming.

Title: Shylock: 'There I have another bad match, if rumour speaketh aright he dare scarce show his face upon the Rialto ...'

28 Brief miming.

Title continued: Shylock: '... a beggar, ... a bankrupt, ... he was want to call me usurer; he was wont to lend money for a Christian courtesy; let him look to his bond.'

29 Close-up of Shylock.

Title continued: '... he hath scorned my nation, ... thwarted my bargains ... cooled my friends ... heated my enemies ... and what's his reasons? *I am a Jew!*'

Title (continued but not roll title): '... hath not a Jew eyes? hath not a Jew hands, senses, ... affections ... passions?'

30 Brief close-up of Shylock.

Title continued: '... hurt with the same weapons ... subject to the same diseases ... healed by the same means ... warmed and cooled by the same winter and summer as a Christian is, ...'

Title continued: '... if you prick us do we not bleed ... if you poison us do we not die ... and if you wrong us ... shall we not revenge?'

31 Close-up of Shylock.

32 Close-up of Salanio and Salerio.

33 Close-up of dagger being drawn.

34 Full shot of Salerio preventing stabbing of Shylock by Salanio. Shylock leaves.

Title: Salanio: 'Here comes another of the tribe a third cannot be matched unless the devil turn Jew.'

35 Tubal approaches Shylock in his room.

Title: Shylock: 'How now Tubal hast thou found my daughter?'

Title: Tubal: 'I often did come where I did hear of her but cannot find her.'

36 Shylock beats his bosom; Tubal comforts him.

Title: End of Reel Two.

Reel III

1 Jessica, Lorenzo, others celebrating, Jessica with wine cup. (New)

Title: Tubal: 'As again I heard a sailor showed me a ring he had of your daughter for a monkey.' (III, 1, continued)

2 Tubal and Shylock talking.

3 Jessica buying monkey from a sailor.

4 Close-up of ring and monkey.

Title: Shylock: 'Out upon her . . . thou torturest me . . ., It was my turquoise; *I had it of Leah when I was a bachelor.*'

5 Shylock sinks to his knees in woe.

Title: Tubal: 'Other men have ill luck too: . . . Antonio the merchant hath an argosy cast away coming from Tripolis.'

6 Shylock exults at the news.

Title: Shylock: 'Good news Tubal . . . Good news . . . I'll plague him, I'll torture him.'

7 Shylock swears vengeance.

Title: 'Bassanio at Belmont.' (III, 2)

8 The choice of the casket. Portia shows her pain or pleasure during the selection.

9 Gratiano and Nerissa, holding hands, embracing.

10 More of casket choosing. Bassanio selects the right casket. Key passed as before. Success; Bassanio reads the letter in the casket.

Title: 'You that choose not by the view / Chance as fair and choose as true / Since this fortune falls on you / Be content and seek no new / If you be well pleased with this / And hold your fortune for your bliss / Turn you where your lady is / And claim her with a loving kiss.'

11 Bassanio kisses Portia's hands. They are interrupted by a messenger, then Lorenzo, Salanio, and Jessica.

Title: Bassanio: 'Lorenzo, Salanio, welcome hither.'

12 Brief miming.

Title: Bassanio: 'What's the news from Venice? How doth that royal Merchant Antonio?'

13 Bassanio sits to read a scroll presented.

Title: Portia: 'With leave Bassanio. I am half yourself and I must have half of everything that this same paper brings you.'

14 She goes to him, stands hand on shoulder.

Title: Bassanio: 'I have engaged myself to a dear friend, engaged my friend to his enemy to feed my means.'

15 Conversation

Title: Portia: 'What sum owes he the Jew?'

Title: Bassanio: 'For me, three thousand ducats.'

16 Conversation

Title: Portia: 'What no more? Pay him six thousand and deface the bond. Double six thousand, and then treble that . . . before a friend of this description shall lose a hair through Bassanio's fault.'

17 Conversation; decorous embrace.

Title: Portia: 'First go with me to church and call me wife, and then away to Venice and your friend.'

18 Embrace

Title: Portia: 'Let me hear the letter of your friend.'

19 Brief relation of content of letter.

Title: 'My ships have all miscarried, my creditors grow cruel, my estate is very low; my bond to the Jew is forfeit and since in paying it, it is impossible I should live, all debts are cleared between you and if I might but see you at my death.'

20 Conversation

Title: Portia: 'O, love, dispatch all business and be gone.'

21 Bassanio kisses Portia good-bye and leaves.

Title: Portia: 'Come on Nerissa, I have work in hand you know not of.' (III, 4)

22 Brief miming.

Title: 'The day of Antonio's trial.' (IV, 1)

23 Shylock arrives at court (outside, stage set), and is reviled by the crowd. (Some long, medium, and close shots in this sequence.)

24 Within the court. The Duke and others arrive.

Title: 'The Trial.'

25 Pan to Shylock.

Title: Shylock: And by our holy sabbath have I sworn to have the due and forfeit of my bond; if you deny it, let the danger light upon your charter and your city's freedom . . .'

26 Close-up of Shylock.

Title continued: 'You'll ask me, why I rather choose to have a weight of carrion flesh, than receive three thousand ducats? . . . I'll not answer that, but, say it is my humour . . . are you answered?'

27 Close-up of Shylock. Bassanio goes to him in expostulation.

Title: Shylock: 'Would'st thou have *a serpent sting thee twice.*'

28 Bassanio offers payment.

Title: Bassanio: 'For thy three thousand ducats here is six.'

29 Close-up of Bassanio and Shylock.

Title: Shylock: 'If every ducat in six thousand ducats were in six parts, and every part a ducat, I would not draw them. *I would have my bond.*'

30 Close-up of Bassanio and Shylock. Bassanio retires.

Title: The Duke: 'How shalt thou hope for mercy, rendering none?'

31 Close-up of Duke.

32 Medium shot of Shylock.

Title: Shylock: 'What judgment shall I dread, doing no wrong? If you deny me, fie upon your law! There is no force in the decrees of Venice. I stand for judgment; answer; shall I have it?'

33 Medium shot of Shylock, speaking.

Title: The Duke: 'Upon my power I may dismiss this court unless Bellario a learned doctor whom I have sent for to determine this, come here today.'

34 Close-up of Duke, speaking.

35 Close-up of Shylock, with Tubal, hearing.

36 Messenger delivers scroll to Duke.

Title: 'Your grace shall understand that at the receipt of your letter I am very sick, but in the instant your messenger came was with me a young Doctor of Rome, his name is Balthazar. We turned o'er many books together, he is furnished with my opinion. I beseech you let his lack of years be no impediment to let him lack a reverend estimation, for I never knew so young a body with so old a head. I leave him to your gracious acceptance, whose trial shall better publish his commendation.'

37 The Duke asks the messenger to bring in Balthazar. He goes and does so. Portia enters and bows to the Duke. Shylock and Tubal talk. Portia goes to Shylock, opens a law book, puts it on a lectern, turns to Shylock.

Title: Portia: 'Is your name Shylock?'

38 Close shot of Shylock and Portia.

Title: 'End of Reel Three.'

If the whole of *The Merchant of Venice* may be judged by these two reels, it is not a ridiculous picture because it is earnest, satisfactorily acted, and a reasonable reproduction of a stage performance of some value, but it is nevertheless a bad film. It is obvious from the analysis that there are almost as many subtitles as there are sequences of action; what is not so obvious to anyone except a viewer is that the titles take more time to read than what is presented in pantomime. Many of them are much too long, especially Shylock's speech, kept in detail because it was famous, from III, 1, and the letter at the end of Reel III. The conversation carried in printed dialogue is meaningless as visual movement. Explanatory titles are useless or should be. Despite some adaptation of Shakespeare's language, *The Merchant of Venice* is far too respectful to Shakespeare's text, and the shots are too brief to do more than illustrate the words. The result is that the words dominate the images, whereas the images should dominate the words. The stage sets, especially of course the outdoor sets, make little contribution to the mobility of the camera; they are simply there to act in. The characters are played without too much exaggeration of gesture, but there is no outstanding performance, as was the case with Baur's earlier Shylock. Almost no emotion is created, partly because of the unemotive acting, partly because the brevity of the shots and the interruption of the titles preclude any building of feeling. The omissions do not matter, and the rearrangement of scenes in Reel II is justifiable. The scene in which Jessica buys the monkey is an interesting flashback, and the presentation outside the court provides a useful prelude to the court room itself. There has been a deliberate attempt, especially in Reel III, to vary the length of shots, and there is even a bit of panning as well as the dissolves mentioned in the review, but the variation relieves little of the monotony and serves largely to highlight acted conversation. Nevertheless the camera work, unimaginative as it is, and the costumes, stage costumes as they are, are the best aspects, unless as a record, of an extremely dull film.

If it is necessary to take the Broadwest picture seriously as an attempt, however banal, to show Shakespeare on film, it is hardly to the point to do much with the Fox *Cleopatra* of 1917. This contrivance, though no doubt a better film, was concocted out of Plutarch, Sardou, Shakespeare, and a lot of Adrian Johnson, who wrote the script, and belongs in the class of the Gardner and Cines revivifications of the past with their emphases on a star, in this case Theda Bara in elaborate dress and undress, and spectacular scenes. Indeed, the Gardner picture was reissued in 1918 in order to compete with it. Since the Fox *Cleopatra* is not available for examination, its content can only be determined by contemporary publicity and reviews; no one wrote about it as an attempt to make a Shakespearean film, and all reports stressed the elaborate and expensive preparations and the pageantry of the finished product, 'a riot of gorgeousness and Egyptian splendour', three thousand extras in one scene, 'regal magnificence', the architecture of Rome and Alexandria, the eighty vessels burned in battle, peacocks and costumes, and so on. There were obvious parallels with Shakespeare, and it may well be that Johnson started with Shakespeare. Witness the characters: Cleopatra and Antony of course, Charmian and Iras, Ventidius, Octavia and Octavius, a messenger who brings to Cleopatra news of Antony's marriage, Julius Caesar and Brutus, but Pharon and Kephren. Pharon was in the Gardner plot as one of Cleopatra's lovers, as he is here, and Kephren is from Sardou. The first part of the Fox film dealt with the affair between Cleopatra and Caesar, only mentioned by Shakespeare, and concluded with the conspiracy and murder of Caesar, Brutus's and presumably Antony's orations over his dead body, and perhaps the rioting and the battle of Philippi – at least in a picture of this sort which ran for ten reels, it is improbable that such opportunities would have been missed. I gather Antony goes to Alexandria with Cleopatra in her barge, subsequently returns to Rome, marries Octavia, is reunited with Cleopatra, is defeated by the forces of Octavius in the naval engagement of Actium, and dies with his enchantress. Several of the subtitles were from Shakespeare. Yet the result must have been not Shakespearean but an eye-filling recreation of glamorous pseudo-history. The film enhanced Theda Bara's reputation and made an enormous amount of money for William Fox, and there's an end on't.

In the records but almost certainly without foundation are two Shakespeare films which starred Armando Falconi and Gösta Ekman. A French periodical in September 1917 indicated that the Italian firm, Savoia, was preparing a *Romeo and Juliet* for the Italian actor, but an Italian trade journal of the same month carries a Savoia advertisement which names two contemporary comedies for him; I have found nothing else in the Italian periodicals I have been able to examine. Perhaps a *Romeo and Juliet* was planned but not produced. Two sources list *Hamlet* (1918) as an early film of the Swedish actor, but I find no confirmation and evidence to the contrary.

There was, however, an authentic adaptation of Shakespeare which came out of Italy in 1917. This was a *Hamlet* from the newly formed Rodolfi-Film, founded by Eleuterio Rodolfi, who had been an Ambrosio director, and who directed this picture. Its star was the eminent stage actor, Ruggero Ruggeri, who when starred in the tragedy at the Teatro Valle di Roma was hailed by the *Giornale d'Italia* on December 5, 1915, as having achieved a triumphant success and as having taken his place beside Tommaso Salvini and Ernesto Rossi. For the new venture the script was prepared by Carlo Chiaves, a man of letters of Torino, where the studio was situated, with the co-operation of Ruggeri and Rodolfi. Mercedes Brignone was to play Gertrude; the Polish-born Elena Makowska, Ophelia; Armando Pouget, the Ghost of the elder Hamlet; Penia, Laertes; Martelli, Claudius; all were experienced players before the camera, and indeed Ruggeri had already appeared in film. Costumes were created by Ditta Zamperoni of Milano, well known as a designer for the theatre and for La Scala. Distribution was to be handled by Alfredo DeRosa. Congratulations were offered to all after the private screening at the Teatro Vittoria, Torino, on November 25th.

Two of the three reels of the Rodolfi *Hamlet*, probably somewhat cut, are available for analysis. I give the usually unlined Shakespearean titles as they appear; misreadings cannot necessarily be blamed on the original film.

Reel I

Title: THE DEATH OF HAMLET'S FATHER, THE KING OF DENMARK
  'Where every God seem to set his seal to give the world assurance of a
  man.' (III, 4)
  1 Hamlet, left in front of a curtain, partially concealed from courtiers to the
    right in the funeral procession for Hamlet's father. A medium shot of a
    non-Shakespearean scene.
  2 A close shot of Hamlet. (New)
  3 Hamlet watches the funeral procession pass and then follows it. Medium
    shot. (New)

Title: HAMLET'S MOTHER MARRIES THE KING
  'A little month or e'er those shoes were old with which she followed my
  poor father's body. – Why she, even she married with my uncle.' (I, 2)
  4 The marriage feast with Claudius and Gertrude at a table. Medium shot.
    (New)
  5 Hamlet seated, front right. Close shot.
Title: 'Frailty thy name is woman.'
  6 Hamlet watching a toast. Medium shot. (New)
    Hamlet rises, obviously distressed, approaches the camera, and moves off
    the scene. Close shot. (New)

Title: POLONIUS THE KING'S CHAMBERLAIN

Title: OPHELIA'S BROTHER LAERTES BEGS HIS FATHER'S CONSENT TO RETURN TO
  FRANCE
  7 The scene of request. Polonius turns to Ophelia and back. Whether this has

anything to do with her relation to Hamlet is not clear. Polonius rises. Close shot. (New)

8 As the others leave, Ophelia, standing behind a chair and leaning on it, is pensive. Close shot. (New)

Title: CLAUDIUS THE NEW KING OF DENMARK

9 Claudius and Gertrude on their thrones are approached by Polonius and Laertes, who asks permission to go to France. Medium shot. (I, 2)

Title: 'Have you your father's leave? Take thy fair hour Laertes. Time be thine.'

10 The permission granted, the King and Queen rise, move toward the camera and out right, followed by the court, Polonius, and Laertes. Medium shot.

11 Polonius blesses Laertes. Close shot. (I, 3)

Title: 'Go not back to school in Wittenburg. Remain here in the cheer and comfort of our eye.'

12 Claudius, unsuccessful in the persuasion urges Gertrude to second him. This scene is not in the throne room but a private chamber. The Queen is seated, Claudius standing by her, Hamlet on the opposite side of the scene. Medium shot.

Title: 'Let not thy mother lose her prayer, Hamlet. I pray thee stay with us.'

13 Hamlet, shown with his mother, consents to remain in Elsinore, and leaves the room. Close shot.

14 Ophelia in a glade or garden, dressed in white, braids forward over her shoulders, is approached by Hamlet from the background. An outdoor scene; medium shot. (New)

Title: Hamlet: 'Doubt thou the stars are fire. Doubt thou the sun doth move. Doubt truth to be a liar. But never doubt I love.' (II, 2)

15 Hamlet presents to Ophelia a necklace, which after coy refusal she accepts. (New)

16 Two characters in a portico, probably Polonius and Laertes watching the previous scene, but it is badly lit and the film has faded. (New)

17 Indoor shot of Ophelia with the necklace, which she kisses. At Laertes' approach she sits in confusion. About to say good-bye, he sees the necklace and shows concern. Close shot. (New)

Title: LAERTES WARNS OPHELIA AGAINST HAMLET'S ADVANCES

18 He does so, kisses her forehead. Close shot.

Title: 'Fear it Ophelia, fear it my dear sister and keep you in the rear of your affections.' (I, 3)

19 Laertes leaves, as Ophelia bows her head, but she again kisses the necklace. Medium shot. (New)

20 Hamlet, sprawled in a chair on a dais, talks with Horatio and Marcellus. The scene is only semi-interior because trees are seen through a large arched opening which forms the background. Hamlet is startled by their information. Medium shot. (I, 2)

Title: 'My lord I think I saw him yesternight . . . the King your father.'

21 More conversation about the ghost. Hamlet rises suddenly. Medium shot.

22 Close-up of Hamlet.

Title: 'I'll watch tonight, perchance 'twill walk again. If it assume my noble father's person, I'll speak to it though Hell itself should gap and bid me hold my peace.'

23 Hamlet, after a pose, comes downstage, an arm on each's shoulder. Medium shot.

24 Hamlet, Horatio, and Marcellus move off. Long shot.

Title: 'Tonight the drunken King mine uncle drains his draughts of Rhenish wine.' (I, 4)

25 Continuation of 24, in a corridor, semi-interior. Long shot.

26 An exterior shot on seashore, looking from shore inland, mostly rocks but also an inflowing stream. Hamlet enters from background, clambering over the rocks. Medium shot. (New)

27 The scene in reverse looking toward the sea, seen through a cleft with rocky cliffs right and left. Hamlet appears on the left with the ghost in double exposure, huge and close, blended with the rocks on the right. Otherwise a medium shot.

Title: 'I am thy father's Ghost doomed for a certain term to walk the night ... if thou did'st ever thy dear father love, revenge his foul and most unnatural murder.' (I, 5)

28 Much emotion shown by Hamlet, who falls to the rock.

Title: 'Tis given out that a serpent stung me ... The serpent that did sting thy father's life now wears his crown.'

29 The murder scene itself is now depicted. The elder Hamlet and Gertrude are affectionate. He leaves her in a chair. Claudius enters. (New)

30 Close shot of Ghost, presumably speaking.

Title: 'Sleeping within my orchard upon my secure hour thy uncle stole with juice of cursed hebanon in a vial and in the porches of my ear did pour the leperous distillment.'

31 Close shot of Ghost.

32 The actual murder in the orchard. Medium shot.

33 The Ghost and Hamlet. Medium shot.

Title: 'Thus was I sleeping by a brother's hand of life, of crown, of Queen at once dispatched.'

34 The Ghost and Hamlet. Medium shot.

Title: 'Taint not thy mind nor let thy soul contrive against thy mother aught; leave her to heaven.'

35 Close shot of Ghost.

Title: 'Adieu, adieu, Hamlet remember me.'

36 The ghost having vanished, Hamlet is shown alone in great perturbation. He is completely prostrate on the rock. (New)

37 A very few frames apparently show the soldiers leaving the scene. There is a shot of the cliff, possibly of the castle in the background, but whatever it is, it looks like a built pile of rocks. Vague, cut long shot. (New)

Title: 'Aye thou poor Ghost remember thee. Thy commandment all alone shall live within the book and volume of my brain.'

38 Hamlet alone, perhaps delivering the above speech. A medium shot but cut and vague.

39 Hamlet, reading, and Polonius. Medium shot. (II, 2)

44. "Palm to palm is holy palmers' kiss." Harry Hilliard and Theda Bara in *Romeo and Juliet* (Fox, 1916). Courtesy of Theda Bara

45. Lear (Frederick Warde) banishes Cordelia (Lorraine Huling) in the Thanhouser *King Lear* (▶
Ernest Warde played the Fool. *Moving Picture World*, November 4, 1916

46. A scene from *The Merchant of Venice* (Broadwest, 1916) with Matheson Lang as Shylock. Na
Film Archive

From the Rodolfi Film *Hamlet*
): Hamlet (Ruggero Ruggeri)
e feet of Ophelia (Elena
owska) in the play-within-the-
cene (*above*); and the closet
with Gertrude (Mercedes
one) (*below*). Museum of
rn Art Film Library

48. Matheson Lang and Hilda Bayley in an *Othello* scene from *Carnival* (Alliance, 1921). Museum of Modern Art Film Library

Title: 'Do you know me, my lord?'
40 Hamlet and Polonius.
Title: 'Excellent well, you are a fishmonger.'
Title: 'Have you a daughter?'
41 Further action of Hamlet and Polonius. Medium shot.
Title: 'Still harping on my daughter. He is far gone, far gone.'
42 Close-up of Polonius.
Title: 'What do you read my lord?'
43 Close-up of Hamlet.
Title: 'Words, words, words.'
44 Close-up of Hamlet.
45 Hamlet flings down the book, and Polonius hurriedly departs. Medium shot.
46 A few frames, apparently of Rosencrantz and Guildenstern with the King and Queen. Medium shot. (Perhaps III, 1)
Title: End of Reel I.

Stills show that Reel II contained the play-within-the-play (III, 2) and the closet scene of Hamlet and his mother with the killing of Polonius (III, 4). The first is very crowded. The camera shoots the backs of spectators in the foreground and through an aisle the play-within-the-play being enacted – the pouring of poison in the elder Hamlet's ear – in the far background. Hamlet is directly centred in the middle distance, Ophelia in a chair beside him, her attendants back of them, soldiers opposite. Hamlet is looking at Claudius and Gertrude somewhat obscured at the left midway between foreground and stage centre. It is a long-to-medium shot. The second starts as a close shot curtain scene, the interview between Hamlet and his mother; it is followed by another close shot, not in Shakespeare, of Ophelia, recumbent on the body of Polonius, which is on a short flight of steps. There is no way of knowing how Hamlet's overheard conversation with Ophelia (III, 1), the prayer scene (III, 3), and the first three scenes of Act IV which deal with the discovery of Polonius' death, the apprehension of Hamlet, and the dictum that he is to be sent to England were handled. If Reel II covered as much territory as Reel I and Reel III, most of these scenes must have been included in one way or another.

Reel III

1 A close shot of Ophelia, mad, toying with hair. (New)
Title: ON A PLAIN IN DENMARK HAMLET MEETS THE NORWEGIAN ARMY UNDER FORTINBRAS CROSSING TO POLAND
2 Hamlet on horseback looking off; no army is shown. Close shot. (IV, 4)
Title: 'To my shame I see 20,000 men that for a fantasy and trick of fame go to their graves – like beds.'
3 A continuation of 2.
4 Laertes, Claudius, and Gertrude in a grove of fir trees. Ophelia enters, mad, and passes through them, without recognition.

I

Title: 'He is dead and gone, Lady
    He is dead and gone
    At his head a grass green turf
    At his heels a stone.' (IV, 5)

5 Laertes storms into the Court to the consternation of the King. Medium shot.

Title: 'Let come what may I'll be revenged most thoroughly for my father.'

6 Ophelia enters, distributing flowers. Medium shot.

Title: 'His beard was white as snow
    All flaxen was his poll
    He is gone, he is gone
    God ha' mercy on his soul.'

7 Laertes is violently shocked at Ophelia's condition; the King restrains Laertes. Medium shot.

Title: 'Laertes your father's death shall be revenged
    Where the offense is let the great axe fall.'

8 Laertes and the King. Medium shot.

Title (crudely printed): 'Horace, kindly do all possible in order that my letters will reach the King. We were on the sea since two days when a pirate ship approached us. I have been taken prisoner. You must secure sufficient money to ransom me and come at once to rejoin me, Hamlet.' (Loosely adapted from IV, 6)

9 Horatio leaves with the messengers who have brought the letter. Medium shot.

10 Ophelia in open woodland. Long shot.

11 A stream which Ophelia approaches with garland; she slips and falls in. Medium shot. (IV, 7, end, but pictured)

12 Claudius and Laertes in an interior. Medium shot.

Title: 'Hamlet who hath your father slain,
    Also pursued my life!
    Your revenge draws near.'

13 A messenger approaches Claudius and Laertes with a letter for the King. Medium shot.

Title (crudely printed): 'Sire, I have the honour to inform you that I have just approached your country. I ask the favour to be introduced to your royal majesty.'

14 Claudius restrains Laertes from impetuously rushing off to find Hamlet. Medium shot.

Title: 'We'll match Hamlet and you in a duel on a wager. A little poison on the point of your sword and you are avenged.'

15 A continuation of 14.

16 The Queen and her attendants in an outdoor shot among fir trees. Laertes and the King approach. Laertes is grief-stricken when he is told of Ophelia's death. He rushes off followed by the others. (Medium shot.)

17 Ophelia's body on the ground, with attendants. (Medium shot.)

18 Laertes arrives, falls in grief on Ophelia's body. The King and Queen approach.

19 A gravedigger digs a grave while Hamlet and Horatio talk with him. (V, 1)

Title: 'I dig this grave for one that was a woman but rest her soul she's dead.'

20 The business of Yorick's skull.

21 More visual conversation, in several medium shots.

Title: 'Imperious Caesar dead and turned to clay
Might stop a hole to keep the wind away.
But soft, here comes the King.'

22 A procession enters rear, as Hamlet and Horatio step behind a rock, right foreground. Laertes goes to the grave, kisses the dead Ophelia, and is raised by the King. The body is lowered into the grave; Hamlet displays surprise and anguish. (Medium shot.)

Title: 'What, the fair Ophelia!'

23 The Queen strews flowers in the grave. (Medium shot.)

Title: 'Sweet to the sweet; farewell!
I hoped thou shouldst have been my Hamlet's wife.'

24 A close shot of the Queen.

25 Laertes moves quickly from the background and jumps into the grave. Medium shot.

Title: 'Laertes: Cursed be the man whose wicked deed deprived thee of thy mind.'

26 Hamlet, though restrained by Horatio, sweeps right to left as Laertes looks out of the grave at him. Hamlet jumps into the grave. They struggle and are parted to opposite sides. Medium shot.

Title: 'I loved Ophelia, forty thousand brothers could not have loved her more.'

27 Hamlet leaves with Horatio, down right. The Queen kneels. Medium shot.

28 Claudius, with Laertes, to Osric. Medium shot. (New)

Title: 'Ask Hamlet if he accepts Laertes' challenge to the fight.' (Coined)

29 Osric departs, as the King and Laertes talk. (Medium shot.)

30 Horatio, standing, and Hamlet, seated, are addressed by Osric with many flourishes, which Hamlet mocks. Medium shot. (V, 2)

Title: 'The King hath wagered with him, six Barbary horses against six French swords that you will win.'

31 Hamlet and Horatio are now both standing. Hamlet shows uneasiness. Close shot.

Title: 'There's a special providence in the fall of a sparrow ... if death be not now, yet it will come – I am ready!'

32 Hamlet and Horatio enter the crowded Court. After talking with Claudius, Hamlet approaches Laertes, hand outstretched. The King and Queen are on thrones at the right. Medium shot.

Title: 'Give me your pardon, Laertes
I've done you wrong ...
What I have done, I here
proclaim was madness.'

33 They shake hands, face the thrones, step back and apart. Osric brings rapiers, hands one to Laertes, one to Hamlet. They try the rapiers. Laertes goes to Osric and picks another rapier. Medium shot. The King speaks.

Title: 'If Hamlet give the first or second hit –
The King shall drink to Hamlet!'

34 Close shot of the King. The focus is on his pouring poison into a cup on a table.

35 Hamlet and Laertes duel, centre, Laertes facing the camera. Hamlet gets the first hit. They part. Hamlet kneels at the thrones. Medium shot.

36 Close shot of Hamlet and the Queen.

Title: THE FATAL DRINK.

Title: 'Here Hamlet, take my napkin, rub thy brows!
     The Queen drinks to thy fortune, Hamlet.'

37 Close shot of the Queen drinking.

38 Close-up of the King, showing consternation.

39 Close shot of the Queen, wiping her lips.

40 The duel is resumed, and Hamlet, now facing the camera, is hit. Medium-long shot.

41 Close-up of Hamlet, hand to heart, face expressing amazement.

42 They fight furiously, and Laertes is disarmed. Hamlet hands him his own rapier, which is taken reluctantly. (Medium shot.)

Title: 'The poisoned weapon with which Hamlet is wounded falls to his own hand.'

43 Hamlet picks up Laertes' rapier. Close shot.

44 Gertrude rises, showing distress. Close shot.

Title: 'O my dear Hamlet, –
     The drink, the drink! –
     I am poisoned.'

45 Hamlet wounds Laertes. The Queen is taken away by her waiting woman, as Laertes falls. (Medium shot.)

Title: 'Hamlet thou art slain,
     The sword is blunted [sic], poisoned. And I am justly killed with mine own treachery.'

46 Close shot of Laertes on the ground, Hamlet kneeling over him.

47 Medium shot of Hamlet, rising, rapier outstretched.

Title: 'Here thou incestuous, murderous, damned Dane,
     Drink off this potion!
        Is thy union here?
     Follow my mother!'

48 Hamlet wounds Claudius with the rapier. The King staggers and falls, mostly offstage, his feet showing. Hamlet is supported by two courtiers, Horatio and probably Marcellus. Medium shot.

49 Hamlet is led to the throne where he is seated. Close shot.

Title: 'Horatio, what a wounded name
     Things standing thus unknown,
        shall live behind me! . . .
     And in this harsh world draw thy breath in pain
     To tell my story.'

50 Close-up of Hamlet on throne, his head crowned, staff of office in his hand.

51 Close shot to include Horatio and Marcellus. Hamlet's head falls forward. Horatio raises the head, which drops again.

Title: 'Now cracks a noble heart
Good night, sweet prince,
And flights of angels sing thee to thy rest.'
52 Horatio and Marcellus kneel before Hamlet. Medium shot.
53 Long shot of courtiers and soldiers, heads bowed. Fortinbras enters, is told
about the events, and outstretches his arm to the dead Hamlet.
Title: THE END

This is a much better script for a silent film version of *Hamlet* than any earlier one. It is not just a visualization of action in Shakespearean lines, but an attempt at making the story and the emotion of the characters clear in pictorial terms to the uninitiated. No doubt it has its deficiencies. There is still too much photographed conversation, the Hamlet–Polonius interview for example at the end of the first reel. Fortinbras is insufficiently identified for his position to be intelligible at the end of Reel III. The court scenes are so crowded that it is not easy to pick out the principals; the play-within-the-play scene especially is so staged that Hamlet is partly lost, and since the guilty Claudius and Gertrude have their backs to the camera, the effect of the 'mousetrap' in the far background cannot easily be made apparent in their reactions. The business of the poisoned cup is obvious enough without the explanatory 'The Fatal Drink'. There may be borrowings from the Forbes-Robertson *Hamlet*, the appearance of the Ghost on the seashore, the crowning of the dead Hamlet, though these are good scenes. But invented scenes based on episodes described or implied by Shakespeare are quite properly shown. The inclusions of the funeral procession of the elder Hamlet and of the marriage feast of Claudius and Gertrude are not merely interpolations of action; they show the effects of action on the protagonist, and do so particularly by shifting from medium to close shots. Laertes is firmly established by a scene in which he asks his father's permission to return to France, and Ophelia is introduced earlier than in Shakespeare so that her role in the play becomes more evident. The outdoor sequence in which Hamlet presents a necklace to her helps to establish visibly their relationship, and since the action is observed by Laertes and Polonius, it prompts Laertes' warning. The portrayed murder of the elder Hamlet springs naturally from the ghost's narration of his death and indicates what Hamlet is hearing, and the pouring of cursed hebona in the porches of his ears here illuminates without further exposition the method of murder in the play-within-the-play. Ophelia over Polonius' dead body directly presents Ophelia's grief. The transfer of Ophelia's mad scene to outdoors prepares for her drowning in a similar setting. Osric's message to Hamlet is prepared for by an episode in which Claudius sends him to the Prince. The editing is another improvement. Titles are cut in, not just at the beginning of action which then becomes a picture of the lines, but in between phases of the action, so that the action remains paramount and the titles merely explain.

Finally, though the camera is stationary, a single episode may contain shots running all the way from long to close up to focus on significant detail.

The Rodolfi *Hamlet* is no masterpiece, nor even a good picture, but it shows an advance in the cinematic treatment of Shakespeare's tragedy. It is less of the stage, in spite of some stagy scenes, and more of the film. Dark and light are contrasted in costumes, and the curtains and rooms will do when outdoor settings cannot be used. Unfortunately Ruggeri's performance is theatrical, perhaps too Italianate. Gestures are violent; facial expressions, too frequently grimaces. Worst of all Ruggeri does not look the part of a Prince, either the young one or the thirty-year-old one whose age is determined by the words of the gravedigger. Some improvement in make-up and constriction might have removed from the merciless eye of the camera the deep lines in his face and the protuberant belly. Ruggeri looks all of his forty-six years, his Hamlet older than Gertrude. The more experienced motion picture actors in the picture are, despite his greater inherent ability, more effective than he is. Still he manages to portray a vigorous, intelligible, deeply moved, and at times moving Hamlet. If the sensitivity and the poetry are not there, as they were to a degree in the Forbes-Robertson version, this is by no means an uninteresting or insignificant presentation of *Hamlet* in the era of the World War.

CHAPTER VIII
Let Me Have Leave to Speak

1920 TO SOUND

THE reaction of cinema to the end of World War I and its development until sound revolutionized it at the end of the 1920's are too complex to epitomize accurately and varied in different areas. Broadly speaking, France recovered slowly but surely, and England returned to its former level, while Italy failed to maintain its prestige. The emergence of imaginative directors in Sweden and Russia brought new excitement and artistic reputation to those countries, and Germany, partly by attracting personnel from Denmark and elsewhere, partly by the conditions during and following its virtual blockade, grew in power and importance. The United States, least hurt by the War, dominated the commercial market both at home and abroad.

The progress of Shakespeare film was, however, not parallel to that of film in general. During these ten years direct adaptations were few indeed, fewer than in any of the three or four year spans which have been covered in the chronological sections already treated. Sweden and Russia showed no interest in Shakespeare on the screen. France and Italy abandoned him as a source, and England was still content with transcription of stage performance or two-reelers. In short, European countries which had produced most of the Shakespeare films withdrew from the field. The United States, concerned first with financial success, found from both its history and its practice that Shakespeare films only rarely paid their way, and that the appeal of its stars was in other directions. Germany was almost alone in experimenting with Shakespeare. There was of course, especially in America, the usual borrowing of the names of characters and motifs, the parodies, the inclusion of excerpts; many of the films were shorts. The major Shakespeare films were confined to 1920, 1922, 1923, and 1925; after 1925 there is temporary oblivion. In addition to the purely economic factors there was a realization as the theory of film clarified and the art of film grew as a possibility that to tell Shakespeare's stories in pictures alone was not appropriate in the developing silent medium and that cinema adaptation would have to wait until the words and music could be heard.

Though the categories are not rigid, it is convenient to divide the films of this period into those which borrow the names of characters or titles but which have no or almost no other discernible relation to Shakespeare, those which parody his plays, those which contain excerpts, announcements of plans for Shakespearean films which were not realized, and those which are more or less direct adaptations. The first group is the largest.

Romeo continued to be a byword by which a producer could indicate a romance of some sort and which he could combine with the rest of his title to convey locale or activity. William Fox found the practice so successful that he made no less than six Romeo films between 1921 and 1925. Thus we have *A Ridin' Romeo*, a Tom Mix western (1921); *A Tropical Romeo*, an Al St John comedy (1923); *Mile-a-Minute Romeo*, again with Mix (1923); *Monkey Romeo*, one of the 'Monkey Comedy Series' (1924); *The Arizona Romeo*, another western but featuring Buck Jones (1925); and *A Spanish Romeo*, a two-reel comedy with Earle Foxe (1925). How ubiquitous or metamorphosed can Romeo be? Even more apparently, if comedy is the chief aim, as witness *Romeo's Dad*, starring Gail Kane and Tom Wise (1920); *Romeo Mixup*, with Edmund Cobb (1924); *Bromo and Juliet*, with Charley Chase (1926); *Roameo*, a Felix the Cat Cartoon (1927); *A Racing Romeo*, in which the football star, Red Grange, drove to the applause of Jobyna Ralston (1927); *Rival Romeos*, an Oswald cartoon about a Lucky Rabbit (1928); *Romeo in the Stone Age* (1928); and *Flying Romeos*, an Irish-Jewish comedy in which Charlie Murray and George Sidney as barbers pursue a beautiful manicurist by emplaning with a pilot who turns out to be an escaped lunatic (1928). There were no doubt better films on other subjects such as Lubitsch's *Anna Boleyn* (1920), alias *Deception*, with Emil Jannings as Henry VIII and Henny Porten as the unfortunate Anne, but equally removed from Shakespeare, and I have to record that Charles Ray appeared in *Alias Julius Caesar* (1922), that there was a *Love's Labour Won* (1922), a *Shylock of Wall Street* (1922), two quite irrelevant *Tempests* (1927, 1929), all long pictures, not to mention *Cleopatra and Her Easy Mark* (1925), which was very short. Toward the end of the period there are innovations, merely transitional: *Cleo to Cleopatra*, a Vitaphone one-reeler in which sound was added to Daphne Pollard, and *Cleopatra*, twice as long, produced by Herbert T. Kalmus in both sound and color; both are of 1928, when the film world was in turmoil, but that is a later story.

Parody is a greater pleasure than casual waywardness and besides is in its way closer to the subject. In this period there were at least twelve parodies; *Romeo and Juliet* was most often the basis of comic comparison; the United States produced the largest number, while England was the most consistent and the only country which produced a planned series. Hepworth was responsible for four one-reel cartoons by Anson Dyer. The first was an animation of *The Merchant of Venice* (1919) which *Bioscope* found to be 'a good-humoured Shakespearean burlesque, full of those ingenious quips and cranks which the inventive cartoonist may introduce with the help of the camera. Antonio, a Venetian ice-cream man, is County-Courted by the rapacious Shylock (enacted with suitable ferocity by that great tragedian, Mr Ward R. Street). After stimulating her window garden to miraculous growth by the flood of her tears, the lovely Portia defends her lover in court, and successfully vanquishes the bloodthirsty Shylock by calling for the production of his ration book, and proving that he has exhausted his meat tickets. This amusing little parody is loaded with novel incidental trick effects whilst the sub-titling (which is made to proceed from a gramophone) is consistently witty.' It is a pleasure to find evidence of original ideas, and the picture was successful enough to prompt two more Dyer cartoons in the same year.

The second, *Romeo and Juliet*, was 'even better than its predecessor' and ran a new tack by introducing Charlie Chaplin as Romeo and Mary Pickford as Juliet. 'With quite extraordinary skill, Mr Dyer has caught the mannerisms of these two film favourites, reproducing in an amazingly life-like way the famous Chaplin walk and the Pickford smile. . . . These vivid studies are the best things of the kind yet done. . . .' Chaplin, as C. H. Aplin, continued in the third animation, this time as 'Amlet. Informed of his uncle's guilt by a spectre, 'Amlet 'shoots' Claudius with a movie camera, as he exults over the rations he has hoarded. A projection of the film confronts Claudius with evidence of his crime, as 'Amlet watches him closely with an electric torch. This ingenious modernization of the play-within-the play was accompanied by clever titling, and the whole proved to be 'consistently entertaining'. The series was concluded with an *Othello* in 1920, in which the Moor, a seaside minstrel, after adventures which humorously parallel the Shakespearean play, smothers Mona 'with burnt cork and kisses. . . .' It was called 'one of the best of the Shakespearean series', but the vein evidently ran out, perhaps because the general public could not be relied upon to know the plots of the other plays.

Other burlesques of 1919–1920 included an Italian *Othello*, adapted, directed, and acted by Camillo De Riso, whose humor was 'incorreggibilmente provinciale', and four American efforts of various types: *A Sage Brush Hamlet*, a Western with William Desmond and Marguerite de la Motte; *Shades of Shakespeare*, a Christie comedy which burlesqued amateur theatricals; a Bud Fisher 'Mutt and Jeff' cartoon called *Cleopatra*; and *Romeo and Juliet* with the plump Walter Hiers as the hero and Dorothy Wolbert as the heroine. In 1923 there was a British *Juliet and Her Romeo*, a syncopated comedy with Queenie Thomas. 1924 saw an 'histerical history' comedy, *Anthony and Cleopatra* and the only one of this group I wish I had seen, a Mack Sennett *Romeo and Juliet* with the hilariously cross-eyed Ben Turpin as Romeo. In one scene he wiggled his ears while he sang Tosti's 'Good-bye' at the family organ.

Another kind of adaptation might be loosely called thematic. From Italy

I*

in 1919 came *Amleto e il suo Clown*, shot by Luciano Molinari for Lucio D'Ambra in which Carmino Gallone directed his wife, Soave Gallone. The script was by D'Ambra. The heroine, Alexandra, was 'a weak, irresolute creature ... doomed to bring unhappiness on herself [and others] ..., a weak nature so inclined to morbid reflection that the mind becomes unbalanced and a tragic end is the only solution'. I quote from *Bioscope*, May 13, 1920, which also summarizes and comments on the English version, *On With the Motley*:

'Alexandra Tranda is in her father's beautiful gardens, awaiting his return home. When his carriage slowly comes up the drive, she is horrified to find his dead body hanging over the splashboard. He has been shot through the head. Within two months Alexandra receives another shock, when her mother marries John Arnold, an old friend of the family. Alexandra broods over this in a morbid way, seeing in its events of her own home a parallel to the story of Hamlet. She induces her mother to give a garden party, and with the assistance of a group of clowns from a circus she gives a version of the play scene from *Hamlet*. Imagining that during the course of the play she detects signs of guilt in her stepfather's conduct, she turns the affair into a veritable tragedy by stabbing Arnold to the heart. She is arrested and while waiting her trial, a young farmer confesses to the murder of her father.

The rest of the story is irrelevant to Shakespeare. Alexandra attempts suicide, is befriended by one of the clowns, becomes seriously ill and overwrought, upon her recovery joins the circus and makes a success. When her mother tries to induce her to return home, she throws herself from on high during a sensational act and dies in her mother's arms. The story is of course no more melodramatic than Shakespeare's, and the review praises the film for 'scenes of exquisite beauty ... photography of the highest quality ... dramatic interest ... violent passions in contrast to light and gaiety of ... native skies'. The company was 'strong', and Soave Gallone particularly commended.

Lighter Shakespearean motifs provided the basis of the last of the short films of Ernst Lubitsch, a winter sports comedy titled *Romeo und Julia im Schnee* (1920). Lubitsch and Hans Kraly wrote the scenario, and Gustave von Wangenheim played Romeo to the Juliet of Lotte Neumann in a snowier clime than Verona. Equally light or more lightweight were two American films of 1921. In *Enchantment*, starring Marion Davies, a father at a performance of *The Taming of the Shrew* conceives the plan of taming his 'flapper' daughter by persuading an actor-friend to be a real Petruchio. The actor succeeds and in the process the two young people fall in love. And Pathé released a film called *The Tempest*, a modernization vaguely related to Shakespeare in which the hero, played by Tom Santschi, is shanghaied, thrown overboard in a storm, finds refuge on an island, and falls in love with the lighthouse keeper's daughter. There is also some mistaken identity about a boy he tries to protect who turns out to be the girl's brother.

Two other films of this sort have or are alleged to have some Shakespearean counterpart. In one case it is difficult to discover just what material was used; in the other, the relationship is if any, even slighter. A Danish comedy, directed in 1922 by Lau Lauritzen for Palladium, called *Han og Hun og Hamlet* (*He and She and Hamlet*) presented the slapstick team of Carl Schenstrøm and Harold Madsen. They were popularly known as 'Fy' and 'Bi', clippings of *fyrtaarnet* and *bivognen*, literally lighthouse and second (trolley) car, or roughly long and short. Schenstrøm was tall and skinny, Madsen tubby. They were a kind of counterpart of Laurel and Hardy and achieved great success in Europe; in Germany they were Patt and Patachon, in France Doublepatte and Patachon. What they did with *Hamlet* I can only guess, since I have found no summary of their jape, but it must have been a hit, since the picture was remade in 1932 with the addition of sound. According to the *Exhibitors Daily Review*, May 22, 1926, the American farce, *Wet Paint*, was 'introduced as having something in common with Bill Shakespeare's *Much Ado About Nothing* ... makes a noble struggle to live up to its reputation [but] ... it completely surrenders itself to slapstick. ...' It is not easy to see from reviews what the parallel was except that put-upon Raymond Griffith is confronted with circumstantial evidence which endangers his romance with Helene Costello and that there is a confusion of identities at the final marriage ceremony. Paint was probably more important than parallel.

The line between thematic adaptation and the inclusion of excerpts is necessarily faint. Theme may be a development of an inclusion, and inclusion may be appropriate to motif. The inclusion in *Carnival* (1921) was decidedly second hand, since the *Othello* interpolation was already in the play by H. C. M. Hardinge and Matheson Lang which Lang and Hilda Bayley had acted on the stage of the New Theatre. Its success there was the impetus for the film directed by Harley Knoles for Alliance, made largely at the St Margaret's-on-Thames studio, partly in Venice, though Lang did not accompany the rest of the company to Italy. Both play and film include a discussion between Silvio Steno, an Italian Shakespearean actor, and Count Andrea Scipione, in which the actor maintains that Othello's jealousy is preposterous. Steno, however, becomes increasingly suspicious during the carnival of the apparent intimacy between his actress-wife and the Count, and he almost strangles her during a performance of the play before misunderstanding is clarified and reconciliation follows. Both theme and excerpt are functional here. The film was widely shown both on the Continent and in America; but it was a poor production in almost every respect.

Much better was Will Rogers' *Doubling for Romeo* of the same year, which Clarence Badger directed for Goldwyn from a script by Bernard McConville with bows to Elmer Rice, Will Rogers, and Shakespeare. 'The reason we made it', said Rogers, 'was that we could use the same costumes that Miss Geraldine Farrar and a friend of hers (at that time) had worn in some costume pictures – all these Shakespearian tights and everything. I don't say this egotistically, but I wore Geraldine's.' *Exceptional Photoplays*, November 1921, said, '*Doubling for Romeo* has what is perhaps the rarest quality in a motion picture story – genuine wit. . . . The whole picture is a delicious burlesque of the conventional film. Will Rogers is a clumsy cowboy who goes to a picture studio in order to learn how to make love in proper movie style to please his girl. He is shown every variety of love-making by the obliging director, and tries his hand at each variety, emerging with a strong preference for the strong-arm method. Presently he falls asleep while reading *Romeo and Juliet* and dreams that he is Romeo, with the girl he loves, but cannot make love to, as his Juliet. Here the fun is at its best . . .', as I can testify, since the Museum of Modern Art has the six-reel film. In the dream various characters in the frame story fade in individually and are transformed into characters of the play. There is a burlesqued balcony scene with Rogers strumming a ukulele for Sylvia Breamer as Juliet above, a quarrel with Tybalt which combines both horse play and sword play and culminates with a blow to the jaw, a Capulet feast from which Romeo escapes in the manner of Douglas Fairbanks by swinging on a rope, a return to the balcony to which Rogers jumps by means of flying apparatus and where he drinks wine with his girl – all this accompanied by frequent subtitle quips. Ultimately Romeo wins his Juliet, and I am glad he did. If the picture needed sound, the movement and action kept it going and Rogers made laughter inevitable in a joyous charade.

The elder Dumas' *Kean, ou Désordre et Génie*, a preposterous mixture of conventionalized heroics and love intrigue, was properly slain by Thackeray in an essay on French drama in *The Paris Sketchbook*, but it was for a century a play which offered a favorable occasion for a romantic star to exhibit a striking and varied characterization of the leading figure, and besides allowed an actor to play an actor who also acted within the context of the plot. Originally it was one of the most successful roles of Frédéric Lemaître. Dumas included in his drama bits and pieces of Shakespeare: two characters named Bardolph and Pistol, who are nothing like the originals; references to *Othello*, *Hamlet*, Falstaff, *Romeo and Juliet*; and in the ninth scene of Act IV an excerpt from the second balcony scene where Romeo takes his departure from Juliet after their marriage night; with such theatrics it was inevitable that the play would be adapted for early film. There was a Danish *Kean* with Martinius Nielsen in 1910, a Brunestelli version from Italy in 1917, and in Germany a UFA production directed by Rudolf Biebrachs with Heinrich George and Alfons Frysland in 1922. How much Shakespeare material these pictures utilized, I cannot say, but there was another film in 1922 which not only kept Dumas' original excerpts but added more, the death scene from *Romeo and Juliet* and an interpolation from *Hamlet*. These bits combined with other roles, Werther, Manfred, and Tristan (not created until some thirty years after Edmund Kean died) exhibited the virtuosity in style and make-up of Ivan Mosjoukine, now in France along with other Russian émigrés. Alexander Volkoff, Mosjoukine, and Kenelm Foss tailored the scenario; Volkoff directed; and Paulina Po played Juliet. This bravura was made largely at the Albatros studio at Montreuil-sous-Bois, once the property of Georges Méliès, but the Drury Lane sequences in the Pathé ateliers at Joinville. Trust an actor to increase the Shakespearean extracts, if opportunity permits.

Other films of 1922 also drew from the wealth of Shakespeare. *Polly of the Follies* allowed Constance Talmadge to play Cleopatra in an amateur show, though her opposite was Julius Caesar rather than Antony, and *The Trouper*, about a general utility girl in a travelling stock company, showed quite incidentally Gladys Walton as Juliet in a balcony scene. More attractive was a Buster Keaton comedy, *Day Dreams*, in which a rural youth tries to make good in the city. As an anticipation of Walter Mitty, he imagines himself as a famous surgeon, and in wide eyed deadpan as Hamlet, complete with sword and skull. There is something like an *Othello* theme, though no direct relation to the play in what was one of the most visually imaginative films of the year, *Warning Shadows*, directed in Germany by Arthur Robison, with Fritz Kortner as a jealous husband, who with his beautiful wife is entertaining a young man and three gallants at supper. 'There arrives at the house a shadow conjurer, who is invited to give his performance. After enacting a Chinese shadow play, the conjurer moves the light backwards, so that the shadows of the spectators are thrown upon the screen where, miraculously, they have a separate existence. As enchanted shadows, the wife and the young man are caught together by the husband, who has the woman bound upon the table, where he forces the three gallants to pierce her with swords. Staggering from the room, he flings himself from the window. Whereupon the conjurer moves back the lights, the spectators finding themselves seated, as they were, at the table. The warning of the shadows has done its work and, while the guests hastily leave, husband and wife embrace in the morning sunlight.' This experimental, atmospheric, and psychological film with 'unusual lighting' and 'pictorial value' – it had no subtitles – is pointed out by J. Isaacs as presenting visually what Shakespeare accomplished with language. The German title was *Schatten eine nächtliche Halluzination*.

Another unusual German film was *Das alte Gesetz* (1923), one of the first directed by E. A. Dupont and based on a scenario by Paul Reno. It told a story laid in Poland and Austria in 1860, about the conflict of a Jewish youth, who wanted to go on the stage, and his father, an orthodox Rabbi. Baruch (Ernst Deutsch) runs away from home to join a travelling company. His performance of Romeo in Reel III is witnessed by the Archduchess Elizabeth Theresa (Henny Porten) who arranges for him to join the Vienna

Burgtheater. He cuts his Jewish locks, and when the Archduchess, who has more than a sponsor's interest in him, flatters the leading actor to taking a drive with her instead of attending an important rehearsal, is offered the role of Hamlet in place of the delinquent player. Opening night is scheduled to take place during the Feast of the Passover. Baruch wishes to decline but is persuaded by the company director and is shown in Reel VI making a sensational success. The indiscreet Archduchess is advised to break with him and does so. Baruch returns home during the Passover and is disowned by his father. Accompanied by his sweetheart, he returns to Vienna and is ultimately reconciled with the Rabbi who has been persuaded to witness his performance as Don Carlos. Deutsch and Porten played well, but *Das alte Gesetz* is most notable for the outstanding direction of Dupont, whose subsequent *Variety* (1925) was to make him famous and bring him from Germany to America.

After two films which are to be taken seriously, it is anticlimactic to name those which need only passing mention. Stills suggest that *The Perfect Flapper* (1924) with Colleen Moore may have had a *Romeo and Juliet* sequence, and Leatrice Joy did two turns as Juliet on a balcony with Rod La Rocque and Victor Varconi respectively, each of whom visualizes himself as Romeo, in a modern romance about a tin can factory called *Triumph* (1924), directed by Cecil B. DeMille. Douglas Fairbanks leaped over a garden wall to woo Mary Astor on a balcony in a Spanish setting in *Don Q*, *Son of Zorro* (1925). Subtitles interpreted him as saying, 'With love's light wings did I o'erperch these walls' and later some minced *Hamlet*; 'O cursed spite that severs those it should unite.' *Bluebeard's Seven Wives* (1925), a spoof on the movies with Ben Lyon as a bank clerk who is made a star by the greatest of all directors contained incidentally both balcony and tomb scenes from *Romeo and Juliet*, relabelled as *Purple Passions*; the Juliet was Blanche Sweet, but Lyon revolted from publicity to marry Lois Wilson.

Scenes from *Hamlet* and *Othello* were interpolated into Robert Wiene's *Der Leibgardist* with Alfred Abel as The Actor and Maria Corda as his wife. Molnar's play known in English as *The Guardsman* was the source of the script by Ludwig Nerz. Molnar had no such scenes though there are references to The Actor's playing Hamlet and Romeo, and *Othello* was presumably added to reinforce his suspicions of his wife whom he tried to seduce in disguise. A German film, *Wie Einst im Mai* (1928) included both theatre and film representations of *Romeo and Juliet* in its story; Karl Harbacher was the Romeo, and Trude Hesterberg the Juliet. Finally for this group was *The Last Moment* (1928), which the National Board of Review magazine, *Exceptional Photoplays*, praised as 'one of the most remarkable and interesting films to appear on this side of the Atlantic.' It was a privately financed experimental film, devised and directed by Paul Fejos, in which a drowning actor, played by Otto Matiesen, sees in flashes a panorama of his life, including a portrayal of Hamlet to the applause of his audience. It is heartening that Shakespeare at least touched such distinguished films as *Warning Shadows*, *Das alte Gesetz*, and *The Last Moment*.

In the decade after the War there were reports of plans for Shakespeare films. They were the product of gossip, rumour, publicity, with here and there a modicum of hope or an indication of initiation of enterprise or an attempt to gauge the reactions of distributors or potential audiences. After John Barrymore's success as Hamlet in New York in 1922–1923, it was bruited about that his performance ought to be transferred to the screen. The *Picturegoer* of January 1923 quotes David Wark Griffith as opposed to a production of the play: 'There are five murders in it. What would the censors say (and do)? Hamlet himself is a very morbid character, who commits suicide, and I fear that not only the censors but the public would ban it without the music of Shakespeare's words.' Other producers, including Goldwyn, Universal, and Warner Bros were said to be favourable to the idea of 'enshrining the best work of America's best actor in celluloid, but doubtful as to its reaction by the public. The scheme, as suggested by Augustus Thomas, is that not one company only, but the entire Producing Managers Association should co-operate in the affair.' Nothing came of this except an announcement in the August issue that though Barrymore would make two films, he was not considering *Hamlet*. In Germany an announcement brochure put out by *Lichtbild Bühne* carried an advertisement of Asta Nielsen-Film for *The Taming of the Shrew* 'nach Shakespearschen Motiven' as the second film for Nielsen for the season of 1922–1923, and No. 25 of the same periodical in 1923 refers to a project to produce the play in Italy with Emil Jannings and Dagny Servaes. Both Asta Nielsen and Jannings had recently made Shakespeare films. These trial flights were the natural consequences.

Jane Cowl's attractive Juliet in New York early in 1923 started a flood of speculation. The *Film Daily Year Book* of 1924 summarizing events of 1923 reported for January that Joseph M. Schenck was after Rudolph Valentino to co-star him with Norma Talmadge in *Romeo and Juliet*, then for December that Norma Talmadge had abandoned the idea and that Lillian Gish would start work on it in the spring. The *Picturegoer* in November 1923 had heard that Talmadge would be starred with Joseph Schildkraut as Romeo and that Conway Tearle would be in the cast. They would be competing with Mary Pickford and Douglas Fairbanks who were planning production for 1924, a plan also reported in the *Year Book*, which added that Ernst Lubitsch would direct. The *Picturegoer* of January 1924 had Lillian Gish playing opposite Richard Barthelmess, then in June 1925 opposite Ronald Colman. The 1926 *Year Book*, however, was back with Talmadge and Valentino. Brusendorff and Knaur both list a *Romeo and Juliet* with Mary Philbin and André Mattoni in 1926, directed by E. A. Dupont, Knaur says in England; I find not the slightest evidence. In the *Motion Picture News*, February 18, 1927, Carl Laemmle was said to be announcing *Romeo and Juliet* with Mary

Philbin and Norman Kerry for Universal. A confusion may have existed with *Love Me and the World Is Mine* in which Dupont did direct these principals in 1927, but the *Film Daily* review of February 12th gives no indication that this picture had anything to do with Shakespeare. All that is clear is that there was talk of doing *Romeo and Juliet* in these years.

The wildest idea, which I find in a scrapbook containing a cutting of the New York *Times* of early 1928, was for Chaplin to play *Hamlet* in a two-reeler, with Pickford, Fairbanks, and Barrymore in supporting roles, the proceeds to go for the construction of the Shakespeare theatre in Stratford-upon-Avon. Imagination staggers. And I can take no stock in a purported film of *Lear* in 1929 supposedly made by the Bayrischen Landesfilmbühne München in 276 metres, listed by Irmgard Thurman.

If the post-war period produced little in Shakespeare film to cheer about, an exception must be made for the best silent *Hamlet* to come from the studios in the twenty years of picture presentation. Produced in Germany in 1920 with the responsibility largely in the hands of emigrés Danes, this version starred as the Prince perhaps the best tragic actress of the silent era, Asta Nielsen. After stage experience at the Royal Theatre of Copenhagen, she found her real métier in her late twenties in films for Nordisk directed by Urban Gad, whom she married. With a style distinctly her own which underplayed gesture and favoured a controlled intensity mirrored in extraordinarily expressive face and body, she soon acquired European recognition which took her with her husband to lucrative contracts in Germany. For Art-Film, her Hamlet was directed in 2367 metres by Svend Gade and Heinz Schall with sets by Gade, camera by Curt Courant and Axel Graatjaer, costumes by Hugo Baruch and L. Verch. Eduard von Winterstein interpreted Claudius; Mathilde Brandt, Gertrude; Hans Junkermann, Polonius; Heinz Stieda, Horatio; Anton de Verdier, Laertes; Paul Conradi, the Ghost; Fritz Achterberg, Fortinbras; and Lilly Jacobsson, Ophelia. All of them effectively played up to the dominance of Asta Nielsen and the conception of the film.

That conception however was not so much Shakespearean as it was a sweeping adaptation of the story on which *Hamlet* was based. It was laid in a cruder and more distant period than the Renaissance and took material from Saxo Grammaticus and at least according to somewhat dubious report other legendary material and the German play, *Fratricide Punished*. In addition the tale was given a violent wrench not found in the background of Shakespeare's play which also changed the motivations of the leading characters. As we have seen, actresses, including Bernhardt, who take the part of Hamlet, ask the audience to assume that they are men and playing a male role. But in this case a woman acted a woman who was disguised as a man. Somehow or other, Erwin Gepard, who wrote the script, or perhaps someone else involved in the planning who brought it to Gepard's attention, had found a copy of a largely unnoticed and forgotten book, *The Mystery of Hamlet* by Edward P. Vining, published by J. P. Lippincott in Philadelphia in 1881, and dedicated to Henry Howard Furness whose New Variorum edition of *Hamlet* had appeared four years before, also through Lippincott. Vining, an interested amateur, had studied the criticisms printed by Furness and found Hamlet more mysterious than the commentators had made him. It is difficult to ridicule ideas presented humbly and earnestly by a writer who recognized in his preface that no views 'could, at first sight, seem more absurd'. That they *are* absurd because illogical and quite contrary to the conventions of Elizabethan playwriting is in this instance less important than the conclusions Vining suggested, that Hamlet is a woman, that Hamlet is in love with Horatio, and that Gertrude, to avoid the problem of succession had passed off a daughter as a son. Starting with conclusions as premises, Gepard wrote a scenario which gave Asta Nielsen hitherto undreamt of dramatic opportunities. How far the story was from Shakespeare may be conveyed by an accurate summary prepared for the American version of the film which appeared in a brochure of Asta Films, the distributor in the United States.

'During the early Middle Ages there was fierce fighting between Denmark and Norway. Fortinbras, King of Norway, and Hamlet, King of Denmark, entered into '*a sealed compact, well ratified by law and heraldry*' whereby it was agreed that the vanquished in a fixed battle to be fought, should '*forfeit all those lands, which he stood seized of, to the conqueror.*' King Fortinbras is killed in this battle by King Hamlet, who is himself wounded.

'While the battle is raging, Queen Gertrude of Denmark gives birth to a daughter in the Royal Palace at Elsinore. A messenger arrives at the Palace with an incorrect report of the death of King Hamlet. The Queen, seeing the crown and throne lost if there is no male issue, is greatly perturbed. Her nurse proposes to the Queen that her subjects be deceived and that they be told that a son has been born. King Hamlet returns from the battle none the worse for his wounds, learns of the Queen's deception but dares not disclose it to his subjects.

'In boy's attire the royal child grows up and bears the name of Prince Hamlet. He is sent to the school for noble youths in Wittenberg. Here among his happy student companions, he meets young Horatio, and also his countryman, Laertes, the son of Polonius, Chamberlain at King Hamlet's Court. He later meets Prince Fortinbras of Norway who is the son of the King who fell in battle against the army led by Hamlet's father. But the royal sons are young and have no desire to keep alive the enmity of their fathers, and a strong bond of friendship is soon sealed between them. Hamlet develops a deep regard for Horatio, the depth of which is never suspected by his young friends.

'In the meantime, foul and terrible deeds are happening at Elsinore. Claudius, King Hamlet's brother, and uncle to Prince Hamlet, has entered upon an illicit love intrigue with the Queen. He murders his royal brother while the latter is asleep in the garden, by means of a venomous snake, seizes the throne and marries the Queen.

'Prince Hamlet at Wittenberg receives the news of his father's death and hastens back to Denmark accompanied by the faithful Horatio. In the King's household Hamlet finds neither sorrow nor mourning. On the contrary, they are celebrating the coronation of Claudius and his marriage to Hamlet's mother. Hamlet finds himself alone in his grief.

'A vision appears to Hamlet which causes a terrible suspicion to take hold of him. Hamlet questions the old gardener who found the body of his father and upon investigation near the pit in the dungeon where the snakes are kept, he finds a dagger which Claudius had dropped there. Hamlet decides to follow this clue and watch his uncle closely for further proof, and conceives the idea of feigning madness to better follow up his clues. Only to his friend Horatio does Hamlet confide his terrible suspicion and the dangerous game he is playing.

'Ophelia, daughter of Pononius, is sent by her father to distract Hamlet and finds herself in danger of losing her heart to the royal youth. Hamlet, however, though pretending love for Ophelia, remains cold and true to his purpose of avenging his father.

'A new pang wrings the heart of Hamlet when he sees his comrade Horatio, whom he has long loved with deep feeling, falling a victim to the charms of Ophelia.

'A wandering theatrical troupe passes the palace and Hamlet conceives the idea of a performance to be given before Claudius in which is portrayed the murder of the King in the manner he suspects his father was murdered. At the presentation of this play, Claudius betrays his guilt.

'Broken in soul, Hamlet goes to his mother, the Queen. He becomes aware that there is a listener behind the curtains in his mother's room. Thinking it is Claudius, Hamlet thrusts his sword through the curtains and kills Polonius, Ophelia's father.

'Claudius realizes that the blow was intended for him and decides to get rid of Hamlet. He commands him, with two court attendants whom he has made aware of his purpose, to deliver a message to King Fortinbras of Norway. Hamlet obeys in silence, but at the first halting place in Norway he obtains possession of the parchment entrusted to his two companions, breaks the seal and reads the order for his own death, which Claudius commands Fortinbras, as his vassal, to execute. Hamlet's quill quickly makes a change in the document, substituting the names of the attendants for his own.

'The journey is resumed and upon arrival at Fortinbras Castle, Hamlet delivers the order to King Fortinbras, his friend of Wittenberg days. The two conspirators are dragged off to the gallows where they expiate their crime.

'Hamlet acquaints Fortinbras with what has happened at Elsinore, and

Fortinbras decides to help Hamlet to his father's throne by leading an army against the criminal King.

'Meanwhile heavy clouds gather around the royal palace at Elsinore. Ophelia's mind gives way at the thought of her father dead by Hamlet's hand and she wanders to her death in a nearby brook. Laertes learns upon his return from Wittenberg of his father's death and his sister's unhappy fate. At the head of an angry mob, already inflamed against the tyranny of the usurping King, Laertes, sword in hand, breaks into the palace seeking vengeance for his father's death. Claudius tells him that Hamlet is the slayer of his father.

'Fortinbras' army is already on the march and is soon camping in the neighborhood of Elsinore. At dawn Fortinbras will resume his march. Hamlet proceeds in advance. He surprises Claudius in the midst of a wild orgy. A drunken stupor overpowers the revelers. Hamlet sets fire to the place and Claudius meets his death.

'Queen Gertrude, forgetting all motherly instincts, seeks revenge for the death of Claudius. When Laertes, seeking vengeance on Hamlet, prepares to fight a duel with him, the Queen prevails upon Laertes to anoint his sword with poison so as to insure the death of Hamlet. To make assurance doubly sure, she prepares a goblet of poison for Hamlet in case Laertes should fail.

'Fate draws near heavy with doom. Hamlet and Laertes begin the duel. Hamlet at first excels his opponent. At a halt in the fight the Queen offers refreshment in the shape of the poisoned cup, which he refuses. An attendant innocently rearranges the wine cups and the Queen herself falls victim to the poisoned cup. Her shriek of 'Poison!' momentarily distracts Hamlet and Laertes pierces him with the poisoned sword.

'Horatio kneels beside the dying Prince, and as he lays him down the steps of the throne, he discovers with deep emotion Hamlet's tragic secret. Too late is Horatio made aware that his comrade was a woman – too late he recognizes that it was a deeper feeling than friendship which bound him to the unhappy Prince.

'King Fortinbras is also to realize the deep tragedy spread before him. As his army enters the palace, he sees at the foot of the throne, which his friend Hamlet was to have ascended, his dead body. Hamlet's body is raised aloft on a shield by Fortinbras' warriors and borne with pomp to its final resting place. [The summary concludes with the first part of Fortinbras' final speech in Shakespeare.]'

It may be useful to present in some detail the provenance of the elements in this amalgam but it would certainly be irrelevant to delve into the relation between Shakespeare's *Hamlet* and its immediate sources, a lost play and perhaps Belleforest's version of Saxo. The enmity between Hamlet's father and the King of Norway involves in Saxo armies which Shakespeare does not mention and may have suggested the initial battle in the film, but in both of the earlier stories there is only single combat. The incorrect report of the death of the elder Hamlet, the Queen's deception about the sex of her child and the King's acceptance of it are invented and from Vining. In Shakespeare, Hamlet and Horatio have been at Wittenberg but not Laertes or Fortinbras; the desire of the two princes to forget the feud may have been suggested by the terms of the earlier single combat in Saxo. The nature of Hamlet's attraction for Horatio is of course from Vining. The illicit relations between Claudius and Gertrude – Belleforest is the most explicit about the adultery – and Claudius' secret murder of his brother are Shakespearean, but Shakespeare's orchard as the scene of the crime gives place to the garden of *Fratricide Punished*, and the means of killing by a snake is a suggestion from the 'forged process' of the elder Hamlet's death, not the actual method used by Shakespeare. Shakespeare's time scheme is changed to allow the showing of Hamlet's reception of the news at Wittenberg and his return for the coronation. The vision seen by Hamlet alone replaces the ghost seen by others as well as Hamlet. The gardener questioned by Hamlet, the snake pit in the dungeon, and the incriminating dagger are invented. The feigned madness is in all the stories, but the use of a girl sent to distract Hamlet may reflect a similar device in Saxo. Hamlet's feelings toward her, his pretended love for her conditioned by his real love for Horatio, and his reaction to her attraction for Horatio are all determined by Vining's theory. The play-within-the-play and the closet scene are in both Shakespeare and *Fratricide Punished*. The journey to Norway replaces the trip to Britain, but the change in the document and the subsequent death of the accessories is Shakespeare's. Fortinbras' decision to help Hamlet to the throne is new, but Ophelia's madness, her death by drowning, Laertes' revolt, and Claudius' allaying of it are all from Shakespeare. Hamlet's return to Elsinore during Claudius' orgy and the destruction by fire are clearly Saxo's. The vengeance sought by Gertrude is new but the methods of its accomplishment are Shakespeare's; on the other hand the accidental shifting of the poisoned cup by an attendant is invented, as is the diversion which causes Hamlet's death. The discovery of Hamlet's sex is inevitably Vining, but the arrival of Fortinbras and the final death-march for Hamlet correspond to the end of Shakespeare's play.

Beyond the shifting of sex for Asta Nielsen, the changes in the story allowed both the return to a violence characteristic of the earlier period in which the action is set and which is more in the spirit of Saxo than Shakespeare, and an opportunity for outdoor scenes and visualization of events Shakespeare did not present on the stage. One remembers a happy Hamlet at Wittenberg, first listening to a lecture by his professor and then after the latter's departure assuming his place at the lectern and mimicking him to the amusement of fellow-students, Hamlet's return to Elsinore, shown as he walks down a long flight of steps toward the camera; the Coronation feast, with Hamlet's dejection; Hamlet and the discovery of the dagger in the dungeon; various shots of Hamlet feigning madness; a close shot of Hamlet meditating suicide; the play-within-the-play in a courtyard; Laertes leading an assault on the castle; Hamlet on horseback on the way to Norway with a fine long shot of lakes and mountains; the rude and murky inn quarters where Hamlet discovers and changes the King's message; Hamlet at the court of Fortinbras; the carousal of Claudius and the fire; an impressive shot at the end of Hamlet being carried on a shield.

The criticism in English which best expresses an intelligent reaction to this film appeared in the organ of the National Board of Review, *Exceptional Photoplays* (January–February 1922):

'Rare is it indeed to see so complete a suggestion of all physical means – appearance, gesture, even the movement of an eye-lid – to the sheer art of showing forth the soul of a character as that which Asta Nielsen accomplishes in her role of Hamlet. . . . For here is a woman whose like we have not on our own screen. Asta Nielsen's art is a mature art that makes the curly-headed girlies and painted hussies and tear-drenched mothers of most of our native film dramas as fantastic for adult consumption as a reading diet restricted to the Elsie books and Mother Goose. . . . It is well . . . to put Shakespeare resolutely out of mind in seeing this production and take it on its own merits, though that is a mental feat made harder than it need have been by the frequent use of Shakespeare's words in subtitles. Considered apart from the great English play, it is a convincing, moving tragedy of a princess who was compelled by reasons of state to be a prince. Thus the old story of avenging a father's 'foul and most unnatural murder' is complicated by feminine scruples and motives – and by a feminine love affair. For Hamlet is in love with Horatio, and his wooing of Ophelia is only the result of his jealousy of the interest Horatio shows in Polonius' daughter.

'Granting its original premise – in which the convincingness of the photo-play persuades one to do – the story moves logically and forcefully through the course of action that Shakespeare has made so familiar, losing much that so enriches the Shakespeare version and gaining much that Shakespeare never thought of.

'The cinema technique of *Hamlet* is often of a high order, though those who prepared the picture for America have thought it necessary, as they invariably do, to gild the lily with superfluous and over-wordy subtitles. Director Sven Gade, the actors and the scene-makers have worked in effective harmony. The sets subtly but powerfully reinforce the action and the acting. And the photography realizes, at times superbly, the mood of the story. In this last regard, one is led to wonder if the picture's grim, tragic atmosphere could have been achieved by the soft effect that seems to be the present ideal of the best camera work.

'Taken all in all, *Hamlet* reaches a level not often seen in our motion picture theatres.'

And the Board of Review includes it among its annual 'Forty Best Pictures of the Year' while the New York *Times*, reviewing fewer films, put it among the first ten. Eleven other New York newspapers carried highly laudatory reviews, and advertisements carried encomia on Asta Nielsen's performance by sculptor Gustave Eberlein, director Ernst Lubitsch, and critic Georg Brandes.

Looked at nowadays, *Hamlet* has serious flaws. The convention that a woman is playing a male role is easily assimilated by an audience, but that none of the characters in the film except those in on the secret recognize that Hamlet is a woman at times strains credulity. Since we are told the truth at the beginning of the picture, it is odd that Hamlet's fellow students at Wittenberg, Ophelia to whom Hamlet makes love, and even the court physician are unable to divine his sex. The final scene in which Horatio makes the discovery by manual examination accompanied by shocked surprise is likely to raise guffaws. Some of the lighting and photography is inadequate, and the exterior scenes are better than most of the interior. The American editing must be held responsible for the titles mutilated from Shakespeare, and those supplied without his assistance can be ludicrous. One is given to Fortinbras after he arrives at Elsinore only to find Hamlet dead: 'I come! To help you to the throne but on the steps your wings did break.' That the picture was not a success in America is understandable. The public was tired of Shakespeare and used to other fare. The trade papers were not encouraging. The distributors publicly protested because it was not housed on Broadway and had to be presented, with the accompaniment of an orchestra playing Tschaikovsky, at the Lexington Theatre. But even at the present time it is apparent why *Hamlet* was widely shown in Europe. It is impossible to be indifferent about it. The story is continuously interesting and frequently exciting; melodrama is raised to a seriousness which creates sympathetic response by emotion and sombre atmosphere. Nothing could be farther from the Forbes-Robertson *Hamlet*, on the whole a record of a great stage performance but admirable in its own way and for its time. Here by adaptation and acting appropriate to pictures in motion, the least Shakespearean *Hamlet* becomes the best *Hamlet* film in the silent era.

Speaking of English stars of the theatre, another of them appeared in 1922, when Sybil Thorndike played Portia in a brief and inconspicuous film of sections of *The Merchant of Venice*. Part of a one-reel series of six produced by Masters Films called 'Tense Moments from Great Plays', this presented bits of Bassanio and Portia which were 'charming as to setting and direction' but chiefly the trial scene in which Ivan Berlyn played Shylock, ending with a shot of the beaten Jew walking out of the court. Unfortunately some of the interiors 'were more reminiscent of Louis XV than the period of the play', but 'a good impression' was given, and Sybil Thorndike made 'a commanding Portia'. I fear this is another example of England's content with recording rather than creating.

The *Luxausgabe der Lichtbild-Bühne | Das Programm* 1922/23 carries an announcement by Caesar-Film for a *Macbeth* as 'das Künstlerische Ereignis der Saison / Regie: Heinz Schall / Künstlerische Bezetzung.' There is no reference to the other participants, but the Wiesbaden brochure lists a production of Elel-Film, Filmindustrie Heidelberg of a 916 metre *Macbeth*. directed by Schall with adaptation by Fritz Kaufmann and Eugen Klöpfer. This is circumstantial enough but maddeningly inconclusive.

A 1922 *Othello* provides much more evidence for a researcher, especially since prints survive, but the film itself is a curious disappointment. The Asta Nielsen *Hamlet* succeeded because it started with, developed from, and adhered to a conception of the *Hamlet* story, which, however unShakespearean, made cinematic sense. Dmitri Bukhovetsky's *Othello* in spite of using such prominent actors as Emil Jannings and Werner Krauss – or perhaps because of them – was much closer to Shakespeare in plot and arrangement, was meant indeed to be a fairly straight version of Shakespeare, but was instead an inartistic distortion of its original. It was made in Berlin in 2662 metres. The scenario was by the director; the photography, largely in studio sets by Fritz Kraencke and Karl Machus, was the work of Karl Hasselmann. Jannings played the title role; Krauss, Iago; Friedrich Kühne, Brabantio; Theodor Loos, Cassio; Ferdinand von Alten, Roderigo; Magnus Stifter, Montano; Ica von Lenkeffy, Desdemona; and Lya de Putti, Emilia. Bukhovetsky had already assisted in the direction of Jannings and Krauss in *The Brothers Karamazov* and had assumed full responsibility for *Danton*. He presumably worked in harmony with his actors so he and they must have been just wrong-headed about the nature of the characters which Shakespeare drew. The best comment I have heard about the film came from a friend who saw it with me, and quoted William Shakespeare himself: '. . . leave thy damnable faces and begin'.

What emerges is more like Cinthio's narrative than Shakespeare's play, a bald and not very well told story of primitive passions without nobility, romance, or poetry, a complicated and unbelievable melodrama of unsympathetic or uninteresting characters. The production was tasteless and unimaginative. The studio settings are ornamental but unatmospheric; the pictures mechanically alternated between long shots architecturally focused and near to close-up which emphasized the actors' grimaces. The subtitles, sometimes semi-Shakespearean adaptations, are far too many, and interrupt the action without adding to it qualities inherent in the play. The cutting is routine and monotonous. The acting in general is incredibly bad in an exaggerated motion picture style which tosses away anything like simple directness for extravagant mumming and mugging. Jannings' Othello has none of the qualities of a first citizen of Venice, but is almost animal, gorilla-like in face and passion without dignity or tragic intensity. Despite a subtitle in Reel I which describes Othello as a worthy and noble person, little or none of these attributes is conveyed, and it is difficult to understand how, as Jannings portrays him, he could be popular with the crowds or, since none of the romantic appeal is there, attractive to Desdemona. Krauss's Iago could not have deceived a lamb. His attempt at joviality becomes buffoonery, and his pop-eyed villainy merely obvious. The handsome Ica von Lenkeffy is only handsome; she does little acting as Desdemona and has no conception of the part. Lya de Putti, whom we remember chiefly for her performance in the frequently shown *Variety*, shows more feeling for the camera and simpler and more facile gestures. The other characters, notably Cassio, are adequately presented, especially when Bukhovetsky allows them to play without inflated emphasis. The version I screened was somewhat cut, but in it, many shots are too short to convey anything and give the impression that the director had used a great deal of film and then tried to cram it into a set playing-time. In short the story seems routine or unintelligible and is told with much posturing and eye-rolling.

Reel I

The point of attack is much earlier than in Shakespeare. The first shot is of the palace of the Duke of Venice, evidently a throne or reception room where Othello is to be welcomed as a victorious warrior. Characters are identified by descriptive titles. Iago and Roderigo discuss the impending choice by Othello of his lieutenant; Iago expects the position. Desdemona is shown sitting on one side of the hall, surrounded by admirers. Roderigo bows to her and receives a distant nod. He and Iago approach her; to Roderigo's annoyance, Iago rudely gets between them. At this point there is some commotion presaging Othello's entrance with Cassio, who is characterized in a subtitle as completely loyal to him. They enter and go to the dais. At the Duke's request for the name of his lieutenant, Othello turns to Cassio, puts his hand on his shoulder affectionately and nominates Cassio. The action here is so slow as to give the impression of a kind of bewilderment in Othello. Iago glowers in surprise and anger; the loss of the lieutenancy in the screen play is the sole motive for his subsequent actions. Othello goes to Desdemona, takes both her hands; she is obviously glad to see him. Brabantio at a distance shows worried disapproval. Iago plots revenge through Roderigo, smitten with Desdemona. It is not clear whether in view of the later action Othello is now planning the elopement. He leaves Desdemona as Brabantio, plainly objecting to their familiarity, approaches her. Othello tells Cassio to take Desdemona and guard her. Desdemona makes an excuse and leaves the room. The next shot is architectural, stairs to the right leading to a portico over a bridge with a canal in the background left and under the bridge; it is a studio construction. Cassio assists Desdemona to a gondola as Iago sneaking through the portico divines what is happening. He tells Roderigo and urges him to call up her father. The next sequence is at Othello's home. Desdemona is already there when Othello enters at the rear. He says, 'Forgive', evidently not knowing her reaction to being brought. She indicates approval, and Othello embraces her violently, an unattractive shot. We then see Brabantio arriving at his house in a gondola. Roderigo, with Iago in the background, apprises Brabantio of the elopement. Brabantio is stormy to Roderigo but calls his servants and finds Desdemona gone (I, 1). In a series of sequences, Othello and Desdemona are married, the Senate and the Duke are called to the council chamber (the same room as before) to receive the message of the Turkish plan to attack Cyprus, Othello is sent for (I, 3), Brabantio arrives at Othello's and is met by Cassio, so that Iago's two-facedness of I, 2 is not shown, thus diminishing his cleverness, and since Othello is not present, the calm dignity of 'Keep up your bright swords . . .' is lost.

Reel II

Cassio sends Brabantio to the Duke. Othello gives Desdemona a handkerchief, stressing its heritage and value, thus introducing the means for later circumstantial evidence much earlier than in Shakespeare. In the council chamber, Brabantio accuses Othello to the Duke (I, 3). Iago tells the Moor the Duke requires him and warns him of Brabantio (I, 2). A crowd is shown cheering Othello as he goes to the council chamber; much the same background as in the earlier scene where Cassio takes Desdemona to Othello, but to emphasize Othello's popularity. Brabantio's accusation of Othello alternates with a scene showing the crowd's objection to Othello's arrest; it is not clear how it knew anything about it. In the council, Othello makes his plea. Here there is a subtitle beginning, 'I am son of Egyptian prince and Spanish princess – my blood is fair like hers . . .', thus playing down miscegenation, perhaps to explain to American audiences that Othello is not a negro. Desdemona publicly acknowledges Othello as her husband. The Duke advises Brabantio to take up this mangled matter at the best. The crowd waits outside. The Duke tells Othello he is to be sent to Cyprus; Othello accepts with alacrity and assigns Desdemona to go in the next galley. Brabantio warns, 'Look to her, Moor', but Othello's 'My life upon her faith' is cut, thereby decreasing our understanding of his belief in her loyalty. Othello leads Desdemona off, 'an hour to spend with thee'. There is acclamation from the crowd. Roderigo threatens to drown himself but is cheered by Iago to put money in his purse and follow to Cyprus. Iago, alone, plots his accusation of Cassio and Desdemona. So far we have much of III, 3, but with crowd shots cut in which on the whole seem unnecessary. Succeeding visualizations are original. Othello and Cassio are shown in the interior of a galley at sea, then Desdemona and Emilia in another ship with the handkerchief much in evidence. Iago sneaks in and sees the handkerchief. Desdemona explains its value to Emilia. On Othello's galley, with Cassio present, it is explained that a storm has scattered the Turkish fleet. Cross-cut to Emilia putting Desdemona to bed; as Emilia leaves the quarters, Iago hides, puts his hand over Emilia's mouth, leads her quickly away, asks her to steal the handkerchief and gives her a present for which she reaches in pleasure before they embrace. At Cyprus there are shots of a square, and battlements through which the sea is visible, the first clearly outdoor photograph in the film. Sentries shoot off a cannon announcing Othello's arrival. Cyprus is announced to Othello on his ship. There is good camera work showing the gathering of crowds on the island and their excitement as all gather to greet and honor Othello, but the scene is short and may be cut (II, 1). Perhaps there was originally also a scene of Othello's arrival with Cassio, but the symbolic separation of Cassio and Othello, on different ships in Shakespeare, could not be there.

Reel III

A public celebration in Cyprus with shots of the crowd cheering, and then scenes of individual and group rejoicing. Iago and Roderigo plot Cassio's disgrace (II, 1). Roderigo, suitable to a night of revelry, will wear a comic-nose mask. Within, Desdemona in a negligee shows considerable leg as she prepares for bed. Othello watches from hiding. Creeping around a curtain, he winds Emilia up in it, as the lovers embrace, a comic scene which does not come off. Outdoor shots show the entertainment around town, including a sword swallower. Othello orders Cassio to look to the guard (II, 3). There is a friendly greeting of Cassio by Desdemona, which Iago ostensibly does not like; it is not appropriate here, but pulled in from III, 3, to provide earlier motivation. More plotting by Iago and Roderigo from II, 3. Othello already has shown signs of jealousy but the bedroom scene which follows is warm. Cross-cutting between Cassio being persuaded to join the revelry; more love making, more roistering with Cassio now definitely drunk. Iago lurks as Cassio and Roderigo fight on steps in the distant background, then calls for help as crowds gather. Montano is hurt. Inside a love exchange is interrupted by the noise. Outside Othello appears, and with much subtitling Iago explains, and Cassio is cashiered (II, 3).

Reel IV

There is news of another Turkish attack, ostensibly to prepare for Othello's later incapability to handle it and his replacement as governor, but III, 2 continues with Cassio's remorse and Iago's urging appeal to Desdemona. It is followed by a kittenish scene between Iago and Emilia which leads up to a statement that Cassio is coming to ask Desdemona's intercession, but that Othello must not know. At this point Emilia has the handkerchief, though we have not seen her take it, and Iago grabs it over her protests (III, 3). The crowd asks, 'Why do they not send Othello against the Turks?' The Cassio–Desdemona interview from earlier in III, 3, is followed by dialogue from later in III, 3, in which Iago identifies the caller and arouses Othello's jealousy. Emilia denies to Othello according to the prearranged non-Shakespearean plan that anyone has visited Desdemona. Othello promptly rushes to Desdemona to inquire who has been with her, and she replies quite simply that it was Cassio and urges Othello to restore him to his post. The reworking of the scene simplifies the motivation, but makes Iago's machinations anything but subtle. The now thoroughly jealous Othello rushes off abruptly as he is summoned to take care of the Turkish danger, while Desdemona is left wondering at Othello's strange change in attitude. Roderigo reproaches Iago (while eating); his jewels and money are gone and he plans to get his presents back from Desdemona and depart (IV, 2). An interview between Montano and Othello shows the latter 'on the rack' and incapable of attending to the business against the Turks. In some non-Shakespearean sequences which are silly, Iago advises Roderigo to serenade Desdemona under her window, and he does so. Iago tells Emilia to bid the serenader be gone. Othello chases Roderigo, not knowing who he is but suspecting Cassio. He then breaks in on Desdemona, as Iago listens. Othello acts strangely and departs.

Reel V

Othello in distraction asks Iago the identity of the serenader, and after a violent struggle Iago gasps 'Cassio'. The facial contortions in this sequence, which again derives from III, 3, are wonderful to behold. Desdemona finds that she has lost her handkerchief (III, 4) and Iago is shown with it. Emilia tries to get it from him but is repulsed. We now see wholly invented sequences. Othello in bed dreams in double exposure of Cassio approaching Desdemona's bed and being greeted with passionate embraces. Othello falls off the bed, heels last, in a ridiculous shot. Desdemona prays (suggested by V, 2). Iago, hearing a noise, goes to Othello, finds him on the floor, raises him to lean on the bed, arranges pillows behind his head, comforts him, wipes his brow with a handkerchief which Othello gradually recognizes. Iago says upon inquiry that he got it from Cassio. The Bianca-business is wholly out as not suitable to the noble Cassio, who is however more absent than anything else. Othello dashes to Desdemona asking for the handkerchief, as Iago listens (partly III, 4). When Desdemona says it is not about her, he thrusts her from him and returns to Iago. Demanding proof of Desdemona's adultery and in a paroxism of rage he tears the handkerchief in his teeth. Othello is summoned to Montano (*vice* Lodovico) to receive a message that he is commanded home and desiring that he approve Cassio for his place. Desdemona adds her plea for approval. Othello strikes her as all show astonishment, and totters off (IV, 1). Iago tells Cassio to go to Desdemona for approval of his governorship – which he does. Iago by way of 'proof' drags Othello to see Cassio leaving Desdemona and to suffer visibly. Emilia is shown in a scene with the frightened Desdemona, who loves Othello despite mistreatment. Iago arranges with Roderigo to attack Cassio in order to keep Desdemona and Othello in Cyprus (IV, 2). With a melodramatic gesture, he gives Roderigo a sword. A part of Iago's soliloquy (V, 1) is given in a subtitle. Emilia denies Desdemona's guilt to Othello, who accuses her of being a bawd and throws her to the ground (IV, 2).

Reel VI

In a very short sequence, Cassio and Roderigo fight, and Roderigo is killed (not apparently by Iago as in V, 1). Othello determines to kill Desdemona in bed and draws a scimitar. He enters the room where she is sleeping, and both are shown in close-up, separately and together. He caresses her lightly, but 'One kiss' wakes her. The sequence follows V, 2, with many titles and much exchange, diminishing the cinematic value of the scene: 'Have you prayed?'; accusation on the evidence of the handkerchief, denial, Othello's report that Iago has killed Cassio; Desdemona's lament which sends Othello into a fury in which he struggles with her on the bed. He apparently strangles her but the actual strangling is below the frame of the picture which is focussed on the upper part of his body. There may be cutting or chopping in the transfer to 16 millimetre film, but as it stands spectators would not know what is happening. Emilia enters to find Desdemona dead and inquires the cause. There are no others present as he names Iago as the accuser, and Emilia denies Desdemona's guilt and explains about the handkerchief. Othello at once accepts the explanation and shrinks from the bed. There is little emphasis on Iago's 'honesty'; as a result his powers of deception are made to seem minimal and he is turned into a stock villain. Iago enters and is reviled as a 'Spartan dog', but there is nothing Spartan and little dog-like in his wide-eyed terror. Othello kills him with the scimitar in a shot hastily cut. In an ante-room, Othello joins Montano, Cassio and others, and is told he must go with them. Cassio's reproach is met by Othello's tender embrace. Othello returns to the bedroom, saying on the way in subtitle: 'Think of me as one who loved not wisely but too well.' A crowd outside wails, 'Othello is arrested; woe woe!' Othello kisses Desdemona in close-up, and falls over her body – on a blade? Cassio enters to find Othello dead. The last shot shows Cassio on a balcony, à la Mussolini, raising his hand for silence and reporting to the people. 'God have mercy on his poor soul', he prays, as he raises his eyes to heaven. O most lame and impotent conclusion!

Yet the fortunes of *Othello* in New York were at first surprisingly high. The trade papers did point out that the film would have to be sold to audiences by special exploitation, particularly the 'educational' appeal, but reviewers almost uniformly praised its quality. The *Film Daily* capsuled its comment to 'a highly intelligent and compelling interpretation of Shakespeare's work', but in detail thought the story 'masterfully handled and wholly absorbing'; the direction, 'superb'. Janning's portrayal was 'as though Shakespeare's character came to life', and Werner Krauss, 'a tremendous hit'. Altogether *Othello* was 'another step in the advancement of the motion picture'. The *Moving Picture World* held it to be 'a well-made and decidedly artistic production [which] holds the interest intensely throughout. . . .' Jannings gave 'a magnificent performance', and Krauss presented an Iago of 'both lightness and depth, power and intense cunning. . . .' On March 10, 1923, it quoted extensively the opinion of critics in the daily newspapers. The *Times* said it had 'vitality' and was 'direct and true'; Quinn Martin in the *World* thought it 'acted with surpassing strength'; Louella Parsons in the *Morning Telegraph*, 'a powerful, efficient work [which] excels in film form'; and Harriette Underhill in the *Tribune* 'a wonderful production . . . superbly acted'. There was certainly unexpected audience interest. Booked for two weeks at the Criterion Theatre where it opened on February 25, 1923, it was, after its box-office success there, transferred by Hugo Reisenfeld for another week to a second Paramount house, the Rivoli, unusual prestige for an independent production and a 'record for a long time to come'. Evidently, however, its appeal was to special groups. It played in Chicago, the Mid-west, and New England but was not widely distributed; the initial interest in it soon died, and Ben Blumenthal ended up losing a considerable part of the money he had invested. In three years it could be rented from the Kodascope Library for nine dollars, later reduced to six and then to $4.50. Its brief glory proved to be a poor index of its permanent value, and the effusive adulations of its critics brief candles in the wind.

In May of 1923 Walturdaw announced that it would present Edward Godal's B. and C. series, Gems of Literature, 'Two Reel Feature Films

Founded on Famous Classics by Well-Known Writers'. A famous British artist was to appear in every Gem with the scenario prepared by Eliot Stannard. At the time the first four were reviewed it was indicated that the next two would be *The Taming of the Shrew* and *The Merry Wives of Windsor* but these short pictures were so inconspicuous that they never received critical notice in the trade papers. By the time it appeared, the second was called *John Falstaff*, and all I know about it was that it contained the basket scene and featured Roy Byford, who had played Falstaff with Ellen Terry in an excerpt of Shakespeare's play at the Coliseum in November 1917 and was to act the whole role at the Winter Garden in April 1924. *The Taming of the Shrew*, directed by Edwin J. Collins, had the Lyceum actor, Lauderdale Maitland as Petruchio and a dancer called Mdlle Dacia as Katherina. Cynthia Murtagh was the Bianca; Gray Murray, the Baptista; Somers Bellamy and Roy Beard acted respectively her lovers, Gremio (here for some reason called Grumio) and Lucentio. By some quirk of survival, this picture can still be seen.

This skeletonized adaptation of *The Taming of the Shrew* minimized the story of Bianca and her lovers and in effect presented parts of five scenes from Shakespeare's play of wooing and submission (I, 1; II, 1; III, 2; IV, 1, 3) with cross-cut glances at the lesser intrigue. After title, production credits, and introduction of each of the characters and actors shown in costume alone and sometimes together to the accompaniment of explanatory captions, Grumio takes Bianca to Baptista and asks for her hand, while Katherina listens and Lucentio watches in the background. When Baptista explains that he will not bestow his younger daughter until he has a husband for the elder, Katherina glares, scolds Grumio, and generally acts the termagant. Exit Bianca to Lucentio in an adjacent study, who tutors her. Katherina continues to rage in the drawing room, then joins Bianca and Lucentio and knocks a book from his hand. A servant announces Petruchio to Baptista and Grumio. He identifies himself and receives permission to woo Katherina. All except Petruchio go to the study, which Katherina after explanations leaves to join Petruchio. Both are wary and stern but when he attempts to embrace her, she breaks away and paces stormily. The ensuing conversation presents Petruchio silently roaring with laughter and the shrew stamping out her defiance. There are cross-cuts to the others, listening. When she slaps him, he holds her hands while she writhes. Baptista and Grumio, entering, are told it will be a match, as Katherina rages. After congratulation and the setting of the wedding day, Petruchio kisses her forcibly, and bows as she runs off.

Reel II begins with the other principals and guests waiting for the arrival of Petruchio for the wedding. Baptista looks out of the window; Katherina in a bridal dress sits in a chair, fretting, and then dashes out to the study where she laments and is comforted by Bianca. Petruchio now appears before the guests in tattered clothing who show astonishment at his costume, and is admonished by Baptista. Bianca and Katherina continue with the same business as before, until they enter the drawing room where Petruchio tosses Katherina a kiss, struggles with her, and pulls her off, as the others follow. Nothing more of the wedding is shown or described. Instead there is an abrupt shift to Petruchio's house where the two arrive after an exhausting journey not depicted. Petruchio berates his servants, shakes one of them, throws him to the floor, and leads his tired and hungry bride to a chair. He calls for supper and beats a servant who takes off his boots, as Katherina tries to calm him. When food is brought, Petruchio throws it in a servant's face, knocks everything off the table, and drives all the servants out. Katherina's outbursts are milder but he tosses her over his shoulder and carries her off to the bridal chamber. Here he seats her in a chair, pushes her back into it when she tries to rise. When she yawns with fatigue he kneels before her in comfort. Laughing behind her back, he throws everything off the bed and out of the room. Katherina protests but is obviously almost asleep in her chair. Petruchio leaves quietly and softly closes the door behind him. In the dining room the next day, Petruchio brings food to a pleading and chastened Katherina who thanks him. Baptista learns that his daughter's tutor is a nobleman in disguise and blesses their union, as Grumio withdraws from the competition. The film ends with a shot of a happy and smiling Katherina sitting on her husband's knee and kissing him. There is no reunion of all the principals.

The coverage of the film, however, conveys little of its quality. The costumes are satisfactory, but the sets, all of rooms, are stagy and cluttered with potted palms. There is variation in the length of the shots, but most are medium to close. Irising is sometimes used at the beginning and end of sequences. The camera is stationary. The acting is theatrical and stresses only one or two notes. Maitland looks both fat and old – he had been on the stage since 1901 – and most of the time simply laughs and strides. Mdlle Dacia is more expressive but there is too much pacing and raising of arms. Worst of all is the number of the subtitles. It is true that the story might be unintelligible without some of them, but there are thirty-eight in the first reel, twenty-five in the second. Fifty-one of these are Shakespearean, more or less, and most of them are merely cues for illustrative pantomime. The effect is both over-literary and uncinematic, especially in the crowded first reel. Inaudible speeches usually supersede the function of the camera, and except for the cross-cutting there is hardly a trace of recognition of the true nature of the motion picture medium. *The Taming of the Shrew* which Griffith, still learning his elements, made in 1908, is more visually appealing than this one fifteen years later.

If *The Taming of the Shrew* was thinned down Shakespeare, *Der Kaufman von Venedig* of the same year is, like the Asta Nielsen *Hamlet*, a kind of expansion and change of emphasis of Shakespeare's plot and its sources. German references indicate it was based not only on *The Merchant of Venice* but on the tales of Ser Giovanni Fiorentino and Masuccio of Salerno, and Christopher Marlowe's *The Jew of Malta*, from all of which Shakespeare probably borrowed for his complex story, and on Pietro Aretino from whom he did not. Peter Paul Felner wrote the script and directed in eight reels of 2806 metres, but it is difficult to unravel into its strands the patchwork he created because the extant print I have examined is a cut version in six reels with English titles which may or may not be translations of the original German. This English copy was released by Stoll on February 1, 1926, in the third year after its first presentation in Germany, and was titled *The Jew of Mestri*, probably in fear lest the public might stay away from another Shakespeare film. The Jew of Mestri is the only name given the money lender in the novella by Ser Giovanni in his *Il Pecorone*, and introductory subtitles in the film, used as a foreword, read, 'Toward the end of the Fourteenth Century when men, after the mental coma of the Dark Ages began again to think for themselves, one, John of Florence, wrote a tale destined to stimulate the imagination of the World's Greatest Dramatist. Two hundred years after John of Florence William Shakespeare wrote his immortal *Merchant of Venice* influenced beyond question by the work of the earlier writer. The original Florentine tale has been slightly modified to not offend the modern standard of good taste.' By whom? Felner or an English adapter? The reference to offensive matter probably is to the winning of the lady of Belmonte by physical possession of her, for which Shakespeare substituted the device of the caskets. The spirit of the film is rather more that of the world described by Ser Giovanni and Masuccio, and the name used for the character corresponding to Bassanio is Giannetto as in the *Pecorone*, but Lorenzo, Arragon, Tubal have their Shakespearean appellations, while Shylock becomes Mordecai; Portia, Beatrice; Jessica, Rachela; Lancelot, Marco; Antonio, Benito. To compound the confusion, the Wiesbaden brochure based on German material uses for its cast names largely Shakespearean: the Doge of Venice, Max Schreck; the Prince of Arragon, Ferdinand von Alten; Antonio, Carl Ebert; Bassanio, Harry Liedtke; Salanio, Gustav May; Salarino, Heinz-Rolf Münz; Graziano, Max Grünberg; Shylock, Werner Krauss; Tubal, Albert Steinrück; Lanzelot Gobbo, Hans Brausewetter; Porzia, Henny Porten; Nerissa, Cläre Rommer; Jessica, Lia Eibenschütz; Marco, Emil Hoffer; Shylocks Mutter, Frida Richard; Elias, Tubal's Sohn, Friedrich Lobe; Beppo, Jakob Tiedtke; Reppo, Carl Geppert; Ali, Porzias Page, Willi Allen. Some of these characters are indistinguishable in the film as it now stands, and others such as Elias and the Jew's wife – not his mother – become important to a story, not in any of the sources, which discards the casket scenes, and puts much emphasis on Shylock's (or Mordecai's) family.

After general and introductory titles and credits to Krauss and Henny Porten, now playing screened Shakespeare far more complicated than her original music-film of *Othello* about sixteen years earlier, the story begins:

1 'On a day in June 1565 in the great city known as "The Queen of the Adriatic" – Venice.' An expansive shot of Venice, then close, through a window, of St Mark's. Men strike a bell on the tower.

2 'The market on the Rialto bridge was alive with traders – Florentines, Sienese, Venetians, men from the east, and Jews.' After this scene is presented, cut to Rachela and Mordecai on a balcony (not quite clear) and then back to the market.

3 'There came in this mart a boy, Marco, the servant of his master, the Jew of Mestri.' So, but what is the purpose? He is shown first in close-up and then looking for someone.

4 'Mordecai, the Jew of Mestri, shrewd with the cleverness of his race, destined to suffer for being a Jew.' The camera picks him in close-up out of the crowd, talking with someone (Tubal?), signing a paper.

5 'Mid-afternoon when most of the people of Venice were asleep.' Pigeons fluttering, close, then long. St Mark's.

6 'Rachela, the daughter of the Jew.' She is seated at a fountain feeding pigeons, close, then longer. A man approaches. She looks up. Another view of the pigeons. As the man comes nearer, we see Rachela's hands suspended. A long shot of the man and pigeons.

7 'Lorenzo, a young nobleman of Venice.' He moves to Rachela, sits beside her.

8 'Sweet Rachela, you are most kind to have come again to our meeting place and for me, a Christian.' Close shot, then long. They rise, walk toward camera. Cut to close-up of pigeons, then back to characters, then to a single pigeon on a post. The symbolism is evident.

9 'And while Lorenzo and Rachela were finding Life's sweetest happiness, Tubal of the Tribe of Benjamin, and the Jew of Mestri were haggling over her dowry.' Thus.

10 'My son is famous for his knowledge of the Scriptures so you must add five hundred ducats for that to her marriage portion.' The haggling is shifted to pictures of Mordecai's wife telling women the secret, as she sews.

11 'My husband, Mordecai, has decided with Tubal that Rachela shall marry Elias, son of Tubal. It is a good match.'

12 'And so when Sabbath came . . .' a betrothal at a Sabbath feast.

13 'This is Elias, of whom I spoke, a young man and very learned.' Elias is introduced to Rachela, but she shows no enthusiasm. They sit at table. Cut to Lorenzo outside, waiting. Back to table, then to Tubal eating, then to Mordecai.

14 'Thus do I betroth Rachela, my only child, to Elias, son of Tubal, friend of mine.' Rachela and Elias, others, eating. Shot of Lorenzo waiting, followed by a close-up of Rachela, seeing him or thinking of him. She rises, leaves. Lorenzo waits. A window, Rachela looking out. The window closes. Her mother appears to the unhappy Rachela.

15 'Do not cry, Rachela. Such is the fate of all the women of our tribe.' After this bit is shown, there is a cut to Lorenzo, still waiting.

16 'Perhaps the gayest blade in all Venice was Giannetto, a nobleman whose poverty weighed lightly on his carefree mind.' We see Giannetto in close up, then drinking with three companions. Iris out.

Will Rogers and Sylvia Breamer in a *Romeo and Juliet* excerpt in *Doubling for Romeo* (Goldwyn, ɪ). Wisconsin Center for Theatre Research

50. Buster Keaton as Hamlet in *Day Dreams* (First National, 1922). Wisconsin Center for Theatre Research

51. The balcony scene of *Romeo and Juliet* with Leatrice Joy and Victor Varconi as the lovers in *Triumph* (Famous Players-Lasky, 1924). Museum of Modern Art Film Library

52. Blanche Sweet and Ben Lyon in a tomb scene from *Romeo and Juliet*, an excerpt in *Bluebeard's Seven Wives* (First National, 1925). National Film Archive

53. Hamlet (Asta Nielsen) contemplates suicide in the Art-Film picture of 1920. Museum of Mode
Art Film Library

17 'From the wineshop to Giannetto's palace the way along the canal spanned by the Bridge of Sighs.' (Symbolism, or just scenery?) Good shots of canals, gondola, bridge, another canal shot, until Giannetto lands. A cut to a bailiff reading an order to seize Giannetto for debt, and Giannetto laughing.

18 'By St. Mary, my dear Bailiff, if I must go to prison, thou must carry me there in a style befitting my rank.' Giannetto lies down on a bench, is picked up by beadles.

19 'Benito, one of the richest merchants of Venice, and the closest friend of Giannetto, the ne'er-do-well.' Ships in a harbour, then Giannetto being carried.

20 'These dear beadles and bailiffs love me so that I have them almost constantly with me.' Benito gets rid of them.

21 'Come Giannetto, I will make you forget your troubles by taking you to meet the Lady of Belmonte. She may show you the way to Fortune.' They go off together. Shot of Lorenzo, waiting.

Reel II

1 'And that same night Lorenzo having heard of Rachela's betrothal determined to press his suit.' He comes to her balcony, climbs up a rope ladder, as if Romeo. Marco watches for intruders while within Lorenzo and Rachela embrace.

2 'Beloved, this dreadful thing shall never be. You are mine. Tomorrow on the Grand Lagoon we will settle all our plans.' Embrace. The Grand Lagoon. They look out the window.

3 'The palace wherein the Lady of Belmonte held her court.' A distant shot of the palace.

4 'The most ardent of the Lady's suitors was the Prince of Aragon, a popinjay whose rich estate hid his poor soul.' Aragon primps before a mirror. Cut to the court of the Lady of Belmonte; courtiers enter, then Aragon, two greyhounds, and the Lady herself.

5 'Beatrice, the Lady of Belmonte.' She is greeted by Aragon, who kisses her hand. Giannetto and Benito watch, not pleased. She turns to see them but goes off with Aragon. Cut to Mordecai's house, Mordecai and Rachela. He realizes something is wrong. Then a pretty shot of Beatrice and Aragon on a balcony overlooking the Grand Lagoon. A shift to Tubal.

6 'They speak in Venice about a Jewish bride who mistook another man for her bridegroom.' Tubal and Mordecai.

7 'Be easy, my good Tubal. Do not listen to the idle gossip of babbling tongues.' Shots of both. To them, Rachela and Marco.

8 'We have arranged things differently, my daughter. Your marriage will be three days hence.' (The hastening of the marriage from *Romeo and Juliet*?) The other characters react as Tubal and Mordecai leave. Marco to Rachela:

9 'Listen mistress. If I were a maid and loved by such a lover as Messer Lorenzo I should become Christian and marry him . . .' Shots of both.

10 '. . . and after you marry you can be a Jew again. Religion, like any other cloak, should be changed with the season.' Individual shots, then cut to Mordecai and his wife.

K

11 'Rachela is to be married in three days and there will be great rejoicings.' Same.

12 'Money will be needed, so I must go to the Rialto, do you go to Benito's and get my ducats back from his friend Giannetto.' She leaves.

13 'Mordecai's wife found his debtors on their way to the Lady of Belmonte.' (For a second visit, or has the earlier sequence been misspliced?) As she approaches, gallants laugh at her.

14 'Contractors of debts, wastrels, revellers, knaves, mockers! Curses on you! Curses on all of you and yours. Curses. . . .' As they laugh, she has a stroke and falls. In swift succession, Marco running, Mordecai on the Rialto, Marco giving Mordecai the news, the gallants leaning over the body, Mordecai hurrying to his wife, reaching her, bending over her.

15 'Oh, you shall pay, you shall pay!' Gallants by Mordecai's wife, then Mordecai picking her up and carrying her off. The gallants at first very serious, then laughing and continuing their way. Mordecai carrying the body. A fade out and in to Beatrice's court, courtiers, greyhounds, Benito, Giannetto.

16 'By your leave, Milady. I want to present my friend, Giannetto, the richest and most powerful merchant prince in Venice.' At the introduction, Beatrice, a forward minx, is quite taken. Cut to Mordecai watching his wife ill, dying. Lorenzo and Rachela embrace in a gondola on the Lagoon; Marco is with them. More dying wife. Mordecai exit. Outside, he meets Rachela and Marco, sends Rachela in.

17 'Never more shall you eat my bread.' Mordecai knocks Marco down. Cut to banquet table at Beatrice's. She and guests enter and sit. She turns to Aragon, seated next to her.

18 'I left my fan on the terrace. Prince, will you get it for me please?' As Aragon goes for it, she motions for Giannetto to take his chair and they chat. Aragon returning with fan, gloves is sent to Giannetto's former place. She drops her handkerchief or napkin. When Giannetto stoops to pick it up, their hands meet, a deliberate invitation. Cut to deathbed scene, now including Rachela, Elias, Tubal. A close up of Elias and Rachela.

19 'Do not weep, Rachela. Comfort yourself with the thought that our wedding is only delayed.' Then cut to Beatrice saying goodbye to Giannetto; they are now on very friendly terms.

Reel III

1 'A few days later the Prince of Aragon has news.' Aragon, Beatrice, attendants.

2 'Benito and Giannetto have played you a scurvy trick! Giannetto I have learned is a pauper – a trickster!' Beatrice shocked, disappointed.

3 'So, Milady, since Giannetto makes a mock of you, marry me if only to shame him for his presumption.' Beatrice sadder but turns to Aragon.

4 'So be it! I shall announce the betrothal at once.' She does so to a cheering court.

5 'That evening Benito held a revel in his palace.' Wine, women, dancing.

6 'Do you know that today the betrothal was announced of the Prince of

Aragon and the Lady of Belmonte?' Shock of Giannetto. Cut to Portia weeping in the arms of an attendant. (Nerissa is never named.)

7 'My heart prompts me to doubt this Prince of Aragon. I shall seek the truth tonight from Benito himself.' Aragon in a garden exulting. Cut to Beatrice and attendant, then to a singer in the garden, cut back to Beatrice and attendant, then again to singer, to a gondola on a canal, to revelry with dancing girls on Giannetto's knees trying to cheer him up, to Beatrice in a gondola, to revelry with Giannetto unconsoled.

8 'The Lady of Belmonte seeks the truth.' Revelry, followed by Beatrice and Benito. She has come veiled, to Benito's palace.

9 'Aragon is jealous! Indeed Giannetto often says in jest that he is poor when half my vessels might well be his.' Beatrice pleased. Revelry. Giannetto approaches, and Beatrice embraces him.

10 'Fair Beatrice thought you had deceived her but I have told her that she deceived herself and that you are indeed a wealthy man.' Giannetto looks unhappy to be so designated, but Beatrice is too desirable for him to make a denial. He kneels before her. She raises him and kisses him.

11 'Benito the following day received an ill turn from Dame Fortune.' Petitioners before him, children.

12 'Help us Messer Benito! One of your ships has sunk and another captured by pirates. Our fathers are lost and we starve.' Benito gives money. Cut to Giannetto at home. Benito arrives.

13 'I told Beatrice you were rich and promised you money today and now, through misfortune, I have none to offer you. Go to the Rialto and borrow, and I will sign your bond.' Giannetto expostulates but is urged. Cut to Beatrice and attendants. Aragon enters and is coldly rejected.

14 'Slanderer! You wished to get my fortune by lying about my friends but you've lost for I have learned the truth.' She returns his ring and dismisses him. Cut to Giannetto meeting Marco.

15 'Lead me to your master, boy, and if I get from him some money, there will be half a ducat for you.' As they move off, shift to Mordecai and Tubal in the marketplace.

16 'See, Messer Mordecai, how I return good for evil; I have brought you a client. For this you should take me back again.' Marco to Mordecai; then Tubal to Mordecai.

17 'Mind, if he wants money, Benito must be his guarantor!' So, then Mordecai to Giannetto:

18 'If you want money come to my house after dinner and bring Messer Benito.' Exit Giannetto.

19 'They killed your wife: they will steal your child! Now is the chance for your revenge.' Mordecai reacts to his tragedy, then:

20 'Under the Roman law there is a form of bond wherein the debtor, if he fails to pay, must make it good with his own flesh.' Conversation thus.

21 'The Bond.' To Mordecai and Elias, enter Benito and Giannetto. Mordecai speaks:

22 'Fair sirs, you many times have mocked and spit upon me and now you wish that I should be your friend and loan you money.' So.

23 'If you lend money do it not as to friends but enemies, and then if I fail to pay, you can with better grace exact the penalty.' So.

24 'Sign the bond then Messer Benito and, in merry sport, let the forfeit be an even pound of flesh cut from what part of your body best suits my jest.' Giannetto protests; Benito replies.

25 'Fear not, man! Long ere the bond falls due my ships will be safe home and the bond paid.' The bond is signed. Benito receives the money which he gives to Giannetto.

Reel IV

Shots of street masques, cross cut with shots of Mordecai, Rachela, and Marco.

1 'What are these masques? Hear me. Rachela, lock up my house and thou, fellow, get outside and guard my door while I am absent at Tubal's house.' Masques, then Mordecai kissing Rachela goodbye. Marco gives a note to Lorenzo in a gondola.

2 'Beloved – Come for me tonight. I shall disguise myself as a boy as though I were one of your masquers. I am yours forever. Rachela.' Lorenzo and Marco, who says:

3 'You had best hurry, Messer Lorenzo, or Mordecai may return early and your bird will be locked in her cage.' Marco picks up coins thrown him by Lorenzo who departs in the gondola. Masquers, then Lorenzo in the gondola, rejoicing crowds, and Giannetto and Beatrice kissing amidst the revelry. She speaks to Lorenzo:

4 'Slip through the masquers and take Rachela to my palace at Belmonte. We will join you there later.' Revelry in front of Mordecai's house. Rachela as a boy preparing to leave. Lorenzo greets her outside the door. They hurry off to a gondola which moves away. Mordecai returns, pushes through the revelers, claps his hands for admittance to his house. When there is no answer, he finds the door unlocked; inside there is no one. He goes out and calls.

5 'Rachela! Rachela! Where have they taken you?' He falls to the ground. The masquers disperse. There is a whole series of reveler shots against Venetian backgrounds to emphasize Mordecai, solitary. He rises, enters his house. More revelry.

6 'On the very day Benito's bond fell due.' Benito, looking grim, talking to someone.

7 'The sinking of your ships has caused terrible distress among your people and in the market.' Tubal in the marketplace is told the news and relays it to a distracted Mordecai.

8 'Benito's remaining ships are wrecked. One of Tripoli, the other near Genoa.'

9 'Jehovah be praised! Run, Tubal, swear out a warrant.' Mordecai laughs madly, shows the bond. Tubal leaves. In his house, Mordecai and Elias, Mordecai reading the bond and gloating.

10 'Your daughter has become a Christian.' Mordecai, overwrought, as Elias leaves. He walks to a niche, knocks a vase off a chest, which he opens, takes out a candle, lights it and puts it in the niche, beats his breast.

11 'Hear me God of Israel. Hear my prayer for the soul of my dead daughter.'

A long sequence cuts to Benito, leaving his palace, met by a bailiff.

12 'Your pardon Messer Benito but I am ordered to arrest you.' They go. Cut to Elias committing suicide by throwing himself into the water. Then to Mordecai and Tubal.

13 'This is the opportunity for your revenge. Not even the Doge himself can deny your lawful claim.'

14 'They killed my wife. They dishonoured my flesh. They stole my daughter. The hour of my revenge is at hand.' Cut to Giannetto and Beatrice, happy at Belmonte.

15 'As long as you love me, Giannetto, wear this ring. When you no longer have it, I will know that you have ceased to love.' Action as implied.

16 'Fair Beatrice, I can no longer keep up the pretence. I would not win you through deception. I am not rich.'

17 'And do you think the love of Beatrice can be bought?' Love-making is contrasted with Tubal and the dead Elias.

18 'Little guessing Benito's fate, Giannetto and Beatrice, Lorenzo and Rachela held high revels.' Enter (apparently) Aragon.

19 'Well may you laugh, Giannetto, for the man who gave you all you have must now give you his life because he cannot pay his Bond.' Consternation.

20 'Hurry Giannetto! Take plenty of my gold and save your friend.' The action shifts to Mordecai reading the bond. Enter Rachela and others; she has come to plead.

21 'Nobody saw her, for no one was she present. She had become a Christian and the prayers for the dead had been spoken.' Rachela goes to Mordecai and kneels but there is no sign of recognition.

22 'I beseech you, my Father, do not do this awful thing. These people are your daughter's friends.'

23 'See, I will give you back all your jewels, if you will do this thing for me.' She puts jewels in his lap, and receiving no reply, slowly leaves.

Reel V

1 'The Day of Judgement.' An elaborate and lofty courtroom with crowds, people at the side, others entering down stairs rear and right, still others standing by balustrades at the mezzanine level. Benito appears. Lorenzo and Rachela look worried at Belmonte, then while Lorenzo stands by, Rachela kneels before the Duke on his way to the court.

2 'I am Rachela, daughter of the Jew of Mestri; and I beg of you pass not this judgment on my father's debtor.' He replies:

3 'Ever has Justice been the pride of Venice, and Justice will be done to Messer Benito.' The Duke passes on. Court-room shots. Benito in the dock. The crowd is angry as Mordecai enters. Lawyers, Duke, much pomp and circumstance. Benito speaks.

4 'If the law protects me not from the consequences of my folly, I shall meet my fate as a man should.' Mordecai holds up the bond.

5 'My deeds shall be upon my own head. I demand the law, I demand the penalty stated in my bond.' Enter Beatrice and a clerk. A letter is delivered to the Duke.

6 'Your Grace, my grave illness prevents me acting as the Judge in the case of Mordecai, the Jew, against Benito, the Merchant. In my stead I am sending a learned young doctor, who will plead the cause. Barratolo.' Beatrice on the judge's bench, standing. Mordecai whets a knife; then Beatrice calls him to the center of the court.

7 'Indeed, Mordecai, your calling is repugnant, yet under the Venetian Law, you are well within your rights.' Close-ups.

8 'I take it that the Bond you hold was duly signed without threat of force or coercion?' Mordecai hands the bond to Beatrice who reads it. Giannetto arrives, breathless.

9 'I offer him, here before this court, thrice the sum, and if that is not enough, I pledge my word to pay it tenfold.' He offers money to Mordecai, who turns away. Beatrice speaks to him.

10 'Then perhaps you may be merciful and save yourself from the obloquy of greed.'

11 'Revenge is sweeter meat than gold, and I demand the forfeit as stated in the Bond.' Various onlookers shout angrily.

12 'Set aside the Law! The law is wrong to permit such an outrage!' Beatrice replies.

13 'The Law is the Law! I have no power to alter a decree established.' Mordecai is pleased.

14 'There speaks the wisdom of old age. Solomon himself would not have given better judgment.'

15 'Are there in the court balances to weigh this pound of flesh.' Mordecai takes balances from under his robe. Benito pleads.

16 'I beg of your Worship to pass judgement. This suspense is keener torture than the usurer's knife.'

17 'Va bene! The Bond is due and is not paid. The Court awards, as stated in the Bond, a forfeit of one pound of flesh from him whose signature is on the Bond.' Shots of court and principals. Mordecai, knife ready, exults.

18 'Prepare yourself for his Knife.' Benito bares his breast as Mordecai advances to him. Giannetto rushes in between them.

19 'Hold! The Jew can have me for his victim, since all he wants is just a pound of flesh.' Close-ups of principals. Benito puts Giannetto aside. Various close and court scenes. Mordecai raises the knife.

20 'Stop Jew. . . . He does so, looking at Beatrice.

21 'The Bond calls for but one pound of flesh, cut then therefore just a pound – no more, no less, and shed not one drop of blood, for that is not specified as a forfeit.' Various reactions.

22 'If by chance you take more than called for in the Bond and thus jeopardize the life of a Venetian citizen all your goods are forfeit and your life is given to the mercy of the Court.'

Reel VI

The reaction of Mordecai, the crowd, Benito, and Giannetto. The court leaves. Benito and Giannetto thank the judges, offer pay.

1 'I will take nothing but your ring and that of your friend can be given to my secretary.' (But there is so far no Gratiano–Nerissa love story and Benito has not been involved so this makes no sense.) After hesitation and urging, the presentations.

2 'A stealthy return.' Beatrice and secretary in women's attire, first in a gondola, then going through a barred door, entering the palace at Belmonte. Fade out and in to a scene at Belmonte with Benito and Giannetto. (There is just a bit of the Gratiano–Nerissa ring business here.)

3 'I am overjoyed to hear of Benito's release but sad to think that you have parted with my ring.'

4 'I love you still, fair Beatrice.'

5 'If you love me show me my ring.'

6 'I swear on oath I have not parted with it to a woman. I gave it to a worthy Doctor of the Law.'

7 'Upon my honour which is still my own, I shall love that Doctor of the Law as dearly as I love myself.' Beatrice turns and leaves. Cut to Beatrice and secretary putting on gowns and glasses, reappearing, disrobing. Recognition and embrace.

8 'And so in a few days the dark canals were gay with the merrymaking of a double wedding.' Spectacle. Cut to Mordecai, alone in his house, his hands over his ears, back to merrymaking, back to Mordecai looking out of a window, his hands over his eyes, then brides and grooms, Mordecai reading the Scriptures, finally Lorenzo and Rachela in a garden.

9 'Beneath the pallid splendor of the crescent moon in far-off Greece, did Venus seek to kiss the timid lips of shy Adonis.' Embrace.

10 'Beneath the silver radiance of the same cold moon Lorenzo, braver than the faint Adonis has won a maid, more beautiful than Venus, for his own.' More of the same.

11 'Desolation.' In close up. Mordecai alone at his door, then walking. Close up. Finis.

I can find in this nothing of Masuccio and *The Jew of Malta* (the Lorenzo–Jessica plot) and little of Giovanni Fiorentino (the wooing of the Lady of Belmont) which Shakespeare had not already taken over. Most of the changes from Shakespeare are sheer invention: the substitution of the jealous Aragon and his attempt to discredit Giannetto for the choice of the caskets; the whole business of the betrothal of Rachela (Jessica) to Elias, son of Tubal, with the inclusion of Rachela's mother, and her and Elias's deaths as motivations for the Jew's revenge. Actually Felner hardly follows Shakespeare at all except in having roughly comparable characters and some parallel situations until the arrangement for the bond in Reel III, where the subtitles, too, pick up a bit of Shakespearean phraseology. From that point he is closer to Shakespeare with the elopement of Rachela, the effect on Mordecai, the report of the sinking of the remaining ships, the love of Giannetto and Beatrice, the attempt to help Benito, the whole courtroom procedure with the discomfiture of Mordecai, the exchange of rings (but evidently so cut as to be unintelligible), and the moonlight love-making. In between are further novelties such as the attempted interventions of Rachela, befitting her greater part in the action. The characters of course are considerably changed, especially those of Giannetto and Beatrice (Bassanio and Portia) into honest ne'er-do-well and knowing pursuer. In fact Benito, Giannetto, and Beatrice all seem generally irresponsible until close to the end. Clearly Felner used parts of I, 3; II, 4, 5; III, 1, 2; IV, 1; and V, 1, filling in with new matter and devising a concoction of his own, laid curiously in 1565, which, however, bears a reasonable resemblance to *The Merchant of Venice*, even though not advertised as such in England.

It is easy to chalk up demerits for *The Jew of Mestri*. Since the action of the first two reels largely concerns the affairs of the Jew's household, there is an uncomfortable shift of interest in Reel III, which is almost wholly devoted to Belmont and gives nothing about Lorenzo and Rachela. Over a reel is devoted to the court scene with its elaborate spectacle in which long shots sometimes dwarf the principals. The cross purposes which replace the winning of Beatrice by the choice of caskets is utterly unconvincing. The artificial revelry becomes tiresome, and some of the crowd scenes contribute nothing to the understanding. Motivations are hazy, and actions illogical. The prettiness of the Rachela–Lorenzo speeches, suggested by V, 1, is intrusive, since there is little action, and it is visibly moonlight anyhow. Shakespeare was careful to separate the moods of his last two acts, but the picture confusedly mixes them. Many of the titles are repetitive or unnecessary. Surely an actor can convey that the character he is impersonating is a ne'er-do-well or a popinjay without captioned explanations to the spectators, and since they know the situation or the state of mind, what are accomplished by 'The Day of Judgement' and 'Desolation'? In general the film is slow and heavy, and too long for its own good.

Yet when the film is compared to earlier Shakespeares, it is equally plain that it had substantial virtues. On the whole the sequences do not merely illustrate titles. The story, the characters, the actions, the emotions are presented in pictures to which the titles are incidental. Some imagination is used in choosing symbols, the pigeons, the Bridge of Sighs, the greyhounds to connote visually attitudes which may be sensed. Best of all are the editing and cutting, which at times almost amount to montage, as in the swift sequences following the heart attack of Mordecai's wife, or in deliberate contrasts between careless festivity and tragic situation, or crowds and loneliness. Certain scenes, for example Rachela's plea to her father and her return of the jewels, are impressive in their own right. Much of the picture was taken in Venice, and the handsome backgrounds lend atmosphere and authority. The director has an eye for pictorial values and composition, and the photography and lighting are good. Werner Krauss, when he does not overact, makes a striking Mordecai; unlike his badly conceived Iago, his creation is made impressive and convincing. Granting a Beatrice unlike

Portia, Henny Porten, except in the trial scene where she is mildly ridiculous, plays effectively an impulsive and provocative woman, and the other parts are adequately mimed and differentiated. Felner's film is not an advance over other films of its immediate period and it evidently made little stir beyond German borders, but it holds interest almost continuously and marks in some respects a forward movement in the development of Shakespeare film. It is often not good Shakespeare, but it is also often good film.

Finally, for silent film, there was another German production which, from what can be gathered, must have included Shakespeare in a stranger mixture than almost any other presented in this chronicle. From criticisms and pictures it is hard to tell whether it was an artistic experiment which failed or just a jumble which was not to be taken seriously. *Ein Sommernachtstraum*, produced, directed, and in part scripted by Hans Neumann in 1925, carried a secondary title *Ein heiteres Fastnachtsspiel*, which suggests a carnival spirit; in England it became *Wood Love*, in the United States, simply *A Midsummer Night's Dream*. The characters were largely Shakespearean in name but the casting is strange indeed. We have had Werner Krauss as Iago and Shylock; here he turns up as Bottom the Weaver. The Puck was Valeska Gert, a dancer specializing in satiric pantomime, who in the same year played the procuress in G. W. Pabst's *Joyless Street*. Oberon was assigned to a woman, the Russian ballet dancer, Tamara. Other actors were Theodor Becker (Theseus), Paul Günther (Egeus), André Mattoni (Lysander), Hans Albers (Demetrius), Ernst Gronau (Quince), Walter Brandt (Snug), Wilhelm Bendow (Flute), Fritz Rasp (Snout), Martin Jacob (Starveling), Ruth Weyher (Hippolyta), Charlotte Ander (Hermia), Barbara von Annenkoff (Helena), Lori Leux (Titania), Bruno Zieger (Milon, General of the Greeks), Armand Guerra (Wenzel, a simpleton?), Alexander Granach (Waldschrat, a sprite or goblin). If the last three seem excrescences, they are no odder than some of the other features. Hans Behrendt collaborated with Neumann on the script; camera was handled by Guido Seeber and Reimar Kuntze; sets and costumes were the work of Ernö Metzner. The subtitles were specially commissioned to Klabund (Alfred Henschke), a poet, novelist, critic, translator, historian, and journalist well known at the time for his association with expressionism.

A Midsummer Night's Dream with its childlike quality, its fantasy, and its fun would seem ideal for children, but we find a clue to this one in the entry in the *Jahrbuch der Filmindustrie*: '5 reels, 2529 metres. Passed by the Berlin Censors. Forbidden for juveniles.' The carnival spirit was evidently robustious. Oswald Blakeston reviewing in England in 1929 is more specific.

'Do chorus girls treading a measure belong to the screen, or even to the stage? They belong to the past. While the maidens foot it lightly this picture resembles the *Arcadians* and certain shorts condescendingly manufactured by a British producer.

K*

'The Gert also in this picture dances her part; and that you may tell me, belongs to the stage. But the camera adds something to the Gert, gives fresh angles in her static poses, on the Gertian tongue lolling from lascivious mouth.

'Krauss is so delighted to be allowed to cast off all restraint and think of himself as a Shakespearian actor that it would be brutal to spoil his pleasure.

' "I draw the line here. I draw the line there. . . ." We all know the respectable whose lives are led in a patch of arid ground shut in by a complicated geometrical pattern of lines. Valeska Gert steps beyond the lines as a hierophant to show what fun one can get from being released; Krauss steps beyond the lines to show what a great actor he is. The Gert puts out her tongue at the audience in devilment; the Krauss puts out his tongue for the audience to see how well he can act the part of a devil.

'For pity for those gentlemen who have spent their money on a private projector let me pass them the "dirt"; there are more things in this picture more ineluctably Rabelasian than I have ever discovered in the most boisterous German comedy.

'Those who demand more from a single movie had better be warned that characters in the wood sequences are superimposed, and a great many of the Gert's double-meanings become indistinguishable, almost lost in double exposure.

'The heartiness in this picture is not biased, it spreads to the simple pleasure of hacking a man in two with a battle-axe.'

This is the second German *Midsummer Night's Dream* to seize on Shakespeare and then treat him brutally. Other sources mention other details. Theseus was shown at the telephone. Amazons and Athenians moved into battle to the accompaniment of Eric Borchard's Original-Jazzband. Klabund's titles were not bridges between sequences but in their smart-alec, sometimes amusing, sometimes banal way directed the spectators to unconventional interpretations and became the centre of the whole film. The court of Athens, man, Shakespeare himself were ridiculed. The tone was mocking, ironical, parodistic. Yet a German reviewer speaks of this film as a really charming version of the play where delicacy and atmosphere create in the imagination a fairy-tale forest populated by elves and dwarfs, the whole whirled about by the grotesqueries of Puck with genuine, mischievous fun. Of a New York showing in 1928 which according to the *Post* substituted Shakespearean titles for Klabund's, the *Times* speaks of this 'old German film translation' as containing despite sections 'somewhat conducive to slumber . . . some passages that have been executed with no little charm. The double-exposure photographics are not without merit; figures appear from the grass and others disappear into the bark of a tree. This subject has been conceived with sincerity and a great deal of ingenuity. The costuming, the make-up of the players, the fading in and out of fairies and other characters has been attended to intelligently. It is true that the result is rather disappointing . . . for despite the camera's magic possibilities, it is something that needs sound and colour.' It is as if we were talking about not one but several films. Clearly Shakespearean titles left an effect wholly different from Klabund's, but it is hard to understand the reported combination of ribaldry and charm within the picture, or the range of estimate from a bluff to be ignored to an experiment in a new form. There are so many contradictions that I fear the film must have been contradictory itself and hence self-defeating.

It is sad to end this part of the story with a note of dubiety about a picture which cannot have represented any height of achievement in the quarter of a century in which an invention became a business of purveying a novelty, business an industry providing entertainment, and entertainment only here and there an encouragement to art. A year later, Warner Bros, on the verge of bankruptcy, took a desperate gamble which had been declined by the major film corporations, and publicly demonstrated on August 6, 1926, at the Manhattan Opera House in New York a short which presented performing musicians who were not only seen but heard, and a feature, *Don Juan* with John Barrymore to which had hurriedly been added a recorded musical accompaniment. There had been sound films before, including Shakespeare films, but no earlier process had solved the problem of proper amplification. Other companies hesitated, but the public did not. More sound shorts and features with synchronized scores soon followed, and on October 6, 1927, the Warners released an otherwise ordinary film, *The Jazz Singer*, which contained audible dialogue and several songs by Al Jolson. It was to make over two million dollars. It turned the industry upside down and then into a scramble to wire theatres and produce sound films. The details are not important to this volume, but in 1928 hastily made sound pictures of generally poor quality, including several vaguely related to Shakespeare, were outdrawing the best silents, and in 1929 silent films began to vanish from the screens. What had been learned about creating only in motion had to be re-examined if sound were to be more than a mere addition and to become a basic part of aesthetic principles, principles soon to be complicated further by a successful three-colour process. The confusions were bewildering but the implications cataclysmic.

From 1925 there were no silent feature films essentially based on Shakespeare's plays. After the Revolution, Shakespeare films were to appear again, but the rest was not silence.

What's Past Is Prologue

SILENT Shakespeare film could not be art, a new art. The aesthetic problem is how to make good film which is good Shakespeare. It could not be good Shakespeare because too much was missing. The poetry with its word imagery, its cadences, its power to stir the emotions and the imagination was absent unless used in brief subtitles. But while the subtitles could do something but not very much, even if properly chosen, they were generally used for direction to the spectators or for a bit of temporary excitement or a hint of characterization. At their worst they merely provided material to be illustrated by pictures. Even at their best, the lines could not be heard, and Shakespeare's lines in his plays were written to be heard.

Another impasse was that film was essentially a business. Most of the manufacturers, however much they employed individuals and adopted elements which in themselves could be capable of transformation into artistic media, could create or re-create, were interested chiefly in using Shakespeare as a means to an end, and the end was an entertainment which would be sufficiently popular to make money. Usually there is nothing illegitimate in making money, and the aim is understandable. Successful film is a property, an asset, and an asset is more viable than a liability. Even when the purpose was as far as possible to reproduce on the screen a stage performance which was artistically important or worth recording, and in spite of much big talk about educational or artistic ends, the end was still financial return. And such film by the nature of film itself with its centre in moving images could not be good film anyway. Good Shakespeare film has to start first with the idea of interpreting Shakespeare, and all other goals become subsidiary. Until commerce decided to collaborate, not much could really be expected.

Moreover the film public was not ready for Shakespeare film. To the large majority of the spectators in the silent era, Shakespeare was a writer of the past; he was not read and known and appreciated. People knew the names of some of his characters, perhaps vaguely even some of the action in which they were intertwined: Romeo, Juliet, love story, feud; Hamlet, tragedy; Othello, jealousy. During much of the period, those who read Shakespeare, those who went to see his plays in the theatre, did not visit the picture houses, were indeed scornful of motion pictures. Under such circumstances, until there was a vast growth in mass education, Shakespeare film could be only a small segment of film, though the segment may be larger than expected. Thirty years ago I asked Terry Ramsaye how films could be so bad; his reply was that he could not understand how they could be so good.

Yet amid this bleak terrain, there were hillocks and ridges. Much was learned about film and therefore something about Shakespeare film and about Shakespeare. Progress comes not in a straight and smooth gradation but by fits and starts. The potentialities of the camera, of the people who used it and the product which emerged had to be discovered and developed. Skill in the use of resources precedes the artistic metamorphosis. It is too easy to denigrate silent Shakespeare film.

Some of the elements of a play by Shakespeare lent themselves to silent film. His point of departure was a story. We sometimes forget that he told good stories. Film too was narrative, and the stories could, at least essentially, be told in pictures. Parts of the tales which Shakespeare in his medium and on his stage left out or described could be included in film, the sequestration of Hermione, Birnam Wood coming to Dunsinane. As story alone it does not matter that in the one case Shakespeare wanted a surprise ending, and in the other the effect of the report on Macbeth. It is better to transform the poetry than not use it at all. The Muse of fire appeals to the imagination but there can be a different kind of imagination in visual images. The battles can be shown, the storm and lightning, the sea voyage. Even what a man is thinking can be caught by the camera, a mental image can become a picture: Macbeth's ambition to be King of Scotland, the bloody dagger. The supernatural indeed naturally lends itself to film, the ghost of Hamlet's father, the transformation of Bottom. Double exposure, superimposition and dissolves were devices film could use to tell a story.

The kind of stage Shakespeare wrote for and the dramatic technique which it occasioned was closer to film than in most periods of dramatic composition. He could use as many scenes as he wanted, could change locales freely, could cover intervals of time. So could film, with its mobility and its flashbacks. It is not tied to large units of continuity, it can move rapidly from one sequence to another, it can cross cut into montage, not only to tell the story but to increase the suspense and to show what characters are doing simultaneously or almost so. Ophelia can drown while Laertes plots vengeance; Shylock can hurry to the Rialto while Portia and Bassanio make love. Rapid shifts are the stock in trade of film.

Shakespeare was not worried about historical authenticity, or actual backgrounds, but film tends to be realistic. On the other hand it does not hurt Shakespeare to show Elsinore or St Mark's or Cleopatra's barge. Film is literally a spectacle; the spectacular becomes important. Crowds massed against architecture, a lonely man in a vast open space can have meaning. We may want Shakespeare's lines, but in lieu of them new values can be achieved.

The camera has another advantage. A member of a theatre audience seldom receives an impression of much depth on the stage. But in silent film a scene could be shown from various distances, from far away to close-up. From the pomp and circumstance of a royal court, a character can be picked out for focus, from the Capulet ball we can move to Romeo and Juliet lost in their sudden love. If the camera was stationary during a good part of the silent era, this meant two shots; as it learned to pan and track it could be one sequence. The camera is movable. Let us see the wonder in Juliet's face.

The silent film did something else. It created an enormous audience, potentially a large audience for Shakespeare. Those who could not afford to go to the theatre went to the cinema. Some of them learned for the first time that Shakespeare was not a far away figure in a distant past but a man who wrote good stories about interesting people wrapped in a varied atmosphere. They could see Venice, and the Forest of Arden, even fairy land and the sea coast of Bohemia. They could witness the performance of actors and actresses they had only heard about, or see in pictures the old familiar faces of the screen smiling or lowering as Shakespeare demanded. My approach has not been sociological, but there must have been some timid consultation of the old and largely forgotten volume of Shakespeare tucked away on the shelf, or a walk to a bookshop for a second hand copy. Schooling and schools helped the young people. The improvement in education and in learning brought more reading. Certainly some who first met with Shakespeare on the screen must have been stimulated to better acquaintance. If the demand for Shakespeare film was small, it would grow larger.

Inadequate, even ridiculous as was Shakespeare on silent film, not art, not often good entertainment, it was the necessary preparation for something better. Trial and error can lead to ultimate success. Sound and to a lesser degree colour were now ready, not as the superimpositions on silent film which they first became, but as elements in a new synthesis which could create a new art from the rough magic of inaudible pictures, Shakespeare was to suffer another sea-change, not always rich and sometimes strange, but with infinite possibilities. There could be good film which was also good Shakespeare.

> If we shadows have offended,
> Think but this, and all is mended.

EXPLANATIONS AND ACKNOWLEDGMENTS

CHAPTER I

Rather than clutter my story with argument and indications of indebtedness, I have preferred to include a supplementary section which can be ignored or referred to at will. To omit these entirely might be to raise doubts of authenticity in an account of a field about which much writing has been anything but accurate. Indeed I correct in the text errors of my own which appeared in earlier articles: 'If We Shadows Have Offended', *The Pacific Spectator*, Winter 1947, pp. 97–104; 'The Shakespeare Film as Record: Sir Herbert Beerbohm Tree', *Shakespeare Quarterly*, July 1952, pp. 227–236; 'Shakespeare in One Reel', *Quarterly of Film, Radio, and Television*, Winter 1953, pp. 139–49. This chapter is a revision of an article with the same title, *Theatre Survey*, 1960, pp. 18–42. I do not flatter myself that I have escaped further mistakes, but I should at least present my evidence, and express my appreciation to the many people who in interview, letter, or print have contributed so much.

1 Tree, *King John* (1899)

Some of the conclusions I have drawn have to be based on what seems to me reasonable inference. Though one would expect notice in the trade papers, I have found no strictly contemporary accounts, and Tree's biographer, Mr Hesketh Pearson, discovered not a jot of relevant material in his examination of the private papers in the possession of Tree's daughter, Lady Cory-Wright; indeed Mr Pearson did not know of the film until I wrote him about it.

I have assumed sunlight because it was necessary for picture taking by the early motion picture camera, and early morning, after it was light enough, for the avoidance of crowds. The date is difficult. 'Alured' in *The Cinema News and Property Gazette*, July 2, 1914, in an interview with Tree quotes him as saying that he first played before the camera 'eighteen years ago in *King John*. We did it down on the Embankment by the Adelphi.' The place is explicit enough but 1896 seems altogether too early. This account may be the source of the date given by Ernest Dench, 'Stage Stars on the Screen', *Pictures and the Picturegoer*, January 29, 1916: 'As far as records go, Sir Herbert Tree is the pioneer. It was as far back as 1896 that he appeared in *King John*, which, by the way, was filmed in London.' Langford Reed and Hetty Spiers *s.v.* Tree in *Who's Who in Filmland*, 3rd ed., London, 1931, repeat the date. On the other hand *The Motion Picture Studio Directory*, 2nd ed., London, October 21, 1916, gives the date for the *King John* film as 1899, and this I have accepted. It seems altogether probable that the film would have been made concurrently with Tree's production at Her Majesty's when cast and costumes were readily available. I have made the season autumn rather than winter as more propitious for filming. Moreover, though one might suspect the time to be the interval when the play was closed during the week before Christmas, the *Era*, which almost regularly details Tree's activities, though maddeningly enough it does not refer to the film, says that Tree was vacationing in Brighton; the cast would have dispersed. He would hardly have done the film after the interval, when he was rehearsing *A Midsummer Night's Dream*, which was to open on January 10, 1900.

An article by Helen Duey, 'Shakespeare in the Films: An Interview with Sir Herbert Beerbohm Tree', which appeared in the *Woman's Home Companion*, June 1916, quotes Tree as saying, '. . . eighteen years ago pictures were made of my performance of "Henry VIII" and "King John". They were merely photographic transcripts of the stage production, entirely without meaning except to those who were perfectly familiar with the play, and could recall the lines appropriate to the action.' Here Tree was either inaccurate or inaccurately quoted. *Henry VIII* was made in 1911; the second statement would apply properly to that film, but not, I think, to *King John*, which must have been extremely brief to have attracted no contemporary notice.

I can only guess at the photographer, but there is one hint. The souvenir program for the sixtieth performance at Her Majesty's on November 13, 1899, of which there is a copy in the Theatre Collection of the New York Public Library, was 'Published for Mr Tree by the British Mutoscope and Biograph Company, Limited, who have received from him sole rights for the photographing at Her Majesty's Theatre.' The still pictures in the programme are from this concern. It was a London branch of the American company and under the direction of E. B. Koopman, who had built a motion picture studio soon after its inception in 1897. Not being sure of exactly who or what was included in the film, I omit here the cast of the stage production; it may also be found in the programme.

My account is tangentially indebted to Terry Ramsaye, *A Million and One Nights . . .* , 2 Vols, New York, 1926; Rachael Low and Roger Manvell, *The History of the British Film 1896–1906*, London, 1948; and Hesketh Pearson, *Beerbohm Tree: His Life and Laughter*, London, 1956. None of these, however, mentions the film.

11 Bernhardt, *Hamlet* (1900)

The material on Bernhardt's life and stage career is derived principally from Ernest Pronier, *Une Vie au Théatre: Sarah Bernhardt*, Geneva, 1942; and Louis Verneuil, *The Fabulous Life of Sarah Bernhardt* (tr. Ernest Boyd), New York [1942]. The first chapter of Forrest Izard's *Heroines of the Modern Stage*, New York, 1915, and William Winter's *Shakespeare on the Stage*, New York, 1911, pp. 431–42 have also been useful.

The fullest account of the Bernhardt film, the Phono-Cinéma-Théâtre, and the people involved is in Georges Sadoul's *Histoire Générale du Cinéma*: Vol I, *L'Invention du Cinéma, 1832–97*, Paris, 1946, pp. 186, 236–7 and Vol II, *Les Pionniers du Cinéma, 1897–1909*, Paris [1947], *passim* but especially pp. 110–14. To him I am especially indebted. The material on Mesguich is from his delightful memoirs, *Tours de Manivelle*, Paris, 1933. Sadoul gives the name of the director of the theatre as Mme Rignault, Mesguich as Mme Marguerite Vrignault. I take the first to be a misprint, the second to include an earlier family name; all other sources, including material in the Museum of Modern Art, refer to her as Mme Marguerite Chenu. The Museum has an original programme. Programmes are reproduced in Sadoul and in a helpful article by H. Cossira, 'La Résurrection des Premiers Films Parlants de 1900,' in *L'Illustration*, April 1, 1933. Sadoul and Cossira reproduce frames of the duel scene.

The announcement of the Kleine Optical Co. is in the *Moving Picture World*, October 24, 1908. Jay Leyda, 'Theatre on Film', *Theatre Arts Monthly*, March 1937, says the sound was supplied by kitchen knives clashed together behind the screen; a similar suggestion is made by Cossira, 'La Cinéma Parlant en 1900', *Le Figaro*, May 1, 1936, who says the sound 'était rendu par des bruiteurs consciencieux'. Other sources speak of cylinder recording, for example, Robert Destez, 'L'Heure Qui Passe: Voix et Gestes D'Autrefois', *Le Figaro*, May 1, 1933; and in view of the other films which required recorded sound, I do not think fallible human agency was likely or desirable for this one, especially on tour. The reference to Bernhardt's faint is from R. E. Whitehall, 'Some Films Called *Hamlet*', *Theatre* (London), Winter 1948. Bernhardt was quite capable of fainting on numerous occasions, but it should be noted that Pronier, p. 228, connects the incident with her later film, *La Dame aux Camélias*.

I do not know whether the *Hamlet* film still exists. In 1951 M. Henri Langlois, Secretary-General of the Cinémathèque Française, wrote me that there was a copy in the archives. When I was in Paris in the fall of 1955, the Cinémathèque was going through a difficult period, and though I received the impression that the negative was extant, I never succeeded in examining it or obtaining any precise information, and subsequent letters of inquiry were not answered. In June 1956, Mr Ernest Lindgren of the National Film Archive of the British Film Institute undertook inquiries in my behalf. The reply from M. Langlois was that the Cinémathèque did not have the film. Nevertheless it was screened at a Unesco Shakespeare Celebration in Paris on November 14, 1964, and Mr Enrico Fulchignoni, Head of the Cultural Film and Television Section of Unesco, writes me that it was lent by the Cinémathèque.

III Vitagraph, *Othello* (1902); *Romeo and Juliet* (1903)
The quotation is from C. A. C. Winchester, *The World Film Encyclopedia*, London, 1933, p. 471. It is apparently echoed by Leslie Wood, *The Romance of the Movies*, London, 1937, pp. 53-4. However the late Albert E. Smith, one of the founders of Vitagraph, told me he remembered no such films, and neither he nor I found supporting records.

IV Pathé, *Cleopatra* (1903)
Francesco Pasinetti, *Mezzo seculo di cinema*, Milano, 1946, p. 19: 'Una *Cléopatra* (1903) publicata da Pathé è quantunque la pellicola sia colorata a mano una ridicola pantomima teatrale fotografata.' A list in the British Film Institute of films in foreign archives gives under the Cineteca Italiana, Milano: 'Marco Antonio e Cleopatra, primitif, France, Pathé, 142 metres', but without date. The historian of the Italian silent film, Maria Adriana Prolo (*Storia del cinema muto italiano*, Milano, 1951, Vol I) wrote me that she did not know of any early Shakespeare films in Italian archives, including the Cinateca Italiana, where she was working at the time. Pathé did release a later *Cleopatra*.

V *King Lear* (1905)
Ernst Leopold Stahl, *Shakespeare und Das Deutsche Theater*, Stuttgart, 1947, p. 682: '*King Lear* ist wohl am allerfrühesten für den Film nutzbar gemacht worden, 1905 in einer (auf 100 Meter Länge!) nur einige Ausschnitte gebenden

Darstellung mit dem grossen italienischen Schauspieler Ermete Novelli.' This may derive from Irmgard Thurman, 'Shakespeare im Film', *Shakespeare-Jahrbuch*, Weimar, 1940, pp. 191–2. Ermete Novelli did appear in a later *King Lear* film.

VI Cines, *Othello* (1907)

Prolo, p. 120, lists under 1907 'Otello (virata), Cines'. Despite the Walturdaw description, *virata* means *toned* in processing, not *tinted*; toning was monochromatic. Sadoul, *Les Pionniers . . .* , pp. 406–10, and *Le Cinéma devient un art*, Vol I, p. 88, gives some history of the company, which I refer to later. Prolo, who also lists a 1909 Cines *Otello*, does not in her book name the director, but in her article in the *Enciclopedia dello Spettacolo* (9 Vols, Rome, 1954–62) on Mario Caserini, who became artistic director of Cines in 1907, she lists him as director for the 1907 picture. Later filmographies apparently follow this account. Prolo (book, p. 38) puts Francesca Bertini, of whom more hereafter, in one of the early Italian *Othellos*, but the date of her cinema début is controversial. Francesco Savio in the *Enciclopedia* article on Ubaldo Del Colle indicates he played in the 1907 *Otello*. A stage actor, he entered film in 1905 and had a long career there, though he was not well known at this time. Presumably he was the Othello. The picture was advertised in the United States in the *Moving Picture World*, April 4, 1908. The description in the text is from the catalogue of *Walturdaw Animated Pictures* (1907), p. 46, in the National Film Archive of the British Film Institute. Cines is not named but there is no other film to which the description can refer. A still of a Cines *Otello*, dated 1908, was shown at the Musée de l'Art Moderne in Paris, which I saw in September 1955.

VII Biograph, *Duel Scene from Macbeth* (1905)

Biograph 1903–1912, Ms. Notebook, pp. 58, 84, Museum of Modern Art. The film was developed on July 17, 1905, and copyrighted July 24th (No. 63805). *Fights of Nations* was copyrighted February 18, 1907 (No. H90564). For both entries, see the volume of copyright registration, *Motion Pictures, 1894–1912*, issued in 1953. There is no longer anything on deposit for either film. It is natural to wonder whether the *Duel Scene from Macbeth* was inspired by the Bernhardt duel from *Hamlet*. It is possible that news of the latter had filtered from abroad, but I find no evidence that the Exposition film arrived in the United States before 1908.

VIII Urban, *The Tempest* (1905)

The trade paper is the *Optical Lantern and Cinematic Journal*. The material on Charles Urban is from Ramsaye, Low and Manvell, and Sadoul, already cited, *passim*, and Low, *The History of the British Film 1906–1914*, London, 1949, see index. The photographer of *The Tempest* may possibly have been F. Martin Duncan, best known for scientific and nature pictures. The Charles Urban Trading Company catalogue of August 1909 is in the National Film Archive of the British Film Institute; Kleine's *Catalogue of Educational Motion Picture Films*, cop. 1910, is in the Museum of Modern Art.

IX Edison, *Burlesque on Romeo and Juliet* (1902)

I should hazard a guess that this is 'derived' from a portion of an original by

Georges Méliès or one of his imitators, with a change to an inappropriate title. Perhaps significantly, the film was not copyrighted. There is an Edison catalogue at Suitland, where some of the films and records of the Library of Congress are stored.

x Vitagraph, *A Midwinter Night's Dream* (1906)
Views and Film Index, January 5, 1907; *Moving Picture World*, March 30, 1907. The picture was copyrighted December 15, 1906.

xi Selig, *All's Well That Ends Well* (1907)
Views and Film Index and *Moving Picture World*, both of August 31, 1907.

xii Harbach, *Merchant of Venice* (1901)
Mimeograph of the Federal Writers Projects, W.P.A., later printed with adaptations in the *Motion Picture Herald*, December 5, 1936.

xiii Edison, *Seven Ages* (1905)
Sadoul, *Les Pionniers* . . . , following p. 583 *s.v.* 1907; Ramsaye, Vol I, pp. 65–73; *Optical Lantern and Kinematagraph Weekly*, June 18, 1908.

xiv Messter, *Othello* (ca. 1907)
Henny Porten, *Vom 'Kintopp' zum Tonfilm : Ein Stuck miterlebter Filmgeschicht*, Dresden, 1932, opp. p. 24, pp. 45–6; Oskar Messter, *Mein Weg mit dem Film*, Berlin [1936,] pp. 64 ff., 108 ff.; Oskar Kalbus, *Vom Werden deutscher Filmkunst*, Altona-Bahrenfeld, 1935, Vol I, pp. 19–20; Sadoul, *Les Pionniers* . . . , pp. 404, 420, and Le *Cinéma devient un art*, Vol I, pp. 288–95; Vol II, pp. 389–90. I am uncomfortable about the date for which the above evidence is contradictory. Charles Reinert, *Kleines Filmlexicon*, Einsiedeln-Zürich, 1946, gives Henny Porten's birthdate as April 7, 1888; she implies she was just under nineteen; and Messter dates her first sound film 1907. Lotte M. Eisner in the article on Porten in the *Enciclopedia* gives her birth date as 1890 and lists *Desdemona* (1908).

xv Méliès, *Cléopatre* (1899), *Le Diable et la statue* (1901), and *Le Miroir de Venise* (1905)
Sadoul, *Georges Méliès*, Paris, 1961, p. 182 lists 'Cléopatre (scène égyptienne)', 1899 but the filmography in Carlos Fernandez Cuenca, *El Mundo de Georges Méliès*, San Sebastian, IX Festival International del Cine, Seccion Actividades Culturales, July 1961, p. 55 makes clear that the subject was *Le Vol de la tombe de Cléopatre*. Sadoul, *L'Invention* . . . and *Les Pionniers*, *passim*, supplies most of the background but I have consulted books and articles too numerous to mention. The second volume, pp. 66–7 summarizes the second film, which I take to be the same as *Le Diable géant* (*le miracle de la Madone*), listed on p. 479. The reference to *Le Miroir de Venise* is from Maurice Bessy and Lo Duca, *Georges Méliès Mage*, Paris, 1945, p. 76. The date is from Jean Mitry, *Filmographie Universalle*, Paris, 1964, Vol II, p. 23.

xvi Méliès, *Hamlet* (1907)
Complete Catalogue of Genuine and Original 'Star' Films (*Moving Pictures*)

Manufactured by Geo. Méliès of Paris . . . , Paris; New York [1908], in the Museum of Modern Art. The price was $68.40. There is another summary, not quite identical, in *Views and Film Index*, October 19, 1907; the same journal, November 2, 1907, has the quoted advertisement. The film was copyrighted October 15, 1907, as *Hamlet*, the title I have used, but there is nothing now on deposit. The catalogue calls it *Hamlet, Prince of Denmark*; it was also named *Hamlet and the Jester's Skull* in an uncatalogued list of Méliès films in the Museum of Modern Art. The negative was for some years the property of Leon Schlesinger, producer of musical cartoons for Warner Bros. After his death, his collection went in 1950 to the Academy of the Motion Picture Arts and Sciences but the *Hamlet* was not among those received. Apparently it had deteriorated and had been destroyed.

XVII Méliès, *Shakespeare Writing Julius Caesar* (1907)

Catalogue cited above. The advertisement in *Views and Film Index*, November 2, 1907, which also has a summary, slightly different from that in the catalogue. The film was copyrighted October 25, 1907, but there is nothing now on deposit. The film sold for $41.28. It is possible that a print still exists, but I have not found it. It was announced for screening at the Shakespeare Film Festival in Wiesbaden (1964) on the basis of a promise from a private archive. The film never turned up and inquiries over the next year by the Deutsches Institut für Filmkunde were futile.

CHAPTER II

The introductory material insofar as it derives from published sources is based largely on Ramsaye; and Lewis Jacobs, *The Rise of the American Film*, New York, 1936, but some of the ideas are my own. For the whole treatment of Vitagraph, I am much indebted to two members of it, now deceased, Paul Panzer and Albert E. Smith. I also interviewed Maurice Costello in 1949 and Edith Storey in 1958, and other people have contributed incidental background. Mr Smith's reminiscences (in collaboration with Phil A. Koury), *Two Reels and a Crank*, New York, 1952, have provided minor details to supplement our correspondence and conversations. Paul Panzer's quoted memories are from the *Moving Picture World*, March 10, 1917.

The Brooklyn studio was constructed between East 14th and 15th Streets and between Locust and Avenue M in what was the old town of Greenfield on the border of Gravesend. When the property was bought by Vitagraph the deed contained a stipulation from the original title, 200 years earlier, that 'Wilhelmina Lot reserves the right to drive her cows through the premises'. I do not know whether the ghosts of Wilhelmina's herd were among Vitagraph's actors but one of the very earliest extras was Leon Trotsky, later tolerably known in other pastures. In 1925 Vitagraph sold out to Warner Bros who used the building for its early sound shorts under the name of Vitaphone and after 1939 as a film-processing plant. In 1954 part of the studio was rented by the National Broadcasting Company for colour telecasts. In 1964 it was acquired from the Technicolor Corporation by two Yeshiva University High Schools. See the *New York Times Magazine* of September 12, 1954; and the *New York Times* of August 31, 1957, and June 3, 1964.

Ranous has been hard digging; much of my information has come from interviews with people who knew him, those above, and Edwin Thanhouser. His name occurs in the indices of George C. D. Odell, *Annals of the New York Stage*, Vols IX–XV, New York, 1937–1949, and in the casts provided by *The Best Plays of 1894 to 1899*, compiled and edited by Garrison P. Sherwood and John Chapman, New York, 1955, and *The Best Plays of 1899–1909*, edited by Burns Mantle and Garrison P. Sherwood, New York, 1944. See also Ramsaye, Vol II, pp. 442, 496. There is something about him in a brief sketch of the life of his wife, by Rossiter Johnson, *Dora Knowlton Ranous : Author–Editor–Translator ; A Simple Record of a Noble Life*, New York, 1916, of which only one hundred copies were privately printed. Dora Knowlton, who wrote *The Diary of a Daly Debutante*, New York, 1910, met Ranous, when she was playing in the spectacular production by the Kiralfy Brothers of Jules Verne's *Around the World in Eighty Days*, in which Ranous acted the part of the detective, Fix. Ranous was 'a man of many attractions, with a remarkable voice for singing, and especially able as a stage manager'. They were married in 1881 when both were playing in Steele McKaye's *Hazel Kirke* in Canada, and Mrs Ranous left the stage shortly after. A few years later she left her husband 'for the best of all reasons, the one indisputable reason' and subsequently divorced him. Their daughter died in 1906, Mrs Ranous in 1916. After directing for Imp, to which he brought Florence Lawrence from Biograph in the spring of 1910, Ranous founded the Manhattan Motion Picture Company, which failed. For the rest of his life he was with the Vitagraph company in California, where he became studio manager, acted in various 'Broadway Star' productions, and in 1913 went on a world tour with a group of Vitagraph players. He died in California in 1915. Vitagraph, with insufficient capital to combat the feature production of competitors, after a temporary merger with Lubin, Selig, and Essanay in 1915 as VLSE, went out of business. To the custodian of its records, Miss Anne Goebel at Warner Bros., I am much indebted.

It was Vitagraph's practice, in addition to protecting itself against illegal duplication by imposing a trademarked 'V' somewhere on as many settings as possible, to deposit in the Library of Congress positive paper film strips of sequences for each picture copyrighted. With the permission and co-operation of Col. Willard Webb, then Chief of the Stack and Reader Division, and Mr James H. Culver, Custodian of the Motion Picture Collection, to whom I owe much, I examined these strips for all the copyrighted Vitagraph Shakespeare pictures which I had not personally seen as full films. Many of them are in good condition but they cannot now be projected, they are too short to form a part of the Library's project of rephotographing paper film deposits, and scanning them with a hand lens is fraught with difficulties. Such magnification seldom makes it possible to identify actors, though it occasionally helps to confirm identifications from other sources. The sequences are in continuous rolls or folds but are frequently out of order. Their helter-skelter arrangement in addition to their brevity has often left me doubtful or baffled about exactly what was being depicted. Sometimes the synopses published by the company in the trade papers can assist in the reasoned or inferred reconstruction of what a film was like, but some of the summaries are suspect because they were prepared not from the film but from the play, and sometimes before the film was made. Reviews which mention details and the few extant stills are more accurate. I have tried to indicate the content of pictures from the assemblage of all the available evidence and to be careful to emphasize my doubts and hesitations, but I should be the first to admit that I may not have achieved complete accuracy. What the paper strips do contribute of great value is information about the number of shots and the settings or locale.

I Vitagraph, *Comedy of Errors* (1908)

There is a summary of this 400 foot bedroom farce in the *Moving Picture World*, February 15, 1908.

II Vitagraph, *Macbeth* (1908)

The picture was copyrighted April 2, 1908. There is what purports to be a summary of the film in *Film Index*, April 18, 1908. I am not at all sure that the film was entirely intelligible. In the *Moving Picture World*, September 5, 1908, there is an article by W. Stephen Bush on 'The Film of the Future' which comments on three of the Vitagraph Shakespeare films, *Macbeth*, *Romeo and Juliet*, and *Othello*: 'Considering the great difficulties in condensation and arrangement, they are probably as good as any that could have been made. . . . The great effects in 'Macbeth' have been preserved with commendable accuracy and distinctness. What the pictures need to make them to the average audience but little less attractive than the play itself is what for want of a better name I may be permitted to call an "epilogue", in part impersonation and in part explanation, carefully prepared to run with the pictures. The three films have all been successful and are still in demand by the moving picture theatres in good neighbourhoods catering to a grade of patrons perhaps a little above the average. . . .' The story of the Chicago film censorship and the quotations from it are from the *Moving Picture World*, June 13, 1908. Identification of the actors is largely from stills which were in the possession of the late Paul Panzer, and in the issue cited of the *Kinematograph and Lantern Weekly*. Mr Panzer did not remember Miss Carver's first name. Mr Smith thought it was Adele and in his book lists a 'Miss Carter'; I cannot help wondering if it was not Louise Carver, who was to obtain success as a comedienne with Mack Sennett. The Miss Carver who was in *Macbeth* was brought to the company by Ranous to ride a horse in some film; she did not stay long either with the horse or Vitagraph. In one still I was delighted to find two stars of the future, Florence Lawrence, later 'the Biograph Girl', and Florence Turner, 'the Vitagraph Girl', as banquet guests. Of course no actors were identified by the company or given screen credits on the film. I am doubtful if the supernatural dagger was handled by double exposure; from the paper strip of this sequence in the Library of Congress, my impression is that it may have been suspended, and either painted or otherwise illuminated.

III Vitagraph, *Romeo and Juliet* (1908)

The picture was copyrighted May 26, 1908. The negative is owned by Mr Walter Greene of Los Angeles. Prints of it were used by RKO-Radio in *Flicker Flashback*, No. 6, Series 3, released March 8, 1946. One print was donated to the National Archives in Washington, where I saw it on December 30, 1946. The positive was clear and in good condition, but perhaps slightly cut; the cutting may go back to the negative. After the initial title, there has been dubbed in typescript indication of the players of the two leading roles, and Shakespeare's prologue. There is a similar typescript insertion of a part of Juliet's speech just before she stabs herself. Since there is no evidence elsewhere of the use of Shakespeare quotations, it is unlikely that these reproduce what was in the original film. I am indebted to Mr Richard O. Fleischer for information about the provenance of the film. In the identification of the cast and locale I have been assisted by Mr and Mrs Panzer. The stills I have seen tend to confirm that the Miss Carver was Louise Carver (see *Macbeth* above). I am quite unable to account for conflicting testimony that the Juliet was Florence Turner. In Florence Lawrence and Monte M. Katterjohn, 'Growing Up with the Movies', *Photoplay*, December 1914, Miss Lawrence is quoted as saying, 'Miss Turner was working in a photoplay version of Shakespeare's *Romeo and Juliet* that day, playing Juliet of course. Paul Panzer . . . was the Romeo of the play.' In Robert Grau, *The Stage in the Twentieth Century*, New York, 1912, is an autobiographical sketch by Florence Turner; she includes Juliet among her cinema parts. (She did appear in an *Indian Romeo and Juliet* in January 1912 but the heroine was called Ethona). On the other hand, J. Stuart Blackton in 'Yesterdays with Vitagraph', *Photoplay*, July 1919, includes a still with the caption: 'The happy family group at the top includes Florence Lawrence as Juliet and Paul Panzer as Romeo. Miss Lawrence at this time was Juliet's own age – sixteen years old.' In addition there is Paul Panzer who certainly knew who was his *vis-à-vis* in the film, and not to mention various other sources, there is the evidence of my own eyes, and those of others who have seen the film and stills. The National Archives print identifies the Juliet as Florence Lawrence. I am also unable to explain a statement by William Shea (the Peter of the film) in 'Twelve Years in One Studio – A Record', *Moving Picture World*, March 10, 1917: 'In this picture *Romeo and Juliet* the balcony scene was forgotten until the last minute, and the actor who was playing Romeo had to build his own balcony.' This contradicts Mr Panzer, the Romeo, and the evidence of the film itself, in which the balcony is on a modern house. I cannot believe there were two Vitagraph films, and can only assume that the testimonies, even the evidence of Miss Lawrence herself (or Mr Katterjohn), are incompetent. The Vitagraph summary and comment is in the *Moving Picture World*, July 4, 1908. Material on the Bethesda Fountain derives in part from 'The Talk of the Town', in *The New Yorker*, July 2, 1955. The film was screened for me through the courtesy of John G. Bradley and Howard L. Walls, then of the Motion Picture Division of the Library of Congress. There is an amusing article which touches on the film, 'Where They Perform Shakespeare for Five Cents' in *The Theatre*, October 1908, by Montrose J. Moses. Most of it is about the audiences of the Tompkins Square Vaudeville, 103 Avenue B, near 7th Street, 'John W. Brownstein, Prop.' but a reproduced bill announces *Romeo and Juliet* 'for one day only', May 12, 1908, 'with an intensly [sic] tragic lecture' by Dr Lamberger, who is called the 'Herr Professor'. The article includes a still of the duel scene from the Vitagraph picture. Stills of *Romeo and Juliet* appear in a number of pictorial books on film, a whole series in '*Pic*', August 23, 1938.

IV Vitagraph, *Othello* (1908)

The Bush and Blackton articles are referred to above. Panzer's mention of the film is in the *Moving Picture World*, March 10, 1917, but most of the details derive from conversation with him. The Vitagraph custodian lists the film, but without date. It is probable that the Vitagraph 'V' was over Desdemona's bed, as it was over Juliet's. So says Sewell Stokes in *Theatre Arts*, May 1946, though in correspondence he indicates he may have been thinking of *Romeo and Juliet*. Probably it was the same bed.

v Vitagraph, *Richard III* (1908)

The paper film strips deposited for copyright in the Library of Congress, September 19, 1908, are not in order and the sequences are almost impossible to follow or to correlate with the synopsis in the *Moving Picture World*, September 26, 1908, but there were apparently seventeen scenes, all taken on the studio stage except those for Bosworth Field. The reference to Linda Griffith is to Mrs D. W. Griffith (Linda Arvidson), *When the Movies Were Young*, New York, (cop.) 1925, pp. 32–3. Linda Griffith and Miss Auer were close friends. Miss Auer in a talk I had with her in 1949 confirmed the statement that she and Tom Ince were in the film, and that Ranous directed and probably played Richard. Panzer agreed about Ranous and added Florence Turner and Julia Swayne Gordon. It is surprising to find Tom Ince in a film so early; Mrs Panzer remembered only his brother, Ralph (who started as a property man), acting with Vitagraph, but Albert E. Smith thought Tom played occasionally. Ramsaye, Vol II, p. 538, says Tom Ince 'chanced into pictures in the fall of 1910', but the whole family was theatrical and frequently in New York, Ralph had been with the company since 1907 and could have got him occasional parts, and Miss Auer was positive. There is a poor still of Bosworth Field in the *Kinematagraph and Lantern Weekly*, November 19, 1908, as part of a Vitagraph advertisement, and a production shot of the offering of the crown in *Long Island* . . . [magazine] March–April 1962, p. 13. See also Blum, below, p. 11. The review is from the *Moving Picture World*, October 3, 1908.

vi Vitagraph, *Antony and Cleopatra* (1908)

Copyright, October 26, 1908. The paper film strips are out of order. Length and release date from *Moving Picture World*, November 7th, which also supplies the American review; the summary is from the London *Bioscope*, December 31st. The quotation about Antony is from W. Stephen Bush: 'Shakespeare in Moving Pictures', *Moving Picture World*, December 5th. Panzer played a lieutenant to Octavius Caesar and identified the others from an old still. Two other stills are reproduced in Daniel Blum's *Pictorial History of the Silent Screen*, New York, 1953, p. 11.

vii Vitagraph, *Julius Caesar* (1908)

Copyright, November 20, 1908. For the Shea article, which is inaccurate as to the date of this film, see above under *Romeo and Juliet*. The synopsis is from the *Moving Picture World*, December 15, 1908. The French journal is *Ciné-Journal*, January 28, 1909; the English, *Bioscope*, January 28, 1909; the American, the *Moving Picture World*, December 5, 1905, and Bush's article in the same, cited under *Antony and Cleopatra* above. The clerical comment is in the WPA article printed in the *Motion Picture Herald*, December 5, 1936, to which I referred under *The Merchant of Venice* (1901).

viii Vitagraph, *Merchant of Venice* (1908)

Copyright, December 9, 1908. The review is from the *Moving Picture World*, January 9, 1909. The scope of the film is based on Vitagraph material in *Bioscope*,

February 18, 1909, and the paper film strips deposited for copyright purposes in the Library of Congress. The *Moving Picture World*, July 11, 1914, says Julia Gordon was in it; she must inevitably have been Portia – as Panzer also thinks – because the autobiographical sketch in Grau, already cited, indicates Florence Turner played Jessica, and Nerissa's part was evidently sharply curtailed. Ranous probably directed. Mr Albert E. Smith tells me that James Young directed the later Shakespeare Vitagraphs, and there is a photograph of him as Shylock in *Photoplay*, February 1916. This, however, may be of a stage characterization, and I do not find that James Young came to Vitagraph until 1912. See Ramsaye, Vol II, p. 606.

IX Vitagraph, *King Lear* (1909)

The paper film strips deposited March 17, 1909, for copyright are in the Library of Congress. The review is from the *New York Dramatic Mirror*, April 3, 1909, reprinted from the *Moving Picture World*. The identifications of director and cast are necessarily somewhat tentative. They are based on Panzer's article in the *Moving Picture World* (March 10, 1917), his own recollections as well as those of Miss Auer, Linda Griffith's book previously cited, and my own exasperated examination of the far from clear film strips. For the possibility that the Ince was Ralph rather than Tom, see under *Richard III*. Edward Wagenknecht, *The Movies in the Age of Innocence*, Norman, Okla., 1962, p. 66, assigns Goneril to Julia Swayne Gordon, and Lear, he thinks, to Charles Kent: 'In the mad scenes, Lear wandered before a painted stagedrop, representing a wave-battered seashore, and at the end, while Edgar and Edmund fought their duel, a tinted sun came up over the cliffs behind them.' I doubt however that Laurence Trimble directed; I cannot place him with Vitagraph before 1911.

X Vitagraph, *A Midsummer Night's Dream* (1909)

Curiously enough, the film was not copyrighted, and its survival may be due to unethical duplication at some early stage in its history. The 16 millimetre positive examined is in the private collection of Mr James Card of George Eastman House, Rochester, New York, who very kindly lent it to me for examination. I sent photographs of some frames to Albert E. Smith for identification of locale and cast. He felt 'reasonably sure' about the actors of Lysander, Bottom, Puck, the fairies, Quince, Demetrius, and Helena. Costello is unmistakable, and Gladys Hulette is named as Puck in the *Moving Picture World*, October 22, 1910. Costello thought Julia Swayne Gordon was Hermia rather than Helena, but he did not see the photographs, and I think his recollection was faulty. It is fair to say also that Panzer gave Ranous as director, but I am not sure Panzer was with Vitagraph at the time; he had been abroad and soon after his return transferred to Pathé. Mr Smith and I examined a catalogue of Vitagraph folders in his possession which contains four stills of *A Midsummer Night's Dream*. He spotted Shea and Rose Tapley as among the participants, and, less surely, Florence Turner, but without assignment to parts. There is an elaborate pre-release summary in the *Moving Picture World*, December 23, 1909; the *Bioscope* review is of March 3, 1910; some of the material on Costello is from Ramsaye, Vol II, p. 441. Wagenknecht, Picture #10, has a still showing Gladys Hulette and a fairy. On p. 66, he speaks of the film as 'An enchanting little primitive with Costello as Lysander and the child Gladys

Hulette as a sweet little bare-legged Puck.' She had already had stage experience in *The Kreuzer Sonata* and *Sapho and Phaon* with Bertha Kalich in 1906 and 1907, in *A Doll's House* with Nazimova in 1907, and was to be Beth in *Little Women* which ran for 184 performances in 1912–13.

XI Vitagraph, *Twelfth Night* (1910)

The 35 millimetre print is in the National Film Archive of the British Film Institute. I am much indebted to Mr Ernest Lindgren and his staff, especially Mr David Grenfell, for their assistance in connection with this film. It was not copyrighted; it was in England offered for outright sale in 1911 (e.g., *Kinemata-graph and Lantern Weekly*, February 23rd, July 20th), and this may have contributed to its survival. It was originally announced (*Moving Picture World*, January 8, 1910) for release on January 8th, but delayed to make room for the third reel of *The Life of Moses*, a five-reel picture directed by Blackton and issued reel by reel, under the supervision of the Reverend Madison C. Peters, D.D., apparently another 'educational service'. The cast identification by Blackton is in an article, 'Yesterdays of Vitagraph', in *Photoplay*, July 1919. The *Moving Picture World*, July 11, 1914, puts Gordon in the picture. Blum, *Pictorial History* . . . , p. 19, has a still of Charles Kent as Malvolio, Gordon as Olivia, and Marin Sais as either Viola or Sebastian. The last identification conflicts with Blackton's and with Miss Storey's identifications. Maurice Costello told me he was probably in the picture, and that it was filmed, presumably in part, on upper Riverside Drive; I do not find him in it, and I doubt the locale; it is more likely to be somewhere on the coast of Brooklyn. I hazard a guess that the shipwreck scene was shot at Bayshore, where Vitagraph occasionally worked on location. See the article in *Long Island* . . . [Magazine], March–April 1962, p. 14. I think Paul Panzer was clearly mistaken when he informed me that Gordon played Viola, and Ranous directed. The Viola does not look like Gordon, and Ranous had already left Vitagraph – so too probably Panzer. In *Screencraft*, New York, 1916, Louis Reeves Harrison analyzes the composition, lighting, action and other values of various stills, including (opp. p. 114) one from *Twelfth Night*; the analysis is of no value, but the still is a good one. Miss Storey also owns a still, and helped me identify the cast; to her my thanks.

CHAPTER III

I Lubin, *Julius Caesar* (1908)

There is nothing on file in the film vaults of the Library of Congress, though the record still exists in the copyright office. Of course there is no evidence that the picture was necessarily based on Shakespeare. A suspicion naturally arises that the film was 'duped' but if so from what? There is to my knowledge no earlier *Julius Caesar* film except Méliès' *Shakespeare Writing Julius Caesar*. Méliès did complain that Lubin counterfeited his films (Sadoul, *Les Pionniers*, p. 228) but if he did so in this case it is strange that Lubin copyrighted the film at all, still stranger that he copyrighted a film which had already been copyrighted the previous October.

II Kalem, *As You Like It* (1908)

The footage and release date are supplied by the custodian at Warner Bros. of the records of Vitagraph, which bought out Kalem in 1916. The announcement is from the *Moving Picture World*, August 1, 1908; the comments in both cases probably by the editor of the journal, J. P. Chalmers, are from a footnote to the article by W. Stephen Bush, 'The Film of the Future', September 5th, and separately, September 26th. Gene Gauntier is quoted from a Ms. in the library of the Musem of Modern Art, which was the basis for 'Blazing the Trail' published serially in *Woman's Home Companion*, October 1928–March 1929. She was probably concerned with the picture as scenarist and perhaps as actress. Sidney Olcott and Robert Vignola, both with Kalem, told me in 1949 that the director might have been Kenean Buel. Certainly he later made several pictures for Kalem which had literary and theatrical sources. Mr Marion wrote me in 1950 that he remembered nothing of the picture. The film was listed in George Klein's *Catalogue of Educational Motion Picture Films*, 1910.

III Biograph, *The Taming of the Shrew* (1908)
The background material is largely from Ramsaye, Linda Griffith, and Jacobs. The release date for the film, which was Biograph's #3487, is given in the *Biograph Bulletin*, a copy of which is in the Museum of Modern Art, which also has valuable manuscript material. I was able to examine the paper roll in the Library of Congress in 1946 with the kind co-operation of John G. Bradley, then Director of the Motion Picture Division, and Howard L. Walls, then its Curator. The criticisms are both from the *Moving Picture World*, November 21st and 28th. A pencilled note on the *Biograph Bulletin* gives the Petruchio as Harry Salter, Miss Lawrence's husband, but the only still I have seen, a small one in the *Bulletin* of the bride and groom returning from their wedding, shows a taller man than Salter, and the assignment of Johnson to the part, as in for example Seymour Stern's 'Index to the Creative Work of David Wark Griffith', Part I, Index Series No. 2, *Sight and Sound*, April 1944, is confirmed by Mrs Stanner E. V. Taylor, who as Marion Leonard was a Biograph actress of the period; I thank her for granting me an interview and for the subsequent correspondence. The film was copyrighted November 11, 1908. I cannot resolve certain difficulties which arise from the Ms. notebook referred to, which gives the dates and locations of shooting. Marvin is credited with taking only 103 feet of film in the studio and Bitzer with 1249 feet at Coytesville (both for Biograph, not Mutascope), yet all but the last scene are interior shots, and it seems unlikely that they would not have been taken in the studio. Another notebook titled 'Photographed by A. Marvin' credits the film to G.B., presumably G. W. Bitzer. Still another, 'Records of Negatives as Rec'd from Operators', gives the following:

> Oct. 2 – 08 – 4 Negs – 545 ft. – Bitzer
> Oct. 7 – 08 – 7 Negs – 549 ft. – Bitzer – M.-Ope. [Mutascope]
> Oct. 8 – 08 – 3 Negs – 258 ft. – Marvin.

The total length here is 1352 ft which agrees with the above but now implies duplication for both Biograph and Mutascope. In any case it looks as though Bitzer was the cameraman for most of the film, and that it was cut from an 'original length' of 1177 ft to a 'corrected length' of 1113½ to a release length of 1048, figures I take in part from the first notebook referred to, headed 'Biograph 1903–1912'.

IV Lubin, *Measure for Measure* (1909)
Copyright, May 18, 1909. Reviewed in *Bioscope*, October 7, 1909.

V Essanay, *Much Ado About Nothing* (1909)
Quotation and summary from the *Moving Picture World*, July 31st. Released August 4th, 510 feet.

VI Edison, *A Winter's Tale* (1909)
Edison, *Kinetogram*, November 15th. Released November 16th, comedy in 250 feet.

VII Imp, *A Rural Romeo* (1910)
Listed in the *Moving Picture World* as released May 9th, not reviewed, 997 feet.

VIII Selig, *Romeo and Juliet in Town* (1910)
Film Index, p. 299, and *Moving Picture World*, June 11th, which gives synopsis, and length as 1000 feet.

IX Edison, *Bumptious as Romeo* (1911)
Summary and comment are based on the *Moving Picture World*, February 11th and 18th. The length and information about Great Britain are from the *Kinematograph and Lantern Weekly*, March 23rd, which also lists the footage, and April 20th. Cumpson is identified in the *Film Index*, p. 354 and Index. There are five stills in the *Motion Picture Story Magazine* for May.

X Kalem, *When Two Hearts are Won* (1911)
Film Index, p. 368, and *Moving Picture World*, September 2nd.

XI Selig, *The Merry Wives of Windsor* (1910)
Moving Picture World, November 24th and December 10th. There is a still in *Photoplay*, March 1911. Some background from Ramsaye.

XII Thanhouser, *A (or The) Winter's Tale* (1910)
The pre-release statement and the advertisements, each with the same two stills, appeared in the *Moving Picture World*, May 21st and 28th; the second issue has the comment. The formal review was on June 11th. I am much indebted to Mr Thanhouser, who died in 1956, for providing me with information not included in the above about this and his later Shakespeare films; there is an obituary in the *New York Times* of March 23rd. He sold out when he felt he had sufficient income for the future and retired. When I met him in 1947 his chief interest was in his collection of paintings of the Barbizon School, rather than his reputation as the producer of the immensely popular *Million Dollar Mystery* (1914) scripted by the Lonergans, Lloyd, Philip, and Elizabeth from a novel by Harold MacGrath. See John William Kellette, 'Makers of Movies: the Lonergans', *Moving Picture World*, September 12, 1914. Mr Thanhouser contributed some written reminiscences to the *Moving Picture World*, March 10, 1917: 'Reminiscences of Pictures' Baby Days'. Mrs Thanhouser, who had created the part of Editha in *Editha's Burglar* (1886) based on Frances Hodgson Burnett's novel – she was six at the time – and who later in the 80's appeared in New York in *Editha's Burglar* and *Little*

Lord Fauntleroy, died in 1951 (obituary, *New York Times*, May 31st). Amelia Barleon was to be Kabirah in the long run of *Kismet*, starring Otis Skinner, which opened in New York on Christmas 1911. About Miss Rosemond (spelled Rosamonde by Blum, p. 18) and Alfred Hanlon Mr Thanhouser remembered nothing – nor do I. Frank H. Crane after New York appearances in 1898 and 1901 had been Thanhouser's leading man in his Milwaukee stock company, later became a director. Martin Faust from Richard Mansfield repertory also turned director. Barry O'Neil went to Lubin; he had been a stage director before the organization of the Thanhouser company.

XIII Thanhouser, *The Tempest* (1911)

There is not very helpful synopsis in the *Moving Picture World* of November 25th, which supplies the release date; the comment is of December 9th. Mr Thanhouser could tell me nothing more about the picture.

XIV Thanhouser, *Romeo and Juliet* (1911)

I was able to see Reel II through the kindness of Mr John E. Allen, Park Ridge, New Jersey, and express my thanks for this and other courtesies; there is another print in the National Film Archive of the British Film Institute. The synopses are in the *Moving Picture World*, August 26, 1911, and *Cinema News and Property Gazette*, February 5, 1913, which prints a still. Other stills are in the Thanhouser advertisements in the first periodical, August 19 and 26, 1911. In this case the company apparently did not announce the cast. The *Film Index*, p. 299, correctly identifies George A. Lessey as Romeo but the Juliet's first name was not Irma. Julia M. Taylor is named as the Juliet in the *Motion Picture Story Magazine*, 'Answers to Inquiries', December 1911; the *Moving Picture World*, 'Inquiries', April 27, 1912; and Mr Thanhouser confirmed. Mrs George W. Walton is identified as the Nurse in the *Motion Picture Story Magazine*, 'Answers to Inquiries', April 1914. Lessey had a long career on the American stage and screen. He was on the stage in New York in plays starring Chauncey Olcott in 1906 and 1907. For a partial list of his appearances, see his obituary in the *New York Times*, June 4, 1947, and the 'Who's Who in the Motion Picture Industry' in the appropriate *International Motion Picture Almanac*. Julia Taylor had been in Richard Mansfield repertory and plays by Leo Ditrichstein in New York; she alternated between stage and film but was still playing in Thanhouser productions in 1914. About Mrs Walton I know nothing; Mr Thanhouser did not remember her. The *Moving Picture World*, October 21, 1911, has a picture of the Gaiety Theatre, Montreal, which shows the three-sheet advertising of *Romeo and Juliet*; the picture cleared $300 in a three-day run and thereby broke all local records. It was released in England on March 8, 1913, and I note that when shown at the Vauxhall Electric Theatre in April, it was 'introduced . . . by a short discourse on the story of the film by the manager, Mr W. T. Bennett' (*Kinematograph and Lantern Weekly*, January 30th, May 1st).

CHAPTER IV

The introductory material is indebted to Rachael Low's sound and perceptive *History of the British Film, 1906–1914* (London, 1949), which also supplies some of the later information.

I Gaumont, *Romeo and Juliet* (1908)

I owe thanks to the late Sir Godfrey Tearle who in 1947 gave me his recollections of the background and some of his experiences. The Lyceum material is from A. E. Wilson, *The Lyceum*, London, 1952, p. 157. The quotation about Ernest Carpenter is from an advertisement in the *Kinematograph and Lantern Weekly*, July 2, 1908. The description of the cricket is from Leslie Wood, *The Romance of the Movies*, London, 1937, pp. 120–1, repeated in *The Miracle of the Movies*, London, 1947, p. 148; Sir Godfrey told me he still had the photograph. He thought the director was Welsh Pearson, but Welsh Pearson was actually Tommy Welsh, who handled the business side of the partnership, and George Pearson. Mr Pearson told me in 1955 that he did not direct the film; Tearle must have confused *Romeo and Juliet* with *The Fool* (1913) in which he played and which Pearson directed as his first production (Low, p. 132). The partial cast is from the periodical above, June 11th, Gaumont advertisement, which provides the release date, length, and price, prints three stills, and is also quoted. The British branch of the French company began operations in 1898. It sold its French films and apparatus and later went into British production and the distribution of its own and others' films. (Low and Manvell, p. 21).

II Clarendon, *The Tempest* (1908)

On the company, see Low, pp. 104–5. The picture is listed in the *Kinematograph and Lantern Weekly*, November 26, 1908, as new and 765 feet. The quotation is from the issue of December 10th. *Bioscope*, December 17th, gives 780 feet, as do two much later issues of the first journal in advertisements for the sale of old prints by Henderson's North of England Film Bureau (February 22, 1912, in which the picture is wrongly identified as by Vitagraph) and Artograph (April 18, 1912).

III Barker, *Hamlet* (1910)

I could write a detective story detailing my pursuit of information about this film, which was probably more elusive than any other treated in the book. It took far more time than it – relatively – deserved, and I kept at it only because it was an annoyance and a challenge. I was even told by reputable collectors and historians that the film was a myth! No doubt much of what has been written about it is inaccurate or repetitive hearsay, and a good deal must remain in doubt, but the film was advertised for sale in the *Kinematograph and Lantern Weekly*, May 16, 1912, by the Globe Film Co., Ltd, and by W. Butcher and Sons; the advertisements were several times repeated. It is specifically listed as Barker's *Hamlet*. Similar advertisements turned up later in the United States by the M. and F. Feature Film Co. of Chicago (*Moving Picture World*, July 12, 1913) and again in London, by the Express Film Service (*Cinema News and Property Gazette*, February 17, 1916). Is not this something more than fantasy?

In 1951 I found that Captain Barker was still alive, and wrote him for information. He kindly replied with his own partial recollections, sent me an article which referred to the film, stated that he had at his retirement in 1918 not kept his records and souvenirs, but indicated that he would search further for information about date, length, etc., and write again. He died on November 5, 1951 at the age of eighty-four before he could do so. Four years later through the Cinematograph Trade Benevolent Fund of London 1 was able to get into communication with a number of veterans who knew or were associated with Barker in the early days: A. C. Bromhead, Reginald Bromhead, W. J. Gell, Frank Bassill, and E. G. Turner, all of whom tried to help but could give me no accurate information from their personal recollections. Mr Bassill, however, referred me to Mr A. P. Smith who had worked for the Warwick Trading Company, Ltd in 1910, and Mr Smith proved to be a gold mine. I thank the gentlemen named above, and I am particularly indebted to Mr Smith for assistance in establishing Captain Barker's connections at the time and date of the film, about which I could find nothing in the trade journals until it was old in 1912.

Accounts of the shooting of the picture may be found in a speech by W. G. Barker, 'Before 1910: Kinematograph Experiences', delivered to a meeting of the British Kinematograph Society, held on February 3, 1936, and printed in the Proceedings of the British Kinematograph Society, No. 38; in Wood pp. 102–3 and his later *The Miracle of the Movies*, London, 1947, p. 146; John H. Bird, *Cinema Parade*, Birmingham, 1947 pp. 39–40; and Charles Graves, 'When British Films *Had* to Pay', *Everybody's Weekly*, December 24, 1949, the report of a personal interview with Barker. There are some discrepancies which I have tried to resolve.

Barker, in his speech, says the film was in one reel, in a letter that it ran about twenty minutes; the advertisements cited above list it variously as 1500 feet, 1325 feet, and in two parts. It may have been a crowded reel, which was later padded to two.

The background material on Barker other than that obtained from him and from Mr Smith is from Low and Manvell, p. 15; Low, pp. 94–5; Wood, *The Miracle . . .* , pp. 145–6; *Cinema News and Property Gazette*, December 12 and December 19, 1918.

As to date, the film was not made by Warwick which Barker had left in August of 1909; it preceded the *Henry VIII* film to be discussed, which was released in February, 1911, and was much more grandiose; it was after Barker opened independent offices in March 1910. The *Kinematograph and Lantern Weekly*, April 21, 1910, said Barker had not yet made his first plot picture. Of course, January 1911 is a bare possibility, but it would have been at that time a cold swim for the Ophelia!

Barker says there were twenty-two scenes requiring backgrounds. Since there are only twenty scenes in the play, some of which occur in the same place, I do not see why so many were necessary. He may have meant twenty-two sequences, or some may have been duplicates in order to save time during the photographing.

Charles Raymond later became a member of Barker's stock company, still later an actor and director for the British and Colonial Kinematograph Company, Motograph, and I. B. Davidson. In the *Kinematograph and Lantern Weekly*, May 2, 1912, which carries a photograph, he claims also to have produced, that is, directed, 'without a previous rehearsal'; 'the adaptation of Shakespeare's immortal tragedy is also the outcome of Mr Raymond's pen'. Perhaps; at any rate both Barker and Smith identified him as the Hamlet in Barker's production.

In the *Everybody's* article, Barker is quoted as saying that the Rosenkrantz 'is the present manager of Wyndham's Theatre'. The manager in 1949 was Arthur Melville; he has written me that he had no connection with the film. Moreover, I doubt Barker's statement which follows:

'Nobody had to learn any lines because those were the silent days. It was largely a question of saying something which approximated in length to Shakespeare's words. I must say, though, that we had a very rude letter from a branch of the Deaf and Dumb Association. The members were horrified by the bad language of my actors and actresses, which they could lip-read.'

No doubt, Shakespeare's lines did not have to be learned, but the length of the apparent speeches could not in so short a film have approximated the duration of Shakespeare's words, and the lip-reading story has been told of countless films and was an 'inside' joke.

How the film was exhibited or distributed I do not know; I find no evidence of advertisement in the trade papers, in fact no reference to the film at all in 1910 or 1911. Mr Smith has suggested that Barker may have sold the negative outright.

IV Barker, *Henry VIII* (1911)

My account follows, but is developed from my article, 'The Shakespeare Film as Record': Sir Herbert Beerbohm Tree, *Shakespeare Quarterly* (July 1952), pp. 230–2. The quotation about Tree's interpretation of Wolsey is from Pearson, who, however, does not mention the film, p. 169. The terms of the agreement have been worked out through a combination of information from the *Kinematograph and Lantern Weekly*, various contemporary issues; Wood, *The Romance . . .*, pp. 108–9; Graves' interview with Barker in *Everybody's*, and Low, pp. 45–6, 95–6, 119. Low, pp. 186, 283, lists Louis N. Parker as producer, that is, director. There cannot have been much direction for the film in the usual sense, and though Parker, dramatist and pageant-master, had conducted the first four weeks of the rehearsals for Tree's stage production, he was in America from December 4, 1910, to March 1, 1911, and could not have participated at Ealing. See his autobiography, *Several of My Lives*, London, 1928, pp. 229–35. Most illustrations of *Henry VIII* I have seen, including the five in Barker's descriptive booklet, are of the stage performance, not the film. London distribution was handled by Barker, provincial by the Globe Film Co., Ltd; rights for Australia, New Zealand, and Tasmania were secured by T. J. West, but was there time? (*Kinematograph and Lantern Weekly*, February 16th, 23rd, March 2nd). G. R. Doyle, *Twenty-Five Years of Films . . .*, London, 1936, p. 203, says weekly film rental was £50; in a suit by Barker against the Bijou Picture Theatre, Camberwell, the hire was given as £40 (*Kinematograph and Lantern Weekly*, March 30th). Excluded by the trusts, the film was not shown in the United States (Same, March 9th).

Information about Tree's adaptation of Shakespeare, and about the scenes photographed is from respectively Tree's souvenir programme and Barker's descriptive booklet. As to the length, the commentator quoted mentions that 'none of the 5000 feet or so . . . was wasted'. He was quite probably present at the filming, and it is more than likely Barker used a roll of 1000 feet for each of his five scenes, but would the visitor have known, and did Barker expose all of it? Added titles would have increased footage. When the prints were destroyed, the *Kinematograph and Lantern Weekly* of April 20th mentions a total of 'some 60,000 feet of film.' If all prints were there, this would make for a three-reel film, but this is problematical, and I am inclined to think it was shorter. The issue of March 2nd says the film lasted about 30 minutes, which would imply two reels. The

Othello (Emil Jannings) strangles Desdemona (Ica von Lenkeffy) in Bukhovetsky's *Othello* (örner-Film, 1922). Museum of Modern Art Film Library

Petruchio (Lauderdale Maitland) and Katherina (Mlle. Dacia) in the bridal chamber scene *The Taming of the Shrew* (British and Colonial, 1923). National Film Archive

56. Shylock (Werner Krauss) displays the bond in the court scene of *The Merchant of Venice* (Peter Paul Felner-Film, 1923); Henny Porten is the Portia, lower left. National Film Archive
57. Snug as a lion (Walter Brandt) attacks Bottom as Pyramus (Werner Krauss) while Snout (Fritz Rasp) impersonates a wall in *A Midsummer Night's Dream* (Neumann, 1925). Museum of Modern Art Film Library

information about exploitation is from issues of the *Kinematograph and Lantern Weekly*, February 16th, 23rd, March 2nd, 9th, 16th, 23rd, April 6th. The quotation about West End theatres is from February 23rd. Taylor's belatedly printed London letter is from the *Moving Picture World*, April 1st. Reports of managers' and spectators' reactions are from the various issues of the *Kinematograph and Lantern Weekly* cited above. The story of the protest against inaudibility is from Wood, *The Romance . . .* , p. 109, but it is reported in the trade journal of March 2nd in somewhat different language. The quotation from the *Cinema News and Property Gazette* is of July 5, 1917. Tree's remarks on the film are from Low Warren, *The Film Game*, London, 1937, pp. 60–1. The burning is described in the *Kinematograph and Lantern Weekly* of April 20th.

There is small chance that the film has survived, and certainly I have been unable to find it. The stories, such as they are, are contradictory and inconclusive. Will Barker wrote me that he would try to answer the question of survival but died before he could do so. Ernest Dench in *Pictures and the Picturegoer*, January 29, 1916, says two prints of the picture were not burned, and that one went to Tree and one was retained by Barker. The account of the conflagration cited above indicates that Barker kept the negative in his safe at Soho Square. Robert Humfrey, *Careers in the Films*, London, 1938, p. 30, says the negative was burned. Taylor, already quoted, implies the negative was to go to Tree: 'Still Barker in filming the picture had another motive than money-making. . . . It is the first permanent record of the Great English actor's art. . . .' Barker in his publicity brochure says one of his aims was 'to hand down to posterity a faithful, silent, and permanent record. . . .' A note in the *Kinematograph and Lantern Weekly* of February 16, 1911, reports: 'Some of the theatrical managers are having their companies filmed, thus emulating the example of my friend Barker, in photographing *Henry VIII*. These films are to be preserved for future reference, so that our descendants may see how our contemporaries comported themselves on the stage.' Does this include Barker's film? In any case, even if there was some survival, unless it were stored properly and regularly inspected, the film in whatever form would have long since deteriorated beyond repair; Hesketh Pearson found no record of it in Tree's effects, and Barker apparently did not after his retirement retain what he may have hitherto saved.

Barker's advertisement in the *Kinematograph and Lantern Weekly* of February 23rd gives the entire cast. In addition to those named in the text it was as follows:

Cardinal Campeius	S. A. Cookson
Cranmer	Charles Fuller
Duke of Norfolk	A. E. George
Duke of Buckingham	Basil Gill
Duke of Suffolk	Edward O'Neill
Duke of Surrey	Gerald Lawrence
Lord Chamberlain	Edward Sass
Capucius	Francis Chamier
Lord Abergavenny	Clarence Derwent
Lord Sands	Walter R. Creighton
Sir Nicholas Vaux	Charles James
Thomas Cromwell	Reginald Owen

L

Griffiths	Henry Morrell
1st Gentleman	Cyril Sworder
2nd Gentleman	Charles Howard
Garter, King-at-Arms	Clifford Heatherly
Surveyor to the Duke of Buckingham	Acton Bond
Sergeant-at-Arms	Arthur Gaskill
Servant	W. B. Abingdon
A Crier	Edmund Goulding
A Scribe	James Smythson
Jester	Ross Shore
An Old Lady	Mrs Charles Calvert
Patience	Miss Lila Barclay

v Co-operative, *Julius Caesar* (1911)

For the background of the company, see Low, pp. 20, 112, 115. She does not mention Barker's connection, but Graves does in the *Everybody's* interview; also Bird, p. 40. Quotations and information about the production are from the company's advertisement in the *Kinematograph and Lantern Weekly*, March 2nd; comment, in the same, March 9th, and *Bioscope*, March 16th. Neither Sir Frank nor Lady Benson mentions the films in respective autobiographies. Later issues of the first journal indicate that on April 13th the film was playing at the Theatre de Luxe, Leeds, and on May 4th at the Polytechnic Picture Palace, Falmouth. A. E. Taylor, foreign correspondent of the *Moving Picture World*, in a 'London Letter' published on April 15th thinks the film 'should be of interest to people on your side of the ocean'. I cannot find that it was.

vi Co-operative, *Macbeth* (1911)

Advertisement in the *Kinematograph and Lantern Weekly*, March 9th; comment in the same, March 16th, and *Bioscope*, same date, which gives cast and two unreproducable stills. This may be the film which was advertised for sale or rent by Bradenburgh in the *Moving Picture World* (August 17, 1912), by Francis Kinematograph Co. (April 3, 24, 1913), and by B. and W. Exclusive Film Proprietors (December 4, 1913), both the last in the *Kinematograph and Lantern Weekly*, and by Harry Ward (later the W. of B. and W.) in *Cinema News and Property Gazette*, November 13, 1913, with two stills which I do not recognize. None of them makes any reasonable identification of what he or it is offering, but the first might mean that the Benson film had gone to the United States, and the last two that it was brought out of the store room to compete with the Bourchier film which was released in the fall of 1913.

vii Co-operative, *The Taming of the Shrew* (1911)

Advertisements in the *Kinematograph and Lantern Weekly*, March 23rd, April 13th; comment in *Bioscope*, April 13th, which, contrary to the company's announcements, gives release date as April 22nd.

viii Co-operative, *Richard III* (1911)

Release dates from advertisements in the *Kinematograph and Lantern Weekly* May 4th, June 1st. I have made my own examination of the film but I am much indebted to Miss Low's analysis with stills, pp. 224–8. The positive print in the National Film Archive has no main title and there is footage missing at the end; it runs to 1327 feet against 1385 as released. *Shakespeare Film*, a publication of the Deutschen Instituts für Filmkunde for the Shakespeare Film Festival in Wiesbaden, 1964, hereafter referred to as the Wiesbaden brochure, gives the cast in addition to Benson and his wife (Lady Anne) as:

King Henry VI	James Berry
King Edward IV	Alfred Brydone
King Henry VII	Eric Maxim
Duke of Buckingham	Moffat Johnston
Duke of Norfolk	James MacLearn
Queen Elizabeth	Violet Farebrother
Duchess of York	Elinor Aicken

CHAPTER V

For various reasons, accuracy in this chapter is peculiarly difficult to achieve. The records for films treated are particularly sparse, and I have sometimes been forced to accept what information I could obtain as true when I have doubts and suspicions, simply because I could not contravene what is stated as fact. It is quite clear that errors have been proliferated by later writers who did not have proper evidence upon which to base their judgments.

The only really satisfactory data must rest upon accounts contemporary with the films discussed, utterances by people directly involved, or upon the trade journals which appeared contemporaneously. Most of such people are dead or remember vaguely; in only a few cases was personal material published early enough to be trustworthy. Files of such journals as the *Ciné-Journal* and *La Cinematografia Italiana* are incomplete both here and abroad, sometimes the only sources which could pin-point a date or provide identification of producing company or participating personnel.

I have seen foreign films in this period which have no indications of place of manufacture, time of production, name of company, or leading members of the cast, not even when the star was a well known theatre personality. Moreover the best film historians contradict themselves or each other.

For example, though Film d'Art was a specific company, *film d'art* was adopted by various organizations not only as a genre but sometimes as a label; the journals compounded the confusion. It was not easy to disentangle Film d'Art from Film d'Arte Italiana when a film by the Italian company was distributed in France, the more so because Pathé was included with both producers and had in addition a Série d'Art and films of the Société Cinématographique des Auteurs et Gens de Lettres. L'Eclair called some of its films *films d'art* because of its association with ACAD (Association Cinématographique des Auteurs Dramatiques); Gaumont produced under the name Film Esthétique; there was also a Film des Auteurs. In Italy, Ambrosio had a Série d'or, and Milano and Aquila produced what were called films d'art or films d'arte. And *série d'art* was used as indiscriminately as *films d'art*. The difficulties with respect to particular films are indicated in the sometimes exasperated text and notes to this chapter.

The introductory material is largely based on Sadoul, *Les Pionniers* ... pp. 528–44 and *Le Cinéma devient un art*, Vol I, pp. 21–38, 86–100, and trade journals. Two articles in the *Ciné-Journal*, June 11, 1910, are especially helpful in distinguishing among the various *film d'art* companies: G. Dureau, 'Films d'Art et "Film d'art",' pp. 3–4 and Georges Fagot, 'Le Film d'Arte Italiana', p. 19. Obviously even the exhibitors were in need of clarification. I have consistently given the name of the French company with an initial capital on the first and last words to avoid any confusion with the genre; the records themselves are inconsistent. Shakespearean titles are in English, regardless of the country of origin, in the following list.

1 Film d'Art, *Macbeth* (1910)

I am grateful indeed to my friend, Jay Leyda, whose letters to me about an original print in the Filmarchiv, Berlin, G. D. R., have prevented me from falling into the errors of most of my predecessors who have dated this film wrongly, who have put Mounet-Sully in the title role, and who in some cases have assumed that there were two films at this time, one of Film d'Art, the other by Pathé. The print is toned, on nitrate stock and carries on one edge: 'Pathé Frères 14 Rue Favart Paris', on the other: 'Exhibition interdite en France en Suisse et en Belgique'. It was then a Film d'Art production distributed by Pathé. This print is the only one I know of which clearly establishes in its introductory frames that the actors were Mounet and Delvair. I first saw this film through the courtesy of Mr Richard O. Fleischer of RKO Pictures, Inc., who in 1947 kindly sent it to me from California for screening at the Museum of Modern Art; he had obtained the print from Pathé News in Paris. It had on it no title or subtitle and no identification of the actors. In 1956 I saw another print at the British Film Institute obtained by Mr Ernest Lindgren from the Cinémathèque Française. This copy, on Pathé safety film, had title and subtitles, not entirely identical with those on the Berlin print, but the actors were not named. The opening title frames contain a minute placard, almost undecicerable, with a date which may be April 10 (20?), 1920 (?). With or without titles the length varies between about 968 and 1000 feet. My analysis is based on all three prints.

The article on Film d'Art by Roberto Paolello in the *Enciclopedia* dates the film 1908, which is too early; Mitry, Vol II, p. 107, says, I believe correctly, 1910. On the other hand, Sadoul, *Le Cinéma devient un art*, Vol I, Chronologie; the article on Calmettes by Bronislaw Horowicz in the *Enciclopedia*; the *Filmlexicon* article by Roberto Chiti on Calmettes; and the Wiesbaden brochure all date 1909. However, there is no mention of a Film d'Art *Macbeth* in the *Ciné-Journal* until a Pathé advertisement in the issue of July 30, 1910, and the Pathé News print is dated 1910 with a figure for the month which is probably meant to designate July (possible January). I should like here to express my indebtedness to Mrs Janou Walcutt, formerly of the American Library in Paris, for searching for issues of the *Ciné-Journal* which I had been unable to locate, finding them in the Bibliothèque de l'Arsenal, examining them, and sending me reports.

Sadoul, above, p. 24, assigns Macbeth to Mounet-Sully, as do Maurice Descotes' article on him in *The Enciclopedia*, Roberto Chiti's in the *Filmlexicon*, Knaur, and Mitry, above; the last unaccountably adds Réjane and Henri Pouctal to the cast and attributes the scenario to Jules Lemaître. The Wiesbaden brochure confounds the two brothers as Paul Mounet-Sully. Neither Mitry nor the article on her in the *Enciclopedia* puts Delvair in the picture, but Coissac, p. 418, indicates she appeared in an early French *Macbeth*. For Paul Mounet, see the unsigned article in the *Enciclopedia*, which, however, does not put him in the *Macbeth* film and Antoine: *Le Théâtre* (*La Troisième Republique de 1870 à nos jours*), 2 Vols, Paris, 1932, *passim*, especially the eulogy at his death in 1922, Vol II, pp. 245–6. On Delvair, see Antoine and the article by Bronislaw Horowicz in the *Enciclopedia*; and for Calmettes, above.

The *Pathé Weekly Bulletin* of May 30, 1910, without mentioning Film d'Art announced a *Macbeth* for release in the United States on June 4th with a puff that 'the best French actors were employed to take the leading part. The whole subject is treated with masterly skill'. The *Moving Picture World*, of June 4th, repeats the announcement. Some have assumed that Pathé, which would be quite capable of it, issued a competing film. Sadoul, above, pp. 34–5 and note, puts it outside S.C.A.G.L. and tentatively assigns the direction to Henri Andréani under the supervision of Ferdinand Zecca, Pathé's chief of production. He is followed by the Wiesbaden brochure, which adds 304 metres. Mitry, Vol II, p. 120, lists an S.C.A.G.L.–Pathé *Macbeth*, dated 1908, directed by Albert Capellani, scenario by Michel Carré, with Edouard de Max as Macbeth. Mitry does not give his sources and I have found nothing to confirm his data. I am pretty well convinced – and so is Jay Leyda – that there was only one *Macbeth* film and that it was made by Film d'Art and distributed by Pathé, which sometimes took the credit.

11 Film d'Art, *Les Enfants d'Edouard* (1910)

The treatment of this film is another example of the exasperation of cinema research. The *Film Index*, p. 437, says, 'Directed by M. Andréani. Original screen play by Casimir Delavigne, with Mlles Delvair, Suterre, Marcelle Fleury, Messrs Toulot [Toulout], Wague, Jacquinet.' Since Delavigne died in 1843, he must have been hard put to it to write a screen play in 1910. Mitry, Vol II, p. 105, dates the film 1909, and gives the scenario to Henri Lavedan, the direction to André Calmettes, and the principal parts to Paul Mounet, Rolla Norman, and Dehelly. I find no evidence for his credits; I cannot place Emile Dehelly in pictures, and Jean Dehelly, born in 1896, did not, to the best of my knowledge, go into film until after World War I. The Wiesbaden brochure, while adding a 1912 Film d'Art *Richard III* directed by Calmettes with Garnier, lists a 1910 *Children of Edward*, without indication of the company, but with a cast containing Jeanne Delvair, René Alexandre, Jean Toulot (sic), and George Wayne (sic). As usual, the only really trustworthy sources are the snippets of information contained in the trade journals. I do not know who wrote the scenario; I doubt if Andréani worked for Film d'Art; the director might, however, have been Calmettes. A good deal of the misinformation has arisen because of the confusion of this film with another with the same title in 1914, which see. The 1910 film was released in England by Cosmopolitan in 1170 feet as *The Princes in the Tower*. (*Bioscope*, June 9, 1910.) The comment in the *Moving Picture World* of June 25th is useless. For a revealing account of Garnier's career, see Antoine, Vol II, pp. 349–50: 'Le cinéma mal organisé à l'époque, ne le fit vivre que malaisément, bien que son masque fût l'un des plus nobles et des plus saisissants que l'on ait vus au théâtre'.

III Cines, *Romeo and Juliet* (1908)

Prolo, Vol I, p. 122, gives Caserini as the director and the length; see also her article on Caserini in the *Enciclopedia*; Lizzani, p. 224, the *Filmlexicon*, Knaur, and the Wiesbaden brochure, which I think confuses this film with a later one in naming Francesca Bertini as the Juliet.

IV Cines, *Hamlet* (1908)

Knaur, followed by the Wiesbaden brochure, lists the director as Giuseppe De Liguoro, but Prolo does not, either in her book or her article on him in the *Enciclopedia*, and de Liguoro was with other firms (Sadoul, *Le Cinéma devient un art*, Vol I, pp. 97–9). Prolo gives the length as 232 metres; *Ciné-Journal* of August 15th as 257 metres; and in America, the Film Import and Trading Company, which represented both Williamson and Cines, as 867 feet (*Moving Picture World*, September 26th). The discrepancy is probably due to separate titling in the different countries.

V Cines, *Un drame judiciare à Venise* (1908)

Sadoul, *Les Pionniers*, pp. 414, 475, groups it with other 'sujets nobles', including *Romeo and Juliet* and *Hamlet*; in *Le Cinéma devient un Art*, Vol I, p. 88, he dates it 1907.

VI Milano, *Hamlet* (1908)

Prolo, Vol I, p. 122, and Sadoul, *Le Cinéma devient un art*, Vol I, p. 97.

VII Pineschi, *The Taming of the Shrew* (1908)

Prolo, Vol I, p. 124, and Sadoul, *Les Pionniers*, p. 416; *Le Cinéma devient un art*, Vol I, pp. 88, 98.

VIII Pathé, *Othello* (1908)

Wiesbaden brochure.

IX Nordisk, *Othello* (1908)

According to the *Moving Picture World* of November 28th, which gives the footage, it was released in the United States on November 14th. *Ciné-Journal* of September 29th lists what must be this picture under the aegis of Raleigh and Robert, 'Fabricants et Representants', for various houses including Nordisk, and gives the length as 95 metres. The quotation is from *Bioscope*, May 25, 1911, when the film was reissued. Arnold Hending, *Da Isbjørnen var lille* (*When the Polar Bear Was Small*. Nordisk's trademark was a polar bear on a globe of the world), Copenhagen, 1945, p. 65, has a still with the caption (translated) 'The film was really called *Othello* – but it was not the Othello Alstrup dreamed of playing in 1907.' This is another film about which the story is told of the protest of the deaf and dumb about what an actor actually said in a silent picture (Hending, p. 74). I reserve treatment of Nordisk until its *Hamlet* (1910).

X Pathé, *All's Well That Ends Well* (1909)

Pathé Weekly Bulletin, March 8th; 497 feet. The summary shows no relation to Shakespeare. I have no idea what its French title was, but it must have been produced abroad, since the issue of May 9, 1910, advises readers to watch for the first American Pathé production.

XI Eclipse, *Henry IV (Henri IV)* (1909)
Ciné-Journal, September 27th–October 3rd; 232 metres; 'drame historique.'

XII Gaumont, *The Daughters of Shylock (Les Filles de Shylock)* (1909)
Ciné-Journal, October 24th–31st, November 1st–7th. The first issue lists it under Théâtro-Films, toned, and somewhat mysteriously '108 m. 238'. Perhaps 108 metres of the 238 were toned. The second issue lists under Gaumont, 'nouveautés: phono-scènes'. Théâtro-Film was a section of Eclair, 'patronné par Maurice de Féraudy, de la Comédie-Française, et dirigé effectivement par Lainé' (Sadoul, *Le Cinéma devient un art*, Vol I, p. 37), but Gaumont was making sound films at the time.

XIII Itala, *Julius Caesar* (also called *Brutus*) (1909)
The *Film Index*, p. 443, lists it under 'History and Biography', rather than 'adaptations from literature', where the Vitagraph *Julius Caesar* is mentioned (p. 292). The sequences in the National Film Archive print were, when I made my examination of it, out of order; my summary restores the original sequence, and is aided by that in the *Cinema News and Property Gazette*, April 16, 1913, when the film was reissued. The print is entitled *Brutus* and bears the Itala trademark; its length is 646 feet, its condition poor; I could examine it only on an Editola and by hand. Prolo, Vol I, p. 128, does not name the director, I think wisely. The film was shown in a film programme of the Cinémathèque Française in 1955 where it was listed as 1907, directed by Pastrone. The Wiesbaden brochure, probably following Knaur, gives the date correctly, but also gives the direction to Pastrone. Mitry, Vol II, p. 88, does not list the film at all, but includes a Pasquali *Julius Caesar* of 1909. The company had been founded in that year by Ernesto Pasquali, but I know of no such film. For Itala, see Sadoul, *Les Pionniers*, pp. 412–13; for Pastrone, *Le Cinéma devient un art*, Vol I, pp. 89–90, 164–72, and the article on him by Francesco Savio in the *Enciclopedia* which does not, however, mention the film.

XIV Cines, *Othello* (1909)
The source is Prolo, Vol I, p. 126, who lists it in addition to the 1907 presentation. See my Chapter I and Explanations. Knaur and the Wiesbaden brochure follow Prolo and list the director as Mario Caserini, who according to Prolo did the earlier version. I cannot help wondering whether it was not merely a question of re-issue.

XV Cines, *Macbeth* (1909)
On Cines and Caserini, see Sadoul, *Les Pionniers*, pp. 406–10; *Le Cinéma devient un art*, Vol I, pp. 88, 95–6. There is an article by Prolo on Caserini which mentions the prize, in the *Enciclopedia*; Dante Capelli, primarily a director, is briefly treated there (in an article on Enrico Capelli), as is Maria Caserini Gasperini. The cost and length of the film are given in Frederick A. Talbot, *Moving Pictures*, Philadelphia, 1912, p. 176. L'Estrange Fawcett, *Films: Facts and Forecasts*, London,

1927, p. 2, mentions its success. The advertisement of the Film Import and Trading Company is in the *Moving Picture World*, December 11, 1909. The picture was first listed in the *Ciné-Journal* in the issue of November 8th–14th, as of 440 metres. I do not find it in the *Kinematograph and Lantern Weekly* until May 4, 1911. Carlo Lizzani, *Il Cinema Italiano*, 2nd ed., Firenze, 1954, p. 225, indicates the presence of Capelli, the *Enciclopedia* that of Gasperini. The assumption that they played the leading roles is my own.

XVI Pineschi (Latium), *Othello* (1909)

Prolo, Vol I, p. 129, 'grande scena tragicomica – parodia del capolavoro di Shakespeare.' See also Sadoul, *Le Cinéma devient un art*, Vol I, pp. 98–9, and the articles on Yambo by Giulio Buccioloni and Francesco Savio in the *Enciclopedia*.

XVII Film d'Arte Italiana, *Othello* (1909)

For Film d'Arte Italiana, I have followed Fagot's article in the *Ciné-Journal*, June 11, 1910, and Sadoul, *Le Cinéma devient un art*, Vol I, p. 95. The detailed account of the company in Venice is a paraphrase and translation of the words of Riccardi quoted in Francesco Soro, *Splendori e Miserie del Cinema*, Milano, 1935, pp. 91–3. Soro gives the cast; see also Prolo, Vol I, p. 127, who identifies the director, and gives the date. The quotation from Parker is from his *Several of My Lives*, London, 1928, p. 208. The American release date is from the *Moving Picture World* of April 16, 1910; the footage, from April 23rd. The *Pathé Weekly Bulletin* of April 11th designates the picture as Film d'Art, with capitals, which it was not. The *Enciclopedia* has articles on Garavaglia by Andrea Camilleri, on Lepanto (unsigned), and on Film d'Arte, by Prolo. The *Filmlexicon* lists the films of Garavaglia, Lepanto, Lo Savio, and Nepoti.

XVIII Deutsche Vitascope, *Romeo und Julia* (1909)

Wiesbaden brochure.

XIX Le Lion, *A Midsummer Night's Dream* (1909)

On Footit, see the article by Alessandro Cervellat in the *Enciclopedia*. The information about Napierkowska is from the clipping file in the Theatre Collection of the New York Public Library. Actually she was born in Constantinople of French and Polish extraction. She played with Henri Krauss in *Notre Dame de Paris* (1911) and *The Anonymous Letter* (1912), and in a number of Max Linder films, and was in 1914 awarded damages against an Italian newspaper which accused her of causing the suicides of her admirers. Le Lion was a small firm which lasted only three or four years. See Sadoul, *Les Pionniers*, index, but especially pp. 363–4.

XX Lux, *Hamlet* (1910)

Sadoul, *Les Pionniers*, pp. 362–3; *Le Cinéma devient un art*, Vol I, p. 209; Mitry, Vol II, p. 147. The picture was distributed in the United States by the Empire Film Company. The film I describe had been acquired by the Museum from the Antique Film Library.

XXI Cines, *Hamlet* (1910)

Prolo, Vol I, p. 132; Lizzani, p. 225; Sadoul, *Le Cinéma devient un art*, Vol I, pp. 95–6. On Capelli, Francesco Savio in the *Enciclopedia*. M. Claude Bance wrote me that at the Unesco Shakespeare Celebration in Paris, a fragment of film was shown on November 14, 1964, which was supposed to be from Caserini's *Hamlet*. The central figure sat dejectedly on a throne while two of his friends tried to cheer him up. I accordingly wrote to M. Sadoul, who was present, for information. He replied that the fragment, projected under the auspices of the Cinémathèque, was not in his opinion a scene from *Hamlet* or from any other of Shakespeare's plays. Let me express here my thanks to M. Sadoul for his kind courtesy in this and other matters he referred to in his letter.

XXII Eclipse, *Hamlet* (1910)

All the external information is puzzling and much of it is contradictory or a repetition of earlier statements without specific indication of the derivation of the data. The article in the *Enciclopedia* on Desfontaines by Francesco Savio and Charles Ford gives him the directorship, Eclipse as the company, and the date as 1910, but without naming the actor. One of the sources cited is the book by René Jeanne and the above Charles Ford, *Histoire encyclopédique du cinéma*, Vol I, *Le Cinéma français, 1895–1929*, 7th edition, Paris, 1947; on p. 128, this work gives Eclipse, Desfontaines, Grétillat, Romano, but no date, and its still #30 on the page following 128 is of Grétillat and Romano in the closet scene. The same still is in *Le Crapouillet* (periodical), November 1932, a special number, 'Histoire du Cinéma'; Henry Fescourt (pref.; no editor named), *Le Cinéma des origines à nos jours*, Paris, [1932], p. 70 (see also p. 185); and Carl Vincent, *Histoire de l'art cinématographique*, Brussels, n.d., p. 13; all three name Grétillat but without date or company. Marcel Lapierre, *Les Cents Visages du cinéma*, Paris, 1948, p. 93, gives Eclipse and Grétillat. An advertisement by George Kleine in the *Moving Picture World*, September 16, 1911, puts Grétillat with Eclipse but not in connection with this film. The *Filmlexicon* says only Desfontaines, 1910; the Wiesbaden brochure, 1910, Eclipse, Grétillat, Romano. Knaur gives Desfontaines, Grétillat, but the date as 1912, which is an aberration. The card file in the information office of the British Film Institute follows Jeanne-Ford. All this information should add up to Eclipse, 1910, Desfontaines, Grétillat, Romano. I am, however, bothered by the fact that Sadoul, *Le Cinéma devient un art*, Vol I, p. 29, puts Desfontaines as a collaborator of Capellani at S.C.A.G.L., nowhere connects him with Eclipse, and names Grétillat as one of the actors hired by Capellani for S.C.A.G.L. He does not mention the *Hamlet* film, and his reference is to an earlier date. Mitry, Vol II, p. 120, is unaccountably circumstantial and different from other sources. He gives 1908, S.C.A.G.L.–Pathé, directed by Capellani, scenario by Michel Carré, with Grétillat, Henri Desfontaines, Benedict. He also, p. 107, lists a 1910 *Hamlet*, directed by Calmettes for Film d'Art, scenario Jules Lemaître, with Sarah Bernhardt, de Max, Charmeroy, and Henri Pouctal, at which I can only throw up my hands in astonishment and dismay. For Grétillat and Romano, see Jules Delini, *Nos Vedettes*, Paris, [1926?].

XXIII Mounet–Sully, *Hamlet* (date?)

I saw Mme Vedrès' film and use information from the programme of the Paris Theatre, New York, 1950. My recollections have been refreshed by a letter from M. Claude Bance, who saw it at the Unesco Celebration. Mr Enrico Fulchignon

L*

of Unesco wrote me that the film had been obtained from the Cinémathèque. The Wiesbaden brochure lists a *Hamlet* film with Paul Mounet-Sully, a confusion of the two brothers, Paul Mounet and Mounet-Sully, as produced by Calmettes for Film d'Art, and dates 1913. A request for the source of this information has not received a reply, and my past experience in trying to elicit information directly from the Cinémathèque has not been happy. M. Bance wrote me that M. Georges Sadoul, who was present at the Celebration, confirmed the information in the Wiesbaden brochure, but I have left the date questionable since I have no documentary evidence. I find no reference to the film in Sadoul or in the other standard histories. There is an excellent account of Mounet-Sully's Hamlet at the Comédie Française by Paul Benchettrit in *Shakespeare Survey*, Vol IX, pp. 63–7. My general information about Mounet-Sully is from Antoine, *passim*; the article by Maurice Descotes in the *Enciclopedia*; and Phyllis Hartnoll (ed.), *The Oxford Companion to the Theatre*, Oxford, 1951, from which I have quoted. The still reproduced was obtained for me by Mrs Walcutt from the Cinémathèque; she also wrote me that the excerpt was in that collection; my thanks to her again.

xxiv Nordisk, *Hamlet* (1910)

The account of the filming is based on Danish sources, and is primarily a paraphrase of the account in Arnold Hending, *Da Isbjørnen var lille*, Copenhagen, 1946, pp. 122–6. I am indebted to Mogens Skot-Hansen, who as United Nations Representative to the Motion Picture Industry, sent me this book in 1952. There are stills of an Ophelia mad-scene and of the ghost's appearance on the ramparts on pp. 125, 127. Two other books by Hending have also been useful: *Stjerner I Glashuse et Causerie over 40 Aars Film* [*Stars in the Glasshouse*], Copenhagen, 1936, still of the end of the play (p. 37), discussion (p. 50); and *Fremmede Fugle : I Dansk Film* [*Strange Birds*], Copenhagen, 1951, pp. 6–10. Ove Brusendorff, director of the Danske Filmmuseum, and author of *Filmen : Dens Navne og Historie*, Copenhagen, 1939 (see p. 184), indicated in 1955 that the film was not in the Filmmuseum and he feared it had disappeared. The best book on Danish film in English translation is by Ebbe Neergaard, Director of the Statens Filmcentral, *The Story of Danish Film*, Copenhagen, 1963 (see p. 20). Stills will also be found in the *Moving Picture World*, April 22, 1911 (closet scene); the *Kinematograph and Lantern Weekly*, March 30, 1911 (Neuss as Hamlet); and *Bioscope*, March 2, 1911 (end of the play). Ole Olsen, *Filmens Eventyr og mit Eget*, Copenhagen, 1940, has a still of the burial of Ophelia, but the film is wrongly dated 1906. The filming at Elsinore preceded by five years the first live performance of *Hamlet* at Kronborg, now a regular procedure. (Alf Henriques, 'Shakespeare and Denmark: 1900–1949', *Shakespeare Survey*, Vol III, pp. 107–15, for this reference, pp. 113–14, and Plate VIIA for a picture of the Castle.)

xxv Pathé, *Cleopatra* (1910)

There has understandably been considerable confusion about the provenance of this film. The keys to accuracy are the *Ciné-Journal* of July 30th which lists it as Série d'Art, Pathé Frères (Lapierre, p. 92, agrees) and the association with it of Zecca in the *Moving Picture World*, March 26th. *The Film Index*, p. 287, says, 'Probably based on Shakespeare's tragedy. Eight scenes. Film d'Art.' This perhaps stems from the *Pathé Weekly Bulletin* of May 9th where the picture is identified as Film d'Art. Pathé had had the distribution rights of Film d'Art (as well as S.C.A.G.L. and Série d'Art–Pathé), but by May 14th had lost them in America to the Motion Picture Distributing and Sales Company (that is, I.M.P.), which did not advertize this film (*Moving Picture World*, May 10th), as it did *The Children of Edward* (same, June 4th). Pathé was by no means averse to trading on the reputation of Film d'Art; as already noted, its *Weekly Journal* of April 11th gave the French company's name to a *film d'art Othello*, which was properly Film d'Arte Italiana, also distributed by Pathé and indeed founded by it. Neither the French, English, or American trade journals speaks of *Cleopatra* as Film d'Art. Zecca had nothing to do with Film d'Art, but as chief of production at Pathé considerable to do with Série d'Art–Pathé Frères, a competing outfit. I doubt however whether Zecca actually staged this film; the director might have been Andréani, as Sadoul conjectures for the Pathé *Macbeth* (*Le Cinéma devient un art*, Vol I, p. 35N1). I think it is confusion between the Série d'Art and S.C.A.G.L. which has led Jeanne and Ford, Vol I, p. 120, to assign an *Antony and Cleopatra*, not dated, to the latter, and therefore to give the director as Albert Capellani, who became artistic director of S.C.A.G.L. in 1908. This ascription is followed in the Wiesbaden brochure, which however calls it Film d'Art, and by Knaur without giving the company, though with the date 1911, but *Antony and Cleopatra* is not included in the filmographies of Capellani and S.C.A.G.L. by Davide Turconi and Francesco Savio in the respective articles in the *Enciclopedia*. It is of course barely possible that there were two films, but I do not believe so.

The footage in the United States is given in the *Moving Picture World*, May 14th (compare *Bioscope*) as 1170 feet. The information on Madeleine Roch is from Antoine, Vol II, p. 443, and Delini, *s.v.* The *Moving Picture World*, May 21st, gives the release date May 21st, not May 11th. *Caesar in Egypt*, which is not Shakespearean, is probably the same film as *Caprice du César Vainqueur* listed in *Ciné-Journal*, July 30th, as Série d'Art–Pathé Frères. There is a piece of it, about 300 feet, in the National Film Archive of the British Film Institute. If one may judge the first in the series by a fragment of the second, *Cleopatra* cannot have been very good, despite its popularity. The Russian reference is from Jay Leyda, *Kino*, New York, 1960, p. 47.

XXVI Pathé, *All's Well That Ends Well* (1910)
Kinematograph and Lantern Weekly, April 21st, released April 7th in 460 feet.

XXVII Brockliss, *All's Well That Ends Well* (1911)
Kinematograph and Lantern Weekly, August 3rd, September 21st; *Cinema News and Property Gazette*, January 1, 1914, on Brockliss. Released August 9th in 839 feet. J. F. Brockliss was the European agent for various firms, Rex, Champion, Imp (American), Milano (Italian), Pharos (German).

XXVIII Cines, *An Adventure of Henry IV of France* (1911)
Kinematograph and Lantern Weekly, July 27th, released August 19th in 698 feet.

XXIX Pathé, *Henry IV et le Bucheron* (1911)
Ciné-Journal, October 28th, 245 metres; *Moving Picture World*, May 4, 1912, released May 10th, as *Henry IV and the Woodchopper*.

xxx Urban, *Katherine Howard and Henry VIII* (1910)
Kinematograph and Lantern Weekly, January 5th, 12th, 19th, April 27th, July 13, 1911. I have dated this film in the year preceding the first reference. The last reference identified it as Urban, 1195 feet. It was probably made in France, so I have included it in this chapter rather than in Chapter IV.

xxxi Pathé, *A Court Intrigue in the Reign of Henry VIII* (1911)
The title above is from the *Kinematograph and Lantern Weekly*, November 9th. In the United States the film was called *Jane Seymour and Henry VIII* (*Moving Picture World*, July 27th, August 3, 1912). All these have summaries. The French reference is *Ciné-Journal*, December 30, 1911; 800 metres, coloured.

xxxii Messter, *Romeo and Juliet at the Seaside* (1910)
Moving Picture World, January 29th, but misspelled Meester. Released January 17th–22nd in 500 feet, but no summary.

xxxiii Pathé, *Romeo Turns Bandit* (1910)
Pathé Weekly Bulletin, May 23rd; *Moving Picture World*, May 28th. Summaries in both, 528 feet, released in the United States on May 23rd, 'extra charge for coloring'. The production was French, not American.

xxxiv Nordisk, *The Taming of the Shrew* (1911)
Cross's Imperial Pictures advertised this film of 912 feet for sale in the *Kinematograph and Lantern Weekly*, April 27th, July 20th. It may well be earlier than 1911. The other Danish picture was in 1914 and is treated later.

xxxv Urban–Eclipse, *A Modern Shylock* (1911)
Kinematograph and Lantern Weekly, January 26th, released February 8th in 705 feet.

xxxvi Cines, *A Winter's Tale* (1910)
Kinematograph and Lantern Weekly, April 21st. Prolo, Vol I, p. 133, says 289 metres.

xxxvii Milano, *Bruto I* and *Bruto II* (1910)
Prolo, Vol II, p. 136, and her article on Liguoro in the *Enciclopedia*. Sadoul, *Le Cinéma devient un art*, Vol I, pp. 97–98, mentions only one *Brutus*, assigns it to Liguoro and implies that he acted in it.

xxxviii Kineto, *Julius Caesar* (1910?)
I am indebted to Mr Sam-Ing The, director of the documentation section of the Nederlands Filmmuseum, for showing me these stills. From his examination of the scrapbook, he thought the date of the film would be 1910–1914. For Kineto, which was also a distributor of foreign films and made films on its own, see Low, index. For details in my account, I make grateful acknowledgment to Mr Denis Gifford of the Central Office of Information, London, who is preparing a complete list of British films. Jeanne and Ford, Vol II, p. 403, indicate Theo Frenkel was

'metteur en scène de théâtre', and directed some Dutch films. His mother's name was Mrs Theo Frenkel-Bouwmeester. She was a well known Dutch actress and sister to an even better known actor, Louis Bouwmeester, who made a sensational film in Volendam in 1912, *L'Or qui brule*, directed by Alfred Machin. Louis Bouwmeester played Shylock in Dutch in Paris and London, while the other actors used their native tongues. I am grateful to Mr E. Alexander of the Toneelmuseum, Amsterdam, for details about Theo Frenkel, Sr, including his identity with Theo Bouwmeester.

XXXIX Cines, *Brutus* (1910)

Prolo, Vol I, p. 132, for date and director; Francesco Savio on Guazzoni in the *Enciclopedia* confirms. I am puzzled, however, by the discrepancy between this date and the evidence for 1911 implied in my text. Kleine's press sheet giving the American footage is in the Theatre Collection of the New York Public Library.

The fragment of film I saw is owned by John Barnes, collector of optical and photographic equipment and owner of the Barnes Museum of Cinematography, St Ives, Cornwall. He acquired the film by chance in the purchase of a job-lot from a junk dealer. I am much indebted to him for telling me about this film and to his brother, William Barnes, for searching it out from storage and bringing it to London, so that it could be shown on the Editola at the British Film Institute. When viewed, the film was in pieces and the sequences in the wrong order. It contains about 340 feet of the original British length of 1187 feet. The film stock is labelled on the titles, 'Societa Italiana Cines Roma'. The film number was on the titles, 658, and they also contain numbers indicating their order. Since the summaries in the text present clearly and in detail the episodes shown, I present here the analysis of Mr Barnes's film in corrected order:

I Title: 'Caesar does not heed the entreaties of his wife Calpurnia who tries to keep him from going to the Senate.' (Not shown.)

II Title: 'Caesar's death – "And thou too! Brutus my son!".' Shown is the beginning of the assassination scene, with the rejection of the petition, but the rest is missing.

III Title: 'Caesar's funeral. The roman people at the ardent words of Marc Antony rises against Caesar's murderers.' Shown are the crowds in the forum, Antony ascending to the rostrum and making his speech as the people show excitement.

IV Title: 'Brutus seeks safety in flight.' Shown is part of the flight through a narrow defile.

V Title: 'Apparition of Caesar to Brutus – "We shall meet at Philippi".' Shown is Brutus, obviously fatigued, at a table. An attendant inquires after his wants but is dismissed. As he leans over the table to study a map, the ghost appears, right. Brutus turns and leans back on the table, left. The ghost vanishes.

VI Title: '. . . and not to be taken alive by his enemies, hurls himself on the sword of a friend.' Shown is a section of the Battle of Philippi, with Brutus and his army fleeing. He finds Cassius' dead body, shows distress and despair, is pulled along unwillingly by his friends. This outdoor scene shows open spaces between trees and rocks.

I do not understand Sadoul's reference to a print, which might be of this film, but which he thinks is not, in the Cinémathèque Française (*Le Cinéma devient un art*, Vol I, p. 96N1).

Four stills of *Brutus* are included in McQuade's article, two in the review in the *Kinematograph and Lantern Weekly*, and one in Kleine's press sheet.

XL Milano, *King Lear* (1910)

Prolo, Vol I, p. 136; Sadoul, *Le Cinéma devient un art*, Vol II, p. 98. Knaur says Liguoro acted in it; Sadoul is vague about the nature of his participation. An advertisement by Brierley and Company in the *Kinematograph and Lantern Weekly*, November 2, 1911, gives the length as 1200 feet, but this may well be padded.

XLI Film d'Arte Italiana, *King Lear* (1910)

Prolo, Vol I, p. 150, gives director, names Novelli and Chiantoni but dates 1912; on the other hand in her article on *Film d'Arte Italiana* in the *Enciclopedia*, she says 1910, and this is confirmed by *Bioscope*, December 8th of that year, which in addition to a summary indicates it was to be released in England on December 21st in 1072 feet. *Ciné-Journal*, January 21, 1911, lists the film, 'Le roi Lear, d'après la tragedie de Shakespeare, interprêté par M. Ermete Novelli, dans le rôle du roi Lear . . . F.A.I – S.A.P.F. – 325', that is Film d'Arte Italiana, released in the Série d'Art–Pathé Frères in 325 metres. In the article by Giuseppe Pastina on Ermete Novelli in the *Enciclopedia*, there is a statement that 'Bertini . . . avera debuttato sullo schermo del' ombre di Novelli in Re Lear', but Francesco Savio in the article on Bertini does not say so. There is much that is shadowy about Bertini's early career, but according to the *Filmlexicon* (Roberto Chiti) she had made a débutante film in Naples in 1904 and *Il Trovatore* in 1909. For Chiantoni, also see the *Filmlexicon*. No doubt because of the identity of first names, Ermete Zacconi has sometimes been listed as the star of *King Lear*. The *Filmlexicon* does so under Lo Savio, but not under Bertini or Chiantoni; the article by Francesco Savio on Zacconi in the *Enciclopedia* indicates Zacconi played Lear on the stage but gives no evidence of a film *King Lear*. E. Ferdinand Palmieri in *Fifty Years of Italian Cinema* (American edition but original, Rome, 1954), p. 28, says, 'I can still see Ermete Zacconi in *Padre* and solemn and raging in King Lear', but in his earlier *Vecchio Cinema Italiano*, 1940, p. 68, he names Novelli as protagonist, which is correct, and Lyda Borelli as also in the film, which is wrong; she had not yet appeared on the screen.

I examined in 1955 a print of the film in the National Film Archive of the British Film Institute. It is tinted, incomplete (807 feet), and marked Pathé along the edges. The main title is a replacement; parts of the film are spotted and tints have faded.

XLII Film d'Arte Italiana, *The Merchant of Venice* (1910–1911)

In the absence of Italian trade journals, I cannot be sure whether the film was made late in 1910 or early in 1911 when it was released in England. Prolo, Vol I, p. 134, says 1910, and this date is accepted by Knaur, the Wiesbaden brochure, and the files of the National Film Archive of the British Film Institute. Yet Prolo in her article on Ugo Falena in the *Enciclopedia* gives 1911, as do Francesco Savio on Bertini and Giuseppe Pastina on Novelli. The filmographies in the *Film-*

lexicon under Bertini, Lo Savio, and Novelli also give 1911. There is no disagreement on the participation of Novelli or of Bertini though only Wiesbaden names her rôle; Pastina's article mentions that Olga Giannini Novelli was in the film with her husband. The reports on the success of the film are from the *Kinamatograph and Lantern Weekly* of March 23rd, April 6th, 13th, 27th, May 4th; it was sometimes shown along with Tree's *Henry VIII*. For the 1913 reissue – it was not called so – see the same journal, July 10th; *Bioscope*, August 14th, where it is listed as Film d'Art; *Cinema News and Property Gazette*, July 9th; the footage checks. *Bioscope*, at this time comments: 'A worthy reproduction of Shakespeare's great work, filmed in Venice itself, and portraying many of its architectural glories. The story is very faithfully followed, considering the limitations of a single reel subject, and a host of people are seen partaking in the general rejoicing over the defeat of Shylock in the final scene (Released Aug. 24th. . . .).'

I examined the film in a viewer at the British Film Institute in 1955. The tinted print was 556 feet long out of the original 890. The can was labelled *Il Mercante di Venezia*, the general title on the positive: The Merchant of Venice / from Shakespeare / Film d'Arte Italiana. The print has been much spliced, especially in scenes where only short strips remain.

XLIII Film d'Arte Italiana, *Romeo and Juliet* (1911)

Curiously enough the film is not listed in Prolo, and I have seen no Italian trade journals so early, but 1911 is given by Francesco Savio on Serena in the *Enciclopedia*, by the *Filmlexicon* on Bertini, by Knaur (though because of the Pathé connection it is listed there as French), and by the Wiesbaden brochure. This film, according to the *Ciné-Journal* of March 30, 1912, was the *Romeo and Juliet* which, along with the Nordisk *Hamlet*, was stolen from M. Coucke of Namur. In the United States – is there a detective story here? – the film was advertised for sale by G. W. Bradenburgh of Philadelphia in the *Moving Picture World* of June 1st, 15th, July 6th, October 12th, as in 3 reels, 2800 feet (coloured), 2700 feet, and 3 reels, 3200 feet. These dates precede the licensed release by the General Film Company. Bradenburgh's reputation was not of the highest, and this looks like piracy and various padding. Francesca Bertini is specifically identified as Juliet in the *Motion Picture Story Magazine*, 'Answers to Inquiries', November, December 1912. The September issue has a fictionalized version of the film with a still. There is also a still in an article by Charles Ford, *Cinema* (Italian), No. 110, 1953, p. 302. Confusion about the date of the film has arisen because it was reissued at various times, even as late as 1917 when *La Cinematografia Italiana ed Estera* of October 1st–10th printed a Pathé advertisement which includes *Romeo and Juliet* with Bertini in a 'Gruppo Ristampe'. I see no need of detailing what Shakespearean scenes were actually used, since summaries are notoriously inaccurate and there is no print.

XLIV Eclipse, *Falstaff* (1911)

Eclipse had absorbed Radios and the Urban Trading Company when Charles Urban founded Kinemacolor. The firm is therefore sometimes listed as Eclipse–Radios, Urban Trading Company, and Urban–Eclipse. Desfontaines is named as director in the article on him by Charles Ford in the *Enciclopedia*; by Jeanne and Ford, pp. 127–8; by the *Filmlexicon*, which dates 1910; Knaur; the Wiesbaden brochure; and Mitry, Vol II, p. 141, who however lists the film as S.C.A.G.L.–Pathé. Articles in the *Filmlexicon* and the *Enciclopedia* on Françoise Rosay date 1913, but this was the date of re-issue, as the *Kinematograph and Lantern Weekly* of October 2, 1913, states. The film was also called *Sir John Falstaff* in the United States, and *The Merry Wives of Windsor* in England. Denis d'Inès was much the most distinguished of the actors. A pupil of Le Bargy at the Conservatoire, he was engaged by Antoine in 1905, acted at the Odéon from 1908, became *sociétaire* at the Comédie-Française in 1920, and *doyen* in 1945. (Bronislaw Horowicz in the *Enciclopedia*). Madeleine Barjac had as a child played with Bernhardt, then was at the Ambigu, with Lucien Guitry, at the Conservatoire and the Odéon in 1906, with Antoine from 1909 to 1911. She made her début at the Comédie-Française in 1919 (Delini). *Bioscope* gave the release date as May 10th, the *Kinematograph and Lantern Weekly* of May 18th as May 17th. The summaries are in *Bioscope*, April 20th; the *Moving Picture World*, June 17th; *Kinematograph and Lantern Weekly*, April 20th, 27th; the last, an Urban advertisement, indicates that Falstaff retains his followers, that Pistol marries Mistress Quickly, and that the last scene is in woodland – perhaps, but I am suspicious of it, as I am of a fictionalized version in the *Motion Picture Story Magazine*, July 1911. Mitry, Vol II, p. 141, says the scenario was by Garbagni after the opera by Verdi; he does not give evidence for the first, and the scenario is closer to Shakespeare than to Boito's libretto. There are stills in *Bioscope* and the *Kinematograph and Lantern Weekly* (2), April 20th; the *Cinema News and Property Gazette*, October 1, 1913; and the *Motion Picture Story Magazine* (3).

XLV Eclipse, *The Taming of the Shrew* (1911)

A Kleine press sheet in the Theatre Collection of the New York Public Library gives the footage as 'about 1020 feet.' The fullest cast is given here also, and includes 'R. Lyon', probably Roger Lion. Didier, Joubé, Lion, and Hervé were also from the Odéon. Joubé had in 1910 achieved a triumph at the Comédie-Française and later replaced Guitry in Rostand's *Chantecler* with great success at the Porte-Saint Martin. (Antoine, Vol II, pp. 66, 73). Hervé, who is mentioned as being in this film only by the *Moving Picture World*, March 1, 1913, where his 'remarkable work . . . remembered by all' is commended, had been a pupil of Paul Mounet at the Conservatoire, but did not make his début at the Comédie-Française until 1919 (Delini). Some members of the cast are named in Lapierre, p. 93; Jeanne and Ford, p. 128; the Wiesbaden brochure; and Mitry, Vol II, who adds Trou-hanova, and assigns the film to S.C.A.G.L. with a scenario by Garbagni. Trou-hanova was a dancer who appeared in an S.C.A.G.L. film, *La Laide*, but I know of no connection with Eclipse (Sadoul, *Les Pionniers*, p. 534; *Le Cinéma devient un art*, Vol I, p. 32). All sources name Desfontaines as director. Knaur wrongly assigns the film to Eclair. My guesses at the scenario are based on Kleine's press sheet, the *Moving Picture World* of July 1st, the *Kinematograph and Lantern Weekly* and *Bioscope* of September 14th, and the fictionalized version in the *Motion Picture Story Magazine*, July, which has three stills, a picture of Petruchio's introduction to Katherina by Baptista with Bianca and Lucentio in the background, another of the wedding with Petruchio in ragged attire, and a third of the dinner being served by three servants at Petruchio's house. There are two stills in *Bioscope*.

XLVI Gaumont, *A Village King Lear* (*Le Roi Lear au Village*) (1911)

For Feuillade and the series, see Sadoul, *Les Pionniers*, pp. 320–1, 323, and *Le Cinéma devient un art*, Vol I, pp. 36, 191–8. A Kleine press sheet in the Theatre Collection of the New York Public Library also has the summary and a still as well. Mitry, Vol II, p. 206, gives the performers as Renée Carl, Alice Tissot, Henri Duval, Henri Gallet, and Suzanne Grandet; I cannot confirm or deny. I examined under difficult circumstances in 1955 an untitled film in the Cinémathèque Française which I believe to be this one.

XLVII Nordisk, *Desdemona* (1911)

I accept the date in the *Enciclopedia* article by Paul Knudson on Valdemar Psilander, who played the principal male role. The Wiesbaden brochure dates 1910 and gives the additional cast as Clara Pontoppidian, Else Fröhlich, Robert Dinesen, and Thyra Reimann; the director is listed as August Blom, who had made the *Hamlet* with Neuss. Knudsen, however, indicates Psilander 'giro ben 80 film: recordiamo in particulare *Desdemona* (1911) dove fu Othello. . . .' The film was copyrighted in the United States by Ingvald C. Oes on April 16, 1912. A complete paper print is on file. In issues of the *Moving Picture World* of August 17th and November 30th, it was advertised for sale by the Federal Feature Film Supply Company, Chicago, and George Kleinke, Berlin (1965 feet). On November 30th Great Northern threatened suit against exhibitors and alleged owners who buy from Kleinke. As a matter of fact a Nordisk advertisement in the *Kinematograph and Lantern Weekly* of March 21st already had indicated that the film may have been 'duped'. I find however no American reviews of *Desdemona*.

CHAPTER VI

1 Vitagraph, *Indian Romeo and Juliet* (1912)

The credits are from the *Motion Picture Story Magazine*, January 1912, which has a fictionalized summary with nine stills, and the *Vitagraph Bulletin* which gives the release date as January 30th and the length as 1000 feet. Hal Reid was James Halleck Reid, who played Rohowaneh. His play, *The Confession*, had been produced at the Bijou Theatre on March 13, 1911. Wallace Reid and Adelaide Ober had appeared briefly on the New York stage. Harry T. Morey, after failing as a hero became a well known screen villain; his stage associations were with George M. Cohan and Anna Held (*Photoplay*, December 1914). Laurence Trimble directed until 1926, for some years in England; he was also the owner, trainer and director of Jean, the Vitagraph dog, and of Strongheart (Obit. New York *Times*, February 10, 1954). Florence Turner in 1913 formed Turner Films, Ltd in England, where Trimble directed her; she returned to the United States in 1916 to play for Universal. Another stint in England where she made films for Ideal and Stoll (1921–4) was followed by acting in America, largely in character roles; she died in 1946. Wallace Reid after a meteoric career as a handsome hero met his untimely death in 1923. On both Turner and Reid see the articles by Davide Turconi in the *Enciclopedia*. Albert E. Smith told me he was sceptical about the Mohawk Valley backgrounds; the outdoor settings were probably more local.

II Vitagraph, *Cardinal Wolsey* (1912)

The summaries in the *Moving Picture World*, March 2nd, and *Bioscope*, May 23rd, are reprints of one in *Vitagraph Life Portrayals*, kindly copied for me by Miss Anne Goebel of Warner Bros. A fictional version by Montanye Perry, with nine stills, appeared in the *Motion Picture Story Magazine* of March. It differs in detail, is closer to Shakespeare, and is less accurate. The complete cast is given in *Vitagraph Life Portrayals*. 'Mr Ober' was George Ober who was with Adelaide Ober in Charles H. Hoyt's *A Contented Woman* at Hoyt's Theatre, opening on January 4, 1897, and in the long run of George Broadhurst's *What Happened to Jones*, later in that year. Logan Paul had been on the New York stage as early as 1895, Robert Gaillard in 1898. For Clara Kimball Young, who had been in stock and vaudeville and starred in films until 1941 (obit. 1960), see the various articles cited in *The Film Index*, p. 158, and index, and Davide Turconi in the *Enciclopedia*. The National Archive print, shrunk and warped, is on film stock of Vitagraph (Paris); it is in 872 feet, with about 125 feet of the original missing. *Bioscope*, April 11th, gives the length as 997 feet for its English release on May 30th. *Vitagraph Life Portrayals* described the film inaccurately for exhibitors as 'An historic incident in the reign of King Henry VIII, of England. The sustaining of the sacredness of marriage by Cardinal Wolsey. The beginning of the establishment of the English Church in Great Britain', and offered suggestions for musical accompaniment. Most of the tunes have been long forgotten, but Karl Hoschna's 'The Birth of Passion' (from *Madame Sherry*) was thought appropriate for the scene where the King spies on Anne at her toilette, and Ethelbert Nevin's 'My Rosary' for the Cardinal in the final scene 'as he stands at the window with a smile of devotion'.

III Vitagraph, *As You Like It* (1912)

My account is indebted both to Albert E. Smith and Maurice Costello, who supplied information in interviews in 1949. The *Moving Picture World* of October 5th gives the footage as 3000 feet and the release date. The credits are from the issue of August 10th, and the *Motion Picture Story Magazine*, October, which has an inaccurate fictionalized version, with stills. There is a still in the November number, and a cast correction in December. The January 1913 issue prints a letter criticizing costumes and properties as a mixture of the fifteenth, eighteenth, and twentieth centuries, though the production was evidently meant to be in terms of Shakespeare's own time. The two periodicals disagree on the assignment of James Young; one of the two stills in Blum, p. 28, makes clear he was Sir Rowland de Boys. I thank Joel Swensen and Anne Goebel of Warner Bros for the title list and the enumeration of title footage. The list includes the parentheses which indicate where the titles were to be inserted. 'Jump' refers to a space between sequences. The print I screened was a 16 millimetre version of about 950 feet with titles 1–3 of Reel I and 1–3 of Part II and the corresponding scenes missing; there may have been other cuts also but they were not obvious. I am indebted to Mr Charles H. Tarbox of the Film Classic Exchange for making it possible for me to examine the print. Rose Coghlan is listed in most of the theatrical biographical directories; information about her performance of Rosalind at Wallack's and quotations from the critics are from Odell, Vol XI, pp. 219–20. Robert McWade, Charles Eldridge, James Morrison, and Frank Mason can be traced on the stage in the early volumes of *Best Plays*. In addition to the fifteen stills in *Motion Picture Story Magazine*, cited above, there are two in the Harrison review, and four in an advertisement in the *Kinematograph and Lantern Weekly*, January 16, 1913. The English footage is from the last named periodical, January 2nd.

iv Thanhouser, *The Merchant of Venice* (1912)

Moving Picture World, June 20th, July 20th; the latter gives release date as July 26th and prints Harrison's review with cast. Other credits and settings were supplied by Mr Thanhouser, who told me he had obtained Flo LaBadie from Griffith; at the same time he turned down an opportunity to hire Owen Moore and his wife, Mary Pickford, because they wanted too much money. There is an account of LaBadie's entrance into films in *Photoplay*, October 1912; she became in 1916 the star of *The Million Dollar Mystery*. According to the *Moving Picture World*, December 28, 1912, both Harry Benham and his wife, Ethyle Cooke Benham were in this picture; perhaps she played Nerissa. On the Benhams, see also *Photoplay*, June 1914. The *Motion Picture Story Magazine*, January 1913, wrongly assigns Portia to Mignon Anderson. The *Motion Picture Studio Directory*, 2nd ed., October 21, 1916, p. 105, has a biographical sketch of William J. Bowman. Harrison's review is accompanied by three stills; consult also the *Kinematograph and Lantern Weekly*, December 19, 1912, and Blum, p. 27. Blum (see Index) has numerous pictures of William Russell; he played manly heroes for many years, was featured in the 60-reel serial, *The Diamond from the Sky* (1915), and was Mat Burke in the first filming of *Anna Christie* with Blanche Sweet and George Marion in 1923. The picture was released in Germany on March 28, 1913, by Lichtbild-Vertrieb (*Der Kinematograph*, February 12, 26).

v Gardner, *Cleopatra* (1912)

Since the film has only Shakespearean bits, I need only comment in brief. No release date is given. The *Moving Picture World* of June 15th gives the length as 5 reels, the issue of January 25, 1913, as 6 reels, the English trade papers as 6000 feet in 5 parts. Evidently about 6000 feet were jammed into 5 reels for exhibition. I saw it through the courtesy of John E. Allen who obtained his 16 millimetre print from James Card of Eastman House; this version, which I think was the 1917 re-issue, ran to the equivalent of about $5\frac{1}{2}$ reels of 35 millimetre film. The transposition has cut frames at the top, sometimes heads, because of the difference in the size of the aperture. Titles give credits in full, which I do not transcribe; the Antony was 'Mr Sindelar'. There are 363 prints in the U.S. Copyright office, and numerous stills in the trade papers mentioned below. My book references are Ramsaye, Vol II, p. 599; Robert Grau, *The Theatre of Science*, New York, 1914, pp. 203–4; Odell, Vol XV, p. 69; Wagenknecht, p. 26. Other material has been derived from or is available in the *Moving Picture World*, above, and November 30th (Harrison review), December 14th, 21st, 28th, 1912; January 4th, 11th, 18th, March 1st, April 12th, May 10, 1913; December 22nd, 29th, 1917; January 5th, March 2 (cast), 1918; *Cinema News and Property Gazette*, February 19, 1913; *Kinematograph and Lantern Weekly*, February 20th, March 6th, 13th, 27th, April 3rd, July 3, 1913; *Bioscope*, March 6, 1913; *Lichtbild-Theatre*, April 3, 1913; *Der Kinematograph*, March 12, 1913. The film was distributed by the United States

Film Company, in 1917 by the Cleopatra Film Company, in England by H. Winik, who sold the continental territorial rights.

VI Alla Nazimova, *Hamlet* (1912)
See the Wiesbaden brochure. I have also seen this film listed in unpublished material as 1914, but I find no substantiation whatever.

VII Lubin, *Love's Labour's Lost* (1912)
Motion Picture Story Magazine, May 1912, with Jack Hawkins and Elsie Glynn. The Lubin advertisement in the *Kinematograph and Lantern Weekly*, January 4th, describes it as 'a laughable comedy in which two fellows, both in love with the same girl, fight a duel and are told in the nick of time that she is married to another'. Released, February 8th.

VIII Lubin, *A Modern Portia* (1912)
Kinematograph and Lantern Weekly, June 20th, 1060 feet, released August 1st.

IX Lubin, *A Midwinter Night's Dream* (1912)
Moving Picture World, February 17th, released February 19th.

X Solax, *A Comedy of Errors* (1912)
Moving Picture World, November 16th, released November 20th. This was probably the picture released in England on May 17, 1913, under American and Continental and distributed by Brockliss, 1000 feet: 'domestic farce' (*Kinematograph and Lantern Weekly*, April 17, 1913).

XI Rex, *Taming Mrs Shrew* (1912)
Moving Picture World, February 12th.

XII Knickerbocker, *The Taming of the Shrewd* (1912)
Kinematograph and Lantern Weekly, June 20th, released July 24th, 750 feet.

XIII Urban–Eclipse–Radios, *All's Well That Ends Well* (1912)
Kinematograph and Lantern Weekly, April 25th, released May 22nd, 865 feet.

XIV Cines, *All's Well That Ends Well* (1912)
Kinematograph and Lantern Weekly, April 25th, released May 25th, 1043 feet.

XV Eclair, *All's Well That Ends Well* (1912)
Kinematograph and Lantern Weekly, August 15th, released August 29th, 720 feet. This was probably the colour film of the same footage advertised for sale by the Kinema Auction Mart and Exchange, as produced by the Tyler Film Company, in the same journal, January 8th, 15th, 1914. Tyler was a renter as well as a part-time producer (Low, p. 117).

XVI Cines, *A Comedy of Errors* (1912)
Moving Picture World, November 30th, released same date, 650 feet. A Kleine press sheet in the New York Public Library gives 663 feet.

XVII *The Jewish King Lear* (1912)

Kinematograph and Lantern Weekly, September 5th. It was filmed at the Pavilion Theatre and shown at New King's Hall. No maker is listed.

XVIII L'Histrionic Film, *La Reine Elisabeth* (1912)

Film Index, p. 448. Distributed by L'Agence Générale Cinématographique. On the film, see Sadoul, *Le Cinéma devient un art*, Vol I, pp. 26–7, 274–6.

XIX Aquila, *Lo Spettro de Iago* (1912)

The Wiesbaden brochure says 800 metres. The English references to *The Vengeance of Iago* are the *Kinematograph and Lantern Weekly*, April 25th, May 9th, 16th, 23rd; Standard Feature Film Company, 'exclusive', released May 27th, 2000 feet.

XX Eclair, *The Tempest* (1912)

For Eclair, see Sadoul, *Les Pionniers*, pp. 363, 393; *Le Cinéma devient un art*, Vol I, p. 37, which lists the principal actors of the company. I have not, however, found any specific identification of who played what in *The Tempest*, and appropriate issues of French trade periodicals are not available. The best summary I have discovered and the one paraphrased is in *Bioscope*, December 12th, which gives footage and release date in England. There are other synopses in the *Cinema News and Property Gazette* of December 25th, and the *Moving Picture World* of April 12, 1913. *Bioscope*, November 21st, and the *Kinematograph and Lantern Weekly*, November 28th, print stills. The picture was copyrighted in the United States on December 26th; the entry includes thirty prints as well as a description, but there is now nothing in the file. It must be this film to which Margaret Thorp refers in her article 'Shakespeare and the Movies', *Shakespeare Quarterly*, Summer 1958, p. 358: 'I remember, among others in the silent days, a two-reel *Tempest* in which fifteen of the twenty minutes was devoted to the shipwreck.' I have no doubt the shipwreck was central, but I doubt whether, in view of the story told, it would have taken such a preponderance of time. The German reference is *Lichtbild Bühne*, December 14th (film distributed by Fritz Holz, Film-Verleih Institut); the American, *Moving Picture World*, April 12, 1913 (Union Features).

XXI Thanhouser, *Cymbeline* (1913)

There are synopses in the *Moving Picture World*, March 29th, and *Cinema News and Property Gazette*, May 7th, but they are not trustworthy guides to content. The list of players and the release date are from the *Moving Picture World*, March 29th; the *Kinematograph and Lantern Weekly* of April 24th gives the English release date of June 24th by the Western Import Co. The above dated *Moving Picture World* has a still. There are other stills in the *Cinema News and Property Gazette*, April 23rd, 30th; the *Kinematograph and Lantern Weekly*, May 15th; and *The Picturegoer*, November 1921, May 1923. The last issue contains an article by Elizabeth Lonergan about Frederic Sullivan. For William Garwood, see the *Moving Picture World*, July 11, 1914, and the *Motion Picture Studio Directory*, 2nd ed., October 21, 1916, p. 110. Cruze's work as a director is admirably treated by Jacobs, pp. 374–9, but for his earlier career, consult Thornton Fisher,

'Off the Screen with James Cruze', *Moving Picture World*, May 16, 1914; Mabel Condon, '"Jimmie" Cruze', *Photoplay*, September 1914; and Alfred A. Cohn, 'Stronger Than Onions . . .', *Photoplay*, September 1919. The reference to English performance of *Cymbeline* is from 'British Notes', *Moving Picture World*, July 12, 1913. Mr Thanhouser thought the continuity was probably prepared by Lloyd Lonergan.

The print, about 1850 feet in length, is an original and in excellent condition with no noticeable cuts. The titles on different stock have shrunk somewhat, but are also original. It was found with other films in the attic of an empty house in Nyack, New York, where it had been the property of a projectionist at the Broadway Theatre, who used it over a long period as a filler, in case an expected film was not delivered, or a delivered film proved shorter than expected. The discovery was the result of the questioning of a friend of the deceased projectionist by John E. Allen, indefatigable in his quest for old films, who bought the lot, sight unseen, and kindly notified me when *Cymbeline* turned up. I am much indebted to Mr Allen for screening the film for me in his private theatre and allowing me to examine it on a viewer in his laboratory.

XXII Sterling, *Richard III* (1913)

The copyright entry says 'Mr Frederick Warde in Shakespeare's Masterpiece *The Life and Death of King Richard III* . . . Sterling Camera and Film Co. (James Keene, author); title, description and 57 prints, September 9, 1913.' There are no stills in the file. There are, however, pictures in the *Moving Picture World*, April 12th (3 including a portrait), September 27th (6), October 11th (4), in the New York Public Library clipping file (5), and in Blum, p. 39 (2). The autobiography is *Fifty Years of Make-Believe*, New York, 1920 (quotation, pp. 305–6); I have also used Hartnoll, *The Oxford Companion to the Theatre*, and John Parker, *Who's Who in the Theatre*, 6th ed., London, 1930. *The Film Index* gives the director as Dudley; the programme in the copyright file lists the producer as M. B. Dudley but for copyright purposes the printed name has been lined through, and the company substituted in handwriting. I know nothing about Dudley, 'Mr Gomp' (who played Edward IV), or the identity of the rest of the personnel involved, not to mention the horses. Incidentally, City Island, though formerly a part of Westchester, became a part of the Bronx in 1895.

XXIII Edison Kinetophone, *Julius Caesar* (1913)

Will H. Hays, *See and Hear*, Motion Picture Producers and Distributors of America, 1929, pp. 41–2. The apparatus is described in Frederic M. Thrasher, *Okay for Sound*, New York, 1936, p. 4. The New York *Times*, February 18th, does not mention the excerpt but the issue of January 4th includes it in a description of a private demonstration at the Edison laboratory in West Orange.

XXIV Mutual Educational, *All's Well That Ends Well* (1913)
Moving Picture World, February 8th; not summarized.

XXV Selig, *Alas! Poor Yorick!* (1913)
Moving Picture World, April 19th; summary.

XXVI Essanay, *Something Rotten in Havana* (1913)
Moving Picture World, July 12th; summary.

XXVII Crystal, *Much Ado About Nothing* (1913)
Moving Picture World, August 30th; summary.

XXVIII Edison, *Othello in Jonesville* (1913)
Moving Picture World, May 13th, 1000 feet; June 7th, summary. The *Kinematograph and Lantern Weekly*, July 10th, shows it was released in England on August 11th in 750 feet. In France the picture was called *Othello au village*; released September 5th in 225 metres. *Le Courier Cinématographique*, August 23rd, says: 'il provoquera une douce hilarité' and indicates Herbert Prior was the actor, Mabel Trunnelle the girl, William West her father, and May Abbey her mother. The director was Charles Seay. Prior, an English actor, also wrote the script.

XXIX Solax, *Romeo in Pajamas* (1913)
Moving Picture World, June 14th; *Kinematograph and Lantern Weekly*, November 27th; 965 feet, released December 25th; summary.

XXX Punch, *A Would-be Romeo* (1913)
Cinema News and Property Gazette, July 16th; summary.

XXXI Selig, *The Galloping Romeo* (1913)
Moving Picture World, August 9th; *Kinematograph and Lantern Weekly*, October 9th; 701 feet, released in England November 13th; summary.

XXXII Cricks and Martin, *Much Ado About* (1913)
Kinematograph and Lantern Weekly, December 19, 1912; *Cinema News and Property Gazette*, January 1, 1913.

XXXIII Cricks and Martin, *All's Well That Ends Well* (1913)
Cinema News and Property Gazette, March 12th; *Kinematograph and Lantern Weekly*, April 3rd. The Artograph advertisement in the second journal on January 15, 1914, describes it as a 'drama'.

XXXIV Gaumont, *Love's Labour Lost* (1913)
Kinematograph and Lantern Weekly, December 26, 1912; *Cinema News and Property Gazette*, January 1, 1913.

XXXV Stratford, *Henry V* (1913)
Kinematograph and Lantern Weekly, May 22nd.

XXXVI Eric Williams, *Henry V* (1913?)
Low Warren, *The Film Game*, London, 1937, p. 180. The only specific references I have to this film are from the *Cinema News and Property Gazette*, September 2, 1915, when it was already 'famous', and February 7, 1918; and *Bioscope*, February 27, 1919, which gives the account of the York performance, but his recital pictures are noted in the *Kinematograph and Lantern Weekly*, November 7th, December 5,

1912; April 24th, June 19th, August 7th, September 18th, December 11, 1913; and January 8, 1914.

XXXVII Gaumont–Eric Williams, *Hubert and Arthur* (1913)

It is clear from the *Kinematograph and Lantern Weekly* of August 7th that the film was made by Gaumont early in that month and exhibited to the trade. The quotation is from the issue of September 18th, when Williams gave his 'remarkable exhibition' in Manchester. *Bioscope*, June 5, 1919, indicates this 'speaking photo-play' was still being presented in that year.

XXXVIII Eclipse, *Anne Boleyn* (1913)

The journal cited indicates release by Gaumont Film Hire Service. The *Moving Picture World*, February 14, 1914, says the release was announced by Eclipse and Pathé, but James S. McQuade's review on May 16th indicates the George Kleine import was to be released by the General Film Company. Henry VIII, he says, was acted by M. Albert Decoeur of the Sarah Bernhardt Theatre and was 'a little lean in his underpinnings'. This must be the film Harry Furniss refers to as '*Henry the Eighth*, presented by a company of French players. . . . Bluff King Hal, the robust and square-set, was played by a tall, dark tragedian, rather slightly built, with a decidedly swarthy head and the manner of an Iago.' (*Our Lady Cinema*, Bristol, 1914, p. 171.)

XXXIX Latium, *Dente per Dente* (1913)

The Wiesbaden brochure lists it as Shakespearean, and derives its information on credits from Prolo, Vol I, p. 162, but though a much later Shakespearean *Measure for Measure* (1942) had this Italian title, the phrase is so proverbial I am suspicious, especially since the brochure also includes in this category the 1909 Lubin *Measure for Measure*, which was not Shakespearean at all. I have found no reviews to resolve the dilemma. If the Italian film was the *Measure for Measure* released by the General Film Agency in England on April 2, 1914, in 2550 feet, then it was the story of a sleep-walker's romance and a quite different 'bed-trick'.

XL Pathé, *A Modern Portia* (1913)

Moving Picture World, December 16th; not an American product since the cast was French.

XLI Projections–A.-G. Union, *Der Shylock von Krakau* (1913)

Der Kinematograph, October 22nd; there are eleven comments from Berlin newspapers in the firm's advertisement, and a review in the same issue; others in the cast were Lia Rosen as a younger daughter and Friedrich Kühne. The issue of February 25, 1914, gives the length. The film was distributed in England as *The Jew* by the Ideal Film Renting Company in three parts; the *Kinematograph and Lantern Weekly* of April 2, 1914, has a summary.

XLII Pasquali, *Bianco contro Negro* (1913)

Wiesbaden brochure, which gives direction by Ernesto Maria Pasquali, book by Renzo Chiosso, camera by Pietro Marelli; Capozzi is assigned to the part of Cassius, Tarlarini is wrongly spelled Tarlini. See also Prolo, Vol I, p. 163, and her article on Capozzi in the *Enciclopedia*; neither Prolo nor Francesco Savio (*Enciclopedia*) lists Tarlarini in the cast. I do not know how much is to be assigned relatively to Chiosso's script, Boito's libretto, or Shakespeare's play.

XLIII Continental Kunstfilm, *Bumke als Othello* (1913)
Der Kinematograph, April 2nd; *Kinematograph and Lantern Weekly*, May 22nd, which has a summary, and August 21st, 28th. Bumke was a variety star who had appeared at the London Hippodrome seven years earlier.

XLIV Savoia, *Iago's Inheritance* (1913)
Kinematograph and Lantern Weekly, December 13th; January 15, 1914, which provides the summary. I do not know the Italian title.

XLV Pathé, *Cleopatra* (1913)
The Film Index, p. 433, says 'not based on the Shakespearean play', but I do not see how any Antony and Cleopatra picture could avoid some influence. The best synopses are in the *Pathé Fortnightly Bulletin*, Vol II, No. 10 (two stills) and the *Moving Picture World*, May 23rd, June 6, 1914. Nothing is said about the cast. Brusendorff, p. 69, lists a *Cleopatra* under Cines, vaguely dated 1910–15, directed by Roger Lion, interpreted by Biscot and Mady Minty. No such French personnel had anything to do with the Cines film; has he confused it with the Pathé? If so and he has grounds for his participants, the Pathé 1913 was something more than a padded re-issue. Roger Lion, however, was associated with Feuillade at Gaumont (Sadoul, *Le Cinéma devient un art*, Vol I, p. 202). Curiously, Mitry, Vol II, p. 214, while not naming a Pathé *Cleopatra*, does list a Gaumont picture with that title, supervised by Feuillade, directed by Maurice Mariaud, with Renée Carl, Henri Keppens, Jeanne Briey, Louise Lagrange, Henri Duval, Yvonne Mariaud; camera by Guérin; in series 'Drames divers'. As in the case of the 1910 *Cleopatra*, the ground is shaky, but I am unwilling to postulate two or more pictures without further evidence.

XLVI Cines, *Antony and Cleopatra* (1913)
The Italian title was *Marcantonio e Cleopatra*; in Germany it was called *Die Herrin des Nils* (*Der Kinematograph*, July 30th). I have been told that the original Italian length was eleven reels. Guazzoni's press release is in the *Giornale d'Italia*, November 4th. The cost is from the *Kinematograph and Lantern Weekly*, October 16th; auction details, October 9th; Paris showings, April 30, 1914; number of personnel, *Ciné-Journal*, July 12, 1913. Details of American presentation are from the *Moving Picture World*, January 17th, 24th, 31st; May 16th, 1914. For American reviews, see James S. McQuade's in the *Moving Picture World*, January 10th, and his report, January 24th, of Amy Leslie's in Chicago. The names of the Italian cast were thought too difficult or inappropriate for the United States. Novelli's first name became Antony or Anthony, and the star actress, in some cases, Jeannette Trimble! (*Moving Picture World*, December 27, 1913; February 28, 1914.) The association with Shakespeare is in George Kleine's *Catalogue of Educational Moving Pictures*, Chicago, 1915, and the *Kinematograph and Lantern Weekly*, October 2, 1913, which reviewed; the latter also mentions Cossa. Summary of the content is based on the Catalogue, the reviews mentioned, and another review

in the *Cinema News and Property Gazette*, October 1st, and my viewing of the film. There are a number of prints of varying lengths available in film collections. The version I used came from the Film Classic Exchange; it was in six reels of 16 millimetre film totalling 2200 feet and was therefore not complete, though sufficient for the purpose. Credits are listed in the references given; the photographer was A. Bona. Articles on the principals may be found in the *Enciclopedia* and the *Filmlexicon*. The quotation from Vachel Lindsay is in *The Art of the Motion Picture*, New York, 1915, pp. 54–5.

XLVII Gloria, *Julius Caesar* (1913)
　　Wiesbaden brochure, but not listed by Prolo.

XLVIII Tommasi-Hübner, *A Midsummer Night's Dream* (1913?)
　　Mr Charles H. Tarbox of the Film Classic Exchange, who kindly lent me a print, wrote that he thought it had been made before 1913, and that some of the positives, though not the one I screened, carried the Warner Features trademark. Early independents like the Warners sometimes distributed foreign films. There was no date or title on the print. The brothers sold out Warner Features in 1915 but retained the trademark and under it issued some pictures until 1918. The *Kinematograph and Lantern Weekly*, April 24, 1913, indicates the first film to be issued by the Warner Feature Film Co., was *The Eye of God* on June 16th. The producing company may possibly have been Artistic Cinema Negatives of San Remo, the foundation of which is announced in the same journal on July 17th. *La Cinematografia Italiana*, September 20th, said 'Socrate Tommasi si produrrá nell' Artistic Cinema Negatives. ...' *Le Courier Cinématografique*, August 30th, in announcing the formation of the firm names personnel as Victor Ralepre, director; Paul Azzuri, formerly of Ambrosio, in charge of *mise en scene*; Novoryta, technical director; and adds that Linda Schwertz and Socrate Tommasi 'ont tourné' the first film. On October 11th, Paulo Azzuri was named 'directeur'; the announcement also appeared in the *Kinematograph and Lantern Weekly*, October 23rd. Azzuri is listed both in the *Filmlexicon* and the *Enciclopedia* (Francesco Savio) but no connection is made with Artistic Cinema Negatives. He founded a cinema school in 1914 at Palermo, which failed in 1915, was revived in Florence in 1916, and had various branches. There is no mention of *A Midsummer Night's Dream*, but he made with his students *La Regina della notte*. Could they be one and the same? Signorina Prolo in correspondence with me did not know of the film but ascribed it to 1919–20. I know nothing whatever about Bianca Maria Hübner, but there is a bare chance that she might have been the daughter of the Czech actress, Marie Rufferová who married a journalist, Vacláv Hübner (Jaroslav Pokorný in the *Enciclopedia*).

XLIX Ambrosio, *The Taming of the Shrew* (1913)
　　The advertisement is in the *Kinematograph and Lantern Weekly*, August 21st, and includes a still. The summary is in the review two weeks later, which gives the footage as 2275 feet. On September 18th under 'The Trade in Italy' by Peyron, it is said that 'during the last few days ... [a] Shakespearean film has been projected in Turin with great success, *The Taming of the Shrew*, an excellent work of the Ambrosio Co.' The footage is variously given in later issues as between 2000

and 3000 feet. *Lichtbild Bühne*, August 30th, calls it a 'Komödie in 3 Akten'. The German periodical has a summary, as does *Cinema News and Property Gazette*, August 20th (still). Knaur and the Wiesbaden brochure list the film as in 604 metres, assign both scenario and direction to Frusta, and list the principal actress as Gigetta Morano. I doubt if Frusta directed. Prolo (*Enciclopedia*) names Morano; were she and 'Mdlle Louise' one and the same? Eleuterio Rodolfi had been in the 1910 Cines *Hamlet*. Background on Ambrosio is from Sadoul, *Le Cinéma devient un art*, Vol I, pp. 86–94.

L Milano, *The Winter's Tale* (1913)

The film was variously titled. Prolo, Vol I, p. 162, under 1913, lists it with perhaps a preliminary title as *Una Novella di Shakespeare*; p. 172 under 1914 as *Una Tragedia alla Corte di Sicilia*, apparently its usual Italian title, though the Wiesbaden brochure calls it *Novella d'Inverno : Una Novella di Shakespeare*. In France, England, and Germany, Shakespeare's title was translated, except that in Germany in 1915, there was a second title, *Zurück ins Leben*, and upon re-issue in England in 1919, it was called *The Lost Princess* (*Erste Internationale Film-Zeitung*, March 13, 1915; information card, British Film Institute). Prolo, Vol I, p. 172, names the two principal actors and Negroni as the director; the Wiesbaden brochure sticks to Sutto. It is not clear to me what their relative responsibilities were as producer, director, adapter. I know nothing about Sutto or V. Cocchi. Baldassare Negroni, who married Hesperia and directed many of her films, started his film career in 1911 with Cines 'come operatore e poi soggettista', directed for Celio in 1912–13 and went to Milano, according to Francesco Savio in the *Enciclopedia*, in January 1914, there directing *Una Tragedia alla Corte di Sicilia* (1914), but as I show in the text there are references to the film before that time. Perhaps they were only advance publicity. Fabbri is a famous name in the Italian theatre from the sixteenth century, but the unsigned article on Pina Fabbri in the *Enciclopedia* does not show her relationship to the family, except that in two of her pictures she was associated with Attilio Fabbri, who is not otherwise identified. Chiefly with Milano, she worked for other companies, too, during a career from 1912 to 1916. There are stills from the film in the *Kinematograph and Lantern Weekly*, April 2, 1914 (4); *Cinema News and Property Gazette*, April 16th; *Bioscope*, April 16th, but I have not found a copy of the brochure, which probably contained more. The positive print in the National Film Archive has a length of 2894 feet; it is in good condition, but a few sequences are out of order.

LI Deutsche Bioscop, *A Midsummer Night's Dream* (1913)

The notices appear in *Der Kinematograph*, July 16, 1913, where it is announced that the film is shortly to appear; August 20, 1913, and March 4, 1914, both by 'J.G.', who comments vaporously about other-worldliness; *Lichtbild Bühne*, August 2, 1913; *Le Courier Cinématographique*, October 25, 1913; and the *Kinematograph and Lantern Weekly*, April 2, 1914, which indicates that the film had recently been presented in the Palace Furstenberg. The picture was copyrighted in the United States on June 5, 1914; the summary is from the copyright file, but the 96 prints deposited at that time are no longer there. There is a still of Grete Berger as Puck in *Der Kinematograph*, July 16th. For Carl Clewing, a stage actor, who played Lysander, see *Who's Who in the Theatre* (1914). The cameraman was probably Guido Seeber, who photographed *The Student of Prague*. There is a sketch of Stellan Rye by Fausto Montesanti in the *Enciclopedia*. On Ewers, if anybody cares, consult *Neue Deutsche Biographie* (article by Karl Richter), Berlin, 1957. I am most indebted, however, to the late Dr Siegfried Kracauer, both for his personal recollections and his book, *From Caligari to Hitler*, Princeton, 1947, pp. 28–31, 153–4; and Sadoul, *Le Cinéma devient un art*, Vol I, pp. 296–7. The copyright material says the film was 'in four acts', which probably means four reels.

LII Eclipse, *Shylock* (1913)

Lapierre, p. 93, puts Denis d'Inès in the cast; the Wiesbaden brochure follows Lapierre in this addition and also names Louis Jouvet. I find no contemporary evidence for the first; and Jouvet, evidently confused with Joubé, was not, I think, in film before 1932. The article on Desfontaines by Francesco Savio and Charles Ford in the *Enciclopedia* names him as director, and indicates Harry Baur made his cinema debut in this picture. Mitry, p. 142, lists the film as S.C.A.G.L.–Pathé, says there were co-directors with Desfontaines, and assigns the scenario to Louis Mercanton. The cast is already familiar except for Pépa Bonafé, about whom I know nothing, and Harry Baur, who was to be prominent; on the latter, see the article by Osvaldo Campassi in the *Enciclopedia*, though there is no mention there of his appearance in *Shylock*. George Kleine copyrighted the film on December 23, 1912. The summary in the *Moving Picture World*, March 8th, indicates the omission of the Lorenzo–Jessica plot. The 35 millimetre print I examined at the National Film Archive has a footage of 1970 out of the original 2040; the main title is a replacement of the 1920's; there is some shrinkage, and the inserted English titles are thrown out of frame. The Library of Congress has three reels of negative and two of positive. The titles filed with Kleine's copyright are different from those in the Archive print; they are much greater in number and more elaborate, but I suspect the English ones are closer to those of the French original, and see no reason for detailing the American extensions. Two of Kleine's press sheets are in the New York Public Library Theatre Collection. One gives a synopsis with six badly reproduced stills; the other has six clearer stills of varying size: (1) Trial scene, (2) Shylock reviled by the crowd, (3) Bassanio's winning of Portia, (4) the wedding, (5) Shylock's grant of the loan, and (6) Bassanio's recognition of Antonio's danger. There is a still of the pound-of-flesh scene in the *Moving Picture World*, February 22nd (and Blum, p. 36), and three stills appear in the issue of March 1st. Pictures of the casket scene and the wedding are in the *Cinema News and Property Gazette*, June 11th and 18th; *Kinematograph and Lantern Weekly*, June 19th and 26th. Nine prints were filed with the copyright.

LIII Film-Industrie, *Macbeth* (1913)

The account of the planning, production, and presentation of this film is based entirely on the trade journals: *Kinematograph and Lantern Weekly*, April 3rd, July 24th, August 7th, September 4th, 25th, October 2nd, 9th, 16, 1913; June 4, 1914; *Cinema News and Property Gazette*, May 7th, July 30th, August 13th, September 24th, October 1st, 15, 1913; *Pictures and the Picturegoer*, January 29, 1916 (by Ernest A. Dench): 'Stage Stars on the Screen', p. 402; 'When *Macbeth* was "captured" for the screen, Arthur Bourchier and his wife, Violet Vanbrugh, journeyed to

Heidelberg, Germany, and received £1000 for their services. When, however, the produced result was seen on the screen it was obvious to all that neither was quite at home in their new surroundings.'; *Moving Picture World*, September 6th, November 8th, 15, 1913; June 24th, July 8th, 15 (by Lynde Denig), 1916. *Ciné-Journal*, August 2, 1913, announces it, as does *Der Kinematograph*, November 5, 1913. The *Descriptive List of Pathéscope Films*, New York, [1918], lists it as 'A Shakespearian production, filmed on the historic site of Dunsinane Castle, in the same environment that inspired Shakespeare in writing the story. The screen lends itself even better than the stage to the mustical scenes with the ghost, etc., and the titles in this production are excellent and fully explanatory. The final attack on the castle, its capture and pillage, with its burning in the last act, together with the combat between Macbeth and Macduff form a fitting climax to the production.' Obviously the inaccuracies form a kind of climax too. The film was still extant on April 2, 1933, when a (London) Film Society Programme indicated that it was shown in part. It was listed as belonging to the Educational Film Bureau. The Film Society later became the New London Film Society. Its secretary knew nothing about the film when I saw her in 1955, and the Educational Film Bureau was no longer in existence. Before it was shown by the Film Society 'at the defunct Tivoli in the Strand' it was screened for the members of the London University Film Society at the first performance given by that organization. I am indebted to Dr G. R. Sedleigh-Denfield, the guiding spirit of the Society, and to Mr Laurence Kitchin who answered my inquiry after I had read his article, 'Shakespeare on the Screen', *Shakespeare Survey*, Vol XVIII, pp. 70–4. On p. 72, he writes of the film, 'Although this ought not to be regarded as a reliable record, the performances are distinctly hammy. . . . The movies take over when Macbeth's attackers camouflage themselves as Birnam Wood. One soldier raises big laughs by getting separated from the main body and scuttling back to them, still holding his branch.' For all I know a piece of this film may still be in existence, but I have not been able to find it. Accounts of Bourchier and Vanbrugh are based on Hartnoll (ed.), *The Oxford Companion to the Theatre*; John Parker (ed.), *Who's Who in the Theatre* (various editions); and Pearson, *Beerbohm Tree . . .* , pp. 169–70, 213.

LIV Gaumont–Hepworth, *Hamlet* (1913)

Forbes-Robertson's modest autobiography, *A Player Under Three Reigns*, London, 1925, is full of anecdotes and compliments to fellow actors, but tells little about his art; for *Hamlet* presentations, see, however, pp. 182–92, 249–54, 297–9, 314–20. His farewell in the United States was three performances of *Hamlet* at Harvard University in April 1916, the last on the 26th. Though he occasionally played other roles for charity after that date, he never played *Hamlet* again. The most convenient source for Shaw's reviews of *Hamlet* is Edwin Wilson (ed.), *Shaw on Shakespeare*, New York, 1961, pp. 85–95. On Shaw's advice, consult William A. Armstrong, 'Bernard Shaw and Forbes-Robertson's *Hamlet*', *Shakespeare Quarterly*, Winter 1964, pp. 27–31. Forbes-Robertson made two films after *Hamlet*, *Masks and Faces* (Ideal, 1917) and *The Passing of the Third Floor Back* (Walturdaw, 1918).

The cast in the National Archive file gives E. Erikson, and spells Montague Rutherford; it indicates the doubling. J. H. Barnes had played Polonius in the 1897 production. The intermediary between Gaumont and Forbes-Robertson was, according to the *Kinematograph and Lantern Weekly* of August 2nd, a 'Mr Wood'. The distributor was Gaumont Hire Service. The issue of October 16th listed the footage as 5800. Some information about the outdoor settings is derived from various articles in the Locke Collection at the New York Public Library Theatre Collection, and *Bioscope*, July 24th. Plumb's article, 'A Peep Behind the Scenes', appeared in the *Kinematograph and Lantern Weekly*, December 4th. The interview with Hepworth is from *Bioscope*, above, later included in his book, *Came the Dawn*, London, 1951, pp. 116–19. Some production details are from the file, one detail from a reminiscence by Maxine Forbes-Robertson; I am grateful too for a letter from Cecil Hepworth in 1951, which, however, supplied no information not already in my possession. The report from Birmingham and the note about advertising in Peckham are from the *Kinematograph and Lantern Weekly*, October 16th and December 4th. I have not included in the text a review quoted by the *Literary Digest* (New York), October 18th, by the dramatic critic of the *Westminster Gazette* because he flaunts his ignorance of the cinema: 'There are variations from accepted ideas. For instance the Ghost makes his famous *ex-parte* statement to Hamlet about the murder on a very pebbly seashore, and not upon "the cellarage". Perhaps this does not matter very much. We watched the characters making faces presumably appropriate to their words, tho sometimes we were in doubt as to the individual speech. We were presented with a synopsis which bravely included what is called the "moral", and I regret that I am unable to give the name of the humorist who wrote it. The pictures I imagine are very good of their kind, and must have cost an immense amount of money. They are affected by the necessary limitations of the medium; the characters are represented on very different scales, and the color is horrible. When the scale is large, the "field" is rather comically small, and, of course, quaint effects are produced by the difficulties due to the employment of a lens less efficient than the human apparatus. The audience seemed impressed . . . To the historian of drama it may be useful to possess these records of a performance but to suggest that the affair from any point of view does justice to the tragedy would be an outrageous absurdity.'

Evidence of the performance and success in Germany is from *Der Kinematograph*, September 17th, and *Lichtbild Bühne*, September 13th and subsequent issues. Performance in India is recorded in *Cinema News and Property Gazette*, July 22, 1915. The American announcement is in the *Moving Picture World*, July 3rd. Material in the Locke Collection of the New York Public Library includes excerpts from the *Literary Digest*, August 2nd; the Cleveland *Press*, August 4th; *Munsey*, September, and *Dress and Variety Fair*, September, but they give only publicity and production details. Retrospective criticism tended to be adverse. Ernest A. Dench in the article cited above (1916) said that 'the eminent actor and his talented wife seemed inclined to rely on "lines" to the detriment of their facial expressions and gestures, while the rest of the players evidently found the motion picture stage a rather cramped affair.' Edward Weitzel, *Moving Picture World*, July 21, 1917, called the screen version a 'woeful spectacle. . . . To recall the sorry figure the English actor presented picking his way gingerly over the real stones on the seashore while following his father's ghost is to be reminded that realism can defeat its own purpose – when the Prince of Denmark's shoes are for the stage only and the soles within them have not been toughened by frequent contact with irregular and unfriendly bits of the solid earth.'

Forbes-Robertson's stage arrangement of *Hamlet* was based on the Cambridge and Variorium texts; it was printed in London by the Nassau Press in 1897; there is a copy at the British Film Institute. Late in 1958 Mr F. G. Miles and his wife, who was Maxine Forbes-Robertson, discovered that they had a print of the film. Correspondence with officers of the British Film Institute led to the examination of the print by the Institute's laboratory, to deposit of the print at the Institute, and to its reproduction on both 35 and 16 millimetre stock. The print delivered to the Institute was a 35 millimetre positive on Pathé stock of the early 1920's based on the original negative, a Gaumont re-issue carrying in its subtitles the Knickerbocker trademark. Some rearrangement was necessitated since scenes and subtitles were out of order. Despite imperfections and some shrinkage, the print, which was 5345 feet long, was in fairly good condition. The print I saw screened at the National Film Theatre on February 15, 1965, had been cut to 4846 feet. I later examined a reproduction of the originally received print, which was on double reels. My analysis is based on the rearranged 5345 feet version without the later cuts, supplemented by whatever information I could obtain from stills and printed sources. I have not thought it necessary to reproduce the subtitles, which are partly Shakespearean.

Stills were reproduced in the *Kinematograph and Lantern Weekly*, July 24th, 31st, August 21st, 28, 1913, and the *Moving Picture World*, July 3rd, 10, 1915, as well as in the more general periodicals cited above and the souvenir programmes; see also Talbot (1923, ed.), opposite p. 322; Blum, p. 76; Hepworth, following p. 104; Sadoul: *Le Cinéma devient un art*, Vol I, opposite p. 230; and the Wiesbaden brochure, opposite p. 68. The *Hamlet* recordings were made about 1928 by the Columbia Gramaphone Company and published by the International Education Society (D-40,006; D-40,007). I am indebted to Mr Patrick Saul of the British Institute of Recorded Sound for the privilege of hearing them.

LV Hepworth, *The Princes in the Tower* (1914?)

Hepworth, pp. 117, 126, but he gives no date. There is no reference to the film in the BFI index to *Bioscope* nor in the *Kinematograph Monthly Film Record* for 1913, 1914, or 1915, but Mr Denis Gifford confirms that it was made. Eric Desmond was the film name of Reginald Sheffield, who had been in Hepworth's *David Copperfield* (1913); born in 1901, he had a long career on stage and screen, mostly in the United States.

LVI Keystone, *A Robust Romeo* (1914)

Moving Picture World, February 7th; *Kinematograph and Lantern Weekly*, May 21st, summary, 1020 feet.

LVII Biograph, *Romeo and Juliet* (1914)

Moving Picture World, May 23rd, summary; June 6th, comment. 'Biograph Stories 1910–1916', a manuscript notebook in the Museum of Modern Art, New York, indicates the story was purchased from Edward Acker for $25.00, and that the picture was finished on April 14th in 508 feet. It was released in 528 feet on July 6th in England, where the *Kinematograph and Lantern Weekly*, May 21st, calls it 'an extremely amusing comedy'.

LVIII American Kinema, *A Modern Romeo* (1914)
Kinematograph and Lantern Weekly and *Cinema News and Property Gazette*, both June 4th. The distributor was Pathé; the English release date, July 9th.

LIX Luna, *Rural Romeos* (1914)
Moving Picture World, January 9, 1915, lists but does not summarize. Luna films were made by the Albuquerque Film Company of Los Angeles and distributed by the United Film Service which included Warner Features. For the actress, see Richard Willis, 'Dot Farley: Comedienne, Tragedienne and Photoplaywright', *Photoplay*, November 1914.

LX Comica, *Romeo geht ins Kino* (1914)
Erste Internationale Film Zeitung, July 18th, pp. 29–30; 175 metres, distributed by Pathé. On Roméo Bosetti, see Sadoul *Les Pionniers*, p. 350; *Le Cinéma devient un art*, Vol I, pp. 123–4.

LXI Kalem, *Nina of the Theatre* (1914)
The review was by George F. Blaisdell. There is a brief summary in *The Film Index*, p. 513. The picture was released on June 8th. There is a still in Blum, p. 37. I should have missed the Shakespeare connection if it had not been for the kindness of Mr Gerald D. McDonald of the New York Public Library.

LXII Planet, *The Seven Ages of Man* (1914)
Low, pp. 195, 292; the trade show was on June 10th. The quotation is from the *Kinematograph and Lantern Weekly*, June 18th.

LXIII Tyler, *All's Well That Ends Well* (1914)
See Eclair, 1912. The *Kinematograph and Lantern Weekly*, January 8th, 15th, indicate the sale was by Kinema Auction Mart of a comedy in colour, 720 feet.

LXIV Princess, *All's Well That Ends Well* (1914)
Moving Picture World, March 7th (quotation); *Kinematograph and Lantern Weekly*, June 4th, released July 6th in 962 feet, handled in England by Thanhauser (summary).

LXV Thanhauser, *Two Little Dromios* (1914)
Moving Picture World, January 24th.

LXVI Neue, *Martin as Hamlet* (1914)
Kinematograph and Lantern Weekly, May 7th.

LXVII Pasquali, *La maschera che sanguina* (1914)
Prolo, Vol I, p. 175; *Ciné-Journal*, May 16th, which prints an advertisement by L. Aubert and two stills of Capozzi as the actor as Hamlet.

LXVIII United, *Love's Labour Lost* (1914)
Kinematograph and Lantern Weekly, September 10th, distributed by R. Prieur.

LXIX Essanay, *When Macbeth Came to Snakeville* (1914)
Moving Picture World, August 29th, September 19th.

LXX Gaumont, *Leonce Plays Othello* (1914)
Kinematograph and Lantern Weekly, June 11th; on Perret and the series, see Sadoul, *Le Cinéma devient un art*, Vol I, pp. 199–201.

LXXI American Beauty, *A Modern Othello* (1914)
Moving Picture World, September 5th, 12th; according to the *Cinema News and Property Gazette*, October 1st, it was to be released in England on November 19th. American Beauty was a brand of the American Film Manufacturing Co. of Chicago; it released through Mutual Film Corp.

LXXII Nordisk, *The Taming of the Shrew* (1914)
The American copyright by Great Northern on November 30th included a description which removes the film from the Shakespearean category.

LXXIII Prieur, *The Tempest* (1914)
Kinematograph and Lantern Weekly, June 4th.

LXXIV Belle Alliance, *The Winter's Tale* (1914)
Wiesbaden brochure.

LXXV Cosmograph, *Les Enfants d'Edouard* (1914)
See Film d'Art (1910). For the record there are reviews in *Ciné-Journal*, March 21st and April 18th; stills, March 14th, 21st, 28th, April 4th. Some of the Cosmograph advertisements list the picture as in the 'Série d'Art B.A.I.' In Italy, the title was *La morte dei figli di Re Eduardo*, in the United States, *The Crown of Richard III*. The *Filmlexicon* adds René Alexandre to the cast; if this is accurate, he must have played Tyrrell. English reviews with summaries may be found in *Bioscope* and the *Kinematograph and Lantern Weekly*, both May 7th. The length is variously given as three and four reels. On Cosmograph see Sadoul, *Le Cinéma devient un art*, Vol I, p. 202, N2.

LXXVI British and Colonial, *The Life of William Shakespeare* (1914)
Pre-release information is drawn variously from the *Cinema News and Property Gazette*, December 11th, 18, 1913, and February 5th, 12th, 19, 1914; the *Kinematograph and Lantern Weekly*, December 25, 1913, and February 5th, 12, 1914; *Ciné-Journal*, March 7th, April 11th, May 2, 1914; *Moving Picture World*, January 31st, March 14th, May 16th, June 13th, October 3, 1914. In the first journal there are stills on February 5th, 12th; in the second, on February 12th. The summary in *Ciné-Journal*, April 11th, provides the name of Grasp. Low, pp. 203, 286, gives the length as five reels in England, and on pp. 97–8 the background of B and C.

LXXVII Universal, *The Merchant of Venice* (1914)
My account is based almost wholly on the *Moving Picture World*, January 17th, 24th (interview), February 14th (review and still), 21st (release date), March 7th

M

(censorship), supplemented by the *Universal Weekly*, February 7th (still), 14th (stills), 21st (posters). The second periodical, February 14th, indicates 'the stage version has not been followed scene for scene, but many scenes which stage limitations bar, have been injected into the piece', and that the 'eminent European authority, Sir James D. Linton, has been consulted' with regard to the costuming. Blum, p. 55, has three stills. In one of them, Douglas Gerrard is shown and named and I have assigned Bassanio to him on this evidence. For Smalley on the New York stage, see *Best Plays of 1899–1909*, pp. 396, 400, 409, 415–16, 541. Lois Weber became better known as the 'highest salaried woman director in the world' and as the director of the controversial birth control film, *Where Are My Children?* (Ernestine Black, 'Lois Weber Smalley', *Overland*, Los Angeles, September 1916). There are other articles about her listed in the *Film Index*, pp. 175, 197. Edna Maison came to the screen from musical comedy (William Richards, 'Carmen Edna Maisonave – Edna Maison "for short",' *Photoplay*, August 1914). Rupert Julian had a longer career as a director; he made *Kaiser—the Beast of Berlin* (1918), completed Erich von Stroheim's *Merry-Go-Round* (1923), and directed Lon Chaney in *The Phantom of the Opera* (1925); there is an article about him by Davide Turconi in the *Enciclopedia*.

LXXVIII Cines, *Julius Caesar* (1914)

See also Cines *Antony and Cleopatra* (1913). Material about the film in the United States is based on the *Moving Picture World*, May 30th, September 19th, November 21st, December 12th, 26th; George Kleine's *Catalogue of Educational Motion Pictures*, Chicago, 1915, pp. 100–1; and his press book in the Theatre Collection of the New York Public Library. There are additional reviews in the *Billboard* and *Variety*, November 14, 1914, and I have profited from information supplied by the National Federation of Film Societies. For England, I have used the *Kinematograph and Lantern Weekly*, June 18, 1914; the *Cinema News and Property Gazette*, April 15th, 29th, July 1, 1915; for Italy, *La Cinematografia Italiana*, November 1–30, 1914, and Prolo, Vol I, pp. 75, 113–14 (N.22), 168; for Germany, *Der Kinematograph*, July 22, 1914, and *Erste Internationale Film-Zeitung*, December 12, 1914, and January 16, 1915; for France, Sadoul, *Le Cinéma devient un art*, Vol I, pp. 162–3; Vol II, p. 269, who puts French exhibition in 1916 and quotes Prolo, pp. 113–14 above who dates a review in August of that year. *Le Courier Cinématographique* lists it on June 2, 1917, and the programme of the Association Cinématographique Parisienne dates a trade showing on June 13, 1917. The print I saw screened was the property of the Museum of Modern Art Film Library; it did not identify the cast except for Novelli. The *Filmlexicon* adds Bruto Castellani. Stills are available in many of the sources listed above, in most film archives, and in Blum, p. 58.

LXXIX Ambrosio, *Hamlet* (1914)

The ground is admittedly shaky. The basis for inclusion is the usually reliable Prolo, Vol I, p. 166, but I have no supporting evidence. Knaur and the Wiesbaden brochure merely follow Prolo. Moreover on the Ambrosio *Othello* below I have to disagree with Prolo as to the inclusion of Revelle. The article on Ambrosio by Prolo in the *Enciclopedia* lists Revelle among Ambrosio actors in 1914, and on pp. 166–7, she names a number of films in which he appeared. Clippings in the

Theatre Collection of the New York Public Library confirm his engagement by Ambrosio and supply other details about his life, but there is no mention of a *Hamlet* film, and none in *Who's Who in the Theatre* (Sixth Edition, 1930), which has a substantial account of his stage appearances. In 1953 Mr James Card of George Eastman House wrote me that in 1952 he had had in for screening an Italian silent production of *Hamlet*. It was the property of Mr Anthony Moscato of Buffalo. An inquiry to Mr Moscato brought the unwelcome news that the 35 millimetre print had so deteriorated that it had to be destroyed for reasons of safety. It was in seven reels, and titled *The Mad Prince* but I have found no record of a film with that title. Mr Moscato had no information about the cast or producer, but just possibly this may have been the Ambrosio film of 1914. There is no clear evidence connecting this *Hamlet* with Photodrama, as there is for *Othello* below, but if it was the later, the assumption is reasonable. Information about the foundation of a Kleine–Ambrosio studio is from the *Kinematograph Year Book*, 1915, p. 97, and there are confusing documents referring to Photodrama in the Kleine file in the Library of Congress film laboratory at Suitland. 'The Trade in Italy', by Peyron in the *Kinematograph and Lantern Weekly*, January 15, 1914, says the Photo-Drama Film Co. has a capital of 2,000,000 francs; general manager, Alfred Gandolfi, formerly of Ambrosio; at Grigliasco [Grugliasco] near Turin; manufactory ready for next Spring. The name of the company is variously Photodrama, Photo Drama, Photo-Drama.

LXXX Ambrosio, *Othello* (1914)

Prolo, Vol I, p. 166, lists under Ambrosio, 'Otello – da W. Shakespeare – riddutore Arrigo Frusta – interprete Hamilton A. Revelle'. In view of the cast listed at the time in *La Cinematografia Italiana*, November 1st–30th, I cannot agree that Revelle was involved. I have supplied first names, when available, from contemporary films listed by Prolo. None of the actors was sufficiently important to be included in the *Enciclopedia*. The synopsis in the *Moving Picture World*, July 11th, is of no value. Kleine's press book is in the Theatre Collection of the New York Public Library. Knaur and Wiesbaden repeat Prolo's information. English trade show and release dates are from the *Cinema News and Property Gazette*, July 1st, 8th, 15th, August 5, 1915. The issues of December 16, 1915, and April 13th, July 20, 1916, report its success; that of August 8, 1918, reports from *Ciné-Journal* the censors' action in Villefranche-sur-Rhone.

The negative is in the film vaults of the Library of Congress at Suitland. At some time sequences had been separated for colouring and then spliced according to tone. The narrative is thus helterskelter. The negative shows some disintegration and can be examined only with a hand-viewer. Without more magnification it is difficult to identify the sequences and next to impossible to put the scenes into their proper chronological or narrative order, especially since there are no subtitles to act as guides. I made what I could out of the picture puzzle in 1958, and express my thanks to Colonel Willard Webb, Mr James H. Culver, and Mrs Linda Coudé for their help. There were actually 21 sequences in Reel I (993 feet), 14 in Reel II (estimated at 800 feet because of the constant need to rewind), 16 in Reel III (629 feet), and 15 in Reel IV (636 feet), some of which I cannot identify or describe. Any given Shakespearean scene may be scattered over the four reels. The total length of 3058 feet is over 1000 feet shorter than the original. Of the 150 prints which Kleine deposited, 75 remain; the others presumably deteriorated and were destroyed. A descriptive folder contains five illustrations. The Museum of Modern Art has ten stills. Others are in the *Moving Picture World*, July 11th; *Ciné-Journal*, April 25th, May 2nd, 16th, 23rd; and the *Kinematograph and Lantern Weekly*, January 22nd.

CHAPTER VII

I Casino, *Ethel's Romeo* (1915)
Produced by Gaumont (Flushing) for the Mutual programme and released on October 17th (*Moving Picture World*, October 30th).

II Edison, *Martha's Romeo* (1915)
Moving Picture World, April 17th; released April 20th.

III Lubin, *Her Romeo* (1915)
Moving Picture World, August 7th, 28th; one reel, released August 14th, story by Epes W. Sargent, with Billie Reeves.

IV Strand, *Her Rustic Romeo* (1918)
Moving Picture World, June 1st: 'Rather a meaningless comedy, featuring Billie Rhodes' for the Mutual programme.

V Rex, *A Seashore Romeo* (1915)
Moving Picture World, August 14th, 28th; released August 22nd, with Ben Wilson and Dorothy Phillips.

VI Star Featurette, *A Prairie Romeo* (1917)
Moving Picture World, October 6th; released the week of October 1st, with George Hernandez as Billy Bones, a western comedy for Universal, in two reels; in England, the *Cinema News and Property Gazette*, February 21, 1918, indicates release in January by Trans-Atlantic in 1160 feet.

VII Kalem, *Romeo of the Coal Wagon* (1916)
Moving Picture World, May 20th, 27th; with Ethel Teare, in one reel, for General Film Service.

VIII Keystone, *A Tugboat Romeo* (1916)
Cinema News and Property Gazette, February 15, 1917. It was released in the United States the previous October 8th in two parts, with Chester Conklin, for Triangle.

IX Nestor, *Two Small Town Romeos* (1917)
Cinema News and Property Gazette, February 22nd; released in England by Trans-Atlantic on March 26th in 930 feet, but the film was American. The Nestor comedies featured Eddie Lyons and Lee Moran.

x Kalem, *Seaside Romeos* (1917)
Moving Picture World, June 30th; a Ham (Lloyd V. Hamilton) and Bud (A. E. Duncan) comedy for General Film, combining a Welsh rabbit dream of buried treasure and a girl's class in aesthetic dancing.

xi Essanay, *A Depot Romeo* (1917)
Moving Picture World, December 22nd; the comic mishaps of a station agent. *Cinema News and Property Gazette*, March 14, 1918; 781 feet.

xii Victor, *A Roaming Romeo* (1916)
Moving Picture World, November 11th; special release on November 8th.

xiii Arbuckle, *A Reckless Romeo* (1917)
Moving Picture World, June 9th; 'Fatty' in an amusement park, released through Paramount, May 21st.

xiv Sennett, *Roping Her Romeo* (1917)
Moving Picture World, September 22nd, October 13th, November 10th, December 22nd; a 'chase' comedy, released through Paramount on October 21st with a familiar Mack Sennett cast: Ben Turpin, Slim Summerville, Charles Murray, Polly Moran, and Mary Thurman. Polly Moran was 'Little Nell', the sheriff, whose horsemanship was featured.

xv Cricks and Martin, *Romeo and Juliet* (1915)
Cinema News and Property Gazette, May 20th, July 1st, 22nd; *Pictures and the Picturegoer*, September 4th. Two reels, 998 feet, released by Davison on August 19th. 'Mr Willie Clarkson, the famous costumier of Wardour Street' was shown in the film making up the Society's actors. 'A real triumph.... It will appeal to every audience, irrespective of any knowledge of the actual play, for, indeed, most of the fun is made out of the audience themselves and the stage effects, and does not in any way depend upon a close reading of the "book",' it was explained, but the WPA card in the Museum of Modern Art says it was 'a poor burlesque' and gives as reference the British Film Institute's National Film Library Catalogue (1938), indicating that there is a print in the Institute's archive. See also below on the Cricks and Martin *Hamlet*.

xvi Crystal, *Romeo and Juliet* (1918)
Moving Picture World, June 29th.

xvii S. S. Film Co., *Romeo and Juliet* (1917)
There were earlier reports in the *Moving Picture World*, September 22nd, November 17th. 'All the sets are specially built and are said to be as correct as the sets used in any stage production of the same play. The costuming of the clay figures will also be historically correct.' The production was under the supervision of J. Charles Davis, Jr and released by the Educational Films Corporation. The sculptor's first name is spelled Helene in a technical article on her films in the *Scientific American*, December 16, 1916.

XVIII Pathé, *Romiet and Julio* (1915)

Summary in the *Moving Picture World*, January 9th; listings on January 16th, 22nd. The film was first listed as Eclectic, which distributed, but the firm was dissolved later in the month. Thereafter Pathé Exchange distributed its own film. There is a still in the *Pathé Fortnightly Bulletin*, Vol III, No. 1.

XIX Fox, *A Footlight Parade* (1917)

Cinema News and Property Gazette, May 10th, 24th; English trade showing May 16th, two reels, with Charles Arling.

XX Cricks and Martin, *Hamlet* (1915)

Pictures and the Picturegoer, May 7th, 15th; *Cinema News and Property Gazette*, April 8th, 29th, May 13th. The brand was Lion's Head, the distributor Davison; released June 7th in 908 feet; stills in *Cinema News*, April 8th, 29th. The writer of the series was Reuben Gilmer; the producer, Will Kellino.

XXI Piccadilly, *Pimple as Hamlet* (1916)

Low (*1914–18*), p. 298, and index; also Low (*1906–14*), index. Denis Gifford writes me that the only reference he has found to this film is an advertisement in *The Cinema* where there is a picture; it was not reviewed; 'it would have been written and directed by the brothers Fred and Joe Evans, with . . . Joe in the cast'. Joe's part was called Joey. Both Fred and Joe were nephews of the well known Will Evans of the music halls and pantomime.

XXII Beauty, *To Be or Not to Be* (1916)

Moving Picture World, January 1st, 8th; released January 8th, with Orral Humphrey as 'the world's greatest Shakespearean tragedian', Gladys Kingsbury, Mary Talbot, Johnny Gough, Ed. C. Watt, 'the popular American players', that is, of American Beauty.

XXIII Lubin, *Hamlet Made Over* (1916)

Moving Picture World, March 4th (summary and advertisement with still), 18th (comment). Earl Metcalfe directed from a script by Mark Swan. Billie Reeves was the tragedian, William H. Turner the manager, Carrie Reynolds the girl, Clarence Jay Elmer the King. In England this 1000 foot film was re-titled *Hamlet Up-to-Date* (*Cinema News and Property Gazette*, June 29th). American release, March 4th; English, August 21st.

XXIV Vitagraph, *Freddy Versus Hamlet* (1916)

Moving Picture World, March 25th, April 15th. This was one of a 'Freddy' series, featuring William Dangman; Tod Talford was Wiggins, William Lytell, Jr the actor, Daisy DeVere the Mabel. The author was Ralph Ince, who ought to have known better.

XXV Bray, *Col. Heeza Liar Plays Hamlet* (1916)

Moving Picture World, September 9th: 'one of the very best comedy cartoons ever made by the distinguished artist', J. R. Bray. Released August 24th by Paramount.

XXVI Powers, *The Barnyard Hamlet* (1917)

I find no such title in the United States, though the film was American. It was distributed in England in 427 feet on November 26th by Trans-Atlantic, which handled the Universal group (*Cinema News and Property Gazette*, October 4th, 11th, 18th).

XXVII Lubin, *Queenie of the Nile* (1915)

Moving Picture World, September 4th, 18th; directed by Arthur D. Hotaling, released September 11th, with Mae Hotely as the mad woman. The scenario was by Epes W. Sargent, who also wrote *Her Romeo*.

XXVIII Pathé–Rolin, *Cleopatsy* (1918)

Moving Picture World, May 25th; two reels. But *Photoplay*, July, gives the title *Cleopatra*, the provenance as the Toto Film Co., and the Cleopatra as Dora Rogers.

XXIX Weston, *Julius Caesar* (1915)

Cinema News and Property Gazette, April 29th; distributed by H. A. Browne and Co.; and see *Pimple as Hamlet* (1916) above.

XXX L-KO, *A Rural Caesar* (1917)

Moving Picture World, August 18th; two reels, released August 29th; still, but no synopsis; distributed by Universal.

XXXI Bamforth, *A Comedy of Errors* (1915)

Cinema News and Property Gazette, July 1st; released by Yorkshire Cine Co., July 12th; 630 feet.

XXXII Edison, *Love's Labour Lost* (1916)

Cinema News and Property Gazette, March 30th; by Raoul Barre, 500 feet, released in England on May 15th. The title is partly, perhaps wholly, English.

XXXIII Judy, *Taming of the Shrew* (1916)

Moving Picture World, June 17th; released June 6th by the newly formed Unicorn Film Service; no synopsis or review.

XXXIV Clarendon, *A Horse! A Horse!* (1916)

The reference is in a communication from Denis Gifford.

XXXV Metro, *The Lady Killer* (1916)

Moving Picture World, October 28th; *National Board of Review Garden of Motion Pictures*, April–October, p. 15.

XXXVI British and Colonial, *The Taming of the Shrew* (1915)

Cinema News and Property Gazette, June 17th; Bertram Clayton, 'Shakespeare and the Talkies', *English Review* (1929), p. 740. The film was distributed by Davison.

XXXVII Beck-Film, *The Merry Wives of Windsor* (1917)
Wiesbaden brochure; Stahl, p. 684, and Knaur, date 1918. The director was William Wauer.

XXXVIII Harmonie-Film, *Elfenszene aus dem Sommernachtstraum* (1917)
Wiesbaden brochure.

XXXIX Thiemann and Reinhardt, *The Picture of Dorian Gray* (1915)
Leyda, *Kino*, pp. 81–2, 420–1; Sadoul, *Le Cinéma devient un art*, Vol II, pp. 138–9. The shot is original, but performances of *Romeo and Juliet*, at which Dorian sees Sibyl Vane as Juliet, are included in Wilde's novel. Since Meyerhold's film has been lost, I do not know whether the stage representation unreflected is also there. Wilde specifically mentions the meeting of the lovers, the balcony scene in the garden, and the tomb. Perhaps bits of the performance also appeared in a Nordisk picture of the story, directed by A. Ström in 1910, and in French and Hungarian versions, but there is no evidence.

XL Film d'Art, *Barbe Russe* (1917)
Le Courier Cinématographique, March 31st; released by Agence Cinématographique.

XLI London, *Love in a Wood* (1916)
This elusive film, as far as I know, was neither listed nor reviewed in the trade journals or year books. All I know about it comes from two sources: the material on file in the United States Copyright Office (though the originally deposited 49 prints, probably on nitrate film, have been destroyed), and Elizabeth Risdon, whom I finally located and to whom I am grateful for taking the trouble at the age of seventy to write me about it. She died a few months later, December 20, 1958, after a long and distinguished career on screen and stage which began when she was twelve. Most of the people who were concerned with the film were well known in the period and some of them later. See Low (*1914–1918*), index, and appropriate *Who's Who in the Theatre*. Miss Risdon wrote, 'It is possible that war-time financial conditions suggested the convenience of a non-royalty script. It was an attempt to present *As You Like It* in modern dress. We had fun doing it, but the press and public *did not like it*, and the result was a failure. Kenelm Foss had an agile mind and probably wrote a literate script, most of which would have been lost in the business of physical action popular in that day.' The quotation in the text is also hers. The film may of course have been made in 1915. The American copyright by Paul H. Cromelin was on March 1, 1916.

XLII British Actors Film Company, *The Real Thing at Last* (1916)
I make grateful acknowledgment to the late A. E. Matthews, Godfrey Tearle, and Edmund Gwenn for information supplied in interviews. There are numerous written accounts of this film which have also served as sources of my treatment and which provide some delightful details I have not included: the fullest are A. E. Matthews: *Matty: An Autobiography* ... London, 1952, opp. p. 96 (still, Barrie Ms.), pp. 153–8 (including cast taken from Barrie Ms.) and Leslie Henson: *My Laugh Story: The Story of My Life: Up to Date*, London, n.d., pp. 287–91. I have also used Low Warren: *The Film Game*, London, 1937, p. 58; J. A. Ham-

merton: *Barrie: The Story of a Genius*, New York, 1929, pp. 413–14; Denis Mackail: *The Story of J.M.B.*, London, 1941, pp. 490–1; and interviews with A. E. Matthews in the New York *Times* and the New York *Herald-Tribune*, both January 17, 1937. Some background is from Low (*1914–1918*), pp. 69–70, but she does not mention the film, which ran only about a half-hour. The long quotations are from the *Cinema News and Property Gazette*, March 16th ('Editorial Chat' by 'Observer') and March 30th (by L.J.S.). In 1956 an inquiry was made for me by Liam O'Leary to Gerald Malvern, former General Manager of BAFC; he indicated that no copy of the film had survived. Presumably this includes a print which Mr Matthews told me had been given to Barrie, who willed it to a hospital or home.

XLIII Triangle, *The Iron Strain* (1915)
  Cinema News and Property Gazette, February 8th, 22nd, 29th (review quoted, still), 1917. Trade showing in England, February 22nd. American review in the *Moving Picture World*, October 9, 1915. Still in Blum, p. 96. *Film Index*, pp. 176, 253, for director and writer.

XLIV Rapf–Pathé, *The Mad Lover* (1917)
  Moving Picture World, April 7th, 21st, May 5th, 25th, June 2nd, July 7th, August 11th (review), December 29th; June 8, 1918. *Cinema News and Property Gazette*, July 11th, August 1 (review), 1918. The American release was reviewed in *Film Daily*, August 2, 1917; the English release by Masterpieces, Ltd was trade shown on July 25th. Rapf was an independent producer who released partly through Selznick, partly as in this case through Pathé. The productions in which Warwick starred were actually under the Robert Warwick Film Corporation. Warwick had been on the New York stage from 1903 until 1914; his career is summarized in *Photoplay*, March 1917. Elaine Hammerstein had taken part in her father's production of *High Jinks* at the Lyric Theatre, December 10, 1913, and allegedly entered films to escape the stage (Arabella Boone in *Photoplay*, November 1919). Pedro Vinzaglio (the villain), Edward Kimball, and Frank McGlinn were also in the picture.

XLV Palatino–Film, *Lady Macbeth* (1917)
  Wiesbaden brochure; Sadoul, *Le Cinéma devient un art*, Vol II, Chronologie, dating 1918.

XLVI Max Mack–Film, *Othello* (1918)
  Wiesbaden brochure; Sadoul, *Le Cinéma devient un art*, Vol II, Chronologie; Knaur places it in Italy. Stahl, p. 682: 'Othello wurde 1918 von Dr Reinhard Bruch, dem damaligen Regisseur am Königlichen Schauspielhaus, für den film bearbeitet. . . .' Jay Leyda in correspondence refers to *Lichtbild Bühne*, January 26th, February 2, 1918, where it is indicated that Montano played both Georg V. Hartung and Othello; Ellen Korth, Prinzessin Lieselotte and Desdemona. Evidently there was a play-within-the-play. Others in the cast were Rosa Valetti, Wilhelm Diegelmann, Max Gülstorff, Jenny Marba, Julius Falkenstein.

XLVII Paul Beckers–Film, *Der Fliegentüten-Othello* (1918)
  Lichtbild Bühne, February 2nd. There is a print in the East German Filmarchiv, Berlin.

M*

XLVIII Thanhouser, *Master Shakespeare, Strolling Player* (1916)

Moving Picture World, March 25th, April 22nd, 29th. The five-reel film was released by Mutual on April 20th.

XLIX Triangle–Reliance, *Macbeth* (1916)

This section is based on my article: *'The Shakespeare Film as Record: Sir Herbert Beerbohm Tree'*, *Shakespeare Quarterly*, July 1952, pp. 227–36, used by permission of the editor. Tree's approval of *Macbeth* is reported in *Pictures and the Picturegoer*, February 5th. The Emerson interview was with Hector Ames, *The Motion Picture Classic*, September 1916, pp. 27–30, 70, which identifies the Fleance as Chandler House. (Quotation by permission: Copyright 1916, *Motion Picture Classic*.) Emerson is further quoted in the *Moving Picture World*, February 19th, and H. E. Aitken, the president of Triangle, on March 18th. The quotation about electrical wiring is from Talbot (1923 ed.), p. 376. The assignment of players is noted in the trade journals as announcements were made but almost the full cast is listed in *Film Daily*, June 8th; those not heretofore named were L. de Nowskowski (Malcolm), Bessie Buskirk (Donalbain), Jack Conway (Lennox), Seymour Hastings (Ross), Jack Brammel (Seyton), Carl Formes, Jr (Bishop), Mary Alden (Lady Macduff); L. Tylden, Scott McKee, Jack Leonard (Witches); Francis Carpenter, Thelma Burns, Madge Dyer (Macduff's children); Raymond Wells (Cawdor); George McKenzie, Olga Gray. The child actor who was Tree's official greeter might have been Ben Alexander. The information from Iris Tree is in her 'Memories' in Max Beerbohm (ed.); *Herbert Beerbohm Tree*, London, n.d., pp. 181–6. Tree on his first day's work is in *Pictures and the Picturegoer*, February 19th. See also DeWolf Hopper and W. W. Stout: *Once a Clown . . .*, Boston, 1927, pp. 158–63. The description of motion picture acting, as Tree saw it, is from his *Impressions of America*, p. 285. He adds, 'The sets for *Macbeth* were all built; the scene of the King's Castle in the last act, solidly constructed in a "location" outside Hollywood, was fully equipped with a moat filled with real water, a drawbridge, and battlements, over which the attacking army clambered, stones being hurled and boiling pitch being poured on them'. For Otis Skinner, see his article, 'The Motion Picture Not an Art', *Ladies' Home Journal*, May 1922. Constance Collier's reminiscences are from her autobiography, *Harlequinade: The Story of My Life . . .*, London, 1929, pp. 243–9. I am much indebted to Miss Collier for granting me an interview in 1949, and to Miss Iris Tree for an informative letter. Edward Weitzel in an obituary of Tree in the *Moving Picture World*, July 21, 1917, adds one useful comment: 'Familiarity even with human slaughter, breeds contempt, and the reproduction in detail on the screen of all the murders in Macbeth turned the poet's work into crude melodrama that lost an impressiveness with each repetition of violent death'. In London, the *Cinema News and Property Gazette* of June 29th called the film a 'Gorgeous Spectacle . . . Shakespeare for All!' and John Emerson's production 'superb'. It also adds some useful details. 'Perhaps the most important modifications of Shakespeare's story are: first, there is no indication of the implication in Lady Macbeth's words, just before the murder; "Had he not resembled . . . done't".' Secondly, there is a quite unwarranted scene showing an apparition of Banquo's ghost to Macduff (while the apparition of Banquo's descendants to Macbeth is strangely omitted); and, thirdly, Lady Macduff does not suppose, as Shakespeare makes her, that her husband has played the coward and deserted her. The domestic scenes at the home of Macduff, with the games of the children, introduce a contrasting element, which, though not Shakespearean, are very pleasant. . . . There is one serious fault in the technique of one scene, used for both prologue and epilogue; the sky in the rugged and weird scene introducing the three witches is obviously a separate photograph from that of the mountain-side itself, and in the epilogue is actually seen to shift as a whole piece in relation to the rest of the scene. . . . It is a little strange that there are too many subtitles, spoiling the dramatic effect of several scenes by breaking their continuity. . . . By a strange irony, the most dramatic scene of this superb and gorgeous production is a simple close-up showing Macbeth . . . and Lady Macbeth . . . waiting (almost without movement) outside King Duncan's door for the opportune moment to commit their crime'. The quick closing of *Macbeth* at His Majesty's was noted in the *Kinematograph Year Book*, 1917, p. 67. For Rupert Hughes, see his 'Early Days in the Movies', *Saturday Evening Post*, April 6, 1935, p. 40; for H. Chance Newton: *Cues and Curtain Calls*, London, 1927, pp. 137–8. Of interest is 'An Interview with Sir Herbert Beerbohm Tree' by Helen Duey in the *Woman's Home Companion*, June 1916, in which Tree gives his views on Shakespeare on film. Mr John E. Allen tells me that the negative of *Macbeth* was destroyed in the Pathé fire in Bound Brook, New Jersey, whither it had been removed from the Fort Lee vault where it had been stored; the Fort Lee vault shortly afterward was damaged by fire and water, and much of the Triangle product ruined. No positive print has been discovered. For this reason and because the only biography of Tree, that by Hesketh Pearson: *Beerbohm Tree : His Life and Laughter*, London, 1956, pp. 224–8, has little about *Macbeth*, I have rightly or wrongly given as much detail as I have found and rather more than usual direct quotation in order to present in their own words what contemporary commentators said, and as clear a view as possible of the nature and content of the film. Numerous pictures eke out our understanding. There are illustrations for example in the Skinner and Duey articles; in the *Moving Picture World*, March 18th, June 24th; in the *Motion Picture Magazine*, August; accompanying an article by Brian Hooker: 'Shakespeare and the Movies', *Century Magazine*, Vol 93 (1916), pp. 298–304; and in Blum, pp. 116, 118. The scrapbooks of the Locke Collection in the New York Public Library contain both illustrations and reviews. The review in the New York *Times*, June 5, 1916, was '© 1916 by the New York Times Company. Reprinted by permission.'

L Metro, *Romeo and Juliet* (1916)

Moving Picture World, April 29th, May 6th, 20th, July 1st, 8th, August 12th, 26th, September 9th, October 14th, 21st, 28th, November 4th, 11th, 18th. According to Miss Bayne, whom I thank for details, extras in the film reported on its progress to Fox, who made his picture in six weeks. Metro's brand name for its Bushman–Bayne series was Quality. The reviews in addition to Blaisdell's are quoted from the *Moving Picture World*, November 18th; there was no doubt some distortion accomplished by the selection. There is another review in *Film Daily*, October 26th, and an article, 'A Moving Picture Romeo and Juliet . . .', signed by Bushman in the *Motion Picture Magazine*, September. It was the president of Metro, Richard Rowland, who indicated that the film was released in forty two cities (*Morning Telegraph*, October 29th). There must have been some opposition to the film from theatre critics to account for the long diatribe of W. Stephen Bush, 'Classics and the Screen', *Moving Picture World*, November 11th, in which he denounces them indignantly for their attitude toward Tree's *Macbeth* and the two *Romeo and Juliet* pictures. He mentions that the Metro version used double exposure to picture Juliet's horror at lying in the tomb with her buried ancestors, and the skill with which suspense is developed in Friar John's failure to deliver the message to Romeo in Mantua. The English distributor was Ruffel's. Illustrations are numerous. There are five in a special number of *Metro Picture News* on file in the Library of Congress, six in the October 14th issue of the *Moving Picture World*, and twenty six in the *Photoplay* still collection, thirteen in *Billboard*, October 28th, six in the *Motion Picture Classic*, September and October, five in Blum, p. 104. Miss Bayne lent me for study some in her own possession. Yet it is difficult to obtain any real idea of what the film was like without examination of a positive print, and there is none. Metro-Goldwyn-Mayer has a negative which I have not been able to get at but about which I have received various reports, sometimes contradictory. The last I knew it was unusable, unavailable, had not been inspected for years, and was somewhere in about eight hundred cases in dead storage in Los Angeles. With modern equipment it is quite possible, though expensive, to step-print shrunken, brittle, and even faded negative, and perhaps one day someone will succeed, as I have not, in persuading MGM to rescue what for its time must have been an attractive film.

There is a good deal of material, much of it silly, on Bushman and Bayne. 'Some Prominent Essanay Players', *Moving Picture World*, July 11, 1914, gives early biographical details; the issue of July 10, 1915, presents the relation between Metro and Quality Pictures Corp., and September 4th the announcement of Bayne's signing with Quality; October 16th has an article on Noble. There is more in Carolyn Lowrey: *The First One Hundred Men and Women of the Screen*, New York, 1920, and the *Motion Picture Studio Directory*, 2nd edition, October 21, 1916. The early volumes of *Best Plays* contain Elsner's credits, and some of the other players had also been on the New York stage. 'Green Room Jottings', *Motion Picture Classic*, September 1916, describes the effect of a storm during shooting at Brighton Beach. It is not clear from the article cited from the *Cinema News and Property Gazette* whether the writer or a correspondent had seen the film, or whether it is based on an American review. Additional members of the cast are supplied by the *Moving Picture World*, August 26th, and *Film Daily*, October 26th: Barry Maxwell (apothecary), Alexandre J. Herbert (Friar John), Ethel Mantell (Rosaline), John Davidson (Paris), Olav Skavlan (Benvolio), Harry Sothern (Abram), Leonard Grover, Leonard Grover, Jr, Lionel Belmore, Marie Booth, Violet Hall-Caine, Edwin Boring, William H. Burton. Camera was by R. J. Berquist. It is only fair to add that *Film Daily* thought the production was slow and tiresome, had too many titles and 'too much Romeo', lacked close-ups, and because of poor lighting did not show Beverly Bayne to the best advantage.

LI Fox, *Romeo and Juliet* (1916)

The *Motion Picture World* references are cited under the Metro picture. The quotation about Theda Bara's conception of the role is from the second of two articles under her name, 'How I Became a Film Vampire', *Forum*, June and July,

1919; the first is supposedly autobiographical. When I talked to her in 1949, Miss Bara, a remarkably intelligent woman, did not remember the articles, and I suspect they were ghosted or the effusions of the publicity department. Almost everything in print about the Bara name is wrong. Ancestors on her mother's side were Italian, Di Bara. She told me she had used Bara, the middle name of her Swiss grand-father, on a collaborated play she copyrighted before she went into pictures. I am much indebted to Miss Bara, who died April 7, 1955, for information. On the actress and the press agentry, see Griffith-Mayer, pp. 66–7, and Wagenknecht, p. 179. The Locke Collection of the New York Public Library contains two vol-umes of clippings about her, pictures, publicity, reviews. There is a review in *Film Daily*, October 26th, and in *Billboard*, October 28th. Also at the Library, see the *Fox Bulletin*, April 17th, on Hilliard, October 23rd on the film. The *Motion Picture Studio Directory*, 2nd Edition, October 21, 1916, contains sketches of Hilliard and Edwards. A check of casts in *Best Plays* shows Alice Gale on the New York stage from 1898 to 1919, frequently in Charles Frohman productions. The relevant issues of the *Cinema News and Property Gazette* are November 9th, 23rd, December 21st. In England the film was in 6994 feet, seven reels. The Stratford and Australian information is from the *Moving Picture World*, February 17th, June 16, 1917. The Library of Congress has Adrian Johnson's script, but it was not published, is still under copyright, and I have not been able to examine it. No negative or print has apparently survived. The film was distributed by the General Vision Co. in 1926 but I gather the company went out of business the next year. I am indebted to A. Sumner Gambee of National Theatres in New York and Col. Jason S. Joy of Twentieth Century-Fox on the West Coast for searching in 1949. There are stills in the *Moving Picture World*, October 21st, November 4th, 11th; in the *Photoplay* still collection, and in Blum, p. 105, but again it is difficult to indicate content except from what little is in the reviews. The *Cinema News* mentions 'armies in opposition'; the 'more dramatic close', quoted in the text, refers to the ending in Luigi da Porto's and Matteo Bandello's versions in which Juliet awakes before Romeo dies. *Film Daily*, October 26th, is specific about some changes from Shakespeare: Romeo climbs vines to Juliet's balcony, the duel with Paris is fought inside the tomb, and Juliet is awakened by Romeo's kiss after he has taken poison. This journal preferred the Fox version to Metro's: the story was 'made human and entertaining by direction' which was 'superb', the street and ensemble scenes were especially good, close ups were used effectively, Shakespeare quotations were used as titles, and the whole was 'impressive . . . splendid enter-tainment'. Camera was by Philip E. Rosen.

LII Thanhouser, *King Lear* (1916)

Warde's background has already been sufficiently treated under *Richard III* (1913), where biographical sources are cited. The references to *King Lear* are from his autobiography, pp. 253–8, 307. I do not know whether Warde used the film to accompany lecture-recital as he had the earlier picture. The progress of *King Lear* is chronicled in the *Moving Picture World*, July 15th, September 2nd, October 7th, November 4th, 18th, 25th, December 2nd, December 23rd (review). There is another review in *Film Daily*, December 14th. Of the personnel involved, Gilmour, except for Warde, was much the best known. He was an old-timer who had acted with Edwin Booth and Lawrence Barrett; he turns up in the pages of Odell as early as 1886 and there are many references to him in the casts of *Best Plays*; he was frequently in Charles Frohman productions and was often second to the lead. Ernest C. Warde, in addition to the *Best Plays* listings, is noticed in the *Motion Picture Studio Directory*, 2nd Edition, October 21, 1916. Whittier, Arey, Huling, Hammer had also been on the Broadway stage, and Boyd Marshall was to appear two years later in *Head Over Heels* with Mitzi, whom he married. Hector Dion had already acted in the Vitagraph Shakespeares. The player of Gloucester was not announced. The film was not copyrighted, was frequently duped, and therefore survived. The 16 millimetre version I screened had no indication of maker or distributor, and some of the misspelled titles were prepared by hand and were not original; there was evidently some cutting, but it was reasonably complete and in satisfactory condition; I obtained it from the Film Classic Exchange. There are stills in the *Moving Picture World*, November 4th, 25th, December 23rd, and in Blum, p. 98. The *Cinema News and Property Gazette*, November 15, 1917, announced a London trade showing for the 14th but did not review. The *Moving Picture World*, July 14, 1917, indicates that the film was used for educational purposes at the Louisiana State Normal School; its president wrote Pathé: 'We were very pleased. . . . In fact, we have had few moving picture shows that have enlisted more favourable comment than did "King Lear" . . .'

LIII Eclair, *Macbeth* (1916)

Cinema News and Property Gazette, April 13th (trade show April 25th, and advertisement), May 4th (review). I have found no other notice of this film. On the performance at Saint-Wandrille, see Georgette Leblanc's ebullient recollections of her love-life – for convenience I have used the translation by Janet Flanner: *Souvenirs: My Life with Maeterlinck*, New York, 1932, pp. 246–52 – and W. D. Halls: *Maurice Maeterlinck: A Study of His Life and Thought*, Oxford, 1960, pp. 98–9. Séverin-Mars had been in the threatre since 1894, and was to appear in films directed by Abel Gance. *Macbeth* was probably his first film; it is not listed in the filmography attached to the sketch of him by Giulio Cesare Castello in the *Enciclopedia*.

LIV Broadwest, *The Merchant of Venice* (1916)

Lang, *Mr Wu Looks Back*, London, 1941, p. 152; other details in his autobiography in the *Sunday Graphic and News*, February 24, 1935, and in 'My Film Memories', *Film Weekly*, December issues, 1939. Broadwest was Walter West and George Broadbridge; the latter became Lord Mayor of London, Sir George Broadbridge, and Lord Broadbridge. The quotations are from the *Cinema News and Property Gazette*, July 20th, August 3rd; release date from July 27th. The *Bioscope* review is of August 3rd; the *Kinematograph Monthly Film Record*, of September. According to the *Cinema News and Property Gazette* of July 27th and January 11, 1917, the film was in six reels, but I think this applies only to the trade showing with its special introductory features. In view of the booking reports, I find it difficult to agree with Miss Low (*1914–1918*), p. 84, that 'the film was widely condemned'; there is no question that the technique was 'out-dated' and 'a disappointment' (p. 185). Walter West said in the *Cinema News* of October 26th: 'It has already been outstanding, the demand for it . . .' and Lang (*Graphic*, above) that 'the film was a remarkable success, not only in England but in the colonies as well. As a result the Broadwest company persuaded me to do some more pictures for them'. This presumably is the film which was advertised without indication of provenance in the *Courier Cinématographique*, September 5th, 12, 1917. Theatrical biographies of Lang, Britton, Hazel Jones, O'Brien, and Skillan may be found in appropriate editions of *Who's Who in the Theatre*, of Lang by Rachael Low in the *Enciclopedia*. There are stills in the *Cinema News*, July 20th, August 10th; *Bioscope*, August 17th; *Picturegoer*, February 1924. The two reels in the National Film Archive are in fair condition, but I looked at it on an Editola. There is not much warping or shrinking but some yellowing either from age or dipping. Reel II runs to about 935 feet, Reel III to about 910; I suspect some cutting, but not much. The BW monogram is in lower corners of titles. I have not bothered to indicate variations from Shakespeare's text in the subtitles. The cast for the stage production listed in *The Era*, December 8, 1915, is not helpful in assigning the other parts for the film, since there were many changes, but Caselli is listed as Cassel. I do not know whether Lang's innovation whereby Shylock makes his first appearance seated cross-legged in his house, bargaining with Bassanio, while Jessica serves wine and admires herself in a handglass, was retained in the picture.

LV Fox, *Cleopatra* (1917)
There is a wealth of material about this film. Its history is covered in the *Moving Picture World* in almost all issues from May 7, 1917, to June 8, 1918. It opened at the Lyric Theatre, New York, on October 14th. Reviews were carried shortly thereafter by all the trade papers and most of the dailies. It was directed by J. Gordon Edwards, and in addition to Theda Bara included Thurston Hall (Antony), Fritz Leiber (Julius Caesar), Herschel Mayall (Ventidius), Henri DeVries (Octavius Caesar), Dorothy Drake (Charmian), Dell Duncan (Iras), Genevieve Blinn (Octavia), Hector V. Sarno (Messenger), Albert Roscoe (Pharon), Art Acord (Kephren). Many of the advertisements contained illustrations, and various archives have stills; the Theatre Collection of the New York Public Library, for example, has over twenty, and the Locke Collection there, clippings, publicity, etc. Five stills are reproduced in Blum, p. 143. Some of my impressions of the film were obtained from Miss Bara.

LVI Savoia, *Romeo and Juliet* (1917)
Le Courier Cinématographique, September 29th: 'La "Savoia" prépare *Roméo et Juliette* avec A. Falconi ... et le *Cercle de la Fortune*.' Savoia's advertisement in *La Cinematografia*, September 15th, announces 'in preparazione: due commedie brillanti di Carlo Zangrini interpretate del Cav. Armando Falconi.' The *Almanacco del Cinema Italiano* (1939), p. 240, has a biographical sketch of Falconi which lists among his films, apparently for Savoia in 1912, a *Romeo and Juliet*, and Pasinetti, *Film Lexicon*, under Falconi, also mentions such a production as before or in 1912. The Wiesbaden brochure repeats the reference, but would Savoia in 1917 have planned another *Romeo and Juliet* film for Falconi if it had made one about 1912? Is there a confusion here with Film d'arte Italiana (1911)? Knaur complicates by listing a 1917 Italian *Romeo and Juliet* with Francesca Bertini. Yet the long article on Falconi by Fausto Montesanti in the *Enciclopedia*, with a considerable bibliography lists no *Romeo and Juliet* in the filmography and does not put Falconi in any film before 1913.

LVII Ekman, *Hamlet* (1918)

Charles Reinert, *Kleines Filmlexicon*, Zürich, 1946, p. 95. According to Stahl, p. 682, Gösta Ekman made a sound film of *Hamlet* in 1934. I suspect confusion with stage performances. Bertil Hagman in the *Enciclopedia* lists *Hamlet* for Ekman in 1918 but Hasse Ekman's book on his father, *Gosta Ekman*, Stockholm, 1938, in a chapter on his early films does not mention it, and Dr Nils-Hugo Geber of the Filmhistoriska Samlingarna, Stockholm, writes me that there is no evidence that Ekman ever played Hamlet on film. Mr Gunnar Lundquist of Film-Index, Stockholm, agrees.

LVIII Rudolfi, *Hamlet* (1917)

La Cinematografia Italiana ed Estera, August 1st–15th, 31st; September 15th, October 1st–10th (stills), December 25th (private showing). The film was also announced in the *Moving Picture World*, October 20th; and the *Cinema News and Property Gazette*, where the cost was estimated at £4000. Signora Prolo wrote me that Enrico Gemelli was also in the film, but she did not identify his role. On Ruggeri, see the article by Guilio Cesare Castello in the *Enciclopedia*; he acted in his long career in both tragedy and comedy, classic and modern, but was perhaps best known for his performances in the plays of Pirandello; he was on the stage for sixty four years before his death in 1953 at the age of eighty one. Ruggeri is also discussed by Alberto Cecchi in *Scenario*, June 1932; his obituary is in the New York *Times*, July 22, 1943. There are biographical sketches of both Ruggeri and Brignone in the *Almanacco del Cinema Italiano*, 1939, of Brignone (by Alberto Casella and Maria Adriana Prolo), and of Rodolfi and Makowska (both by Francesco Savio) in the *Enciclopedia*. A brochure on the film is in the Museum of Modern Art, New York; the text in both Italian and French gives the credits, four coloured drawings by Carlo Nicco, and six stills. I traced the surviving 16 millimetre print, which has no indication of cast or copyright, through various hands, and ultimately obtained the two reels from Modern Sound Pictures, Omaha, Nebraska. In the search I was aided by William H. Dudley, *The Educational Screen*, and Institutional Cinema Service. The footage was Reel I, 380 feet; Reel III, 385 feet. The film at the beginning has the title: 'Institutional Cinema Service, Inc. Presents *Hamlet*'; at the end of Reel I: 'Dudley Circuit Service'. Some of the titles suggest this print derived from France.

CHAPTER VIII

I Fox, *A Ridin' Romeo* (1921)

Film Daily, June 5th; *Kinematograph Weekly*, August 25th; *Picturegoer*, August 1922. Mix wrote the story himself for a film of 4750 feet; Rhea Mitchell was the heroine.

II Fox, *A Tropical Romeo* (1923)

Kinematograph and Lantern Weekly, November 1st, two reels.

III Fox, *Mile-a-Minute Romeo* (1923)

Film Daily Year Book lists as 1923 but no review in *Film Daily*; *Picturegoer*, July 1924, identifies Mix; *Kinematograph Weekly*, February 28, 1924, 5250 feet.

IV Fox, *Monkey Romeo* (1924)
Film Daily, August 24th, *Kinematograph Weekly*, September 25th. The two-reel comic shorts in this series used live monkeys; this one featured Max Moritz and Pep.

V Fox, *The Arizona Romeo* (1925)
Film Daily, January 18th, directed by Edmund Mortimer; *Kinematograph Weekly*, March 19th, 4600 feet; *Picturegoer*, August.

VI Fox, *A Spanish Romeo* (1925)
Film Daily, February 15th; National Board of Review, *Selected Motion Pictures* (*1925–1926*): 'Van Bibber attends a bull fight and again becomes a hero. Story by Richard Harding Davis'.

VII Universal, *Romeo's Dad* (1919)
WPA card index at the Museum of Modern Art, and copyright entry. Based on a story by Calder Johnstone, it was directed in two reels by George W. Terwilliger.

VIII Arrow, *Romeo Mixup* (1924)
Moving Picture Almanach, 1929.

IX Pathé, *Bromo and Juliet* (1926)
The film was available some years ago at a local Camera Exchange; I thank Harold Osborn for the reference. It was probably a Roach production for Pathé release.

X Educational, *Roameo* (1927)
National Board of Review, *Magazine*, June, one reel; Pat Sullivan was the cartoonist. 'Felix woos his way around the world but comes back to his first true love. . . .' Ideal (Willoughby) lists the title as *Romeeow*.

XI FBO, *A Racing Romeo* (1927)
Film Daily, October 23rd, directed by Sam Wood; *Kinematograph and Lantern Weekly*, September 27, 1928, 5366 feet.

XII Universal, *Rival Romeos* (1928)
National Board of Review, *Magazine*, January, one reel; 'The Lucky Rabbit goes a courting and so does his rival.'

XIII Pathé, *Romeo in the Stone Age* (1928)
Jason, Vol II, p. 217. Released in Germany by UFA as *Romeo in der Steinzeit*, 159 metres, censorship date June 1st. I find no other reference to the title, which I have merely translated.

XIV First National, *Flying Romeos* (1928)
National Board of Review, *Magazine*, March; *Film Daily*, April 8th, 6184 feet. Mervyn LeRoy directed a screen story by John McDermott.

v UFA, *Anna Boleyn* (1920)

Deception in the United States, *Anne Boleyn* in England. For reviews, see for example *Film Daily*, April 24, 1921; *Exceptional Photoplays*, April 1921; *Bioscope*, January 24, 1924. Prints of this historically important film are available at the Museum of Modern Art, New York, and the Cineteca Italiana, Milano. It deals with Henry's repudiation of Queen Katherine, his excommunication and establishment of the Church of England, his marriage to Anne who fails to produce a male heir, her execution and his marriage to Jane Seymour.

xvi First National, *Alias Julius Caesar* (1922)

National Board of Review, *Selected Motion Pictures 1922–1923*, 5 reels: 'comedy of a young man who succeeds despite frame-up of chums, in taking his sweetheart to a dance'. Ray himself directed.

xvii British Exhibitors, *Love's Labour Won* (1922)

Presumably an Italian film but my only reference is the *Kinematograph Year Book*, 1923, which lists it as 5000 feet, with Linda Pini, released by the above on May 30th, and reviewed in the *Kinematograph Weekly*, May 25th. I cannot find a copy.

xviii Burton King, *Shylock of Wall Street* (1922)

Film Daily Year Book, 1944.

xix United Artists, *Tempest* (1927)

Copyright October 11, 1927, by Feature Productions, Inc. Presented by Joseph M. Schenck, produced and directed by Sam Taylor, script by C. Gardner Sullivan, 10 reels, with John Barrymore and Louis Wolheim. *Film Daily*, May 27, 1928: 'Romantic drama of the Russian Revolution.'

xx Wufku, *The Tempest* (1929)

Close Up, April 1929, with stills. Scenario by N. Bijazy, camera by I. Houdyma, directed by P. Dolyna, with Samytchkovsky.

xxi Pinellas, *Cleopatra and Her Easy Mark* (1925)

Pinellas Films was the distributor of the New Redhead Comedies. *Film Daily Year Book*, 1926, says released on October 1st in 650 feet as *Cleopatra and Her East Mark*, probably a misprint.

xxii Vitaphone, *Cleo to Cleopatra* (1928)

Copyright June 30th, one reel. Vitaphone was the sound system adopted by Warner Bros.

xxiii MGM, *Cleopatra* (1928)

Copyright July 7th, two reels, directed by R. William Neill, story by Natalie Kalmus, scenario Lou Abrams, edited by Aubrey Scotto. The Kalmus process was Technicolor; the company had been formed in 1917 but was not to bring out a successful three-colour process until 1932 (Jacobs, p. 446; see also George

Gordon, 'Painting the Shadows ...' *Photoplay*, April 1930. and 'What? Color in the Movies Again', *Fortune*, October 1934).

XXIV Hepworth, *The Merchant of Venice* (1919)
Bioscope, August 28th. Ward R. Street of course equals Wardour Street.

XXV Hepworth, *Romeo and Juliet* (1919)
Bioscope, October 23rd.

XXVI Hepworth, *'Amlet* (1919)
Bioscope, December 11th; *Kinematograph Monthly Record*, February 1920.

XXVII Hepworth, *Othello* (1920)
Bioscope, July 29th.

XXVIII Caesar, *Othello* (1920)
My thanks to Signora Prolo for the original reference. The quotation is from the article by her and Francesco Savio on De Riso in the *Enciclopedia*.

XXIX Exhibitors-Mutual, *A Sage Brush Hamlet* (1919)
Wid's Year Book, 1919, but not reviewed in the *Film Daily*; Wiesbaden brochure. The director was Joseph J. Franz.

XXX Christie, *Shades of Shakespeare* (1919)
National Board of Review, *Garden of Motion Pictures*, April 19th–December 31st. It was according to a programme at the Museum of Modern Art playing at the Rialto Theatre, New York, the week commencing July 27th.

XXXI Fox, *Cleopatra* (1920)
Moving Picture World, December 25th.

XXXII Universal, *Romeo and Juliet* (1920)
Copyright November 15th, one-reel Star Comedy, directed by Vin Moore, story by Maynard Laswell; Wiesbaden brochure; produced by Al Christie, 518 metres.

XXXIII Butcher, *Juliet and Her Romeo* (1923)
Picturegoer, June, July. Queenie Thomas 'particularly liked' this film, directed by her husband, Bertram Phillips, who was also responsible for this 'joyous series of burlesque comedies'.

XXXIV Universal, *Anthony and Cleopatra* (1924)
Copyright October 23rd, 1 reel, directed by Brian Foy.

XXXV Sennett, *Romeo and Juliet* (1924)
Copyright July 31st by Pathé Exchange, which released. *Film Daily*, August 3rd; *Moving Picture World*, August 2nd; *Kinematograph Weekly*, August 24th. Mack Sennett advertisement, two reels. Alice Day was Juliet in a rustic stage

performance. In Germany, the picture, released by UFA, was titled *Ein schöner Romeo*. (Jason, Vol II, p. 217.)

XXXVI D'Ambra, *Amleto e il suo Clown* (1919)
Distributed in England by London Independent Film Company in five reels; the office information card of the British Film Institute says 6000 feet. There are articles in the *Enciclopedia* on Molinari and the Gallones. See also Sadoul, *Le Cinéma devient un art*, Vol II, pp. 280–2, and E. F. Palmieri, *Vecchio cinema italiano*, Venezia, 1940, p. 172.

XXXVII Maxim-Film, *Romeo und Julia im Schnee* (1920)
Special Supplement to *Sight and Sound*, Index Series No. 9, 'An Index to the Films of Ernst Lubitsch', by Theodore Huff, January 1947, according to which it was released on March 28th. The *Revue du Cinéma*, September 1948, includes the picture in the 'Liste des Films d'Ernst Lubitsch établie par Jean Mitry et annotée par Amable Jameson'. There are prints in the Oesterreichische Kinemathek-Filmmuseum, Vienna, and the Cinemateca Brasileira, São Paulo. According to the Wiesbaden brochure, which labels it a 'parodie', others in the cast were Jacob Tiedtke, Josefine Dora, Julius Falkenstein, Paul Biensfeldt, and Hermann Picha, with camera by Theodor Sparkuhl and length of 964 metres. The material in *Lichtbild Bühne*, March 27th, indicates it was a well acted and directed rural comedy which included parental deception, a dance, and supposed poison; it was forbidden for children by the censor. Falkenstein was the Paris, Tiedtke and Marga Köhler a peasant couple, Biensfeldt and Picha country officials. Dr Ludwig Gesek of the Österreichische Gesellschaft für Filmwissenschaft, Vienna, who gives the original length as 825 metres, kindly sent me the following summary: 'Die beiden Bauern Capulethofer und Montekugerl sind gegeneinander wegen eines verlorenen Prozesses verfeindet. Julchen, die Tochter Capulethofers, in den jungen, von langer Abwesenheit zurückgekehrten Montekugerl verliebt, ist dem geistig beschränkten Sohn Mosers versprochen. Als sie sich verloben soll, beschliessen beide Selbstmord zu begehen. Aber das "Gift" (der Dorfapotheker füllte Zuckerwasser in die Flasche) wirkt nicht. Deshalb stellen sich beide tot, als sie vom ganzen Dorf gesucht werden und bewirken damit die Versöhnung der beiden Elternpaare angesichts der beiden "Leichen".'

XXXVIII Cosmopolitan, *Enchantment* (1921)
Film Daily, November 6th, released by Paramount in 6982 feet, directed by Robert G. Vignola; *Moving Picture Stories*, October 14th, says that 'an entire theatre was built in the studio' for the Shakespeare scene. I am indebted to Mr Gerald D. McDonald for drawing this reference to my attention.

XXXIX Pathé, *The Tempest* (1921)
Copyright March 9th with a description from which I borrow. This was not a French film, though Margaret Lilich so classifies it in 'Shakespeare on the Screen', *Films in Review*, June–July 1956, pp. 247–60. The other actors were Harry Lonsdale, Patricia Palmer, Strake Patteson, and George Kunkle. The story was by Howard North Bradbury and Frank M. Clark; the length, 2000 feet.

XL Palladium, *Han og Hun og Hamlet* (1922)

Brusendorff, pp. 184 ff. with stills; *50 Aar I Densk Film*, Copenhagen, 1956, p. 87; Carl Schenstrøm, *Fyrtaanet Fortæller*, Copenhagen, 1943, pp. 48–9; Sadoul, *Le Cinéma devient un art*, Vol I, p. 189. I gather from stills that there was a *Hamlet* scene, but not how it related to the plot. Beside his autobiography, see the article on Schenstrøm by Fausto Montesanti and Paul Knudsen in the *Enciclopedia*. Other members of the cast were Olga Svendsen, Lissen Bendix, Oscar Stribolt, Christian Gottschalk, Jørgen Lund, Lauritz Olsen, Mathilde Felumb.

XLI Famous Players-Lasky, *Wet Paint* (1926)

Moving Picture World, June 5th; *Film Daily*, June 23rd. The Wiesbaden brochure describes it as 'groteskkomödie nach Motiven von Shakespeare's "Viel Lärmen um Nichts".' The German title was *Eine tolle Brautjagd*. Arthur Rossen directed from a script by Lloyd Corrigan after Reginald Morris. Camera was by William Marshall, and Bryant Washburn was also in the cast.

XLII Alliance, *Carnival* (1921)

Kinematograph Weekly, February 10th; *Bioscope*, February 17th; *Picturegoer*, March, May (still of Lang as Othello); *Film Daily*, July 3rd; Lang, pp. 153, 159; see also Blum, pp. 206, 207. Lang said that the London Film Company was the producer; the catalogue of the British Film Institute names H. K. [Harley Knoles] Productions and gives Alliance as the distributor. Probably there was some sort of combination for an individual venture which was financed by Lord Rothermere. The cast included Ivor Novello as the Count, Maria de Bernaldo, and Clifford Gray. Photography was by Philip Hatkin; the length upon release, May 28th, was 6500 feet, but the print in the National Archive is only 4835. I saw the film when it was first shown in the United States and quite agree with Sadoul's judgment of it (*Le Cinéma devient un art*, Vol II, p. 181). According to the Wiesbaden brochure, the film adaptation was by Adrian Johnson and Rosina Henley.

XLIII Goldwyn, *Doubling for Romeo* (1921)

Film Daily, October 30th; Blum, p. 208, still. Rogers is quoted from Samuel Goldwyn, *Behind the Scenes*, New York, 1923, p. 231. Art direction and sets were by Cedric Gibbons, camera by Marcel Le Picard; others in the cast, Raymond Hatton, Sydney Ainsworth, John Cosser, Al Hart, and Kate Lester.

XLIV Albatross-Sequana, *Kean* (1922)

Oscar M. Sheridan, 'Romeo Deserts Juliet', *Picturegoer*, August 1923; Paul Rotha, *The Film Till Now*, London, 1932, p. 326; Leyda, p. 117; Jean Arroy, *Ivan Mosjoukine*, Paris, 1927. Sheridan's article includes *Romeo and Juliet* stills, and Arroy's book, pp. 2, 56–7, pictures of Mosjoukine as Hamlet and Romeo. I have not seen the film, which was in nine reels, but there is a print in the Jugoslovenska Kinoteca, Beograd. It was reviewed in the *Kinematograph Weekly*, May 15, 1924. Others in the cast were Kenelm Foss, Nicolai Koline, Nathalie Lissenko, Mary Odette. Camera was by J. Mundviller and F. Bourgassoff. In 1956, *Kean* was to emerge again in an adaptation by Jean Paul Sartre as a vehicle for Vittorio Gassman with excerpts from *Hamlet* and *Othello*.

XLV First National, *Polly of the Follies* (1922)
   Film Daily, March 5th; *Picturegoer*, May 1923 (stills). I regret to say that John Emerson who directed, and with Anita Loos wrote the story allowed Julius Caesar (John Daly Murphy) a caption, 'You're the cat's whiskers, Cleo, old dear', as I learned from one of six stills in the now dispersed *Photoplay* collection.

XLVI Universal, *The Trouper* (1922)
   Film Daily, July 23rd; *Picturegoer*, August (still). Jack Perrin played the male lead; direction by Harry B. Harris; about 5000 feet.

XLVII First National, *Day Dreams* (1922)
   National Board of Reviews, *Selected Motion Pictures, 1922–23*, three reels. J. P. Coursodon, 'Keaton et cie.', *Cinéma d'aujourd'hui*, 1964, says two reels. At any rate this was one of the last of Keaton's short films; Renée Adorée was in it. There are *Hamlet* stills in Blum, p. 214, and Griffith-Mayer, p. 159.

XLVIII Dafu, *Schatten eine nachtliche Halluzination* (1922)
   J. Isaacs, 'Shakespeare as Man of the Theatre', reprinted from *Shakespeare and the Theatre* by Members of the Shakespeare Association (1927) in Anne Bradby (ed.), *Shakespeare Criticism 1919–35*, London, 1941, p. 316. The quotation is from *Bioscope*, November 20, 1924. There were reviews by Iris Barry in the *Spectator*, November 15, 1924; by Celia Simpson in the same, August 18, 1928; and by G. W. Stonier in the *New Statesman*, August 11, 1928. Design was by Albin Grau, camera by Fritz Arno Wagner; other parts by Alexander Granach, Fritz Rasp, Ruth Weyher.

XLIX Comedia, *Das alte Gesetz* (1923)
   Also called *Baruch* and in English speaking countries *The Ancient Law*. There are prints in the National Film Archive of the British Film Institute and the Filmhistoriska Samlingarna, Stockholm. Reviews: *Kinematograph Weekly*, May 15, 1924; *Film Daily*, December 7, 1924. I have availed myself of the summary in the National Film Archive; photography was by Theodor Sparkuhl; nine reels, 7532 feet, but commercial versions in England and the United States were cut to, respectively 6500 and 5500 feet.

L First National, *The Perfect Flapper* (1924)
   Film Daily, June 29th; *Picturegoer*, July 1925 (still). Sydney Chaplin was in this one, directed by John F. Dillon, 7000 feet.

LI Famous Players-Lasky, *Triumph* (1924)
   National Board of Review, *Selected Motion Pictures, 1924–25*, *Film Daily*, April 27th; pictures in Blum, p. 260; Taylor, Hale, and Peterson, p. 153. The eight-reel picture was based on a script by Jeanie Macpherson after May Edginton; Bert Glennon was at the camera.

LII United Artists, *Don Q, Son of Zorro* (1925)
   Film Daily, June 21st, directed by Donald Crisp.

LIII First National, *Bluebeard's Seven Wives* (1925)

I should have missed this if it had not been for the capacious memory of Liam O'Leary, who dug up some stills. Reviews in *Film Daily*, January 3, 1926, and *Exhibitors Trade Review* (later *Motion Picture Daily*), January 2nd. Al Santell directed in 7774 feet.

LIV Pan-Phoebus, *Der Leibgardest* (1925)

Molnar's play in Hungarian is *A testör* of which the title of this Austrian film is an exact translation, but bodyguard has quite other meaning in the United States; consequently Philip Moeller's version for Alfred Lunt and Lynn Fontanne made a change. Lunt and Fontanne in 1931 appeared in a sound film of the play which they had acted so deliciously in 1924. The Wiesbaden brochure gives the length of the Austrian film as 2520 metres; others in the cast were Anton Edthofer, Alice Hechy, and Karl Forest.

LV Ellen Richter, *Wie Einst im Mai* (1926)

Wiesbaden brochure. Directed by Willi Wolff in 2665 metres from a script by Wolff and Rob. Liebmann; camera by Axel Graatjaer; sets and costumes by Paul Leni; with Ellen Richter, Adolf Klein, Paul Heidemann, Walter Rilla, Hugo Fischer-Köppe, Frida Richard, Julius von Szöreghy, Alice Torning.

LVI Freedman-Spitz, *The Last Moment* (1928)

Made in Hollywood, distributed by Zakoro, camera by Leon Shamroy, six reels; others in the cast, Lucille La Verne, Isabel Lamore, Georgia Hale, Amielka Eltar, Reviews in *Exceptional Photoplays*, February; *Film Daily*, March 11th; Clifford Howard in *Close Up*, August (still); *Bioscope*, October 3rd; Gilbert Seldes in the *New Republic*, March 6, 1929.

LVII Art-Film, *Hamlet* (1920)

There is a good deal of material about Asta Nielsen and the film; most useful have been Sadoul, *Le Cinéma devient un art*, Vol I, pp. 178–9; Bardèche and Brasillach, pp. 56–7, 194; Kracauer, see index but especially pp. 26–27; Herbert G. Luft, 'The Career of Asta Nielsen', *Films in Review*, January 1956; Iris Barry, Museum of Modern Art Film Library programme, 'The Film in Germany and the Film in France', Series III, Programme 2; material prepared for the National Federation of Film Societies; relevant articles in the *Enciclopedia*; and the Wiesbaden brochure. The Museum of Modern Art has 6803 feet of film out of the original 7768 feet; it ordinarily screens only 1049 feet from the last three reels. I have seen both versions several times, but since there has been cutting use the summary in the Asta Films brochure by Francis Trevelyan Miller. On the other hand, the print contains some sequences not in the summary, for example, Claudius with Gertrude in the dungeon picking a snake out of the pit for his projected murder, an interior play-within-the-play scene (in addition to the one in the courtyard) which must be an interpolation from some other *Hamlet* film, possibly Ruggeri's, and the altar and graveyard scenes, but does not include Hamlet's so-called 'vision' or Laertes' assault on the castle. There were other reviews and comments in the New York *Times*, the *Tribune*, the *American*, the *Daily News*, the Evening *Journal*, the Evening *Mail*, the Evening *Telegram*, the *Herald*, the

World, the *Telegraph*, *Staats-Zeitung*, the *Dramatic Mirror*, *Variety*, the *Film Daily*, the *Moving Picture World*, all of November 9th or shortly after; see also Oswald Blakeston, 'Film Curiosities', *Close Up*, March 1929. Stills appear in Vincent, p. 140; Blum, p. 204; the *Enciclopedia*, accompanying the biography of Asta Nielsen by Guilio Cesare Castello; the Asta Films brochure; and the Wiesbaden brochure.

LVIII Masters, *The Merchant of Venice* (1922)
 Kinematograph Weekly, July 13th.

LIX Elel-Film, *Macbeth* (1922)
 Wiesbaden brochure; *Lichtbild Bühne*, No. 18 (?). I owe the second reference to Jay Leyda. It is an advertisement for Caesar-Film: 'Nicht nur das Werk Shakespeares wird hier verfilmt, die Regie Heinz Schalls ist darauf bedacht, Shakespearishen Atem durch jede szene wehen zu lassen. Unter Mitwirkung erster, hingebungsvoll gestaltender künstlerischer Kräfte soll die Tragödie der Lady Macbeth zu unerhörter Wucht und wundervoll geschlossener Wirkung gesteigert werden. Die Mitwirkung ernsthafter Historiker bürgt für absolute Stilreine.' The article on Klöpfer by Francisco Savio and Lotte Eisner in the *Enciclopedia* mentions no such film; Stahl, p. 682, says Klöpfer had an interest as a collaborator. Lapierre, p. 464, lists a *Macbeth* as a German film adaptation of this period.

LX Wörner-Film, *Othello* (1922)
 The Wiesbaden brochure gives the credits in full; an announcement by UFA, which distributed, for its releases of 1922–23 says the picture was 'nach Shakespeare und Cinthio' and indicates Bukhovetsky was assisted by Stats Hagen. The *Jahrbuch der Filmindustrie*, 1923, notes *Othello* was passed by the censors, February 23, 1922. On Bukhovetsky, see Leyda, pp. 118–19, and Harry C. Carr, 'How the great directors work', *Motion Picture Magazine*, May 1925. The film was partially financed by Ben Blumenthal, who founded the Export and Import Film Co. He had opened the first German two-dollar-admission picture house in Berlin in 1913 and imported American films into Germany; when the War broke out he came to America and imported German films into the United States. With a friendly competitor, David P. Howells, he held the American rights to *Othello*, which was copyrighted as '*The Moor*, presented by David P. Howells . . . adapted from *Othello*, Export and Import Film Co., 5 December, 1922'. I am much indebted to Mr Blumenthal, who granted me an interview in 1947. At the time the negative was at Lloyd's. From 1926 to 1936 a positive print in 5552 feet on six reels was available through the Kodascope Library, New York, a subsidiary of Eastman Kodak, but was then withdrawn from circulation. It was located for me in Rochester by the Secretary of Eastman, Mr Milton K. Robinson, who kindly sent to me for screening a 16 millimetre positive of 2221 feet. The 35 millimetre print for public distribution was of 6385 feet, considerably shorter than the original as a result of American editing by Don Bartlett. The version released in England on July 16, 1923, by Goldwyn as *The Moor* was in five reels (*Kinematograph Year Book*, 1923, under May). It was reviewed there in the *Picturegoer*, July 1923. American comment appeared in the *Film Daily*, February 2, 1923; the *Exhibitors*

Trade Journal, March 10th; the *Moving Picture World*, March 3rd, 10th, 17th, 24th. Material on Jannings and Krauss is voluminous; see the articles with bibliography in the *Enciclopedia*, and the listing on Jannings in the *Film Index*, p. 138. There are stills in his autobiography, *Theatre-film: Das Leben und ich*, ed. C. C. Bergius, Berchtesgaden, 1951, p. 56; Kalbus, Part I, pp. 67–9; Pasinetti, p. 88; *Picturegoer*, December 1923 and November 1925; the *Moving Picture World*, as above; the Wiesbaden brochure; Blum, p. 251. Jean Mitry, *Emil Jannings*, Paris, 1928, has a picture of Jannings as Othello (p. 13) and a brief criticism of his interpretation (p. 30).

LXI British and Colonial, *John Falstaff* (1923)
Bioscope, May 3rd, 10th; November 1st, 8th. The film was probably shot soon after May 10th and certainly before November 1st. The studio was at Walthamstow. For information about this and the other Shakespeare in the Gem series, I am indebted to Arthur Kingston, who was the cameraman. For Byford, see *Who's Who in the Theatre*, 5th ed., 1925.

LXII British and Colonial, *The Taming of the Shrew* (1923)
I saw a cut down version without identification except for the actors, made available by the Film Classic Exchange in a 16 millimetre length of about 675 feet, before the full film turned up in the National Archive of the British Film Institute in 35 millimetres, 2056 feet, which includes all credits. My summary is based on the second, which indicated the participation of Mr Kingston, now a collector and inventor of motion picture apparatus. He was able to give me the approximate date, which I was ultimately able to verify in *Bioscope*, May 3rd, 10th; November 1st, 10th; and kindly supplied three stills. For Maitland, see *Who's Who in the Theatre*, 5th ed., 1925; Reed and Spiers, *Who's Who in Filmland*, 3rd ed., 1931. George Pearson, *Flashback*, London, 1957, p. 112, lists Dacia as 'The Dancer' in his Betty Balfour film, *Love, Life, and Laughter* (1923). Most of the personnel appear in Low, *History of the British Film (1914–1918)*; see her Index. The picture was probably made just before *John Falstaff*.

LXIII Peter Paul Felner-Film, *The Merchant of Venice* (1923)
The references to German sources are to the Wiesbaden brochure, both in the list of Shakespeare films and in the article by Steffan Wolf, 'Geschicte der Shakespeare-Verfilmung (1899–1964)', p. 22; see also Stahl, p. 683, who is earlier. The Wiesbaden brochure gives the length in metres, and assigns the camera to Axel Graatkjaer and Rudolf Mayer; the sets to Hermann Warm. The *Jahrbuch der Filmindustrie 1923–1925* gives the length also as eight reels and indicates the film was passed by the censors on August 31, 1923. The positive print of *The Jew of Mestri* in six reels is in the National Archive of the British Film Institute. That I saw it on an Editola explains some of my own confusions and queries in the analysis. The information card in the Archive and *Bioscope*, May 21, 1925, disagree on the players of Antonio and Bassanio; the card names Harry Liedtke as Giannetto (Bassanio), and Ferdinand von Alten as Benito (Antonio); the journal, Carl Ebert as Giannetto, Harry Liedtke as Benito. The Wiesbaden brochure does not name Lorenzo at all and places von Alten as Aragon. Stahl gives Albert Steinrück as Morocco, who is not in the picture I saw. For British comment see *Bioscope*,

above; also July 30, 1925; January 21, 1926; *Kinematograph Weekly*, August 6, 1925. We have met the principals before, but there is a sketch of Felner in Kurt Mühsam and Egon Jacobsohn, *Lexicon des Films*, Berlin, 1923. There is, or was, a film strip biography, *Henny Porten, life and career of a film artist*, compiled and edited by Oskar Kalbus in 1928 (UFA). I take it that Knaur's listing of a Felner *Romeo and Juliet* is in error. There is a still of Krauss in character in the Wiesbaden brochure.

LXIV Neumann, *A Midsummer Night's Dream* (1925)

Credits from the Wiesbaden brochure. Some of the participants were concerned in much different and more important films (see Kracauer, index). Neumann is included in the Mühsam-Jacobsohn *Lexicon*. Blakeston's review of *Wood Love* is in *Close Up*, June 1929. I have shamelessly cribbed from the German reviews in the *Nürnberger Zeitung*, October 29, 1928, and the *Essener Anzeiger*, April 15, 1929, both of which are quoted by Thurman, pp. 190–91, who also supplies additional information. The New York *Post*, January 30, 1928, praised the photography, but in a generally unfavorable review said the picture was 'done in a stodgy, dull fashion'. The New York *Times* review of the same date was '© 1928 by The New York Times Company. Reprinted by permission'. Another estimate is in Kalbus, Part I, p. 68. The Wiesbaden brochure, p. 22, includes illustrations by Ernö Metzner from Klabund's *Wie ich den Sommernachtstraum im Film sehe* (1925), which I have not seen. *Film Photos Wie Nach Nie*, p. 182, has a picture of Krauss as Bottom. The Museum of Modern Art has stills.

BIBLIOGRAPHY

The bibliography below is confined to books and articles of general interest or comprehensive coverage to which reference has been made. It does not include the many items which have been consulted during the investigation which were rejected as repetitive, irrelevant, or superfluous. References to trade journals, serial newspapers and periodicals, house organs, catalogues, and year books which have provided information about a particular film, for example announcements, production details, synopses, credits, and reviews, are cited with the dates in connection with the discussion of that film, sometimes in the text but usually in the section, Explanations and Acknowledgments; the specification of pages, numbers, and volumes, since the publications are brief in compass or material is listed alphabetically, has not in most cases seemed necessary. When a short title or designation has been substituted after a first citation or when the name of an author of more than one work is given without title, identification is provided in brackets following the entry in the Bibliography.

ANTOINE, *Le Théâtre* (*Le Troisième République de 1870 à nos jours*), 2 Vols, Paris, 1932

ARMSTRONG, WILLIAM A., 'Bernard Shaw and Forbes-Robertson's *Hamlet*', *Shakespeare Quarterly*, Winter 1964, pp. 27–31

ARROY, JEAN, *Ivan Mosjoukine*, Paris, 1927

BALL, ROBERT HAMILTON, 'If We Shadows Have Offended', *Pacific Spectator*, Winter 1947, pp. 97–104

——, 'Pioners and All: The Beginnings of Shakespeare Film', *Theatre Survey*, 1960, pp. 18–42

——, 'The Shakespeare Film as Record: Sir Herbert Beerbohm Tree', *Shakespeare Quarterly*, July 1952, pp. 227–36

——, 'Shakespeare in One Reel', *Quarterly of Film, Radio, and Television*, Winter 1953, pp. 139–49

BARKER, W. G., 'Before 1910: Kinematograph Experiences', *Proceedings of the British Kinematograph Society*, No. 38, 1936

BEERBOHM, MAX, (ed.), *Herbert Beerbohm Tree*, London, n.d.

BENCHETTRIT, PAUL, '*Hamlet* at the Comédie Française: 1769–1896', *Shakespeare Survey*, Cambridge, Vol IX (1956), pp. 59–68

BESSY, MAURICE, and LO DUCA, *Georges Méliès Mage*, Paris, 1945

Best Plays of 1894 to 1899, ed. Garrison P. Sherwood and John Chapman, New York, 1955

Best Plays of 1899–1909, ed. Burns Mantle and Garrison P. Sherwood, New York, 1944

Biograph 1903–1912. Ms. Notebook. Museum of Modern Art, New York

BIRD, JOHN H., *Cinema Parade*, Birmingham, 1947

BLUM, DANIEL, *A Pictorial History of the Silent Screen*, New York, 1953

BRUSENDORFF, OVE, *Filmen: Dens Navne og Historie*, København, 1939

COLLIER, CONSTANCE, *Harlequinade: The Story of My Life ...*, London, 1929

CUENCA, CARLOS FERNANDEZ, *El Mundo de Georges Méliès*, San Sebastian, July 1961

DELINI, JULES, *Nos Vedettes*, Paris, [1926?]

DOYLE, G. R., *Twenty-Five Years of Films* . . . , London, 1936

DUEY, HELEN, 'Shakespeare in the Films: An Interview with Sir Herbert Beer-bohm Tree', *Woman's Home Companion*, June 1916, p. 8

DUREAU, G., 'Films d'Art et "Film d'art",' *Ciné-Journal*, June 11, 1910, pp. 3–4

EKMAN, HASSE, *Gösta Ekman*, Stockholm, 1938

Enciclopedia dello Spettacolo, dir. Silvio d'Amico, 9 Vols, Roma, 1954–62. Appendix, 1963. [*Enciclopedia*]

FAGOT, GEORGES, 'Le Film d'Arte Italiana', *Ciné-Journal*, June 11, 1910, p. 19

FAWCETT, L'ESTRANGE, *Films: Facts and Forecasts*, London, 1927

FESCOURT, HENRI (pref.; no ed. named), *Le Cinéma des origines à nos jours*, Paris, [1932]

Filmlexicon degli Autori e della Opera, dir. Michele Lacalamita, 5 Vols, Roma, 1958–62

50 Aar I Densk Film, København, 1956

Film Index, The: A Bibliography, Vol I, *The Film as Art*, New York, 1941 [*Film Index*]

Film Photos Wie Noch Nie, Giessen, [1929]

FORBES-ROBERTSON, JOHNSTON, *A Player Under Three Reigns*, London, 1925

FURNISS, HARRY, *Our Lady Cinema*, Bristol, 1914

GOLDWYN, SAMUEL, *Behind the Scenes*, New York, 1923

GRAU, ROBERT, *The Stage in the Twentieth Century*, New York, 1912

——, *The Theatre of Science*, New York, 1914

GRAVES, CHARLES, 'When British Films Had to Pay', *Everybody's Weekly*, December 24, 1949, pp. 11–13

GRIFFITH, Mrs D. W. (LINDA ARVIDSON), *When the Movies Were Young*, New York, [1925]

GRIFFITH, RICHARD, and MAYER, ARTHUR, *The Movies* . . . , New York, [1957]

HALLS, W. D., *Maurice Maeterlinck: A Study of His Life and Thought*, Oxford, 1960

HAMMERTON, J. A., *Barrie: The Story of a Genius*, New York, 1929

HARRISON, LOUIS REEVES, *Screencraft*, New York, 1916

HARTNOLL, PHYLLIS (ed.), *The Oxford Companion to the Theatre*, Oxford, 1951

HAYS, WILL H., *See and Hear*, Motion Picture Producers and Distributors of America, n.p., 1929

HENDING, ARNOLD, *Da Isbjørnen var lille*, København, 1945

——, *Fremmede Fugle: I Dansk Film*, København, 1951

——, *Stjerner I Glashuse et Causerie over 40 Aars*, København, 1936

HENRIQUES, ALF, 'Shakespeare and Denmark', *Shakespeare Survey*, Cambridge, Vol III (1950), pp. 107–15

HENSON, LESLIE, *My Laugh Story: The Story of My Life: Up to Date*, London, n.d.

HEPWORTH, CECIL, *Came the Dawn*, London, 1951

HOOKER, BRIAN, 'Shakespeare and the Movies', *Century Magazine*, Vol 93 (December 1916), pp. 298–304

HOPPER, DEWOLF, and STOUT, W. W., *Once a Clown* ..., Boston, 1927

'Histoire du Cinéma', spec. no., *Le Crapouillet*, November 1932

HUMFREY, ROBERT, *Careers in the Films*, London, 1938

ISAACS, J., 'Shakespeare as Man of the Theatre', reprinted from *Shakespeare and the Theatre* by Members of the Shakespeare Association (1927) in Anne Bradby (ed.), *Shakespeare Criticism, 1919–1935*, London, 1941, pp. 292–326

IZARD, FORREST, *Heroines of the Modern Stage*, New York, 1915

JACOBS, LEWIS, *The Rise of the American Film*, New York, 1936

JANNINGS, EMIL, *Theatre-film: Das Leben und ich* (ed. C. C. Bergius), Berchtesgaden, 1951

JASON, ALEXANDER, *Handbuch der Filmwirtschaft*, Vol II, Berlin, [1930]

JEANNE, RENÉ, and FORD, CHARLES, *Histoire encyclopédique du cinéma*, 5 Vols, Paris, 1942–62
Vol I, *Le Cinéma Français*, 1895–1929, 7th ed., 1947

JOHNSON, ROSSITER, *Dora Knowlton Ranous: Author-Editor-Translator; A Simple Record of a Noble Life*, New York, 1916

KALBUS, OSKAR, *Vom Werden deutsches Filmkunst*, Vol I, Altona-Bahrenfeld, 1935

KITCHIN, LAURENCE, 'Shakespeare on the Screen', *Shakespeare Survey*, Cambridge, Vol XVIII (1965), pp. 70–4

Knaurs Buch vom Film, ed. Rune Waldekranz and Verner Arpe, München, 1956. [Knaur]

KNOWLTON, DORA, *The Diary of a Daly Debutante*, New York, 1910

KRACAUER, SIEGFRIED, *From Caligari to Hitler*, Princeton, 1947

LANG, MATHESON, *Mr Wu Looks Back*, London, 1941

LAPIERRE, MARCEL, *Les Cents Visages du Cinéma*, Paris, 1948

LEBLANC, GEORGETTE, *Souvenirs: My Life with Maeterlinck* (tr. Janet Flanner), New York, 1932

LEYDA, JAY, *Kino: A History of the Russian and Soviet Film*, New York, 1960

——, 'Theatre on Film', *Theatre Arts Monthly*, March 1937, pp. 194–207

LILICH, MARGARET, 'Shakespeare on the Screen', *Films in Review*, June–July 1956, pp. 247–60

LINDSAY, VACHEL, *The Art of the Motion Picture*, New York, 1915

LIZZANI, CARLO, *Il Cinema Italiano*, 2nd ed., Firenze, 1924

LOW, RACHAEL, and MANVELL, ROGER, *The History of the British Film 1896–1906*, London, 1948

——, *The History of the British Film 1906–1914*, London, 1949. [Low]

——, *The History of the British Film 1914–1918*, London, 1950. [*1914–1918*]

LOWREY, CAROLYN, *The First One Hundred Men and Women of the Screen*, New York, 1920

MACKAIL, DENIS, *The Story of J.M.B.*, London, 1941

MATTHEWS, A. E., *Matty: An Autobiography*, London, 1952

MESGUICH, FELIX, *Tours de Manivelle*, Paris, 1933

MESSTER, OSKAR, *Mein Weg mit dem Film*, Berlin, [1936]

MITRY, JEAN, *Emil Jannings*, Paris, 1928

——, *Filmographie Universelle*, Paris, 1963–
Tome II, *Primitifs et Précurseurs, 1895–1915*
Première partie: France et Europe, 1964

Motion Picture Studio Directory, 2nd ed., London, October 21, 1916

Motion Pictures 1894–1912 : Identified from the Records of the United States Copyright Office by Howard Lamarr Walls, Washington, 1953

Motion Pictures 1912–1939 (Catalogue of Copyright Entries, Cumulative Series), Washington, 1951

MÜHSAM, KURT, and JACOBSOHN, EGON, *Lexicon des Films*, Berlin, 1923

NEERGAARD, EBBE, *The Story of Danish Film*, Copenhagen, 1963

NEWTON, H. CHANCE, *Cues and Curtain Calls*, London, 1927

ODELL, GEORGE C. D., *Annals of the New York Stage*, 15 Vols, New York, 1927–49

OLSEN, OLE, *Filmens Eventyr og mit Eget*, København, 1940

PALMIERI, E. FERDINAND, *Fifty Years of Italian Cinema*, Rome, 1954

——, *Vecchio Cinema Italiano con Diciannove Tavole*, Venezia, 1940

PARKER, JOHN (ed.), *Who's Who in the Theatre*, 5th ed., London, 1925; 6th ed., London, 1930

PARKER, LOUIS N., *Several of My Lives*, London, 1928

PASINETTI, FRANCESCO, *Mezzo seculo di cinema*, Milano, 1946

PEARSON, GEORGE, *Flashback*, London, 1957

PEARSON, HESKETH, *Beerbohm Tree : His Life and Laughter*, London, 1956

'Photographed by A. Marvin'. Biograph Ms. Notebook. Museum of Modern Art, New York

PORTEN, HENNY, *Vom 'Kintopp' zum Tonfilm : Ein Stück miterlebter Filmgeschicte*, Dresden, 1932

PROLO, MARIA ADRIANA, *Storia del cinema muto italiano*, Vol I, Milano, 1951

PRONIER, ERNEST, *Une Vie au Théâtre : Sarah Bernhardt*, Geneva, 1942

RAMSAYE, TERRY, *A Million and One Nights : A History of the Motion Picture*, 2 Vols, New York, 1926

'Records of Negatives as Rec'd from Operators'. Biograph Ms. Notebook. Museum of Modern Art, New York

REED, LANGFORD, and SPIERS, HETTY, *Who's Who in Filmland*, 3rd ed., London, 1931

REINERT, CHARLES, *Kleines Filmlexicon*, Einsiedeln-Zürich, 1946

ROTHA, PAUL, *The Film Till Now*, London, 1932

SADOUL, GEORGES, *Georges Méliès*, Paris, 1961

——, *Histoire Générale du Cinéma*

  Tome I, *L'Invention du Cinéma, 1832–1897*, Paris, [1946]. [*L'Invention*]

  Tome II, *Les Pionniers du Cinéma, 1897–1909*, Paris, [1947]. [*Les Pionniers*]

  Tome III, *Le Cinéma devient un art, 1909–1920*

    Vol I, *L'Avant-Guerre*, Paris, [1951]

    Vol II, *La Première Guerre Mondiale*, Paris, [1952]

SCHENSTRØM, CARL, *Fyrtaanet Fortæller*, København, 1943

Shakespeare Film, ed. Max Lippman, Deutsches Institut für Filmkunde, Wiesbaden, 1964. [Wiesbaden brochure]

SMITH, ALBERT E. (with Phil A. Koury), *Two Reels and a Crank*, New York, 1952

SORO, FRANCESCO, *Splendori e Miserie del Cinema*, Milano, 1935

STAHL, ERNST LEOPOLD, *Shakespeare und Das Deutsche Theater*, Stuttgart, 1947

TALBOT, FREDERICK A., *Moving Pictures*, Philadelphia, 1912

THORP, MARGARET FARRAND, 'Shakespeare and the Movies', *Shakespeare Quarterly*, Summer 1958, pp. 357–66

THRASHER, FREDERIC M., *Okay for Sound*, New York, 1936

THURMANN, IRMGARD, 'Shakespeare in Film', *Shakespeare-Jahrbuch*, Vol 76, Weimar, 1940, pp. 189–98

VERNEUIL, LOUIS, *The Fabulous Life of Sarah Bernhardt* (tr. Ernest Boyd), New York, [1942]

VINCENT, CARL, *Histoire de l'Art Cinématographique*, Brussels, n.d.

VINING, EDWARD P., *The Mystery of Hamlet*, Philadelphia, 1881

WAGENKNECHT, EDWARD, *The Movies in the Age of Innocence*, Norman, Okla., 1962

WARDE, FREDERICK, *Fifty Years of Make-Believe*, New York, 1920

WARREN, LOW, *The Film Game*, London, 1937

WHITEHALL, R. E., 'Some Films Called *Hamlet*', *Theatre* (London), Winter 1948, pp. 39–40

WILSON, A. E., *The Lyceum*, London, 1952

WILSON, EDWIN (ed.), *Shaw on Shakespeare*, New York, 1961

WINCHESTER, C. A. C., *The World Film Encyclopedia*, London, 1933

WINTER, WILLIAM, *Shakespeare on the Stage*, New York, 1911

WOLF, STEFFAN, 'Geschicte der Shakespeare-Verfilmung (1899–1964)' in *Shakespeare Film* (ed. Max Lippman), Wiesbaden, 1964, pp. 15–33

WOOD, LESLIE, *The Miracle of the Movies*, London, 1947

——, *The Romance of the Movies*, London, 1937

INDEX OF FILMS

N

INDEX OF NAMES

SHAKESPEARE ON SILENT FILM

A